ROUTLEDGE LIBRARY OF BRITISH POLITICAL HISTORY: LABOUR AND RADICAL POLITICS 1762–1937

VOLUME VIII

ROUTLEDGE LIBRARY OF BRITISH POLITICAL HISTORY: LABOUR AND RADICAL POLITICS 1762–1937

VOLUME I
A Short History of the British Working Class Movement I, 1789–1848
Edited by G. D. H. Cole

VOLUME II
A Short History of the British Working Class Movement II, 1848–1900
Edited by G. D. H. Cole

VOLUME III
A Short History of the British Working Class Movement III, 1900–1937
Edited by G. D. H. Cole

VOLUME IV
A History of British Socialism I
Edited by M. Beer

VOLUME V
A History of British Socialism II
Edited by M. Beer

VOLUME VI
English Radicalism 1762–1785
Edited by S. Maccoby

VOLUME VII
English Radicalism 1786–1832
Edited by S. Maccoby

VOLUME VIII
English Radicalism 1832–1852
Edited by S. Maccoby

VOLUME IX
English Radicalism 1853–1886
Edited by S. Maccoby

VOLUME X
English Radicalism 1886–1914
Edited by S. Maccoby

VOLUME XI
English Radicalism: The End?
Edited by S. Maccoby

ENGLISH RADICALISM 1832–1852

Edited by
S. Maccoby

Taylor & Francis Group
LONDON AND NEW YORK

First published 1935 by George Allen & Unwin Ltd.

Published 2018 by Routledge
2 Park Square, Milton Park, Abingdon, Oxon, OX14 4RN

Simultaneously published in the USA and Canada
by Routledge
52 Vanderbilt Avenue, New York, NY 10017

First issued in paperback 2018

Routledge is an imprint of the Taylor & Francis Group, an informa business

All rights reserved. No part of this book may be reprinted or reproduced or utilised in any form or by any electronic, mechanical, or other means, now known or hereafter invented, including photocopying and recording, or in any information storage or retrieval system, without permission in writing from the publishers.

Notice:
Product or corporate names may be trademarks or registered trademarks, and are used only for identification and explanation without intent to infringe.

British Library Cataloguing in Publication Data
A catalogue record for this book is available from the British Library.

Library of Congress Cataloging in Publication Data
A catalog record for this book has been requested.

English Radicalism 1832–1852

English Radicalism: 6 Volumes
ISBN 0-415-26570-3

Routledge Library of British Political History: Labour and Radical Politics 1762–1937: 11 Volumes: ISBN 0-415-26562-2

Publisher's Note
The publisher has gone to great lengths to ensure the quality of this reprint but points out that some imperfections in the original book may be apparent.

Typeset in Times by
Keystroke, Jacaranda Lodge, Wolverhampton

ISBN 13: 978-1-138-86760-4 (pbk)
ISBN 13: 978-0-415-26573-7 (hbk)

ENGLISH RADICALISM 1832-1852

by
S. MACCOBY, Ph.D.

LONDON
George Allen & Unwin Ltd
MUSEUM STREET

PREFACE

THIS study arose from dissatisfaction with existing accounts of nineteenth-century political history. Adequate explanation of the course of events in the decades following 1832 seemed to be unobtainable. Even the great work of Elie Halévy, a work of which the maturest of English historians might be proud, leaves some questions unanswered and others unasked. But that is, perhaps, inevitable in so bold a piece of pioneering, and it keeps the way open for further essays in reinterpreting a period which was often grotesquely mishandled in the "standard histories" of the past. Particularly did earlier writers tend to the error of viewing the rapid political and legislative changes of the 1830's and 1840's not primarily from the standpoint of the forces compelling their adoption, but rather from that of the legal machinery registering them, and registering them in very resistive fashion. There have actually been historians ready to assign the major "credit" for the "reforms" of the epoch to the coroneted Cabinets and the landed Parliamentary majorities of the time. Even in political history little is explained by mere *personalia*, and the ascription of "reform" to such causes as the "views" of Grey, Brougham, and Russell on the one hand or those of Peel, Shaftesbury, and Stanley on the other seems singularly superficial and unhistorical.

Of the imposing list of "reforming" Acts, drafted in Downing Street and passed at Westminster, a deeper explanation is necessary than one conceived mainly in terms of Cabinet or Parliamentary personalities. Both the Acts and their limitations call, indeed, for a different kind of analysis. The nature of that analysis may be suggested, at least in part, by the querulous words of Earl Grey of the Reform Bill himself. "We should not be urged," he declared at a critical moment in 1834, "by a constant and active pressure from without to the adoption of any measures the necessity of which has not been fully proved, and which are not strictly regulated by a careful attention to the settled institutions of the country both in Church and State." Whigs and Tories alike were now being subjected almost without intermission to "a constant and active pressure from without": alike they were moved by it to adopt measures of reform. It is that very "pressure from

English Radicalism 1832-1852

without" which calls for definition and for due recognition among the constructive historical forces of the period. But any full picture of Whig and Tory "reforming" activity recalls other and complementary circumstances. When "pressure from without" had become highly inconvenient and even positively dangerous, a modicum of sedative legislative compromise was prepared in which all "the settled institutions of the country" were most carefully safeguarded. Even then, whether the legislation was drafted by Whig Cabinets or Tory, further rigid safeguarding was usually insisted upon by the Ultra-Conservatives of the Lords. "Public opinion," finally, in the shape of *The Times* newspaper and the like, hastened to congratulate an often dubious, jeering, or actively hostile populace on living in the liberal and progressive era which permitted "great changes" to take place peacefully almost every year.

It is then to the evokers, sustainers, and supporters of "pressure from without" that it is necessary to turn for completer knowledge of what were the motive forces in nineteenth-century politics. And it is impossible to turn a great way before reaching conclusions. So far from accepting, with the Tories, "the settled institutions of the country both in Church and State" as divinely ordained, or believing, with the Whigs, that they needed only an occasional cautious re-adaptation, the exponents of "pressure from without" were labouring for the "radical reform" of these institutions, and often enough for their total abolition. "Radical reformers," or plain Radicals as they had soon come to be, were almost universally agreed on one constitutional creed however much their various schools might differ as to its proper fiscal, economic, social, and religious application In constitutional politics virtually all Radicals pursued the same aims. They pressed for the creation of a fully democratised House of Commons, a House of Commons democratised not merely to the point of representing, without property qualification, constituencies organised on the system of equal manhood suffrage and vote by ballot, but democratised even to the point of needing most frequent renewal of its electoral mandate.

Practically all Radicals demanded such a House of Commons because they wished to make it their instrument for effecting great changes in the ordering of society. And it was exactly for the same reason that the ruling classes, Whig and Tory alike,

Preface

resisted its creation so strenuously. Side by side, moreover, with the great Suffrage struggle for the legislative machinery of the State, the different Radical schools undertook much other collateral campaigning for "radical reform" of the economic and social order. These "radical reform" pressures on a community whose political machinery had been far less democratised in 1832 than had at first been believed are the subject of this book.

It should be said at once that attention has not been confined to "Parliamentary Radicalism," and its Elections, Motions, and Divisions. Benthamites, moreover, and Utilitarians, Free Traders and Anti-Corn Law Leaguers, Dissenters and Disestablishers, Owenites and Trades Unionists, Ultras and Chartists are not treated in separate compartments, but are handled together in relation to the movement of "public opinion" under their total pressure.

The "public opinion" of convention, again, the "public opinion" of *The Times* and the "respectable Press," of *Hansard* and the Reports of Royal Commissions and Select Committees, is not taken at its own valuation. Its bias, conscious and unconscious, has incessantly to be allowed for, and a whole Ultra-Radical world, which it would fain have ignored or misrepresented, has to be revalued in juster terms. Fortunately there is a wealth of material permitting qualitative and even to some extent quantitative revision of the judgments passed by the "public opinion" of 1832–52 upon the Radicalism and Ultra-Radicalism of its time. This material ranges from police correspondence to Parliamentary petitioning, from the files of struggling Ultra newspapers to the records of Chartist National Conventions, from Reports of Congresses of "Rational Religionists" to programmes adopted by Conferences of the National Association of United Trades. From the correlation of such largely unworked sources with others better known, a fuller and more balanced view of the age emerges.

Much more than a short concluding paragraph of acknowledgment is the due of the friends who have made this work possible. For two years, for example, Mr. H. L. Beales of the London School of Economics tirelessly lent himself to the work of improving the present volume and preparing the way for its two projected successors. The staff of the Bishopsgate Institute, again, have done everything in their power to make fully available

English Radicalism 1832-1852

the wealth of Radical material of which they are the custodians. Professor Harold Laski, too, has always been ready to give advice and encouragement, and the Senate of the University of London has made a valuable grant in aid of publication. Finally Dr. J. L. Hammond, Mr. C. A. Furth, and Miss Mildred Willson must be warmly thanked for valuable suggestions at the pre-publication stage.

CONTENTS

CHAPTER		PAGE
	PREFACE	7
	INTRODUCTION: ORIGINS OF "RADICAL REFORM," 1768–1831	13

PART ONE

I	RADICALS AND THE REFORM BILL, 1831-2	31
II	THE CONSTITUTION OF 1832	48
III	ELECTION PLEDGES IN 1832	62
IV	THE REFORMED PARLIAMENT	74
V	CORN LAW, SINECURE, AND PENSION LIST GRIEVANCES	91
VI	END OF THE GREY GOVERNMENT	104
VII	POOR LAW AND MUNICIPAL REFORM	120
VIII	RADICALISM FAILS TO IMPOSE ITS PROGRAMME	139
IX	THE PEOPLE'S CHARTER AND THE NATIONAL PETITION	157
X	OASTLER, STEPHENS, AND FEARGUS O'CONNOR	171
XI	FAILURE OF THE CHARTIST CONVENTION OF 1839	186
XII	CHARTISM SURVIVES	203
XIII	PEEL'S ADVENT TO POWER	220
XIV	THE AGITATIONS OF 1842 AND 1843	236
XV	RADICALS AND GOVERNMENT POLICY, 1844–6	251
XVI	PARLIAMENTARY RADICALISM AN INCREASING FORCE	269
XVII	THE CONTINUED PRESSURE FOR INNOVATION, 1848	283

CHAPTER		PAGE
XVIII	THE PROTECTIONIST "REACTION" OVERCOME, 1849–52	298
XIX	SUFFRAGE, EDUCATION, AND NEWSPAPER TAXATION	313
XX	RELIGION, LANDOWNERSHIP, AND THE FAMILY	332

PART TWO

XXI	RADICALS AND THE EMPIRE	349
XXII	RADICALS AND FOREIGN AFFAIRS	365
XXIII	RADICALISM AND LOCAL GOVERNMENT	380
XXIV	THE WORLD OF LABOUR	396
XXV	THE NEWSPAPER PRESS	410
XXVI	RADICALISM'S SEARCH FOR LEADERSHIP AND PARTY ORGANISATION	425
	SELECT BIBLIOGRAPHY	439
	APPENDIX A	449
	APPENDIX B	452
	INDEX	454

INTRODUCTION

ORIGINS OF "RADICAL REFORM," 1768-1831

"My sentiments on the subject of Parliamentary Reform are formed on the experience of TWENTY-SIX YEARS, which, whether in or out of Government, have equally convinced me that the restoration of a genuine House of Commons, by a renovation of the rights of the people, is the only remedy against that system of corruption which has brought the nation to disgrace and poverty, and threatens it with the loss of liberty."
> *The Duke of Richmond to William Frankland, High Sheriff of Sussex, 1783.* (Quoted in Henry Brookes's Introduction (*1859*) to the Duke's "Right of the People to Universal Suffrage and Annual Parliaments clearly demonstrated. 1783.")

"Never did so great an opportunity offer itself to England, and to all Europe, as is produced by the two revolutions of America and France. By the former, freedom has a national champion in the Western world; and by the latter in Europe. When another nation shall join France, despotism and bad government will scarcely dare to appear. To use a trite expression, the iron is become hot all over Europe. The insulted German and the enslaved Spaniard, the Russ and the Pole all begin to think. The present age will hereafter merit to be called the Age of Reason. . . ."
> *From* PAINE's "Rights of Man," *Second part, 1792.*

". . . before a labourer can have a loaf of bread, he must give a quantity of labour more than the loaf costs by all that quantity which pays the profits of the farmer, the corn dealer, the miller and the baker, with profit on all the buildings they use; and he must moreover pay with the produce of his labour the rent of the landlord. How much more labour a labourer must give to have a loaf of bread than the loaf cost, it is impossible for me to say. I should probably underrate it were I to state it at six times; or were I to say that the real cost of that loaf, for which the labourer must pay sixpence, is one penny. Of this, however, I am quite certain, that the Corn Laws, execrable as they are in principle, and mischievous as they are to the whole community, do not impose anything like so heavy a tax on the labourer, as capital. . . ."
> *From* "Labour Defended against the Claims of Capital or the Unproductiveness of Capital Proved," *by a Labourer* (THOMAS HODGSKIN), *1825. Second edition.*

AMONG the dates which make possible starting-points for a brief historical introduction to Radicalism, March 28, 1768, has special claims. On that day the "independent" freeholders of Middlesex elected John Wilkes as one of their members and unconsciously expedited the domination of British politics by the subject of Parliamentary Reform. Wilkes's past career made his election the aptest possible expression of the discontent of vast metropolitan populations with the corrupting control of Parliament established by a Court enjoying neither popular favour nor popular esteem. On February 3, 1769, nevertheless George III's royal will was duly registered by a subservient majority of the House of Commons and John Wilkes was expelled. There followed a turbulent period of constitutional agitation by the aristocratic politicians of the Whig Opposition connexions and by large sections of the "independent" electorate, helped by the mob. It was in this agitation that the desirability of effecting large changes in the constitution of the House of Commons was first mooted in the eighteenth century. In the beginning the subject was treated not in terms of fundamental human and civic right, but rather as a practical matter of freeing the Commons' House from the vitiating presence of the Crown's placemen and pensioners. It was the great stirring of political thought caused by the American troubles which gradually widened the range of discussion until some were considering the complete democratisation of the representation.

The ill success of Court policy proved a special stimulus to such discussion. The country had rarely known so dangerous and distressful a season as the winter of 1779–80 when the Court and its "rotten borough" majority were involved in war with France, Spain, and the Americans, and when relations were strained with a number of European Courts besides. It proved possible, indeed, to launch at this season a most remarkable political movement embracing some of the most conservative sections of the country.[1] County meetings were held in twenty-seven English and three Welsh shires, similar meetings took

[1] The inner history of this movement is unfolded in the *Political Papers* of the Rev. Christopher Wyvill. They were issued between 1794 and 1804 by this well-connected Yorkshire clergyman and landowner, from whose sagacity, public spirit, and energy the Parliamentary Reform agitation of 1779–82 derived much of its strength.

Introduction: Origins of "Radical Reform" 1768-1831

place in eleven English municipalities, and deputies from most of these areas were authorised to assemble in the capital for federated action.[1] More remarkable even than this was the growing acceptance of extreme notions of political egalitarianism by powerful sections of the Opposition Whigs who had yet no reason to suspect that egalitarian ideas might next invade the field of property rights. The Chartists of the nineteenth century were never tired of proving that all their six points of Ultra-Radical Reform had been elaborated by Opposition Whigs in 1780.

The Gordon mob-riots, the return of peace, the political mistakes of Fox, and the Court's alliance with Pitt the younger produced for a time a notable change in the political situation. There was virtually a disappearance of the pressure for what had already been called "radical reform" by Major Cartwright, that most persistent of its propagators, whose agitation, begun in 1776, was only to close with his death in 1824. Indeed, Pitt's own majority was suffered to defeat his very moderate Reform Bill of 1785 without any semblance of a public stir ensuing.

The outbreak of the French Revolution, however, revived the ardour of Reformers in England, and the very complete democracy soon being planned in the French Constitution was not of a nature to damp it. One specially significant feature of 1792 was in fact to be the appearance of Reforming Clubs in provincial and Scottish centres which had never yet known political activity. Another was to be the spirit with which social grades, incapable hitherto of any political expression save mob rioting, entered into plans for organised reforming effort. Burke's attack on what was being done in France had, it is plain, far less influence on artisans and small tradesmen than Tom Paine's *Rights of Man*.

Of the new political organisations the most epoch-making was certainly the London Corresponding Society wherein metropolitan artisans were gathered for a political part which was to outdo both that of the Foxite "Friends of the People" and that of the more middle-class "Society for Constitutional Information." The founder of the London Corresponding Society was the shoemaker, Thomas Hardy, and his aim was to unite the voteless working men of the metropolis in a suffrage agitation which was to be linked with similar agitations outside the capital. It is

[1] *Annual Register*, 1780, History, p. 87.

English Radicalism 1832-1852

interesting to observe that Hardy's original impulse came not, as might have been expected, from Paine, but from earlier Reform advocacy, English and Irish, of the American War period. In 1791 Hardy had been re-perusing some of the pamphleteering of Price, Jebb, and others which had been distributed gratis a decade before by the Society for Constitutional Information.[1]

Launched at a meeting of eight persons on January 25, 1792, the London Corresponding Society was soon in relations with similar societies at Sheffield and Manchester. In April, using the weekly pennies of an increasing membership, it published its first Universal Suffrage manifesto,[2] a document gratuitously distributed and voicing effectively the demand for a "fair, equal, and impartial representation of the people in Parliament." Adherents now began to come in very fast as more and more artisans were attracted by the Society's aims and its weekly meetings. Indeed, arrangements had soon to be made for assembling the members in local divisions with a delegate from each sitting in a central managing committee. By November the number of enrolments amounted according to Hardy's account to twenty thousand.[3] Rapidly as the society was growing, this number seems altogether too large and the careful Hardy for once to be in error.

Yet the publication and enormous sale of the Second Part of Paine's *Rights of Man* had undoubtedly had an astonishing effect throughout the spring and summer of 1792. There could certainly have been no better way of arousing artisan enthusiasm for a Universal Suffrage Republic than Paine's far-sighted fiscal proposals to benefit the labouring classes and to force on the division of great estates. Paine was driven abroad by a Government prosecution, but the effect of his work was seen in the bold tone taken in a congratulatory Address to the French National Convention which was adopted by the London Corresponding

---

[1] Add. MSS. 27814, f. 5. But Hardy's first political apprenticeship had, it seems, been served with the "Protestant Association" gathered round Lord George Gordon. At one time eighty-five "corresponding societies" were attempting co-operation on a plan doubtless suggested to them, as to the Irish Volunteers by the successful activities of the American "Committees of Correspondence" of the pre-rebellion stage.   [2] Add. MSS. 27811, f. 6; 27814, f. 14.

[3] Add. MSS. 27814, f. 26. The number of local divisions was just then being increased to twenty-four (*Ibid.*, f. 100), and according to the rules no division should have met more than forty-six strong without arranging to throw off a new division. In 1794, however, the Government was to allege that some divisions numbered hundreds.

Introduction: Origins of "Radical Reform" 1768–1831

Society on September 27th, and subsequently adhered to by four other societies.¹ In November another London Society ventured even further. The Society for Constitutional Information, revived in 1791 among active middle-class supporters of "radical reform" and now doing its best for the dissemination of Paine's views, sent two envoys, who were allowed to address the Convention on November 28th. Congratulating the French on their Republicanism, the envoys announced the formation of "innumerable societies" of British Reformers and predicted that "it would not be extraordinary, if in a much less space of time than can be imagined, the French should send Addresses of Congratulation to a National Convention of England."²

When Anglo-French war began in February 1793, British democrats held on their way though it became steadily more dangerous. Thus after the savage sentence of fourteen years' transportation had been inflicted on Muir at Edinburgh late in August 1793 and another of seven years on Palmer at Perth, the London Corresponding Society did not shrink from assembling a large general meeting in the open air³ for the purpose of choosing two delegates to be despatched to a general convention which the Scottish societies were assembling. These two delegates together with the Secretary of the Convention became additional victims of the Scottish judges when the "British Convention of the Delegates of the People associated to obtain Universal Suffrage and Annual Parliaments" was forcibly dispersed at its fifteenth sitting. They were sentenced to fourteen years' transportation.⁴

The brutality of these sentences failed to intimidate the democrats of England. With remarkable courage the London Corresponding Society held on its course. Before long it was approaching not only the Society for Constitutional Information, but also the Foxite Friends of the People in order to arrange the assembly of a "Convention of the Friends of Freedom, for the purpose of obtaining, in a legal and constitutional method, a full and effectual representation."⁵ The Friends of the People thought it wise to hold off, but the Constitutional Information Society, now much guided by Wilkes's old ally, the fearless Horne Tooke, was

---

¹ *A Collection of Addresses transmitted by certain English Clubs and Societies to the National Convention of France*, 1793 (2nd Edn.), pp. 15–18.
² Ibid., pp. 24–5.   ³ Add. MSS. 27814, ff. 56–7.   ⁴ Ibid.
⁵ Ibid., ff. 70–1; *Ann. Register*, 1794, History, p. 269.

apparently readier to undertake joint approaches to the provincial societies on the subject of a Convention. But no Convention was allowed to meet. On May 12th Hardy was arrested, later a number of other arrests followed including that of Horne Tooke, and in October nine prisoners were facing their trials for high treason. On a lesser charge it is very possible that well-to-do Middlesex jurors would have elected to follow those of Scotland and would have facilitated the Government's suppression of the democrats by convicting the prisoners.[1] But the result of Hardy's eight-day trial proved that the jurors were not inclined to condemn even a political shoemaker to the dreadful penalties of treason because of Crown scaremongering about pikes in Sheffield. After the explosion of joy excited by the verdict in Hardy's case, the acquittal of his fellow-prisoners was certain, though the Crown persisted with the treason charge against Horne Tooke and Thelwall, the pioneer of professional Radical "lecturing."[2]

For a time the triumphant issue of the State Trials gave the London Corresponding Society a great impetus. Its surviving papers for 1795[3] show a flourishing organisation arranged in seventy divisions[4] and capable of gathering so huge a public meeting prior to a critical reopening of Parliament that the numbers present were estimated at 150,000.[5] A furious mob demonstration against the King followed, however, and allowed the Ministry to enact legislation making the use of expressions adverse to the King or the Constitution heavily punishable and forbidding meetings of more than fifty persons. The Ministerial programme was only placed upon the Statute Book against a storm of public protest, to which the London Corresponding Society contributed two great open-air meetings and a petition purporting to be from "nearly 400,000 Britons" but actually bearing no more than 12,113 signatures.[6] Yet the Society was still

---

[1] W. Massey, *A History of England during the Reign of George the Third*, iii, 340-51, for a recital of cases tending to prove that Middlesex juries were readier to convict in political cases than juries in the City of London.

[2] H. Jephson, *The Platform*, i, 254-5. Thelwall's lectures were given twice a week, each being part of a course. His average audience in 1794 was 430, and in 1795 520, though admission to each cost 6d. The demand for political discussion by lecturers and debaters arose all the more easily in 1792 because of the absence of a "radical reform" Press.

[3] Add. MSS. 27808 and 27813. The Society published *Correspondence of the London Corresponding Society* at the end of the year containing communications from Bradford, Sheffield, Portsmouth, etc.

[4] *Ibid.*, f. 28.   [5] *Ibid.*, f. 39.   [6] H. Jephson, *The Platform*, i, 276.

Introduction: Origins of "Radical Reform" 1768-1831

intrepid enough to attempt another new departure in politics, the despatch of two Deputies to address provincial gatherings. The Deputies were arrested in Birmingham. Authority, indeed, was waiting its chance, and fear of its informers was doubtless one of the factors tending to drive out of the Society in despondency some of its steadiest elements, afraid of being compromised by the false and the headstrong. Thus in the summer of 1797 when funds were already low, the holding of another huge meeting like the monster assembly of 1795 was resolved upon in order to revive interest and support. The plain illegality of the project led, however, to a new batch of secessions by members[1] who at the same time protested their fidelity to the political principles of the Society.

The end came in April 1798 when the General Committee incautiously decided to advise the members to join the armed volunteer corps which were being formed to meet possible invaders. Bow Street officers immediately entered the room and arrested all present,[2] presumably because the decision of the Committee was regarded as an insidious preparation by potential revolutionaries to possess themselves of arms. Under Habeas Corpus Suspension some of the unfortunates were long imprisoned without being brought to trial. In the penal legislation of 1799, moreover, the Corresponding Society was specifically suppressed by name, and similar organisations for federating the activities of distinct associations were put under the ban of the law.[3]

In Francis Place the Corresponding Society left an heir fitted to win a Parliamentary position for Radical Reform as soon as the heavy years of work should have gone by which permitted him to win a competence as a Westminster tailor. In Burdett, a baronet whose wife's wealth had made possible the winning of a Middlesex seat in 1802 and the revival there of the tumultuary politics of the Wilkes era, Place found in 1807 a first Radical member for Westminster.[4] Ultimately he succeeded in adding in Hobhouse one who seemed at first likely to become an even more manageable second.[5]

Invaluable as the political command of the Westminster citadel

---

[1] Add. MSS. 27815, ff. 165-6.
[2] Add. MSS. 27808, ff. 88-90.
[3] 39 Geo. III, c. 79.
[4] Add. MSS. 27850; G. Wallas, *Life of Place*, chapter 2; M. W. Patterson, *Sir Francis Burdett and his Times*, I, 132-218.
[5] Add. MSS. 27837; Wallas, *op. cit.*, chapter 5.

English Radicalism 1832-1852

proved to the Radical Reform agitation between 1807 and 1832, its tangled history cannot here be followed. Nor can space be spared to record individual exertions on behalf of Radicalism as important as those of Cobbett, Hunt,[1] and Bentham. Suffice it to say that in Cobbett Radicalism won a journalist of unparalleled power, in Hunt a demagogue of matchless impudence and energy, and in Bentham a legal reputation greater than that of any other contemporary in the world. A few words, however, may be devoted to the second burst of working-class political initiative which in the distressful years after Waterloo studded the industrial areas with Hampden Clubs officered by men like William Benbow and Samuel Bamford.[2] Readers of Cobbett, followers of Hunt, and admirers of the aged but still active Cartwright, leaders of this type promoted the extensive meetings and petitionings of the winter of 1816-17. Afterwards near a score of them arrived in the capital to sit with the national and metropolitan leaders of Radicalism in a species of Convention which superintended the presentation of the petitions and drafted a Reform Bill. Ultimately these men arranged in 1819 the great meetings of the unenfranchised[3] which permitted the Tories to disgrace and weaken themselves by Peterloo.

Peterloo was followed by a general outburst of indignation all over the country[4] against the callous brutality which had been dealt out to a peaceful meeting. When the Eldons and the Sidmouths replied with the rigid repression of the Six Acts, a temper grew which permitted the Radicals of the capital to produce the men of Cato Street and those in Scotland the rebels of Bonnymuir.[5] Normally Cato Street and Bonnymuir might have brought powerful reinforcement to the unyielding High Toryism, which had so long defended a State full of abuses by police spies and yeomanry sabres. The temper of the increasingly numerous, increasingly independent, and increasingly wealthy body of the professional and commercial classes standing immediately below the ruling landed caste was now the decisive factor in political development, for without its support the Old Order could not stand for long. Antagonised though these middle classes might

---

[1] *Hunt's Memoirs*, 3 vols., 1820-22, tell a story less known than Cobbett's and Bentham's.
[2] Bamford's *Passages in the Life of a Radical*, i, chapters 2, 4.
[3] *Annual Register*, 1819, History, chapter 7.   [4] Ibid., History, pp. 112-13.
[5] Ibid., 1820, History, pp. 37-9.

Introduction: Origins of "Radical Reform" 1768-1831

be by Pension List, rotten borough and State Church abuses, Ultra-Radical insurrectionism frightened them and Ultra-Radical journalism made them uneasy. If Cobbett's *Political Register* and Wooler's *Black Dwarf*[1] were rarely to middle-class taste, Carlile's *Republican*[2] was even less so. It was a journal aiming openly at supporting the anti-Christian polemics of Paine's *Age of Reason*, polemics which thanks to Carlile's reprints were already exercising an increasing effect on the working classes.

In the summer of 1820, however, High Toryism was fated to be injured, seemingly beyond repair, by the well-nigh incredible incidents connected with George IV's attempt to win a divorce.[3] On the other hand, populace and middle classes were united in enthusiastic defence of an unfortunate Queen whose answers to a prodigious and long-continued stream of loyal addresses grew in Radical readiness to associate her cause with that of the nation's imperilled liberties.[4] The Liverpool Cabinet might well have given way under the strain if an alternative Government had been possible not committed by the participation of Lords Grey and Holland, the Foxite heirs, to the consideration of Catholic

[1] A second ably written weekly with considerable circulation among Ultra-Radical operatives. It lived from January 1817 to November 1824, and was first issued at 4d.

[2] The new name given by Carlile in August 1819 to *Sherwin's Weekly Political Register*, a 2d. Ultra-Radical paper first issued in April 1817. Carlile had been engaged on it for some time. It may be noted that during Carlile's long incarceration between 1819 and 1825 the *Republican* was continued despite the greatest difficulties.

[3] The position in Edinburgh is especially interesting, for after the Scottish Radical trials of 1793-4 all independent political life there had been crushed out of existence. "Nothing was viewed with such horror," writes Henry Cockburn in his *Memorials of his Time*, "as any political congregation not friendly to existing power. No one could have taken a part in the business without making up his mind to be a doomed man. No prudence could protect against the falsehood or inaccuracy of spies; and a first conviction of sedition by a judge-picked jury was followed by fourteen years' transportation." Yet in December 1820, after "the proceedings against the Queen had thrown the whole nation into a ferment," Edinburgh held a great meeting, the first for twenty-five years, "in direct and avowed opposition to the hereditary Toryism of government." The resultant petition asking for the dismissal of the Government was actually signed by 17,000 of Edinburgh's 20,000 male adults, while the Tory counter-petition only "got about 1,600 or 1,700 names." "The influence of all this," concludes Cockburn, "can scarcely be overstated. Old Edinburgh was no more."

[4] Cobbett's *Political Register*, xxxvii, July-December 1820, contains a veritable literature of Queen's Answers. The *Register* for November 25th particularly has some most Radical denunciation of Government corruption and tyranny, and even a plea for "timely reform" (p. 1336). E. Halévy, *A History of the English People*, 1815-1830, p. 100, n. 1, believes that Cobbett had himself been called in to compose the Queen's Answers.

English Radicalism 1832-1852

Emancipation, Dissenters' Relief and Parliamentary Reform. But the death of the Queen in August 1821 and the passing of the industrial areas in the meanwhile from "bad times" to good greatly eased the strain on Authority. The Prime Minister, too, proved sufficiently sensible of the need of winning middle-class confidence to resist the pressure of the "landed interest" for Corn legislation which would have provoked graver discontent than the Corn Law of 1815. Finally good fortune brought his Government the notable Budget surpluses of 1823, 1824, and 1825, and a combination of dexterity and chance served to associate his Cabinet with the talents of Canning, Huskisson, and Peel and to dissociate it from the unpopularity of Castlereagh, Sidmouth, and Vansittart.

Despite the apparent tranquillity of much of the British political scene for several prosperous manufacturing years after 1821,[1] the vast and virtually unrepresented forces[2] making for radical political changes could not for ever be averted from the so-called British Constitution by Canning's "liberal" foreign policy and the laudable activity of his colleagues at the Board of Trade and the Home Office. It is true that the serious financial crisis of 1825-6 was marked by no new mass outcry for Universal Suffrage. But millions of Catholic Irish, organised by Daniel O'Connell, were demanding Emancipation with a new insistence, and during the Session of 1826 House of Commons Whigs were to return anew to the subject of Parliamentary Reform.

A temporary disturbance of Parliamentary alignments was caused by the Canning Premiership of 1827, but soon afterwards the Whigs were fated to resume their part of moderate opposition. Supported by popular forces from without, they promoted the liberation of Dissenters from the Uniformity and Corporation Acts, agitated the enfranchisement of Birmingham, Leeds, and Manchester, and helped the Wellington Government to carry Catholic Emancipation against its own Ultras.[3] The surprising sequel is well known. In bitter anger at a Ministerial "betrayal" which would have been impossible if there had been the anti-

---

[1] The *Black Dwarf* ceased publication at the end of 1824 with a sorrowful complaint of the indifference of the public towards Parliamentary Reform (Introduction, xii).

[2] Radical representation did not really extend beyond the Westminster members and occasional allies from similar wide-enfranchised "open" boroughs.

[3] S. Walpole, *Life of Lord John Russell*, i, 136-7.

Introduction: Origins of "Radical Reform" 1768-1831

Catholic prejudices of popular majorities to appeal to, the Ultra-Tory Marquis of Blandford set himself to invent a Radical Reform usable by the High Tories to secure Wellington's ejection. In the Session of 1830 neither the advent of Irish Radicalism with O'Connell's advocacy of Universal Suffrage, Triennial Parliaments, and Vote by Ballot, nor the Whigs' persistence with much milder proposals was as calculated to arouse public interest as Blandford's sweeping Reform suggestions. They were as portentous as the increasing activities of the Birmingham Political Union wherein the middle and working classes of that memberless town had bound themselves for the advancement for Radical Reform.[1]

The death of George IV on June 26, 1830, followed as it had speedily to be by a General Election, permitted Radicalism to progress another stage. The return of Henry Brougham for Yorkshire and that of Joseph Hume for Middlesex were only the two most remarkable of the "open" elections which revealed the advance that was being made in "public opinion" by Radical causes.[2] Moreover, stirring events on the Continent, beginning with the overthrow of the reactionary Charles X in Paris,[3] kept newspaper readers excited and unwilling to accept stationary policies in England. An especially important development was that among the working men of the metropolis. There was a school of London artisans, deeply read in Paine and Cobbett, trained to discussion in Mutual Improvement Societies and with revolutionary notions on the economic malorganisation of Society,[4] derived from Owen and confirmed by Hodgskin's lectures at the London Mechanics' Institution. Deeply stirred by the part the Paris workmen had taken in the overthrow of Charles X, these potential revivers of the cherished traditions of the London Corresponding Society were further stimulated by two new phenomena. At the Blackfriars Rotunda Carlile launched a series of Ultra-Radical meetings and debates[5] which, continued in one

---

[1] C. M. Wakefield, *Life of Thomas Attwood*.
[2] Cf. Harriet Martineau, *History of the Thirty Years' Peace*, ed. 1877, ii, 385-6.
[3] Cf. *Courts and Cabinets of William IV and Victoria* by the Duke of Buckingham and Chandos, i, 25, 42, 46, 100-1, for the effect of this in England.
[4] Cf. *Life and Struggles of William Lovett*, chapters 2 and 3.
[5] *Dictionary of National Biography* under Richard Carlile. Of the lectures and debates the *Quarterly Review* wrote (January 1831, p. 300): "Blasphemy was soon found to be a more attractive commodity than treason, as well as an approved preparation for it.... The reader would be not more greatly astonished than shocked were we to relate what passes at these meetings; the revolting

form or another for years, provided operative leaders with meeting-places and policies. In the *Penny Papers for the People*, again, commenced by Henry Hetherington on October 1st, was laid the foundation of a new and intensely class-conscious Ultra-Radical Press.

What gave these developments an especial importance was the Parliamentary situation which arose during the ensuing winter. When the Wellington Government faced Parliament again in November it was not necessarily doomed because there had been a number of Ultra-Whig and Radical successes in "open" boroughs and large counties.[1] The general composition of the House of Commons had not been vitally altered, there was no obvious alternative Government and a little "moving with the times" in the direction of Parliamentary Reform would probably have saved it. Had Wellington, indeed, only made a reasonably politic declaration on November 3rd instead of his ludicrously unguarded refusal to consider the British Constitution as anything but perfect, events were moving to his rescue. There was already grave anxiety in the North over a great Trades Combination fostered by the cotton spinners,[2] in the South the "Last Labourers' Revolt" was about to break out and everywhere from among the "respectable classes" support for Authority would have been forthcoming.

As things were, the somewhat ignominious fall of the Wellington Government certainly played its part in releasing the general unrest among the "lower orders" which was to be such a marked feature of British politics for years to come. Without it, the Government Reform Bills of the Grey Ministry might not have been so far-reaching[3] nor the General Election of the spring of 1831 have permitted that astonishing breakdown of the "nomination" and "influence" system of returning members which allowed several scores more of Whigs and another contingent of

ribaldry, the nefandous impiety, the daring and rabid blasphemies.... Large as the theatre is, it is crowded."

[1] Cf. the contemporary pamphlet *Parties and Factions in England at the Accession of William IV* and the editorials of *The Times* for August 1830.
[2] C. L. Sanders, *Melbourne Papers*, pp. 120–31.
[3] 645 Reform petitions, it should be remembered, reached Parliament between November 5, 1830, and March 4, 1831. Of these, 280 specifically demanded Vote by Ballot, and over 150 "short Parliaments." The Cabinet majority, though it refused to entertain such Ultra demands, probably went considerably further in pocket borough suppression than might have been the case if there had been no pressure of this kind.

Introduction: Origins of "Radical Reform" 1768–1831

Radicals into the Commons. In that House at least the Reform Bills were safe and consideration could accordingly be given to the problem of forcing them through the Lords.

In their early enthusiasm for the Ministerial proposals the great majority of operatives had followed the lead of middle-class friends of "Radical Reform." But gradually operatives' views changed as the very scanty measure of enfranchisement offered them was fully grasped. But despite the formidable shape taken on by the Ultra-Radical Press and the National Union of the Working Classes before the Reform struggle was over, no changes in the Ultra-Radical direction were secured. A Parliamentary representation virtually confined to Henry Hunt[1] needed less conciliation than the embattled hosts of Tories in both Houses. A party, moreover, which added to Paine's Anti-Christianity and Spence's abhorrence of the private appropriation of land, the more modern dislike of the industrial capitalist and the "£10 shopocrat" was devoid of allies. Men as ready as Place and James Mill to engineer Radical crusades against the surviving ecclesiastical and territorial idols of past ages were aghast at the hatred equally meted out by working-class Universal Suffragists to the industrial and commercial institutions of their own day.[2] Their attitude makes clear the main basis of the distinction made in the parlance of the day between Radicalism and Ultra-Radicalism.

Indeed, when exact definitions of Radicalism are essayed appropriate to the political situation arrived at in 1831, the degree and nature of the anti-property animus of some of Radicalism's strongest divisions make conspicuous difficulties. When in 1780 Cartwright treated of "radical reform" in his best pamphlet, *The People's Barrier against Undue Influence*, and demanded Universal Suffrage and Annual Parliaments on mixed grounds of natural and constitutional right, he was joining in an agitation motivated on the economic side by mere primitive dislike of rising taxation. If Cartwright's Radicalism remained economically undeveloped to the end,[3] Paine's was very different. Both in the *Rights of Man* of 1792 and the *Agrarian Justice* of 1796 Paine allied "radical reform" with schemes of property-taxation on behalf of the propertyless. In the *Agrarian Justice*, for example, property was to pay a

[1] Elected M.P. for Preston late in 1830.
[2] G. Wallas, *Life of Place*, pp. 273–4.
[3] As evidenced by the long letters sent by him to the *Black Dwarf* in the years preceding his death in 1824. They are almost purely political.

10 per cent inheritance tax[1] to finance a scheme of benefits to the poor, who were thus to be compensated by landowners for the extinction of their natural rights in the soil and by the owners of personal property for the inadequate remuneration of labour which had made accumulation possible.

Thomas Spence's crude scheme of expropriating landowners and substituting parish ownership and letting deserves only to be mentioned as illustrating the particular Ultra-Radical animus against the private appropriation of land especially in the form of large estates.[2] That animus was certainly not less in 1831 than it had been in 1817 when the Spenceans had been deemed sufficiently dangerous to have their organisation suppressed by law. William Godwin's attack on all private property, again, though it made a great noise after its first appearance in 1793, was altogether too anarchical to form the basis of any large political school, however extreme.[3] Very different was the Communism of Robert Owen which certainly had the widest of Ultra-Radical followings in 1831. Beginning in 1817 with a scheme for settling some of the numerous unemployed of the time in Villages of Unity and Co-operation, Owen's theories had rapidly risen to embrace the Communistic reconstruction of the whole of Society on a basis wherein the elimination of private property figured largely.

Next to the landed estates the "Funds" made the most conspicuous species of private property open to Ultra-Radical attack. Right up to 1832 and beyond, Cobbett conducted an untiring agitation against the huge annual levy made on the national income by the "Funds," swollen as they were to dangerous heights by twenty years of war-finance and currency depreciation between 1793 and 1815. As the fundholder's claims increased in "real" weight with the return to gold in 1819, Cobbett's army of "equitable adjustment" was a political factor to be reckoned with in 1831. Moreover, there were important auxiliaries like Attwood,[4] founder of the Birmingham Political Union, and there was even a

---

[1] As reprinted in *Pioneers of Land Reform* (Bohn's Popular Library), p. 204. Paine's Preface gives the winter of 1795-6 as the period of composition, and an early copy shows J. Ashley (of the Corresponding Society) as publisher.

[2] For the Spenceans, see Place's collection of their documents in Add. MSS. 27808, ff. 255 sqq.

[3] Cf. *Inquiry into Political Justice*, Book VIII, of Property.

[4] Who had, however, his paper money differences with Cobbett. See the 1832 pamphlet, *Report of the Discussion at Birmingham between Attwood, C. Jones, and Cobbett*.

Introduction: Origins of "Radical Reform" 1768–1831

school of the landed, attracted by the parallelism which Cobbett and Attwood were prepared to draw between the fundholder, who had lent depreciated pounds to the State and took gold reckoning for interest, and the mortgage-holder who levied similarly usurious toll on private estates and ruined the countryside. Cobbett, it should be remembered, had no Spencean quarrel with private landed property as such, holding, indeed, that it was socially mortgaged with becoming heaviness by the Poor Laws and that even Corn Law Repeal should not be considered apart from his "equitable adjustment." That is why during the remarkable "distress" agitation of 1822–3 by the "agricultural interest" Cobbett and Hunt were repeatedly able to carry "county meetings" for astonishingly Jacobinic programmes.[1] That is why the numerous "distress" Petitions of 1830 still bore frequent marks of Debt and Currency studies in the *Political Register*.[2]

If the "Funds" represented a species of private property under conspicuously hot attack in 1831 from very varied angles, industrial capital was a kind of property the attack on which was confined to operative Ultra-Radicals. Holding that industrial profits represented no less than Fund-interest and rent an unjustifiable toll on the actually productive classes, they demanded Universal Suffrage principally with a view to obtaining legislative domination over the economic field. The actual balance of political forces prevented Universal Suffrage from obtaining any serious consideration in 1831. If it had been under such consideration middle-class Radicals as thorough-going as Mill and Place would have seen ample reason for caution in the views expressed by the National Union of the Working Classes as to the working-man's right to the "whole produce of labour."[3] In the field of property rights, at least, Mill had gone no further than to maintain against McCulloch the expediency of appropriating for the community what later ages came to call the "unearned increment of land

[1] Cf. the Norfolk County meeting of January 3, 1823, where Cobbett's Parliamentary Reform Petition was adopted with a view to obtaining a Parliament which should undertake: an appropriation of a part of the public property, commonly called Church property, and also the sale of Crown lands to the liquidation of the Debt; a reduction of the standing army, and a total abolition of all sinecures, pensions, grants, and emoluments, not merited by public services; an equitable adjustment with regard to the public debt, and also with regard to all debts and contracts between man and man, etc. (H. Jephson, *The Platform*, i, 576).

[2] *England in 1830* is the title of a useful collection of the "distress" petitions of the year.   [3] G. Wallas, *Life of Place*, p. 274 n.

English Radicalism 1832-1852

values."[1] Even landed property, in his view, largely represented capital invested in land improvement, and for the workman to quarrel with this or other forms of capital which permitted his being set to work was fatal. The labourer's road to well-being lay along the path of birth-limitation. When his numbers began decreasing relatively to the accumulation of capital, he would command the economic situation more and more.[2]

[1] James Mill, *Elements of Political Economy*, ed. 1826, pp. 251-5.
[2] *Ibid.*, pp. 65-7.

PART ONE

CHAPTER I

RADICALS AND THE REFORM BILL, 1831-2

2nd October 1831.
. . . on the 8th (September) saw one of the great Glasgow processions. . . . All the villages within many miles were in motion early in the morning, all pouring with devices and music into the Green. . . . I don't believe that there were, including spectators, fewer than 100,000 persons on that field. . . . The procession took above two hours to pass, walking four abreast. Those engaged were about 12,000. They were divided into crafts, parishes, towns, mills, or otherwise, variously and irregularly, each portion bearing its emblems and music. The carters to the number of nearly 500 went first, mounted, their steeds decorated with ribbons. . . . The banners were mostly of silk, and every trade carried specimens of its art, many of which were singularly beautiful. . . . Nothing surprised me so much as the music. . . . There could not be under fifty really good bands. . . ."
"Journal of H. Cockburn."

"I am convinced that we are indebted for the preservation of tranquillity solely to the organisation of the people in political unions. All the other unions look to the Birmingham one, and that looks to its half-dozen leaders, who consequently act under the most intense consciousness of moral responsibility, and are very careful neither to do nor say anything without the most careful deliberation. I conversed the other day with a Warwickshire magistrate who told me that the meeting of 150,000 men a few days previous would have done any thing without exception which their leaders might have proposed. . . . The agricultural people are as determined as the manufacturers. The West is as exalté as the North. . . ."
"Letters of J. S. Mill," *i, 7, October 20-22, 1831.*

"The Reformers (Place, etc.) talked to by me—felt assured of success. The run upon the banks and the barricading of the populous towns would have brought matters to a crisis and a week they—the Reformers—thought would have finished the business. They meant so to agitate here that no soldiers could have been spared from London and the army is too small elsewhere to have put down the rebels. In Scotland I think the most effectual blow would have been struck. . . ."
YOUNG, *confidential agent to the Home Secretary, on the crisis of May 1832 in* MISS J. BUCKLEY'S "Joseph Parkes of Birmingham," *pp. 195-6.*

IN view of the deep popular passions which had been roused, many acute observers of the political situation in the closing months of 1831 considered that Reform could not stop short at the Parliamentary Reform Bill which was being pressed against the Peers' hostility. The compelling forces in the nation were for the time indubitably the fast-spreading Political Unions,[1] warmly befriended by the bulk of the newspapers,[2] and the new working-class Press whose cheap sheets, successfully distributed in tens of thousands in defiance of the Stamp Law, kept the operative world in the most insurrectionary of tempers.

Such figures as those of Thomas Attwood, the remarkable banker-demagogue who had founded the now mighty Birmingham Political Union,[3] and of Francis Place, manœuvre master of well-entrenched Westminster Radicalism and organiser of a new National Political Union,[4] represented the most influential of the elements directing the Political Unions. A mere cautious redistribution of Parliamentary seats or hesitant extension of the franchise seemed hardly likely to be the ultimate goal towards which they were working.

Still less likely was this to be the case with such extremer working-class leaders as Richard Carlile,[5] the tried hero of a six years Press imprisonment in Tory days and now imprisoned once more by Whig hands, or Henry Hetherington,[6] proprietor of the *Poor Man's Guardian*, the most widely circulated working-class newspaper of the day. The objects to which this school of Ultra-Radical leaders was trying to conduct the nation may, indeed, be found frankly set out in the announcement heralding the appearance in March 1831 of a new Hetherington paper, the *Republican*, at ½d. per copy instead of the 1d. charged for the *Poor Man's Guardian*. The list runs as follows:

Extirpation of the Fiend Aristocracy; Establishment of a Republic, viz. Democracy by Representatives elected by Universal Suffrage; Extinction of hereditary offices, titles, and distinctions; Abolition of the

---

[1] J. R. M. Butler, *Great Reform Bill*, pp. 311–12.
[2] Cf. *The Times*, November 1st; *Morning Chronicle*, November 19th.
[3] J. Buckley, *Joseph Parkes of Birmingham*, pp. 85–6.
[4] For Home Office disquiet even before it was set up, see *Melbourne Papers*, p. 138. [5] B. 1790, d. 1843. G. J. Holyoake's *Life*, p. 15.
[6] B 1792, d. 1849. See the *Life and Character* issued by G. J. Holyoake in 1849.

Radicals and the Reform Bill 1831–1832

unnatural and unjust law of primogeniture; Equal distribution of property among all the children; Cheap and rapid administration of justice; Abolition of the Game Laws; Repeal of the diabolical imposts on Newspapers, Almanacs, and other channels of knowledge; Emancipation of our fellow-citizens, the Jews; Introduction of Poor Laws into Ireland; Abolition of the Punishment of Death for offences against Property; Appropriation of the Revenues of the "Fathers in God," the Bishops, towards maintenance of the Poor; Abolition of Tithes; Payment of every Priest or Minister by his Sect; The "National Debt" not the debt of the Nation; Discharge of the Machinery of Despotism, the Soldiers; Establishment of a National Guard.[1]

All this, however, was merely the doctrine of Paine or its elaboration, and, in point of fact, would in milder language have won the assent of the Political Union Schools of Parkes and Place as a list of ultimate objectives. But operative Ultra-Radicals had also adopted revolutionary anti-capitalist views from Godwin, the Owenites, and Hodgskin's remarkable *Labour Defended against the Claims of Capital*, and these served to open the widest of gulfs between their National Union of the Working Classes[2] and the Political Unions, between their *Poor Man's Guardian* and the middle-class Radicals' *Morning Chronicle*.[3] Operative Ultra-Radicals of the class-conscious school wanted Universal Suffrage at once so that a working-class majority might be obtained for the widest alterations in the social and economic fabric of society. But Political Union Radicals, though admitting Universal Suffrage as one of their ultimate objectives, accepted the Whig Reform Bill as a stage in its attainment. They were, perhaps, secretly thankful that there promised to be ample time in the future for preparatory Diffusion of Useful Knowledge effort and other types of educational endeavour[4] before working-class majorities were enfranchised.

There were other Radicalisms also pressing themselves on the public attention. No one had a greater following in the English villages than William Cobbett. His *Political Register* had been

---

[1] *Poor Man's Guardian*, March 8, 1831.
[2] Which, thanks to men like Hetherington, Lovett, Watson, and Cleave, grew to importance with surprising rapidity after its foundation in the spring of 1831. Add. MSS. 27791, ff. 243 sqq., and *Life and Struggles of William Lovett*.
[3] A powerful daily, written in the "philosophic Radical" tone of the "liberal" members of the professional classes.
[4] The Mechanics' Institutes, grown numerous since Birkbeck's London foundation of 1823, the growingly active Society for the Diffusion of Useful Knowledge, and the increasing school provision for children were encouraging phenomena.

English Radicalism 1832-1852

thundering near thirty years, and to such purpose that in July 1831 he was facing his trial for the part the *Register* was deemed to have played in provoking and maintaining that extraordinary revolt of half-starved labourers which had startled Southern England at the end of 1830. The trial had given Cobbett a great opportunity of denouncing a Whig Government responsible, he claimed, for more political prosecutions in seven months than the Tories had undertaken in seven years.[1] His triumphant acquittal left him free to continue his furious and widely relished lashings of sinecurism and jobbery, fundholders and political economists, the Wen and the Rev. Mr. Malthus.

Then there was what might be called a Factory Radicalism. On the one hand the cotton districts had produced under the able leadership of John Doherty a National Spinners' Union, whose formation had promoted the wide-spread wage-combativeness of 1830 and provided the basis for the United Trades General Union, so disquieting to the Home Office of 1830-1.[2] The Yorkshire woollen districts, on the other hand, were in the autumn of 1831 organising that Factory Ten Hour Day movement, which led on through the Factory Select Committee of 1832 and the Royal Commission of the following year to the 1833 Factory Act. It was a peculiarity of the Ten Hour movement, that though manned by plebeian Radicals as politically agitated as the rest of the country, it was led by religious philanthropists from the opposite political camp. But even a Sadler, for all his devotion to factory children, was not prepared to carry his High Tory defiance of "Malthusian Political Economy" to the legislative limitation of adult hours of factory labour, the ulterior aim, of course, of the most Radical of the operatives.

The factory districts, too, were the strongest home of a commercial Radicalism whose central principle was hostility to the corn laws. Divided on so much else, masters and men agreed on the fundamental inequity of the corn legislation which kept bread dear so that rents might be high for the landlord class that dominated Whig and Tory party alike. There was similar agreement on the unfairness of the "provision laws" by which the import of other staple foods than bread was restricted or prohibited, again, it was held, in the interests of landlords. Election proceedings in

[1] *Annual Register*, Chronicle under July 7th; "A full and accurate report of the Trial of W. Cobbett," pp. 9-10.   [2] *Melbourne Papers*, pp. 120-32.

Radicals and the Reform Bill 1831–1832

1832, moreover, were to reveal working-men's discontent with the heavy burden imposed on them in protecting the "colonial interest" in sugar and coffee and granting the East India Company a monopoly in the import of tea. Nor was it merely the inequitably high price-level of leading articles of consumption that was complained of. The restriction of export openings involved in a system which impeded so seriously returns by food importation was already making in the factory districts the readiest pupils of the Free Trade propaganda of "Philosóphic Radicalism."[1]

Less spectacular but more persistent, less impassioned but more adjusted to penetrate Government, less popular but vastly more elaborated intellectually than any other Radicalism, "Philosophic Radicalism" was the fruit of the marriage of two rare minds, those of Jeremy Bentham and James Mill.[2] From the time of James Mill's alliance with the already world-famous legal thinker, a campaign must inevitably have been shaping itself to turn upon all the oppressive, irrational, and selfishly maintained archaisms of English society a stream of the same type of deadly ammunition which had already made Bentham the most formidable foe of Eldonian Law. After Mill had completed the great *History of British India*, destined soon to take him and his more famous son after him into controlling places at East India House, a steady flow of Benthamic criticism of existing stupidities in society began. It ranged from the *Church of Englandism and its Catechism Examined* of 1818 to that famous exposure of clap-trap in politics, the *Book of Fallacies* of 1824, wherein every rhetorical and emotional trick of the anti-reformers was ruthlessly exposed and publicly dissected.[3] It is worth noting that Bentham was enlisting a new generation of disciples to help in the work. The eye which in the past had chosen a Dumont, a Romilly, and a James Mill had now lighted on Place, Grote, Bowring, and John Stuart Mill.

Bentham and James Mill in their constructive as in their destructive work had a noble idea before them, to secure the greatest happiness to the greatest number. Some of Mill's most influential work went into a series of articles for the Supplement to the *Encyclopaedia Britannica* in which he dealt with Government,

---

[1] A. Prentice's *History of the Anti-Corn Law League*, chapter 1.
[2] J. S. Mill's *Autobiography*, chapters 2, 3, and 4.
[3] Sydney Smith gave the readers of the *Edinburgh Review* an admirable condensation, reproduced in *Essays Social and Political, 1802–25*, by Sydney Smith, pp. 30 sqq.

English Radicalism 1832–1852

Education, Jurisprudence, Liberty of the Press, and other public topics on very Radical lines, the Government article, for example, advocating universal suffrage on the ground that to leave a man without a vote was to leave him liable to oppression.[1] Another important piece of work by Mill was the *Elements of Political Economy*, in which the labourer was assured a brighter future if he adopted birth-limitation, the State was invited to annex the unearned increment of land values, and the "middling classes" were treated as the highest and most desirable product of civilisation. Mill's trenchant thinking and writing also served "Philosophic Radicalism" in the *Westminster Review*, whose successful launching, indeed, in 1824 as a Radical organ of equal pretensions with the Whig *Edinburgh* and the Tory *Quarterly* was largely due to his biting examination of the *Edinburgh's* political record.[2]

Bentham, meanwhile, though farsightedly financing the *Westminster Review*, urging on Brougham to Law Reform and encouraging Poulett Thomson into Parliament as a Free Trade advocate, was giving the last years of his old age to a great project of his own. He was working at a massive *Constitutional Code for the use of all Nations and all Governments professing Liberal Opinions* and enlisting minds as pregnant of the future as Edwin Chadwick's and Southwood Smith's to help in its prophetic elaboration of the political and administrative equipment which would be needed by the coming completely democratised State of free peoples. In praising Bentham's foresight it is usual to concentrate on his proposals to set up Ministries of Interior Communications, Indigence Relief, Education and Health, to recruit the Civil Service by examination, and to give Central Government departments "inspective, statistic, requisitive, officially informative, information-elicitative and melioration-suggestive functions" in regard to local administration.[3] But there was much else of the highest importance in a work of 1830 which has been ever since a quarry for Constituent Assemblies and Commissions of Inquiry into the organisation of Local Government and Courts of Law.

---

[1] The article, when reprinted, was hotly attacked largely on this very ground, in the *Edinburgh Review*, March, June, and October 1829.
[2] J. S. Mill's *Autobiography*, ed. 1908, pp. 53–5.
[3] A large part of the *Constitutional Code* was published in 1830 under the title of *Official Aptitude Maximised, Expense Minimised*. See this book, chapter ix, for the inspective, etc., functions.

Radicals and the Reform Bill 1831-1832

Busy and aged as Bentham was in 1830, he could not forbear from venturing right into the forefront of the democratic battle when the French Revolution of 1830 provided him with the opportunity. As an honorary citizen of the French nation since 1792 he addressed a remarkable letter to his fellow-citizens of France avowing the wisdom of abolishing the Second Chamber and the Monarchy.[1] It was the completion of an Ultra-Radical declaration of faith which he had begun with his "Radical Reform Bill" of 1819.

These, then, were the Radicalisms fermenting in the country when the Lords on October 8, 1831, rejected the Reform Bill by a majority which included twenty-one bishops, against whom the full force of public fury was turned with special venom.[2] There followed the Parliamentary exchanges to be expected. On the 10th the Commons replied to the Peers with a strong vote of confidence in the Grey Ministry which encouraged an already nervous monarch to continue his support despite great misgivings in his immediate entourage. Next day there were heated scenes in the Lords, called out by the dangerous mobbing which anti-Reform Peers were already suffering. Then on the 12th indignant Tory Commoners were discussing the huge metropolitan Reform procession held earlier that day[3] and the strong letters of thanks addressed by two Ministers to a previous and even larger demonstration in Birmingham.[4] That same night Place made part of a deputation which went to the Prime Minister's house and tried to force an assurance that Parliament would resume Reform proceedings speedily and conduct them to a finish. Grey gave them an unbending reception, but aroused such popular suspicions that he was seeking a long Parliamentary adjournment in order to come to terms with the Tories[5] that he quickly took another tone. Before Parliament suffered prorogation on October 20th, both Grey and Brougham had made some disarming assurances.[6]

Out of doors, meanwhile, Political Unions were forming even in cathedral towns and villages, and there was a serious danger of

---

[1] In pamphlet form as *Letter to the French Nation on a House of Peers.*
[2] Add. MSS. 27790, f. 9; *Morning Chronicle*, October 19th.
[3] A very remarkable affair whose success impressed Place so much that he obtained special details of its organisation for his projected *History*, Add. MSS. 27790.   [4] Add. MSS. 27790, f. 81.
[5] W. N. Molesworth's *History of the Reform Bill of 1832*, pp. 277-8.
[6] *Ibid.*, pp. 278-9.

mob disorders spreading widely. Bad trouble had commenced at Derby as soon as the news of the Reform Bill's rejection arrived.[1] Worse followed at Nottingham, where the Castle, owned by the notoriously anti-Reforming Duke of Newcastle, was fired and similar violence undertaken in the neighbourhood. Most critical of all was the situation which developed at Bristol at the end of the month. There the gaols were forced open, the town hall fired, and the bishop's palace burnt to the ground.[2]

What such an acute and instructed observer as John Stuart Mill thought of the political situation even before the bloody Bristol affrays should here be quoted. In a letter dated October 20th to 22nd he wrote as follows:

> You may consider the fate of the Church as sealed. Only two bishops voted for the Bill, about five more stayed away, the rest voted against it. The hierarchy being thus, as a body, hostile to it while the temporal Peers were almost equally divided, the first brunt of public indignation has fallen upon the Prelacy. Every voice is raised against allowing them to continue in the House of Lords, and if I do not express my conviction of their being excluded from it before this day five years, it is only because I doubt whether the House itself will last so long. I cannot say I regret either the approaching downfall of the Peers or that of the Church. . . .
>
> If the ministers flinch or the Peers remain obstinate, I am firmly convinced that in six months a national convention chosen by universal suffrage will be sitting in London.[3]

Ultra-Radicals were, indeed, waiting for a fortunate chance which might open them a road to effecting revolutionary changes. On October 1st the *Poor Man's Guardian* hoped somewhat naïvely that on the approaching rejection of the Reform Bill the Whigs would "promote a lawful rebellion in which we shall stand a chance of demanding our own terms." On October 29th the *Prompter's* hopes took a somewhat different turn: "Lord Grey will make a few more despicable shuffles and contradictions, and then be kicked out of office, amidst the hootings of every man of every party in England. The nation will then cry: 'No more Whigs—no more middlemen—no more constitutional reformers. Let us have a fair battle with the Tories.'" Nor, in point of fact, did fighting seem very far off for a few agitated weeks while harassed Tories made arrangements for defending their house-

---
[1] Rev. T. Mozley, *Reminiscences*, i. 252–64.
[2] W. N. Molesworth, *op. cit.*, pp. 283–98.
[3] J. S. Mill, *Letters*, i, 4, 7.

Radicals and the Reform Bill 1831–1832

holds by force,[1] the middle-class Press agitated the question of arming the Political Unions as a National Guard against aristocracy above and rabble below[2] and Ultra-Radicals brought their talk of a "Popular Guard" somewhat nearer by organising great demonstrations in the metropolis and elsewhere for November 7th.[3] Ultra-Radicals wanted not the Reform Bill, which enfranchised the whole of the middle class and only a very small proportion of the "productive" classes, but Universal Suffrage and the Ballot to make it freely usable.

Yet the very confusion and alarm of October and November 1831 probably did a great deal to smooth the eventual path of the Reform Bill. On the one hand it seems certain that those Cabinet forces which would have been only too glad to surrender essential portions of the Bill on the excuse of facilitating the passage of the rest through the Lords were kept from gaining predominance in the Government.[4] On the other hand Whig Ministers could in such circumstances act unitedly in making a vigorous display against "anarchy." First, despite their protests the leaders of the National Union of the Working Classes were compelled to cancel their great demonstration of November 7th by Home Office preparations with police and military to treat it as seditious if not treasonable.[5] Later followed the proclamation of November 21st against "political unions composed of separate bodies with various divisions and subdivisions under leaders with a graduation of ranks and authority." It proved an effective deterrent to any renewal of such attempts as had been made at Birmingham to subdivide the Unions for drilling[6] and incidentally conveyed an official hostility to all Unions which the timid found disconcerting. Indeed, but for Place's prompt posting of bills announcing that the proclamation did not apply to the National Political Union "nor to the great majority of the Unions now in existence"[7] its effects on middle-class Radicalism might have been serious. Finally, Ministers hurried forward the organisation of Special Commissions to try the rioters of Derby, Nottingham, and Bristol

---

[1] *Croker Memoirs*, ii, 138, for Peel's case and his views of the unwisdom of some Tory plans of going farther and forming armed Associations.
[2] Cf. *The Times* and *Morning Chronicle*, October 27th.
[3] *Poor Man's Guardian*, October 29th, pp. 139–41.
[4] *Melbourne Papers*, p. 140.
[5] J. R. M. Butler, *Passing of the Great Reform Bill*, p. 317.
[6] *Correspondence of Earl Grey with King William IV and Sir H. Taylor*, i, 413 sqq.; Add. MSS. 27790, f. 242.   [7] Add. MSS. 27790, f. 242.

in a manner calculated to intimidate those prepared for further disorders.

By means of this kind it was that the King was reassured as to the ability of the Ministry and the machinery of State to ride the storm and persuaded not to press his dislike of such speechmaking Army Radicals as Colonel Napier to the point of dismissal.[1] Meantime he was further soothed by the knowledge that ministerial representatives were entering hopefully into private conversations designed to forward agreement with such moderate Tory Peers as were sobered by the popular determination to have Reform.[2] When on December 12th the Ministry again brought the subject of Parliamentary Reform before the Commons these conversations appeared not to have been without effect. On the one hand the Government had introduced some conciliatory changes into their measure, and on the other the group of Tory "Waverers" announced their readiness to accept the principle of Reform if not the detailed applications.

Yet the bulk of the Tory majority in the Lords continued hostile, and even the Waverers were only prepared to vote for a greatly restricted Bill. So soon as the measure, therefore, should have left the Commons another Parliamentary crisis was to be expected in the Lords, and perhaps even more dangerous popular demonstrations in the country than had occurred in the previous October. In these circumstances the close of the year 1831 found Lords Brougham and Durham pressing the Prime Minister, as Sir James Graham had already done some time before, to face the King with the necessity of creating Peers to overcome Tory resistance.[3] It is significant that all these three members of the Cabinet had a Radical past and that events were moving sufficiently in their direction to induce the Cabinet majority of January 2nd to commission the Premier to open the matter with the King. Reluctantly the monarch gave a very qualified promise that if it should prove necessary sufficient Peers would be created to carry the Bill.[4] What the "movement men" in the Cabinet would have liked—the instant creation of a batch of Peers to intimidate Tory

[1] *Correspondence of Earl Grey*, i, 368–70. The management of the King was vital at this stage, for the Tories, elated with a couple of by-election successes, were ready for a "call" to the Palace and a new General Election under their own auspices.
[2] *Ibid.*, 464–79, for the minutes of one of Grey's conversations.
[3] J. R. M. Butler, *op. cit.*, pp. 328–30.
[4] *Correspondence of Earl Grey*, ii, 68 sqq.

Radicals and the Reform Bill 1831–1832

Lords in advance of discussion in their House—was beyond constitutional reach. The Cabinet would not have united to press it upon the unwilling King, and even if it had, the King would probably have allowed Ministers to resign rather than give way. He was not being left unaware by Tory circles that they were ready to form a Government and had what they held to be the best of prospects of reimposing nomination and influence on the rebel constituencies of 1831.[1]

The Cabinet waited, therefore, until the prolonged proceedings in the Commons should have ended and the Reform Bill should approach its critical stages in the Lords. In the interval the leaders of the Political Unions gave very little trouble partly, perhaps, because of the arrival of cholera and partly the enthusiasm of their followers was not to be kept at fever-heat for months at a time. Even the Birmingham Political Union, for example, sank surprisingly low pending the arrival of the next crisis.[2] The working-class Ultra-Radicals proved more active. In December their extremists had assembled a "National Convention"[3] which drew up a Radical Reform Bill of its own, and in January their Manchester Political Union was voicing the general indignation of the populace at the severe sentences passed by the Special Commissions on the October rioters. The cries of "Murder" and "Blood" which issued from the sombre Nottingham crowd watching three rioters executed on February 1st[4] certainly instanced no operative love for the Whig Ministry or its Bill.

There are indications, indeed, that the Ultra-Radical demand for Universal Suffrage in place of the Whig Reform Bill was acquiring ever greater weight during the agitating suspense between October 1831 and May 1832. Hetherington, for example, was able to issue yet another paper, the *Twopenny Dispatch*, and such a violent extremist as William Benbow, beside whom Hetherington was a moderate, was encouraged to bring forward his plan for establishing working-class power by means of a Grand National Holiday (working-class general strike) of a

---

[1] *Wellington Despatches*, viii, 30, 142–3, 166.
[2] Lord Broughton (J. C. Hobhouse), *Recollections of a Long Life*, iv, under January 26, 1832, for its precarious finance; also Add. MSS. 27792, ff. 305–7, for Parkes's money-begging in London to get "steam up" again.
[3] *Poor Man's Guardian*, December 10, 1831.
[4] *Annual Register*, 1832, Chronicle, p. 18.

English Radicalism 1832-1852

month's duration.[1] On April 11th, again, the *Poor Man's Guardian* reprinted in a special supplement the principal portions of Macerone's *Defensive Instructions for the People* with its information on barricade construction, movable barricades, the fabrication of long pikes, and the use of acids. It was a plain intimation that the Ultra-Radicals hoped to be prepared in case the Tory majority in the Lords again showed sufficient obstinacy to provoke the Whig Cabinet and the middle classes into bitter hostility. The most remarkable manifestation, however, of the temper of Ultra-Radicals at this stage is to be found in the events of March 21st. Yielding to religious pressure, a rather unenthusiastic Government had arranged for that day to be observed as a General Fast Day of supplication against the cholera scourge then rampant. The National Union of the Working Classes succeeded in organising the workmen laid idle that day into a vast holiday procession through the London streets, each member being pledged to make a joyful dinner afterwards as befitted the "General Farce" day.[2] Never had infidelity raised its head in England so openly before or so combatively.

On April 14th, thanks to the support of some "Waverers," the Whig Government obtained a majority of 184 against 175 for the Second Reading of the Reform Bill in the Lords. It was a success which stimulated the Political Unions into renewed activity, and vast and joyful meetings were held throughout the country. Nor were threats lacking of what could happen should the Tory leaders attempt trouble on the Committee stage which was arranged to open on May 7th. Indeed May 7th was the day deliberately chosen by the leaders of the Birmingham Political Union for the greatest of their demonstrations, when thirty neighbouring Unions[3] helped them to mass 200,000 people and pledge them to unceasing agitation for more radical reform if the Bill before Parliament failed of enactment. The special strength of the Birmingham Union had always been the Ultra-Radical fervour of its middle-class leaders headed by Attwood, a fervour which had prevented the opening of any differences among the medley of commercial men, professional men, shopkeepers, small

[1] Announced in the *Poor Man's Guardian*, January 14. It was later to be the basis of much Chartist planning.
[2] *Poor Man's Guardian*, March 24th, which quotes the *Morning Chronicle's* statement that 100,000 must have been afoot in connexion with the procession
[3] Add. MSS. 27792, ff. 305-7.

Radicals and the Reform Bill 1831-1832

masters and artisans which composed their following. That fervour was admirably expressed in two parts of the proceedings of May 7th whose dramatic appeal to the entire nation may well have been a deciding factor in the agitated weeks which followed—the singing of the Union Hymn and the vow of self-dedication. The vow was taken in the following words: "With unbroken faith, through every peril and privation, we here devote ourselves and our children to our country's cause." The two most striking verses of the Union Hymn ran as follows:

> God is our guide! from field, from wave,
> From plough, from anvil, and from loom,
> We come our country's rights to save,
> And speak a tyrant faction's doom.
> And hark! we raise from sea to sea
> The sacred watchword Liberty!
>
> God is our guide! no swords we draw,
> We kindle not war's battle fires;
> By union, justice, reason, law,
> We claim the birthright of our sires.
> We raise the watchword, Liberty!
> We will, we will, we will be free![1]

On the very day when these striking democratic scenes were being enacted at Birmingham, the first step was taken by the majority of the Lords to execute the carefully considered plan of the Tory leaders[2] to whittle down the Reform Bill. But when the Government was prevented from taking the Bill into Committee in its own way, Grey was stung to a resolve to end the uncertainties of the situation. After an almost unanimous Cabinet had met next day, the King was asked to create fifty[3] Peers or accept the resignation of his Ministers. Taking only a night to consider his course, the King resolved to accept the resignations.

There followed probably the most critical days in the more modern history of English politics. On the one hand, invited thereto by the King, the Tory leaders in the Peers attempted in the face of a hostile House of Commons to construct a Government on a basis of modified Parliamentary Reform. On the other

---

[1] For the Birmingham meeting of May 7th, C. M. Wakefield, *Life of Thomas Attwood*, pp. 192, 197-206. [2] *Wellington Despatches*, viii, 272-98.
[3] *Correspondence of Earl Grey*, ii, 415, from which it seems that Grey and Brougham had told the King that even fifty might not prove sufficient.

English Radicalism 1832-1852

hand, the leaders of the Political Unions began to prepare for open armed resistance to the return of the Old Order as represented by the Duke of Wellington, the centre of all the Tory combinations. On May 11th deputies from Birmingham and other places were rapturously welcomed in Westminster and the City of London, and on May 12th under Francis Place's direction a plan of campaign was arranged which was to be brought into operation as soon as a Tory Government attempted to take office.[1] There are numerous indications that the lower and middle classes were now prepared for a common effort. The Birmingham Union, for example, was receiving vast accessions of membership,[2] at Manchester a great and harmonious meeting was arranged of sections hitherto on terms of enmity,[3] and the City of London saw the Livery appealing to the Commons to vote no supplies to a Tory Government and the Court of Common Council setting up an emergency committee to meet from day to day.[4]

Though, to quote Place, "numbers of military men of all ranks and many naval men, all men of experience,"[5] were ready to give professional leadership to the popular cause, it was hoped that matters would not go as far as that. The organised refusal of taxes[6] and the deliberately planned run for gold on the banks would, it was expected, add so violently to commercial alarm, already great, as to close the banks and produce a revolution of themselves[7] in the great centres of population whose industry would have been brought to a standstill by commercial uncertainty. The two bankers present at Place's meeting planning the offensive against a Tory Ministry must be held to have known their business well enough to make a substantially accurate forecast of what would happen when the placard "To stop the Duke Go for Gold"[8] made its appearance all over the country. A Tory Government facing a hostile House of Commons and agitated provincial centres full of angry Radical "laid off hands" would certainly have found it extremely dangerous to try to use the Army. If Wellington,

---

[1] Add. MSS. 27793, ff. 99 sqq.
[2] *Poor Man's Guardian*, May 19th, quoting the last *Birmingham Journal*.
[3] *Ibid.*, pp. 395-7, Hetherington was among the speakers.
[4] *Annual Register*, 1832, History, p. 170.
[5] Add. MSS. 27793, f. 142. Cf. Parkes in *Personal Life of George Grote*, pp. 78-80.
[6] The placard "No Taxes Paid Here until the Reform Bill is Passed" was already widely displayed. Add. MSS. 27793, f. 88.
[7] Add. MSS. 27795, f. 147. [8] *Ibid.*, f. 148.

Radicals and the Reform Bill 1831–1832

however, had attempted to brave all dangers, if he had dissolved the Reforming Parliament and ordered out the tiny professional Army to uphold the "King's Government," the Reformers would not have been unprepared. Birmingham would have given the signal to the rest of the country by helping the leaders of the Political Union there to take charge of the town and possibly the whole surrounding area. Professional military advice would have been available[1] in case the 150 troopers barracked locally had attempted suppression, but there is evidence to show that the rank and file would not have allowed themselves to be used against such an orderly movement as was planned.[2] Once a number of provincial and Scottish centres were in Reforming hands Wellington with a seething metropolitan population of near two millions round him would have been helpless. His Government might have collapsed even before that massed Radical march on the capital, already loosely projected on several occasions,[3] had been undertaken. If events, however, had actually been allowed to get as far as this, incidents might have occurred with irrevocable consequences. When the Duke of Wellington was contemplating the issue of warrants for the arrest of the leading Reformers and they in their turn were planning the seizure of Tory hostages,[4] the likelihood of a chance incident leading on inescapably to a great breach with the past was not to be ignored.

But the Tory Government was never formed after all. There was great hesitation among Tories invited to take office in the face of an angry country and a hostile House of Commons. They would have to rely on troops whose numbers were patently insufficient and whose loyalty might not stand the strain of the employment to which they would be quickly put. To dissolve the House of Commons and plunge the excited country into new elections opened up dangers of the most widespread disorder. To face the existing House of Commons with a modified Reform Bill was scarcely more promising. Throughout its long resistance to every proposal of Parliamentary Reform, the Tory party had committed itself so thoroughly to the defence of every noxious constitutional survival, that a Tory Reform Bill was impossible.

---

[1] See note 5, p. 44.
[2] Alexander Somerville, *Autobiography of a Working Man*, p. 248. Cf. Add. MSS. 27794, f. 10.
[3] Cf. Alexander Somerville, *op. cit.*, pp. 245–6, for the 1832 projects of a march from Birmingham.   [4] Add. MSS. 27794, f. 282.

Peel, the ablest Tory Parliamentarian, felt this so keenly that he declined a place in the Tory combinations.¹ When during the agitated proceedings of May 14th in the Commons, Peel's view of the essential immorality of a Tory Reform was urged from every side of the House² the possibility of a Tory Government's taking office was virtually over.

Directly the King turned to Lord Grey once more, the problem of an extensive creation of Whig Peers again became urgent. In procuring for the Cabinet information from Place as to the Radical plans for barricading provincial cities Hobhouse, now a Minister, may have helped the Government to resolve upon a bold step.³ Despite the danger of provoking another constitutional crisis with the King, Grey and Brougham, his Chancellor, were authorised to insist on an unqualified royal pledge to create any number of Peers necessary to carry the Reform Bill. There was a painful interview whose adverse outcome would have plunged government into chaos again and the country into disorder. The King gave way, however, though by personal appeals⁴ he arranged that a sufficiency of Peers should abstain from voting on Reform and so help him to avoid the necessity of being asked to fulfil his pledge. On June 7th the English Reform Bill became law and later in the summer corresponding measures for Scotland and Ireland. A General Election could not long be denied to the new voters and the new constituencies. It took place in December.

Mr. J. R. M. Butler in the very stimulating chapter with which he concludes his book on the "Passing of the Great Reform Bill" has attempted to estimate how near to civil war the country actually was in the critical May days of 1832. He allows great authority to the views of Place, who was convinced that the metropolitan and provincial commotions would have ended in a few days with a Reform victory though not before much irreparable damage had been done.⁵ Mr. Butler is something less optimistic, grounding himself partly on evidence that the Whig majority in the Commons would not have refused Wellington the supplies⁶ as the Political Unions were hoping. Yet it seems difficult to believe that the House of Commons would have stood by while

---

¹ *Croker Papers*, ii, 177; *Peel Papers*, ii, 205.
² Hansard (3rd series), xii, 947, for a Tory opinion.
³ Add. MSS. 27794, ff. 278-80.
⁴ *Correspondence of Earl Grey*, ii, 421; *Memoirs of Baron Stockmar*, i, 322.
⁵ *Op. cit.*, pp. 416 sqq.   ⁶ *Ibid.*, pp. 419-20.

Radicals and the Reform Bill 1831-1832

sanguinary conflicts between troops and civilians spread through the land. Another surmise made by a Whig Minister before the crisis was over presents a view perhaps more inherently likely than any other despite its neglect of the possibility of military refusal to obey orders. Jeffrey, Lord Advocate of Scotland, considered that the first step of a Tory Government at this stage would have been to dissolve Parliament. "Then would follow the dispersion of unions, and meetings, and petitions by soldiery; and vindictive burnings; and massacres of anti-Reformers in all the manufacturing districts; and summary arrests of men accused of sedition and treason; and shoals of persecutions for libels, followed by triumphant acquitals; and elections carried through amidst sanguinary tumults; and finally a House of Commons returned to put down that brutal administration, but too late to stay the torrent it had created."[1]

[1] Lord Cockburn's *Life of Jeffrey*, ed. 1872, pp. 325-6.

CHAPTER II

THE CONSTITUTION OF 1832

"Our readers know that we are advocates of the broadest possible suffrage, of the annual exercise of the elective right, and of the protection afforded to the electors by secret voting, and that consequently no scheme of reform which does not embrace these points can receive our unqualified approbation. . . . We did not, of course, expect that even the most zealously reforming administration, considering the strength of the adverse interests which would have to be encountered, would venture to propose anything like a perfect scheme. We have it now before us, and though it falls far short of what we demand . . . it is a great deal better than we expected. . . ."

ARCHIBALD PRENTICE *in the* "Manchester Times," *March 1831.*

"To populous places, they had not deemed it fit to give that share in the representation to which they would be numerically entitled, because it was considered that a preponderance of newly popular representatives in that House might have the effect of making the machine of State move with too great a velocity. For this reason, too, they had retained a number of small boroughs."

LORD JOHN RUSSELL.

"It is settled by both sides of the House, that the people are of two sorts—those that are disposed to go too fast, and those that are disinclined to move. The rate of speed is in proportion to the density of population."

The irate FONBLANQUE *in the* "Examiner" *during the Reform Debates of 1831 (from* "England Under Seven Administrations," *ii, 90–1).*

"The county of Galway had a larger population than Worcestershire; but Worcestershire had four members and Galway only two. The Protestant county of Down was no better treated than the Catholic county of Galway; . . . the county of Cork had nearly as large a population as the principality of Wales; Wales had twenty-eight representatives and Cork had two. So with the boroughs. . . . The same deliberate injustice ran uniformly through the whole scheme. . . ."

O'CONNELL *after he had turned to Repeal (from* GAVAN DUFFY'S *paraphrase in the* "Nineteenth Century," *December 1883).*

THE "Great Reform Bill" on which the Lords' resistance had been beaten down in the manner just described was the measure reforming representation in England, but it was accompanied to the Statute Book by corresponding Scottish and Irish Reform Bills whose real handling only commenced after the crisis of May 1832 was over.[1] To a generation long accustomed to vigorous Tory clamour of the approaching advent of red revolution and general confiscation of property directly it was proposed to transfer two members from a petty borough, convicted of gross corruption, to Manchester, Leeds, or Birmingham, the first Ministerial Reform proposals of March 1831 had caused a first thrill of genuine delight. Not one but sixty petty boroughs with fewer than 2,000 inhabitants had been marked down for total loss of members and a long list of forty-seven others with fewer than 4,000 inhabitants had been sentenced each to lose one member.[2] Not Manchester, Leeds, and Birmingham alone were to gain Parliamentary representation for the first time, but twenty-eight English urban areas more besides others designed in Scotland.[3]

But the first Tory struggle in the Commons terminated by the spring General Election of 1831, the renewed struggle during the summer months after the election culminating in the Lords' rejection of a second Reform Bill in October, the rumours of Whig readiness to compromise current before a third Reform Bill was introduced in December—all these had gone far to end the original temper in which the Whig proposals had been received. When sober citizens, leaders of Political Unions, were discussing means of coercing the Lords by force, it was inevitable that talk should grow of the Reform Bill being but a beginning of the cleansing of the State and the giving to every man of his due.

Strange as it may seem to modern eyes, it is hard to find evidence that there was any audible Radical demand in 1831–2 for the democratic equalisation of constituencies which would make every member of the House of Commons represent an approximately equal population.[4] By the third and final Whig Reform Bill

[1] The English Bill is 2 & 3 Will. IV, c. 45; the Scottish and Irish are c. 65 and c. 88 of the same year.
[2] *Speeches and Despatches of Earl Russell*, i, 321–2.   [3] *Ibid.*, pp. 315, 325.
[4] Even an examination of the file of the *Poor Man's Guardian* and of Henry Hunt's *Addresses* of late 1831 yielded nothing tangible.

English Radicalism 1832–1852

143 seats were to be gained from small borough disfranchisements and reallotted as follows: 44 to 22 new English two-member boroughs of widely varying population and importance, 21 to a corresponding number of one-member boroughs, 65 to the English counties, 8 to Scottish boroughs, and five to Ireland. Though the new arrangements would still leave Parliamentary representation a mass of inconsistencies and injustices if viewed from the democratic standpoint of population, it was the Tories, anxious to discredit the whole principle of Reform, who advanced the most damaging evidence to display this. Croker, for example, the principal demonstrator of Whig inaccuracy and partiality in the disfranchisement of small boroughs, indulged also in such dangerous queries as why the 700,000 Irishmen in Cork County were to keep merely two members while the representation of Cumberland's 160,000 was increased to four,[1] why among the English counties themselves the grossest disproportion of representation to population was suffered to be set up by a scheme which allowed the two Devonshire divisions, for example, two members each and three to a number of undivided counties of population altogether inferior to either Devonshire half.[2] Other Tories, arguing against the new metropolitan boroughs, were incautious enough to point out that on ministerial notions of basing representation on population and wealth the metropolitan area ought to have been given at least fifty members.[3] Peel, too, saw no good reason on ministerial grounds why Liverpool and Tamworth, for example, should both retain their two members of pre-Reform times despite the immense differences which had grown up between them or why Dublin was left with the two-member representation only to which less populous and less influential Limerick, Waterford, Galway, and Belfast were being promoted.[4]

That Tories should have felt it safe to argue in public on these lines after many months of Reform debate is a testimony to the comparative absence even among the Radical Reformers of any desire systematically to revise the representation arrangements on a logically defensible plan. It was Tories, even, who were left to ask what was to happen when new populations began clamouring

---
[1] *Hansard* (3rd series), January 19, 1832, ix, 626.
[2] *Ibid.*, January 27, 1832, 1000–1.
[3] *Ibid.*, February 28, 1832, x, 923.
[4] February 28, 1832, Peel's Speech.

The Constitution of 1832

for Parliamentary representation,[1] and the efforts of Merthyr, Stockton, and Toxteth Park, for example, to prove marked superiority to other areas recommended by the Whigs for constitution as Parliamentary boroughs gave special point to the argument. Macaulay's heated query of July 5, 1831: "Are you prepared to have after every decennial census, a new distribution of members among electoral districts?" wrecking Tory Parliamentarians had long been allowed to ignore. Indeed, in their anxiety to put no obstacles in the way of the Reform Bill, Radical members of Parliament not only refrained from pressing such "crazy projects of the disciples of Tom Paine"[2] as the decennial revision of electoral districts but accepted in virtual silence the Parliamentary equalisation of Manchester, Glasgow, Leeds, and Birmingham with Horsham, Shoreham, Andover, and Thetford.[3]

Even when O'Connell and the Irish Radicals came to the discussion of the markedly unsatisfactory Irish Reform Bill after May 25, 1832, their criticism was rather one of detail than of principle. Ireland was the principal sufferer from the changes admitted by the Whigs into their original Reform plans, for instead of returning 105 members to a House of 596 it was to return 105 members to one of 658—and this though its population of 7,839,514 was nearly a third of the United Kingdom census total of 24,205,525. What, however, excited the bitterest Irish Radical feeling was that of the insufficient increase of five members finally allowed Ireland above its original 100, the Whigs took one for Dublin University where a constituency of 96 Protestants already possessed one member. It is typical of the mentality of Whig ministers that they defended this addition to Dublin University's representation partly on the ground that the Irish Protestant interest needed strengthening in view of more democratic arrangements in other parts of their scheme and partly because they were making arrangements to expand the University

---

[1] Cf. Peel, *Hansard* (3rd series), March 9th, xi, 68.
[2] Canning as rendered by Macaulay on July 5, 1831, *Writings and Speeches*, ed. 1878, p. 499.
[3] These were not, of course, the only instances, nor even the worst, of gross over-representation. The following also returned two members, after 1832 as before, though only the ludicrous number indicated actually voted in December 1832: Bodmin, 217; Chippenham, 172; Cockermouth, 227; Devizes, 360; Harwich, 183; Knaresborough, 207; Lyme Regis, 183; Marlborough, 163; Tavistock, 193; Totnes, 193. The *Quarterly Review*, April 1833, p. 263 (complaining of Reform Bill discrimination in favour of Whig "nomination boroughs").

English Radicalism 1832-1852

constituency to what they hoped would be 600. It was in vain that the superior claims of the huge population of Cork County were pointed out or the extra member demanded for Kilkenny City, or the transfer of the seat suggested to a Protestant yet populous place like Londonderry.[1] Dublin University got its two members, and O'Connell hating this and much else in the Irish Reform Bill yet voted for it against the Tories, because it did at least release Dublin representation from the toils of a corrupt Corporation and give Belfast a constituency of 2,300 £10 householders instead of 13 tools of the Marquis of Donegall.[2]

The ministerial success in relation to Dublin University had, perhaps, some influence on a Tory plan to achieve something similar in Scotland where a two-member Glasgow and Edinburgh on a £10 householder basis and a one-member Paisley, Greenock, Aberdeen, Leith, and Dundee called loudly on the best ministerial principles for the special representational entrenchment of the minority counter-interest. Even after the Tory defeat on the "Great Reform Bill," therefore, there was still a Tory attempt made in the Lords to secure part of Scotland's representation for a University constituency specially to be created. In a sardonic refusal to accept this Tory suggestion, Brougham declined to allow academic quiet to be broken in upon and expressed regret that Scottish religion, too, had not been set free from political stirs.[3] He obviously sympathised with an attempt made earlier in the Commons by the Scottish Radical Gillon to keep the Scottish clergy out of politics even to the extent of denying them the vote.[4]

It is interesting to turn to one side of redistribution on which Tories and advanced Reformers had both attacked the Government plan though from differing motives. In dividing many larger English counties for election purposes, Ministers had aimed at reducing the often enormous burthen of costs imposed upon candidates by the attempt to canvass a whole county and bring its voters to the poll cheered by inevitable and illegal refreshments en route. Indeed, it had been partly to meet the "treating" evil that Ministers had inserted into their Reform schemes provision for the establishment of branch polling places even in the county

---

[1] Coming from an English Whig-Radical of repute like Sir Robert Heron, this carried more weight than if it had come from O'Connell, Sheil, or Leader, Hansard, June 13th, xiii, 597. [2] Hansard, May 25th, xiii, 158.
[3] Ibid., July 9th, xiv, 182. [4] Ibid., June 6th, xiii, 476-96.

The Constitution of 1832

divisions. When the average voter, moreover, had had his road to his polling place greatly reduced, it became fairer to request him to record his vote within a two-day polling period instead of one of fifteen days.

But despite the admitted evils against which Ministerial division plans were directed, there were Whig-Radical and Radical members who felt that they brought dangers of their own. In an undivided county returning four members the pressure on an individual voter from his social superiors would, it was felt, be less serious than in a county division where a few large proprietors acting together would be in a position to nominate two candidates and coerce opposition.[1] The position was graver from the fact that Ministers had decided against their original intention to allow the county franchise to the £50 tenants-at-will, a class which was at the mercy of its landlords. Already in February 1832 the not unfounded fear was expressed in Parliament that as leases and other tenures fell in, landlords, in the interests of their electoral power over a county division, would decline to consider any other tenure than tenancy-at-will.[2] In these circumstances some members, who might have been prepared to leave open voting without question in undivided counties, were driven to consider whether the more rigid landlord-dictation made possible by county division did not call for tenant-protection by means of the Ballot.[3]

The Ballot, fated for so long to be demanded in vain from Tory and orthodox Whig alike, might very easily have been conceded to Radicals in the Reform Act itself. Certainly the ministerial committee which under the Radical Lord Durham's chairmanship drafted the Reform plan recommended the Ballot.[4] Though it was struck out later by the conservative section of the Cabinet, there is evidence that it might have been conceded to a great public outcry.[5] Thus would the whole problem of the landlord's intimidation of his tenantry and the rich customer's threats to his tradespeople have been prevented from poisoning the political development of the next forty years. Thus, too, would the dis-

[1] *Hansard*, ix, 988; Cutlar Ferguson, 997, Ewart.
[2] *Ibid.*, 1116–17, Lord Milton.
[3] E.g. Sir Robert Heron and Cutlar Fergusson, February 1st.
[4] Earl Russell, *English Government and Constitution*, ed. 1865, p. 228.
[5] "I object to the Ballot, and would rather be forced to yield to it than introduce it in the Bill." Grey to Lansdowne, January 15, 1831. Quoted from Howick Papers, J. R. M. Butler, *op. cit.*, 184, n. 2.

couraged payer of bribes in the many small constituencies allowed to survive have been prevented from learning whether he had really got the votes he had paid for or not.

Unfortunately, the average Whig Peer or country gentleman hardly considered it safer than did the Tory to release the constituencies from that rigid supervision of the individual voter by the "property" of his neighbourhood which was made possible by the open voting system. Accordingly when Lord John Russell opened the Parliamentary history of the Great Reform Bill on March 1, 1831, he announced that it did not embrace Vote by Ballot and began, indeed, the work of building up the huge Whig prison of objections in which the project was confined for more than forty years.[1] The Ballot, he said, would afford a cover "to much fraud, to much deceit, private hatred, treachery, and falsehood" because, forsooth, a voter worried by influential canvassers or intimidated by his landlord or a rich customer would promise to poll one way and actually poll another. Again, argued Lord John Russell, it was doubtful whether voters accustomed to open voting would ever avail themselves of the secrecy of the Ballot; men of rank and title would turn from the mere capture of men's votes to that more enslaving capture of their minds necessitated by secret voting; and, finally, it was not desirable to make voters "irresponsible in the exercise of a vast power." This, however, was but a beginning of the Whig sophistries on the subject. By January 1833 the *Edinburgh Review*[2] was conjuring up nightmare visions of a Ballot system under which every individual voter was likely to be subjected to such minute scrutiny of his acts and opinions that tenants, liable to ejection on mere suspicion of having voted the wrong way, shopkeepers, fearful of desertion by their wealthiest customers, and Irish voters, exposed to being waylaid by a lawless peasantry on their road to the poll, would all demand with one voice the return of open voting. Under open voting, they would argue, it was at least possible to escape penalisation arising from mere malicious gossip, tale-bearing, or electoral espionage.

Had the Radical handful in Parliament and the Political Unions outside foreseen the future, they would doubtless not have allowed the Ballot to go almost by default in 1831. But the Reform Bills promised them a new type of Parliament in which not merely

[1] Earl Russell, *Speeches and Despatches*, i. 330–1.   [2] Vol. lvi, 552–64

The Constitution of 1832

the Ballot but Household Suffrage, Triennial Parliaments, Abolition of the Members' Property Qualification, and Equalisation of the Constituencies seemed likely to be quickly carried. Rather than imperil the Reform Bills, therefore, they waited to press these things upon a new Parliament only to be grievously disappointed with the result. In 1833 Whig Ministers began to talk of the unwisdom of making new changes until the full effect of those already conceded was ascertained. Stanley, indeed, their rashest if most eloquent speaker, was already being quoted in the Tory *Quarterly* as committed to the Reform Bill as a final[1] settlement of the Constitution allowing of no further concession to the Radicals.

As the one Ultra-Radical in close touch with the populace, Henry Hunt had endeavoured to stretch the Whig Reform Bill farther than the £10 householder. Adapting his own Universal Suffrage principles to the necessity of winning Whig attention, Hunt had asked for the suffrage to be bestowed on everybody who paid direct taxation.[2] When this was refused, he proceeded with democratic logic to move that those not enfranchised should be exempted from rates, taxes, the militia ballot, and sea-impressment, but failed to win any support.[3] A last attempt made by Hunt on the Suffrage issue concerned his own Preston constituency of seven to eight thousand potwallopers which would eventually be reduced by the Reform Bill to eight to nine hundred £10 householders. In view of this and the absence of corruption in the borough, Hunt asked unsuccessfully for the maintenance of the old wide enfranchisement practices.[4]

If Hunt failed to prolong the existing electoral practices of Preston into the indefinite future, the Tories had been more successful in their venture on behalf of an important group of special protégés. Lord John Russell's first proposals involved the termination of the freeman qualification in the important group of freeman boroughs. Existing resident freemen whether by right of birth, apprenticeship, or otherwise would like potwalloping and scot-and-lot voters elsewhere[5] have retained their

[1] *Quarterly Review*, January 1833, xlviii, 549.
[2] *Hansard*, February 2, 1832, ix, 1209 sqq.
[3] *Ibid.*, February 3, 1832, ix, 1258–9.   [4] *Ibid.*, 1259–60.
[5] For details of the voting conditions in different boroughs, see E. and A. Porritt, *The Unreformed House of Commons*. Dod's *Electoral Facts, 1832–1866*, has useful indications of the proportion of these types of voters surviving in the years after 1832.

English Radicalism 1832-1852

franchise for life even in the absence of a £10 household qualification. But admissions to the voting registers after March 31, 1831, would with certain exceptions have been solely dependent on the householder qualification. In many Parliamentary boroughs the class of poor hereditary freemen was thoroughly corrupt, and their votes were always at the disposal of the highest bidder. Stout Tory support, however, was forthcoming for a set of electoral clients of this amenable class and they were helped also by Radical dislike of cutting off any class of poor man voter. The final Reform Bill, therefore, did nothing to prevent new batches of bribable poor freemen from being added to the electoral rolls every year.[1] It contented itself with extinguishing the Parliamentary franchise of non-resident freemen, imported in shoals by wealthy candidates, to record a vote in boroughs which their fathers might have quitted scores of years before.

It was, perhaps, some justification for the Whig acquiescence in the indefinite perpetuation of a thoroughly debauched category of voters that the Government was pledged to produce stronger and more effective anti-bribery legislation than any yet on the Statute Book. Lord John Russell, indeed, busied himself with a Bill which proposed to make petitions against an alleged corrupt election receivable for as long as two years afterwards instead of the actual fourteen days and also offered compensation at public expense to petitioners who succeeded in substantiating their charges.[2] It was a Bill which might conceivably have improved Radicalism's electoral results very conspicuously in the years after 1832. Indeed, if Radicals had also obtained that reform of Election Petition procedure which was only partially conceded them in 1840[3] it would almost certainly have done so. Russell, however, had some trouble in dealing with "practical" objections to his Bribery Bill from members who had the best of reasons for fearing the suspension of a sword of Damocles over their heads for two years after elections. Finally he allowed the Lords to block the passage of his measure to the Statute Book.[4] The reign of money was not to be lightly removed from a host of constituencies. On the contrary, even when beaten at the poll,

---

[1] The Tory defence of this useful electoral class was renewed in 1835 on the Municipal Reform Bill. See *Croker Papers*, ii, 280.
[2] *Hansard*, July 30, 1832, xiv, 956.
[3] Spencer Walpole's *History of England*, iii, 515-16.
[4] *Hansard*, August 13th, xiv, 1354.

The Constitution of 1832

money had in the Election Petition a dangerous weapon of financial coercion.[1]

Another check inflicted by the Lords on the Ministerial Reform plans even in the midst of the triumphant summer of 1832 concerned the Irish freeman vote. In view of the dangerous Protestant sectarianism of the Irish corporations and freemen, the Government had declined to sanction for Ireland that indefinite perpetuation of the freeman vote which it had conceded in England. The Lords, aware of the Government's reluctance to undertake a distasteful contest late in the session, insisted that in Ireland also[2] newly fledged freemen should continue to be added year by year to the electoral register, though they possessed no £10 householder qualification. As matters stood, the main weight of the Irish freeman vote was even more likely to be obtainable for a Tory and against a Radical than the similar poor freeman vote, say, of Liverpool, Bristol, and Norwich. Both in England and Ireland there was normally greater financial inducement to vote Tory, and besides Corporation charities were usually reserved for trusty Tory electoral clients.

Some features of the borough Reform debates still remain for mention. In their Scottish Reform Bill proceedings of 1832 the Whigs allowed themselves to be won over to restricting Scottish Burgh membership for the first time to those with the £300 per annum landed qualification.[3] Within a few days a Radical uproar had been excited before which the Government withdrew.[4]

It certainly was a most inept time to have chosen to impose upon Scottish boroughs the ideas of Queen Anne Tories still governing the representation of the rest of the nation. The fact that Scottish Burgh representation was left unguarded by any qualification whatsoever was to form a useful precedent after 1832 for all those Radical forces calling for the complete abolition of the property qualification not only in regard to borough membership, but shire membership also. Ingenious as were the legal devices employed to create nominal landed properties of £600 per annum for shire members and of £300 per annum for

---

[1] E.g. after the Radical Perronet Thompson had been elected for Hull in 1835, he was put to thousands of pounds of expense in beating off what he claimed was a "frivolous" petition. In 1837, again, Tories raised a large sum to petition against O'Connell's election and that of his followers.
[2] *Hansard*, xiv, 822–4.   [3] *Ibid.*, 982.
[4] *Ibid.*, 1057–69.

English Radicalism 1832–1852

borough members,[1] it should be remembered that Feargus O'Connor could still lose his County Cork seat for lack of qualification in 1835, and Sir Samuel Whalley his Marylebone seat in 1838 for a similar cause.

The great complaint of the Irish Radicals in regard to the borough provisions of their Bill was that in a number of instances they would serve not to increase but to decrease the number of voters. Undoubtedly in several impoverished Irish boroughs a constituency composed of householders occupying premises of £10 annual value or over would be the reverse of a large and representative one, whatever might be the case in London or the prosperous provincial cities of Great Britain. Even in the larger Irish cities the £10 occupier vote could hardly be expected to yield a proportion of enfranchisement comparable with what was expected in England, and especially in the metropolis. Indeed, the Tories were in a continuous panic about the effect of the £10 occupier vote in the metropolitan boroughs[2] where they expected wild scenes of demagogy at the hustings and Jacobinic leaders issuing from the pollings of tens of thousands of the horny-handed. Though the Grey Government was only prevented from making them concessions by fear of a Radical explosion, it realised also that the Tories were making insufficient allowance for the effect of Whig precautions. A very marked curtailment in the number of poorer voters was, in fact, to result from the disfranchisement of "paupers" and from the imposition of a year's residence and the satisfactory discharge of house-tax and rate-payments due as conditions precedent to registration.

In point of fact the English Reform Bill had not been on the Statute Book two months before a Radical clamour began as to the extent to which disfranchisement had been inflicted on the "ten pounders" by the "ratepaying clauses." A high proportion of artisan ten pounders lived in yards, courts, and other blocks for which their landlords were accustomed to pay a "compound" rate collected in the rent. To obtain admission to the register ten pounders of this class had been required to tender to the overseers the rates due on the premises they occupied and had been left to make their own difficult rent-readjustments with

---

[1] The minima under the 9 Anne, c. 5.
[2] For a calculation by Peel as to the huge measure of enfranchisement to be conceded, *Hansard*, x, 948.

The Constitution of 1832

their landlords. Moreover, as the Reform Bill came to be interpreted the occupier of this class had to pay more in rates than his landlord had done. Whereas the landlord was normally allowed "compound" terms, generously covering the trouble of collecting the rates through the rent, the ten pounder was expected to pay the full rate. Apart, therefore, from the difficulty of finding unwonted sums in cash for rates, the ten pounder was often asked to tax himself considerably if he desired to vote. It is little wonder, then, if at the beginning of August 1832, wild figures were circulating among Radicals as to the measure of disfranchisement which had been wrought by the detested "ratepaying clauses." One Radical estimate ventured in Parliament was to the effect that 200,000 of the 300,000 new £10 householder eligibles had not been registered for voting.[1]

The situation seemed serious enough for the Government to offer an extension of the time for registration if it could be carried by agreement.[2] When the Tories, however, declined to consider any further change, the Government gave way, though not without another Radical protest as to the ills[3] which would follow at the General Election already being busily prepared for. Till 1851 the "ratepaying clauses" were destined to continue a bitter Radical grievance, especially in the Metropolis with its relatively high percentage of artisan £10 occupiers who year after year found it impossible to become voters. The legal interpretation of the Reform Act, indeed, was to put still another obstacle in their way to the voting registers. Every time a rate was struck, they were not only required to tender payment, but also to renew their claim for a vote.[4]

To be registered cost a voter a shilling in England and two shillings in Scotland.[5] It had been originally intended in the English case to make registration a public charge and to defray the costs of preparing the voting register from local rates. Unfortunately, the defenders of local property were allowed their way and the preparatory costs of the register were thrust on the voters themselves.[6] One result of this particularly mean economy was to disfranchise a very considerable number of the poorer or more

---

[1] *Hansard*, xiv, 1230–1.   [2] *Ibid.*, 1235.   [3] *Ibid.*, 1292.
[4] Cf. *Hansard*, July 24, 1850, Sir W. Clay moving the Second Reading of the Compound Householders Bill.
[5] Thanks to O'Connell Irish "certification" cost 1s.
[6] Schedule H, Reform Bill, *Statutes at Large*.

59

conservative English county voters of the 40s. freeholder class, or alternatively to make them look to the party agents for money.¹ Fortunately, the county registers were swollen by the many thousands of £10 copyholders, £10 leaseholders on long term, and £50 leaseholders on shorter term of twenty to sixty years, who though now admitted to vote for the first time, made an admirable set of "independent" voters. Unfortunately, the value of their "independence" was liable to be lost through being overborne by the heavier vote of the £50 tenants-at-will which was plainly at the command of the landlords in the absence of the Ballot.

It was in the Scottish counties that the new voting arrangements were to have the largest comparative effect.² There the right of voting had been attached not to the freeholder class as in England, but to the even smaller class holding feudal superiority over land, though not necessarily the land itself. Accordingly such amazing things had become possible as the confinement of the Banff vote to nineteen individuals, only two of them with land in the county, the restriction of the Ross and Cromarty vote to twenty-nine persons, only eight of them with local land, and the exclusion of all but 2,340 superiority holders, half of them without land in their counties, from a voice in the choice of the Scottish shire representatives.³ To enfranchise the ordinary £10 freeholder for the first time, to add to him the £10 copyholder and the £50 leaseholder for nineteen years or more meant an altogether greater degree of change in the electoral conditions of rural Scotland than that effected in rural England.

While England and Scotland were rejoicing in the creation of vast new electorates, Ireland was still mourning a late mass disfranchisement and seeking a restoration. In 1829 the Tories had insisted on accompanying a Catholic Emancipation Bill permitting Catholic members of Parliament with the disfranchisement of the large if impoverished 40s. freeholder class most likely to elect them. It is true that the votes in question represented either poor squatter holdings on bare hillsides or faggot voting lots created by political landlords among their peasant dependents before these had been turned against them by the Catholic

---

[1] *Abridgement of Evidence before the Select Committee appointed in 1835 to consider Bribery, Corruption, etc.*, pp. 17-18.
[2] Though the Scottish boroughs were also to see vast changes. For pre-Reform election monopoly by co-opted Town Councils, see *Hansard*, vii, 529. September 23, 1831.   [3] Earl Russell, *Speeches and Despatches*, i, 324.

The Constitution of 1832

Association. In view, however, of the maintenance of the 40s. freehold franchise in England O'Connell was justified in asking for equality for Ireland, where according to his fellow-Irishman, Leader, county constituencies totalling 216,000 in 1829 would number 26,000 in 1832[1] under Whig "Reform."

Yet in view of the Irish Tithe resistance perturbing the Parliamentary majority ever more seriously as its sway increased, O'Connell could hardly have expected democratic concessions. The Whigs professed satisfaction with a Bill which they claimed would give the seven million Irish in the counties as many as 52,162 voters, 22,000 of them, as they pointed out conciliatorily to the Tories, freeholders of property worth above £50 annually.[2] Indeed, the Irish Secretary had weighted things so nicely that he felt able to doubt whether his Bill would give the "Catholic interest" more than seven new seats.[3] It was a calculation which doubtless underwent revision after O'Connell's persistence necessitated a concession by which the £10 leaseholder for twenty years was added to the classes already proposed for enfranchisement. Even before this, Tories had been so nervous of what might come from Irish constituencies admitting £10 freeholders, copyholders, and sixty-year leaseholders, and £50 leaseholders for above fourteen years that they had predicted that the "Protestant interest" must despair of 76 of the 105 Irish seats.[4]

The nice political weighting of Irish constituencies to prevent any alarming gains by O'Connellite Radicalism did not, of course, dispose of the Irish problem. While Parliament was in prorogation between August 16th and December 3rd and British attention was largely concentrated on such things as the lists of voters finally passed by the Revising Barristers and the geographical limits assigned to the new boroughs and county divisions, the Irish masses had their principal concern with very different things. In September military shot down a crowd of anti-tithe demonstrators at Doneraile, Co. Cork, and it was sought to avenge the deaths there by two murders.[5] In October worse occurred in Co. Waterford where a police party, posting tithe notices, extricated itself from a perilous situation by shooting which killed more than a dozen people and wounded twenty.[6]

[1] *Hansard*, xiii, 580.   [2] *Ibid.*, xii, 122.   [3] *Ibid.*, 125.
[4] *Annual Register*, 1832, History, p. 202.
[5] *Ibid.*, Chronicle, pp. 117–23, 127.   [6] *Ibid.*, Chronicle, pp. 131–2.

CHAPTER III

ELECTION PLEDGES IN 1832

"1. Will you pledge yourself to propose or support a measure to obtain for the nation an effectual reform in the Commons House of the British Parliament: the basis of which reform shall be short parliaments, extension of the suffrage to every male, vote by ballot and especially No Property Qualification for Members of Parliament?
"2. Will you propose or support the total abolition of all taxes on knowledge?
"3. Will you propose or support the total abolition of tithes and the dissolution of the alliance between Church and State?
"4. Will you propose or support a measure to restore to the people the right of electing Sheriffs and Magistrates?
"5. Will you propose or support a Bill to exclude from the House of Commons placemen and pensioners?
"6. Will you propose or support a measure that will render justice cheap and expeditious, so that the poor man may no longer continue the victim of oppression?
"7. Will you propose or support the abolition of all monopolies, the repeal of the Corn Laws, and of all the taxes pressing upon the necessaries and comforts of the labouring man?"

Pledges suggested to its readers by the "Poor Man's Guardian" as suitable to be required of candidates. July 21, 1832, p. 466.

"In travelling lately, through some of the great manufacturing towns of Lancashire, I was struck by the various placards on the walls in every quarter, relating to the ensuing election; and if one opened a newspaper, its columns were full of the same subject. . . . Who are the new boroughmongers whose influence threatens the real liberty of election as much as it was ever threatened by the old ones? Who are now setting up tyrants over us. . . . They are the agitators of the Political Unions, and of the newspaper press—the brazen, shallow, and insolent speakers—the ignorant, lying, and malignant writers, known for nothing but their turbulence and their libels. . . ."

August 10, 1832. The Whig ᴅʀ. ARNOLD (*of Rugby*) *in the* "*Sheffield Courant.*"

EVEN before the "Great Reform Bill" of 1832 was on the Statute Book, Radical Reformers were organising for the inevitable elections to follow. To them the Bill was only a beginning, a means to a number of ends which they were confident of attaining, and for the most part of attaining quickly. John Stuart Mill, for example, may be found writing to his friend Carlyle on May 29, 1832: "There is now nothing definite and determinate in politics except Radicalism, and we shall have nothing but Radicals and Whigs for a long time to come."[1] This was something too optimistic as events were before long to prove. The great bulk of the Whig majority which had carried Reform through the Commons would certainly be returned once more, reinforced no doubt by scores of fresh accessions of Whig country gentlemen, members for new county divisions or older boroughs wrenched from Tory control. The quality of these men's Radicalism was very doubtful, and many felt that even the more earnest Radicals to be expected from the large centres of population might, once seated in Parliament, all too easily forget the ardent reforming temper which animated the people outside. Great efforts were therefore made by more earnest Radicals to bind candidates in advance to specific Radical programmes.

It is unlikely that the England of 1832 possessed many men more capable of discerning the limits of the practically possible in politics than Francis Place, the acute and patient father of Westminster Radicalism. He had already made in 1831 a first remarkable if unsuccessful attempt to secure a central Radical party organisation in the Parliamentary Candidates' Society.[2] Later in the year he had founded the National Political Union, now, after essential services in the Reform struggle, available for use as an agency for nation-wide Radical electoral propaganda.[3] It is singularly enlightening, therefore, to turn to the pamphlet entitled *On Pledges to be Given by Candidates*, which was issued in July 1832 by the National Political Union and certainly expresses views held by Place.[4] Pledges should be sought from candidates, urged the pamphlet, which would bind them to

---

[1] *Letters of J. S. Mill*, I, 31, p. 31.   [2] Add. MSS. 27789, ff. 350 sqq.
[3] Thus the National Political Union's pamphlet on the Taxes on Knowledge and that on the Ballot, also, seem to have been very widely diffused.
[4] Graham Wallas, *Life of Place*, p. 366.

English Radicalism 1832–1852

further reform of Parliament[1] and to Law Reform, Financial Reform, Trade Reform, Church Reform, the Abolition of Slavery, and the Abolition of the Taxes on Knowledge.[2] It was a programme less vast than that being called for by the Ultra-Radicals, but still one which must have appeared much too all-embracing for immediate practical politics even in the eyes of "movement" Whigs. To be pledged to it by constituents, moreover, would not only go far to make impossible those compromises with strong vested interests so dear to the "practical" politician's heart but would serve also to degrade the Parliamentarian from the position of legislator to that of popular delegate.[3] Accordingly, Radical pledging effort was but too often made in vain wherever candidates felt relatively sure of their seats.

It is revealing to follow, if only in a few instances, the Radical attempts to impose their policies on the politicians. In few constituencies, apparently, should success have been more certain than in Westminster. In that densely populated borough which had always enjoyed what was practically household suffrage Place had perfected a Radical organisation which had successfully captured both borough seats for its nominees, who had long held them unchallenged. But the Radicalism of the wealthy sitting baronets, Sir Francis Burdett and Sir J. C. Hobhouse, was what had passed for Radicalism with Wellington and Peel before 1830. Both now refused to be pledged to advanced Reforming activity in the new Parliament, and so set their most energetic Radical constituents the gravest of problems.

Burdett, who had represented the borough for twenty-five years, was not pressed hard, but Hobhouse, who had taken office, underwent different treatment. A committee of electors sent a deputation of three to see him on Sunday, November 18, 1832, when the elections were fast approaching. The deputation was charged with the four following questions:

1st.—As you, Sir John, have maintained the propriety of voting by Ballot, will you move for or support a motion to accomplish that purpose?
2nd.—As you were returned to Parliament to procure short Parliaments,

---

[1] The Ballot and Shorter Parliaments are among the points raised. For a time the position was not unhopeful.
[2] The effective Radical name for the heavy newspaper Stamp Duties and the high Paper Duty.
[3] Cf. Trevelyan's *Life and Letters of Macaulay*, ed. 1889, pp. 202-3.

Election Pledges of 1832

will you move for or support a motion for the repeal of the Septennial Act?

3rd.—As you made a motion in 1822 for the repeal of the Assessed Taxes, will you repeat that motion?

4th.—As you have advocated the repeal of the Taxes on Knowledge, will you move for or support a motion to repeal the Stamp Tax on Newspapers and the Excise Duty on Paper?[1]

Hobhouse's refusal to give the pledges required led to the adoption of the Ultra-Radical, Lieut.-Colonel De Lacey Evans, as a rival candidate. Though unsuccessful in December 1832, he ousted Hobhouse at a by-election in 1833, when the whole of shopkeeperdom had gone Radical on the Assessed Taxes question.

None of the new constituencies created by the Reform Bill was expected to be more Radical than Finsbury, Lambeth, Marylebone, and Tower Hamlets, four new two-member metropolitan boroughs with a higher proportion of £10 householders of the working and small shopkeeper class than was to be found anywhere else in the country. Throughout the Tory attempts to secure changes in the Reform Bill these constituencies had been the objects of special dread as breeding centres of an English Jacobinism. But a rank-and-file Radicalism was singularly difficult to organise in these huge aggregations of streets, courts, yards, and alleys suddenly set up as Parliamentary boroughs, and in 1832, at least, there issued no Dantons and Marats from their polls. On the contrary, the small shopkeepers and publicans suddenly promoted to political importance showed a keen desire for candidates of the most eminent "respectability." The vastest and dingiest urban constituency in the country, Tower Hamlets, sent to the Commons Lushington, a Whig ecclesiastical lawyer, and Clay, a wealthy merchant of no very decided politics. Finsbury, which ran Tower Hamlets close in point of dinginess, sent even milder politicians in the lawyers Robert Grant and Spankie. Here, however, an Ultra-Radical medical candidate made a good showing, thanks to the discovery of first-rate organising talent in a local shopkeeper of Ultra views. But Ultra-Radical money and "respectability" both proved insufficient for victory.

At first sight Marylebone, composed as it was of the reputable parishes of Marylebone, St. Pancras, and Paddington, hardly

[1] *Report of a meeting of electors held at the Salopian Coffee House, Charing Cross*, the 19th day of November, 1832 (printed).

seems as proper a home for combative Radicalism as Finsbury or the Tower Hamlets. Here, moreover, there were a couple of very strong Whig candidates in the field; Mr. Portman, a large landowner with extensive property in the borough, and Sir William Horne, the Attorney-General. Yet there were local reasons which contributed to make a democratically organised Ultra-Radicalism a strong electoral force in Marylebone even in 1832.

Nothing makes Radicals so quickly and so extensively as corrupt and costly ecclesiastical administration. In a metropolis where the most vigorous and influential working-class leaders had long been disciples of Paine and avid readers of the *Age of Reason*, such ecclesiastical jobbery as had been perpetrated in the parishes of St. Pancras and Marylebone was certain to arouse the strongest feeling. In the parish of St. Pancras the Church Trustees levied between May 1816 and March 1833 £130,104 of Church rates, and borrowed £85,000 in addition.[1] The ratepayers' money had been spent largely in erecting, furnishing, or repairing churches at jobbed figures which, it was alleged, would not bear the light of day. The salary figure for ministers, clerks, organists, etc., was also a grossly extravagant one.[2] In the Marylebone parish a Select Vestry had carried on similar enterprises, and had only been stopped with difficulty from pushing through Parliament in 1827 a Bill to erect for its rector a £4,000 parsonage, and to bestow on him compulsory "Easter offerings" of £2,000 per annum besides.[3] Even good Marylebone churchmen had turned and appealed to Parliament, and they turned still more when it was made plain that the Select Vestry had accumulated £227,000[4] of debt to the charge of the parish, largely on account of its loosely audited church-building. One item in the account for church furniture was actually £213 for two chairs. It is no surprise to find a local churchman ruefully reflecting that such chairs should have been fit for the Pope himself.[5]

A Vestries Act of 1831, sponsored by Hobhouse, had offered relief in these and other parishes by giving charge of parochial business to Vestries elected on a broad representative basis. Parochial committees of a Radical cast had quickly arisen, one in

[1] J. W. Brooke, *The Democrats of Marylebone*, 1839, p. 7.
[2] *Ibid.*, pp. 22–3.   [3] *Ibid.*, p. 2.   [4] *Ibid.*, p. 7.
[5] *Ibid.*, p. 7.

Election Pledges of 1832

Marylebone, several in St. Pancras, to arrange the first Vestry elections in May 1832,[1] and stayed in being for years afterwards engaged in capturing parochial machinery and patronage. These committees naturally formed the nucleus of a Radical constituency organisation. Indeed, when the Parliamentary election approached nearer, and a public meeting was called with the famous Joseph Hume in the chair, the pledges which it was resolved to demand from candidates eclipsed in democratic thoroughness those to be found in most other parts of the country. If returned, candidates were to promote:

> A sound and rational system of National Education free from pecuniary barriers or sectarian exclusion and by legislative enactments to prevent rather than punish crime.
> A Revision of the Poor and Excise Laws, and those affecting the administration of Justice and the election by the people of their own magistrates.
> The Abolition of the Punishment of Death except in cases of Murder.
> The Abolition of Tithes and all Abuses in the Church Establishment.
> The Abolition of all Slavery.
> The total Abolition of the Corn Laws and the Repeal of all Taxes that press on the Industry of the People.
> The Removal of all restriction on the Press and on the Diffusion of Knowledge.
> The Abolition of all Useless Offices and Repeal of Unmerited Pensions.
> A Reduction of the Staff and Standing Army; the Abolition of Impressment in the Navy, and of the Punishment of Flogging both in the Navy and Army.
> A Sufficient Control of the Parish Authority over the Police Force and a Reduction in its Expenditure.
> A Definition of the Law of Libel and the Punishment thereof.
> The Repeal of the Septennial Act.
> Equal Rights for Ireland with England and Scotland.
> The Establishment of the Ballot at all Elections.
> To do away with all Property Qualifications in the Elected and Electors.

Finally, candidates were to undertake "constant attendance to the House of Commons and at the Committees and to resign their seats when called upon to do so by a majority of their constituents at a public meeting duly convened."[2]

The list given above expresses without extravagances, Republican or Owenian, a Radicalism subscribable alike by Hume and O'Connell, Cobbett and Hunt. On a free vote every one of its

---

[1] J. W. Brooke, *The Democrats of Marylebone*, pp. 26–39, 58–82.
[2] *Ibid.*, pp. 140–1.

clauses would probably have won a numerical majority of a nation anxious for the future to have a large elimination of the cruelties and injustices of the past. But the problem of its imposition on the politicians was not thereby solved. In Marylebone, for example, there was no hope of committing the Whig candidates, Portman and Horne, to any part of such a programme. But Marylebone conditions encouraged more Radical candidates to appear and risk their money in a contest. A Sir Samuel Whalley presented himself with some of the prestige lent by a title, and, though declining to commit himself to the pledges, made it obvious that he was prepared to go much farther with Reform than the official Whigs. More advanced than Sir Samuel were two other candidates —Murphy, the Catholic oracle of the Radicals of St. Pancras, and Lieut.-Colonel Jones, who had done some useful agitation for Parliamentary Reform between 1830 and 1832. The election figures are interesting in view of the difficulty of campaigning in an eminently respectable constituency against candidates who, like Portman and Horne, had wealth, Parliamentary experience, and the prestige of having voted for the Reform Bill. The result was as follows: Portman 4,317; Horne 3,320; Whalley 2,165; Murphy 913; Jones 316.[1] In 1833, however, Whalley was to be more successful at a by-election, and in 1835 both seats were to become Radical.

The impression so far given of Radical electoral chances in 1832 is, perhaps, misleadingly depressing. There were, after all, hundreds and even thousands of wealthy or influential men in the country who had experienced a veritable sense of intellectual release when the old, hard High Toryism had been finally driven from power in November 1830. No more were the maddening old platitudes on the glorious British Constitution, "the wisdom of our ancestors," the special virtues of pocket boroughs, and the rare merits of Anglican Christianity to be mouthed at them with unctuous evangelical rectitude by Percevals and Liverpools. From this band of wealthy or influential Radicals, composed as it was of barristers, merchants, writers, military and naval officers, doctors, bankers, squires, and Whig peers' sons, a quite formidable corps of candidates emerged, prepared for extensive reconstruction of the political superstructure of society, if not of its economic basis. George Grote, for example, who had rendered great services

[1] J. W. Brooke, *op. cit.*, p. 143.

Election Pledges of 1832

in the City during the Reform crisis, and who was to top the City poll, announced that he stood for such things as Vote by Ballot, Triennial Parliaments, Abolition of the Taxes on Knowledge, Speedy Inquiry into the Constitution and Revenues of the Church of England, and a substitution of Moderate Fixed Duties on Corn for the existing Corn Laws.[1] John Humphery, again, who was successful at Southwark, was more radically explicit on Church matters than Grote ventured to be. He supported not only the Abolition of Tithes without Grote's mention of compensation, but talked of the appropriation of Church lands for the purposes for which they were originally intended, of the removal of the bishops from their share in temporal government, and of vesting the right of appointing clergy in the parishioners.[2]

Ireland witnessed peculiar election phenomena unparalleled elsewhere. Irish Radicalism did not principally interest itself with the giving and taking of pledges on Ballot,[3] Triennial Parliaments, Church Reform, Corn Law Repeal,[4] Free Trade, Termination of the East India and Bank Monopolies,[5] Abolition of Slavery, Reduction of Taxation,[6] Firm Handling of Sinecurism and of the Pension List, and such other topics of the kind as monopolised the attention of British Radicals. O'Connell was making Repeal of the Union the great issue in Irish politics, and thirty-eight of the successful Irish candidates were fully pledged to it.[7] Others for whom this was too radical had offered to consider it if Ireland was denied justice by the Reformed Parliament.[8] Irish election addresses are eloquent on what was the justice expected. They are full of demands for the Abolition of Tithes, Repeal of Vestry and Church Cess, Radical Change in the Grand Jury Laws, and

---

[1] From his Letter to the Electors, October 23rd, as reproduced in the Press.
[2] Letter to the Electors, November 26th.
[3] Major Beauclerk, successful candidate for East Surrey, issued a very Radical address more definite on this point than that of some urban Radicals. Letter to the Electors, October 25th.
[4] Fryer, elected for Wolverhampton, made this the principal point of his campaign. Letter to the Electors, June 12th.
[5] M. D. Hill, elected at Hull, put this into the forefront of his address of August 25th.
[6] Sir John Key, elected for London, offered to move the repeal of the House Duty, and pledged himself against the Assessed Taxes generally, the Malt Tax, the Soap Duty, Tithes, and the Corn Law. Address of October 27th.
[7] Cf. Fitzsimon, King's Co., Address, December 6th; Lynch, Galway City.
[8] Cf. Cornelius O'Brien's Address in Co. Clare, December 6th.

similar matters of burning interest to the Catholic masses.[1] Sometimes they promised action in regard to Irish development and the setting up a system of Poor Laws.[2]

A last look may be taken at the election issues of 1832 from the standpoint of Lambeth, where there was a particularly interesting contest. Lambeth was a borough composed of the parishes of Lambeth, Camberwell, and Newington; its population totalled 154,163, and the registered electors numbered 4,768. A local group of moderate Radicals, attracted by the political record of Tennyson D'Eyncourt, Member for Stamford, decided to invite him to contest the populous new borough the representation of which naturally brought more political weight than that of Stamford. D'Eyncourt was a landed gentleman of Lincolnshire who had sat in Parliament since 1818, and who at the age of forty-eight had just been bold enough to lay down his office in a Whig Government not apparently altogether to his liking. His election address issued on June 29, 1832, certainly announced a programme which might have been deemed over-bold in a minor Minister. Some quotations will illustrate its spirit.[3]

"Although we have obtained a Reform of the House of Commons," wrote D'Eyncourt, "Reform in its more extended and substantial sense is yet to be effected. . . . The new Parliament must anxiously devote itself to remove all evils and abuses . . . in the law, the Church, or the Executive Government and those which encumber our commercial and monetary systems . . . its earliest efforts must be directed to accomplish the abolition of slavery . . . to effect a fair commutation of tithes, a reform of corporations, an alleviation of the severities of the criminal law and of that military punishment which dishonours the soldier and degrades the nation."[4] By September 25th D'Eyncourt's Radicalism had grown more pronounced. To a meeting held that day he announced his conversion to vote by Ballot, his readiness to devote any Church surpluses available after Church reform to non-ecclesiastical purposes, his opposition to taxes on the Press, and his view that a graduated property tax might be substituted with advantage for some of the existing taxes.

---

[1] Cf. A. H. Lynch's Address in Galway City.
[2] Cf. T. B. Martin's Address in Galway Co. (From Press cuttings in the Howell Collection.)
[3] G. Hill, *Electoral History of the Borough of Lambeth*, pp. 19-20.
[4] A reference to flogging.

Election Pledges of 1832

It is, perhaps, unjust to suppose that D'Eyncourt's Reforming zeal was somewhat quickened by the fact that in addition to a strong local candidate, Hawes,[1] two advanced Radical barristers were in the field for the two Lambeth seats. Yet extracts from the Radical barristers' programmes would serve to show that it is by no means impossible that D'Eyncourt was pushed farther forward by their competition than might have been the case otherwise. One of them, for example, had announced: "The assessed taxes ought to be instantly repealed, the malt tax also: all taxes upon knowledge of the means of acquiring it ought to be abolished: tithes ought also to be abolished, and a better arrangement of the Church establishment and its revenues effected: all monopolies in trade and commerce should be thrown open: the corn laws should be revised; all useless places and unmerited pensions should be swept away: the duration of Parliaments should be shortened."[2] It was certainly a programme which seemed likely to have a wide appeal.

At the hustings D'Eyncourt went farther than ever before. Household franchise and triennial Parliaments were added to his programme, and his constituents were warned to "keep their eye on the landed aristocracy of the country" and its electoral bullyings stifling the popular voice.[3] Benjamin Hawes, the strong local candidate, hedged on the Ballot as he had already done on Church questions. No doubt he realised how large a proportion of the voters of Lambeth were not "ten pounders" merely, but fifteen, twenty, thirty, and forty pounders very apt to be disturbed by programmes whose principal appeal was to the lower depths beneath enfranchisement level altogether. Then followed one of the Radical barristers, Moore, with a full-throated denunciation of the bishops. "The extravagant manner in which the bishops were paid," he said, "excited universal indignation. One bishop, when accused last year of receiving £100,000 a year, modestly replied that he had not quite so much. What did the bishops do for their money? . . . They sold their votes in order to be translated to richer sees . . ."[4]

Finally spoke the second Radical barrister, Mr. Daniel Wakefield, who but for a family name laden with a good deal of scandal

---

[1] Whose address of June 23rd was indefinitely "liberal" save on the Corn Law and Free Trade, where a timid Radicalism was ventured. Hawes wanted the "respectable" vote. [2] *Electoral History of Lambeth*, p. 21.
[3] *Ibid.*, p. 33. [4] *Ibid.*, p. 36.

—utilised naturally by the Hawes party—might have had a fair chance of being returned with his friend D'Eyncourt. "It was now generally acknowledged," runs the report of his speech, "that the Reform Bill had failed to accomplish all that had been expected from it. . . . He thought that no man could be a real reformer who would not constantly demand the vote by ballot. Secondly, he was an advocate of that measure upon which the minds of the millions had long been made up, namely reform of the overgrown Church establishment. As to a commutation of tithes, any person who supported that was no better a reformer than Lord Henley, who was trying to turn Joseph Hume out of Middlesex. A commutation was only a new distribution of the mass of ill-gotten wealth. He would cut at the root of the tithe system and would sever the Church from the Government."[1]

The show of hands at the hustings was overwhelmingly favourable to D'Eyncourt and Wakefield, but the result of the polling demanded by the Hawes committee made it very plain that many of the hands raised for Wakefield at least must still have been unenfranchised. The voting figures were: D'Eyncourt, 2,716; Hawes 2,166; Wakefield 819; and Moore 155. The indications are that the balance of feeling among the voters was towards distrust of Ultra-Radicalism, and that D'Eyncourt's poll represents Tory homage to a Privy Councillor and Whig respect for one of the Ministry of 1830 as well as Radical support for "advanced reform." Certainly the Hawes vote must be interpreted as indicating a strong desire for caution in effecting legislative changes, a desire very widespread among moderate "respectables" if not among the populace. It is a commentary on the oligarchic political stratification represented by the Whig and Tory parties that Hawes as the son of an important commercial figure in Lambeth was often counted as a "moderate Radical" in his first years in the House of Commons. To derive an income from trade rather than from land, to wish revision of the Corn Laws and a remodelling of the Church of England, and to be dubious about the Church of Ireland's claims are the sum of Hawes's Radicalism.

From the after-the-poll speeches of the successful candidates it seems plain that they expected the problem of the State Churches to play a very prominent part in the debates of the first Reformed Parliament. According to D'Eyncourt, "a most extensive reform

[1] G. Hill, *op. cit.*, pp. 36–7.

of the Church was required—an end must be put to private patronage—the possessions of the Church must be redistributed —and the ministers of every parish must be elected by the people." Hawes, too, had evidently made some progress during an election campaign in a constituency whose populace had in Lambeth Palace and the income of the Archbishop of Canterbury who lived in it symbols of what they resented most keenly in the organisation of national life. "He wished to see Deans and Chapters swept away," announced Hawes, "and the funds possessed by the lazy drones given to the industrious clergy."[1] Strong language like this certainly mollified the dissenters, the religiously indifferent, and the anti-religious, even if it did not give them what they wanted.

[1] G. Hill, *op. cit.*, p. 40.

CHAPTER IV

THE REFORMED PARLIAMENT

"Sunday, *February* 3, 1833.

"Sir Robert Peel said to me that he was very struck with the appearance of this new Parliament, the tone and character of which seemed quite different from any other he had ever seen; there was an asperity, a rudeness, a vulgar assumption of independence, combined with a fawning reference to the people out of doors, expressed by many of the new members, which was highly disgusting. My friend R——, who has been a thick-and-thin Reformer, and voted with the Government throughout, owned to me this evening that he began to be frightened."

"Journal" *of* T. RAIKES, *Esq.*

"The Budget has been opened and the hocus-pocus of Downing Street let loose . . . the whole thing is from beginning to end, humbuggery of the worst description. . . . One thing is self-evident that there is not the slightest pretence to make even an attempt at relieving the suffering millions from any portion of their burdens. . . . We are then right glad to perceive that the National Union of the Working Classes think with us and have felt themselves compelled to call upon the 'people' in all parts of the country to prepare themselves for a National Convention."

"The Working Man's Friend," *April 27, 1833, p. 149.*

"The population of Ireland has doubled since the Union. Has her capital increased in the same proportion—and is there not a far greater mass of misery than there was before? . . . We propose repeal—others propose poor laws. What does he (the Secretary of the Treasury) suggest? All that Ireland requires is good government! . . . Let us pass over smaller details—the Arms Bill, the jury packing, the exclusion of Catholics on tithe questions, the infusion of theology into the police; let us go to great and essential incidents. . . . Your Reform Bill . . . adopted population as a standard here: you did not employ it in Ireland. . . . Your Coercion Bill . . . put upon the Statute-book a precedent for tyranny. . . . Your Tithe and Church Bills, your 147th clause, and those absurd and cruel experiments . . . to reconcile that most monstrous of all anomalies—a Church of one religion, and almost an entire nation of another. . . ."

SHEIL *on the Whig record in Ireland and urging Repeal, The House of Commons, April 25, 1834.*

M. HALÉVY has argued in his famous history of the years 1830–41 that the House of Commons gathered in 1833 contained like its predecessors an "overwhelming majority" of country gentlemen and members of the aristocracy. This is comment which may be dangerously misleading. It is true enough, of course, that such Ministers as Lord Althorp, Lord John Russell, Lord Howick, Lord Duncannon, and the Honourable Edward Stanley were scions of noble houses, and that behind them sat other scions like Lord Milton and Lord Molyneux. Yet it does not need a profound acquaintance with the life history, say, of Russell, Howick, and Milton to understand how the long period of Opposition to which they had been bred had trained them to a considerably deeper understanding of the deficiencies of the existing institutions of society than was normally to have been expected from aristocratic occupants of the Treasury Bench. The same deeper understanding may be found in many of the "country gentlemen" of old lineage who were to exercise more than average influence in the 1833 Parliament, whether a Cabinet Minister like Sir James Graham is considered or a Privy Councillor like Tennyson D'Eyncourt, a wealthy littérateur like Edward Bulwer or an economist of repute like Sir Henry Parnell, a widely travelled soldier like Sir Ronald Ferguson, or a benevolent "friend of the poor" like Robert Aglionby Slaney. All the considerable personalities named above, for example, show altogether wider individual deviations from the stock pattern of "country gentleman" than might be expected from the simple label. What, too, is to be said of Sir J. C. Hobhouse, son of a self-made lawyer, or Henry Labouchere, Francis Baring, and Edward Ellice, gentlemen all no doubt in the sense of landed qualification and all soon to stand high in official Whiggery, but with personal experience of the bank and the counting-house?

It is possible to blur the distinction between the Reformed Parliament and its predecessors in yet another way. It may be pointed out, for example, that such a Radical notability as Joseph Hume had first been elected to Parliament in 1812, and that the firebrand Daniel Harvey, the philosophic Henry Warburton, and the humanitarian William Ewart had all had long membership of the unreformed Parliament. But this again is not to allow for the fact that in the unreformed Parliament they had been voices

English Radicalism 1832–1852

crying in the wilderness, while now they were senior members of a formidable Parliamentary section and in close touch with vast popular forces outside. The prospect of the Radicals dictating the course of legislation and administration seemed to many to be very near.

Reform, indeed, permitted altogether new social layers and new Radical viewpoints to find expression. Brotherton, for example, the advanced Bible Christian vegetarian, was able to give Salford distinctly unusual representation. Fielden of Todmorden, the great employer who was soon to advocate a universal eight-hour day, brought Cobbett in with him for the representation of Oldham. In his *Journal*[1] the Tory, Raikes, made a special note of the return for Brighton under the nose of the Court of Faithful and Wigney, two "most decided Radicals talking openly of reducing the allowance to the King and Queen." The Brighton return takes precedence even of the election of Gully, the ex-pugilist and Newmarket betting man who surpassed the Tory Lord Mexborough in the favour of Pontefract. Dundee, again, celebrated the election of Kinloch, one of the Scottish Radicals who had been put under the ban of the law in 1819, and Cork City that of Dr. Baldwin, the medical Radical Repealer who added to his other interests one in the *Cork Mercantile Chronicle*.

The counties, too, the strongholds of the landed, witnessed not merely a fair number of Radical candidatures,[2] but a number of unusual returns. The most striking was, perhaps, that of the Quaker Joseph Pease for South Durham, for the very problem of his entry into the Commons bristled with oath difficulties. If it is wrong to describe John Walter, proprietor of *The Times*, as a Radical, it is none the less true to assert that his return as a member for Berkshire represented almost as great an electoral innovation as that of Pease, Darlington industrialist and railway promoter, for South Durham. Some Irish counties, of course, enacted complete electoral revolutions. The return of Feargus O'Connor at the head of the poll for County Cork was one of the most notable of these. Two others were the return of Finn of the *Dublin Comet* for Co. Kilkenny and Patrick Lalor of the *Carlow Post* for Queen's Country,

---

[1] Under December 15, 1832.
[2] E.g. in North Warwickshire and North Leicestershire which had industrial sections.

The Reformed Parliament

Another type new to Parliament was such a university professor as George Pryme, Professor of Political Economy at Cambridge. He reaped the reward of long attention to municipal interests when, in breach of the Duke of Rutland's long domination of the representation, he was returned as Cambridge's senior burgess. In Matthew Davenport Hill, one of the Hull members, advanced educational practice in schools received representation as well as Benthamic law; in William Tooke, member for Truro, friends of the new University of London, dreaded at Oxford and Cambridge as a potential seminary of godlessness, had a member very determined to press for a Charter. Richard Potter, elected for Wigan, and Attwood and Scholefield, elected for Birmingham, represented a very different Radical interest, that of the Political Unions. Sheffield, again, returned in James Silk Buckingham one of the most unusual men in the first Reformed Parliament. Successively sailor, printer, bookseller, merchant captain, and Oriental trader, he had passed on to issue a Calcutta newspaper whose bold attacks on East India officialdom had led to his expulsion. Converting himself into an Oriental traveller, he had finally reached London, and opened himself a way with his pen broad enough to make him the Ministerial choice in 1831 for "working the Press."[1] In Parliament he was to become the advocate of a number of advanced causes. Principally he pressed for the supersession of the East India Company, the abolition of "pressing" for the Navy, the establishment of Public Walks and Recreation Grounds, the provision of Literary and Scientific Institutes and Museums, and the official promotion of Temperance.

It is, of course, impossible to pass under close review the whole of the five hundred members returned to the 1833 Parliament as Reformers, or the fractions of that huge host who might be claimed as evident Radicals. Indications, however, have been given as to how it might be proved that the Reform Bill had done something to alter the social composition of Parliament, and even more the range of views it embraced. In this latter connection a study of the intellectual and social positions of the small group of Benthamite Radicals, denominated the Philosophic Radicals, would be found specially revealing. Four of their members were destined to leave substantial traces in the history

[1] J. R. M. Butler, *Passing of the Great Reform Bill*, pp. 151-2.

of the succeeding decades—Grote, Roebuck, Molesworth, and Buller—and the first three entered Parliament for the first time in 1833 in circumstances with whose recapitulation this section of the chapter must end. In the City Grote's candidature had made such an appeal that, though he had had none of their aldermanic and other local government experience, he yet left his fellow-members, Waithman, Wood, and Key, well behind on the poll; in Bath Roebuck, arriving with little more recommendation than an introductory letter from Joseph Hume, became an exceedingly popular member with its workaday population; and in north-east Cornwall Sir William Molesworth's wealth and family name permitted him to join the small company of English county Radicals.[1]

A preliminary investigation of the kind just attempted will do something to make it easier to follow the calculations which were made by contemporaries on the subject of the party composition of the 1833 Parliament. Party organisation was altogether looser than it is to-day, but both Whig and Tory authority can be found for estimating the vastly diminished Tory membership at about one hundred and fifty. More than five hundred members, therefore, were to be accounted either good Ministerialists, normally ready to follow the Government's lead, or more advanced Reformers determined to press that Government forward in the path of change faster than it would be willing to go of its own accord. One Tory estimate of January 1833 actually gave Ministerialists only 320 members as against 190 Radicals of varied types.[2] It seems hardly possible to-day to reach the latter figure, save by adding to the professed Radicals of different schools every Reforming member capable on occasion of giving one anti-Government vote. To the Attwoods and Cobbetts, the Grotes and the Roebucks, the Buckinghams and the D'Eyncourts must be added all the Dissenters, all the manufacturers, all the humanitarians, all O'Connell's "tail," and finally all such occasional remonstrants as Ingilby of Lincolnshire and Key of London.

[1] This section of the chapter has been based on biographies or autobiographies of Althorp, Russell, Graham, Hobhouse, Cobbett, Pease, Pryme, Attwood, Silk Buckingham, Grote, Roebuck, and Molesworth; notices in the *Dictionary of National Biography* and Press cuttings on the 1832 election in the Howell Collection.
[2] Lord Mahon to Sir R. Peel in C. S. Parker, *Peel Papers*, ii, 209-10, speaks of not less than 190 "thick-and-thin Radicals, Repealers from Ireland; members or friends of the Political Unions, and so forth."

The Reformed Parliament

The proceedings of Parliament were soon to make it plain that the Government would rarely need to fear any combined demonstration from the discordant groups of more advanced Reformers. On such questions, too, as might lead to a junction of Radical groups against the Government the support of Sir Robert Peel's followers would often be forthcoming.

It did not take the more pugnacious Radicals long to find out that they would be quite incapable of seizing control in the new Parliament by frightening the Ministers into subserviency. Hume made the first demonstration when he tried to impose a new Speaker upon a Government which had already determined to retain Manners Sutton's experience to control a probably difficult House. Though Manners Sutton had played a considerable part in Wellington's plans to form a Tory Government in May 1832, the Government succeeded in beating off Hume's attack by 241 votes against a mere 31.[1] Another trial of strength came not long afterwards when O'Connell, not without a measure of justification, voiced his indignation at the severity of the references made to Irish agitation in the King's Speech, and tried to get the formal Address to the Crown, moved by Ministerialists in reply, referred to a committee of the whole House. Though O'Connell had obtained strong debating support from British Radicals in his attacks on Stanley's coercive administration as Chief Secretary, he obtained but 40 votes all told against the Government's 428.[2]

Cobbett's "violence and unmannerliness," again, soon made it plain that he could never hope to carry any great Parliamentary weight despite the eager attention with which his doings were at first followed out of doors. Though his first scanning of the election results had led him to hope for a possible following of 100[3] in attempts to coerce the Government, his thoroughgoing amendment to the Address raised only a division of 23 against 323.[4] Cobbett's attempts to punish Peel proved specially unfortunate, for Peel succeeded in impressing the new House from the very first, and to an almost sensational degree. To what standing the anti-Peel vendetta reduced Cobbett can be seen from the five supporters he raised against 298 when he moved

---

[1] *Hansard* (3rd series), xv, 76.
[2] *Ibid.*, p. 455. D'Eyncourt's milder tactics won 60 votes against 393.
[3] *Working Man's Friend*, January, 5th, p. 22.   [4] *Hansard*, xv, 549.

English Radicalism 1832–1852

in May to expel Peel from the Privy Council.[1] It was the inevitable fate of one whose mind was composed of little but passionate and contradictory prejudices—prejudices which had already ranged him against the removal of Jewish disabilities, and were soon to set him in opposition to another great Radical cause, that of Popular Education.

The Government seems to have been considerably relieved by the early Radical failures to establish a grip on the House. Their relief is most graphically evidenced, perhaps, in a letter of Creevey's dated February 22nd.[2] Creevey, an old Parliamentary ally of Grey's turned placeman-toady, wrote as follows in reviewing the Parliamentary situation of the opening weeks in the Commons. "The start the other day was most favourable for the Government. Hume boasted beforehand that he was sure of 100 followers: so that 31 only was a woeful falling-off. It seems to be put beyond all doubt that Cobbett can do nothing. His voice and manner of speaking are tiresome, in addition to which his language is blackguard beyond anything one ever heard of. O'Connell too was disgustingly coarse . . ." and again, "It is made perfectly manifest by their first vote that the reformed Parliament is not a Radical one, when Joe Hume and the Right Honourable Tennyson, all the O'Connells and all the Repealers with Cobbett to boot could only muster 40 against 400."

Another observer reporting from a different angle found the situation the same. On March 9th J. S. Mill wrote to Carlyle as follows: "The Reformed Parliament has not disappointed me any more than you: it is so ridiculously like what I expected: but some of our Utilitarian Radicals are downcast enough, having deemed that the nation had in it more of wisdom and virtue than they now see it has, and that the vicious state of the representation kept this wisdom and virtue out of Parliament. At least this good will come out of their disappointment, that they will no longer rely on the infallibility of Constitutionmongering; they admit that we have as good a House of Commons as any mode of election would have given us, in the present state of cultivation of the people. They are digging a little nearer to the root of the evil now, though they have not got to the tap-root. Read Roebuck's article on National Education in Tait's last number."[3]

Yet if Radical leaders were not able to dictate their own

[1] *Hansard*, xvii, 1324.   [2] *Creevey Papers*.   [3] *Letters of J. S. Mill*, I, 39.

The Reformed Parliament

conditions to Whig Ministers, they were a formidable force for criticism. On February 14th, for example, Hume raised 138 votes against 232 in pressing against sinecures, on March 21st Attwood divided at 158 against 192 on the subject of current distress, and on March 26th George Robinson had a division of 155 against 221 for a proposition to substitute a tax on property in place of the fiscal burdens pressing most heavily on "productive industry." Out of doors, also, the populace was waiting impatiently for tangible results from Parliamentary Reform; the Radical Press, stamped and unstamped, was still growing in power,[1] and the Political Unions remained a rallying-point for Radical and Ultra-Radical dissatisfaction.[2]

When the Whig Government capped a thoroughly unpopular record of Irish Coercion, Sinecure Retention, and Currency and Taxation Conservatism with a Budget which drove farmers and metropolitan shopkeepers into furious revolt, a dangerous situation developed. For a time Parliament threatened to pass out of Ministerial control,[3] and out of doors meanwhile the Birmingham Political Union tried to organise a vast national demonstration against Ministers,[4] and the National Union of the Working Classes to stage a National Convention. The preparatory meeting for the Convention was forbidden, but crowds assembled nevertheless, whose dispersal by the still very unpopular Metropolitan Police was the reverse of gentle.[5] For weeks afterwards there was a tense atmosphere in the capital as the Crown attempted to secure the conviction of one of the public, who was alleged to have stabbed a policeman to death. But danger passed as first a coroner's jury found justifiable homicide,[6] and then the jury empanelled for the murder trial found Not Guilty. In eagerly following these proceedings plebeian discontent with the achievement of the Reformed Parliament found a not very reputable vent. It is significant, perhaps, that during this time criticism of

---

[1] E.g. Early in 1833 there first appeared the very ably produced *Working Man's Friend* as an unstamped 1d. weekly, and the more licit *True Sun* followed with morning, evening, and weekly editions despite the crushing taxation which had been designed to make such things impossible.
[2] Cf. notices in Raikes's *Journal* under February 25th and April 26th.
[3] See *Hansard*, April 26th, for its defeat on the Malt Tax.
[4] Raikes's *Journal* under May 3rd. The Birmingham meeting was on the 7th.
[5] For the events of May 13th, *Working Man's Friend*, May 18th, pp. 169–73.
[6] *Working Man's Friend*, May 25th, pp. 178–83. The murder trial was in July, *Ibid.*, pp. 236–7.

the proceedings of the Political Unions is to be found even in the democratic Press.[1] Most of them were, indeed, very rapidly to lose their importance as increasing dominance by violent and vulgar clap-trap drove forth the last middle-class elements and some of the best working-class elements from their midst. But, as will be shown later, decline among the Political Unions in 1833 denoted no abatement in Radicalism's pressure on existing institutions. Working-class Radicalism, for example, was turning increasingly during the closing months of the year towards the vast conception of the Grand National Consolidated Trades Union.[2]

Against this general background the efforts of Parliamentary Radicalism during the 1833 Session can be better evaluated. The "organic reform" which Conservatives, whether of Whig or Tory complexion, most feared was the liberation of the voter from the "legitimate influence" of property by means of the Ballot. On April 25th Grote's motion to introduce a method of polling employed in France and in twenty of the twenty-four states of the American Union as the surest guarantee of individual political liberty was rejected by 211 votes against 106.[3] On July 23rd D'Eyncourt led an attempt for Triennial Parliaments which raised a vote of 164 against 213,[4] and secured a Treasury Bench admission that the existing system, which left the voter exposed to seven years of impotence to change his member, was not in the abstract the most desirable one. Two Radical efforts to secure changes of detail in the Reform Bill had meanwhile been defeated.[5]

On July 30th Roebuck in a most notable speech launched what "philosophic Radicalism" was beginning to consider the most promising way of remoulding the national future, a project "for the universal and national education of the people." The Government persuaded Roebuck to desist from pressing his elaborate and startling plan for a Central Education Department under a Cabinet Minister who would organise Teachers' Training and Text Book Composition, and would supervise also the work

---

[1] *Working Man's Friend*, June 15th, p. 204. Cf. E. L. Bulwer on Political Unions in *England and the English*, i, 188–90.
[2] William Lovett, *Life and Struggles*, ed. 1920, i, 88, ascribes the decline of the powerful National Union of the Working Classes to this cause.
[3] The pamphlet reproductions of Grote's speech give a list of 137 Ballot supporters among M.P.'s.
[4] *Hansard*, xix, 1107.   [5] *Ibid.*, May 22nd, June 17th.

The Reformed Parliament

of elected District School Authorities administering a series of infant, industrial, and evening schools.[1] On August 17th was announced its own contribution to the education of England and Wales. The Treasury proposed to subvention the existing religious societies founding schools to the extent of £20,000 during the year 1834.

That no greater result had come from impressing a Whig Government with the fact that Prussia had built up a remarkably organised national scheme of universal education, and that France was following on similar lines with effects that might become startling in the industrial sphere, needs, perhaps, a little explanation. Philosophic Radicals might be dreaming of producing a new nation after their own heart in schools of their own peculiar design, but the stubborn fact remained that they got virtually no help from working-class agitation. Nor can working men be blamed for concentrating their agitation on subjects which promised them relief in their own time and not in their Benthamised children's or grandchildren's. Besides, their most trusted leaders in politics, Cobbett and O'Connell, were both enemies of the new projects. Rising soon after Roebuck, O'Connell, the typical Catholic democrat, had objected to State education of the Prussian model as "regimental," and to State education of the French type as organised to "unchristianise the country."[2] To the vote of £20,000, again, for "teaching reading and writing" Cobbett objected not only because the older race of unlettered fathers worked better than their lettered sons, but because the money would go "but to increase the number of schoolmasters and schoolmistresses, that new race of idlers."[3] Hume, too, managed to find a reason for disliking the vote of £20,000 which should go with a general attitude of Benthamism. The amount was too small to be useful, and there was, besides, £500,000 of income from ancient endowment which could be made available when a proper scheme should be planned.

The Radicals, then, had had little success with the particular innovations for which any section of them had stood. In regard to them "public opinion" out of Parliament had failed to rise to the heights necessary to operate large conversions within. It should be remembered, however, that Radical motions after all were only short breaks in a Parliamentary process which turned

[1] *Hansard*, xx, 139 sqq.   [2] *Ibid.*, p. 169.   [3] *Ibid.*, pp. 734-5.

English Radicalism 1832-1852

primarily about the critical Irish situation and the Budget. In regard to the Budget proposals, certainly the public outside Parliament showed no apathy. Indeed, it may almost be said that the Radical forces which had carried Reform in 1831 and 1832 were in 1833 largely absorbed in the work of forcing the Government to surrender unpopular items of taxation. There was great farming agitation, supported by the Radicals, against the Malt Tax which Tories might approve as yielding an indispensable five millions of the fifty millions of national revenue, but which the farming community counted as one great source of "agricultural distress." But Malt Tax troubles even in barley areas were surpassed in intensity by House Duty troubles in the towns.

The most vexatious branches of inland taxation in the country were the notorious House and Window Duties, grouped in the fiscal division of the Assessed Taxes. There were few Radical pledge-lists of 1832 which had not, therefore, condemned the Assessed Taxes to destruction. The universal dislike of the Window Duties' taxation of light and air is explicable enough in the crowded and insanitary towns, but assessment on the monstrously inequitable basis of the detested House Duty arrangements noticed below[1] made them particularly provocative. House Duty to the extent of an annual £1,200,000 was raised on a system of assessment which allowed huge mansions like Raby and Lambton to be returned as below £100 in annual value, while crowded urban tenement houses with a poverty-stricken family to each room were often rated higher than large country houses.

It is not surprising, then, to find the Assessed Taxes agitation rising high in the early spring of 1833, and heavy enough petitioning to Parliament being organised by the particularly irritated shopkeeping community to affect many urban members. Having already sustained an awkward Parliamentary check on the Malt Tax, Ministers had good reason to give thought to the Parliamentary move threatened against the House and Window Duties on April 30th. They gave plain notice to the Commons

[1] The following comparative table of House Duty Assessments, as they had existed in 1833, was still being used in 1846 after their abolition to stimulate anti-aristocratic prejudice. Chatsworth, £400 per annum; London Tavern, £1,000 per annum; Stowe and Blenheim, £300; White Hart, Bath, £900; Eaton Hall, £300; Plough, Cheltenham, £850; Alnwick and Belvoir, £200; Old Ship, Birmingham, £750; Hatfield House, £200; Laing's Hotel, Manchester, £200.—*The Aristocracy of England*, by John Hampden, Junior, ed. 1846, p. 247.

The Reformed Parliament

that such major dislocations of their Budgetary plans as were being contemplated by some of their habitual supporters would involve the reimposition of the dreaded Income Tax.[1] By such means did Ministers prevent more than 157 members from insisting on large changes in the Budget. But the shopkeeping community, though offered some concession, refused to be content, and persisted with an agitation which raised one dangerous situation in May and was again provoking formidable lawlessness in the autumn and winter.[2] In February 1834 the Government, in possession of an opportune Budget surplus, decided at length to dispense with the House Duties. It was wise. A very critical temper had been developing in normally "respectable" circles towards the financial demands of the State, and the "property tax" was being called for increasingly as a method of winning relief both from unjust fiscal imposts and the heavy Poor Rate.[3]

Of the Irish affairs which figured so prominently in the Parliamentary business of 1833, only the briefest mention can be made. The Government's policy was twofold. On the one hand there was a severe Coercion Bill to deal with the grave agrarian lawlessness, born in tithe resistance to the alien State Church and nurtured in the resentments evoked by a most oppressive system of tenures. On the other hand there were Irish Church proposals designed to make the apparatus of the State Church in Ireland somewhat less grievous and provoking to the immense Catholic majority.

On Irish Coercion, Radicals helped O'Connell to contest the need for taking powers to transfer whole Irish districts to military control by proclamation. Owing to the Government's ability to make play with the swollen statistics of crime,[4] the rally of sufficiently imposing numbers to make the Ministers revise their policy proved impossible. On Irish Church questions the Radicals would have been prepared to go farther altogether than a Government which contained zealous churchmen, and was fearful

---

[1] For the critical situation in politics, see *Journal* of T. Raikes, April 26th–30th.
[2] *Ibid.*, for May. For later developments involving police concentrations and the use of troops, *Annual Register*, Chronicle, pp. 142, 151, 155. Cf. *Poor Man's Guardian*, November 2nd, for an Ultra-Radical view of the Marylebone situation in which workmen were assisting tradesmen to resist distraint for non-payment of Assessed Taxes.
[3] Sir J. S. Lillie, *Observations on the Reformed Ministry and Reformed Parliament*, 2nd ed., 1834, pp. 77–80.
[4] E.g. *Hansard*, February 27th, xv, 1216–62.

English Radicalism 1832–1852

too of becoming involved in another conflict with the Lords. Yet, on the whole, they were ready to take the original Whig Bill with moderate thankfulness. It did after all reduce the Irish Episcopate from twenty-two to twelve,[1] end cathedral and other ecclesiastical sinecurism, pay for church repairs by a levy not on ratepayers but on a central fund raised by the taxation of the higher Church incomes, and finally, and most hopefully, promise to leave an annual £60,000 from Church properties available for general Irish purposes. By August the moderate Radical satisfaction of March was largely over. Valuable provisions had been dropped[2] and important principles sacrificed in order that the remainder might make their way to the Statute Book through ecclesiastical bigotry, Court dislike, and Upper House ill will.[3]

It is necessary to turn to two activities of the Parliamentary Session of 1833, more significant for posterity at least than any so far discussed, the Abolition of Colonial Slavery and Factory Reform. Abolition, it is plain, primarily owed its position on the Parliamentary agenda of 1833 to the fervent plebeian interest the subject had excited during the election campaigns of 1832. Thereafter less was heard of the West India interest's special pleadings against Abolition, ranging from the sanctity of a class of property recognised in the Bible to the certainty of commercial ruin and black insurrection if Abolition were carried even with compensation.[4] But if the West India interest now resigned itself to the necessity of liberating the slaves in name, it enforced nevertheless very heavy compensation in taxpayers' money and in compulsory labour from the "liberated" slaves. Indeed, but for a revolt of the chapel Radicals outside the House producing marked effects within, slave-owners would have received both twenty millions in cash and in addition twelve years of compulsory "apprenticeship" from their ex-field slaves. Though the compulsory "apprenticeship" was finally reduced to a period of seven

---

[1] Though there was one Radical suggestion of a reduction to four bishops, and Hume (May 13th) thought one would suffice. Again, even the very moderate Pryme was anxious to take the opportunity of providing for the displacement of Irish bishops from the Lords.
[2] Cf. *Hansard*, June 21st, for one Radical attempt to stay this, which raised 148 votes against 280.
[3] For a critical Government defeat in the Lords, *Hansard*, xix, 1232. There were already Tory schemes to force a dissolution and reinstate Conservatism (*Raikes's Journal* under November 5, 1833).
[4] For a typical statement of the West India interest's standpoint, see the article on "Negro Emancipation" in *Blackwood's Magazine*, February 1832.

The Reformed Parliament

years, chapel Radicals continued to conduct a bitter agitation for some time in an effort to free the slaves sooner. Even Hume was moved to preach them caution.[1]

The Factory Act of 1833 has a very special history. The way, it is true, had been prepared by Owen's long agitation between 1815 and 1819, and Hobhouse's subsequent legislation of 1825 and 1831. But ultimately the strongest force which impelled the Act of 1833 to the Statute Book was not the philanthropy of the wealthy but the persistent ten-hour pressure of the relatively well-paid and well-organised operative spinners.[2] Anxious to stem the "over production" certain to bring in its train a period of depression with reduced pay and unemployment, the operative spinners saw in the sentimentality excited by the overworked factory child the very thing which might give them the victory they had failed to win by strike methods in 1829–30. They pressed, indeed, for nothing less than the legal prohibition to work factory machinery for more than ten hours a day. So complete, too, was their capture of operative and philanthropic feeling in the factory districts that, with some assistance from the Evangelical Tory Chairman of the Commons Factory Committee of 1832, it proved possible to draw up what moderate opinion considered an altogether exaggerated indictment of the normal effect of factory

---

[1] Halévy's *History of England*, 1830–41, p. 86. For the throwing over of Buxton's leadership by the Abolition zealots see *Memoirs of T. F. Buxton*, pp. 338–9. For fuller treatment, see chapter xxi below.

[2] Cf. that able, if hostile, pamphlet of 1834, *Character, Object, and Effects of Trades' Unions*, pp. 28–9. "From the evidence relating to the cotton trade taken before the Factory Commission, it appears that the spinners were invariably the most strenuous, and in many cases the only supporters of the Ten-Hour Limitation Bill. It is also shown by the Report of the Commission that the spinners are nearly the sole employers of the children, and consequently answerable for the cruelty, if any there be, in their treatment. Why then, it may be asked, did they not leave the promotion of this Bill to those of their fellow-workmen, who could support it with a decent regard to consistency? Those who have not penetrated their secret motives may think this surprising; the circumstance, however, admits of an easy solution. The effect produced by the Spinners' Union affords an explanation of this anomalous conduct. It has been before stated that the high wages given in this business cause a greater number of persons to enter it than the trade can employ, and that these superfluous labourers receive a weekly stipend from those who are in work to prevent them from engaging themselves under the combination prices. The Union calculated that had the Ten-Hour Bill passed, and all the present factories worked one-sixth less time, one-sixth more mills would have been built.... The effect of this would have been to cause a fresh demand for workmen; and hence those out of employment would have been prevented from draining the pockets of those now in work.... Here we have the secret source of nine-tenths of the clamour for the Ten-Hour Factory Bill."

English Radicalism 1832–1852

labour on the child. It was not difficult, therefore, for the protesting factory owners to obtain the Royal Commission of 1833 designed to go into the factory situation more scientifically and impartially than had been done in 1832. This was a result which caused great chagrin among the baffled operatives, and led them to attempt the organisation of a veritable boycott of the Commissioners sent to the factory districts.[1]

The outcome was strange. Two of the three members of the Central London Commission of the Factory Inquiry were the Benthamite Radicals, Chadwick and Southwood Smith, who, it is obvious, secured large changes in the scope of the contemplated legislation. Their social and economic doctrines prevented the Benthamites' solicitude in regard to hours from extending beyond the child worker proper below the age of thirteen.[2] But for these was obtained a minimum age of entry into the textile factory, a maximum working day of nine hours and working week of forty-eight hours, and finally that famous compulsory provision for two hours' schooling every working day, which reconciled to the Bill many of the more kindly adherents of non-interference in industry. Another Benthamite innovation was the appointment of a professional Home Office Factory Inspectorate,[3] a service which in the hands of men like Leonard Horner, commissioned in October 1833, was to exercise such influence for the humanisation of industry. Again, if the Benthamites had had their way, the Act of 1833 would have legislated more widely than it did in regard to factory ventilation and cleanliness, and a limited employers' accident liability might have found its way sooner to the Statute Book.[4] Benthamites allowed State solicitude for adult workers to function in the sphere of health if not in that of hours.

A concluding glance may be bestowed on the progress of some other Radical causes. The famous Poor Law Commission on which Chadwick's influence was increasing was inquiring into the abuses of poor relief administration, and the Corporation Commission with Parkes as a leading figure was about to undertake another epoch-making inquisition into the English municipal

---

[1] For details, see Alfred, *History of the Factory Movement*, ii, 35–55. For the whole Ten-Hours movement, see Hutchins and Harrison, *A History of Factory Legislation*, chapter 4.

[2] *Factory Commission Report*, pp. 50–3, Parliamentary Papers, 1833, xx. The Government nevertheless very wisely decided on giving some legal safeguards to a new class of "young persons" between thirteen and eighteen years of age.   [3] *Ibid.*, pp. 68–9.   [4] *Ibid.*, p. 73.

The Reformed Parliament

corporations. Armed with the findings of still further Commissions, Brougham was continuing his efforts at legal reform. Unfortunately, his major projects of setting up a Land Register and Local Courts of the nature of the later County Courts broke against too many interested prejudices for success.[1] The Land Register fell a victim in the Commons to the dislike of country gentlemen for the publicity it would give to their property transactions, and to the allied resentment of attorneys, fearful apparently of losing those invaluable conveyancing perquisites which made it impossible for any but the very rich to acquire real property safely. The Local Courts Bill, on the other hand, was killed in the Lords by Tory Law peers, whose hostility to Brougham led them to disregard the very urgent need of providing tribunals where tradesmen's small debt business might be cheaply done.

A humaner criminal justice as well as a cheaper civil justice had been one of the most persistent Radical demands from the candidates of 1832. Though, therefore, the year 1832 had itself seen important deductions from the offences deemed capital, pressure on the Government for more continued, accompanied by such things as calls for a Prisoners' Counsel Bill. Military and naval flogging, too, was an aspect of State brutality to the socially humble for whose abolition all Radicals called. On the Mutiny Bill proceedings, therefore, Hume was able to divide the House at 140 against 151 on the subject.

Finally, it must be remarked that Radicals found an opportunity to express their hatred of commercial monopolies during this same wholly unprecedented Session of 1833.[2] The approaching expiration of the Charters of the Bank of England and the East India Company had attracted wide attention among Radicals in the 1832 election. Repeal of the Bank and East India Charters had, indeed, often stood in Radical pledge-lists cheek by jowl with Repeal of the Corn Law and Abolition of Sinecures. In point of fact the Bank of England, which had hitherto monopolised joint-stock banking within a sixty-five miles radius of the City,

---

[1] *Hansard*, xviii, 1010, for defeat of the Land Register project. *Hansard*, xix, 372, for the defeat of the Local Courts Bill. Another project of Brougham's to abolish the vast bulk of the Ecclesiastical Courts was never pressed.

[2] It was the Radical energy in contesting "abuses" of every kind which was mainly responsible for the hitherto unexampled figure of 1,270 hours of sitting spent by the Commons during this Session (*Hansard*, xx, 907).

was compelled for the future to allow other joint-stock companies to compete for ordinary banking business if not for note issue. The East India Company, too, surrendered its last monopoly—the China trade. Radical economists taught, and Radical politicians and voters believed, that thenceforth tea would be cheaper and more efficiently distributed and joint-stock banking accommodation more widely available in the former Bank of England monopoly area. They were right.[1]

[1] In regard to the chapter's whole content that well-known Whig Government "puff" of itself, its views, and its record, *The Reform Ministry and the Reformed Parliament*, has its uses. It was very widely distributed.

CHAPTER V

CORN LAW, SINECURE, AND PENSION LIST GRIEVANCES

"The principal obstacle to a more extended sale of our manufactures was the high price of corn for the food of the people. ... It was not on the article of corn alone that these most mischievous and most impolitic restrictions were imposed. ... No manufacture was protected above 30 per cent with one exception whilst there was a long list of articles of agricultural produce which the people of this country were absolutely prohibited from importing—imported beef, pork, black cattle of any kind, fish with one exception. ..."
    March 6, 1834, HUME, *moving the undertaking of a Corn Law Inquiry,* "Hansard," *xxi, 1202 sqq.*

"THE QUARTERN LOAF, Flour and Baking . . 4¾d.
                    Landlord's Tax . . . . 3¾d.

                                               8½d."

Title section of a cheap Anti-Corn Law periodical on sale in 1834 and advertised in the "Poor Man's Guardian," *March 29th, p. 64.*

"... the Black Book, as it is called, in which all places and pensions are exhibited, has struck terror into all who are named and virtuous indignation into all who are not. Nothing can be more malapropos than the appearance of this book at such a season, when there is such discontent about our institutions and such unceasing endeavours to bring them into contempt. ..."
    C. C. F. GREVILLE'S "Memoirs," *December 5, 1830.*

A SPECIAL chapter has been reserved for detailed consideration of two subjects which were to be among the most difficult for a Reformed Parliament to handle: Agriculture and the Corn Laws on the one hand, and on the other a large reduction of State expenditure, which would permit extensive remissions of taxation. Among the factors which had contributed to the growth of Parliamentary Reform fervour few should rank higher than hatred of the expensive and corrupting Sinecures and Pensions associated with the old régime, and detestation of the Corn Laws which seemed to urban Radicals to be that régime's most characteristic fruit. Certainly few subjects figure more prominently in Radical resolutions as to the future, and few had contributed more to the solidarity of the alliance of middle-class and artisan elements in so many scores of Political Unions.

Since 1815 the Corn Laws had been one of the sorest points in the national life—a permanent irritant of urban, manufacturing, and exporting interests against the politically dominant landlord caste which had imposed them. Even before the 1815 Act had been put upon the Statute Book, 42,473 Westminster petitioners, representative of many thousands of others, had voiced their dislike to its provisions in language as trenchant as the following:

> Your petitioners have noticed with extreme concern and anxiety the introduction . . . of a Bill relative to the importation of corn, which, if passed into a law, must necessarily and directly produce, and in the judgment of your petitioners is intended to produce, a great and permanent increase in the price of one of the first necessaries of life, for the sake of enabling the proprietors and cultivators of land to maintain undiminished a splendid and luxurious style of living, unknown to their fathers, in which they were tempted to indulge during the late war, so highly profitable to them, and so calamitous to most of their fellow-subjects.[1]

The particularly anxious corn year of 1826–7, which served to convince even the Liverpool Government that some modification of the existing Corn Law was necessary, saw the appearance of a work destined to be a rallying-point of opposition to the Corn Laws until their repeal. It was Perronet Thompson's famous *Corn Law Catechism* which destroyed much of the huge erection of irrelevant argument which had been thrown like a sheltering wall round the central position of the Landed Interest. Such

---
[1] *Hansard*, xxx, 110–11.

Corn Law, Sinecure, and Pension List Grievances

propositions and answers as those which follow show how easily anti-Corn Law propaganda developed into a complete frontal attack on the whole of the social position and activities of the governing caste, an attack which promoted that hatred without which neither Parliamentary Reform nor Corn Law Repeal could have been carried.

That the race of English gentlemen, English farmers, and English yeomen is worth preserving.
A. Not if they are kept at the public expense. As long as they keep themselves everybody is glad to see them.
That they are a source of light and knowledge to the lower orders.
A. They teach them what they are anxious they should learn; and others do the same.
That they have sound political principles.
A. They take the side which they think best for themselves; and others do so too.
That they fought the battle against the Jacobins.
A. Which other people are to pay for.
That they kill foxes and others.
A. The mole-catcher would do it better.
That they sit at Quarter Sessions.
A. And strange things they sometimes do there.[1]

Another work of 1827 which served as a permanent incitement of the populace against the Corn Laws was Ebenezer Elliott's *Corn Law Rhymes*.[2] A single stanza may be taken to illustrate the kind of attack to which the "Landed Interest" laid itself open by its stiff-necked attitude on the Corn Laws.

> Bread-Tax-eating absentee,
> What hath bread tax done for thee?
> Cramm'd thee from our children's plates,
> Made thee all that nature hates,
> Fill'd thy skin with untaxed wine,
> Fill'd they breast with hellish schemes,
> Fill'd thy head with fatal dreams—
> Of potatoes, basely sold
> At the price of wheat in gold,
> And of Britons sty'd to eat
> Wheat-priced roots instead of wheat.[3]

Nor were there lacking voices on the landlords' side which

---

[1] *Catechism on the Corn Laws*, 4th ed., 1828, pp. 117-19.
[2] First Series "printed by order of the Sheffield Mechanics' Anti-Bread Tax Society" reappeared in paper covers at 9d., 1831. A second series was printed in London, 1833.   [3] From the famous "Black Hole of Calcutta" Rhyme.

urged a modification of attitude. Sir James Graham, the Cabinet Minister of 1833, had put the seal on his importance when in his *Corn and Currency* of 1826 he had pressed his fellow-landlords to come to an agreement with the middle classes on the subject of the Corn Laws. For propagandist purposes, however, no work proved more deadly than Lord Milton's famous *Address to the Landowners of Great Britain*. Coming as it did from the heir to one of the most important landed properties in the country, it made peculiarly impressive material for Anti-Corn Law agitation during the whole period between 1831 and 1846.[1] Though in 1828 the "Landed Interest" had permitted apparently fairer sliding-scale schemes of corn duty to replace earlier corn importation prohibitions and restrictions, Milton urged upon his fellow-landowners the common justice and prudence of giving up their whole machinery to keep corn prices high and rent rolls swollen. He argued that the Corn Law policy was actually harming the tenant farmers and the agricultural labourers whom the "Landed Interest" was affecting specially to protect. The one class was kept on the stretch by high rents which constantly had to be reduced by favour on term-day, and the other class was paying far too much of its scanty wages for high-priced bread. Meanwhile the whole of the urban and manufacturing interests were forced by high food prices on to a scale of money wages which raised the price of their manufactures, restricted their export markets, and reduced that demand for farm products which was the surest foundation of rent.[2]

And with the "Landed Interest's" special pleading Milton dealt as follows: "By some, however, I am told that the charges upon landowners are heavy: that their estates are loaded with mortgages and family settlements: that they are called upon to maintain a certain state in the country; that for these purposes their rents must be kept up; and that, to keep up rents corn must be dear. I hope that these difficulties of the landowner are exaggerated by imprudent advocates of the Corn Laws; for, depend upon it, no impartial judge can ever think that such arguments justify the imposition of a heavy tax upon the community."[3]

Nor were opponents of the Corn Law in 1833 confined to

[1] Anti-Corn Law Societies may be found circulating the *Address* in the form of the February 1831 edition during the winter 1833–4.
[2] Milton's *Address to the Landowners of Great Britain*, ed. January 15, 1834, pp. 9–12.   [3] *Ibid.*, p. 8.

Corn Law, Sinecure, and Pension List Grievances

such sources as those which have been enumerated. Landlords' patriot anxiety about the probable subservience of British policy to foreign Powers, if the nation should become dependent on them for any considerable portion of its food supply, could be countered by the arguments of the great Ricardo in that moderate and illuminating essay of 1822, *On Protection to Agriculture*. Ricardo had urged that if Britain should come to look to Prussia and Russia for a portion of its supplies, those countries would have the greater motive for keeping on good terms.[1] He had been sceptical, too, concerning the likelihood of any great flow of cheap foreign corn into the country directly importation was made somewhat less difficult, and his scepticism was borne out by the reports of the official investigator William Jacob as published in 1826 and 1828.[2] That the miserably inefficient and largely serf-conducted agriculture of North-Eastern Europe, barely capable of producing from the ground four times the seed sown,[3] could ever under existing conditions export more than a thin stream of corn was shown to be impossible. The "Landed Interest's" nightmare, that is, of ten million quarters ready to flood England at forty shillings below the home price was revealed as a very baseless ground for allowing landlord and farmer a panic code. And the general problem of foreign retaliation against the Corn Law might be found popularly handled as follows:

>Hopeless trader, answer me!
>What hath bread-tax done for thee?
>Ask thy lost and owing debts,
>Ask your bankrupt-thronged Gazettes.
>Clothier, proud of Peterloo!
>Ironmaster, loyal too!
>What hath bread-tax done for you?
>Let the Yankee tariff tell,
>None to buy, and all to sell:
>Useless buildings, castle strong,
>Hundred thousands worth a song;
>Starving workmen, warehouse full,
>Saxon web, from Polish wool,
>Grown where grew the wanted wheat,
>Which we might not buy and eat. . . .[4]

[1] David Ricardo, *On Protection to Agriculture*, 4th ed., pp. 85-6.
[2] *Report on the Trade in Foreign Corn and on the Agriculture of the North of Europe*, 2nd ed., 1826. *A Report respecting the Agriculture and the Trade in Corn in some of the Continental States of Northern Europe*, 1828.
[3] William Jacob, *Tracts Relating to the Corn Trade and Corn Laws*, 1828, p. 140. [4] *Corn Law Rhymes*, 3rd ed., 1831, pp. 38-9.

English Radicalism 1832-1852

Sight should not be lost, moreover, of other factors contributing still further to that profound dislike of the Corn Law which had made it a theme of heated oratory from most of the Radical candidates at the elections of 1832. Anything which savoured of landlord oppression at once tended to bring to Radical lips that challenge to the legitimacy of the private appropriation of land which Thomas Spence had made so resoundingly in a previous generation. How at least one Manchester Ultra-Radical of 1832 felt on the subject may be learnt from a letter printed in the *Poor Man's Guardian* of April 14th, and signed *One of the Oppressed*. Arguing the inadequacy of the Reform Bill, the correspondent wrote: "It is supposed that the members for the manufacturing towns will be enabled successfully to attack and abolish the Corn Laws. Nothing can be more delusive. They must be holders of stolen land themselves before they can become members. Besides, if they were not, a sufficiency of land-stealing members has been secured by the division of counties to make head against the large towns, and for the loss of the rotten boroughs, so that in short the corn laws will be equally secure as ever . . ." And though middle-class Radicals might take a less severe view of private property in land than this, the gloomy forecast of Ricardo concerning the inevitability of rent swallowing an ever-increasing proportion of the national income as the growth of population forced the cultivation of ever poorer soils was a standing incitement to contest the "Landed Interest's" position on the Corn Laws. Many might well feel that such slackening in the pace of the inevitable rent increase as was obtainable from foreign importation ought not to be denied.[1]

Yet, strange as it may seem after all this prologue, the Reformed Parliament, though it contained so large a representation of advanced Whiggery and urban Radicalism, hardly produced any immediate danger for the Corn Law of 1828. Indeed, the abundant harvest of 1832 had brought corn prices so perilously low for farmers burdened with heavy rents, tithes, poor rates, and county rates that on April 26th many Radicals may be found enlisting in the attempt to procure them a large reduction of the Malt Tax.[2] On May 3rd, again, the Chancellor who had had to beat off the

---

[1] This view was given a terrible emphasis in Ebenezer Elliott's *Corn Law Rhyme*, "Caged Rats."   [2] See Division List, *Hansard*, xvii, 716-18.

Corn Law, Sinecure, and Pension List Grievances

attempt was nevertheless offering a Select Committee on Agriculture.[1] Since the populace was in a contented enjoyment of cheap bread, and the admittedly distressed farmers believed the impugned Corn Law vital for their interests, the political atmosphere was now the reverse of favourable for a downright Anti-Corn Law attack. Even the motion of May 17th to substitute fixed corn duties, suspensible in time of dearth, for the existing sliding-scale duties which made corn importation an unending speculation full of dangers, failed to win more than 106 against 305.[2] The Select Committee on Agriculture, again, when it reported in August gave the Corn Law Repealer nothing of cheer. "Practical agriculturists" saw nothing for it but to let Rent, Wages, Currency, and Corn Law alone, and set to nibbling at County Rate, Tithe, and Poor Law modifications in aid of the farmer's struggle to pay his rent.[3]

During the recess many politicians were facing their constituents to explain their conduct through a most eventful Session. Macaulay, as an urban Whig member connected with the Government, found it necessary to give his Leeds constituents among other things an explanation of the Reformed Parliament's failure to move on the Corn Import legislation, which had for so many years been condemned as unjust to urban interests. A quotation from his speech will show the type of apologetics indulged in even by the Anti-Corn Law section of official Whiggery until the "low fixed duty" was adopted officially in 1841 as the one chance of averting electoral disaster. "I believe," said Macaulay, "we have the truth and reason of the case on our side; I believe it is possible in time to enlighten the agricultural interest, and by free discussion, and the inculcation of sound principles, they may be brought round to as complete an agreement with you on the subject of the Corn Laws as they have been on the subject of the Reform Bill. . . . I hold the Corn Laws to be one of the greatest possible evils. But I do not think the public mind ripe for putting this question on a sound footing. It would be towns against country—a certain victory for the agriculturists in the House of Lords—a doubtful contest at a general election—and I will not say what would be the effect of violence." Well might Albany Fonblanque bitterly comment in the Radical

---

[1] *Hansard*, xvii, 958.   [2] *Ibid.*, 1378.
[3] Report, Parliamentary Papers, 1833, v.

English Radicalism 1832–1852

Examiner, "Was Reform carried by the folding of hands, and a hope that boroughmongers would see the error of their ways?"[1]

As the corn prices ruling in the winter of 1833–4 had, thanks to another abundant harvest, fallen below those of 1832–3, the cry of agricultural distress failed not to be raised again. Anxious to secure some portion of the Budget surplus for itself, the "agricultural interest" strongly supported a motion made on February 21st by the Marquis of Chandos to the following effect: "That in any reduction of the burthens of the country which it may be practicable to effect by a remission of taxes, due regard should be had to the necessity of relieving, at the present period, the distressed condition of the agricultural interest."[2] The fact that this motion won 202 votes against 206 gave Ministers abundant reason to press on the preparation of the Poor Law Amendment Bill with its promise of lower Poor Rates for the corn-farming of pauperised Southern England. Projects for tithe commutation were also among the ministerial plans of bringing relief to a farming community whose main trouble was, of course, over-high rents, fixed by the standard of the great gains possible in a succession of dear corn years.

Though a "distressed agriculture" and relatively cheap bread did not offer Radicals the best campaigning conditions against the 1828 Corn Law, the winter of 1833–4 saw nevertheless quite vigorous Anti-Corn Law activities.[3] Particularly marked were the efforts of the Radical daily, *The Morning Chronicle*, to prove to working-class Ultra-Radicals that a steep downward revision of corn-import scales would give them through cheap bread and a quickened flow of trade the practical benefits they were then vainly seeking from the formidably swelling Owenism of the time.[4] On March 6, 1834, Hume, supported by a considerable volume of petitioning, moved for the substitution of a fixed duty in place of the existing scales which virtually prohibited foreign importation until home prices approached scarcity level, and even

---

[1] Quoted from A. Fonblanque, *England under Seven Administrations*, ii, 395–6.   [2] *Hansard*, xxi, 659.
[3] Including some pamphlet distribution by Anti-Corn Law Societies, the gathering of petitions to Parliament, and the publication of a cheap sheet, *The Quartern Loaf*, for Ultra-Radicals.
[4] Especially in inserting a series of *Letters on the Corn Laws and on the Rights of the Working Classes*, by H. B. T.

Corn Law, Sinecure, and Pension List Grievances

then made it a highly speculative enterprise. Sufficient Anti-Corn Law sentiment was stirred to provoke two nights of debate and a division of 155 against 312,[1] and a feature of the discussions was the unflinching condemnation of the Corn Laws uttered by Poulett Thomson, Vice-President of the Board of Trade. That Minister, who together with some less important colleagues had won Cabinet leave to speak and vote as he wished, denounced the Corn Laws as the principal cause which had spurred on countries, denied reasonable admission for their corn, to undertake "prohibitory tariffs" and to "manufacture for themselves."[2] The receipt of a huge Liverpool petition, moreover, permitted the renewal of Parliamentary debate later in the month.[3]

But this was to be the end of effective Anti-Corn Law pressure for a very considerable time. Political factors denied the first Reformed Parliament a third Session in which the issue might again be raised, and its successor, issuing from the elections of January 1835, contained a far stronger Tory representation. Not, therefore, till serious manufacturing decline set in and corn prices began to mount to substantial figures did Clay, the representative of the terrible poverty of the Tower Hamlets, renew the Anti-Corn Law challenge on March 16, 1837.

It was not on the Corn Law alone that Whig Ministers failed to do anything to redress the pressing grievances of those to whom they principally owed their political triumphs. On Budgetary matters also the significant gesture to the liberated people of 1833 was withheld and the prompt remission of the hated House, Window, and Newspaper Duties denied. Ministers failed to see that it was the wrong time to continue their Budgetary courses of 1831 and 1832, and to search conscientiously in the Customs and Excise Lists for small items, trammelling the course of commerce, upon which to expend their surplus. Anxious not to seem to merit Tory criticisms of truckling to the mob, they had to be drawn from their preoccupation with such Budgetary items as the shopmen and marine insurance duties, and the soap, raw cotton, and tiles imposts[4] by the House Duty revolt of the autumn of 1833. The terms in which the subsequent Whig

---

[1] *Hansard*, xxi, 1345. [2] *Ibid.*, p. 1286.
[3] March 19th, 20th, and 21st.
[4] Items abolished or reduced in the Budget of 1833. *Hansard*, xvii, 326

surrender of February 14, 1834, were announced are significant: "If I were to look at the question simply as a financial question," the Chancellor told the Commons, "I think that there are other taxes the repeal of which is more desirable. . . . But I feel it very strongly that it is one of the ingredients in the impropriety of a tax, that it is most exceedingly unpopular. Taking all the circumstances into consideration . . . I do think that the best suggestion I can make is that the House Tax should be repealed."[1] He was right, even if the sum of duties remitted or reduced had to sink from the 217 of 1832 and the 63 of 1833 to the mere 16 of 1834.

The Whig handling of the Sinecure and Pension List situation, again, was not one to placate Radicals deeply read in the extraordinary details which had provided unending matter for a generation of Radical journalism and had created the taste for *Black Books*.[2] At the very opening of the Reformed Parliament, Hume produced some facts concerning sinecure appointments in the army which involved two of the King's natural sons with Tower of London appointments, and took 138 members into a division against the Government's 232.[3] It was not a comfortable situation for the Ministers, who found it wise to accept two of Hume's resolutions on April 18th which prohibited future sinecure appointments or the award of emoluments to persons executing duties by deputy.[4] Moreover, to ward off the dangerous Radical attacks still possible on sinecure holders already appointed, Treasury speeches on the important occasions of April 19th and July 16th were well packed with figures of offices abolished and economies made. Only the most imposing façade of this kind would, it was justly felt, withdraw animosity from much of the rottenness Whig Ministers still felt themselves bound in honour to shelter within.[5]

---

[1] *Hansard*, xxi, 365. This attitude, of course, brought Tory reproof.
[2] The taste for *Black Book* matter had been particularly strong between 1830 and 1832. Carpenter's *Political Letters*, again, of the winter of 1830-1 are typical of democratic literature, and contain much of the same Pension List, etc., material. Cf. issues December 4th, December 7th, February 4th.
[3] *Hansard*, xv, 713.   [4] *Ibid.*, xvii, 298-303.
[5] E.g. such a sinecure as that of Greville of the *Memoirs*, who, besides his Clerkship to the Privy Council, held the Secretaryship of Jamaica at £2,000 per annum as the result of an appointment "in reversion" made in 1801, when he was seven. The *Memoirs* reveal Greville's successful defence of his "property."

Corn Law, Sinecure, and Pension List Grievances

One of the greatest of Whig mistakes after the Reform Bill was the obstinate attempt to leave the Pensions List position untouched out of an exaggerated deference to the sovereign and an exaggerated chivalry to the beneficiaries of the old régime. A firm but decorous handling of the worst of the admitted scandals in a long-odious institution still in 1830 absorbing £180,944 annually[1] would have done much to ease the relations between Whigs and Radicals between 1833 and 1837, when the Pensions List inquiry was at length conceded. To maintain that it was right to put a man as wealthy as Lord Eldon on the Pension List for a retiring pension, to put there not only Mr. Croker but Mrs. Croker also, not only such left-handed royalties as the Fitzclarence ladies or such dubious Dublin Castle protégées as Madam Fitzhum and Lady Hill, but the Countess of Mansfield and the Duchess of Manchester as well,[2] was impossible. Again, such hereditary pensions as those awarded in past times to Graftons, Schombergs, and Ginckells plainly called for liquidation. But the Whigs professed to be content with the measures taken by the Wellington Government, which had divided the pensionaries of 1830 between the Consolidated Fund and the £75,000 Pension List of the future. As old annuitants dropped off from the Consolidated Fund their pensions would not be available for new grants. These would be confined to the sums freed by the death of pensionaries on the £75,000 list. No constitutional security, however, was given that this new list would not repeat the scandals of the old, though on a smaller scale.

The Radical attack on Pension matters was conducted by the eloquent and virulent Daniel Whittle Harvey, who year after year was to bring the Government into difficulties. What made his eloquence the more formidable was the unrelaxing attention paid by the populace outside Parliament to a subject which showed the ruling classes at their worst. Thus before the opening of the 1834 Session the Ultra-Radical public was being offered for twopence "the amount of each pension continued on the Civil List" and "in a few days, at the same price, the Pensions on the Consolidated Fund, forming a companion to the above and showing the amount taken by the aristocracy out of the pockets

---

[1] *Hansard*, xxi, 497, 3.   [2] Extracted from the *Black Book*, ed. 1832.

English Radicalism 1832-1852

of the labouring people."[1] On February 18th, therefore, when Harvey moved for a Select Committee to inquire into the grounds on which the pensions on the £75,000 List had been granted, the Government made a concession. It offered to be bound by a Resolution of the House reserving future recommendations to the Pension List to "such persons only as have just claims on the royal beneficence or who, by their personal services to the Crown, by the performance of duties to the public, or by their useful discoveries in science and attainments in literature and art, have merited the gracious consideration of their sovereign and the gratitude of their country."[2] In effect, past pensions were to be screened from inquiry and the first call on future pensions was still to be reserved to the Fitzclarences,[3] Court ladies, military gentlemen, and the like. Scant wonder, then, that Harvey raised a vote of 182 against the Government's 190.[4]

Before Harvey finally forced the Whigs to give way in 1837 he had had to use some very plain language, hailed with delight outside Parliament by Ultra-Radicals infuriated by the new Poor Law. Speaking of the "300 titled paupers" on the Pension List, Harvey waxed sarcastic that "able-bodied paupers were no longer to live upon the parishes, but strong-boned peers were to live upon the state." He defied the Government to show in the list "a dozen names of persons who could be said, even on the most charitable construction of their acts, to have deserved their pensions by services rendered to the country in the field or at sea, but numerous were the names of those who had earned this reward by great political profligacy or gross personal vice. . . ." His crowning audacity was a direct attack upon the King. "The list contained five daughters of the King of England, possessed though he was of such extensive private revenue. That it should be so was a monstrous insult to the people of England. The amount of private revenue was very great and but little known. The incomes derived from the duchies of Cornwall and Lancaster, what were they, could any one tell?"[5] Yet even after this "scurrilous" language of April 19, 1836, Harvey was able to raise

---

[1] Advertisement in the *Poor Man's Guardian*, January 4th, p. 428.
[2] *Hansard*, xxi, 498.
[3] William IV's family of ten by Mrs. Jordan, the actress.
[4] *Hansard*, xxi, 546.
[5] Extracted from the *Annual Register's* excellent summary of the speech, History, pp. 230-2.

Corn Law, Sinecure, and Pension List Grievances

in Parliament a vote of no less than 146 against the combined Whig and Tory 268. Plainly, Radical and Ultra-Radical constituents were still agitated by the Pensions question.[1]

[1] But the Pension List was to give trouble to the end. The Government had to fight the Tories (December 8, 1837, *Hansard*, xxxix, 933) to carry the inquiry into past pensions, which they at length conceded to Radical pressure. On the other hand, they created Radical discontent by omitting Harvey from the inquiry on the ground that he declined to pledge himself not to divulge its proceedings during their course (December 18, 1837, *Hansard*, xxxix, 1273). Harvey, no doubt, declined to tie his hands in advance because he had a shrewd idea that Whigs and Tories would combine on the Select Committee conducting the inquiry, and would save all but the most patently indefensible of the pensions. This is in fact what finally happened (see the very moderate *Black Book of England*, 1847, pp. 182–222), so that a Pensions List question of a kind survived for the Chartists to agitate. Additional matter for criticism came from the survival of the hereditary pensions unscathed, and the occasionally dubious use to which it was found possible to put the truncated Pension powers allowed Victoria by the 1 Vict. c. 2, clauses 5 and 6 (*Black Book of England*, 1847, pp. 223–50).

CHAPTER VI

END OF THE GREY GOVERNMENT

"Society in this country exhibits the strange anomaly of one part of the people working beyond their strength, another part working at worn-out and other employments for very inadequate wages, and another part in a state of starvation for want of employment.

"Eight hours' daily labour is enough for any human being, and under proper arrangements sufficient to afford an ample supply of food, raiment, and shelter, or the necessaries and comforts of life, and to the remainder of his time every person is entitled for education, recreation, and sleep.

"The productive power of this country, aided by machinery, is so great, and so rapidly increasing, as from its misdirection to threaten danger to society by a still further fall in wages, unless some measure be adopted to reduce the hours of work, and to maintain at least the present amount of wages."

Foundation Axioms of the Owenite Society for National Regeneration, adopted November 25, 1833, "Morning Chronicle," *December 7th:* "Cobbett's Register," *December 7th.*

"The Dissenters are not satisfied—they *cannot* be satisfied with their present position. They claim the *equality* of citizens. They do not ask to be placed above the Churchman, they cannot *submit to be placed* beneath him."

"The Case of the Dissenters," *5th edition, 1834, p. 9.*

"Mr. Howitt.—They had prayed for the separation of Church and State. Earl Grey said he was sorry for it. The expression of such sweeping desires for the destruction of the establishment would embarrass ministers, alarm both Houses of Parliament, and startle the country. He wished they had confined themselves to the removal of disabilities connected with marriage, burial, registration, and such matters. . . .

"It was replied that neither Parliament nor the country was now so easily frightened—all that concerned Dissent was whether these measures were just. . . ."

Report of a Dissenting deputation to Earl Grey, January, 1834. Extracted from the "Annual Register," *Chronicle, pp. 7–8.*

SUCH Corn Law and Pension List agitations as have been dealt with in the previous chapter were no novelties to the British politicians of 1834. In the Parliamentary recess of 1833-4, however, the seething Radical world of which most of the politicians understood so little was big with two newer agitations which are to form the subject of the present chapter, the operative effort to gather the entire working class into one gigantic Trades' Union, and the Dissenting effort to gather a movement which should force the surrender of Church privileges.

First must be examined the way in which the impoverished working-class multitudes, bitterly disappointed with the record of the Reformed Parliament, saw a new hope of altering the world quickly in rallying to Robert Owen's project of the Grand National Consolidated Trades' Union. Owen's social views had penetrated deeply through the working classes, but before 1832 positive action had virtually been confined to the limited field of the co-operative consumers' store, though eventual co-operative production was nearly always an ulterior aim. Of such co-operative stores hundreds had been founded since Mudie had organised co-operation amongst the London printers in 1821,[1] but many staggered rapidly into commercial pitfalls or those constituted by negligent or dishonest store-keeping. Yet the ideal possessed an ever-fresh attraction, and the amount of co-operative enthusiasm to be found in these years may be judged not merely from the biography of Lovett but from a study of the issues of the *Brighton Co-operator* (1828-30), the *Birmingham Co-operative Herald* (1829), the *Chester Co-operative Chronicle* (1830), and the *Lancashire and Yorkshire Co-operator* (1831-2), which the zeal of local societies produced. Co-operator enthusiasm rose particularly high when in the summer of 1832 Owen made a considerable effort to grapple with the co-operative problem from the angle of production and exchange. The National Equitable Labour Exchange with a supporting newspaper in the *Crisis* certainly appeared for a time to be a portentous economic phenomenon.[2]

---

[1] M. Beer, *A History of British Socialism*, 1921, i, 200-6.
[2] The first number of the *Crisis* at 1d. appeared on April 14, 1832, and was evidently connected with the Third Co-operative Congress arranged to open in London on April 23rd (p. 4). The first announcement of Equitable Banks of Exchange appeared on June 16th (*Crisis*, p. 50), and on June 30th followed an elaborate explanation, with examples, of book-keeping and store-keeping

English Radicalism 1832–1852

Owen was soon carried forward on the wave of the active and optimistic Trade Unionism of 1833[1] to contemplating that idea of a federal junction of all trades already projected by Doherty in the National Association for the Protection of Labour. As forecast by Owen, however, the new scheme envisaged nothing less than the enrolling of the entire working population into Co-operative Productive Unions federated together to arrange distribution and manage the State. A Congress of Owenite Societies, for example, was thus addressed by Owen on October 6, 1833: "I will now give you a short outline of the great changes which are in contemplation, and which shall come suddenly upon society like a thief in the night. It is intended that national arrangements shall be formed to include all the working classes in the great organisation, and that each organisation shall become acquainted with what is going on in other departments; that all individual competition is to cease; that all manufactures are to be carried on by National Companies. . . ."[2]

The characteristic weakness of all Owenite apocalypticism is obvious at once to modern eyes. In this instance it is the lofty disregard of the certainty that the State and the interests controlling the industrial apparatus of society would neither be converted to the Owenite revelation nor allow themselves to be quietly superseded. For many years, indeed, the whole police mechanism of Home Office, Lords-Lieutenant, and Justices of the Peace had been largely trained upon the detection, in conjunction with industrial employers and farmers, of combination perils and illegalities.[3] That is why, through the stirring times which followed, the *Poor Man's Guardian* was consistently to preach that Owen was making a mistake in leading his Consolidated Union movement away from politics, and especially

---

mechanism which would have to be set up (pp. 62-3). But already on September 29th (p. 120) the Central Labour Exchange was overcrowded with deposited articles, and a fortnight later it was advertising a drastic change in its acceptance policy. Yet even after it had been compelled to announce that the Labour Notes issued in return for manufactures accepted from artisans had to be used with equal quantities of cash in the purchase of meat and coals (p. 155), enthusiasm was still running high enough to project Branch Exchanges for the East End, Deptford, and Birmingham. For an unfavourable notice even from an unorthodox economist-politician, see Poulett Scrope's *Principles of Political Economy*, ed. 1833, p. 243.

[1] Best mirrored in James Morrison's famous builders' weekly, the *Pioneer*.
[2] *Crisis*, October 12th, iii, 42.
[3] Cf. *Melbourne Papers*, pp. 147-51, for the watching of the agricultural labourers of Hampshire in 1832.

End of the Grey Government

away from the universal suffrage demand whose fulfilment would be necessary for final success.[1] Yet that working-class politicians took the movement seriously almost at once and rallied to its support is evident from the very *Poor Man's Guardian* which reported the Congress. Other factors, too, were making important allies for Owen just at the time when he must have been occupied with the task of launching his Consolidated Union. Thus in November Fielden, the Oldham M.P., and Doherty, the remarkable organiser of the cotton spinners, were associated with the Manchester movement for "National Regeneration" to which Cobbett gave publicity in his *Register*, and which sought to establish itself nationally in alliance with Owen. Its programme was an eight-hour working day to begin from March 1, 1834, and to be accompanied by a system of national education.[2]

Meanwhile the Owenite propaganda among the Trade Societies was mightily assisted by a bitterly contested Derby trade dispute which lasted throughout the winter and enlisted the sympathy of the entire working-class world.[3] At Derby came to a head that bitter antagonism between an over-confident Labour, undiplomatically blunt, perhaps,[4] in its attempt to dictate wages and conditions, and irritated employers who had already been stung in the Manchester building trades, for example, and in the Yorkshire dyeing trade to attempt the demolition of the formidable Trades' Unions facing them by refusing work to all who were members.[5] The *Pioneer* newspaper, as befitted the organ of the

---

[1] E.g. in the issues of December 7th and December 14th.
[2] *Cobbett's Register*, December 7th; *Morning Chronicle*, December 7th; *Pioneer*, December 7th, December 21st.
[3] *Poor Man's Guardian* and *Pioneer*, January 1834 issues.
[4] Cf. *Character, Object, and Effects of Trades' Unions* (1834), pp. 32–3: "Mr. Leatham, a master mason at Liverpool, having discharged a workman from his employ, the Committee of the Union suspected that he had done so with a view to punishing the man for his supposed activity in managing the affairs of the combination. They accordingly sent him a letter *ordering* him to appear before the Committee the same evening, and to give up the name of the person who had communicated to him the information respecting the part his discharged workman had taken in the Union. . . . Messrs. Patteson, master masons at Manchester, discharged a couple of men because they had refused to work at a building at which bricklayers not belonging to the Union were employed. They received in consequence a long remonstrance from the Society, from which the following is an extract: 'Unless you take them again into your employ, on Saturday afternoon next, at one o'clock, all your hands will withdraw themselves . . . and so remain until you do reinstate the above-mentioned R. and W., and further that each and every one in such strike shall be paid by you the sum of four shillings per day for every day you refuse to comply.'"
[5] *Poor Man's Guardian*, July 1833, pp. 238, 254.

English Radicalism 1832-1852

most powerful of the Trades' Unions, that of the builders, was especially energetic in the dispute.[1] Indeed, it evolved that ambitious scheme of setting all the Derby "turnouts" to work again as co-operative producers which the Grand National Consolidated Trades' Union had to take over almost at birth. Meanwhile the Grand Consolidated organisation was not merely being born, but was growing to portentous size with great rapidity by receiving the affiliation of all manner of Trade Societies, those already in existence before its appearance, and those whose creation[2] had been stimulated by the great working-class enthusiasm attending its birth.

The first Convention of the new monster organisation took place in February 1834. It resolved not only to support the Derby strikers by a shilling per head levy throughout all its affiliated organisations, but also made arrangements to grow bigger still. Miscellaneous lodges, embodying several crafts, were to be formed in areas where such organisation was most suitable, and women's lodges also were to be set up. Nor did these resolutions remain unfulfilled, as the prompt formation of such lodges as that of the Chelsea Gardeners and Labourers, and the Grand Lodge of the Female Shoe Binders showed.[3] The *Pioneer's* comment on the Convention, indeed, made while it was sitting, may well have been disturbing to such official eyes as scanned it in search of information on a movement which was disquieting authority. "There are two parliaments at present sitting, and we have no hesitation in saying that the Trades Parliament is by far the most important: and will in a year or two be the most influential. It is more national than the other . . . and the constitution is much larger. The Union is composed of nearly a million of members, and Universal Suffrage prevails among them."[4]

Among those who had been attracted to adhere to the new movement were the farm labourers of the Dorsetshire village of Tolpuddle, threatened as they were with a reduction of wages to the monstrous level of six shillings a week.[5] The local Methodist chapel supplied a central core of stalwarts and a leader, George Loveless, who obtained the Flax Dressers' Union rule book from

[1] *Pioneer*, December 7th, 14th, 21st, 28th, January 4th, 11th, 18th.
[2] E.g. Saddle, harness, and collar makers, *Pioneer*, February 22, 1834.
[3] *Ibid.*, March 15th, p. 249.   [4] *Ibid.*, February 22nd, p. 214.
[5] George Loveless, *Victims of Whiggery*, ed. 1875, p. 5.

End of the Grey Government

Leeds,[1] and even procured the visit of "two Trade Society delegates"[2] to initiate in Tolpuddle a Grand Lodge of the Friendly Society of Agricultural Labourers. By the end of January 1834 the local magistrates were in possession of some information concerning the grisly though customary rites attending the swearing in of new members,[3] and had rumours, too, of a project for a labourers' strike to be assisted by strike pay from Manchester.[4] They approached Lord Melbourne at the Home Office, and were encouraged to proceed.[5] On February 24th, accordingly, six of the labourers in the Union were arrested for "administering unlawful oaths," and at Lord Melbourne's suggestion, and "for the sake of promptitude in bringing the offenders to justice," prosecution proceedings were hurried forward to permit of a trial at the approaching Assizes.[6] On March 19th, therefore, the six arrested labourers received the astounding sentence of seven years' transportation from a judge anxious to intimidate the growing membership of the Grand National Consolidated Union. Greville's entry of April 3rd, made after he had spoken with a friend back from the Dorchester Assizes, shows the temper of the Court. "On the event of the trial," he was told, "the lower and labouring classes had their eyes fixed, and the conviction was, therefore, of great consequence: any relaxation would have been impossible under the circumstances." When Lord Melbourne, the Whig Home Secretary, ignoring all the journalistic and political protests[7] made, hurried the prisoners off to Australia before a sufficiently imposing national remonstrance could be staged, he did much to sever the last hold of House of Lords Whiggery on the populace.

It seems obvious from the whole history of the Dorchester case that the portentous growth of the Grand National had excited not merely the apprehension of local authorities but also of the Home Office. "The proceedings in your county," wrote Melbourne

---

[1] J. Frampton, J.P., to Viscount Melbourne, March 29th, Add. MSS. 41567, L. No. 23.   [2] *Victims of Whiggery*, p. 5.
[3] For an Exeter swearing-in where two wooden axes, two large cutlasses, two masks, two white garments, a large figure of Death with the dart and hour-glass, etc., were seized by the authorities (*Poor Man's Guardian*, January 25th). This was more imposing material than was used in Tolpuddle.
[4] Add. MSS. 41567, L. No. 1.   [5] *Ibid.*, No. 3.
[6] *Ibid.*, No. 8, March 6, 1834.
[7] Even *The Times* thought the sentence "too severe" on March 21st, and on April 1st was still hoping for mercy. For the first of numerous petitions presented by the Radicals, see *The Times*, March 26th.

to the Dorsetshire magistrate chiefly responsible for the prosecution, "are a part of the general system which is now attempted to be established in many other parts of the Kingdom, and they proceed from a general directing Authority . . ."[1]

The savage Dorchester sentence, however, did not break up the Grand National as Melbourne seems to have expected.[2] Indeed, the great Union never seemed more powerful than when it staged the imposing protest demonstration of April 21st in Copenhagen Fields, a very disciplined affair for all the huge crowds gathered[3] and the tens of thousands of Trades' Unionists wearing their trade colours in their button-holes. But on the one hand the Government declined all concession, and on the other, despite the efforts of the Owenite *Crisis* to secure the deferment of all strikes until the Grand National was solidly organised,[4] such strikes were already afoot. At Oldham twelve thousand men had struck after the arrest of two men at a lodge meeting had led to bloodshed in an attempt at rescue, and there followed the pillage of an employer's house. The London tailors, again, who had been specially prominent at the great Dorchester labourers' demonstration, launched only four days afterwards their move for a ten-hour day at six shillings during the four summer months and an eight-hour day at five shillings during the rest of the year.[5]

The *Pioneer* and *Crisis* of ensuing weeks must have made rather cheerless reading for fervent Trades' Unionists. A great delegate meeting, indeed, was summoned for the beginning of August, but the complete collapse of the Derby strike, the successive defeats of the London tailors and the London shoemakers,[6] who had found the Grand National no help, and finally the widespread employers' measures to force their men out of Unions of whatever kind, seem to have broken up the Grand National completely even before that date. It certainly seems

---

[1] Add. MSS. 41567, L. No. 8.   [2] *Melbourne Papers*, p. 160.
[3] The *Poor Man's Guardian* estimate of the crowd was 120,000, 70,000 of them with union ribbons (April 26th, pp. 91–2). The *Times* allowed the gathering to have numbered between 27,000 and 30,000 (April 22nd).
[4] The *Crisis*, issues for April 26th, May 3rd. The latter number spoke in severe terms: "We are merely a band of foragers and marauders. We are sadly annoying and alarming all the peaceable inhabitants of the land: but we have not sufficient unity of action to take possession of the country, or to govern it when taken."
[5] For the hostility of the "public," see *The Times*, April 29th and 30th.
[6] The Journeymen Cordwainers, who quarrelled with the Grand National because their strike was not approved.

End of the Grey Government

hard to believe that a genuine trades assembly would have consented to alter the name of the Grand National Consolidated Trades' Union, and adopt instead the style of "The British and Foreign Consolidated Association of Industry, Humanity, and Knowledge." The florid official report to be read in the *Crisis* of August 23rd must, therefore, refer not to the meeting of trades delegates originally intended but rather to the activities of a gathering of Owenite partisans probably assembled instead. Many strong Trade Society groupings, of course, survived the bursting of the great Trades' Union bubble and pursued their old local lives.[1] And until they were able to produce the next and very different working-class movement of 1837, operative leaders of the calibre of William Lovett and Robert Hartwell found ample occupation in continuing the battle for the unstamped Press or building up a movement for requiring the return of the Dorchester labourers from transportation.

While the Trades' Union agitation had been increasing in intensity during the winter of 1833-4, the Dissenting sects had been organising against the most hateful badges of their subjection to the State Church. M. Halévy has traced with remarkable clearness how the much stronger political position of Nonconformity after Parliamentary Reform had led to the swift gathering among Dissenters of a powerful agitation against Church privileges.[2] Numerous meetings were held, widespread petitioning was organised, and the attention to the political world was effectively enough captured to make Dissenting grievances loom very large in the proceedings of the Parliamentary Session of 1834. But the bulk even of middle-class Dissent, it would appear, wanted no mere parleying about grievances but the end of State Churches. This stands out very clearly from the moderately phrased *Case of the Dissenters*, of which a fifth edition was being printed early in 1834 for gratuitous distribution. The franker opinion held of the existing State Church of England by the

[1] Nor did all the new Societies born in 1833 and 1834 uniformly collapse. Thus the later Amalgamated Union of Cabinet Makers traced its origin to a Society founded in 1833, and Societies founded in 1834 were to develop into the United Society of Boilermakers and Iron and Steel Ship Builders, and the United Kingdom Society of Coachmakers. The foundation dates are from the *Report of the Chief Registrar of Friendly Societies for 1896*, Part C, Appendix M.
[2] *History of the English People, 1830-41*, pp. 152-4. Cf. S. Skeat, *History of the Free Churches in England*, pp. 588-95. Baptists and Congregationalists were the most combative sects, and official Wesleyan Methodists the most averse to entering Radical Politics.

English Radicalism 1832–1852

Dissenting stalwarts is, however, rather to be sought in William Howitt's savagely combative *Popular History of Priestcraft in all Ages and Nations*, a work first issued at this time and destined for many years afterwards to be an armoury for plebeian Disestablishers. Howitt put at its strongest the Dissenting case for considering the Church of England as the greatest drag on the effective Christianity of the country.

One of the principal Dissenters' grievances—the levy from them of Church Rates for such things as church repair and maintenance—was already causing commotions in many parishes. It is related, for example, of Jacob Bright of Rochdale that he had allowed his property to be distrained upon more than twenty times between 1811 and 1833 rather than pay Church Rates,[1] and the example of such stout-hearted Friends was likely in post-Reform times to be widely imitated. In other parishes it was becoming difficult to secure a vestry meeting which would authorise Church Rates at all, and where the collection of the clergyman's Easter offerings[2] had not been abandoned, that too was certain to lead to resistance from those who believed that Churchpeople should meet their own expenses as Dissenters met theirs. Tithes, too, were most unpopular even with Anglican farmers, and there is abundant evidence to show of the particularly ugly contention which often went on between pastor and flock in "cases in which the Church had," according to Lord John Russell, "insisted unwisely on its full rights, or a combination of farmers had determined to vex and worry a clergyman."[3]

But Dissenters had other grievances besides the financial exactions made from them on behalf of Churchpeople whom they now claimed to outnumber. One cause of never-failing embitterment against the Church was its complete monopolisation of the ancient universities. Nor was the Dissenting temper towards Anglicanism improved by the pertinacious opposition that zealous Churchmen thought it right to offer to the conferment of degree-granting powers on the new University College of London, founded in 1826 by the joint efforts of "schismatic" Dissenters

---

[1] W. Robertson, *Life and Times of John Bright*, ed. 1912, p. 34.
[2] W. Howitt, *Popular History of Priestcraft*, 8th ed., p. 243, for the Burton list of Easter dues: For every householder, 2d; for smoke, 1d.; for garden and orchard, 1d.; for every son, etc., over sixteen, 4d; for every daughter or servant maid over sixteen, 2d.; for every foal, 2d., etc.
[3] Earl Russell's *Speeches and Despatches*, Introduction, i, 108.

End of the Grey Government

and "infidel" Philosophic Radicals. Then there was the legal compulsion to employ the services of an undesired Anglican cleric at the most solemn ceremonies of family life, marriage and burial.[1] The command of the parish churchyard which the law bestowed upon the Anglican clergyman was constantly causing "incidents" with Dissenting families who had no other place of burial, and who would in any case have desired to be buried with their forbears.[2] The virtual Anglican monopoly of the marriage service seems often to have proved as provoking to Nonconformists. That intelligent Conservative Greville, anxious above all to cut the "Conservative" party free from old High Tory lumber, has a very striking passage on the subject. Its temper may be judged from the following extract: "This (the question of Dissenters' marriages) has been an enormous scandal, and its continuance has been owing to the pride, obstinacy, and avarice of the Church; they would not give up the fees they received from this source, and they were satisfied to celebrate these rites in church while the parties were from the beginning to the end of the service protesting against all and every part of it, often making a most indecent noise and interruption."[3]

Moreover, the Church which imposed these humiliations on millions of English Dissenters, and whose tithes in Ireland necessitated the constant calling out of horse, foot, and artillery, was rotten with the corruptions of time and the workings of worldly interests. The inequitable maldistribution of its vast income, the scandals of cathedral sinecurism, pluralities, and non-residence, the indefensibility of the existing workings of lay patronage and lay impropriation of tithe shocked even its more far-sighted defenders into considering drastic plans of reform. When Lord Henley called among other things for the removal of the bishops from their lay concerns in the Lords, and Dr. Arnold advocated the sharing of church buildings with all Christian denominations,[4] it is understandable why Nonconformity, aware

---

[1] *The Case of the Dissenters*, 5th ed., 1834, pp. 10–12, mentions also baptism. The Church baptism register formed the only authorised register of births.
[2] W. Howitt, *op. cit.*, pp. 242–3.
[3] The *Greville Memoirs* under February 15, 1835.
[4] Lord Henley's *Plan of Church Reform*, 1832, and Dr. Arnold's *Principles of Church Reform*, 1833, are two of the most revealing indications of Church-people's awareness of the need to go a great way to meet popular feeling if the Church was to be saved. Cf. also Arnold's letters of 1833 in Dean Stanley's famous *Life*.

English Radicalism 1832-1852

like them of the dangerous unpopularity of the Church, was tempted to call for more than a mere redress of its most pressing grievances. When the Dissenting campaign reached its height, therefore,[1] on May 8, 1834, and a united committee, representative of the leading Dissenting organisations,[2] met the hundreds of delegations it had convened in an imposing convention, there took place what had already occurred at many of the preliminary meetings in previous months. Almost unanimously a call was made for severing the union between Church and State. And though a Dissenting majority was obviously in favour of leaving Church estates with the Anglicans, one influential section favoured so Ultra-Radical a policy as their nationalisation.[3]

After the Dissenting activities out of doors have thus been sketched the course of the troubled Parliamentary Session of 1834 becomes more explicable. On February 20th were introduced certain Government proposals for altered arrangements in regard to the Irish tithe which, after being cast and recast during an anxious Session, were doomed to extinction at the hands of the Lords. The experience of several successive years had now proved abundantly even to Whig "conservatives" that the good old days, when the Irish parson's tithe proctor was able to drive hard bargains and get his value or distrain, must be regarded as gone for ever. By the spring of 1833, indeed, Irish tithe-resistance had become so widespread that there were arrears of £1,200,000 of tithe, and some of the poorer clergy were destitute. At this stage the Government had stepped in,[4] had advanced a million to tithe-owners, and had then attempted most unsuccessfully to

---

[1] The most useful barometer of public feeling available is the total of signatures procured for Parliamentary petitions. Anglicans, who were already being animated by the Oxford Movement, obtained during the Parliamentary Session of 1834 155,783 signatures in support of the Church of England, and 52,909 in support of the Church of Ireland, while the Church of Scotland obtained 21,839 signatures. Against these figures stand the 352,910 for the Relief of Protestant Dissenters (367,032 for the Abolition of Tithe), the 110,699 for the alteration of Lay Patronage in Scotland, and the 538,978 for the Repeal of the Union with Ireland. It may be pointed out that the organisers of petitions normally liked to confine signatures to heads of households, or at least to adult males.

With the 155,783 Anglican and the 352,910 pro-Dissenting signatures it is interesting to compare other petition signature totals. During the 1834 Session there were 152,819 petitioners against the Corn Law, and 221,517 in favour of the Dorchester labourers (from *Companion to the British Almanac*, 1835, pp. 224-6).

[2] S. Skeat, *History of the Free Churches in England*, pp. 593-4.
[3] *Ibid.*, p. 595.   [4] *Hansard*, xx, 341, 345

End of the Grey Government

deal with the arrears itself. By February 1834, therefore, the Whig Government was prepared partly to cajole and partly to force the twin Protestant interests of the Land and the Church to stand together. Substantially the Government plan aimed at inducing the Irish "landed interest" either to redeem its land from tithe on generous terms,[1] or to take over tithe responsibility from the tenantry in return for their land being burdened to only 80 per cent of the extent of the old tithe. The landowner would reimburse himself and possibly earn some compensation for tithe responsibility by collecting the higher rents to be expected from a tithe-freed peasantry.

Ingenious as the scheme appeared, it failed to win any warm support. Many Churchmen in the Tory ranks argued that to reduce Irish tithe claims to 80 per cent of their value at the bidding of Irish agitators was the first step to their total repudiation. O'Connell, on the other hand, though he got no support from British Radicals for the repeal agitation which he was now conducting, could rely on their aid in resisting all Irish tithe proposals which represented no real gain for the people of Ireland themselves. O'Connell began the Session with a demand for the wiping off of two-thirds of the tithe and the conversion of the rest to the "benefit of the working classes,"[2] a suggestion so alien to the Whig mind that Lord John Russell denounced it as proposing "a direct act of robbery."[3] Many Radicals, and even Lord John himself, tended to seek a benefit for Irishmen in a different way, at once more likely to be adopted as a statute and free from the objection that decrease of tithe meant increase of rent. If the personnel of the Irish Church were reduced to the modest size sufficient for the reasonable service of Irish Episcopalians, and if the utmost use were made of the vast Irish Church estates, Church revenues (including, of course, the 80 per cent landlord-paid commuted tithe) could be made to yield a very considerable surplus for the common benefit of all Irishmen, Catholic and Protestant alike.

The second reading of the Irish Tithe Bill did not take place till May, but in the interval Parliament had had the opportunity of discussing other aspects of the hotly assailed union of Church and State. On February 25th Lord John Russell introduced a Dissenters' Marriage Bill in an effort to placate Nonconformists

[1] *Hansard*, xxi, 591.   [2] *Ibid.*, 598.   [3] *Ibid.*, p. 620.

in regard to one of their grievances.¹ His proposals would have allowed the Dissenting minister to celebrate marriages in duly licensed Dissenting chapels, but only after receiving a certificate from the parish clergyman, who would also continue to read the banns as before. This suggestion, at once assailed by Radical members on behalf of the Dissenters, had to be quickly withdrawn, as it became plain that Dissenters would operate no statute which still contrived to give Anglican clergymen supervision of their marriages. On March 13th a Radical proposal "to relieve the archbishops and bishops of the established church from their legislative and judicial duties in the House of Peers" obtained as many as 58 votes against 125.² Later in the month the Government showed its readiness to forward the Dissenters' aspirations in regard to the universities. On March 21st Lord Grey himself laid before the Lords a petition from the more liberal elements in the University of Cambridge advocating the admission of Dissenters to the colleges and to the degrees.³ A Bill on these lines, supported by the Government and applying to Oxford also, was carried through its readings in the Commons by majorities of 185 against 44, 371 against 147, and 164 against 75. The Lords killed it at a time when the Whig Government, breaking to pieces on the Irish question, was incapable, even if it would, of expressing its resentment.

Meanwhile, on April 21st Lord Althorp, Chancellor of the Exchequer and Leader of the House, though occupied with the reconstruction of English tithe proposals first introduced in 1833, was able to acquaint the Commons with a new Government plan in regard to Church Rates. But again the Radicals inside Parliament and the Dissenting organisations outside saw reason for violent objection. They were determined that Churchmen should in future pay themselves for the upkeep of their churches, and were hostile to a suggested solution which proposed to end Church Rates but provided compensation in the shape of £250,000 per annum from the Treasury. Churchmen probably did not relish Althorp's assurances that his new scheme did not allow of the organs, the peals of bells, and the other ecclesiastical luxuries which they had once voted themselves from the Church Rates, nor his references to the church repair jobbery which was now to be checked by closer supervision. But Tories nevertheless saw

---

[1] *Hansard*, xxi, 776.   [2] *Ibid.*, xxii, 153.   [3] *Ibid.*, p. 497.

End of the Grey Government

reason to vote with the Whig Government and make up their division total to 256 against the 140 Radicals who objected as much to putting church repair on the taxes as they did to leaving it on the rates.[1] In the result the Government decided to leave the thorny problem alone for a time, and the parochial Church Rate wars were resumed with results that could only profit Radicalism so long as Churchmen maintained their old claims. From the notable Rochdale Church Rate contest, for example, issued John Bright.

In May came the momentous debates on the Government's Irish Tithe Bill. An intervention by Lord John Russell on May 6th proved that some members of the Government at least were determined that the Cabinet's pro-Church wing led by Stanley should no longer be allowed to dictate a policy of refusal even to examine whether Irish Church revenues might not on suitable rearrangement yield a surplus for general Irish purposes.[2] The issue was brought to a head when Ward, Radical member for St. Albans, prompted from without by Durham,[3] who was anxious to enter a Government reconstituted on a more Radical basis, introduced a famous resolution on May 27th. The House was invited to declare "that the Protestant episcopal establishment in Ireland exceeds the spiritual wants of the Protestant population, and that it being the right of the state to regulate the distribution of church property in such a manner as Parliament may determine, it is the opinion of this House that the temporal possessions of the Church of Ireland ought to be reduced." Proceedings had not gone far[4] when Lord Althorp asked for the adjournment of the House. The Cabinet's pro-Church wing led by Stanley had resigned.

Though four Cabinet Ministers in all withdrew, it proved possible to reconstitute the Government on the basis of sending out to Ireland a Commission of Inquiry into the Church revenues. But Durham himself was not admitted, nor the more Radical programme accepted, which would have eased the strain in the Commons. Indeed, Lord Grey virtually committed the recon-

---

[1] *Hansard*, xxii, 1059. [2] *Ibid*, xxiii, 664–6.
[3] H. L. Bulwer, *Life of Palmerston*, ed. 1870, ii, 197.
[4] *Hansard* gives only the speeches of Ward, the mover, and Grote, the seconder, both notable efforts. According to Mrs. Grote's biography of her husband, however, Grote's speech was not spoken owing to Althorp's request for the adjournment.

stituted Government to a contrary course in acknowledging a widely signed entreaty to stay at the head of the Ministry. "We should not be urged," he claimed, "by a constant and active pressure from without to the adoption of any measures the necessity of which has not been fully proved, and which are not strictly regulated by a careful attention to the settled institutions of the country both in Church and State."[1]

This was hardly the temper which augured well for a Government soon to approach yet another set of Irish difficulties. Some of Grey's own Ministers, indeed, were engaged at this very time in a manœuvre to edge their chief and the Cabinet into requiring a less stringent Irish Coercion Bill for the ensuing year than that made in 1833.[2] So was it hoped to recall O'Connell from the open onslaughts upon the Grey Government which he was now making, and for which he would assuredly recruit some British Radical support if the Coercion Bill were not modified. O'Connell's flaming anger is evidenced in an *Address to the Reformers of England and Ireland* prepared at this time. "Is it just," he cried, "that Ireland should be insulted and trampled on, merely because the insanity of the wretched old man who is at the head of the ministry develops itself in childish hatred and maniac contempt of the people of Ireland? . . . There appear to be but two leading ideas in his mind. The first regards the procuring for his family and relations the greatest possible quantity of the public spoil. . . . The second, but subordinate, sentiment in Lord Grey's mind is hostility to Ireland."[3]

After O'Connell had been appeased by the private promises of the Irish Secretary the miscarriage in the Cabinet of the manœuvre for a less stringent Coercion Bill[4] led to Lord Grey's innocently introducing the original Bill. O'Connell, considering he had been tricked, thereupon made revelations which led to Lord Grey's resignation and a break-up of the Government. In sending for Lord Melbourne, and suggesting a combination of Whig Ministers with Tories and Stanleyites, the King now attempted to dam the

---

[1] *Annual Register*, 1834, History, p. 43.
[2] Earl Russell, *Speeches and Despatches*, Introduction, i, 95–6. W. Cory, *Guide to Modern English History*, pp. 389 sqq., Part 2, gives an interesting review of most of the available evidence which includes the *Brougham Memoirs*, and similar Ministerial biography.
[3] Quoted in W. N. Molesworth, *History of England*, 1830–71, i, 373.
[4] D. Le Marchant, *Memoir of Viscount Althorp, Earl Spencer*, pp. 511–12.

End of the Grey Government

modest current of Reform which even Grey had approved.[1] He was not successful, and Melbourne constructed a Government much on the lines of Grey's. In the circumstances it was a Government without great authority. But it modified the Irish Coercion proposals[2] in a way which avoided a Radical storm and proceeded with the harassing labour of the enormous and complicated Tithe Bill.

On this measure O'Connell with Radical support succeeded in carrying an amendment which completely altered the Government Bill.[3] In the hope of easing the situation of the Irish peasantry the Commons now resolved to ask landlords to pay not 80 but only 60 per cent of the former tithe, and to find the extra 20 per cent for the tithe receiver from the Church Fund to be accumulated from the suppressed bishoprics. The Tory peers, however, now definitely turned against the Bill, though its rejection promised to leave Irish clergymen without any tithes at all. Fresh from the slaughter of the Dissenters' University Admission Bill, they turned successfully upon the Irish Tithe Bill also. By humiliating the Government they were bringing its end nearer and pushing forward the day when Wellington and Peel could be called for without any serious departure from the constitutional conventions. Then could come the long-planned-for Dissolution[4] and the full use of every electoral "influence" calculated to restore a Tory majority and "firm government."

---

[1] *Peel Memoirs*, Part 2, pp. 1–13.
[2] *Hansard*, xxv, 32.
[3] *Ibid.*, 757.
[4] *Brougham Memoirs*, iii, 278, 296, 362.

CHAPTER VII

POOR LAW AND MUNICIPAL REFORM

"Not a week passes, nay not a day or even an hour, that does not witness the death of one or more victims in consequence of that atrocious Bill (Poor Law Amendment Act). Take up any one number of our *Twopenny Dispatch*—we care not what number within the last six months—and it teems with the horrors of this Bill. . . . All we can say is that if it works well, so do plague, pestilence, and famine work well, and so does the Devil and Swing work well and so does everything else work well that works death and destruction."

"*Poor Man's Guardian*," *October 17, 1835, p. 704.*

". . . To take away the veto now possessed by the House of Lords in all legislative measures; and to substitute in lieu thereof a suspensive veto in that House; so that if Bills which have been passed by the House of Commons be rejected by the House of Lords and again during the same session be passed by the Commons, such Bills shall become law on the royal consent being thereunto given. . . ."

Notice of motion by ROEBUCK *after the controversy with the Lords on Municipal Reform (Pamphlets for the People,* "The Conduct of Ministers, etc.," *p. 11).*

"*September 9th.*

"Lyndhurst . . . said there was no chance of the House of Lords surviving ten years, that power must reside in the House of Commons as it always had. . . .

"*September 27th.*

"The papers are full of nothing but O'Connell's progress in Scotland, where he is received with unbounded enthusiasm by enormous crowds.

"*February 12th.*

"Lord William Bentinck has published an address to the electors of Glasgow which is remarkable, because he is the first man of high rank and station who has publicly professed the ultra-Radical opinions. . . ."

Extracts from GREVILLE, *1835–6.*

ON April 17, 1834, when a relatively united Grey Government still appeared to dominate the political scene, Lord Althorp had introduced a Government Poor Law Bill soon to become notorious. It put into legislative form the recommendations of the Commission appointed in 1832 to inquire into and report upon the abuses connected with the old parochial Poor Law system. Through Assistant Commissioners, among whom the area of England and Wales had been divided, a most exhaustive collection of facts had been procured, the mere necessity for whose publication and subsequent correlation had delayed the appearance of the Commissioners' Report until the opening of 1834.

The Report was largely the work of Chadwick, who had been promoted from Assistant to full Commissioner during the investigation, and who with Nassau Senior[1] had virtually taken charge of its composition. For the first time the general public received a comprehensive view of the worst effects of the principles upon which Poor Relief was being administered, and the waste, corruption, and inefficiency attendant on unsupervised, unregulated, and unco-ordinated parochialism. It became plain why it was that poor Irish flowed more readily to the centres offering prospects of employment than English agricultural labourers, chained still by Settlement Laws, and at once debased and debauched by Speenhamland Pauper Family Scales;[2] why an unmarried labourer of thrifty habits was an exception amid the improvidently married and the carelessly breeding;[3] why strong parochial interests—the house-owners, for example, the grocers and the tavern-keepers—approved the system of generously administered relief in aid of ludicrously inadequate farmers' pay; why farmers and others liked a system which enabled them "to dismiss and resume their labourers according to their daily or even hourly want of them, to reduce wages to the minimum or even below the minimum of what will support an unmarried man, and to throw upon others the payment of a part, frequently of the greater part and sometimes almost the whole of the wages actually received by their labourers."[4]

---

[1] 1790–1864, an acute lawyer and political economist, whose opinions carried considerable weight with the Government.
[2] *Poor Law Commission's Report*, 1834 (edition of 1905), pp. 156–7.
[3] *Ibid.*, p. 30.   [4] *Ibid.*, p. 59.

English Radicalism 1832-1852

In regard to the other main side of Poor Relief, that in the so-called workhouse, more strong criticism was voiced of the actual results of parochial administration. "In by far the greater number of cases," says the Report, "it (the workhouse) is a large almshouse in which the young are trained in idleness, ignorance and vice; the able-bodied maintained in sluggish sensual indolence . . . the aged and more respectable exposed to all the misery that is incident to dwelling in such a society, without government or classification, and the whole body of inmates subsisted on food far exceeding both in kind and amount not merely the diet of the independent labourer, but that of the majority of the persons who contribute to their support."[1] This was, perhaps, greatly to overrate both the "sluggish sensual indolence" and the fare allowed in the average workhouse; to build up a case from a few notorious instances, and even then to omit essential facts. The very high proportion of imbeciles and mental deficients among the workhouse population, for example, would have gone far to explain the "sluggish sensual indolence" complained of, while to judge of actual workhouse fare by what a contractor had undertaken to provide was hardly legitimate.

Yet on Outdoor and Workhouse Relief alike Senior and Chadwick must have been conscious of the need to put their colours on thick, for they were asking for a very radical departure from tradition, a Benthamite Poor Law Department with the widest powers to remodel and control local Poor Law administration beneath it. They were asking for it, too, on grounds which made a special appeal to moderate Radicals of the schools of Hume and Grote, the protection of the "independent labourer" from pauper competition and of the plundered ratepayer from coalitions of vestry "interests." The situation, however, was not so morally simple as it appeared to Chadwick, Grote, and Hume.[2] Under a close examination by modern eyes the "independent labourer" class becomes a small minority whose stoic virtues "property" was anxious forcibly to multiply in the interests of net receipts. The plundered ratepayer, again, even in his most aggrieved shape takes on the aspect of the resident rentier or the tithe-owner, forced by selfish but highly rented farmers to assist in the work of keeping labourers from starvation.

[1] *Poor Law Commission's Report*, 1834 (edition of 1905), pp. 53-4.
[2] Cf. Poulett Scrope's *Principles of Political Economy* (1833), pp. 304-16.

Poor Law and Municipal Reform

The great defect of a Report, admirable as a piece of administrative criticism and suggestion, is the very narrow social viewpoint from which it was written. Before John Stuart Mill undertook his wide criticism of the British system of land-tenure and property distribution, "practical men" even in the Radical camp seem to have had little conception of that system's formidable contribution to the poverty problem.[1] Yet the revolt against the New Poor Law led by the Cobbettites was to show how strongly the poor were aware of it, how tenaciously they held that they were entitled to compensation in the shape of kindly Poor Relief administration for the crippling of all their opportunities involved in the land monopolisation which had been increasingly effected by "property" since the abbey, guild, and common land seizures of the sixteenth century. Again, the Report ignored the very practicable schemes which were current for a large supersession of the Poor Law machinery in favour of National Insurance against sickness, old age, and widowhood.[2] Yet Chadwick would no doubt have organised National Insurance as ably as he did the New Poor Law administration.

The Report, too, is impregnated with the bleakest Malthusianism. It is true, of course, that the Commission had not considered the most far-reaching of the suggestions made by Malthus. "I should propose a regulation to be made," Malthus had written in the best-abused passage of his *Essay on Population*, "declaring that no child born from any marriage taking place after the expiration of a year from the date of the law, and no child born two years from the same date, should ever be entitled to parish assistance."[3] The mere proposition of a social experiment of this type entirely at the expense of the poor would have

---

[1] The Poor Law Commissioners did, indeed, instruct their Assistant Commissioners to obtain information concerning the effect on Pauperism of "facilitating the occupation, and even the acquisition, of land by labourers" (*Instructions from the Central Board of Poor Law Commissioners to Assistant Commissioners*, subject vi). But it was obviously intended for treatment merely as an allotment problem, and even so the final Report is against public action because it would lead to wasteful expenditure.

[2] Poulett Scrope, for example, gives a scheme under which employers would be required to pay the following contributions: 4d. per week for a male employee, 2d. for a female, and 1½d. for young persons between ten and twenty years of age. Benefits for a man would be 6s. per week for bed-lying sickness, 3s. per week for walking sickness, 3s. per week pension after sixty, and a funeral benefit of £10 commutable into a widow's pension. Employers would be recompensed for their payments in the lower rating demands made of them for Poor Relief (*Principles of Political Economy*, pp. 316–20).

[3] Malthus, *Essay on the Principle of Population*, 6th ed. (1826), ii. 319.

provoked the gravest unrest. It would have been completely inadmissible, moreover, to any Government conscious of the British population's special exposure to unpredictable trade depressions and, so long as the Corn Laws lasted, to the calamitous effects of a bad British harvest. But within the limits of the politically possible the Commission, which undoubtedly eyed working-class marriages with Malthusian disquiet as to their possible prolificacy,[1] made recommendations of dangerous severity. Nor could a Commission containing the Bishops of London and Chester be expected to have made inquiry concerning the extent to which the need for such severity might be abrogated by the working-class's use of artificial means of birth control. Birth control of a rudimentary kind already had its open Radical advocates anxious to allow working men to marry young and to control the number of their family with a view to modest comfort and security.[2] It took many long decades, however, to force the subject into the arena of admissible discussion.

It is time to turn to the actual recommendations of the Commission which were so largely adopted in the epoch-making Government Bill of 1834. All but the largest parishes were to lose their Poor Law independence and be grouped together to form Unions substantial enough to permit the organisation of

[1] Cf. the following instructions to their Assistant Commissioners inquiring into population "redundancy": "He will endeavour to ascertain how far it (population redundancy) has been occasioned by the stimulus applied to population by the relief of the able-bodied: and for that purpose inquire into the frequency of marriages where the husband at the time or shortly before or after the time of marriage was in receipt of parish relief and into the proportion of the number of such marriages to those of independent labourers: and compare the average age of marriage among paupers and among independent labourers" (*Instructions*, p. 21).

[2] Place in his *Illustrations and Proofs of the Principle of Population* of 1822, section iii, chapter 5, had argued the working-class need for birth control without, however, giving direct instruction as to methods. But to Place rather than to Owen has recently been ascribed the responsibility for the first Birth Control propaganda attempted in England, the circulation of the handbills of 1823, which contain such instruction (article by Norman E. Himes in the *Lancet*, August 6, 1927). Later landmarks in Birth Control history are Carlile's *Every Woman's Book* of 1826 and Robert Dale Owen's *Moral Physiology* of 1831. The latter book was widely enough advertised in the *Poor Man's Guardian* to suggest that it was influencing Ultra-Radical thought and family practice. So long, however, as the sheath remained dear (in 1831 the American price was a dollar), very coarse, and only obtainable surreptitiously, neither the pamphlets mentioned above nor such successors as the famous *Fruits of Philosophy* of 1833 could advance matters very far. But by 1854, when Dr. George Drysdale's very influential *Elements of Social Science* first appeared, there is evidence that considerable progress had been made.

Poor Law and Municipal Reform

efficient workhouses. At suitable dates the payment of outdoor relief allowances to able-bodied persons and their dependents would cease, and relief would only be obtainable in severely disciplined workhouses. Workhouse conditions, indeed, were to be frankly deterrent at least for the able-bodied, and it was to be made plain that existence within the "house" was altogether less eligible than the life procurable by labour outside.

The local direction of the system would be in the hands of Boards of Guardians, elected for the most part by rate-paying occupiers and their landlords on a scale of differentiated voting power tending greatly to strengthen the "interests" most concerned in checking Poor Law "extravagance." But to maintain national standards of working management and local relief administration, to keep down local corruption, and to prevent the development of that "undue neighbourliness" which had raised the Poor Rates of the past, the working of the new system was to be directed by three central Poor Law Commissioners and a staff. These Commissioners were in the first instance to act for five years, but in point of fact central auditing of Poor Law accounts, central direction of Poor Law methods, and central inspection of Poor Law administration were never afterwards surrendered. Chadwick, too, as secretary to the Commissioners was to build up a model Benthamite department with methods which were strongly to influence all the subsequently created departments of social scope, the Science and Art Department, for example, the Committee of Council on Education, and the Central Health Board.

The Bill, which for all its lack of appreciation of the claims of the poor introduced modern administration into Britain, was brought into the Commons on April 17th. On April 30th came the first formidable declaration of war. After some initial hesitation the important *Times* newspaper opened a pertinaciously pressed resistance,[1] continued for years, which at once induced circles behind the Government to acquire the *Morning Chronicle* as a

[1] Its tendency to a conservative-humanitarian angle had already appeared on April 19th, and its suspicion of the newly proposed Control Board on April 22nd. But on April 30th came the two-column attack which launched it on its long crusade. The responsibility for this course was with the proprietor, John Walter, M.P. for Berkshire, the peasantry of which seemed particularly threatened. Certainly Walter was simultaneously moved to issue a *Letter to the Electors of Berkshire* hostile to the new Poor Law proposals (*The Times*, April 30th).

English Radicalism 1832-1852

counter-organ.[1] The hostility of *The Times* undoubtedly helped Ultra-Radicalism to hearten itself for a Parliamentary struggle on behalf of the poor. In Committee, certainly, Cobbett was able to lead a very pertinacious struggle hardly to be expected after the Government's Second Reading victory of 319 against 20,[2] and the determined lead in favour of the Bill given by Hume and Grote to their schools of middle-class Radicalism. By the time the Third Reading was carried on July 1st by 157 votes against 50[3] it was already obvious that Cobbett had found a cause to his taste and one dangerously liable to become an Ultra-Radical rallying-point. Cobbett's speech of July 1st, for example, forecast that the projected workhouses would contain military and police; that husband and wife would be separated therein from one another and from their children; and that the harsh workhouse régime was intended to force labourers to accept "potatoes and seaweed" outside in Irish fashion rather than venture into the humiliations and privations within.[4]

Fortunately for the Government, the Tories, conscious of the services of the Bill to "property," made no attempt for the time to make party capital from the discontent.[5] The one serious trouble arising in their citadel in the Lords concerned the Bill's bastardy proposals, and on this the Lords and the populace seemed to think alike. In view of the immense amount of perjury and vindictiveness associated with bastardy proceedings, the Commissioners had recommended and the Government had adopted the heroic plan of ceasing all legal proceedings to compel the alleged fathers of illegitimate children to assume a financial responsibility which might otherwise fall on the Poor Rate. In the eyes of the multitude, however, this seemed to throw the whole punishment on the woman, and to allow the father to go scot-free

---

[1] Harriet Martineau, *Autobiography*, ed. 1877, i, 222–6, as corrected by Mackay's account in the *Hist. of the English Poor Laws*, iii. Miss Martineau, who had been encouraged by Brougham to write her famous *Poor Law Tales* in order to prepare the public for the New Poor Law, was in a position to know.

[2] *Hansard*, xxiii, 806.   [3] *Ibid.*, xxiv, 1061.

[4] *Ibid.*, 1050–1. Cf. also Cobbett's *Weekly Political Register* during June and July.

[5] It was, indeed, slow in rising into tangible shape partly, perhaps, from the inability of rural districts to organise Parliamentary petitioning under the suspicious eyes of their superiors. The petitioners against the New Poor Law during the session of 1834 were 16,157. When the industrial districts were threatened with its approach in 1837, they raised 201,967 petitioners for its repeal and 63,796 for its amendment.

Poor Law and Municipal Reform

when the mother was forced to enter the workhouse for lack of a little support in keeping the child. The Lords did no unpopular thing when they insisted on amendment in this respect.[1] In the following winter, indeed, when Peel was struggling at the head of a Tory Government against Whig and Radical hosts, Cobbett was tempted to offer him an alliance in return for repeal of the New Poor Law.[2] A Disraeli would have been tempted as Peel was not.[3]

Cobbett, who died in June 1835, never lived to lead the vast Ultra-Radical movement which was eventually organised against the New Poor Law after the onset of industrial depression during the winter of 1836–7.[4] But as it was a movement which followed the lines of advocacy he had marked out, it may be well to summarise here Cobbett's final Anti-Poor Law position as set out in the *Legacy to Labourers* issued by him in the winter of 1834–5. In his savage *History of the Protestant Reformation* Cobbett had already once drawn a striking picture of corrupt and wicked Tudor courtiers possessing themselves of the vast lands which the Church had received from pious donors principally for the use of the poor. This picture was now repeated in brief with its sequel. As some compensation, Cobbett urged, for the loss of their endowment the poor had been offered the Elizabethan Poor Law,[5] whose benefits were now to be withdrawn without consideration of the rights which had been tacitly surrendered in exchange. This was being done, Cobbett insisted, because there was alarm that annual Poor Rates of £6,700,000 should be swallowing up the yields from landlords' estates. Yet it was possible to pay an annual thirty millions to the usurers holding National Debt, another seven millions to sinecurists, and altogether raise an annual revenue of fifty-two millions without

---

[1] *Hansard*, xxv, 1097. [2] In the *Legacy to Labourers* discussed below.
[3] But even Peel was ultimately to displease some of the more alert defenders of "property." During the elections of 1837 and 1841 he was held not sufficiently to have discountenanced "Tory-Radical" attempts to use Poor Law discontent against the Whigs. Such attempts, it was thought, might yield immediate political profit, but only at the cost of making "paupers" as "exigent" as they had been before 1834.
[4] Even in relatively prosperous 1835, and among the cowed peasantry of the South, mindful of the Special Commissions of 1831 and of Dorchester, the introduction of the New Poor Law was far from untroubled (cf. T. Mackay, *Hist. of the English Poor Laws*, iii, 177, 196, etc.). But opposition was sporadic and unorganised, and was dealt with piecemeal in a way which the abundant political Radical leadership available in industrial areas did not allow to be repeated there. [5] Cobbett, *Legacy to Labourers*, p. 116.

exciting the slightest uneasiness![1] Were not landlords, too, drawing ten and twenty times their former rent-rolls while Poor Rates had increased far less in proportion? The object of the New Poor Law was to force down the labourer's standard of living, maintained hitherto by Poor Law allowances, to the dreadful Irish level.[2] In order to effect this the "old neighbourly system of relief" was to be abandoned and a tyranny by three commissioners and a secretary installed in its place.

Further weapons of assault, it should be remembered, would come to hand as the enforcement of the Bill began and the "three bashaws of Somerset House" proceeded with the aid of assistant commissioners eventually numbering twenty-one to organise the new "bastilles," as the workhouses were dubbed.[3] Even Cobbett, who on June 12, 1834, had sought by an amendment to prevent the separation of husband and wife in workhouses, might have been amazed by the anti-Malthusian frenzy which Stephens succeeded in raising on the subject in Northern England during 1838. But for the enforced separation of husband and wife, indeed, it may be doubted whether a long-continued storm of any size could have been raised against the New Poor Law, despite the Radical attacks on the workhouse dietary scales and on the workhouse classification which separated children from their parents. Yet, though supporters of the New Poor Law could not openly avow it, the deprivation of sexual and domestic gratifications in the workhouses was their principal reliance, and could not be surrendered.

The story of Poor Law developments must, however, be left to a later chapter, and for the present it is desirable to return to the political crises of 1834, the story of which has been recounted down to the Parliamentary recess of 1834. Though the unimpressive Melbourne Cabinet had been compelled to stomach in its first few weeks of office the defiant rejection by Tory Peers

---

[1] Cobbett, *Legacy to Labourers*, pp. 13–14.
[2] Cobbett, *op. cit.*, p. 28. The problem of the competition of poverty-stricken Irish, who in the absence of an Irish Poor Law had to come over to Britain or starve, seemed a very grave one to British operatives. Poor Laws for Ireland had figured among Radical demands for some time, and, in point of fact, an official inquiry had been proceeding on the social condition of Irish labourers in Britain during the very passage of the Poor Law Amendment Act. See G. C. Lewis, *Letters*, pp. 28–35.
[3] The complete Anti-Poor Law Armoury may be studied in G. R. W. Baxter's *The Book of the Bastilles, History of the New Poor Law* (1841). For an Assistant Commissioner's own account of his proceedings, see Sir F. B. Head's *English Charity*, i, Descriptive Essays, pp. 46–150.

Poor Law and Municipal Reform

of the Universities Bill to placate the Dissenter Radicals and of a Tithe Bill to placate the Irish Radicals, Ministers might yet have hoped to enjoy some freedom from acute political troubles during the Parliamentary recess. The very reverse proved to be the case. The unaccountable if brilliant Brougham, in a Scottish political tour undertaken prior to attending a Grey banquet in Edinburgh,[1] chose to make a series of unbalanced speeches, a prominent feature of which, continued at Edinburgh, was criticism of Radical "impatience." This roused Lord Durham, who, since his departure from a Whig Cabinet which he had found too Conservative, had been qualifying more and more for Radical leadership.[2] He sounded a note in reply which aroused Radical enthusiasm. Deploring the "clipping, and paring and mutilating" to which Reforming proposals, just in themselves, were constantly subjected in the "attempt to conciliate enemies who are not to be conciliated," he spoke of himself as viewing with regret "every hour which passes over the existence of reorganised and unreformed abuses."[3] An immense weight of Radical feeling was instantly recruited to Durham's banner by this plain expression of dissatisfaction with Whig half-heartedness. A huge Glasgow demonstration of October 29th,[4] held in Durham's honour and presented by him with a moderate Radical programme, showed the official clique that if such a not unlikely political crisis occurred as allowed the Radical majority of the nation a voice in its destinies, Durham and not Brougham would be its candidate for the Premiership.[5]

[1] Both tour and banquet, it should be noted, are landmarks in the history of political democratisation as important as the issue in 1833 of a remarkable Ministerial "account rendered" in a famous pamphlet, *The Reform Ministry and the Reformed Parliament*. Brougham tried to take the pamphlet's confident tone even after the great disappointments of 1834, and made other mistakes besides (cf. Raikes's *Journal* under September 24th).

[2] See chapter xxvi below. Though still young, Durham had a Radical record going back to his very democratic Reform Bill of 1821. It was known that he had been a forceful Chairman of the Ministerial Committee which had prepared the Reform Bill. After his resignation in March 1833 he had announced his willingness to go farther. In 1834, moreover, he had disapproved the Irish Coercion Bill, though Grey was his father-in-law.

[3] *Speeches of the Earl of Durham delivered at public meetings, etc., in 1834* (J. Ridgway, 1835), pp. 5–6.

[4] *Ibid.*, pp. 36 sqq. The whole town was on holiday, and parts of the adjacent counties also, headed by the Renfrew Political Union, the Kilmarnock Political Union, the West District of Stirlingshire Political Union, etc. The numbers in the streets were estimated at 120,000.

[5] Brougham's attempt to discredit Durham's claim of having pressed for a more democratic Reform Bill in 1831 did him no good. Nor was he helped by his ludicrous efforts to win Court favour.

English Radicalism 1832-1852

But the whole political situation was suddenly altered by the intervention of the Crown. The King had long been anxious to take refuge in the haven of a Tory Ministry from the democratic political storms which bewildered and frightened him, and which Whig Ministers rode so imperfectly. In the first half of November he got his chance. Lord Althorp, Leader of the Commons since November 1830, had, thanks to his high Whig birth and Radical opinions, been trusted by Whigs and Radicals alike. His removal to the Lords by the death of his father faced Melbourne with the difficult problem of replacing him and executing the third Whig Cabinet reshuffle of the year. The King, however, declined to accept Lord John Russell as an adequate substitute for Althorp in the Leadership of the House. What is more, he proceeded with unconstitutional haste to treat Melbourne's dutifully phrased account of his Cabinet's difficulties as sufficient warrant for turning to Tory advisers who did not enjoy the support of a quarter of the House of Commons.[1]

There followed Wellington's unprecedented Prime Ministership *pro tempore* while the indispensable Peel was brought back from an Italian holiday and preparations were hurried forward for a General Election permitting the full exercise of Tory "influence." For a considerable time it appeared likely that, using the "Church and King" cry with one section of the limited electorate, "Conservative and not Destructive Reform" with another, and supplementing them both with money for the bribable and "influence" for the intimidable, a Tory majority was procurable. An important section of the Press, for example, changed sides headed by *The Times*,[2] and indulged in bitter assaults upon Anti-Property Ultra-Radicalism from which England was to be saved by the Great Duke and Peel of the adroit *Tamworth Letter*.[3]

---

[1] W. M. Torrens, *Melbourne Memoirs*, ed. 1890, pp. 309-11; *Peel Memoirs*, ii, 1-33; *Memoirs of Baron Stockmar*, i, 329-30. There is no doubt a "backstairs" part to the story which these *Memoirs* do not give. "The Queen has done it all," wrote *The Times* just before changing sides.

[2] *Greville Memoirs*, November 19th-December 2nd; *Poor Man's Guardian*, January 3rd.

[3] *Peel Memoirs*, ii, 58-67. The *Letter's* most effective section ran as follows: "If by adopting the spirit of the Reform Bill it be meant that we are to live in a perpetual vortex or agitation—that public men can only support themselves in public estimation by adopting every popular impression of the day; by promising the instant redress of anything which anybody may call an abuse; by abandoning altogether that great aid of government, more powerful than either law or reason, the respect for ancient rights, and the deference to pre-

Poor Law and Municipal Reform

In this clever electoral appeal, indeed, Peel nearly decided the issue, the more so as while he was taking the opportunity of tempting High Toryism to give up its most hated positions for the chance of electoral triumph, Melbourne was blunderingly attempting to screen the King from the proper blame attachable to his unconstitutional dismissal of the Whig Ministry. So tame, in fact, had been Melbourne's first public declaration of November 26th that private remonstrances had forced him to attempt something more spirited on December 1st. Even then it was singularly unprofitable in him to criticise "the bitter hostility and ulterior designs against the Established Church which have been openly avowed by several classes and bodies of Dissenters" and to stress "the great alarm" occasioned "in high and powerful quarters" thereby and "the life and spirit and courage" aroused in the political adversary—"a party powerful in numbers, powerful in property, powerful in rank and station."[1]

Only the utmost exertions of Radicalism, British and Irish, prevented the anticipated victory of the Tories. For British Radicals the return of the men of 1815–30 to office meant the imperilment of all the democratic causes which had been so sensibly advanced in Church and State since 1830; for Irish Radicals it meant Orange administration, and the multiplication of such dreadful affairs as the Rathcormac tithe-shooting of December 17th,[2] when a Catholic crowd's resistance to a tithe-distraint brought twelve deaths and twenty-six woundings. Accordingly, the Ultra-Radical *Poor Man's Guardian* may be found supporting the Whigs against the Tories despite the "Poor Law Starvation Bill,"[3] and Dissenting committees were so busy in the constituencies that even Cobbett was threatened with

---

scriptive authority: if this be the spirit of the Reform Bill, I will not undertake to adopt it. But if the spirit of the Reform Bill implies a careful review of institutions, civil and ecclesiastical, undertaken in a friendly temper, combining with the firm maintenance of established rights the correction of proved abuses and the redress of real grievances, in that case I can, for myself and colleagues, undertake to act in such a spirit and with such intentions."

[1] W. M. Torrens, *op. cit.*, p. 325. These speeches, it should be pointed out, were not made in the modern political manner at public meetings, but in answer to deputations of supporters. They were, however, very widely reported.

[2] *Poor Man's Guardian*, January 3rd, pp. 379–80.

[3] "The Whigs were cashiered because they felt some scruples of conscience, some pangs of remorse in carrying on the system. . . . The Tories are called in because they are men without scruples, without remorse, without humanity. . . ." (*Poor Man's Guardian*, January 3rd).

English Radicalism 1832–1852

opposition till a Disestablishment pledge was given.[1] In Ireland, again, despite great and confident efforts on the part of Protestantism, Landlordism, and the Government, more than sixty[2] members were returned to join with British Radicals and Whigs in ejecting the Peel Government, which for all its large number of gains in landlord-controlled counties and corrupted boroughs was in a definite minority.

For some three months after the Elections were over Peel continued as Prime Minister. Dexterous as he proved with his offers of Church Reform, a Tithe Bill, and a measure for Dissenters' Marriages, he was faced by a solid Coalition in Parliament which was determined to prove that the day had passed in England for Crown-imposed Ministries. There were members of Melbourne's Cabinet who were ready for a Royal abdication and a struggle with the Lords on the issue,[3] and most of the others felt that the Government which succeeded Peel's would have to impose a more Radical policy on Crown and Peers than had yet been attempted. There were alarmed Tories, indeed, who, pointing to the much greater relative strength of Radicalism in 1835, entreated Peel not to resign despite successive defeats on the Speakership, the Address, the Russian Ambassadorship, the London University Charter, and the Irish Church. They hoped to the last that Whigs, if not Radicals, would vote the Supplies rather than court anarchy.[4]

In quitting office on April 8th, however, Peel showed himself wiser than his more anxious partisans. To have persisted in defying a majority of the Commons would have been to play right into Radicalism's hands, and to forfeit for Conservatism a large amount of the "moderate" goodwill which had been won by the *Tamworth Letter* and the altered policy it had announced. To leave office was to permit Whiggery to expose itself once more to the "impatient" demands of Radicals and Repealers and to the futility of constant rejection of its Bills at the hands of the Tory majority in the Lords. From Peel's point of view the whole episode of November 1834 to April 1835 had been profitable in vastly strengthening Toryism in the Commons. If some very

---

[1] *Poor Man's Guardian*, January 10th, p. 389.
[2] W. J. Fitzpatrick, *Correspondence of D. O'Connell*, i, 521.
[3] Greville, *Memoirs*, under January 15, 1835.
[4] *Raikes's Journal* under April 2nd.

Poor Law and Municipal Reform

Radical language had fallen in private from irate Whig lips, the controlling elements in the Whig successor Cabinet could still be relied upon never to attempt to lead the populace against the Lords and the Monarchy, if only because the consequences of victory would spread to property, the Church, the Irish Union, and their own power. Most official Whigs would have abandoned the Corporation and Church reforms they still had in mind rather than have allowed a situation to develop where Daniel Harvey really threatened to control the Pension List, Hume the Army Estimates, O'Connell the Irish Police, and Dr. Bowring the Corn Laws. Indeed, a Whig-Tory coalition against Radicalism would probably have been formed under Grey[1] the moment Radicalism became unduly alarming.

The second Melbourne Government of April 1835 approached its critical sessional business in June. On the 2nd it coalesced with the Tories to defeat Grote's Radical motion for the Ballot, on the 5th Lord John Russell introduced the famous Municipal Reform Bill, and on the 26th Lord Morpeth brought in an Irish Tithe Bill. Among English Radicals the demand for the Municipal Reform, undefiled by Tory amendments, was the greatest political manifestation of the year, and by the end of the Session 260,129 petition signatures had reached Parliament in its favour against the 26,534 hostile signatures. But the 154,447 petitioners on behalf of the Dorchester labourers and the 57,848 petitioners for the repeal of the newspaper duties also represented active forces on the Radical side, as did the 129,493 Scotsmen who petitioned Parliament against making the Church Extension grant asked for by all sections of the Kirk.[2] Scottish Radicals, who had received their advanced Burgh Reform in 1833, were now deep in their own State and Church controversy.

The English Municipal Reform Bill was based on the Report of a Commission which had been appointed in 1833, after a Select Committee had grasped the magnitude of the investigations

---

[1] Cf. Greville under April 9, 1835.
[2] *Companion to the British Almanac*, 1836, pp. 212 sqq., for the petition statistics. The Kirk was, of course, already involved in its internal controversy between Conservative pro-lay patronage and Radical anti-lay patronage sections. Both had nevertheless united to seek State money for building extra churches in the large towns where crime and infidelity could be plausibly explained by the lack of sufficient Church sittings. The Peel Government had offered a grant, but Melbourne was induced by the heavy petitioning to go no further than offer a Commission of Inquiry. (*Memoirs of Dr. Chalmers*, iv, 18–21.)

required, and the necessity for taking evidence in the towns affected and not at Westminster.¹ Beginning in the autumn of 1833, the Commission's inquiries had only terminated in the spring of 1835. In its first Report,² available soon afterwards, the anachronisms, abuses, and corruptions of near two hundred municipal corporations were laid bare by a Commission whose alleged bias to Radicalism may be admitted, since Parkes, its secretary, was very satisfied with its work, and Place was ready to assume journalistic defence of its recommendations. Whiggery, moreover, was the readier to legislate on the basis laid down by Radical barrister-commissioners because the existing corporations were strongholds of Tory influence of deservedly unpopular kinds.³

Radicals, then, heartily supported the Government's Bill for abolishing the corrupt old municipal oligarchies and substituting for them elected councils, chosen by all the ratepayers on equal terms and possessed of full police powers and the control of finance and charitable trusts. Indeed, the only improvements suggested by the Radicals were that the new municipalities should possess the right of adopting the Ballot for local voting if they so desired,⁴ and that they should be furnished with "local judiciaries" appointable by some democratic method. The Government, however, made no concessions either to Radicals or Tories on Municipal Reform or on the Tithe Bill for Ireland which was being advanced by parallel stages. That they came through without mishap on a single division suggests that Ministers employed the correct tactics.

Matters were very different in the Lords, where the able, combative, and unscrupulous Lyndhurst meant to inflict a thorough humiliation on the Government, and could rely on finding a majority of coroneted Tories to support him.⁵ For a

---

¹ The Report figures as Parliamentary Papers, 1835, xxiii.
² There was a Second Report in 1837 dealing with London. It may be noted that Irish Corporations were also ready for legislative treatment before the end of the 1835 Session as the result of an inquiry parallel to the English. Though an Irish Municipal Corporation Bill was introduced by the Government in 1835, it was finally remitted to the 1836 Session.
³ Cf. Lord John Russell in *Hansard*, xxviii, 541-8.
⁴ Cf. Grote, *Hansard*, xxix, 159.
⁵ *Courts and Cabinets of William IV and Victoria*, ii, 204-07, shows the unteachable Tory elements for whom Lyndhurst had consented to act. The Londonderrys, Buckinghams, and Newcastles found Peel too "liberal," and were trying to obtain another Tory Premier-designate. Lyndhurst, who was

Poor Law and Municipal Reform

whole month the impotent Government was compelled to look on while the Peers first conducted a Corporation Inquiry of their own, and then riddled the Government Bill with anti-democratic amendments which roused the Radicals of the Commons to fury.[1] If Peel had not been far-sighted enough to see that mere Tory partisanship would not do, a dangerous Radical storm would undoubtedly have swept the country. Even after Peel had helped the Government to save all the vital parts of the Bill a powerful Radical movement for the drastic Reform of the Lords could still be launched, and widespread Radical triumphs mark the first municipal elections held at the end of 1835.[2]

On Church matters, however, Peel was apt to be less clear-sighted than on temporal. In the very moderate Irish Tithe Bill of the Government Whigs, Radicalism, British and Irish, was really being quieted with very little. A great British majority and an overwhelming Irish majority were to acquiesce in replacing a Tithe system which had broken down with one which would work, and were to receive in return a few clauses permitting some annual thousands of tithe revenue to lapse from the Irish Church to Irish education. New appointments were to be suspended in the case of 860 parishes with fewer than fifty Protestant inhabitants, whose spiritual oversight, however, was not to be neglected. A first charge on the annual £58,076[3] eventually obtainable from the suspension of clerical appointments would, indeed, be the payment of neighbouring clergymen for their services, and a second would be the construction costs of approved ecclesiastical buildings. Only what was left after these deductions

---

alleged to have been a Radical himself in his early days at the Bar, has been whitewashed in a biography by Sir T. Martin (2nd ed., 1884, pp. 330–44), but it is not convincing as compared with Lord Campbell's famous *Life*.

[1] Cf. *Hansard*, August 31st–September 2nd, for Radical comments on the proceedings of the Lords from July 28th to August 25th.

[2] The following Tory comment on the election result even in a cathedral city like Lichfield is revealing. It is from (General) *Dyott's Diary*, ii, 221.

"January 1836. On the 1st of the month the Lichfield Radicals usurped the municipal power in the city, having succeeded in the choice of the new council according to the provisions of the Municipal Act. They proceeded this day to nominate the Mayor in the person of Dr. Rowley. These worthies also nominated the new aldermen from the scum of democracy and radicalism. Poor Lichfield, respectability has flown from thy people, distrust and hatred must dwell in thy community."

It was not till November 1843, and after great Tory effort, that the *Dyott Diary* reports: "The Conservatives victorious after eight years of tyrannical sway by the Radicals."

[3] *Hansard*, xxviii, 1334.

would be used for "general moral and religious instruction" in Ireland.¹

This most modest approach to Irish appeasement it was which Peel could not stomach, and which gave delighted Tory Ultras in the Lords the opportunity of reducing the Government to futility on the Irish question for a second time.² There were Ultra-Tory circles, indeed, round the royal Duke of Cumberland who, thanks to Hume, were detected in the work of setting up Orange Lodges in the Army³ for ends which might well have embraced a large return to the conditions of 1830. After such a Session as that of 1835 a Radical campaign against the Lords was inevitable. Indeed, it had already been opened in the Lower House by Hume, Duncombe, and Roebuck during the final proceedings on the Municipal Reform Bill, and Roebuck, too, was assailing the Peers in his widely read *Pamphlets for the People*.⁴ But it was O'Connell who was to demonstrate what feelings against the Peers could be mobilised in the populace. He had good reason for launching his sensationally successful campaign. The Lords had rejected not merely the Irish Tithe Bill, but also a Constabulary Bill, a Marriage Bill, a Dublin Police Bill, and a Voters' Registration Bill, all interesting Ireland.

O'Connell's remarkable speech-making tour in denunciation of the Peers, his huge and wildly enthusiastic audiences at Manchester, Newcastle, Edinburgh, Glasgow, and Dublin (not to mention numbers of smaller places through which he passed en route),⁵ the speedy reproduction of his speeches and political letters in large quantities for sale at one penny each—all these bear witness to the fact that the great democratic tide of 1831-2 was very far from having spent its force, as so many Tories were fond of believing. Indeed, in alarm at the wilder storms which

---

¹ Spencer Walpole, *Life of Lord J. Russell*, i, 264.
² See Lords' proceedings on August 24th in *Hansard*.
³ *Hansard*, August 4th, August 11th. For later allegations that William IV's deposition in favour of Cumberland had been mooted in 1832, see an article, "The Orange Exposure," in Roebuck's *Pamphlets*.
⁴ Under titles like "Of what use is the House of Lords," "The Crisis," and "The Peers and the People." Hotter than Roebuck was Publicola of the *Weekly Dispatch*, who in one August article proclaimed "The Last Hours of the Peerage" (quoted *Poor Man's Guardian*, August 22nd).
⁵ *Ann. Reg.*, 1835, History, pp. 367-71, a hostile account; *Poor Man's Guardian*, September 26th, October 3rd, October 10th, is unfriendly, but makes interesting incidental admissions of the vast stir O'Connell had made on what it held to be a relatively unimportant issue compared with the Poor Law, the Dorchester Labourers, etc.

Poor Law and Municipal Reform

O'Connell seemed to be conjuring up with his plans of setting a small elective House of Lords in the place of the existing body,[1] a very influential section of moderate Radicalism rallied to the traditional institution. Gratitude for Whig services in the past, fear of driving the Whig nobility into the Tory camp, hope that Tories would realise the dangers that the heated partisanship of the Peers entailed, dislike of O'Connell and the mob—all these had their part.[2] Before long, moreover, moderate Radicals were confirmed in their dislike of O'Connell's propaganda by some revelations in the O'Connell-baiting *Times* concerning the electioneering methods necessarily used by him in Ireland.[3]

Reform of the Lords, nevertheless, lingered on for a couple of years as a cause which Radical Parliamentarians, flouted on Irish Church adjustments and Irish Corporation Reform by a partisan majority in the Peers, might have to press on British constituencies, absorbed though these were with their own grievances. If, indeed, a British Radical grievance could have been found on which it would have been possible to raise a Lords and Commons controversy, Reform of the Lords would have become an immediate issue. There were British Radical grievances enough, of course; that of shopkeeper Radicals, for example, who were denied the Ballot, that of Dissenter Radicals who wanted the abolition of Church Rates, and that of working-class Radicals who demanded the repeal of the New Poor Law.[4]

---

[1] Manchester Speech, September 10th, p. 5; Letter to the *Leeds Times*, November 10th, p. 6. O'Connell contemplated a House of 150 elected from among 800 Peers, British, Scottish, and Irish, existing or to be created.

[2] Cf. E. Baines, M.P., Leeds, in *Remarks on the Proposition to re-model the House of Lords*. This pamphlet exercised a great influence.

[3] *Annual Register*, 1835, Chronicle, pp. 146-53, reproduces the Carlow election revelations, which were also extensively reprinted in pamphlet form. O'Connell had guaranteed a wealthy London Catholic banker, Alexander Raphael, a Co. Carlow seat in return for a very substantial sum towards expenses, but did not return the money when Raphael failed to win, as Raphael claimed he had promised to do. Though much prejudiced by the immense Tory use made of the matter, O'Connell, who did not have a Carlton Club election fund at his back, issues respectably from the situation in the eyes of the historian.

[4] Thus, in the 1837 Session, even with the improvised organisation of enthusiasts, there were 147,556 petitioners for the Ballot, and over 260,000 against the New Poor Law, while the Dissenters with the chapel machinery behind them raised the colossal and possibly unprecedented total of 674,719 petitioners against Church Rates. But when the Government, whose acceptance of this popular pressure was confined to some aspects of the Church Rate demand, attempted legislation, it was foiled by a drift of their own Churchman followers into the Tory division lobby. The 1837 Session, it should be noted, was the last

Poor Law and Municipal Reform

So long, however, as the existing electoral system permitted combinations of Whigs and Tories to refuse redress even in the Lower House, it was impossible to persuade the aggrieved that Reform of the Lords was the vital immediate issue. The bulk of them, indeed, preferred to be led first against the oligarchic ramparts thrown up round the House of Commons.

when an anti-Lords campaign on the Irish issue remained a possible political development (the petition numbers above are from the *Companion to the British Almanac*, 1838, pp. 215 sqq.).

CHAPTER VIII

RADICALISM FAILS TO IMPOSE ITS PROGRAMME

"The people are entitled to household suffrage, vote by ballot and triennial parliaments.

"These three great principles form the groundwork from which we expect a good and cheap government, not supported by a State Church, profligate patronage, pensioners, and a standing army in the time of peace, but based on the affections of an industrious and intelligent people...."
   Address of Newcastle working-class Radicals to the Earl of Durham, October 19, 1834. (From "Speeches of the Earl of Durham delivered at Public Meetings ... in 1834," J. RIDGWAY, *1835.)*

"We pledge ourselves to exert the best energies we possess to elevate Lord Durham to the Premiership of England. (Carried with three times three.)"
   Placarded resolution of the Dudley Political Union, Thursday, December 2, 1834.

"I beg to call the attention of the Cabinet to the position in which the present conduct of the House of Lords may place the Ministry and the country, It is evident that a majority of that House are combined, not to stop or alter a particular measure, but to stop or alter all measures which may not be agreeable to the most powerful, or in other words, the most violent among their own body.... The Radicals complain of a mischievous obstacle to good government, and propose an elective House of Lords. The Ministers stand in the position of confessing the evil and not consenting to the remedy...."
   June 5, 1836. A Cabinet paper circulated by Lord John Russell. In the "Life" *by* SPENCER WALPOLE, *I, 277.*

"It is not at all worth while to undergo the fatigue of nightly attendance in Parliament for the simple purpose of sustaining Whig Conservatism against Tory Conservatism."
   The despondent Grote, February 1838. (From MRS. GROTE'S "Personal Life of George Grote," *p. 127.)*

IT has been made plain in the preceding chapter that the critical Parliamentary situation arrived at by the close of the 1835 Session did nothing to dampen the combative Radical section in the Commons. Its pugnacity, indeed, was increased by the apparent inevitableness of the process by which power seemed destined to fall into its hands. The elections of the previous winter might have led to the defeat of many Whig members especially in the county divisions, but British urban Radicalism had kept its hold and O'Connellism had again proved the greatest electoral power in Ireland.[1] The result, naturally, had been to strengthen Radical influence with the Whig Government since the support of the Radical contingents had become vital to its life. The increase of Radical influence was best evidenced, perhaps, in the new direction given to Irish administration by Mulgrave as Lord Lieutenant, Morpeth as Irish Secretary, and Drummond as Irish Under-Secretary. It was obvious enough also at the famous meetings of Government supporters called on August 31 and September 7, 1835, meetings in which the Radical leaders spoke with marked authority[2] on the Municipal Reform dispute with the Lords.

One important element in the political situation was the complete electoral dominance Radicalism had been able to establish in the metropolitan area since 1832. Of this Radicalism represented by such "Ultras" as De Lacy Evans, Whittle Harvey, and Duncombe, Wakley, junior member for Finsbury, may be taken as a specially interesting leader. Having made himself a power in his own profession of medicine with the iconoclastic *Lancet* journal, he entered Parliament at his third attempt, committed to the abolition of Tithes, Corn Laws, the Malt, Soap, and Newspaper Taxes (which taxes and others unfairly burdening the productive classes, were to be replaced by a real property tax), and, of course, the New Poor Law also. The *Lancet* and his place in Parliament were to make him a most dangerous foe of workhouse "economies" whenever a careless dietary scale could be seized on or there occurred a pauper death ascribable

---

[1] The Radical strength, British and Irish, mobilisable in this Parliament was about 150. In the Ballot division of March 7, 1837, 153 votes were raised against the 265 of Whigs and Tories. The party composition is very similar in the Whittle Harvey Pension Division of April 19, 1836, when voting was 146–268.

[2] *Melbourne Memoirs*, ed. 1890, p. 385.

Radicalism fails to impose its Programme

to malnutrition or neglect. Deaths after army floggings, again, allowed him to tilt with special advantage against the Horse Guards' long resistance to the surrender of a brutalising corporal punishment, debasing to the lower ranks. It was on the Dorchester Labourers question, however, that Wakley was first to make his Parliamentary mark, and his forceful intervention on the unfortunates' behalf during his opening Parliamentary Session of 1835 undoubtedly expedited the ultimate Cabinet decision to repatriate them all.[1]

Other Radical causes also received notable recruitment in the 1835 Parliament. In Bowring, the well-known commercial negotiator with foreign Powers,[2] Perronet Thompson, the soldier-author of the *Corn Law Catechism*, and Villiers, the aristocratically connected member for Wolverhampton, the Anti-Corn Law cause obtained three notable recruits. In Wyse, Waterford landowner, historian of the Catholic Association and son-in-law to Lucien Bonaparte, popular education, especially in Ireland, won a vigilant and instructed friend. In Sharman Crawford, like Wyse an Irish Protestant landlord of advanced opinions, a Radical cause virtually new to Parliament raised its head, Tenant Right.[3]

The state of the Press, too, offered no discouraging view for Radicalism. One analysis of the Newspaper Stamp Return for the two years ending June 1835 produced the following averages for London-produced stamped newspapers: Subscribers to Tory dailies 25,798, to Tory weeklies 39,365; subscribers to Reforming dailies 18,915, to Reforming weeklies 85,088. Moreover there were, according to the same authority, four Ultra-Radical unstamped weeklies which alone issued 100,000 copies in successful defiance of the law, and altogether the total circulation of the Unstamped was over 200,000 weekly.[4] Specially cheering to

[1] S. Sprigge, *Life of T. Wakley*, is the principal source used; for an impression of Wakley's great power in the Dorchester Labourers debate of June 25, 1835, see the Roebuck *Pamphlet* on the Dorchester Labourers, pp. 5–6.

[2] With an extraordinary career as independent merchant, self-taught linguist, translator of Russian, Spanish, Serbian, Bohemian, Polish, Magyar, and Dutch poetry, Benthamite editor, Commissioner for the reform of the Public Accounts, etc., behind him.   [3] *Dictionary of National Biography*.

[4] Roebuck, *Pamphlet for the People*, "Democracy in America," article, "The Newspaper Stamp Return" by H. S. Chapman. The Roebuck weekly *Pamphlet* was undated to escape liability to a Newspaper Stamp, which would have increased its price form 1½d. to 5d. It achieved a large circulation while it ran between June 1835 and February 1836. Roebuck finally found the extra strain too great.

English Radicalism 1832-1852

Parliamentary Radicals was the progress of their "opinion-making" Press with circulation among the political classes and the professions. The *Morning Chronicle* was believed to be approaching the circulation of the apostate *Times*;[1] some of the *Examiner*'s own subscribers had by advance subscriptions helped it to acquire new printing machinery and thereby improved its prospects; and thanks to such moneyed Radical politicians as Strutt, Warburton, Marshall, and especially Molesworth, a new Radical review had made its appearance under the notable editorship of John Stuart Mill. Mill was aiming very high with the *London Review*—"to throw the combined strength of the most thoughtful and fertile-minded of the Radicals into one publication, of a more weighty and elaborate character than any magazine can be; allowing itself to treat subjects at greater length than the *Repository* or *Tait*; excluding altogether things which compromise the Radical cause by platitude or mediocrity or ignorance or subservience to any popular delusion."[2]

Despite the abundance of Radical energy available, the Session of 1836 was to prove disappointingly unfruitful of Radical measures. On the one hand, no measure obtaining the adhesion of Lords Melbourne, Holland, and Lansdowne, the most influential Cabinet representatives of pre-Reform Whiggery, could be expected to contain any but the most cautious proposals for the redress of the acutest grievances.[3] On the other hand, the increasing drift of alarmed "moderates" towards Peel's skilfully elevated standard,[4] a movement manifest already in the widespread formation of Conservative constituency organisations,[5] encouraged

[1] The average circulation of *The Times* for the first half of 1835 was 7,353 and that of the *Morning Chronicle* 5,490. The June figures, it was believed, would be nearer together (*Ibid.*).

[2] *Letters of J. S. Mill*, 1, 82-3, 93-4. Carlyle was the recipient.

[3] The high aristocratic character of this controlling triumvirate is plain, not only from the English sources, but from the observations of foreigners, the American Ticknor, for example (G. Ticknor, *Life and Letters*, i, 408 sqq.), or the French Guizot (*Embassy at the Court of St. James's in 1840*, chapter 4, English Society).

[4] Cf. *Speeches by the Rt. Hon. Sir Robert Peel, Bart., during his Administration 1834-5*. The publishers, announcing an "extensive demand" for them, "not only when printed separately, but also in a collective form," issued a second edition in August 1835 at 10s.

[5] In Staffordshire, for instance, the Conservative Association had been launched in April 1835 with a membership of 400. In the very month following it had been able to wrest a seat from the Whigs at a by-election, in which the Conservative candidate is reported to have been attended at nomination by "a vast string of carriages extending more than a quarter of a mile" (*Dyott's Diary*, ii, 201).

Radicalism fails to impose its Programme

the Lords to reject even such Reform as had passed through the Whig Cabinet sieve, if it was but judged inimical to the interests which Peers desired to preserve.

Thus it was that a Bill for the commutation of Irish Tithe was rejected because it envisaged the eventual diversion to Irish education of a small fraction of Irish Church revenues deemed "surplus." On the other hand, an English Tithe Commutation Bill was accepted because it treated the question of Tithe merely as one of adjustment between the "landed interest" and the Church. The Government's Irish Municipal Reform Bill, again, was rejected because Catholic influence would displace Protestant and the Charitable Trusts Bill "on account of the vicious principle that Dissenters should be eligible as trustees of old foundations."[1] The Bill, however, for setting up the permanent Ecclesiastical Commission was accepted, and the Commission's activities in gradually securing a more defensible distribution of Church income and a more effective distribution of Church effort have proved a principal cause in laming Dissenting efforts for Disestablishment. The Lords, indeed, were not averse to more change of this "conserving" kind. At the close of the Session Lyndhurst may be found complaining that the Ecclesiastical Courts Bill "had been allowed to slumber"[2] and that the Church Pluralities and Regulation of Fees Bill had been abandoned by harassed Ministers.

The two most Radical pieces of Government legislation which the Lords admitted to the Statute Book during the Session of 1836 were the Bill for Dissenters' Marriages and that for the establishment of Civil Registration of Births, Marriages, and Deaths. It was very plain, for one thing, that till this legislation was conceded vast Dissenting numbers would never be won from their embittered Radicalism. Even Wesleyan Methodism had lately split in such a way as to reveal the danger of a large part of its following turning from the political indifferentism it inculcated to the more robust politics of the rest of non-Churchmen.[3] There was, moreover, the best of practical cases for the

---

[1] This is the version of Lyndhurst's speech summing up the Session in the *Melbourne Memoirs*, ed. 1890, p. 414. *Hansard*, xxxv, 1289, is more discreetly worded. [2] *Ibid.*, 1285.
[3] For Ultra-Radical interest, see *Poor Man's Guardian*, September 5, 1835. Primitive Methodism, too, it should be remembered, differed widely from its parent in its political tendencies. If in the latter 1830's Wesleyan Methodist congregations were inclining markedly towards political Conservatism, Primi-

143

English Radicalism 1832-1852

Registration proposed in the manifest unsatisfactoriness of a system which made the State depend on incomplete ecclesiastical registers of baptisms and marriages for essential vital statistics.[1] In regard to Dissenters' Marriages, again, Peel during his bid for power in 1835 had committed himself in a way which confined unsuccessfully attempted Tory amendments to such irritating suggestions as that those who desired marriage without the intervention of the parish clergyman should be compelled to make a formal declaration of conscientious objection to Anglican rites.[2] It was fortunate, too, that many Dissenters in revolt against sacramental ideas of the marriage service wanted not chapel but civil marriages.[3] It would certainly have been impossible otherwise to get the Lords to consent to a Bill affording incidental marriage facilities to conscientious "infidels."

It should not be forgotten, however, in assessing the scant measure of Radical satisfaction with the Government that the Whig Ministers had deliberately refrained from pressing a good deal of the full Dissenting case. In the very speech, indeed, in which Lord John Russell had introduced the Marriage and Registration Bills, Dissenters had been asked to forgo their hopes of opening the gates of Oxford and Cambridge speedily to their sons. In regard to Church Rates and Burial Services they had been admonished to live at greater peace with the Church. If they did, urged Lord John, "a clergyman living in harmony with his parish and having feelings of goodwill to all classes of his parishioners might be induced to allow a funeral ceremony to be performed by a Dissenting minister in whom he had confidence and with whose piety and devotion he was satisfied, and from whom he did not anticipate anything obnoxious or insulting to his feelings."[4] If this was the Whig tone, it can be

---

tive Methodist local preachers were in Northumberland and Durham often the leaders of miners' combinations and strikes (cf. J. Ritson, *The Romance of Primitive Methodism*, pp. 280 sqq.). There is, indeed, something of a case for the contention of certain Primitive Methodists that it was their "camp meetings" which were to suggest the Chartist mass demonstrations of 1838-9, and certainly their hymns, altered to fit the Chartist case, were often used by the Chartists. Moreover, when Chartism was being reconstructed for a long agitation in the year after 1839, an organisation on a basis similar to the Methodist "class" was frequently attempted.

[1] Lord J. Russell, *Speeches and Despatches*, i, 438 sqq., February 12th.
[2] See *Hansard*, June 28th, for proceedings on Goulburn's amendment rejected by 68 against 132.   [3] *Baptist Magazine*, May 1837, pp. 192-7.
[4] Lord John Russell, *Speeches and Despatches*, i, 452, February 12, 1936.

Radicalism fails to impose its Programme

understood how completely insufferable was that of the Tories and how inevitably spirited Dissent was driven into Radicalism.[1]

Combative Parliamentary Radicalism had other causes of discontent with official Whiggery besides the non-redress of Dissenting wrongs.[2] Imperfect as was the representation of the people in the existing House of Commons, small as was the real share that the will of the nation as a whole played in its legislative programme, the Lords were yet being allowed to destroy whatever of Liberalism emerged, while Ministers looked on, helpless or unwilling to provide effective remedy.[3] It was not merely that the Peers nullified the main Bills of the Session, those on Irish Tithes and Irish Municipal Corporations. They went further and in the case of the Registration of Voters Bill, the Post Office Bill, and the Catholic Marriages Bill, they rejected measures which, as Lord Melbourne bitterly complained, the Tories in the Commons had accepted.[4] On a third class of Bills, moreover, like the Prisoners' Counsel Bill the Lords introduced amendments so unacceptable as to tempt Radicals to send them back and make a display of readiness to prolong the Session. But thanks to the system of proxy voting in the Upper House, another "abuse" marked down for destruction by the Radicals,[5] the Lords majority had all the advantages in a struggle of endurance with the Commons. A group of the more belligerent Tory Peers could, when duly armed with the proxies of their friends, release the

---

[1] The relations between Anglican clergymen and Dissenting ministers often made great trouble, the Dissenting ministers usually having to complain of the "haughty monopolising spirit" of the Anglicans (cf. *Baptist Magazine*, February 1837, p. 54, and October 1837, pp. 446-7, for evidence of how Anglican "pride" and "assumptions" confirmed Dissenting ministers in urging the need for Disestablishment).

[2] E.g. *Annual Register*, 1836, History, pp. 140-9, shows very vividly the great trouble there was over the "Bishops Bill" with its schedule of high salaries for Bishops, who had been persuaded to make over the episcopal estates to the management of the new Ecclesiastical Commission.

[3] The Irish Municipal Corporations controversy with the Lords will be found specially rich in recrimination. See the proceedings of May 19th, June 9th, June 10th, and June 30th in the Commons. Hume attempted a summing-up speech for the whole Session just prior to the prorogation on August 20th.

[4] *Melbourne Memoirs*, ed. 1890, p. 414.

[5] One of the most "liberal" of the Whig Peers, the Marquess of Westminster, may be found raising the subject in the Upper House itself on August 6, 1833, and in the Commons Duncombe rallied a vote of 81-129 against Peers' proxies on May 9, 1837. It should nevertheless be remembered that the use of "proxies" in the Lords was limited by the Standing Orders—not theoretically irrevocable, it is true—which allowed each Peer personally voting the use of two "proxies" only, and not on Committee stages.

English Radicalism 1832–1852

rest of the party in Commons and Lords from the painful necessity of spending the hot August weeks "in town."

But serious as Radical discontent with Whiggery tended to become in these conditions, there were factors working strongly to prevent such a breach as would allow the Tories to return to power. It was widely known, for example, that Ministers were finding the King so hostile[1] that the question of creating new Peers in sufficient numbers to intimidate Lyndhurst and his following could not be raised without provoking a grave constitutional crisis. Virtually no Parliamentary Radicals were yet prepared lightheartedly to court the risk of a Tory Administration by pressing the Whig Ministers so hard on the Peerage question that they would be compelled to resign. O'Connell, too, was using all his great weight in the Radical ranks on behalf of the Ministers. British Radicals, moreover, like Irish, did not lack tangible proof that a Whig Government, even if weak legislatively, had very real Executive capacities useful to Radicalism. Thus Silk Buckingham's crusade for the abolition of naval "pressing" had certainly advanced a long way by 1836[2] and army flogging, too, had been brought under much humaner regulation.[3] In the new English municipalities, again, the appointment of borough J.P.'s had been such as to give rise to vigorous Tory complaints that a clean sweep of Tories from the borough Benches had been made.[4]

The Government's Budgetary control, finally, permitted Radicals to advance a great step towards that "Abolition of the Taxes on Knowledge" which many had been making their principal aim since 1832. The decisive factor was not, perhaps, the Parlia-

---

[1] Cf. Greville under August 30, 1836. Hobhouse, a Cabinet Minister, reports Melbourne as saying on the Cabinet tension with the Court, "in 1834 the dismissal was the result of a scheme. Now there was no scheme, but His Majesty was all but crazy. . . ." (*Recollections*, ed. Lady Dorchester, v, under August 20, 1836).

[2] J. S. Buckingham, *National Evils and Practical Remedies*, xxiv–xxv. In 1836 Buckingham secured an Admiralty admission that voluntary enlistment under the improved conditions newly offered had fully answered the Service's need (cf. *Hansard*, xxxii, 1108).

[3] The arrival of Lord William Bentinck in the Radical ranks re-inforced Radical pressure. As Governor-General of India, Bentinck had lately abolished flogging in the sepoy regiments (*Hansard*, xxxii, 1041–3). The Horse Guards issued almost simultaneously with the anti-flogging debates of 1836 a revised flogging schedule confining regimental courts-martial to 100 lashes, district courts-martial to 150 lashes, and even general courts-martial to 200 lashes (cf. *Hansard*, xxxii, 1049).

[4] Cf. Wharncliffe in the Lords, February 23rd, and Peel in the Commons, March 29th.

Radicalism fails to impose its Programme

mentary demonstrations led by Lytton Bulwer but rather the great working-class support for the "Unstamped" before which the Revenue efforts at arrests and prosecutions were proving punily ineffective.[1] Indeed, the position of the legal Stamped Press was becoming so dangerously undermined by 1835[2] that Spring Rice as Whig Chancellor of the Exchequer was at last allowed to promise consideration for the Radical case if the next Budget were drawn up in favourable conditions.[3] Place, however, recognised that it would be fatal for Radical efforts to slacken at this critical stage, and it was primarily under his guidance that working-class volunteers in the metropolis arranged the widespread Parliamentary petitioning from all over the country which made the Anti-Newspaper Stamp Petitions with 130,766 signatures one of the important political manifestations of the year.[4] The result was that Spring Rice resolved to devote very nearly the whole of the surplus, for which prosperous conditions allowed him to budget, in halving the excise duty on paper of printing quality and in pulling the newspaper duty down from 4d. to 1d.[5] On this matter, at least, the Government was able to ignore the clamour of *The Times*, to resist the Tory pressure to make health-giving soap and not debauching news-sheets the object of tax remission[6] and to enjoy Lord Lyndhurst's

[1] Though there were hundreds of prosecutions (e.g. 219 in 1835, Wallas, *Life of Place*, pp. 348–9). Thanks to the generosity of the remarkable Julian Hibbert, the Ultra-Radicals had a Victim Fund for the fined, the imprisoned, and their dependents (Lovett, *Life and Struggles*, ed. 1876, p. 89).

[2] Especially in the case of the weeklies trying to sell at 8½d. against the "Unstamped's" price of 2d. For the appeal of *Bell's New Weekly Messenger* to the Chancellor, see *Poor Man's Guardian*, July 18, 1835, pp. 604–5; July 11th, p. 596, for the danger of the dailies.

[3] C. D. Collett, *History of the Taxes on Knowledge*, ed. 1933, p. 28. For Spring Rice's speech, *Hansard*, August 21, 1835.

[4] *Companion to the British Almanac*, 1837, pp. 226–8, for the petition figures of 1836, which had been raised from the 57,848 of 1835. Place claims (Add. MSS. 27819, f. 26) that "a correspondence was opened with nearly three thousand respectable persons," and the working men concerned formed the nucleus for the famous London Working Men's Association of 1836. When J. S. Mill was concerned for the Ballot motion of 1837 he tried to get Place to set up the machinery once more. Place, however, seems to have been angry because, though he had kept the costs down to £110, the promoting committee had been left £20 in debt (*Life and Labours of Albany Fonblanque*, pp. 30–1).

[5] Spencer Walpole, *History of England from 1815*, iii, 366 sqq., for a lucid summary of his proposals. It should be remembered that the 4d. had been subject to 20 per cent discount.

[6] *Hansard*, xxxiv, 613–63. Wallas's *Place*, p. 350, for the Radical opposition which was raised to the 1d. duty, even though it gave free postage. Place understood well the dangers of adding the 1d. tax to the 1d., 1½d., or 2d. price of the "Unstamped."

English Radicalism 1832-1852

constitutional inability to defeat in the Lords a reduction of taxation voted by the Commons.

This is not the place to relate how the Whig Government, so often baffled and humiliated in the Lords and so frequently worried at Court by personal discourtesies and difficulties over Honours Lists, was called upon in the autumn of 1836 to face the beginning of a great economic storm. To know, however, that after a series of bounteous harvests the British autumn crops of 1836 were disappointing; that after years of great commercial and industrial activity (which included some risky railway and joint-stock bank financing at home and heavy advances abroad) the country went into a long period of depression with only five millions of bullion at the Bank[1] and some of that quickly called upon, is to understand what powerful economic factors were henceforth at work upon the transformation of the political scene. There was some revival of Anti-Corn Law agitation, for example, during the ensuing winter and a vast increase in the volume of petitioning for repeal or amendment of the New Poor Law.[2] In the industrial North, indeed, threatened with the advance of workhouse-erecting Assistant Poor Law Commissioners who had finished their work in the South, the year 1837 was to see Ultra-Radicalism particularly concentrated on the Poor Law question.

During the 1837 Session, meanwhile, the Melbourne Ministry had perforce to devote its principal legislative attention to a renewed effort to pass its Irish Tithe and Corporation proposals. The critical Corporation division of February 23rd with its high majority of 80 for the Government[3] showed rank-and-file Tories, hungry for office, that they were farther from power than they had confidently imagined. In fact, by objecting to granting the Irish towns similar municipal privileges to those enjoyed in England and Scotland they had taken the very course to bind impatient Parliamentary Radicals closer to the Government. For the Radicals a vital day in the Session was March 7th, when their Ballot motion was made. Outside Parliament heavier peti-

---

[1] *Melbourne Memoirs*, ed. 1890, p. 421.
[2] *Companion to the British Almanac*, 1838, p. 217, shows that during a Session ending on July 17, 1837, 201,967 petitioners had asked for the repeal of the New Poor Law, and 63,796 for its amendment.
[3] *Hansard*, xxxvi, 958. The voting was 322–242.

Radicalism fails to impose its Programme

tioning had been organised than ever before,[1] and inside a number of Whigs, anxious to help Whig-Radical relations to smoothness, abstained from the anti-ballot lobby.[2] The resultant division at 153–265 was not unhopeful.

It was the Government's Church Rate Bill of 1837, however, which most markedly brought the Whig position closer to the Radical for a space. On its announcement, indeed,[3] the nation was organised for petitioning *pro* and *con* more extensively than had ever been the case before. The total of petitioners for the Government's proposals before the end of the Session was no less than 674,719, and the adverse total of 330,123 was itself greater than any previously collected by Churchmen.[4]

In Parliament, however, sentiment proved to be very differently balanced. Churchmen were furious when they found that Spring Rice, departing from the Whig plan of 1834, suggested not an annual Treasury grant of £250,000 in lieu of Church Rate levies, but an annual £250,000 to be taken from the profits made by the Ecclesiastical Commission in its management of episcopal estates.[5] So that Dissenters might have a legal veil thrown over their immoral and unchristian resistance to an immemorial impost of the most moderate proportions and devoted to the most sacred purposes, argued Churchmen, the Government was preparing to annex Church money, needed for church and school building and the augmentation of poor livings. Events certainly proved that the Government had overcalculated the Church's readiness to retreat from the still rapidly spreading Church Rate contentions. Indeed, with a majority falling as pro-Church temper rose from the initial 273 against 250 of March 15th to the 287 against 282 of May 23rd,[6] Ministers' position became ever more serious.

[1] *Life and Labours of Albany Fonblanque*, pp. 30–1. The actual numbers who petitioned during the Session were 147,556 (*Companion to the British Almanac*, 1838, p. 217). In 1836 the numbers had been 11,770.
[2] *Melbourne Memoirs*, p. 430. Radicals were very anxious to improve their figures of June 23, 1836, when they had divided at 88–139.
[3] *Hansard*, xxxvi, 1207.
[4] The petition figures are from *Companion to the British Almanac*, 1838, p. 215.
[5] *Melbourne Memoirs*, pp. 429–30. *Hansard*, xxxvii, 147–50, for the Archbishop of Canterbury's lead to the Opposition, and *Ibid.*, pp. 155–8, for the influential Bishop of London's. The Church case, of course, was that when the Bishops had consented to make over the episcopal estates to the Ecclesiastical Commission, and to take in return the "moderate" fixed salaries of the "Bishops' Bill," they had done so in the full belief that the surplus would be devoted to such purposes as Church Extension and the augmentation of poor livings.
[6] *Ibid.*, 549; xxxviii, 1073.

English Radicalism 1832–1852

Nor was their situation improved by such other contemporary events as grave troubles in the Canadas, deepening depression in commerce and trade[1] and the defeat of the Radical-led British Legion intervening for Spanish Liberalism under Government auspices.[2] When, moreover, the old Radical Burdett, complaining of Ministers' subservience to O'Connell and the Ultras, resigned his Westminster seat to refight it on a Conservative basis, his victorious emergence from a hot electoral contest with the advanced Radicals, seemed to set the seal on a long series of by-election misfortunes.[3] But doubtless there was a good deal in such Radical explanations of Tory strength as were made by Roebuck in a notable fighting speech of June 9th.[4] According to him, it was the constant Whig hedging between aristocracy and democracy which was reducing the popular weight behind them and only the adoption of a bold forward policy into democratic government would recruit sufficient popular enthusiasm to save them. At such a Radical price, of course, the greater part of the Cabinet did not desire to be saved.[5]

Indeed, it may almost be assumed that a Whig Cabinet, which a single important resignation might have brought down,[6] would ere this have made way for Peel had it not been for a common determination to decline to surrender to the unscrupulous tactics of Lyndhurst in the Lords. The whole State was discredited by a political situation which the exulting Lyndhurst was able, on June 23rd, to describe virtually as follows: "During a session which wanted only a few days of five months' duration, only two Acts of distinct and special legislation had been passed—the Post Office Contracts and the Scottish Sedition Bills—while

---

[1] Raikes under April 11th and 12th. The depression was aggravated by tendencies to financial panic for which Tories blamed the unsound methods which had been pursued by the Joint Stock Banks, whose foundation had been facilitated by the Whigs.
[2] Raikes under March 19th and 22nd. For the resultant Tory attempt to defeat the Government on its Spanish policy, Raikes under April 22nd and 24th
[3] Raikes, under May 12th.   [4] *Hansard*, xxxviii, 1337 sqq.
[5] Thus Melbourne had not mourned the Radical defeat at Westminster overmuch (*Memoirs*, p. 434). A success would have raised the Radical demands on the Whigs.
[6] Spencer Walpole, *Life of Lord J. Russell*, I. 277-8, and Melbourne, *Memoirs*, p. 425, suggest that Lord J. Russell was dangerously dissatisfied with the lack of Cabinet spirit in Peerage creation. Lord Lansdowne, on the other hand, was the reverse of eager to engage in hostilities with the Peers. It would appear from Hobhouse that the Government was not far from collapse during the summer of 1836 (*Recollections*, ed. Lady Dorchester, v, 59).

Radicalism fails to impose its Programme

there were at present no fewer than seventy-five public Bills depending in the other House. So far as the foreign policy of Ministers was concerned, it elicited the pity of their friends and the scorn and derision of their enemies."[1] The Palmerstonian Foreign Office, still concerned for Spanish and Portuguese constitutionalism, not freed yet from Greek, Belgian, and Turkish troubles, anxious about the repercussions of Canadian events on Anglo-American relations, was not yet apparently an institution which reconciled the stoutest Tories to Whig administration. On the other hand, Radicals like De Lacy Evans, O'Connell, and Attwood had frequently voiced their anger with its inability to stay the course of Russian repression in Poland and of Russian aid for "despotism" everywhere.[2]

In some respects, however, the Ministerial situation had already been improved before Lyndhurst made his contemptuous speech of June 23rd. William IV had died on June 20th, and instead of a hostile monarch whose fits of ill-temper and obstinacy had sometimes gravely inconvenienced the Ministers, Melbourne had the youthful and soon very friendly Victoria to deal with.[3] The royal demise, again, temporarily extracted the Ministry from a Parliamentary deadlock likely to become every day more damaging to its position. The law still required the demise of the Crown to be followed within six months by the gathering of a new Parliament. In view of the approaching General Election, therefore, Ministers had a good case for confining their Parliamentary efforts to the rapid passage of non-contentious legislation and of the Budget.

The election campaign found Ministers directing their appeals not so much to the often voteless Radical as to the hesitant "moderate" so assiduously wooed by Peel. Radicalism, indeed,

---

[1] *Hansard*, xxxviii, 1837-8.   [2] E.g. *Ibid.*, xiii, 1137, 1143.
[3] The Duchess of Kent, Victoria's mother, had not without astuteness leaned to the "popular" side during William IV's closing years (cf. Greville, under September 9, 1835; June 2, 1837). Durham, again, the most Radical of those promotable to the Premiership, is noted as "a manifest favourite" in 1832 (Hobhouse, *Recollections*, ed. Lady Dorchester, iv, under March 26, 1832), and his possible rise to power in a new reign was a matter of some speculation (cf. *Courts and Cabinets of William IV and Victoria*, ii, 125-6, by the 2nd Duke of Buckingham and Chandos). By 1837, however, Victoria had come to have a very real respect and liking for the Melbourne Ministry (*Letters of Queen Victoria*, April 28, 1837, May 2nd), and as Queen she rapidly learned under Melbourne's guidance to view Radicals and Tories with his eyes (cf. *Ibid.* Letter, August 9th).

stood to fare ill when Peel stressed his fair-mindedness in having given zealous support "to a weak and inefficient Government whenever it has offered an opposition, however lukewarm and hesitating, to projects of further change in the system of representation or in the balance of the constituted authorities of the State"; when Lord John Russell was anxious to go on record as considering the Reform Bill "a final measure" and as being permanently opposed to "any proposition for the adoption of an elective House of Lords or of the voluntary principle in religion" (Disestablishment); and when even Lord Durham, returning from the Petersburg Ambassadorship in hopeful quest of power, defended such further reforms as he desired because their effect would be "to rally as large a portion of the British people as possible around the existing institutions of the country —the Throne, Lords, Commons, and the Establishd Church."[1] The remarkable outburst of sentimental loyalty towards the charming and unspoiled young girl who had ascended the throne was not, it is plain, the most auspicious of accompaniments to the agitation of Radical causes.

In point of fact, the elections of the summer of 1837 gave Parliamentary Radicalism a violent set-back. Such typical men of 1832, for example, as Daniel Gaskell and William Tooke, friend of the now chartered London University, were swept for ever from the Parliamentary scene. That active, wealthy, and experienced Parliamentarian, the humanitarian Ewart, failed to secure re-election for his native Liverpool, largely responsible though he was for the 1834 Act abolishing hanging in chains, the 1836 Act allowing the use of counsel to those accused of felony and the considerable deletions from the list of capital crimes made in 1837. Perronet Thompson, author of the *Corn Law Catechism*, and a member of the 1835 Parliament, failed at Maidstone against so notorious a political adventurer as Disraeli. The formidable Hume himself was defeated in Middlesex though the opponent by whom he was ousted was a man of no eminence. Wigney, again, of Brighton and Roebuck and Palmer of Bath were among the vanquished.[2]

The Bath election may be chosen to illustrate the factors

---

[1] J. Irving, *Annals of Our Time*, ed. 1871, p. 3.
[2] See Dod's *Electoral Facts, 1832–1866*, under Wakefield, Truro, Liverpool, Maidstone, Middlesex, Brighton, and Bath.

Radicalism fails to impose its Programme

contributing to the electoral set-backs of Radicalism in 1837. Major-General Charles Napier, one of the Radical pillars at Bath,[1] ascribed Roebuck's failure there to Tory bribery and intimidation, to Whig jealousy, to Dissenting discontent with Roebuck's opposition to the Sabbatarian crusade,[2] and finally to Roebuck's support of the New Poor Law. It is a convincing catalogue which may serve to explain other Radical defeats than Roebuck's and other Tory victories than Lord Powerscourt's. There were additional reasons for such Tory gains as there were in the counties. Not only were many tenantries intimidated by fear of incurring the displeasure of their landlords, but there was real rural discontent with the repeated refusals of Whig Chancellors to repeal the Malt Tax or to do more for the "land" then relieve county rates of half the cost of prosecutions.

Despite some of the surprising election results recorded, Peel failed to obtain a majority. In England, it is true, the Conservatives established by means, often far from reputable,[3] a clear superiority of numbers but the very different position in Scotland and Ireland turned the balance against them. Middle-class Scotland could not yet be induced to forget the long Tory misuse of power and patronage before 1830,[4] and in Ireland O'Connell's influence was in 1837 greater than ever before. In view of the Whig Government's diminished and now very precarious majority, it was particularly fortunate in retaining the unwavering support

[1] W. Napier, *Life of Gen. Sir C. Napier*, i, 466.
[2] A crusade under the Parliamentary direction of Sir Andrew Agnew aiming at the passage of Lord's Day Observance Bills which would effectually prevent "desecration" of the Sabbath. Not merely Sunday railway travelling was aimed at, but even the holding of markets on Saturdays and Mondays, because Sabbath desecration was inevitable for some of those who attended. The great bulk of Dissent favoured Sabbatarian legislation, despite the "conservative" politics of its principal proponents. Most Parliamentary Radicals, however, resisted the Sabbatarian movement, though such conduct facilitated the bringing of dangerous charges of "infidelity" against them. The best Radical line of approach proved to be to stress the need of Sunday morning food sales for the very poor, the need of trips into the country by boat, coach, or train for dwellers in the unhealthy quarters of the towns, the commercial need for Monday morning mail deliveries involving though they did Sunday coaches and trains, the popular need of Sunday newspaper reading, etc. Included in the wealth of literature on the subject is one meritorious poem of 1837, " Sunday, a poem in defence of the reasonable enjoyments and recreations of the Toiling Classes of London—by a Friend to Humanity."
[3] Greville, under July 28th, estimates Norwich to have cost £50,000 to the two victorious Tories. For Pontefract conditions, see T. W. Reid, *Life of R. M. Milnes*, i, 198.
[4] Best pictured in H. Cockburn's *Memorials of His Time*. For Scotland and the 1837 election, see Cockburn's *Journal* (1831-54), i, 145 sqq.

of O'Connell, the more so as the reduced band of British Radicals was to show the greatest restiveness under a Parliamentary system which allowed Conservative membership to increase while the unrepresented majority of the nation was becoming more Ultra in its Radicalism. O'Connell, of course, sympathised with the grievances of the British Parliamentary Radicals but was never, like them, prepared to press demands for political democratisation to the point of imperilling a resisting Whig Ministry. Ireland, after all, was O'Connell's first interest, and in Irish administration and legislation the Whigs were doing everything he could reasonably desire.[1] Indeed, in the matter of the Irish Poor Law finally passed in 1838, they were preparing to go farther than O'Connell himself desired.[2]

The mutiny of British Radicals against Ministers refusing to advance a single step in the direction of democratisation began at the very commencement of the new Parliament when Wakley and Molesworth attempted to amend the Address by making it promise juster representation to the people. Russell held that "entering into this question of the construction of the representation so soon again would destroy the stability of our institutions" and led a majority of 509 against the rebel Radical vote of 20.[3] When on December 15th Hume, now by the grace of O'Connell member for Kilkenny, attempted to reduce by £50,000 Victoria's suggested Civil List income of £385,000 he could only divide at 19 against 199. Though, again, a Select Committee was at last granted on the Pension List which had so long provoked the masses, means were found to exclude from the inquiry the Ultra-Radical D. W. Harvey, who had made the subject peculiarly his own.[4]

On these and later matters wherein a small muster of combatant Radicals openly resisted the Government, they did not endanger its existence because the Tories were in favour of what it proposed to do. Moreover, there was a strong body of influential Radical

---

[1] Moreover, the whole O'Connellite following needed Whig protection from an extreme Tory attempt to challenge the legality of their elections. The large Spottiswoode fund had been raised for this purpose (*Hansard*, xxxix, 788 sqq.), and a case based on priestly cursings and admonitions, mob violence, etc., was possible.
[2] On April 28, 1837, O'Connell had resisted the Second Reading of a Government Irish Poor Law Bill. For consequent British Radical animadversion, see W. Napier, *Life of Gen. C. Napier*, i, 464.
[3] *Hansard*, xxxix, 81.   [4] *Ibid.*, p. 1273.

Radicalism fails to impose its Programme

opinion which disliked and opposed such resistance as tending to disintegrate a Parliamentary majority from which much was yet to be hoped.[1] "Public opinion," indeed, was inclined to measure the strength of Radicalism not by the small vote obtainable on Ultra motions but rather by the annual division on the Ballot.[2] When the 1838 Ballot division of February 15th with its vote of 198 against 315 showed that 200 M.P.s were now committed to the Radical panacea, many felt the continuous rise in the pro-Ballot vote to indicate the likelihood of a Ballot Act being inscribed before long on the Statute Book.[3] As it was universally assumed that Ballot voting would dry up the main sources of Tory and even of Whig Power, the dislike of some Radicals for violent Ultra courses of opposition, which might bring the Government down before the Whig conversion to Ballot was complete, becomes understandable.

On March 6, 1838, nevertheless, Molesworth opened an assault on the Whig Colonial Secretary which, in view of the Tory readiness to attack him on grounds different from those of the Ultras, presented long-awaited possibilities of combining sufficient Radical votes with Tory to overthrow the Government. The complaints of both Radicals and Tories had reference to a critical Canadian situation with dangerous American extensions. But where the Tories complained of administrative inefficiency, the Radicals complained also of the neglect of colonial claims to self-government which had led to rebellion in both Canadas. Once more, however, the Government escaped defeat by a narrow margin[4] and staggered on for fourteen weary months longer, able to pass only such legislation as the Tory majority in the Lords accepted. Thus in 1838 after five Sessions of contention, the Whig Cabinet at length allowed the Peers to dictate an Irish Tithe Bill from which all provision for the appropriation of surplus Church revenues had been removed.[5] But neither on

---

[1] *Personal Life of George Grote*, p. 127, for bitter complaint of "the degeneracy of the Liberal party and their passive acquiescence in everything good or bad which emanates from the present Ministry."

[2] Raikes under March 9, 1837; Greville under February 18, 1838.

[3] Greville (February 18th) reports Brougham as predicting the carrying of the Ballot in five years. One prominent Tory, Lord F. Egerton, may be found calling the division the "commencement de la fin," and advocating "a coalition with the remnant of the sounder Whigs" (*Peel Papers*, ii, 359–60).

[4] By 316 against 287. Hansard, xli, 684.

[5] *Melbourne Memoirs*, ed. 1890, pp. 451–2.

English Radicalism 1832–1852

the fourth Government Bill of 1838 for Irish Municipal Reform nor on the fifth of 1839 could the expected counter-concessions be obtained from the Tories.[1]

Indeed, in 1839 the Lords made a frontal attack on the whole of Irish Whig Administration and by resolving to set up their own Select Committee on the subject in defiance of the Government produced a considerable political crisis.[2] There was for a time a possibility that the outraged Whig Cabinet would, in view of the Anti-Corn Law and Chartist tempests now raging out of doors, agree to a moderate composition with Parliamentary Radicalism[3] which would strengthen its hands against the Lords on the one hand and assist in pacifying the country on the other. The Radical terms for a hearty alliance would have been far from high and yet would have made a popular appeal which would have exposed the groundlessness of the Tory claim that there was a "national reaction" against Reform. But Cabinet agreement on the abolition of the "ratepaying clauses," the disfranchisement of boroughs with fewer than 300 voters and the making of the Ballot an "open" question was impossible.[4] Accordingly ten Radicals refused to swallow their scruples of conscience on a Government Bill for suspending the Jamaica Constitution which the Tories were also opposing. As the Government majority was thereby reduced to five,[5] Ministers decided to resign and retire from difficulties growing ever more serious.

[1] For a useful summary of many weary scores of Hansard columns, see Spencer Walpole's *History*, iii, 456, 457, 482.
[2] Cf. Lord John Russell's Speech of April 15, 1839, initiating an Irish debate lasting till the 19th.   [3] Cf. Greville under April 6th and 21st.
[4] Greville under April 22nd gives these three conditions as the "minimum of concession that would do." His informant on the attitude of the moderate Parliamentary Radicals was Fonblanque. The principal Cabinet opponent of concession was Lord J. Russell, who at this stage opposed even the "opening" of the Ballot. He was apparently afraid of what would happen if the Whigs consented to the modification of the Reform Bill, and it is certainly hard to believe that even moderate Radicals would long have been content with Fonblanque's programme.
[5] The Jamaica division of May 6th was 294 against 289.

CHAPTER IX

THE PEOPLE'S CHARTER AND THE NATIONAL PETITION

"Parliamentary Radicalism, while it gave articulate utterance to the discontent of the English people, could not by its worst enemy be said to be without a function.... How Parliamentary Radicalism has fulfilled this mission, entrusted to its management these eight years now, is known to all men. The expectant millions have sat at a feast of the Barmecide; been bidden to fill themselves with the imagination of meat. What thing has Radicalism obtained for them; what other than shadows of things has it so much as asked for them? Cheap Justice, Justice to Ireland, Irish Appropriation Clause, Rate-Paying Clause, Poor Rate, Church Rate, Household Suffrage, Ballot Question 'open' or shut: not things, but shadows of things: Benthamee formulas, barren as the east wind."

From CARLYLE'S "Chartism" (*1839*).

"Of the six millions of adult men in the United Kingdom, it has been calculated that about five millions assist in producing and distributing wealth; and that of this number four millions belong to the division called the working class. It has been shown that by the present arrangements of society this last great division receive scarcely £200,000,000 of the £500,000,000 of the wealth annually created which averages about £11 per head for the men, women, and children comprised in this class; and that for this miserable pittance they toil, on the average, 11 hours per day. . . .

"If there be any among them who are contented with their position in society and their future prospects—who believe that their Creator made them to be the slaves and the prey of their fellow-men—who are willing when worn out by years of toil to lie down on the highway side and die like dogs—if there be any such among working man, they will not ask for a social change; but if there be those who believe that the rights of men are equal—that man may claim no dominion over man—that life was given for another purpose than that of being spent in one unwearying round of incessant toil, then will they demand and they will have a change in the present state of things. . . ."

J. F. BRAY'S "Labour's Wrongs and Labour's Remedy" (*1838–9*), *pp. 155, 209. The book is a plea that the expected popular triumph should be used for setting up the Owenite state.*

It may, perhaps, be considered partial to regret the opportunity which was lost between 1832 and 1837 to undertake some far-going renovations in the faultiest parts of England's social system. There was certainly a House of Commons majority in being which, thanks to the pressure to be expected from the populace, would have responded well to far-sighted and adroit Radical leadership. Indeed, it is not too much to say that even apart from such pressure the Commons majority of the period was further in advance of the actual institutions of its own day than has probably ever been the case since.[1] But it was the Greys, the Lansdownes, and the Melbournes who were in the strategic commanding positions at Whitehall. Though willing to undertake an unenthusiastic removal of the worst anachronisms from British politics, they were strongly opposed to instituting a Radical democracy.

By 1837, as has been seen, a section of Parliamentary Radicalism was already in revolt. Between 1837 and 1839 it was energetically trying to force Whiggery forward to what the Tories considered the most dangerously Ultra of programmes because tending to weaken the forces defending "Property." A quotation from an illuminating speech made by Molesworth in January 1837 at the beginning of the "Ultra" campaign will show, however, that the Westminster Ultra-Radicals at least had few *arrière-pensées* on property in undertaking their democratic crusade. "It is said we ought to overlook minor differences of opinion," retorted Molesworth upon the moderate Radicals who were criticising the Ultra readiness to attack the Whigs. "But is the ballot merely a minor difference of opinion? Is the repeal of the ratepaying clauses—is an extension of the suffrage—is an abolition of Church-rates—of the Irish Church—of the Corn Laws—is a reform of the army—is a reform of the universities—above all a reform of the House of Lords—are all these questions of minor importance?"[2] It may be safely assumed, indeed, that Molesworth and the

---

[1] Irish Disestablishment and the Ballot, for example, the work of the notorious Radical majority of 1868, could have been achieved with a Government lead in 1833. In 1836, again, the Government could have led the House of Commons in imposing a more satisfactory solution of the House of Lords problem than was even attempted by the Radicals of 1906-11.

[2] *Annual Register*, History, p. 12, 1837. It may be noted in addition that on February 14, 1837, Molesworth divided the Commons at 104 against 133 for abolition of the property qualification of M.PS.

The People's Charter and the National Petition

Parliamentary Ultras confined their immediate "Property" ambitions very largely to the readjustment of income and purchasing power which would follow on the Corn Law Repeal to be expected from a democratised political system.

For some two years and a half after the Ultra declarations of January 1837, the relations between advanced Parliamentary Radicalism and the Government continued to provide problems for the political tacticians. But long before a cessation of hostilities was arranged on the basis of the Government's allowing the Ballot to become an open question[1]—a decision not without its importance at the time since it allowed the pro-Ballot vote of 1839 to rise to 216[2]—popular Ultra-Radicalism had developed its own Chartist programme and agitation. To the history of this development it is now necessary to turn, noting, of course, that it was fundamentally based on hopes of effecting altogether larger changes of Income Distribution than were in the mind of the Molesworths.[3]

For the origins of the powerful Chartist movement of 1838-9 it is first necessary to examine the activities of a central knot of London working men who since 1830 had been able to play a very considerable part in national politics. Educated in the Mutual Improvement Societies and the Coffee House Debating Clubs of the 'twenties,[4] brought together in the London Mechanics' Institution and in the Owenite Movement they had been able to found a National Union of the Working Classes in March 1831 with a programme of universal suffrage. Though unable to carry their programme, the Ultra-Radicals of the National Union of the Working Classes were probably the main factor which prevented a Whig retreat from the original principles of the Reform Bill in order to effect a compromise with the Lords and the Court. After the passage of the Reform Bill had left the majority of working men without votes, the best energies of Ultra-Radical leaders had been thrown into the struggle for the "Unstamped" Press. Hetherington, Cleave, and Watson, indeed, the three most notable publishers of "Unstamped" newspapers, were

---

[1] Greville under June 7, 1839.
[2] The division figures on the Grote Ballot motion of June 18, 1839, were 216–333.
[3] Max Beer, *Hist. of British Socialism*, i, 146, 194, 213, 239, 248, 250, for the powerful effects on Radicalism of such glaring statistics on Income Inequality as those of Patrick Colquhoun's *Resources of the British Empire*, 1814.
[4] *Life and Struggles of William Lovett*, ed. 1876, pp. 34–6.

English Radicalism 1832–1852

genuine working-class crusaders of fine character, who well deserved the working-class loyalty which was shown them.[1]

Closely associated with the trio of Ultra-Radical working-class publishers was William Lovett, the Cornish-born cabinet-maker who had been prominent in the Ultra politics of the capital since 1831.[2] His share in the "Unstamped" struggle had taken the shape of administering the "Victim Fund" for the prosecuted Vendors and their dependents;[3] and in agitating to the end even against the penny duty of the Whig Newspaper Stamp Bill of 1836,[4] which was allowed to settle the "Unstamped's" war with the Revenue. But in the closing stages of the "Unstamped" struggle Lovett was also busy with plans to keep together the nucleus of public-spirited operatives who had been associated with him in the contest. On July 17, 1836, a London Working Men's Association was set up after careful preparation, and with Hetherington, Cleave, Watson, and Lovett as its central core.[5]

The aims of Lovett's Association were far-reaching, but designed as they primarily were for a working-class *élite* they proved far from impracticable. The "intelligent and influential portion of the working classes" were to be united not merely to secure equal political and social rights for their class and the removal of "the cruel laws that prevent the free circulation of thought,"[6] they were also to promote juvenile education, to collect labour statistics and digest them, to undertake the publica-

---

[1] For Hetherington, see the small *Life and Character of Henry Hetherington*, edited by G. J. Holyoake, 1849; for Watson, see W. J. Linton's *Memoir* of 1879; for Cleave, see scattered notices in the *Poor Man's Guardian* of 1831 and 1832.

[2] A careful checking of his well-known autobiography reveals Lovett's fundamental veracity. The *Poor Man's Guardian* for September 10, 17, and 24, 1831, for example, reveals how enthusiastically the working-class world hailed his stand against Militia liability on the principle of "No vote, no musket"; the issues of March 24, April 14, and April 21, 1832, again, confirm his large responsibility for the famous "General Farce Day."

[3] He was active very early in this sphere (cf. *Poor Man's Guardian*, September 2, 1831). For the important sums raised and distributed, see a Victim Fund Audit, *ibid.*, October 13, 1832, p. 567.

[4] In conjunction with such men as Dr. Birkbeck and Place, C. D. Collett, *History of the Taxes on Knowledge*, ed. 1933, p. 31.

[5] Add. MSS. Brit. Mus. 37773, f. 6. There is evidence that Feargus O'Connor and his friend, Beaumont of the "Radical" newspaper, gauged almost simultaneously the possibility of launching a powerful Ultra-Radical Association. Add. MSS. 27819, ff. 32–4.

[6] To be understood probably as indicating opposition to more than the penny newspaper stamp. There were blasphemy laws on the Statute Book hindering free comment on religion, and Birth Control Pamphlets were also assailable. Watson's Printing Press, for example, was never really secure from prosecution.

The People's Charter and the National Petition

tion of their views, to form a library of reference, and to maintain a meeting-place for themselves where country brothers could be received also.[1] Almost from the first, it would appear, Lovett recognised the unique opportunity which existed for a group of widely known and widely trusted working men of character and intelligence to assume the political leadership of the working classes.[2]

With the relatively high subscription of one shilling per month and a strenuous intellectual programme to boot, the London Working Men's Association was not aiming at numbers. Between July 1836 and June 1837, indeed, while it was winning for itself an undisputed position at the head of working-class agitation, its membership was only allowed to rise from the original thirty-three to one hundred.[3] There was besides a list of thirty-five honorary members who, not being of the working class, were not eligible for ordinary membership. In this list stood the names of a batch of Ultra-Radical Parliamentarians, and also those of other Radical notables like Place, Owen, and W. J. Fox.[4] Feargus O'Connor was also among the honorary members,[5] a six-foot Irish lawyer-squireen professing extreme democratic opinions, and for whom some sympathy was felt because he had lost his Co. Cork seat after two and a half years' tenure for lack of sufficient property qualification. O'Connor, however, did not relish being forced into the background by Lovett and his friends and was looking for an opening where he might exercise unchecked the remarkable demagogic qualities which had made him an Irish popular politician with pretensions only below those of O'Connell himself.[6]

[1] *Life and Struggles of William Lovett*, pp. 92-3.
[2] *Ibid.*, p. 91, for his innate distrust of upper-class leadership.
[3] Add. MSS. 37773, f. 58. This is the Association Minute Book.
[4] A notable Unitarian preacher and a political writer for the Radical Press. See *William Johnson Fox (1786-1864)*, by Graham Wallas, 1924.
[5] Add. MSS. 37773, f. 24.
[6] J. O'Connell, *Life and Times of Daniel O'Connell*, i, 24-7, 97-109, 141-50, for O'Connor's electioneering prowess. O'Connor had already made a fool hardy attempt in 1835 to succeed to Cobbett's Oldham seat, and his position in British Radicalism. Since that time he had been in close relations with Augustus Beaumont, a wilder democratic adventurer than himself, who must have lost much of his money in launching about this time an ill-fated *Radical* newspaper. Before successfully launching themselves upon the Northern Anti-Poor Law movement in 1837, O'Connor and Beaumont had attempted to set on foot a scheme for Universal Suffrage Clubs. Nor were other adventurers lacking seeking to direct Radical unrest: the persistent promoter of a farmer-operative alliance, J. B. Bernard, and the unlucky projector of unsuccessful Radical newspapers, John Bell.

English Radicalism 1832–1852

In conformity with its aims, the London Working Men's Association set itself almost at once to study and publication. The most surprising result, perhaps, of the first phase of the Association's activities was the appearance in November 1836 of an address to the Working Classes of Belgium.[1] This generous display of interest in the fate of some arrested Belgian workmen was symptomatic of the wide range of view which the Association allowed itself, a range, indeed, which was to permit it shortly afterwards to espouse publicly and warmly the cause of full self-government in the agitated Canadas.[2]

But the most important of the earlier activities of the Association was the issue of its famous and widely circulated pamphlet, *The Rotten House of Commons*.[3] Here there were levelled against the Constitution of 1832 and on behalf of the working classes exactly similar weapons to those which had been employed by the Foxite Friends of the People against the old Constitution. In a Parliament elected by 839,519 privileged only out of the 6,023,519 of adult males, in a Parliament still so weighted by petty borough representation that 151,492 electors controlled 331 out of the 658 seats, in a Parliament, in short, which allowed one-fortieth[4] of the total of male adults in circumstances peculiarly favourable to all the exclusive interests to dictate the course of legislation, there could be no justice to the working classes. To have added the manufacturer, capitalist, master, and "the whole host of Moneymakers, Speculators and Usurers" to the "immense number of Lords, Earls, Marquises, Knights, Baronets, Honourables, and Right Honourables," "the multitude of Military and Naval Officers," and "the multitude of Barristers, Attorneys and Solicitors, most of them seeking places" customarily in the Commons meant, it was urged, no measure of fitter representation "for the sons of labour."

Indeed, "the infamous Acts" passed since "the monied and commercial classes" had obtained a portion of political power[5] only confirmed their bad record in past struggles over wages and

---

[1] Lovett, *op. cit.*, 98–9; Add. MSS. 37773, f. 22.   [2] *Ibid.*, f. 49.
[3] It will be found in Add. MSS. 27819, ff. 195–204. It is a pamphlet of twenty pages giving the exact numbers of voters and male inhabitants in every electoral division in the country. The figures are accompanied by an *Address* penned by Lovett.
[4] These striking deductions from the constituency figures were repeated in a Petition to the Commons, Lovett, *op. cit.*, Appendix A.
[5] A reference particularly to the New Poor Law.

proved that they were not to be looked to for "more leisure, less toil." What was needed was universal suffrage, vote by ballot, annually elected Parliaments, equal electoral divisions, abolition of the members' property qualification, and above all a perfectly free Press.

It is not surprising that a body as vigorous as the London Working Men's Association soon had applications from provincial Radicals anxious to set up similar bodies in their own towns. As early as December 28, 1836, a special sub-committee had been set up to deal with requests for copies of the Association's rules;[1] in April a first batch of Northern democrats were elected honorary members, and in August Messrs. Vincent and Cleave set out on an organised missionary endeavour to promote Working Men's Associations in Yorkshire.[2] These were stages in a movement which was before long to cover Britain with a vast network of Working Men's Associations all of whom looked to the senior body in London for political guidance.[3]

Concurrently with its proselytising activity the Association was undertaking the preparatory work for organising a great petition to Parliament. On February 28, 1837, it called an important meeting at the Crown and Anchor Tavern in the Strand where a petition embodying all the constitutional proposals later put forward as the People's Charter was signed by about 3,000 persons.[4] Later Roebuck was approached on the subject of its presentation to the Commons, and as it was found that he would be prepared to go further and move a Universal Suffrage Bill, it was resolved to circularise all the Radical members who might be looked to for support. The outcome was a meeting of May 31st between representatives of the Association and the following Parliamentarians: Hume, O'Connell, Bowring, Leader, Perronet Thompson, Hawes, Sharman Crawford, and Hindley. Though the Association was disappointed by the cautious attitude of some of the politicians and their advocacy of gradual measures, a further meeting was arranged for the following week. At this

---

[1] Add. MSS. 37773, f. 28.
[2] *Ibid.*, f. 62. Printed placards announcing meetings during this tour will be found in Set 56 (Place Collection) at Hendon, 1837 volume.
[3] Late in 1838, when it was a question of rallying Ireland to the Charter against O'Connell's influence, 135 Secretaries of provincial societies joined Lovett in an appeal to the Irish People, Add. MSS. 27835, ff. 89-90.
[4] *True Sun*, March 1, 1837.

meeting the Parliamentarians agreed to the formation of a joint committee of six members and six representatives of the London Working Men's Association. The committee was to draw up a Bill "embodying the principles of universal suffrage, equal representation, free selection of representatives without reference to property, the ballot and short Parliaments of fixed duration, the limit not to exceed three years."[1] Before this committee set to work, the death of William IV precipitated the general elections of 1837, and a grave Radical electoral setback took place which put a stop to Bill-drafting activities on the suggested lines.

Though the London Working Men's Association had itself entered into the electoral struggle with an Ultra-Radical Address to Reformers which was very widely circulated,[2] the election's unfortunate outcome was not allowed to dampen its ardour. In August a successful Association-founding mission was at work in Yorkshire, and in September the Association's Address to the Queen on Political and Religious Monopoly was making a good deal of noise in the Press.[3] Other activities of the Association embraced the publication of an Address to the Citizens of the American Republic, the issue of a notable plan for the organisation of National Education,[4] and in December the drawing up of a reply to the revived Birmingham Political Union's Address to the Reformers of Great Britain and Ireland.[5] The Association joined the Union in calling for "another enthusiastic effort for freedom," and advocated the reconstitution of the Political Unions of the Reform epoch as well as the formation of "Working Men's Associations in every district, town, and parish in the country."

The Association was here entering into friendly contact with another strongly based body intent on stirring up a vigorous Radical movement. The onset of the great industrial depression which broke up the boom conditions ruling between 1833 and 1836 had affected no places so severely as great manufacturing centres like Glasgow and Birmingham. In the Glasgow area it led to those great strikes in many trades which culminated in the savagely conducted dispute in the thirty-eight cotton spinneries

[1] Add. MSS. 37773, 53.
[2] Add. MSS. 27819, f. 220; Lovett, *op. cit.*, pp. 115-21.
[3] Lovett, *op. cit.*, p. 128. The attempt of the Association to present their very unorthodox Accession Address through a deputation not in Court dress was very widely noticed. [4] Add. MSS. 27819, ff. 225-7.
[5] Add. MSS. 37773, f. 83; Lovett, *op. cit.*, pp. 148-50.

The People's Charter and the National Petition

and Sheriff Alison's bold arrest of the whole operative spinners' committee.[1] In Birmingham, however, the abundant Radical middle-class leadership available was to be responsible for totally different results. Round Attwood and Scholefield, Birmingham's Radical M.P.s, Douglas of the *Birmingham Journal* and manufacturers like Salt and the Muntz brothers, the middle- and working-class alliance of the Birmingham Political Union was reconstructed in the spring of 1837.[2] A huge meeting of 50,000 was held on June 19th and committed the Black Country to Household Suffrage, the Ballot, Triennial Parliaments, Payment of Members, and Abolition of the Property Qualification.[3]

Though these things would give assurance that future Administrations would follow the wishes of the neglected "producing classes" in framing their financial policies, the Birmingham meeting urged more immediate remedies also. Attwood had long been a critic of the rigid restriction of the currency ensured by giving its units a gold value, and was now pressing for a departure from gold in order to permit the issue of the extra currency needed to vitalise trade and diminish unemployment. The meeting of June 19th sent a deputation to harangue Melbourne on the subject,[4] Attwood made it the principal topic of the Birmingham election of 1837[5] and on November 2, 1837, another Birmingham deputation rained arguments upon the Prime Minister and his Chancellor of the Exchequer.[6]

The Birmingham Union, however, was soon driven to centre its main energies upon Suffrage propaganda by the blunt Whig "finality" stand upon the 1832 Reform Bill which was made at the opening of the Session of 1837-8. On December 7th the Birmingham Union retorted with a very effective appeal to the Reformers of Great Britain and Ireland, and on December 19th Attwood, passing beyond denunciation of Whiggery, openly declared for Universal Suffrage and angrily attacked the species of Radicalism affected by the greater portion of Radicals in Parlia-

---

[1] Sir Archibald Alison's *Life and Writings*, ed. Lady Alison, i, 371 sqq.
[2] Add. MSS. 27819, ff. 73-181, gives the history of the reconstruction as written by Place. The Birmingham middle-class leadership was always so Radical that independent working-class organisation, though once attempted in 1832-3 in a Midland Political Union, was before long abandoned.
[3] *Ibid.*, f. 99. [4] *Ibid.*, pp. 111-13.
[5] C. M. Wakefield, *Life of Attwood*, p. 307.
[6] Add. MSS. 27819, ff. 137-53.

ment.[1] The Birmingham Union had thus come to set itself very similar aims to those of the London Working Men's Association. The parallelism became closer when Douglas set to work to draft a National Petition, and Collins, a working man, was in April 1838 sent as a missionary to Glasgow. The Glasgow mass meeting of May 21st which followed witnessed the powerful Ultra-Radicalisms of London, Birmingham, and industrial Scotland working together. 150,000 Radicals gathered to hear Attwood and other delegates from Birmingham, two delegates from the London Working Men's Association and M'Nish, the local hero of the Cotton Spinners' struggle.[2] Nor was it a mere feast of oratory. That day the popular Radicalism of the entire country was offered Birmingham's National Petition as a rallying-point for nation-wide petitioning activity and London's People's Charter as the democratic enfranchisement scheme to be pressed to the Statute Book. The two documents rapidly and completely captured the popular imagination.

The People's Charter as published on May 8, 1838, was the result of many months of effort on the part of Lovett.[3] The choice of name was singularly apt and so was the Act of Parliament form in which the People's Charter was drawn up. But the Charter's most striking appeal lies in the clarity with which had been envisaged all the practical arrangements which would be necessary to implement Universal Manhood Suffrage.[4] How the three hundred equal electoral districts of the democratic future were to be based on the figures of every decennial census; what irreproachable arrangements would be made for the registration of electors, the nomination of candidates and the polling of voters;

---

[1] Add. MSS. 27819, ff. 162-4. Attwood, it should be remembered, was poles apart from the Hume School on other matters than currency. For one thing he was opposed to the New Poor Law.

[2] C. M. Wakefield, *op. cit.*, pp. 333-5.

[3] The actual Charter occupies pp. 13-36 of the 36 pp. pamphlet in which it was issued. Lovett's account of its drafting is in his autobiography, pp. 164-5. The 1848 editions contain introductory sections confirming it. Accordingly Place's claim to the main credit of authorship (Add. MSS. 27835, f. 160) cannot be accepted, though it may be allowed that he made useful suggestions.

[4] Lovett's original draft had provided for Women's Suffrage too, but as there were strong objections in the joint committee of six M.P.s and six members of the London Working Men's Association which examined Lovett's plan, Woman's Suffrage was dropped. (Lovett, *op. cit.*, p. 170.) The objectors were probably right in estimating the harm that would be done by including Woman's Suffrage in the project. Even working-class opinion might have tended to regard it as visionary.

The People's Charter and the National Petition

when the annual elections would take place and between what dates the salaried Parliamentarians would sit—all these details and many more were put with a vivid terseness which fascinated workmen politicians into seeing the whole system at work if they could but raise the necessary agitation. For a whole generation, indeed, the placing of the Charter upon the Statute Book was to be the principal end of all working-class politics.

The National Petition of Birmingham had great merits of another kind which were having their effect even before the tremendous Birmingham meeting of August 16th formally approved and adopted its text. Douglas's wording achieved a homely sonorousness very appealing to vast popular audiences; there were simple and effective dramatic passages made the more telling by the repeated recapture of Biblical cadences; a note of high seriousness and measured resolution pervaded the whole. It was probably by hearing a solemn reading of the Petition at a public meeting rather than by perusing a copy of the People's Charter that most Ultra-Radicals were introduced to the new "Chartist" movement of 1838–9. Accordingly considerable quotations from this quite short[1] but very remarkable document become the more justifiable.

It opened with the following skilful attempt to associate harassed traders and worried manufacturers with their underemployed workmen:

"We, your petitioners, dwell in a land whose merchants are noted for enterprise, whose manufacturers are very skilful, and whose workmen are proverbial for their industry.

"The land itself is goodly, the soil rich, and the temperature wholesome; it is abundantly furnished with the materials of commerce and trade; it has numerous and convenient harbours; in facility of internal communications it exceeds all others.

"Yet with all these elements of national prosperity, and with every disposition and capacity to take advantage of them, we find ourselves overwhelmed with public and private suffering.

"We are bowed down under a load of taxes; which, notwithstanding, fall greatly short of the wants of our rulers; our traders are trembling on the verge of bankruptcy; our workmen are starving; capital brings

---

[1] It is most readily accessible in Lovett's *Life and Struggles*, where it is printed as Appendix C, pp. 469–73. Its author, R. K. Douglas, was making the *Birmingham Journal*, which he edited, a power not merely in Birmingham. One official investigator of 1839 found seventy-one weekly copies in Dunfermline (*Parl. Pap.*, 1839, xlii, 203).

no profit and labour no remuneration; the home of the artificer is desolate, and the warehouse of the pawnbroker is full; the workhouse is crowded, and the manufactory is deserted.

"We have looked on every side, we have searched diligently in order to find out the causes of a distress so sore and so long continued.

"We can discover none in nature, or in Providence.

"Heaven has dealt graciously by the people; but the foolishness of our rulers has made the goodness of God of none effect."

Another striking set of passages coming somewhat later in the Petition voice resolute determination in regard to the Corn Laws and the Currency Laws. "We tell your Honourable House," they run, "that the capital of the master must no longer be deprived of its due reward; that the laws which make food dear, and those which by making money scarce, make labour cheap, must be abolished; that taxation must be made to fall on property, not on industry, that the good of the many, as it is the only legitimate end, so must it be the sole study of the Government." Then the Petition passes on to consider the means necessary to effect these and other requisite changes. It is concluded that a law must be passed "granting to every male of lawful age, sane mind and unconvicted of crime, the right of voting for members of Parliament; and directing all future elections of members of Parliament to be in the way of secret ballot; and ordaining that the duration of Parliaments so chosen shall in no case exceed one year; and abolishing all property qualifications in the members; and providing for their due remuneration while in attendance on their Parliamentary duties." One point put forward by the London Working Men's Association is not specifically included in the Petition, equal representation, or in modern phraseology, equal electoral divisions. There is reason to believe that Birmingham did not desire to commit itself to the doubling of Irish Parliamentary strength which would ensue, if the principle were adopted. Certainly in 1839 Attwood would be found to object very strongly to a representational scheme which would entitle Ireland to a third almost of the total seats in Parliament.[1]

After the great Glasgow meeting of May 21, 1838, wherein both Petition and Charter were made public, rapid support for their aims was systematically enlisted. Before returning home

---

[1] *The Charter*, May 12, 1839. O'Connellite political management in Ireland aroused distaste even among British Radicals. A Parliament with over two hundred Irish members would, moreover, have rapidly broken down.

The People's Charter and the National Petition

Attwood and the Birmingham deputation made an extensive Scottish tour, and afterwards Collins, the shoemaker who had roused Glasgow so effectively, was left to enlist support for the Petition at meetings in industrial Lancashire and Yorkshire.[1] But the Petition and Charter could not have grown to great importance solely on missionary eloquence of this type. In the network of Working Men's Associations, however, there existed permanently organised supporting forces and these were strengthened, moreover, by an important Press. The winter of 1837-8, it should be remembered, had seen the foundation of three important new weeklies circulating extensively among the Ultra-Radicals of the industrial areas. At Leeds Feargus O'Connor had launched the *Northern Star*, at Newcastle Beaumont had founded the *Northern Liberator*,[2] and at Manchester the sons of Cobbett were interested in the *Champion*. Quite soon after the new Ultra-Radical movement had begun all these journals were "Chartist" as was also the older *Hetherington's Dispatch*[3] with its important national circulation.

Meanwhile the Birmingham Political Union was planning the next step in the agitation. On July 17th it resolved on arranging the assembly of a General Convention of the Industrious Classes. To avoid the legislation against Corresponding Societies still on the Statute Book, each centre of population, acting for itself, was advised to arrange open and legally conducted meetings for the purpose of nominating delegates to such a convention, the total number not to exceed forty-nine. Birmingham would lead the way in a great meeting where its delegates would be elected and commissioned to act with similar delegates from other areas in forwarding the new Ultra-Radicalism. On the due date of August 6th, and amid the plaudits of a vast assembly gathered at Newhall Hill, Attwood, supported by the representatives of London, Scotland, Lancashire, and Yorkshire, unfolded the case against the Government and forecast a popular victory. Eight delegates from the Birmingham area were chosen,[4] and the

---

[1] Mark Hovell, *The Chartist Movement*, p. 106, where evidence from Add. MSS. 27820 is correlated with that from the *Northern Star*.
[2] Whose columns give evidence of a sphere of influence embracing Tyneside, Wearside, the Durham and Northumberland colliery areas, and pockets of weaving populations reaching into Lowland Scotland.
[3] The old *Twopenny* of Unstamped days, now the *London Dispatch*.
[4] Add. MSS. 27820, f. 176.

work of gathering a National Convention had begun. In the remarkable six months of agitation which followed, Chartism spread very rapidly till it ranged from Aberdeenshire and Forfarshire[1] in the North to as far as Devonport[2] in the South. When the Convention assembled contemporaneously with the opening of the Parliamentary Session of 1839, its constituency could justifiably be counted as vastly exceeding that of the House of Commons.

[1] Add. MSS. 34245 B, f. 290-1, for evidence, for example, of Montrose. Chartism in such communities was based on the weavers.
[2] R. G. Gammage, *Hist. of the Chartist Movement*, p. 81, ed. 1894.

CHAPTER X

OASTLER, STEPHENS, AND FEARGUS O'CONNOR

"If they will not reform this, aye uproot it all, they shall have the revolution they so much dread. We shall destroy their abodes of guilt, which they have reared to violate all law and God's book. If they will not learn to act as law prescribes and God ordains, so that every man shall by his labour find comfortable food and clothing—not for himself only, but for his wife and babes—then we swear by the love of our brothers—by our God who made us all for happiness—by the earth He gave for our support—by the Heaven He designs for those who love each other here, and by the hell which is the portion of those who violating His book, have consigned their fellowmen . . . to hunger, nakedness, and death; we have sworn by our God, by heaven, earth, and hell, that from the East, the West, the North and the South, we shall warp in one awful sheet of devouring flame, which no arm can resist, the manufactories of the cotton tyrants, and the places of those who raised them by rapine and murder. . . ."
    Rev. J. R. Stephens at Glasgow, January 1838. From GAMMAGE, *"History of the Chartist Movement," p. 57, ed. 1894.*

"As respects general politics I see nothing in the present radical outbreak to cause alarm or make one dread the fate of liberalism. On the contrary it is preferable to the apathy of the three years when prosperity (or seemingly so) made Tories of all. Nor do I feel at all inclined to give up politics in disgust as you seem to do because of the blunders of the Radicals. They are rash and presumptuous or ignorant if you will, but are not the governing factions something worse? Is not selfishness or systematic plunder or political knavery as odious as the blunders of democracy? We must choose between the party which governs upon an exclusive or monopoly principle, and the people who seek, though blindly perhaps, the good of the vast majority. . . . I think the scattered elements may yet be rallied round the question of the Corn Laws. It appears to me that a moral and even a religious spirit may be infused into that topic, and if agitated in the same manner that the question of slavery has been, it will be irresistible!"
    Richard Cobden, October 5, 1838. From MORLEY'S *"Life," ed. 1903, p. 126.*

AMONG the areas which were most enthusiastically to adopt the National Petition and the People's Charter were the suffering textile districts. In a time of deep economic depression, when wages even in an advancing machine trade like cotton-spinning had by the summer of 1837 already tumbled catastrophically enough to cause the celebrated Glasgow Spinners' Dispute, the plight of hand-loom weavers rapidly became pitiable. The lot of the 840,000[1] hand-weavers in cotton, wool, linen, and silk, fatally committed for the most part to a losing race against power-weaving, had engaged the attention of Parliament even in the prosperous days of 1834-5.[1] In 1838, when conditions had become worse, an inquiry by Royal Commission was opened, and the desperate poverty of such leading hand-weaving communities as those of Glasgow, Manchester, Carlisle, and Ashton-under-Lyne became plain. Silk-weaving, again, had its hosts of unfortunates in Spitalfields and Bethnal Green; and the ribbon-weaving area round Coventry, if not Coventry itself, was also sunk in poverty and degradation. Yorkshire and other woollen weavers, if suffering less seriously than those engaged in cotton, had a multitude of grievances, and the stockingers of the Midlands had more. Populations enduring as much as these,[2] and dreading the substitution of Poor Law Commission workhouses for outdoor relief, were splendid raw material for the agitator.

The Lancashire and Yorkshire textile areas, indeed, possessed indigenous agitations of their own and special leaders before the rise of Chartism.[3] Of these leaders Richard Oastler, the steward of the Thornhill estates near Huddersfield, was the most notable, always surpassing in importance even figures as prominent as Fielden of Todmorden and Cobbett's lawyer sons settled in

---

[1] See Report from the Select Committee on Hand-loom Weavers, Parl. Papers, 1834, x; Parl. Papers, 1835, xiii. The Committee's estimate of 840,000 is in the 1835 volume, p. xi.

[2] The Parliamentary Papers with Hand-loom Commission Reports are 1839, xlii, and 1840, xxiv; for a Report by a Commission on the conditions of the stockingers, see Parl. Papers, 1845, xv. It is almost impossible to understand the geographical distribution of Chartism and the measure of its local intensities without correlating the data of political agitation with the industrial data of these Reports and similar information from other industries, especially mining.

[3] The hand-loom weavers' agitation for Boards of Trade with statutory wage-fixing authority is one of these movements which deserves more exploration than it has received. Its petitioning strength in 1835 was, for example, as great as 74,253.

Oastler, Stephens, and Feargus O'Connor

Lancashire. Oastler had been the most powerful orator of the Short Time movement, and probably the greatest single force in raising an agitation great enough to secure the child-protection clauses of the 1833 Factory Act. Since then he had been co-operating with Lord Ashley in the difficult task of obtaining the enforcement of the 1833 Act, had joined full-bloodedly in the revived Short Time (ten-hour factory day) agitation of 1835 and 1836, and had bitterly resisted the Government's unsuccessful attempt to beat a partial retreat from the child-protection standards put on the Statute Book in 1833.[1] More than this, though professing a Throne and Altar Toryism for himself, he had yet led some powerful Ultra-Radical agitation on such un-Toryish causes as the return of the Dorchester convicts.[2]

It was on the New Poor Law, however, that Oastler's platform violence first began to approach sedition. There is, perhaps, no short extract from his speaking which will give a better idea of the temper with which he resisted that law than the following passage from a letter dated April 17, 1835, and addressed to Lord Ashley:[3]

> What care the People of England about the Dissenters? or the Corporations? or O'Connell? Not one rush,

wrote Oastler, dismissing the principal contentions of the day.

> They want bread, and the Whigs and Tories and Radicals join together in robbing the pauper!!! Oh, shame, shame. And refuse to protect Labour!!! Oh, what folly. It is labour that supports the Throne—not your Jew with his £10,000,000!! Oh, my Lord, do excuse me. I must write as I feel. I write not for myself. No, my Lord. I expect nothing but poverty and want and death. I look forward to the assassin's knife, or a cold stone bed in a dungeon, but I will never hold my peace so long as I have power to speak. When I am dead, and the Throne and Altar are levelled, then, perhaps, I shall have been known to speak the truth....

This was the style which the operative of the 1830's expected in his best platform speakers.

---

[1] Alfred, *A History of the Factory Movement*, is the main authority. Also *Northern Star*, March 31, April 7, April 14, April 21, 1838.
[2] *Poor Man's Guardian*, July 11, 1835.
[3] E. Hodder, *Life and Work of Lord Shaftesbury*, i, 215. See T. Mackay, *History of the English Poor Laws*, iii, 250–4 for Oastler's influence in raising disturbances which prevented the introduction of the new Poor Law machinery at Huddersfield in June 1837. Bradford and Todmorden followed the example.

English Radicalism 1832–1852

Another northern speaker who came into prominence in the revived Short Time agitation of 1836 was the Reverend J. R. Stephens. As a Wesleyan minister, who declined to sever his connexion with a proscribed Disestablishment movement in Ashton-under-Lyne, Stephens had been deprived of his charge in 1834.[1] He maintained a following in the town, nevertheless, and passing on from the denunciation of factory conditions to that of the New Poor Law[2] won increasing fame throughout the North. On January 1, 1838, he may be found speaking as far afield as Newcastle, and in a meeting called to demand the repeal of the Poor Law Amendment Act of 1834 outdoing the fury even of the violent and unbalanced Beaumont, proprietor of the *Northern Liberator*.[3] The whole of the industrial North was then aflame with the determination to resist any attempt which might be made by the Poor Law Commissioners to prohibit outdoor relief to the able-bodied as they had already done in the agricultural South. Such prohibition, it should be remembered, would have entailed more than the quick transference to the workhouse of thousands of families of underpaid weavers and sweated stockingers, always liable to be driven "on the parish" by the stress of any sudden emergency. In times of acute commercial depression like those actually prevailing, the prohibition of outdoor relief might have come to involve the ordering of similar transferences to the workhouse from normally prosperous sections of the working class.

In point of fact the Poor Law Commission did not commit the dreadful folly of treating the industrial districts of the North, dependent as they were on fluctuating foreign demands, as they had done the agricultural areas.[4] Instead it promoted the establishment in suitable industrial centres of Poor Law labour yards, where task-work like stone-breaking might be offered instead of

---

[1] G. J. Holyoake, *Life of J. R. Stephens*, pp. 47–55.
[2] *Northern Star*, October 6, 1838, for a Liverpool speech with Stephens's own account.
[3] Beaumont died some weeks afterwards when only thirty-seven (Add. MSS. 27821, ff. 14–24). He was ready for open revolution.
[4] T. Mackay, *History of the English Poor Laws*, iii, 245–9, for early problems in this connexion. This book, however, offers the discerning reader ample proof of the reluctance at Poor Law headquarters to take due account of Unemployment, resulting from trade depression, as one of the factors of the Poor Law situation. This was partly due to the fact that scientific Political Economy, as understood by Chadwick, was still very far from an adequate realisation of the full implications of the industrial process.

Oastler, Stephens, and Feargus O'Connor

entry into the workhouse during times of acute industrial depression. But it is distinctly doubtful whether this departure from the rigidity previously shown by the Poor Law Commission would have been obtainable but for the success of such inflammatory oratory as that of Stephens. "If the people who produce all wealth," declaimed Stephens at Newcastle, "could not be allowed, according to God's word, to have the kindly fruits of the earth which they had, in obedience to God's word, raised by the sweat of their brow, then war to the knife with their enemies, who were the enemies of God. If the musket and the pistol, the sword and the pike were of no avail, let the woman take the scissors, the child the pin or needle. If all failed, then the firebrand—aye, the firebrand—the firebrand, I repeat. The palace shall be in flames. I pause, my friends. If the cottage is not permitted to be the abode of man and wife, and if the smiling infant is to be dragged from a father's arms and a mother's bosom, it is because these hell-hounds of commissioners have set up the command of their master the devil, against our God."[1]

During the course of 1838 a new method of rousing popular hate against the Poor Law Commissioners was being brought into use, especially in the North, where it was adopted among others by Stephens.[2] Ever since 1834 Poor Law administration had been credited with the most satanic intentions in regard to the families of the poor. Thus one Assistant Poor Law Commissioner preparing a Devonshire area for its Union workhouse reported the peasantry as believing "that all the children beyond three in a family were to be killed: that all young children and women under eighteen were to be spayed; that if they touched the (Poor Law) bread they would instantly drop down dead."[3] Whether by accident or design, a work was published in 1838 well calculated to foster dangerous popular credulity of this type.[4] Certainly the pseudonymous Marcus's discussions on how to limit population by adopting socially decorous methods of public infanticide were taken with the greatest apparent seriousness by

[1] *Northern Star*, January 6, 1838.
[2] Cf. J. Irving, *Annals of Our Time*, ed. 1871, p. 32.
[3] T. Mackay, *op. cit.*, pp. 238–9.
[4] *On the Possibility of Limiting Populousness*, by Marcus, p. 46, with which was printed *An Essay on Populousness*, pp. 27. The work was reproduced for Chartists as *The Book of Murder: a Vade Mecum for the Commissioners and Guardians of the New Poor Law*, by Marcus, one of the three. It gained an ample notoriety.

English Radicalism 1832–1852

Stephens, who sought to identify "Marcus" with the Poor Law Commissioners' Department.[1] The greater the tyranny and the inhumanity which could be ascribed to the Poor Law Commission, the easier Stephens and Oastler must have found it to adopt the Universal Suffrage Chartism of the bulk of their audiences. A Parliament elected under the People's Charter would assuredly at once have ended the Commission and its methods of treating the poor.[2]

It is time to trace how the personality of Feargus O'Connor became the link between the Anti-Poor Law agitation of Oastler and Stephens and the Universal Suffrage agitation of the Working Men's Associations. In more than two years of London effort between 1835 and 1837 O'Connor had failed to establish any considerable independent position for himself in metropolitan Ultra-Radicalism. It is true that in 1837 he gathered a London Democratic Association, with the fire-eating young Harney as

[1] Even when Chadwick officially denied that any of the three principal Poor Law Commissioners had been connected with Marcus's book, Stephens was not at a loss for a retort. "There were other Commissioners," he asserted, "a score or two—besides these three, and then there were Mr. Chadwick himself, his patron, Lord Brougham, and his bosom friend, Mr. Francis Place, and their 'female assistant,' Miss Martineau" (*The Times*, January 15, 1839).

[2] No epithet of abuse was more readily and more deservedly applied to the Commission than "Malthusian." Malthus had suggested a practical application of his Population doctrine, whose harsh inequity to the Poor had roused Cobbett to unceasing fury, and had made working men bitter opponents even of Malthusian doctrine. The doctrine, too, was being "scientifically" demolished at the very time when the Commission was enforcing as much of its application on the poor as it dared. An examination of such a book as Poulett Scrope's *Principles of Political Economy* (1833) will reveal the nature of the "scientific" attack possible upon Malthusianism. Surveying the vast expanses of yet unpeopled lands, the great multiplication of agricultural yield already obtainable from improvements in actual use, the almost infinite expansion certainly to be expected from the further "progress of agricultural chemistry, the science of manures, and vegetable and animal physiology," Poulett Scrope saw no present reason "to consider the propriety of restraining the inclinations of young men and maidens to marry and be given in marriage" (pp. 274–5). So long as in some quarters of the globe next neighbours were separated by an interval of leagues, the progress of civilisation was being delayed, "not by a redundancy, but a deficiency of hands." Moreover, for the time and even without recourse to the vast possibilities of emigration, Poulett Scrope was prepared to argue that it was exceedingly doubtful whether there was "any one country in Europe whose internal resources for the employment and comfortable maintenance of its population would be found *as yet* deficient" were it not for fiscal and currency malorganisation (pp. 399 sqq.). Ultra-Radicals with altogether vaster changes in view than those suggested by Liberal Humanitarians like Poulett Scrope could even more conscientiously pooh-pooh the "over-population panic" of the Malthusians. Thus, the finest Ultra-Radical production of 1838–9, J. F. Bray's *Labour's Wrongs and Labour's Remedy*, took the view that an Owenite State would not need to fear over-population "for thousands of years" (p. 189).

Oastler, Stephens, and Feargus O'Connor

secretary, but it never seriously challenged the great authority of the London Working Men's Association, which had little use for an O'Connor.[1] In the autumn of 1837, however, the persistent Irishman at last found the opening for which he had been feeling since his disqualification from Parliament in 1835. There was £800 at Leeds awaiting investment in the foundation of a working-class newspaper, a helpful publisher ready in Joshua Hobson, and a willing editor in Hill, a one-time Swedenborgian minister.[2] Astute enough to take advantage of his apparent position as a moneyed Ultra-Radical, O'Connor was given sole charge of the enterprise on guaranteeing to find interest on capital already raised and to supply any new capital which might be required. Possibly without needing to pay out any money of his own, O'Connor was able during the course of November 1837 to launch from Leeds a new working-class weekly at a price of $4\frac{1}{2}$d. per copy.[3] The paper was named the *Northern Star*, and rapidly achieved great success.

In their histories of Chartism, Hovell and West have followed Place[4] in attempting to account for the *Northern Star's* remarkable good fortune. They have noticed Hill's capable editorship, Bronterre O'Brien's informing and well-written contributions from London, and O'Connor's own untiring attendances at working-class meetings in the North, where his distinguished presence, his ample claims, and skilled demagogy gave him a rapid ascendancy over audiences less critical than the Lovetts and the Hartwells of London.[5] They have noticed also the

---

[1] Julius West, *History of the Chartist Movement*, p. 86.

[2] Hobson, who had been twice imprisoned during the "Unstamped" struggle, was, like his fellow-publisher, Abel Heywood, of Manchester, an important Radical force in the North. He was a Socialist as well as a Chartist, and wrote in 1838 *Socialism as it is*, pp. 144. A grammar book and sermons by Hill were occasionally advertised in the *Northern Star*. Gammage describes him as "an acute and clever, but not very agreeable writer" (*History of the Chartist Movement*, ed. 1894, p. 17).

[3] Lovett, *op. cit.*, p. 173, quotes an account to the effect that O'Connor ventured no money of his own. This is possibly unfair to O'Connor. The whole matter became a subject of dispute later, and O'Connor's own account, as given to the shareholders of his Land Co. on October 26, 1847, assigned an altogether larger part to his financing. But it is hard to accept his story undiluted, alleging, as it does, that in 1837 he possessed two incomes from land, one of £400 and another of £900, that he was earning £2,000 per annum at the Bar, and that he had £5,200 in hand from timber-sale transactions on his property.

[4] Add. MSS. 27821, f. 22.

[5] A quotation from a Dewsbury Poor Law speech of December 11, 1837, will give a specimen of his platform style. "When this Bill was in the House of Commons, I supported the immortal Cobbett, and raised my voice against the

177

English Radicalism 1832–1852

Northern Star's readiness to give generous space to the reporting of quite small local meetings. Other points might, perhaps, be made, such as the *Northern Star's* unstinted support for the Anti-Poor Law crusade of Oastler and Stephens,[1] its lavish supply of just the suitable vulgarity on Universal Suffrage,[2] and the business acuteness with which it hit upon the device of occasionally presenting to readers an engraving with the likeness of a popular Radical hero.[3]

O'Connor was lucky enough, moreover, to get an early opportunity of distinguishing himself in the eyes of the zealots of the trades clubs. The notorious Glasgow Spinners case, which had been dragging on since the summer of 1837, had fortunately ended with a January trial producing not sentences of death but only of seven years' transportation.[4] That much at least could now be effected when all working-class Britain grew excited about a trades case; when the immediately affected areas too—in this instance Glasgow and Edinburgh—waxed specially explosive under the stimulus of oratory from O'Connor, Stephens, and Beaumont to supplement their own native supply from Dr. Taylor

monopoly of wealth, to advocate the rights and inheritance of the poor and industrious. I voted against every [sic] clause of this measure. . . . But let me ask, had you any voice in the passing of this law? Was it enacted at your instigation and with your consent? Did you send representatives to Parliament there to betray you and rob you of your inheritance? . . . Are you half as bad as the aristocracy, to save whose purses this law has been enacted? No, your morality and general demeanour are altogether untarnished, when contrasted with the very men who passed this law. . . . You ask to return to the 43rd of Elizabeth. I would not have it. While all other sciences are going on to perfection, surely the science of legislation should not for ever stand still (hear), and while luxury is going on apace, and depravity and dissipation are looking for means on which to support themselves, let us also have an extensive improvement in the condition of the working classes of the people (tremendous cheers)." (from Baxter's *The Book of the Bastilles*, pp. 392–3).

[1] *Northern Star*, March 31st to April 21st, gives a Life of Oastler. Stephens's notorious Newcastle speech of January 1, 1838, is reported in the next number of the *Northern Star*, and on February 10th he is hailed as "our pride, our boast, and our Radical."

[2] *Ibid.*, February 18th, May 12th, has articles on Universal Suffrage, concluded as follows: "Laws made by all, would be respected by all. . . . Universal Suffrage would, at once, change the whole character of society from a state of watchfulness, doubt, and suspicion, to that of brotherly love, reciprocal interest, and universal confidence." "Give us, then, the only remedy for all our social and political maladies; make every man . . . his own doctor by placing the restorative in his hand, which is Universal Suffrage!!!" These are by O'Connor himself, who was plainly developing a capacity for the "stirring" leading article.

[3] *Ibid.*, March 31st, for Oastler portrait; June 23rd for Henry Hunt. On June 2nd, meanwhile, its circulation was announced as 9,822.

[4] J. Irving, *Annals of Our Times*, ed. 1871, pp. 12–13.

Oastler, Stephens, and Feargus O'Connor

of the Glasgow *Liberator*.[1] But the Cotton Spinners' Association had undoubtedly been proved to have been ready over a long period of years to countenance the use of violence, arson, and assassination in the course of trade disputes.[2] After the Parliamentary Session recommenced, therefore, a possibly dangerous Select Committee on Combinations was asked for and obtained, and the London Working Men's Association set itself to organising the arrangements to defend the interests of Labour. O'Connor hotly attacked their conduct in thus countenancing what was certain to be a partisan inquiry with Labour on the defensive, and forced a London meeting to listen to his by no means pointless criticisms of the Association's policy. In the following number of the *Northern Star* three columns were occupied by a report of O'Connor's speech and about a dozen lines given to the rest of the proceedings.[3]

For all O'Connor's independent platform feats, for all his original launching of the *Northern Star* rather into the vigorous Anti-Poor Law current set flowing in the North by Oastler and Stephens than into the democratic Ultra-Radicalism of the London Working Men's Association, the great demagogue was astute enough to associate himself prominently with the Charter and the National Petition as soon as their inescapable attraction for the working masses was made plain. Thus he took a personal

---

[1] "The Radicals denounced the prosecution as a mere attempt by a base Whig Government, moved by rich and vindictive master manufacturers, to oppress free and virtuous workmen. There were public meetings in all our manufacturing towns in favour of these indicted conspirators and murderers, from which petitions were sent to Parliament commiserating them, and abusing the law of Scotland and its administrators. One of these was actually signed by about 20,000 people.... The populace was addressed both here (Edinburgh) and in Glasgow by four persons, who for some time have been practising for hire the profession of itinerant corrupters of the manufacturing population. A person, calling himself the Rev. Joseph Stephen, openly preached to the people of Glasgow the propriety of burning the mills of the 'cotton tyrants,' and in November, when the first diet of the trial took place, a person named Beaumont and Feargus O'Connor harangued a meeting in the Waterloo Hotel here on the proceedings, when one of their finest flights consisted in contrasting the 'five villains in scarlet' (the Judges) with the 'five respectable gentlemen in black' (the prisoners). I don't understand why these direct interferences with a pending trial were allowed, or have not been punished" (*Journal of H. Cockburn*, under January 15, 1838). Cockburn was a Scottish Judge and a Whig.

[2] A. Alison, *My Life and Writings*, i, 394–9. Working-class fears of trouble to follow for their Trade Clubs were considerable (cf. O'Brien's remarkable message from London in the *Northern Star* of January 31st, with its counsel that "every moment that the producers can steal from their tasks and meals ought to be religiously concentrated to plans of mutual defence against the enemy").

[3] Lovett's account in *op. cit.*, ed. 1920, i, 166.

English Radicalism 1832–1852

part in the great Leeds meeting of June 5th, wherein a Great Northern Union[1] was formed behind the National Petition, and he was soon, against some protest, fighting a way into the new agitation for the avowedly non-political Stephens and the confessedly Church and King Oastler.[2] It was the worst service which he could have rendered to the responsible Chartism of London and Birmingham. Oastler and Stephens were orators of the most unbalanced class, and their feverish mouthings on pistols, swords, daggers, and death,[3] hitherto confined to Anti-Poor Law agitation, were now imported into Chartism and took on the great and dangerous vogue which led the movement so woefully astray in 1839.

Another dangerous feature of North of England Chartism, as distinct from that sponsored by London and Birmingham, was the O'Connor worship already beginning in the summer of 1838. As early as July 1838, for example, O'Connor amid loud Carlisle cheering could permit himself such debasing prating as the following: "He had never travelled a mile or eaten a meal at the expense of either Whig, Tory, or Radical, nor would he, as pledged to his constituents, ever accept place, pension, or employment from any Government save that which was erected by Universal Suffrage. He was the unpaid, undeviating, unpurchasable friend of liberty, and servant of the people."[4] Another side of O'Connor is revealed if attention is paid to how cleverly and successfully he imparted to his Birmingham speaking of August 6th, when a huge assembly was gathered to open the choosing of delegates to the Convention, touches of the heady Northern revolutionary manner, highly relished apparently by the groundlings if not by the platform.[5] O'Connor's energy, moreover, permitted him to

---

[1] *Northern Star*, June 9th, Collins of Birmingham spoke on the Petition. It may here be noted that there was also an important Union in Northumberland and Durham known as the Northern Political Union.

[2] *Ibid.*, June 30th, reporting O'Connor at a Newcastle meeting.

[3] *Ibid.*, August 4th, reports Oastler, addressing a great Halifax meeting as follows: "He would recommend them every one before next Saturday night to have a brace of horse pistols, a good sword, and a musket. . . . Did anyone tell him that he had no right to these tools? It was the right and duty of every man to have them." *Ibid.*, June 9th, reports Stephens saying: "Unless the people of England arm—and use their arms if need be, there will be no doubt of the fact that the New Poor Law Bastilles are intended to be a chain of barracks round the country, each capable of holding 500 to 1,000 men, and each intended to be garrisoned in part by regular military and in part by the Russelite military police. . . ."

[4] *Ibid.*, July 14th, 21st.   [5] *Ibid.*, August 11th.

go everywhere. He must have known how intensely the London Working Men's Association disliked such pearls of his Birmingham oratory as "fleshing swords to the hilt"[1] and "Come he slow or come he fast, it is but death that comes at last." Yet he did not intend to be absent from a principal place at the Association's public launching of Chartism in the capital. The important Palace Yard meeting of September 17th, therefore, found Feargus O'Connor, as the most popular provincial delegate present, able to indulge in a speech containing more "physical force swagger."[2]

In the autumn of 1838 a new stage of Chartist agitation began. Following the lead of Birmingham and London, other industrial areas called mass meetings to choose their delegates to the National Convention. The huge Manchester meeting of September 24th[3] gave a Stephens in somewhat milder vein than usual the chance of addressing a vast audience from the cotton area on the Charter as a knife and fork question. On September 25th, again, Sheffield held its meeting under the chairmanship of Ebenezer Elliott, who declared that the people demanded Universal Suffrage so that they might further Abolition of the Corn Laws, a National System of Education, Disestablishment, Facilities for forming Co-operative Communities, and Abolition of Joint-stock and Private Banking in favour of a National Bank.[4] While mainly moderate notes of this kind prevailed, Russell, the Whig Home Secretary, declined to allow Tory criticisms to force him into repressive courses. At a Liverpool banquet of October 8th, indeed, he proclaimed his Whig faith in the constitutional propriety and the social efficacy of free meeting and free discussion in good set terms. If there were popular grievances, he declared, the people had a right to meet and make them known so that

---

[1] These are extracts from the disgusted Lovett, *op. cit.*, p. 189 (cf. Place, Add. MSS. 27820, f. 211). [2] *Ibid.*
[3] Held on Kersal Moor, it witnessed possibly the largest political assembly ever held in the country. Even the cautious Place was disposed, after a study of the newspapers, to accept the numbers present as exceeding 200,000 (Add. MSS. 27820, ff. 221–2).
[4] *Northern Star*, September 29th. The Corn Law Rhymer's impression of the use which would be made of Universal Suffrage has its importance as illustrating the different factors contributing to the growth of Chartism. The mention of Co-operative Communities, for example, makes clear the importance of the Owenite factor, and indeed, Owenite Socialism was now undergoing a remarkable revival (cf. Lloyd Jones, *Life, Times, and Labours of Robert Owen*, 2nd ed., 1895, pp. 294–350; J. F. Bray's *Labour's Wrongs and Labour's Remedy*, 1839). Though Owen disapproved political action, multitudes who accepted his social system as the ideal one were Chartists.

they might be redressed; if there were no popular grievances, common sense might be relied on to put a speedy end to the meetings being held.[1]

But the excitements of agitation were already rising quickly, and such perfervidly enthusiastic torchlight meetings as soon began to be held in the evenings on the moors outside impoverished industrial towns were not of a kind to breed restrained oratory. After the great West Riding meeting of October 15th had heard O'Connor on tyrannicide, and Stephens on the five thousand brave men in his district who had already armed themselves,[2] further violent oratory came at Bolton on October 29th during what may be regarded, perhaps, as the first of the specifically torchlight meetings.[3] The Chartists might claim that they held torchlight meetings because their long working hours gave them no opportunity of coming together save at night. But undoubtedly they relished the subtle flavour of revolution and incendiarism which such assemblages conveyed to worried "respectables." That flavour affected their leaders, too, as may be seen from perusing O'Connor's Preston speech of November 5th, with its harping on "physical force" and its implied threat to the Government that the first shot from its troops would set fire to Preston.[4]

That O'Connor was himself in danger of being carried away by the excitement he was so powerfully stimulating seems obvious from a speech he made at Manchester on November 6th. Decrying the estimate of Douglas, author of the Petition, that three years of agitation would be required to carry the Charter, he ventured to fix September 29, 1839, as the date beyond which a delay in its enactment should not be allowed without the assurance of trouble on the 30th.[5] "For himself," he added, "he knew that nature would be exhausted if it were longer protracted," and in any case he may have felt that a quick and violent agitation with

---

[1] J. Irving, *Annals of Our Time*, ed. 1871, p. 26.
[2] *Northern Star*, Extraordinary, October 16th. The meeting had been vast enough to warrant a special number.
[3] *Ibid.*, November 3rd, used the headlines: "The ever-glorious Bolton Demonstration; 50,000 Hardy Northerners demand the Rights of Freemen by Torchlight." The contagious excitement was, of course, good for the sale of the *Northern Star*, which, on November 17th, before the end of its first year, was reporting a circulation taken to the then extraordinary height of 11,932.
[4] Place in Add. MSS. 27820, f. 287. [5] *Ibid.*, f. 292.

such a time-limit would bring better results than one in which greater opportunity was allowed for the dissipation of hope. Stephens, too, after a notoriously lurid speech at Norwich, told a Wigan audience on November 12th that the London and Birmingham leaders, then wisely seeking to ban talk of "physical force," were old women. "The firelock must come first," announced this rabid convert to Universal Suffrage, "and the vote afterwards. Universal Suffrage might be a very fine thing, but as yet it was all in the moon, and they must have a very long pike with a hook at the end of it to pull it down."[1]

O'Connor, however, understood if Stephens did not that neither in London nor in Birmingham could he yet afford to be excommunicated by the strongly entrenched local leaderships, which were growing ever uneasier in his company.[2] Earlier in the year he had adroitly held his own in London despite the manifest dislike and suspicion of the Lovett circle, and in November he repeated the feat in Birmingham, where Douglas of the *Birmingham Journal* had been the leading critic of his "physical force" tendencies. Three times in successive weeks did O'Connor appear before the Birmingham Political Union, and his appeal to the working-man rank and file proved so strong that an apparently cordial alliance was re-established.

The reluctance of the Birmingham leaders to undertake the responsibility of a breach with O'Connor is understandable. It would have broken up a great agitation which was still making remarkable progress, as the foundation of further Chartist newspapers illustrated.[3] A movement, moreover, which could gather on November 14th a Radical meeting of more than five thousand even at Blandford in Dorsetshire, and which could follow this up on the 17th with a meeting at Colchester and on the 21st with another at Lewes,[4] was not without its chances of winning considerable concessions from a House of Commons whose Radical contingents seemed always on the point of forcing Lord Durham nearer the centre of affairs.[5]

---

[1] Add. MSS. 27820, f. 300.
[2] Cf. *Operative*, December 16th, p. 97, article, "Treachery in the Camp."
[3] *The True Scotsman* of Edinburgh and *The Operative* of London were new foundations of this time. Moreover, such papers as the *Ayrshire Examiner* and *Brighton Patriot* had adopted Chartist principles (cf. *Northern Star*, November 17th).   [4] Add. MSS. 27820, ff. 306-9, 310, 326.
[5] *Northern Star*, December 7th, for Molesworth's letter "To the inhabitants of Leeds." This did much to prevent the Canadian situation from counting to

O'Connor's "moral force" assurances, therefore, were accepted with good grace, and O'Connor on his part tried to do something to live up to them. Thus proceedings at the Bury torchlight meeting of December 8th were somewhat more restrained, and in the *Northern Star* of December 15th O'Connor was found discountenancing violence. "I have been arraigned as a physical force man," he wrote in one article, "when I can confidently appeal to all who have heard me that in my speeches and writings I have been the first to portray the horrors of confusion and civil war."

If O'Connor thus kept one eye on London, Birmingham, and a Government which issued on December 12th a proclamation hostile to the nocturnal torchlight assemblies, the other had to be kept on a Northern operative following, accustomed by Stephens to the unceasing contemplation of a final resort to violence. Anxious as O'Connor might be not to jeopardise the prospects of the forthcoming National Convention, he could not afford to leave his own following dishearteningly destitute of their favourite reading matter. Besides, as an Irishman and a student of O'Connell's methods he doubtless appreciated such means of pressure on the Government and the classes behind it as was offered him by an agitation threatening at every moment to boil over into actual violence.[1]

It is perhaps not surprising, therefore, to find that the same *Northern Star* of December 15th which contained O'Connor's reassurances on the subject of "Confusion and Civil War" contained also a discussion by him on "Physical Force." In this O'Connor argued that not military and police but "the arming of the whole community capable of bearing arms" would be "the finest means of preserving peace abroad, and harmony and satisfaction at home." Pending this consummation, such of his followers as legally possessed themselves of arms were advised never to use them as individuals even for defence, and never unitedly in any unconstitutional cause. But the definition of

Durham's discredit. In the next Ministerial crisis of May 1839, therefore, Parliamentary Radicals like Attwood still hoped for a Durham Ministry (*Life*, pp. 367-8). Melbourne, however, had cautioned the Queen against considering it (*Letters of Queen Victoria*, 1837-61, i, 155).

[1] As the Chartists were to have good reason to know, O'Connell had just launched the "Precursor" agitation. Despite Chartist appeals, it was to keep Ireland completely aloof from the agitation for the National Petition and the People's Charter.

Oastler, Stephens, and Feargus O'Connor

constitutional and unconstitutional made at Huddersfield or Ashton-under-Lyne was apt to differ from that maintained at the Home Office or the Poor Law Commissioners' Department, and O'Connor knew it. When working men turned back far enough to the seemingly rosier past, it was not merely brand-new Poor Law bastilles which took on an unconstitutional appearance. The "standing army" still had but a dubious position in the "Constitution," and new brands of professional police, Metropolitan or otherwise, were several centuries younger than the very non-professional parish constable. There was plenty of warrant still in obsolescent legal and constitutional dicta to allow an "armed freeman" to state a case for resisting military or police "illegalities."

CHAPTER XI

FAILURE OF THE CHARTIST CONVENTION OF 1839

"Weekly meetings are held in Loughborough and very seditious language used in the Chair by Skevington, the husband of a respectable bonnet-maker. He and Smart, once a supervisor in the lace trade where he was unfortunate, now a schoolmaster, are their chosen delegates. . . . Thirty pounds each have been collected by pennies . . . to defray their expenses to London. They are both reckless men, destitute of character...."

    C. M. PHILLIPS, J.P., *to the Home Secretary, January 30, 1839. H.O. 40, 44, Leicestershire.*

"John Bright's motion at a large Rochdale meeting on February 2nd. 'That the Corn Laws have had the effect of crippling the commerce and the manufactures of the country, have raised up rival manufactories in foreign countries, have been most injurious and oppressive in the operation with the great bulk of our population, and the working classes have been most grievously injured by this monopoly of the landed proprietors.'

"Chartist amendment carried by an overwhelming majority: 'That it is the opinion of this meeting that though the Corn Law is an injurious tax, yet the present House of Commons or any other House of Commons constituted on the present suffrage will never repeal that so as to be beneficial to the working classes, and this meeting is of the opinion that the present Corn Law agitation is made up for the purpose of diverting the minds of the people from the only remedy of all political grievances....'"

    G. M. TREVELYAN'S "*Life of Bright*," *pp. 30–1.*

"Mr. Wm. Townshend, Jr. (who I am told is treasurer of the Chartist Society held in this place and is a dealer in provisions and iron) on Saturday last offered a Mr. Johnson . . . an order for 300 muskets, 600 cutlasses and a great quantity of pistols to be delivered here within a week...."

    The MAYOR OF NEWPORT, *Monmouthshire, to the Home Secretary, April 30th. H.O. 40, 46.*

THE winter of 1838-9 was a time of great excitement among working-class Radicals, who cherished the fondest hopes of the results which would follow on the meeting of their "National Convention." The excitement was not lessened by the apprehension on December 27th of Stephens, the favourite orator of the North, for seditious speaking. But for the magistrates allowing him to find bail for his appearance at the still distant Assizes, there might have been serious trouble in the Manchester area thus early in the history of Chartism.[1] His release on bail, however, allowed pacified Chartists to add the raising of a Stephens Defence Fund to their other absorbing causes. Signatures were being gathered for the National Petition; "National Rent" was being raised for the Convention's expenses;[2] and plans were being completed for the Convention's coming together in the capital almost simultaneously with Parliament. Often the Chartist "constituencies" had the further task of completing internal arrangements to raise the money necessary for sending their Convention delegates to London and for maintaining them there afterwards.

The tens of thousands of readers of the *Northern Star*, meanwhile, were following also one of the most extraordinarily taxing personal campaigns attempted even by O'Connor. As he summed it up for the *Northern Star*, now circulating over fifteen thousand copies,[3] O'Connor wrote as follows: "From the 18th of December to the 15th of January, I have attended in London, Bristol, Manchester, Queenshead, Bradford, Leeds, Newcastle, Carlisle, Paisley, and Edinburgh twenty-two large public meetings and have travelled over 1,500 miles, and I can safely say that your moral philosophy has been the greatest enemy of our cause."[4]

[1] *Northern Star*, January 5, 1839, which quotes also the London *Sun*.
[2] The Birmingham delegates, who had been the first chosen, and who had announced their intention of guiding the agitation by advertisement in the Press, had early pressed the necessity of the "National Rent" (cf. *Northern Star*, September 1st).
[3] As many of these copies were sold to public-houses, or were otherwise circulated, this figure should be multiplied many times to obtain its circle of readers. For the importance of the public-house sale to newspapers, cf. O'Connor at Liverpool: "He charged them never to drink a drop of beer where the *Mercury* (Liverpool), or *Sun*, or *The Times*, or *Chronicle* were taken" (*Northern Star*, September 29, 1838).
[4] *Northern Star*, January 19th. It may be noted that on January 15th O'Connor had opened at Leeds resistance to the new Anti-Corn Law campaigners, the most dangerous "moral philosophers" of them all, as it proved.

English Radicalism 1832–1852

"Moral force" Birmingham, indeed, had once more become uneasy over O'Connor's "physical force" alliances.[1] In London and Scotland, again, though O'Connor had easily carried audiences with him against "moral force" opponents, his personal ascendancy was not yet established. But against the astonishing activity and plausibility of O'Connor the attempts of Lovett in London, Douglas and Salt in Birmingham, and Brewster in Scotland to keep the moral appeal of Chartism at a high level seemed increasingly doomed to failure.

Yet it is characteristic of Lovett that he should have been organising for months the means which he hoped might serve to steady Chartism as it approached the critical Convention stage of its activities. With admirable thoroughness and caution he had interested the London trades in a plan for a newspaper under their control, and had secured support which ensured an opening circulation of five thousand even at the price of sixpence. Under the editorship of the well-known William Carpenter the responsibly written *Charter* made a meritorious first appearance on Sunday, January 27, 1839, in sixteen large and well-printed pages, full not only of Chartist news but also of the items usually expected of a good Sunday paper.[2] Lovett might well hope that, in combination with Hetherington's *London Dispatch*, Douglas's *Birmingham Journal*, and the *True Scotsman*, he had secured the means of neutralising the worst violences which might come from the *Northern Star*, the *Northern Liberator*, and the *Operative*. From the only other avowedly Chartist organ of importance, the *Champion* of Manchester, incendiarism was much less to be feared.

On February 4th, the day before Parliament assembled, the Convention met at the British Coffee House in London to transact preliminary business. Fifty-three delegates had been elected at mass meetings, of whom the greater part now came together to hear that 500,486 signatures had so far been obtained for the National Petition, that £967 of National Rent was collected, and

---

[1] *Northern Star*, December 15, 1838, expresses anxiety lest Birmingham should cut adrift from O'Connor and Stephens, and rally round O'Connell and Lord Durham.

[2] Add. MSS. 27821, ff. 22–3, for Place's criticisms, which seem very harsh. Place did not like Carpenter. Yet it may be admitted that there was a certain flatness of tone about the *Charter*, which did not help its competition with the *Weekly Dispatch*.

Failure of the Chartist Convention of 1839

that arrangements were being made for the further conduct of the Charter campaign.[1] Next day Parliament was opened with a Queen's Speech containing a comminatory passage condemnatory of the Chartist agitation. But the delegates to the Convention were already occupied with current business and a discussion of the advisability of dividing themselves into sub-committees among whom the labour of interviewing every single member of the Commons should be apportioned.[2]

Except, indeed, for the passage bearing on themselves which they animatedly discussed, there was little enough to interest Chartists in the Queen's Speech. Apart from the expected platitudes on foreign and colonial affairs the Sovereign had said little save to announce that the Ministerial legislative plans were virtually confined to a fifth Irish Municipal Reform Bill and a Bill dealing with the Ecclesiastical Commission. Justly considering themselves representatives of a far greater constituency than a House of Commons occupied with matters like these, most members of the Convention were disposed to take a high line. On February 13th, for example, Bronterre O'Brien carried a resolution inviting the House of Commons to meet the Convention.[3] On February 14th, again, J. P. Cobbett on moving a series of resolutions aimed at confining the business of the Convention to a mere superintendence of the Petition's progress and presentation found himself repulsed by thirty-six votes against six.[4] The majority plainly desired a rapid presentation of the Petition and the consideration of coercive "further measures" if it should be rejected.

Yet, thanks mainly to Birmingham, matters did not proceed quite so fast. Delegate Salt in a missive and Delegate Douglas in the columns of the *Birmingham Journal* succeeded in convincing the Convention's majority that the mere 600,000 of signatures so far obtained by the National Petition was altogether insufficient.[5]

---

[1] *Northern Star*, February 9th; *Charter*, February 10th, pp. 44-5.
[2] Cf. Disraeli's *Sybil*, book iv, chapter 5, for a rendering of such interviews as ultimately took place.
[3] *Charter*, February 17th, p. 52.   [4] *Ibid.*, p. 54.
[5] Attwood, who knew something of agitation, had set very different standards. "Only let two millions of men lay down 1s. each," he had said, "that will produce £100,000, and if your delegates in London with that sum at their back do not carry Universal Suffrage in one year, I will forfeit my life, provided only the people will not break the law" (*Operative*, January 27th). After this a National Rent figure standing on February 4th at only £967 lent itself to

Accordingly the date of its presentation was deferred beyond the originally mooted February 28th, and an extensive missionary campaign involving fifteen delegates in widespread peregrinations for a month was resolved upon.[1] Soon the violent section of the Convention, which chafed at the resultant delay, made a demonstration. At a meeting of the extremist London Democratic Federation, Delegates Harney, Ryder, and Marsden made violent speeches which forwarded the passage of resolutions to following effect: That if the Convention did its duty the Charter would be law in less than a month; that there should be no delay in presenting the Petition; and that all acts of injustice and oppression should be met by resistance. Readiness for promoting open revolution could hardly have been less disguised.

Three days of excited debate followed in the Convention, where sufficiently prudent counsels still reigned to ensure the censure of the three offending delegates if not their expulsion.[2] But revolutionary sentiments soon found open expression once more when Delegates Harney, Sankey, Rogers, and Feargus O'Connor addressed a public meeting at the "Crown and Anchor" on March 16th. Harney created the phrase of the evening. Initiated into revolutionary journalism by serving as Hetherington's shopboy and undergoing several arrests, Harney was now at twenty-two the delegate of Northumberland, Norwich, and Derby, and the fieriest member of the Convention. Before the end of the year he told his audience in his best revolutionary style, "the people should have universal suffrage or death."[3] He already saw himself in the Paris of Marat, his ideal.

On March 18th the Convention itself became the scene of violent speech-making as discussion turned on a projected "Rural Police Bill," whose remission to Parliament Chartists were expecting.[4] Ultra-Radicals who still regarded even the Metroderision. One influential Radical journal (H. G. Ward's *Weekly Chronicle*, February 24th) used the opportunity to urge the abandonment of the agitation and the substitution of a powerful rally to Lord Durham.

[1] *Operative*, March 3rd.
[2] Add. MSS. 27821, ff. 42–8; *Charter*, March 10th, pp. 108–9.
[3] J. Irving, *Annals of Our Time*, ed. 1871, p. 37. Add. MSS. 34245 B, f. 239, for Harney's attempt to commit the Convention to nation-wide "simultaneous meetings" to be called on Good Friday, March 29th.
[4] It was put on the Statute Book as the County and District Constables Bill, 2 & 3 Vict. c. 93. It may be noted that a Constabulary Commission appointed in 1836 was recommending the wholesale adoption of police professionalisation (for Abstract of its 1839 Report, see *Companion to British Almanac*, 1840, pp. 109–30).

Failure of the Chartist Convention of 1839

politan Police as an instrument of tyranny, who saw rather its disciplined potency for suppressing discontent than its utility for diminishing crime, were moved to fury by official plans of extending professional police all over the country. In Chartist eyes the County J.P.s were to be invited to saddle the helpless ratepayers with the cost of a mercenary force which would provide spies upon workmen's meetings, hired bullies to beat down Anti-Poor Law organisation, and armed gendarmerie to act in advance of the military against popular movements. It was Dr. Fletcher, delegate for Bury, Heywood, Prestwich, Ratcliffe, and Ramsbottom, who made the most sensational speech of the day. "He would not recommend," he said, "the use of daggers against the Rural Police, but he would recommend every man to have a loaded bludgeon as nearly like that of the policeman's as possible; and if any of these soldiers of the Government, for soldiers they would really be, should strike him, to strike again, and in a manner that a second blow should not be required."[1]

Next day the Ministerial daily, the *Morning Chronicle*, contained a hostile account both of the "Crown and Anchor" speeches of the 16th and the Convention speeches of the 18th. The Convention retorted by proving that during the tense autumn days of 1831 the *Morning Chronicle* had itself suggested the arming of householders as a means to Reform. But matters were now going too far for an important middle-class section of the Convention. Dr. Wade, Vicar of Warwick and delegate for Nottingham, Sutton-in-Ashfield, and Mansfield, now abandoned it as J. P. Cobbett had done earlier. Salt, Douglas, and Hadley of Birmingham, moreover, were soon to announce a similar resolution.[2]

Meanwhile the core of the Convention hardly had reason for delight in the reports which were coming in from their missionaries. Before his resignation the equivocal Salt sent a disheartening account of the lukewarmness of Warwickshire, Worcestershire, and Staffordshire towards the Chartist agitation.[3] If the delegate at work in the Potteries sent more cheerful news, the delegates in the south-west could report no welcome from Dorsetshire, and from Devon and Cornwall only that Chartism needed building

---

[1] *Charter*, March 24th, p. 140. [2] *Ibid.*, April 17, p. 172.
[3] Add. MSS. 34245 A, ff. 107–10. Salt and his friends of the Council of the Birmingham Political Union were already despondent, for they professed that only three millions of signatures would give the National Petition a chance.

up virtually from the beginning.¹ Later news was for a time more cheerful until some disheartening information came from Devizes in Wiltshire. On April 1st Henry Vincent, delegate for Hull, Cheltenham, and Bristol, and Chartism's most winning orator, had entered Devizes at the head of a large party in order to give an address in the market-place. But so violent had been the concerted local opposition that he had had to be conducted outside the town under constabulary protection. Almost at the same time local Sheffield Chartists were reporting apathy, even in an industrial area.

But if Chartism was failing to penetrate uniformly throughout labouring Great Britain, the larger half of the Convention nevertheless had good reasons for staying hopefully together. Considerable sections of the population, indeed, seemed to be ready even to rise should the Convention give the word. The best proof of this is, perhaps, to be found in General Napier's journal and correspondence. At the end of March Napier had been preparing to take over the Northern Command and the oversight of eleven shires. On March 30th he remarked on the trade proceeding in six-foot pikes, which were selling at 3s. 6d. each.² During April he reported variously on the "funk" of the magistrates who were calling for troop parties to be posted near their homes; the watch which was being kept on a plot to assassinate the Duke of Portland; the talk in Halifax public-houses of the ease with which the troops, separated in their billets, might be disposed of; and the circulating of cheap copies of Macaroni's book on pike exercises.³

At the beginning of May, again, Napier was anxiously considering whether the expected popular outburst would take place on May 6th, the date fixed on by the Convention for presenting the National Petition, or whether it would be delayed until the following Whit-Monday.⁴

What serves to give Napier's reports special authority as compared with the panicky mayoral and magistrates' reports which had been streaming into the Home Office, is the calm

---

¹ Add MSS. 34245 A, f. 120. The information following is from the same volume of the Convention's correspondence.
² In W. Napier's *Life of Gen. Sir Charles Napier*, ii, 6.
³ *Ibid.*, pp. 7–23. For the hopes of some extremists that the soldier would not fight "the people," see the *London Democrat*, May 4th, "What will the Soldiers do?" pp. 30–1. ⁴ Napier, pp. 24–5.

Failure of the Chartist Convention of 1839

assurance he maintained of his complete ability to deal with any manner of rising whatsoever. When, therefore, Napier gives approval to the Government's proclamation of May 3rd against the practice of military exercises, when on May 9th he expresses a desire for so unusually serious a measure as a disarming Bill, his view of the imminence of grave troubles carries greater conviction to the modern investigator than that of the magistrates of Loughborough and Barnsley, for example, or that of the Mayors of Newcastle-on-Tyne and Newport, Monmouth.[1]

While Napier at Nottingham had been drawing up his plans for the Northern Command area, the Convention had been spending an agitated month awaiting May 5th and the closing of the list of signatures to be appended to the Petition. On April 9th Delegate Richardson of Manchester had forced to the fore the burning question of the Chartist's right to possess arms. In a speech in which a multitude of authorities were cited in evidence of "the fact that the possession of arms was the best proof of men being free, and the best security for their remaining so," he initiated a long and important debate. It concluded with the determination "that we should not take any legal advice; but that this Convention is fully convinced that all constitutional authorities are agreed in the undoubted right of the people to possess arms."[2] Lovett, who was acting as the Convention's secretary,[3] had been in favour of a somewhat less trenchant conclusion. The resignation of Delegate Wood of Bolton on April 18th and of Delegate Matthew of Perthshire and Fife on April 22nd would seem to show that he was right.

April 23rd was another important day in the Convention's history. In a speech denouncing the cowardice of the "deserters" and reproving the lukewarmness of other delegates, O'Connor asked for the recall of delegates on missionary work. He went on to consider what the Convention should do after Parliament rejected the Petition, and advocated the declaration of a permanent sitting and an invitation to the country for direction.[4]

[1] Cf. Hovell, *The Chartist Movement*, pp. 137–8.
[2] *Charter*, April 14th, pp. 188–9.
[3] A capacity which allowed him to direct a characteristic circularisation of Chartism's constituent bodies with a view to ascertaining their local strength, numerical and financial, and the political, industrial, economic, and journalistic conditions ruling in their areas. Such fragments of the information elicited as survive (Add. MSS. 34245 B) suggest that a compendium would have been a most useful guide not only to the Convention, but to the historian.
[4] *Charter*, April 28th, pp. 219–20.

English Radicalism 1832–1852

It was time, indeed, to initiate discussions on the manner of the Petition's presentation and the measures to be taken thereafter. Attwood and Fielden were chosen for the honour of presenting the Petition, but they gave the Convention some trouble by trying to impose conditions. They asked, in fact, for a resolution condemning the inflammatory speeches which had been made by some members of the Convention and a letter promising that the future exertions of the Convention on behalf of the Charter would be governed by "the principles of peace, law, and order." This was altogether too much for the Convention, which determined to find other members to present the National Petition rather than give way. In the end Attwood and Fielden yielded, and on May 7th the Convention marching two abreast escorted the National Petition with 1,283,000 appended signatures[1] to Attwood.

The Petition, however, was not fated to be presented to Parliament till June 14th nor debated there till July 12th. On May 7th, it should be remembered, Parliament was in the full throes of a Ministerial crisis. After four years of office and frustration at the hands of the Lords, the Whig Government of Lord Melbourne had at length seen its precarious working majority in the Lower House practically wiped out on May 6th. Not, perhaps, without political calculation, the baffled and discredited Ministers resolved to take the opportunity to transfer to their Tory critics the responsibility for grappling with serious difficulties at home, abroad, and in the colonies. On the afternoon of May 7th, therefore, a Government under Peel and Wellington seemed about to take over the administration.

This unexpected political development had an important effect upon the Convention. O'Connor, who had once before asked the Convention to transfer itself to enthusiastic Birmingham, now returned to the plan. On May 8th he pointed out the danger which was to be apprehended from a Tory Government if the Convention remained in London, but asserted that in Birmingham delegates would be safe.[2] In view of its late incorporation, indeed, police power in Birmingham had passed into the hands of Attwoodite Radicals, who would hardly make the best instruments for executing a possible Tory policy of arresting some delegates

---

[1] *Charter*, May 12th, p. 252. For an adaptation of the scene to fiction, see Mrs. Gaskell's *Mary Barton*, chapter 9.   [2] *Ibid.*, May 12th.

Failure of the Chartist Convention of 1839

and dispersing the rest. Birmingham's working classes, too, were of a Chartist temper which promised to give trouble if a Tory Home Office attempted strong measures. It is not surprising, therefore, that O'Connor's plan of moving to Birmingham should have been accepted by a large majority of the delegates.[1] May 13th was fixed as the date when the Convention should begin its business at Birmingham. To that date was remitted the consideration of a list of "ulterior measures" to be taken if and when the Petition should be rejected.

More surprising political developments had taken place, however, before thirty-five Convention delegates arrived in Birmingham by train to receive a great working-class welcome. The Bedchamber squabble between Peel and the Queen had led to the recall of the Melbourne Ministry, which on the 13th and 14th was busy explaining to Parliament its resolve not to abandon the Sovereign "in a situation of difficulty and distress."[2] But it was becoming plain that Whig Ministers, too, were now readier for stronger measures against Chartism than had been the case hitherto. At the end of April it had been resolved to move troops from the relatively untroubled South to the particularly agitated Monmouthshire area[3] as a supplement to the greater troop movements taking place further North. Early in May, moreover, a Proclamation was published against illegal drilling, and the Government invited magistrates in areas where life and property were imperilled to form "civic forces" for whom arms would be provided. This gave the signal for more than a vast swearing-in of propertied special constables all over the country. Batches of Chartist arrests began in different parts, and a harsher official attitude was adopted towards Chartist meetings.[4]

The Convention assembled in Birmingham, nevertheless, and continued with confidence its leadership of the Chartist agitation.[5]

---

[1] 27–10, with six abstentions, a vote explained by the fact that the first arrest of a Delegate, that of Henry Vincent, had just taken place.

[2] Melbourne, in *Mirror of Parliament*, 1839, iii, 2424.

[3] The Home Office Records may be supplemented from the *Charter*, p. 248, which reveals how the troops were hurried from Plymouth.

[4] For arrests at Manchester, Ashton-under-Lyne, Westbury and elsewhere in Wilts, Clerkenwell in London, Newport in Monmouth, and Llanidloes in Montgomeryshire, see *Charter*, May 12th and 19th. Among the meetings forbidden were those in the Bull Ring, Birmingham, and Smithfield, London.

[5] The number of Working Men's Associations, Radical Associations, and Charter Associations behind it seems still to have been growing fast. Moreover, some Chartist "constituencies" had already replaced "deserters" from the

English Radicalism 1832–1852

Its first and principal business was the study of a list of "ulterior measures" to be adopted when the Petition should have been presented and rejected. A committee with Lovett as secretary had already been preparing such a list before the Convention left London, so that rapid progress proved possible. Pending the presentation of the Charter, the committee advocated the holding of simultaneous mass meetings in the different centres of population.[1] At these meetings, conveniently fixed for the approaching Whitsuntide, the populace would be asked to pledge itself to a number of courses designed to bring the greatest possible pressure on the authorities and the classes supporting them. A run on the banks and the conversion of paper money into gold and silver; the holding of a Sacred Month of abstention from labour and taxed liquor; the refusal of rents, rates, and taxes; and preparation "with the arms of freemen to defend the laws and constitutional privileges their ancestors bequeathed to them" were indicated as the principal courses to which the Chartist Convention desired to commit its constituents. Besides these pledges, Chartists were also to be invited to give others. They were to be invited to pledge themselves to support Chartist candidates only at the next General Election; to deal exclusively with Chartist tradesmen; to resist the attractions of rival agitations;[2] to refrain from reading hostile newspapers; and to obey the "just and constitutional requests of the majority of the Convention."

The Convention adopted all these suggestions save two.[3] It adopted also the very eloquent conjoined appeal to the masses which had been penned by Lovett's committee. The ten thousand copies of the combined document which were ordered to be printed must indeed have made most effective propaganda, and have represented possibly the most valuable single item of outlay in all the Convention's expenditure of "National Rent." "We see victim after victim selected," runs one salient passage, "and witness one constitutional right after another annihilated; we

Convention, and some, not represented, were showing eagerness to be allowed Delegates.
[1] "Simultaneous meetings" were not only inspiring, but had the special advantage, long recognised by Ultra-Radicals, of keeping troops, yeomanry, and constabulary in small parties in their own areas.
[2] O'Connor had feared the counter-attractions of the Anti-Corn Law agitation from the first (cf. *Northern Star*, January 19th).
[3] *Charter*, May 19th, for the excision of the suggestion as to the non-payment of rents, rates, and taxes, and the boycott of hostile newspapers.

Failure of the Chartist Convention of 1839

perceive the renegade Whig and the shuffling professor of Liberalism uniting their influence to bind down the millions and, if possible, to stifle their prayers and petitions for justice. Men and women of Britain, will you tamely submit to the insult? Will you submit to incessant toil from birth to death, to give in tax and plunder out of every twelve hours' labour the proceeds of nine hours to support your idle and insolent oppressors?" Next follow a running criticism of the factory employment of women and children, the New Poor Law and the projected police plan, a frightening picture of what would happen to the middle classes if the people should turn to "wild revenge," and an appeal to them to aid in the attainment of the Charter. Finally comes the list of "ulterior measures" to be suggested to the simultaneous meetings then being arranged, and an assurance that after July 1st the Convention would immediately "proceed to carry the will of the people into execution."[1]

This able document laid down the lines which were followed by the vast and enthusiastic "simultaneous meetings" of the Whitsuntide season at the end of May.[2] It was in order that its members might direct these meetings and the subsequent Scottish oratory arranged for June that the Convention after less than a week in Birmingham adjourned until July 1st. Before dispersing it had decided that the people should regard any serious Government measures for interfering with the Chartist programme by prohibition of meetings or arrest of delegates as a signal for the commencement of "ulterior measures." On the other hand it had asked those in charge of the meetings to consult beforehand with the local authorities, and had condemned the carrying of staves, pikes, pistols, and other weapons to the meeting-grounds.

The meetings indeed, for all the huge numbers present, produced so little dangerous disturbance that General Napier was complaining to a correspondent on June 29th that both the Home Office and the Horse Guards were over-optimistic as to the situation.[3] Certainly very desperate talk had been going on in some Chartist circles. Even in the Metropolis, whose apparent apathy had disappointed the Chartist Convention in its early weeks, the ultra-revolutionary *London Democrat* had revealed for

[1] *Charter*, May 19th.
[2] Cf. R. Gammage, *History of the Chartist Movement*, ed. 1894, pp. 113–23.
[3] Napier, *op. cit.*, ii, 50.

a space the real sentiments of many in the Tower Hamlets, Clerkenwell, and other working-class quarters.¹ An examination, again, of the well-known Somerville's *Warnings to the People on Street Warfare* will show how in May and June 1839 insurrection in Glasgow and Birmingham was being treated as a contingency whose perils for the populace itself needed vivid illustration.²

The Convention reassembled in Birmingham on July 1st. There were the inevitable glowing reports of the great meetings, but also on July 2nd the decision to remove to London for the 10th. Attwood's motion on the National Petition was to be taken in the Commons on the 12th, and Delegate Moir of Glasgow and Lanarkshire successfully urged that the Convention should be at hand. On July 3rd and 4th the advanced party in the Convention pressed a demand for early decisions on the "ulterior measures" which had been adopted with such enthusiastic readiness by the great meetings in the country. Though Delegate Craig of Ayrshire questioned the preparedness of the populace, a run on the banks, the boycotting of anti-Chartist tradesmen, and use of the constitutional privilege of arming were approved for an early date, and a decision on the Sacred Month was only deferred until after the Commons had dealt with the Petition on July 12th.³

Meanwhile the action of Birmingham's magistrates was precipitating grave local disorder. With the return of the Convention to Birmingham, local working-class extremists had grown dangerously excited,⁴ and, ignoring a magistrates' ban on meetings in the Bull Ring, had held them almost continuously. Pending the passage of a Birmingham Police Bill by Parliament, the Mayor had only a score of street-keepers and a handful of constables at his disposal for the professional enforcement of his orders. He travelled to London with two brother magistrates, and brought back on July 4th sixty Metropolitan Police who had been placed at his disposal.⁵

---

¹ It ran between April 13th and June 8th, and preached arming and insurrection vigorously. (See especially pp. 29, 41, 51.) Its disappearance is possibly not unconnected with the police, who filed most of its numbers.
² This publication was issued in seven weekly numbers.
³ *Charter*, July 7th, p. 381.
⁴ One of their leaders, sent by them to the Convention in place of the Birmingham Political Union "deserters," was under arrest, Brown. Another leader, Fussell, was on bail (cf. Hovell, *op. cit.*, pp. 144–5, for the situation in Birmingham). ⁵ *Charter*, July 7th, p. 382.

Failure of the Chartist Convention of 1839

Almost as soon as they arrived the London police were set to clear the Bull Ring, where a meeting was in progress. No warning had been given by the flustered magistrates, the angry crowd fought hard, and military assistance was finally necessary. Some hours later renewed trouble broke out, and the police made more arrests of Chartists, including this time the two energetic delegates, Drs. Taylor and M'Douall, who claimed, however, to have been engaged in dissuading a violent crowd from taking action.

Next morning the Convention condemned the action of the Birmingham authorities in strong terms,[1] and decided to placard the town with five hundred copies of its resolutions. The placards appeared on the 6th, and as a result the authorities, who had been provided with the services of forty more London policemen, proceeded to the arrest of Delegate Collins of Birmingham and Delegate Lovett of London, who had given the printer the order for the placards. Even before the Convention returned to London, therefore, the treatment meted out to some of its members had stirred anew the fires of Chartist agitation. On July 10th, for example, General Napier reported to the Home Office that Nottingham Chartists had considered the plan of marching to Birmingham's assistance. On July 15th, again, a day of serious Birmingham rioting, he reported the following areas in his Northern Command to be agitated: the Durham colliery districts, Newcastle, Carlisle, Cockermouth, Bolton, Stockport, and Sutton-in-Ashfield. The indignant Convention's attempt to retort upon the Government which had permitted the use of the Metropolitan Police in Birmingham was not apparently without effect. But though the Convention had recommended the immediate resort to all the "ulterior measures," save the Sacred Month, the arming figures supplied to Napier must have been exaggerated. A hundred pistols for distribution in Nottingham, the introduction of three hundred stand of arms into Stockport in a single week,[2] these and similar accounts elsewhere bear the mark of credulous or interested informers.

[1] *Charter*, July 7th, p. 380.
[2] Napier, *op. cit.*, ii, 52–3. Home Office, 40, 49, however, shows that at least one Chartist attempt to procure firearms in considerable quantities was made. There is a deposition from a Birmingham gunmaker to the effect that on May 9th a score of muskets and bayonets was ordered from him, and an order for hundreds more promised if the first batch was satisfactory. Dr. M'Douall, a Delegate to the Convention, was one of the two persons involved, and the other came from Ashton.

English Radicalism 1832-1852

Meanwhile the Convention itself, thinned by arrests, desertions, and hesitations, was facing its sternest test. On July 10th a mere twenty-four members had begun business in London, and on the 12th an appeal had been sent out to the Chartist following. The election of delegates-substitute was asked for so that arrested members members might be replaced, and new delegates were invited from areas which had not yet sought representation.[1] On the same day, July 12th, the Commons at length reached the business for which the Chartists had so long been waiting, Attwood's motion to go into Committee of the whole House to consider the National Petition. Though the Government had not opposed the holding of a debate, it cannot be said that Lord John Russell treated Attwood's opening speech, Fielden's speech as seconder or the National Petition itself with any real seriousness.[2] O'Connell, too, took the line that the Chartist agitation had ruined the best Radical prospects by alienating the middle classes. Only forty-six members finally voted with Attwood against a hostile majority five times as large.[3]

On July 13th, 15th, and 16th, therefore, thirty delegates of the Convention anxiously debated whether to use their last and oft-flourished weapon, the declaration of a Sacred Month of abstention from labour. After three days of debate a mere rump of a majority, composed of thirteen delegates only out of twenty-four present, determined to declare a Sacred Month to begin on August 12th, and one committee began the preparatory work and another undertook the drafting of a manifesto to the middle classes inviting their support. This was not merely to ignore the advice of Attwood and Fielden to keep calm and organise another and even more extensively supported National Petition.[4] This was also to ignore the counsel of cautious and experienced members of the Convention like Carpenter, editor of the *Charter*, who pointed out how little reason there was to expect that even convinced Chartists would be able to pay any heed to the Convention's desperate resolution and stay away from work for a month.[5]

Second thoughts came after it appeared obvious that the

---

[1] *Charter*, July 14th, p. 379.
[2] Cf. Disraeli, *Mirror of Parliament*, 1839, v, 3891.
[3] The division was 46-235; a Chartist summary of the debate is Gammage, *op. cit.*, pp. 138-44.
[4] Gammage, *op. cit.*, p. 145.   [5] *Charter*, July 21st, pp. 412-13.

Failure of the Chartist Convention of 1839

destructive Chartist rioting of July 15th at Birmingham had more than ever antagonised the "public." On July 22nd, therefore, the normally combative O'Brien took the lead in asking for a revision of the Sacred Month decision. Amid some recrimination and opposition a majority was secured for such a course, and a partially new direction was given to Chartism.[1] In effect it was decided that leaving a Central Council in London the delegates should disperse to their constituencies and ascertain at specially convened meetings just how long a period of "abstention from labour" Chartists were prepared for. With such information available the Central Council would decide Chartism's future course.

On August 5th, 6th, and 7th Chartism's small Central Council was actually sitting and examining the missives to hand from fellow delegates and from local Chartist leaders on the subject of the attitude of the rank and file towards the Sacred Month. To collate these missives[2] with the Home Office records[3] is to be satisfied that the recommendation finally made by the Council was in the circumstances the most justifiable one. It was recommended that the Sacred Month should be abandoned but that endeavours should be made to secure as from August 12th abstention from work "for two or three days, in order to devote the whole of that time to solemn processions and meetings." There was certainly sufficient operative response on August 12th and the days following to keep many sets of magistrates alarmed. At Nottingham, for example, both on August 12th and 13th the magistrates issued proclamations against the meetings designed, and when this proved vain asked for troops and read the Riot Act.[4] At Barnsley, too, the Riot Act was read and troops called out on the 12th, while at Sheffield much the same thing happened on the 13th. At Bolton, where the "solemn processions and meetings" had been celebrated with especial unction,[5] street affrays broke

[1] *Charter*, July 28th, pp. 428-9.
[2] Surviving in Add. MSS. 34245 B, ff. 72-129.
[3] The Home Office series of Records on the "disturbances," H.O. 40, 37-58, will often be found to provide an invaluable check on the statements of Chartist orators and newspapers. Though largely consisting of mayoral and magistrates' communications to the Home Office, they make a very complete picture of the disturbed England of the time.
[4] Napier, *op. cit.*, ii, 71-2. Cf. H.O. 40, 53.
[5] H.O. 40, 44, Bolton, Mayor's letter, August 12th. "Parties began to assemble before 6 a.m., and have perambulated the town ever since, occasionally collecting in the market place, where they are addressed by some of their leaders."

*

201

out on the 14th which necessitated the use both of military and yeomanry. On Tyneside, led by the resolute Northern Political Union, the colliers attempted a "General Strike."[1] Even London showed surprising amount of effervescence, which had not vanished as late as the 20th.[2]

But undoubtedly this widespread excitement was very soon succeeded by a remarkable calm, to which Ministers contributed very effectively by mitigating the death sentences which had been passed on three Birmingham rioters of July. Scottish Chartism, too, virtually separated itself from coercive tactics when its large delegate meeting of mid-August formed a Scottish Chartist organisation on a very "moral force" basis indeed. The Scots recognised that a determined effort to educate "public opinion" would be required before the Charter could be won.[3] In England, however, conditions were far from similiar, and "physical force" notions were still widely entertained. Moreover, the discredited Rump of the Convention, which was slowly being assembled at the end of August, was incapable of united action in any direction. Rent by the internal feuds inevitable in a body which had achieved neither success nor credit, it did not even attempt to organise Chartism's future. Indeed, most of its time prior to the dissolution of September 14th was occupied in miserable squabbling over the accounts of the expenditure of "National Rent."[4] It was a sordid, even a disgraceful end to the body which only a few months before had taken on the airs of a legitimate Parliament. But Chartism did not die with the 1839 Convention. All over the country loyalty to the People's Charter lived on, and such loyalty was reinforced by the thought of the many scores of Chartist martyrs in the gaols. London, for example, did not forget Lovett, nor Wales and the West, Vincent. The gathering of a second Convention, indeed, was already being debated on the same Chartist pages which reported the end of the first.[5]

---

[1] H.O. 40, 46, Northumberland, for Northern Political Union's placard headed "General Strike." Few colliers were at work on the 12th, and some were still out on the 15th.
[2] Ibid. 40, 44, Metropolis, for Police Reports on meetings, August 12th-20th.
[3] Hovell, op. cit., pp. 192-3; Gammage, op. cit., pp. 155-6.
[4] Charter, September 15th, p. 533.
[5] Cf. Northern Star, September 21st.

CHAPTER XII

CHARTISM SURVIVES

"We are aware that according to the newspapers Chartism is extinct; that a Reformed Ministry has put down the chimera of Chartism in the most felicitous effectual manner. So say the newspapers: and yet, alas, most readers of newspapers know withal that it is indeed the chimera not the reality of Chartism which has been put down. . . . The matter of Chartism is weighty, deep-rooted, far-extending; did not begin yesterday; will by no means end this day or to-morrow. Reform Ministry, constabulary, rural police, new levy of soldiers, grants of money to Birmingham . . . all this will put down only the embodiment or chimera of Chartism. The essence continuing, new and ever new embodiments, chimeras, madder or less mad, have to continue. The melancholy fact remains that this thing known at present by the name of Chartism does exist; has existed; and either 'put down' into secret treason, with rusty pistols, vitriol-bottle and match-box or openly flourishing pike and torch is like to exist till quite other methods have been tried with it."

T. CARLYLE, "Chartism" (1839).

"Not that Corn Law Repeal is wrong; when we get the Charter, we will repeal the Corn Laws and all the other bad laws. But if you give up your agitation for the Charter to help the Free Traders, they will not help you to get the Charter. Don't be deceived by the middle classes again. You helped them to get their votes—you swelled the cry of 'The Bill, the whole Bill, and nothing but the Bill!' But where are the fine promises they made you? Gone to the winds! They said when they had gotten their votes they would help you to get yours. But they and the rotten Whigs have never remembered you. Municipal Reform has been for their benefit—not for yours. All other reforms the Whigs boast to have effected have been for the benefit of the middle classes—not for yours. And now they want to get the Corn Laws repealed—not for your benefit—but for their own. 'Cheap bread,' they cry. But they mean 'Low wages.' Do not listen to their cant and humbug. Stick to your Charter. You are veritable slaves without your votes!"

A Chartist speech of the winter of 1840–1 reported in the "Life of Thomas Cooper," *pp. 136–7.*

WHILE Chartism had been rising to the optimistic heights of May and June 1839, and falling again into the slough of despond of September, official Whiggery had seemed increasingly incapable of undertaking anything but a Tory policy. Even before Chartism had risen to its apogee Leader, one of the most forceful of the Parliamentary Radicals, had complained bitterly of the fact that Peel it was who governed England. Peel, indeed, had dominated the Commons for years, and only when he disapproved of some particularly outrageous piece of partisan warfare in the Lords was the Ministry able to make any headway there. The whole Bedchamber incident, too, served to weaken the credit of official Whiggery still further, while its dependence on O'Connellite votes became the more damaging as "moderate" British opinion increasingly tired of the methods by which O'Connellite political supremacy was maintained in Ireland.

Two pearls of O'Connellite eloquence may here be quoted. They may serve to explain why no overwhelming indignation was aroused among British "Reformers" by the Lords' persistence in repeating in 1839 their previous wreckings of the Government's central legislative plan for elected Irish municipalities. Addressing a Dublin meeting called to congratulate the Queen on her Bedchamber stand against the Tories, O'Connell's fervour overflowed. "May the great God of Heaven bless her who did it!" he ranted, "that creature of only nineteen—lovely as she is young, and pure as she is exalted. She was something which might be dreamed of in chivalry or fairyland." Grattan's eloquence took a darker turn as he pointed to Orange regrets that Cumberland, King of Hanover and heir-presumptive, was not on the throne in place of his niece. "If her Majesty," he said, "was once fairly placed in the hands of the Tories, I would not give an Orange Peel for her life. If some of the miscreants of the party got round her Majesty, and had the mixing of the Royal bowl at night, I fear she would have a long sleep."[1] Ever since Queen Victoria's accession O'Connell had been converting the Irish Radicals into Queen and Government men of a zealotry which even the Whigs found embarrassing. When British Ultra-Radicalism, moreover, had offered Irishmen the Charter as the surest means of ending Irish woes, O'Connell had taught them

---

[1] J. Irving, *Annals of Our Time*, ed. 1871, p. 43.

to have nothing to do with it. That was doubtful wisdom even from the Irish point of view.

While expending months of Parliamentary time Session after Session over an Irish Municipal Reform Bill which the Lords refused to accept, official Whiggery sought neither the means to coerce them nor offered the concessions to Radical causes which would have strengthened its hands. On March 18th the whole Radical Parliamentary strength, backed now by an increasingly organised Anti-Corn Law movement outside,[1] began a strong demonstration on Villiers's motion to go into Committee on the working of the Corn Law. But though the debate stretched over five sittings, and 195 votes were won in the division,[2] the Radicals failed to make Corn Law revision part of the Government's programme. On March 21st, again, Hume proposed a Household Suffrage motion which would have gone far to lay the Chartist agitation, but the Government had no welcome to give to any departure from the principles of the Reform Bill. On June 4th the Radical educationists, whose Select Committee of 1837-8 had done something to stir the Government to educational resolves, had the chagrin of listening to Lord John Russell throwing the projected State Normal School to the wolves of inter-sectarian jealousy[3] so that he might save the imperilled Committee of Council on Education. On June 18th, again, Grote's Ballot motion, for all the 216 votes obtained on the division, was still opposed by all the essential forces of Whiggery and Toryism combined.[4]

The Government, which declined so persistently to give any welcome to Radicalism's most moderate and most responsibly urged proposals, had before the end of the Session to take the additional onus of legislating to renew the powers of the detested Poor Law Commissioners. Nor was this all. Under the threat of Chartism it was increasing the army and laying down the basis for the professionalisation of the police system. The extensive

[1] During the Session 516,568 persons petitioned against the Corn Laws, and 318,723 for them. For the formation of the Anti-Corn-Law League, normally dealt with satisfactorily in the text-books, readers are referred to Prentice's well-known *History* of the League.
[2] *Hansard*, xlvi, 859.
[3] *Ibid.*, xlvii, 1381 (June 4th). The terms on which Dissenting Ministers were to be allowed to undertake the religious instruction of denominational pupils, though arousing Church wrath, were unacceptable to the denominations.
[4] *Ibid.*, xlviii, 504.

new police legislation of 1839, moreover, was based on Tory models. Thus in the counties the Justices, uncontrolled by representation even of the rate-paying population, received the widest powers of enrolling new police forces,[1] and in the new Charter-created boroughs, Manchester, Birmingham, and Bolton, the town councils were for the time allowed nothing to do with the police save to pay for them.[2] Rarely had Peel and Property so obviously dictated the course of Whig legislation as when Russell altered the Birmingham Police Bill on July 29th to secure the support of the Conservative leader.[3]

Meanwhile the miserable work of trying arrested Chartists had already begun at the July Assizes in Montgomeryshire, a county sufficiently moved by Chartism to permit its towns of Newtown, Welshpool, and Llanidloes to elect a representative to the convention. Amid a large batch of lighter riot sentences one term of fifteen years transportation for stabbing was awarded, and three others of seven years for training and drilling to use arms.[4] The Warwick trials of Birmingham rioters followed with three death sentences, fortunately commuted, and in addition the conviction of Stephens at Chester, of Vincent at Monmouth, and of Lovett and Collins at Warwick. Less important Chartist notabilities were meanwhile being apprehended in wholesale fashion at Manchester and Newcastle. Nor were arrests confined to leaders, national or local. The attempts of workmen to celebrate a National Holiday on August 12th and the days following caused scores of rank-and-file Chartists to find their way into the gaols.

After the miserable end of the Convention in September, nevertheless, the Government Whigs seem to have found some comfort in the thought that belligerent Chartism was dead. On October 24th, for example, Campbell, their Attorney-General, told a meeting of his Edinburgh constituents that Chartism as an agitation had passed away.[5] Yet all over the country there were still physical force Chartists in possession of weapons of a kind and convinced that a well-planned local blow might raise

[1] 2 & 3 Vict. c. 93.   [2] 2 & 3 Vict. c. 87, 88, 95.
[3] *Hansard*, xlix, 938–65.
[4] Returns relating to prisoners, etc. (publication ordered August 5, 1840), show that there had been fifty Montgomeryshire Chartist prisoners, mainly weavers. For further details of arming and drilling H.O. 40, 46, Montgomeryshire. One Home Office correspondent announced that 1,500 were armed with pikes at Llanidloes, and 1,700 at Newtown.
[5] J. Irving, *Annals*, p. 54.

Chartism Survives

all labouring Britain. Such a blow was actually attempted early in November in Monmouthshire, and there is some evidence to suggest that Bradford and Birmingham might have seen similar efforts if the first had been more successful.[1]

Monmouthshire became the scene of the first and only Chartist rising in arms for a variety of reasons. There was a reputable local Chartist leader available in the Newport draper, John Frost. Not only had Frost been the delegate in the Convention for Newport, Pontypool, and Caerleon, but he was also an ex-Mayor of Newport, and had been on the local Bench till the Government had removed his name in the spring for sitting in the Convention. Then there was a special local cause of excitement. Henry Vincent, the Chartist orator imprisoned in Monmouth, had made himself immensely popular amongst the colliers and iron-workers of Monmouthshire, and his memory was kept green by the weekly he had founded, *The Western Vindicator*. From the time of his first committal to prison in May ideas of rescue appear to have been entertained and the authorities to have been apprehensive.[2] Finally, John Frost, who seems to have been the leading man in the closing stages of the Convention,[3] was not a mere braggart and knew that the colliers and iron-workers of Monmouthshire and South Wales could be raised in suitable circumstances for a Chartist blow.[4]

Amid the maze of accounts as to what actually happened on November 3rd and 4th it is extremely difficult to ascertain the truth. One extreme report of the numbers engaged speaks, for example, of 20,000 Chartists, whereas one modern historian ventures rashly to write this down to 200, and another more prudently hesitates between 1,000 and 3,000.[5] It would appear certain, nevertheless, that on Sunday evening, November 3rd,

---

[1] H.O. 40, 50, contains a long series of police reports on Birmingham drilling, etc. Attacks on the new Birmingham police were meditated there, while in Bradford the attack would have been on the barracks (H.O. 40, 51, York, November 29th, Deposition of Sarah Ward).

[2] *Rise and Fall of Chartism in Monmouthshire* (1840), p. 17, speaks of three hundred special constables sworn in and a military detachment held in reserve on the day when Vincent was committed for trial.

[3] Cf. *Northern Star*, September 21st.

[4] Thus one Glamorganshire Bench reported on September 6th: "that the working people are constantly practising firing at targets, and that meetings are frequently held on the Mountain." H.O. 40, 51.

[5] Gammage, *op. cit.*, p. 265, reports the 20,000 estimate, though his own is 10,000. The 200 figure is from Julius West's *History*, p. 144. The other estimate is Hovell's, *op. cit.*, p. 179.

very considerable bodies of armed colliers, blast-furnace workers, and others from a wide area round Newport were preparing for a night march on that town. There was apparently some immediate intention of punishing the Newport magistrates for their persecution of Vincent, and a further intention of raising the whole of the county for the rescue of Vincent from Monmouth Gaol.[1] Moreover, in view of the accounts of excitement from Breconshire and Glamorganshire[2] it must be assumed that the Monmouthshire preparations enjoyed the sympathy of neighbouring areas which would doubtless have quickly joined a successful movement.

Success, however, was not forthcoming. The Chartists had intended to seize Newport in the darkness and by surprise, and had they been able to carry out their plans they might, perhaps, have found the Newport magistrates, their special constables, and the twenty-eight soldiers in the town no great obstacle. But the columns from the different villages neither collected so rapidly as had been planned nor found night-marching as expeditious as they had hoped. Indeed, the final descent into Newport was not made until nine o'clock in the morning, and by men who were tired and had been drenched by a night's steady rain. Again, the authorities, so far from being taken by surprise, had received intelligence of Chartist preparations even before the march began,[3] so that Chartist precautions on the road had been vain. Accordingly when the Chartists attempted to break into the Westgate Arms Inn, where military and magistrates were stationed, they were received by heavy musketry fire at close range. After a struggle lasting only twenty minutes, and during which nearly every military bullet fired seems to have made a casualty, the beaten colliers drew off leaving nine dead bodies, but carrying their wounded and some of their dead with them.[4] Numerous arrests quickly followed, including that of Frost, who was taken with three pistols and ammunition on his person. On December 10th a Special Commission took the first stage of the trial of the

---

[1] "Some say they are going to Monmouth to liberate Vincent and Edwards ... others that they are going to Newport to seize the magistrates who had been most active in arresting them. . . ." Message from the manager of a large ironworks near Pontypool whose men had gone, November 3rd, H.O. 40, 46.

[2] H.O. 40, 31, Wales.

[3] *Ibid.* 40, 46, for Lord-Lieutenant's Letter of November 3rd. It mentions that the combative Mayor of Newport knew what was happening.

[4] F. F. Rosenblatt, *Chartist Movement in its Social and Economic Aspects*, gives the total Chartist dead as twenty-two.

Chartism Survives

thirty-eight prisoners referred to it. Against Frost and thirteen others the charge preferred was high treason, and the trials proper were fixed to begin on December 31st.[1]

One of the unexpected results of the Newport fighting was a sudden revival of Chartist zeal. All over the country Chartists found a new energy in determining to save the life of Frost and his fellow prisoners. Many of the Radical and Working Men's Associations, however, did not merely begin energetically to hold pro-Frost meetings, raise Frost Defence subscriptions, and prepare to send delegates to a second Convention.[2] Some certainly went on to more planning of armed movements on Frost's behalf. The Metropolitan Police, for example, were called upon to deal with an informer's reports of East End conciliabula, whose aim was to "fire shipping in the River and Docks" and to "kidnap the principal men in the State." "Their [sic] is to be a general rise," wrote the informer in the same letter, "the day before the execution of Mr. Frost . . . there is to be a rise in Manchester and Newcastle upon the same day."[3] In Birmingham, again, the police had very definite proof that the Radical Association's organisation was being used partly for drilling purposes.[4] The arrests, trials, and sentences of the previous months, indeed, were serving to drive a large part of Chartist activity underground. Organised in classes of eight or more, with class leaders in charge of drilling and inter-communication, Chartism in some areas assumed for a time the most dubious of aspects.[5]

Naturally the usual alarm reigned among magistrates, mayors, and lord-lieutenants. Monmouthshire and South Wales were conspicuous centres of such alarm,[6] the more so as Chartist inter-communication between Merthyr and Birmingham was held to have been established with a view to a combined rising.

---

[1] *State Trials*, 1839–43, iv, 85 sqq.
[2] H.O. 40, 51, York, for example, gives the Bradford Working Men's Association meeting of December 14th to elect a Delegate. The Convention was to begin on December 19th.
[3] *Ibid.* 40, 44, Metropolis, November 15th.
[4] *Ibid.* 40, 50, Police Report, December 19th. The police informant was apparently a zealous driller, in police pay.
[5] *Ibid.*, and H.O. 40, 44, Leicestershire, November 28th, which gives a police report of "Class" meetings in the Loughborough area with designs of night operations.
[6] *Ibid.* 40, 46, for example, shows the military commander at Newport saying, "The Mayor here is in great alarm, and has, he says, the best information that there is to be a general rising . . .," December 20th.

English Radicalism 1832-1852

Authority ventured even upon admittedly illegal seizures of packages of the *Western Vindicator* at Cardiff and Newport in its anxiety to prevent that paper's "dangerous" influence on the working population.[1] In the North the greatest panic was perhaps at Bradford, where unemployment was serious and the firing of mills was dreaded. As usual, General Napier kept his head. Writing to the Home Office on December 10th he would admit no more than that "taking the cream of the many informations received from various parts, it is possible that some ill-arranged commotion may take place in Frost's favour; but nowhere is there evidence of an organised plan." In regard, again, to the panic among the Bradford magistrates he reported very coolly to the Home Office on the 22nd. An efficient police force, he said, would certainly be an advantage, but with thirty-two watchmen under a chief to serve as a magistrates' bodyguard, with 1,800 special constables ready to assemble on the ringing of the parish bells, and with a military party in the background, no mischief would take place, especially if the Poor Law Guardians avoided parsimony in the grant of poor relief.[2]

Meanwhile O'Connor was bestirring himself to utilise the renewed opportunity which Frost's trial gave him. He assured Chartists he would save Frost's life, briefed two eminent counsel on behalf of Frost and his comrades, and raised a large defence fund to which he himself contributed a whole week's profit of the *Northern Star*.[3] When the Special Commission's proceedings reopened at Monmouth on December 31st the defence was able to begin with a responsibly urged technical objection which was serious enough to warrant remission after the trial to the Bench of Judges in London.[4] For the time, however, the trials proceeded, and in all the cases in which the Crown persisted with the high treason charge a verdict of guilty was returned, though always with a recommendation to mercy. There was naturally no question of execution until the defendants' objection on the manner of delivery of the witness list had been disposed of in the Exchequer Chamber. Here a majority of the Judges held that the witness list had been

---

[1] *Western Vindicator*, December 14th, for a vigorous counter-attack and some fierce writing on the subject of the trial. At 2d. the *Vindicator* had been good value even before the December 14th appearance at 1½d. and "unstamped." It was now doomed.   [2] Napier, *op. cit.*, ii, 95–8.
[3] *Northern Star*, December 7, 1839.   [4] *Charter*, January 5th, pp. 795–7

Chartism Survives

improperly delivered, though not to the extent of invalidating the trials.[1] It was a fortunate finding which helped the Government to agree to commute Frost's sentence to transportation for life. The announcement of the reprieve on February 1st allowed the Queen's wedding to be celebrated on the 10th in an atmosphere which had lost much of its tenseness.

There can be hardly a shadow of doubt but that serious trouble would have followed on the three executions which the Whig Government had contemplated and from which Melbourne was only with great difficulty dissuaded. Not only had there been a tremendous volume of petitioning for a reprieve,[2] but active preparations to wreak vengeance if Frost's life were taken. During the Monmouth trials Napier, not usually an alarmist, reported to the Home Office the heavy sale of gunpowder in Nottingham, the posting of Chartist sentinels, and the manufacture of a large quantity of fireballs for purposes of arson.[3] On the night of January 11th, again, there was considerable trouble in Sheffield involving many arrests of armed men, and muffled stir also in other parts of the West Riding, especially Dewsbury and Heckmondwike.[4] Then on the night of the 15th there was an attempt to fire the barracks at Barnsley, and on the 16th arrests by the Metropolitan Police in Bethnal Green. In the latter half of December, indeed, a sort of convention had gathered in London to deal with Frost's case, a second of thirty-three delegates assembled in Manchester early in February, and even in April another could be collected in Nottingham.[5] The execution of Frost, Williams, and Jones, it is plain, would have provoked untold bitterness in working-class hearts for many a year.

The Chartist reprieves, however, quickly effected a notable change of atmosphere, and so allowed a revived Chartism to undertake a rapid and yet not insincere change of front. The example had long been given in Scotland, where a Convention of

---

[1] *The Times*, January 30th.
[2] *The Charter*, February 2nd, reports 30,171 signatures obtained in Birmingham in six days, and 13,166 in Merthyr. London, too, was very moved (cf. W. J. Linton's *Recollections*, pp. 43–4), and altogether it seems that the Dorchester Labourers' figures were far exceeded. [3] Napier, *op. cit.*, ii, 107–9.
[4] *Sheffield Iris*, January 14th; *Charter*, January 19th.
[5] *Charter*, December 29th, January 5th, for first Convention; *Ibid.*, February 9th, for second; Napier, p. 122 for third. After the reprieve Chartists aimed at bringing Frost and the others back from transportation. Frost's return, conceded in 1856, marks the end of one of the most pertinaciously pressed of Chartist efforts.

fifty-six delegates which had met in Glasgow on August 14, 1839, drew up plans for a national Scottish organisation on a purely "moral force" basis. On a foundation of local societies, divided into "classes" of ten for collecting purposes, was to be reared a superstructure of an executive meeting weekly and a committee meeting monthly for the transaction of such central business as the conduct of petitioning, the organising of lecturing and agitation and the issue of literature.[1] Among English Chartists it was a considerable time before organising activity of this type developed. Indeed, there is reason to believe that while the stalwarts continued "physical force" preparations, a considerable section of their less violent brethren were attracted by the growing Socialist propaganda of the Owenites[2] or by the Anti-Corn-Law League lecturing of men like Paulton and Sydney Smith.[3] After the Newport reprieves, however, English working-class Radicalism proved more capable of adapting itself to the necessity of organising for a possibly lengthy political crusade on behalf of the Charter. As was inevitable after the misfortunes and disasters of 1839, "physical force" was only mentioned to be disowned. "Moral force" was summoned instead to aid the Chartist cause.

Two prominent examples may serve to illustrate the altered temper abroad. When in the early spring the Northern Political Union was reorganised the objective aimed at was described as "the attainment of Universal Suffrage by every moral and lawful means, such as petitioning Parliament, procuring the return of members who will vote for Universal Suffrage, publishing tracts, establishing reading rooms."[4] When Hetherington, again, took the leading part in founding a Metropolitan Charter Union about the same time his experiences in the Convention seem to have taught him how essential it was to deprecate from the first all inflammatory language and all concealment of ulterior views and objects. The federation of all Radical and Chartist associations,

[1] *Charter*, August 25th; September 1st. The fortunes of the organisation may be followed in the Scottish *Chartist Circular* from September 1839.
[2] Cf. *Charter*, September 1st, for notices of Socialist meetings at Edinburgh, Northampton, and Bradford. Though it was an Owenite principle not to put faith in political action, Chartists were unceasingly and irresistibly attracted to the co-operative community preached by the Owenites, and to the Owenite ideals of education and morality. It may be noted that Hobson, who published the *Northern Star*, published also the Socialist *New Moral World*.
[3] *Charter*, February 23, March 1, 1840, shows men like Hetherington were ready to come to terms with the League. League meetings had already made a great impression. [4] *Northern Liberator*, April 11, 1840.

Chartism Survives

the circulation of tracts and a weekly, the formation of co-operative stores, coffee-houses, and reading-rooms—these were the principal activities which Hetherington's Charter Union wished to see undertaken.[1]

It was, of course, much easier to launch local Chartist organisations than to found a co-ordinated national party. This was, however, being attempted against great obstacles in 1840. For months before twenty-three Chartist delegates assembled at Manchester for the purpose (on July 20th), the *Northern Star* had contained proposals from a variety of sources. O'Connor's proposal merits particular mention. He planned a daily paper to be called the *Morning Star*, which he was ready to launch with £3,500 of his own and subscriptions to a much larger amount from readers of the *Northern Star*, who would be allowed special facilities for becoming shareholders.[2] Shareholders were optimistically promised 10 per cent, though not in the first year, when £2,000 would be allotted to the holding of a Chartist Convention, the payment of Chartist lecturers, the needs of a Chartist defence fund, and less important miscellaneous purposes. Considered though it was by the Manchester meeting of July 1840, it was not the scheme ultimately adopted. The perils of committing the fortunes of Chartism to a risky speculation were perhaps obvious, and also the unwisdom of bringing Chartism before the public as completely dominated and financed by Feargus O'Connor's newspaper office.

The Manchester meeting, therefore, leaving on one side O'Connor's and other schemes, adopted a straightforward plan.[3] The National Charter Association was to rest on a basis which was to some extent already prepared. The towns were to be organised into wards with a ward collector to each, and further subdivided into classes of ten, each with its own class leader responsible for collecting the penny a week Chartist subscription. Both in the towns and in the counties there were to be local councils in touch with the National Executive of seven which was to be annually elected by the members. This Executive, responsible for direction and agitation, was to be paid for time

---

[1] *Northern Liberator*, May 2nd.
[2] *Northern Star*, July 18th. O'Connor was prepared to appoint local collectors to receive 6d. a week for forty weeks from would-be shareholders.
[3] *Ibid.*, July 25th, August 1st

spent in the service of the Association at the rate of 30s. per week for ordinary members and £2 per week for the secretary.

The effort necessary to launch and operate the National Charter Association was immense, the more so as the original rules had to be altered so that members might avoid the far-flung nets of the Anti-Corresponding Society legislation of 1799 and 1817.[1] Thus on December 11, 1841, sixteen months after the effort to launch the National Charter Association had begun, the *Northern Star* could only report a total membership of 13,000 distributed between 282 "localities." Again, if a rapid increase to 40,060 and beyond then set in, it is yet quite obvious from the Executive's financial plight that subscription payments were all too often in arrears.[2] It is difficult, indeed, not to assume that it was only the exceptional Chartist who religiously renewed his twopenny membership card every quarter and paid his weekly subscription besides. It is from this position, therefore, that Lovett's famous educational plan for Chartism must be judged, a plan noble in its conception but making one difficulty the more for the Charter Association by raising an influentially supported rival movement.

In their prison Lovett and Collins had collaborated in the production of a book called *Chartism. A New Organisation of the People*, which appeared soon after their release in July 1840, but too late to be considered by the Manchester meeting that launched the National Charter Association. It was urged in this book that if all who had signed the National Petition would agree to pay a penny a week, the resultant yield of £256,600 annually would suffice to finance an enormous scheme of education, juvenile and adult, and would permit also the establishment of travelling libraries, the circulation of political tracts, and the employment of paid lecturers.[3] If, indeed, the Chartists had been capable of rising to the heights which Lovett here sketched for them, the speedy attainment of the Charter would have been assured. But a movement of hungry working-class Radicals, who demanded political powers in order to improve their economic lot, could not be converted into a vast and costly educational crusade.

[1] 39 Geo. III, c. 79; 57 Geo. III, c. 19.
[2] *Northern Star*, February 19, 1842, for Executive's Address announcing that 40,060 membership cards had been issued; but *Ibid.*, July 9th, for a list of 170 branches three months or more in arrear with their payments of 1d. per member per month to an Executive, now £50 in debt.
[3] Lovett and Collins, *Chartism*, pp. 54-5.

Chartism Survives

Besides launching the National Charter Association, the Manchester Chartist Conference of July 1840 had given a number of significant directions to Chartists. Political meetings were to be attended so that Chartist resolutions might be carried against their promoters; sobriety was to be maintained among the Chartist following; and at the election hustings Chartist candidates were to be carried at the show of hands, who though they did not proceed to the poll were yet to be regarded by Chartists as their representatives. The mention of sobriety is a reminder of the rapid growth of temperance propaganda at this period; that of the election hustings is a reminder that notions of setting up another Convention with the claims of a legitimate Parliament were far from ended. But it is the mention of meetings which is the most significant. It is evidence of Chartism's rivalry with the other great British secular agitation of the time, that conducted by middle-class Radicalism against the Corn Law. Under the auspices of the Anti-Corn-Law League eight hundred lectures were delivered during the course of the year; $1\frac{1}{4}$ million handbills and tracts were issued, and 330,000 copies of the fortnightly *Anti-Corn-Law Circular* were distributed.[1] Thanks also to the support of a very powerful newspaper Press, a remarkable petitioning power was being developed. Indeed, during the Parliamentary Session of 1840 Anti-Corn Law petitioners totalled 1,398,523,[2] and so considerably outnumbered those who had signed the Chartist National Petition. Moreover, but for the unceasing opposition of the Chartist leadership, Anti-Corn Law agitation might already have achieved even more conspicuous results.

The quarrel between Chartists and Leaguers was no doubt inevitable. When the manufacturers and merchants of the industrial areas offered to lead the populace against the Corn Laws, when they pointed to the disastrous effects on industry of a code, imposed by and for the politically dominant landlord caste, the Chartists had very relevant counter-matter to urge. To most Chartists the manufacturer and merchant was after all much more the industrial opponent than the political ally. Moreover, even as political ally against the territorial aristocracy, Chartists held the middle-class Radical to have played a most treacherous

---

[1] A. Prentice, *History of the Anti-Corn-Law League*, i, 173.
[2] *Companion to the British Almanac*, 1841, p. 224.

part. Though popular help had taken him to an influential place in Parliament from 1833, and to the domination of town councils and borough benches from 1835, he had, it was urged, repaid it in 1839 and 1840 by undertaking or permitting the wholesale repression of Chartism. If now he again professed sympathy for the people on the Corn Law question, it was only for the sake of increasing unrighteous profits. When bread was cheaper he hoped to be able to pay lower wages. To help the Anti-Corn-Law League, therefore, was to co-operate in another colossal middle-class cheat from which the working classes would not be allowed to benefit as they would from a Corn Law revision undertaken after the enactment of Universal Suffrage. Such was the dominating strain of Chartist oratory and journalism in regard to the League.

If Suffrage conditions bred one kind of Radical agitation and the Corn Law another, the connexion between State and Church unceasingly bred a third. In England the opposition to Church rates remained the principal local problem in many parts of the country, and two famous cases brought it into high relief. On May 2, 1840, the Anti-State Church majority at Braintree obtained from the Court of Queen's Bench the reversal of an ecclesiastical court's judgment that churchwardens might levy a rate which was opposed by a majority of the vestry.[1] At the end of July, again, Parliament was discussing repeatedly the Church rate case of John Thorogood, who as a result of ignoring a demand for 5s. 6d. of Church rate had already spent some eighteen months in Chelmsford Gaol.[2] But besides cases of this type there were other factors stimulating Dissenters to Radicalism. There was still, for example, a large Church party hopeful of obtaining financial support from the State for projects of church extension in the crowded new industrial areas which had inherited insufficient church provision from the past or none at all. During the Session of 1840, indeed, Parliament received 2,577 petitions with 216,176 signatures asking for State support for such church extension.[3] It was a movement which some Dissenters at least

[1] J. Irving, *Annals of Our Time*, p. 65. *Ibid.*, p. 388, for the Church party's renewed attempt of 1841, which caused litigation not ended until August 12, 1853. The final decision for the vestry majority made the collection of Church rates more then ever impossible in most parts of the country.
[2] Cf. *Hansard*, July 24th, 25th, and 30th (Commons).
[3] *Companion to the British Almanac*, 1841, p. 223. One considerable Parliamentary struggle of 1840 went on over the Weaver Churches Bill, which allowed the profits of the Weaver Navigation to be applied to church construction

considered threatening enough to warrant countering with 1,360 petitions bearing 202,586 signatures.

In the Commons the year 1840 found the Radical Parliamentary groups something less aggressive than before. The hope of effecting large constitutional changes which had animated some Radicals from 1833 to 1839 was now vanishing. Chartism had sundered them from the people, and without the heartiest popular support the prospect of their being able to force Conservatism to concessions was very remote. Moreover, politicians in all parties were tending to turn from the purely political disputes of the last decade to what Carlyle in a work of genius had dubbed the "Condition-of-England Question."[1] Thus the housing and sanitary conditions of the working classes were already beginning to attract some attention, thanks to Chadwick and Southwood Smith.[2] But till the politicians were provided with such a basis as Chadwick's Famous Reports of 1842, the possibility of preparing for remedial legislation was absent. It is but just, however, to admit that Radical politicians had already approached the public health question, though only from the open spaces standpoint. Both in 1837 and 1839, for example, they[3] had committed the Commons to the refusal of any Enclosure Bill which did not leave sufficient open space for the exercise and recreation of the neighbouring population.

Since the basis for sanitary legislation on behalf of the working classes had not yet been prepared in 1840, the principal gainers from the new "Condition-of-England" temper among public men were the already established types of humanitarianism. Thus when Lord Ashley appealed for a Child Employment Commission on August 4, 1840, he met with no opposition, though he pointed to the following trades as revealing harmful and sometimes scandalous conditions of child labour: earthenware, porcelain, hosiery, pin-making, needle-making, manufacture of arms, nail-making, card-setting, draw-boy weaving, ironworks, forges, iron foundries, glass trade, collieries, calico-printing, tobacco manufacture, button factories, bleaching, and paper mills.[4] On May 5,

---

(cf. *Hansard*, May 18th, June 26th, July 2nd, for Churchmen's victories on strongly contested divisions).
[1] T. Carlyle, *Chartism*, chapter 1.
[2] Cf. Slaney's speech in the Commons, February 25, 1840.
[3] Hume on March 9, 1837, D. W. Harvey on April 9, 1839.
[4] *Hansard*, lv, 1262.

1840, again, Molesworth made a remarkable and generally approved speech which called for the abolition of transportation, so that the possibilities of emigration to Australia might be fully developed, possibilities that many considered full of promise for portions of England's population.[1] Another political manifestation, not confined to one political camp, was the attempt to reduce the list of capital crimes. It was an attempt, ended by the Government on Third Reading, after the humanitarians had succeeded in Committee with the proposal to take from the dread list even rape and the firing of Queen's ships.[2] Finally, the Grammar Schools Act, permitting the partial diversion of grammar school revenues to the teaching of modern subjects, and the Infant Felons Act, allowing the courts to remove children who had come into serious conflict with the law into other guardianship than that of their parents, may be cited as useful specimens of a type of virtually non-contentious social legislation which was about to become more common.[3]

Of the contentious political legislation of 1840, Ireland as usual provided the principal subject-matter, and as usual the British Radicals were associated with their O'Connellite allies and the Whigs in resisting Tory attempts to "refuse justice to Ireland." On August 7, 1840, nevertheless, the Whig Ministers, after a weary struggle with the Peers going back to 1835, at length felt constrained to accept the conditions dictated by the Tories on the subject of Irish Municipal Reform. These included many features provocative of Irish resentment such as the confinement of the new municipal franchise to the householder rated at £10 or over, when in England and Scotland the smallest rating did not bring exclusion. Such a franchise, it was hoped, would give the Protestant communities in the towns an influence altogether disproportionate to their numbers and might even safeguard their old supremacy.

Even more likely to revive the Irish Radical cry for Repeal was another Tory legislative activity of 1840, the pressure to enact Lord Stanley's Irish Registration Bill.[4] The Irish Catholic majority was undoubtedly more effectively represented in Parliament than

---

[1] *Hansard*, liii, 1236. [2] *Ibid.*, July 15th, July 29th.
[3] The Acts are 3 & 4 Vict. c. 77, c. 90.
[4] *Companion to the British Almanac, 1841*, p. 223, gives the number of petitioners against this Bill as 415,788, and the number for it as 67,903.

Chartism Survives

the framers of the Irish Reform Bill had intended in 1832, and this was made possible by devices which had long been the subject of Tory attack.[1] The Tory Registration Bill, however, would have "purified" Irish elections by adopting a harsh registration system which would certainly have exposed poor Irish voters to risks of wholesale disfranchisement. As a check on the primary rulings of Revising Barristers, who might too often be suspect Whig nominees, it was to be made possible, for example, to drag the claimant to a vote to face an appeal before a Judge on Assize.[2] Radical voting strength was, of course, uniformly thrown against this Tory Bill, but its good strong party flavour served to rally Tories so extensively to its support that after a long and striking succession of victorious divisions Stanley promised its reintroduction in 1841.

Though they resisted the Registration Bill, virtually no British Radicals had any sympathy for the Repeal agitation whose revival was being accelerated by Tory conduct. Only too often the calamities of the Irish agrarian situation were ignored and a bland assumption made that Ireland's best hopes lay in as close a connexion with Britain as was possible. The one justification for British Radical blindness is that O'Connell himself, adept politician though he was, had virtually no remedy for Irish economic ills to propose save such heavy taxation of absentee landowners as should force them to come back and spend their money in Ireland.

---

[1] Leading eventually to the appointment of a Fictitious Votes Committee (Ireland), whose proceedings in 2562 pages far from exhausted the subject.

[2] Cf. *Familiar Epistle to Mr. Sergeant Jackson*, M.P. (1837), for Tory distrust of Whig-appointed Revising Barristers, pp. 64–71. For the O'Connellite view of the 1840 Bill see the pamphlet, *Report of the Committee appointed at a public meeting held in Dublin, March 19, 1840, to consider the effect of Lord Stanley's Irish Registration Bill.*

CHAPTER XIII

PEEL'S ADVENT TO POWER

"When I go down to the manufacturing districts I know that I shall be returning to a gloomy scene. I know that starvation is stalking through the land and that men are perishing for want of the merest necessaries of life. . . . When I see a disposition among you to trade in humanity I will not question your motives but this I will tell you, that if you would give force and grace to your professions of humanity it must not be confined to the negro at the antipodes, nor to the building of churches, nor to the extension of church establishments, nor to occasional visits to factories to talk sentiment over factory children . . . you must untax the people's bread."
    COBDEN *in the Commons, September 17, 1841.*

"I shall take the first opportunity in the House of avowing myself for the suffrage to every man. After all, I hardly entertain a hope that we shall effect our object by old and regular methods; accidents may aid us, but I do not see my way in the ordinary course of things to beating down the power of the aristocracy."
    Cobden, February 27, 1842. (MORLEY's "Life of Cobden," p. 229.)

> Dire oppression, Heaven decrees it,
> From our land shall soon be hurled;
> Mark the coming time and seize it—
> Every banner be unfurled!
> Spread the Charter!
> Spread the Charter through the world.
> *From the* "Shakespearean Chartist Hymn Book," *1842.*

"Look at the proprietor of great territorial possessions, encompassed with every advantage. . . . Turn from him to the professional man, who is engaged from morning till night, and from night almost till the break of day, in the exhausting occupations from which his precarious subsistence is derived; . . . do you, I say, declare whether it be just, whether it be fair, whether it be humane, that upon these men, and in the same proportion, the same impost should be infflicted. . . ."
    The Irish Whig-Radical SHEIL *arousing middle-class hostility to Pitt's Income Tax, in the Commons Debate of April 8, 1842.*

In the autumn of 1840 a plan was being prepared for bridging the gulf which the Chartism of 1839 had opened up between the Radicalism of the masses and that of the middle class.[1] A great meeting at Leeds was proposed where some of the most popular of the Radical politicians would once again declare their perfect democratic faith and pledge themselves to the cause of the people. Leeds, the home of the moderate *Leeds Mercury*, the more advanced *Leeds Times*, the Chartist *Northern Star*, and the Socialist *New Moral World*, was a very capital of all the Radicalisms. Moreover, in the Messrs. Marshall, the great mill-owners, Leeds possessed some Radical politicians who were willing to provide a Chairman and very large premises for a meeting, which it was hoped might turn the course of politics. O'Connell, Hume, Roebuck, Perronet Thompson, and Sharman Crawford were the nationally-known Radical figures who were picked upon to give a lead to the new movement. The great meeting was arranged for January 21, 1841, and would thus have the character of a united Radical demonstration prior to the opening of the Parliamentary Session of 1841. In 1840 the Anti-Corn Law Radicals at Manchester had carried out an even more ambitious demonstration on their special question which provided the promoters of the Leeds meeting with a model.[2]

The scheme hardly worked according to plan. Chartism had by now acquired an identity of its own, had its own leaderships, loyalties, and martyrs,[3] and was by no means ready to sink itself into a following of Radical Parliamentarians, however eminent. The summons of O'Connell to the meeting, again, was a cause of offence to Chartists, who could not forgive his assault on Combinations in 1838 and his damaging criticisms of Chartist activities in 1839. Accordingly, though numbers of influential Chartist leaders, including O'Connor, were still in prison, the Chartists were able to organise and use the Leeds demonstration

---

[1] *Leeds Times*, September 15, 1840.

[2] Cf. L. Apjohn, *Richard Cobden and the Free Traders*, pp. 95–6. The Manchester demonstrations of January 1840 had been housed in the specially erected "Pavilion" so lavishly noticed in the Press.

[3] *Return relating to Prisoners, etc., ordered to be printed on August 5, 1840*, shows 380 sentences in England and 63 in Wales; the prison treatment of Lovett, Collins, Vincent, and O'Connor, immured in local gaols supervised by unsympathetic J.P.s, had also been inconsiderate enough to excite ample Parliamentary attention.

for their party propaganda. Delegates from a large number of industrial centres were sent to Leeds, who, after holding Chartist demonstrations of their own, attended the Radical meeting with their following. Their representatives seem to have shared the speaking equally with the notabilities and to have had a much better reception. The notabilities certainly had no great success in persuading the meeting to accept a wide Household Suffrage as the greatest instalment of Universal Suffrage which could be practically agitated for the time.[1] A meeting, ending in hearty hooting for the absent O'Connell and enthusiastic cheering for O'Connor and the transported men of Newport, hardly served the purpose for which it had been called. The Radical Parliamentarians would not be able to intervene in the approaching Westminster debates with the assured authority which is born of the consciousness of widespread popular support.

When Parliament opened, Irish Registration once more became the leading subject of party contention. Stanley again brought forward a Bill whose effect would have been to strike large numbers of poorer Irish voters from among the enfranchised, and again British Radicals inevitably associated themselves with a resistance which in Ireland was nation-wide.[2] A Bill which proposed to guard the electoral registers from improper additions by decreasing the facilities for registration and increasing the facilities for challenge, was quite unacceptable even to the Whigs. Indeed, it needed not O'Connell's statistics to show that, in proportion to the population, the standard of Irish enfranchisement was already vastly inferior to that of Britain. Accordingly, in introducing Registration provisions of their own for Ireland, Ministers associated them with electoral proposals warmly supported by the O'Connellites and by the British Radicals. It seemed so certain, in fact, that the net effect of the Ministerial Bill would be to increase and not to reduce the number of voters that one Irish Tory spokesman affected to believe that Universal Suffrage was at hand. Though Ministers secured a Second Reading for their

[1] R. Gammage, *History of the Chartist Movement*, ed. 1894, pp. 190–2. The Parliamentary Radicals were ready to agitate the enfranchisement of all adult male householders and all heads of families.

[2] *Companion to the British Almanac, 1842*, p. 198. During the Parliamentary Session Repeal petitioners numbered 102,002; petitioners against the Stanley Bill, 358,245; and petitioners against the Stanley Bill and for the Government Bill proposed instead, 374,522. Many Irishmen may, perhaps, have signed both the latter types of petition.

Peel's Advent to Power

proposals by a division of 299 against 294, their plan of enfranchising the Irish £5 leaseholder for fourteen years was too bold for some of their Whig followers. Indeed, before the Ministers abandoned the Bill in Committee, it had become so altered that the Radicals were dividing against the Government in an effort to restore the Bill's original virtues.[1]

Another proposal of the Government's had, meanwhile, been meeting with tough resistance from a Radical section headed by Wakley and Fielden. It was the plan of extending for ten years the functioning of the hated New Poor Law machinery. As a philanthropic Tory section had also been antagonised by the harsh attitude towards pauperism adopted by the Poor Law Commission, the division lists will be found to contain an odd conjunction of Radical and Tory names.[2] Disraeli, for example, the most far-sighted and adventurous of the "Tory Radicals" in Parliament, increased the effect which he had already produced in 1839 by the adoption of a sympathetic attitude towards the Chartists. But Sessional events were to lead to the Government's abandonment of its Poor Law Bill also. The Chancellor's Budget statement of April 30th precipitated an absorbing taxation dispute which culminated in a General Election.

The financial statement given to the House was not a cheerful one. Despite the new imposts of 1840 the Whig Government had to report a deficit for the fourth successive year, and this time one for so comparatively large a sum as £1,842,000. Moreover, on the basis of existing taxation, the deficit for the ensuing year was estimated at no less than £2,421,000. If this were to be avoided, therefore, it would be necessary to take far-reaching steps, and those proposed by the Whig Chancellor were along the lines which had been consistently advanced for many years by Radical Free Traders. The timber and sugar duties, a Customs sphere with Colonial preferences huge enough to divert trade very widely from "natural channels," were to be readjusted to permit the foreigner a more "natural" share of the market, the home con-

---

[1] *Hansard*, Ap. 28, for Radical divisions against the Government.
[2] G. R. W. Baxter, *Book of the Bastilles*, pp. 548–9. The Government, however, carried the Second Reading on February 9th by 201–54. In Committee more dangerous opposition developed as some Radical elements, which accepted the need for the Poor Law Commission, questioned the necessity for conferring ten years' authority. On March 22nd an amendment to make the term five years won 135 votes against 174.

sumer a more competitive price, and the Exchequer a larger yield from the increased consumption. The details of the complementary scheme to increase the yield from the duties on Corn Import were announced a week later. In essence they were based on the assumption that the Tory Corn Law of 1828 unwisely reduced Corn Importation to over-small proportions, and so a part of the thesis of the Anti-Corn Law League Radicals was admitted. Ministers proposed, however, to institute not Free Trade in corn but trade on a basis of fixed duties of 8s., 5s., 4s. 6d., and 3s. 6d. on the quarter of wheat, rye, barley, and oats respectively.

Though accepted by the Anti-Corn Law League Radicals as better than the existing law, the Whig Corn Law proposals by no means satisfied them.[1] Indeed, they continued their propaganda with an energy which is revealed by their ability to raise the number of petitioners for Total Repeal from the 474,448 of May 14th to the 1,144,380 at which their Sessional total stood on June 15th.[2] The achievement is the more remarkable from the fact that Anti-Corn Law meetings were suffering from disturbances by the Chartists who had been conducting a petition campaign of their own for the release of Chartist prisoners and had gathered over 1,300,000 signatures.[3] Meanwhile, the Whigs, who had undergone two damaging defeats in Parliament, decided to appeal to the country on their new fiscal policy. Elated by the consciousness of having taken their boldest step forward since the Reform Bill, some Whig Ministers were not without hopes that it might bring back a portion of their long-lost popularity with the masses. Certainly the General Election was fought with greater spirit and harmony by Whigs, Whig-Radicals, and Radicals than would have seemed possible before. J. S. Mill, for example, editor of the Parliamentary Radicals' review, was completely won by the new Ministerial step. "A Radical," he wrote, "unless he be a Chartist, must be worse than mad if he does not go all lengths with them. . . . The moderate Radical Party and moderate Radical Ministry which I so much wished for, and of which I hoped Lord Durham would have made

---

[1] Cf. J. Morley, *Life of Cobden*, pp. 172-3, ed. 1903.
[2] J. Irving, *Annals of Our Time*, pp. 84-6.
[3] *Companion to the British Almanac*, 1842, p. 200. The matter was debated in the Commons on May 25th, and Duncombe obtained a division of 59 against 59 for an Address to the Crown. The Speaker gave his casting vote against it.

Peel's Advent to Power

himself the leader, were merely a party and a Ministry to do such things as these are doing, and in the same manner."[1]

The General Election of 1841, however, yielded Tory gains considerable enough to put the Whig Ministers into a minority of 91 on the assembly of a new Parliament. The conspicuous increase of corruption had told apparently mainly in a Tory direction and so had the Protestant fervour which had been assiduously invoked against O'Connell's influence and that of the Irish priests. The farming element, moreover, had objected to the proposed changes in the Corn Law, and middle-class country-town moderates had found it more and more impossible to avoid yielding to the decorous wooing of Peel. To crown all, the Chartist unenfranchised, after "showing hands" for their own candidates, had almost universally passed on to demonstrate against candidates who had supported the Whig Ministers guilty of imprisoning or transporting their leaders.[2]

The strength of Peel's position when he was called to office on August 30th has often been exaggerated. He had certainly obtained an apparently invincible working majority and was not the man to miss his chance of forming an effective if over-aristocratic Ministry. But his majority of members stood primarily for over-protected interests like the home "agricultural interest" and the colonial sugar and timber interests. On the other hand, the extraordinarily depressed exporting interests had virtually no representation at all either in the majority or in the Ministry. In these circumstances Peel's hands were dangerously tied in relation both to Corn Law revision and to the far-reaching Customs changes which had been recommended by the Hume Committee of 1840 and eagerly accepted by the commercial world.[3]

---

[1] *Life and Labours of Albany Fonblanque*, p. 32.
[2] Cf. *Life of Thomas Cooper*, 4th ed., p. 152 sqq., for events at the elections for Leicester City and the two county divisions. Thomas Cooper, the gifted new journalistic recruit to Chartism in Leicester, was the Chartist "show of hands" candidate in all three divisions. Of the Scottish elections the Whig *Journal of H. Cockburn* reports: "The Radicals and Chartist votes were courted wherever there was a contest by Tories, to whom these votes were almost invariably given; and in return, wherever the struggle was between a Radical and a Whig, the Tory votes almost always strengthened the former."
[3] Joseph Hume had taken the leadership of the Parliamentarians interested in carrying into effect the Report of the Import Duty Committee of 1840. It had been found that 94.5 per cent of the Customs revenue was produced by the duties on 17 classes of articles, and that trade on nearly nine hundred other

English Radicalism 1832-1852

The Corn Law situation, indeed, rendered Peel's position critical from the very first. On August 14th, for example, a short time before Peel took office, wheat had risen to the calamitous price of 86s. per quarter,[1] a price graver from the fact that distress and pauperism were still mounting fast.[2] On August 17th, again, Richard Cobden, Stockport's new Radical member and a power in the Anti-Corn Law League, had given an imposing display of the League's growing power by addressing a great conference of some 650 ministers of religion and enlisting their unanimous support for Corn Law Abolition.[3] As soon, therefore, as Peel took office, he was to find the Radicals dangerously insistent on immediate steps to meet the growing distress and prepared, in fact, to divide the House against the granting of supplies before the distress was inquired into.[4] But Peel with a party to prepare and to educate for large and unpalatable changes, could only hurry forward the long prorogation, necessary for the purpose, in a fashion which seemed for the time to play into the Radicals' hands. Yet before effecting the bitterly-criticised prorogation of October 1841,[5] Peel took some skilful steps to abate two of the greatest difficulties facing his Ministry. On September 20th he announced that the Government would not adopt Stanley's partisan Irish Registration Bill and thus he avoided the peril of an immediate Irish crisis. On September 27th again, his Home Secretary, in asking for a year's renewal of the New Poor Law machinery, was allowed to promise a complete re-examination of the whole Poor Law situation within that period.

The distressful winter of 1841-2 saw, nevertheless, the development of a most determined Anti-Corn-Law agitation by League Radicals, who had some striking concrete figures to use against the Government. On October 23rd, for example, a Leeds meeting heard of 4,752 local families containing 19,936 individuals with only 11¼d. per head per week to live on because only 3,780 were

---

classes could be unshackled without any appreciable revenue loss. The trading towns, led by Liverpool, opened a supporting agitation (cf. *Companion to the British Almanac*, 1842, p. 235).

[1] *Irving's Annals*, p. 89.
[2] Cf. G. R. Porter, *Progress of the Nation*, ed. 1851, p. 90, for the increase in pauperism. [3] Place Collection, Hendon, 1841, Press Cuttings.
[4] *Hansard*, September 17th. The Radicals were outvoted by 149 against 41.
[5] A protest was arranged even in Tamworth, Peel's constituency. The Tamworth petition against prorogation was treated in a way which led to hostile comment in Parliament (October 6th).

Peel's Advent to Power

employed.[1] On December 1st, again, the Lord Provost of Glasgow called a meeting to consider the problem of the complete destitution of 14,000 persons in the Paisley area.[2] Figures such as these could have been used with marked effect even by less skilful agitators than the men of the Anti-Corn Law League had now become. Their resourcefulness, indeed, was already presenting the Government with its major problem. Widespread meetings to demand the immediate convocation of Parliament; a commercial convention of the Midland counties at Derby on December 10th; an important Edinburgh Conference of Dissenting Ministers on January 11th; a remarkable Anti-Corn Law Bazaar at Manchester early in February; a gathering of 600 Anti-Corn Law deputies in London to coincide with the opening of Parliament[3]—all these represent when added to the normal Anti-Corn Law lecturing and pamphlet distribution a sum of activity threatening to dominate the political life of the country.

Many of the middle-class industrialists who contributed to the League, were, like Cobden, now the soul of its Executive Committee, professors of a political Radicalism advanced almost to the point of Chartism. In these circumstances it was inevitable that the possibility of making an entente with Chartism should have suggested itself to those anxious to enlist the full weight of the operative world in the Anti-Corn Law agitation. Cobden, after a little exploration, decided that the League had everything to lose and very little to gain from a Chartist alliance. "The Feargusites," he decided, had "no organisation, no membership, no pecuniary resources, no moral influence,"[4] and even Chartist leaders as reputable as Lovett and Collins were both unequipped and unwilling to throw a proper emphasis on Corn Law Repeal. But though he decided to keep the League itself free from the Chartist associations, which would have imperilled both its subscriptions and reputation while bringing no compensating

---

[1] *The Nonconformist*, October 27th, p. 488.
[2] Cf. *Greville Memoirs*, under November 30th and December 3rd, for Government discredit in this connexion caused by Wellington's refusal to see a Paisley deputation.
[3] J. Irving, *Annals of Our Times*, pp. 95–9. Cf. *Companion to the British Almanac, 1843*, p. 257, for the sessions of the Anti-Corn Law deputies, which were renewed later in the year.
[4] E. W. Watkin, *Alderman Cobden of Manchester*, pp. 82–3. Watkin at this time was organiser of the Manchester Operative Anti-Corn Law Association, and pressing for an understanding with the Chartists.

advantage, Cobden did not discourage a great League party from venturing as individuals into the remarkable movement of 1841–2 for reconciling the differences between the middle and working classes.[1]

The primary motivation for the new effort had come from the *Nonconformist London Weekly Newspaper*, which, thanks to vigorous Disestablishment and Anti-Corn Law writing, had quickly penetrated extensive circles of Radical Dissenters. During the autumn of 1841 Miall, its editor, wrote a special series of articles pressing the moral benefits which might be expected to accrue from the grant of full civic and suffrage equality to the working classes.[2] In attracting the enthusiasm of Alderman Joseph Sturge of Birmingham this series went far to alter the shape of Radical movements in 1842. Sturge, a wealthy and philanthropic corn-miller and Friend, had already proved his capacity for organising most effective agitation against slavery before 1833 and against the "Apprenticeship" of ex-slaves afterwards.[3] Now he was stimulated to opening the matter of "Complete Suffrage" among his fellow-deputies to a Manchester Anti-Corn Law Conference of November 17th. The result of the separate conference which ensued on the subject was the issue of a Declaration on the Suffrage[4] that was circulated throughout the country and most extensively signed. On the list of signatories in each town Complete Suffrage Unions were constructed during the opening months of 1842. By the end of March such Unions existed in the most important towns of England and Scotland.

Meanwhile Sturge used the opportunity afforded by the great

---

[1] A. Peckover, *Life of Joseph Sturge*, pp. 66–7.
[2] E.g. *Nonconformist*, November 10th, p. 521. "Education will not need then to be forced upon the poor. They will pant for education . . . and religion itself will appeal with much greater probability of success to the myriads who now suspect it to be an instrument of oppression. . . ."
[3] Henry Richard, *Memoirs of Joseph Sturge*.
[4] "Deeply impressed with conviction of the evils arising from class legislation, and of the sufferings thereby inflicted upon our industrious fellow-subjects, the undersigned affirm that a large majority of the people of this country are unjustly excluded from that fair, full, and free exercise of the elective franchise to which they are entitled by the great principle of Christian equity, and also by the British Constitution, for 'no subject of England can be constrained to pay any aids or taxes, even for the defence of the realm or the support of the Government, but such as are imposed by his own consent, or that of his representative in Parliament.'" See Blackstone's *Commentaries*, vol. i, book 1, chap. 1.

Peel's Advent to Power

League gathering at London in February 1842 to bring about an exchange of views between League notables and Lovett and Hetherington. Many other species of Chartist leadership were also interested in the reconciliation of middle-class and working-class Radicalism which was going forward. Arthur O'Neill and Collins in Birmingham; Vincent, Roberts, and Philp in Bath and the West; Richardson and Mills in Lancashire; Williams in Sunderland; Lowery and the Rev. Patrick Brewster in Scotland; and even the great Bronterre O'Brien himself may be quoted as examples.[1] Indeed, it is worthy of notice that when the preliminary Complete Suffrage Conference of April 1842 was gathered in Birmingham no fewer than nine of the Chartist Convention of 1839 were present.

It remained to clarify the terms of association between middle-class and working-class Radicalism in a definition of Complete Suffrage which both could accept. Though freely denounced by O'Connor and the *Northern Star*, the Chartists who were present at the Birmingham Conference had no intention of making any sacrifice of their principles. They were there to persuade the middle-class Radicals to accept the Charter as the basis of the Complete Suffrage agitation which they were designing. Lovett and O'Brien, indeed, were successful in forcing the adoption of all the "six points" enshrined in the Charter and only desisted from pressing the immediate acceptance of the Charter as a whole, when it became plain that even the most patient of the Complete Suffragists would rather abandon the Conference than give way. To some of the Complete Suffragists the Charter must have been a name most repulsively associated with ruffianism and mob disorder, while most of the rest probably felt that the last hope of making a successful Complete Suffrage agitation would have been removed if it were directly associated with the Charter.

Indeed, it seems plain that such members of the Conference as Sturge, Miall, and Bright felt that the Chartist pressure for all their "six points" had been politically unwise.[2] A cheerful face

---

[1] M. Hovell, *The Chartist Movement*, p. 245 sqq.
[2] *Nonconformist*, April 13th and 20th, for full reports of the Conference attended by over one hundred delegates, April 9th to 13th. It should be remembered that Complete Suffrage was under attack from the "moderate" Leaguers led by the very influential *Leeds Mercury* (cf. issue for February 19th). Some Chartist concession would, therefore, have been politic.

was put on the matter, however; it was agreed to arrange a larger and more representative Conference later and meanwhile to organise a National Complete Suffrage Union with all the organs of agitation. In fact the Complete Suffrage movement was formally brought under the notice of the House of Commons as early as April 21st, when the sympathetic Sharman Crawford, Radical member for Rochdale, moved for an inquiry into the reform of the repesentation. He obtained a division of 67 against 226, the Whigs abstaining.[1]

All this time the main Chartist body, guided by O'Connor and the *Northern Star*,[2] had persisted in regarding the Complete Suffrage movement as nothing but another piece of middle-class trickery to gain indispensable support against the Corn Laws. O'Connor's release from prison on August 30, 1841, had, it should be remembered, allowed him to undertake some remarkable touring, which had more than ever confirmed his hold on the Chartist rank and file.[3] In the National Charter Association, moreover, he had a party organisation of which he was still hopeful and which had adopted a second National Petition whose forwarding was to be the main Chartist business of 1842.[4] In these circumstances the Complete Suffrage movement more than ever took on the appearance of a treacherous diversion by the Leaguers, and the rally to it of considerable sections of Chartist leadership seemed little less than high treason in eager Chartist eyes. This rally, however, hardly seems to have affected the fortunes of the National Petition of 1842. Violent, ill-phrased, and vulgar though the document was,[5] impolitic though it had seemed to the point

[1] Hansard, lxii, 982.   [2] *Northern Star*, March 12th.
[3] Cf. *Northern Star*, November 13th, for O'Connor's own account of his Scottish visit. O'Connor's immense popularity at this stage is mirrored in the best-known of the Chartist songs, *The Lion of Freedom*. The first two verses run as follows:

> "The Lion of Freedom is come from his den;
> We'll rally around him, again and again;
> We'll crown him with laurel, our champion to be:
> O'Connor the patriot: for sweet Liberty!
>
> "The pride of the people—He's noble and brave—
> A terror to tyrants—a friend to the slave:
> The bright star of Freedom—the noblest of men:
> We'll rally around him again and again."

[4] *Ibid.*, October 16, 1841.
[5] Hansard, lxii, 1376. From a House of Commons standpoint its most objectionable passages were those treating of the incomes of the Queen, Prince Albert, the King of Hanover, and the Archbishop of Canterbury, and the

of driving Scotland to long-sustained mutiny,[1] it was to all appearances much more numerously signed than the National Petition of 1839.

Inevitably there is suspicion of the total 3,317,702 signatures which, it was claimed, were attached to the Petition.[2] Moreover, the small Convention, which had been brought together for three weeks on April 12, 1842, hardly contained elements parallel to those which had made the use of inflated numbers impossible in 1839. Yet it would appear from the proceedings of the House of Commons on May 3rd, when the Petition was debated, that members were not prepared to cast serious doubt upon the figures put forward by the Chartists. The floor of the House had, perhaps, been too effectively covered with petitioners' signature sheets on the previous day.[3]

The debate of May 3rd took place on Duncombe's motion that the petitioners "be heard by themselves or their counsel at the Bar of the House," and he closed an effective speech by giving an assurance that not more than six Chartists would address them nor occupy more than two days in doing so. The two classic speeches of the debate were, however, those of Macaulay and Roebuck. As a rhetorical effort Macaulay's speech must take high rank, but the intense vividness and conviction with which he was prepared to argue that the enactment of Universal Suffrage would be followed by universal confiscation of private property and the collapse of civilisation give the measure of its intellectual profundity. Civilisation is, after all, a very tenacious plant, and as to property, Roebuck, while refusing to concern himself with the "trashy doctrine"[4] of the "malignant and cowardly demagogue" who had drawn up the Petition, felt able to assure the

concluding demand "that your Honourable House ... do immediately without alteration, deduction, or addition, pass into law the document entitled the 'People's Charter.' "

[1] *Northern Star*, November 27th, for Scotland's dislike of the demand for Repeal of the Union and of the Poor Law Amendment Act, which did not concern the Scots; *Ibid.*, January 8th, for a Scottish demand for the inclusion of Corn Law Repeal; *Ibid.*, January 15th and 22nd, for trouble from a Glasgow Convention of sixty-three. [2] *Ibid.*, May 7, 1842.

[3] *Ibid.*, May 7, 1842. Its account of the Chartist procession to take the Petition to Parliament is exaggerated. It is plain, however, that the breaking up of the six-mile roll of signature sheets, wound on a frame too huge for admission to the House, had its effect.

[4] The Petition had complained of the interest payment on "what is called the national debt" and of "the existing monopolies of paper money, of machinery, of land, of the public Press—of the means of travelling and transit. ..."

English Radicalism 1832–1852

House that it was not regarded with hostility by the petitioners. If they were admitted within the pale of the Constitution and allowed thereby to secure for themselves the proceeds of their own labour, it would be the best guarantee of property. Finally a not unworthy debate[1] ended with a division of 49 Radical votes in favour of hearing the petitioners against 287 Tory and Whig votes cast in opposition to such a course.

The second National Petition was, therefore, dead and O'Connorism, though still recruiting new leaders and supporters,[2] was without a stimulating practical activity to which to set its hand. This time, of course, no "ulterior measures" had been drawn up, and there were no transportation and death sentences against which to protest. Before long, indeed, O'Connor himself deemed it wise to take a favourable opportunity of making some approach to the Complete Suffragists who were continuing their campaign. This he did by coming with other Chartist leaders to assist Sturge at a notable and long-drawn-out Nottingham by-election wherein Sturge's opponent was Walter of *The Times*, the greatest power in Anti-Poor Law Toryism.[3] Had Sturge not been narrowly defeated by the Tory use of bribery, very interesting developments among Anti-Corn Law politicians might have been possible. Business in the manufacturing districts had now fallen to catastrophic depths, and industrialists were watching with increasing anxiety the growth of foreign factories behind rising tariff walls[4] whose best justification had always been the British "Corn and Provision Laws."[5] Though marking a departure from the Tory tradition of well-nigh exclusive concern for the "landed interest," Peel's policy during the 1842 Session was altogether below what the League politicians considered necessary for safety. What Peel had done must now be examined.

The Prime Minister had opened with a modification of the 1828 Sliding Scale of Corn Import Duties which he succeeded in imposing upon a somewhat suspicious "landed interest" and in defending from the Moderate Fixed Duty projects of the

---

[1] *Hansard*, lxiii, 13–91.
[2] R. Gammage, *History of the Chartist Movement*, pp. 210–17.
[3] *Life of Thomas Cooper*, pp. 156–61. Walter was unseated for bribery.
[4] An American Bill for higher tariffs, which became law on August 30th, after two Presidential vetoes, was the particular anxiety of 1842.
[5] *Companion to the British Almanac, 1843*, gives the petitioning of 1842 as 810,301 for Repeal of the Corn and Provision Laws, 503,662 for Repeal of the Corn Laws, and 276,713 for Corn Law Repeal and Free Trade.

Peel's Advent to Power

Whigs and the Anti-Corn Law attacks of the Radicals.[1] Next had come the project of an Income Tax of sevenpence in the pound from incomes of over £150. Not only was it to be the Government's principal resource in restoring the deranged balance between national revenue and expenditure, but it was to yield a handsome surplus over and above what this demanded and thus allow an immediate if partial application of the Import Duties Report of 1840. A great step towards the Free Trade so long and so ardently preached by powerful Radical schools would have been taken when Peel carried through the Customs revision he was proposing in his third large-scale measure of the Session, the Customs Bill. In this measure 750 of the 1,200 articles on the Customs list were to be treated on a plan by which "the duties upon raw materials would only in a few instances exceed 5 per cent; and those on partially manufactured articles would never exceed 12 per cent; and on completed manufactures the maximum duty would not exceed 20 per cent."[2] The "agricultural interest" was, moreover, being required to forgo the complete prohibition which existed upon the entry into the British market of foreign cattle, bacon, cheese, butter, and vegetables and to accept moderate duties instead.

"The great Parliamentary middleman" had here taken up an almost impregnable position from which he dominated Parliament during the rest of the Session following on his remarkable Budget speech of March 11th. Yet his Government was, perhaps, more markedly successful in disarming or discrediting Tory critics in Parliament[3] than in preventing Radical assaults on the new Corn Law and Whig and Radical objections to the Income Tax from making their way in the country. The Whig objections to the Income Tax, which was far from popular even with Conservative shopkeepers and professional men, were grounded partly on the argument that the Whig plans for corn, sugar, and timber would make its levy unnecessary. From among the Radicals also a more desirable substitute for the

[1] *Hansard*, February 9th, for Peel's plan of duties which Cobden at once denounced as an "insult to a suffering nation." Next day more than seven hundred Anti-Corn Law deputies proclaimed it "a denial of the just demands of the people, and a selfish and unrighteous proposal, destructive of every interest in the country."   [2] *Ibid.*, March 11, lxi, 450-1.
[3] *Ibid.*, May 23rd, for the voting down by 380 against 113 of Tory objections to the Customs Bill conditions for the admission of live cattle, perhaps the greatest subject of nervousness to the "agricultural interest."

*

233

Income Tax was suggested in an inheritance duty on real estate.[1] It was Roebuck, however, who led the main Radical objection to Peel's Income Tax proposal. He contended in effect that incomes precarious because earned by personal exertion should pay at only half the rate imposed on those secure incomes which came from property.[2] A propertied House found the best of reasons for rejecting this proposal in a division of 258 against 112.

Meanwhile there was no sign that the Anti-Corn Law League had accepted Peel's modified Corn Law as a concession of any real moment. Industrial depression was still profound, pauper numbers were still rising, and the high price of corn meant bitter privation to independent labourer and pauper alike. The great distress of the time was made obvious to the "public" when in cities like Leicester and Glasgow[3] the unemployed formed themselves into begging parties traversing the town. The Anti-Corn Law deputies, who came together again in London towards the end of the Session, had very grim accounts to give of conditions in other stricken areas also, and measures were taken to see that Ministers and members of Parliament were not spared the information.[4] In the House of Commons too the Radicals assiduously agitated the question of distress as the closing stages of the Session approached in July.[5]

Ministers, however, professed to see signs that industrial conditions were brightening[6] and were hopeful, also, of the effects of what promised to be a remarkable harvest. No further concessions were, therefore, made and, indeed, the mere mention of them might have broken up the Tory party, a large section of which was already very fearful of what would happen when foreign meat and cattle began entering the home market under the Peel tariff.[7] On the Anti-Corn Law side, meanwhile, feelings steadily grew more strained and language of open or muffled

---

[1] *Hansard*, lxii, 231, 1139.   [2] *Ibid.*, April 29th.
[3] J. Irving, *Annals*, p. 111.
[4] A. Prentice, *History of the Anti-Corn Law League*, i, 337 sqq. Cf. H. Ashworth, *Recollections of Cobden and the League*, pp. 55 sqq.
[5] *Hansard*, July 1st–8th, 11th, 21st, 22nd.
[6] Peel, July 21st, *Hansard*, lxv, 463
[7] *Croker Papers*, ii, 383–4, for Peel's impatience; "I say to the agriculturists. . . . Your apprehensions about fat pigs and fat cattle from Hamburgh are absurd—when farmers were whimpering over fresh meat . . . from Hamburgh —at 3d. a pound, which meat costs 5½d. in the Hamburgh market, I said the alarm is groundless. . . ."

Peel's Advent to Power

menace became more common. One speaker at the Conference of Anti-Corn Law deputies spoke of setting up a Committee of Public Safety. Another, the Rev. W. Bayley of Sheffield, professing to report his constituents, said: "It was not words would move Parliament but Force they should have, if they did not change their system. He had heard of a gentleman who in private company said, that if a hundred persons cast lots among them, and the lot should fall upon him, he would take the lot to deprive Sir Robert Peel of his life."[1] In closing four weeks of eventful if fruitless activity, the deputies still displayed undiminished pugnacity. "Your own intelligence, your own virtue, your own energy must deliver you," they said in a final address to the nation. "We now separate, but are prepared to reassemble at such time and place as the Council in Manchester may determine. Providence has given plenty. A few men of wealth and title have opposed their mandate to the will of Heaven. Shall mortal man be more just than God?"[2]

All this time industrial depression and the accompanying wage reductions were leading to danger of extensive strikes. The Midland colliery districts and the Potteries, homes of a vigorous Chartism, had been centres of industrial trouble since the beginning of June,[3] and the trouble spread steadily. By August 12th, the day of the Parliamentary prorogation, a situation totally unexpected by Westminster politicians even of the most advanced Radical brand had been created. Large sections of the populace in different parts of the country were ready to strike "till the People's Charter became law of the land." Under the stimulus of all the agitation of the past few years, Chartist, Socialist,[4] and Anti-Corn Law, the urge to liberate their souls from the feeling of oppression and their bodies from ill-requited labour had taken possession of them. Even the Chartist leaders were taken by surprise.

---

[1] *Quarterly Review*, December 1842, lxxi, 280. The well-known article from which this is drawn is full of similar matter.
[2] L. Apjohn, *Richard Cobden and the Free Traders*, pp. 128-9.
[3] *Companion to the British Almanac, 1843*, p. 258.
[4] *The Social Reformers' Almanack, 1842*, pp. 56-8, shows some sixty branches. For their vigorous leadership, see G. J. Holyoake's *Sixty Years of An Agitator's Life*, i, 141-3.

CHAPTER XIV

THE AGITATIONS OF 1842 AND 1843

"Yesterday Oldham, Crompton, and the neighbourhood were visited by the mob Government, all the mills of every description were stopped—all the men were turned out, and as far as could be, persuaded to join the general body. This morning about ten o'clock they entered Rochdale from Oldham, turning out the hands at all the mills and workshops in their progress. At eleven they had passed through the town and were approaching our premises—some turned down to the Engine House and boilers to let the water out. They had a very large meeting close to the gates leading up to my house. I think 6,000 or 8,000 present. They said the population were starving, wages falling, and ruin before them—machinery robbed them . . . they would work no more until the wages of 1840 were guaranteed them with ten hours labour per day and no more. . . . They had several hundreds of women with them . . . they sang songs, Chartist hymns I believe. . . ."

John Bright to a correspondent, August 11, 1842. (From G. M. TREVELYAN'S *"Life of Bright," p. 80.)*

"*May 7, 1843.*

"Great excitement existing in Parliament and in the country respecting the Corn Laws. The truth is the subject is become a *fight* between the manufacturing and the agricultural interests, or rather with the Radicals to upset the Government of the country. The only hope left us is the firmness and excellent talent of Sir Robert Peel.

"*May 14th.*

"The landed interest alarmed relative to the importation of corn from Canada, perhaps without reason. The subject has been the effect of lowering Sir Robert Peel's popularity, and raising the expectations of the blustering Corn League."

DYOTT'S *"Diary."*

"Whereas meetings of large numbers of persons have been already held in different parts of Ireland, at several of which meetings, language of a seditious and inflammatory nature has been addressed to the persons there assembled, calculated and intended to excite disaffection in the minds of her Majesty's subjects, and to bring into hatred and contempt the government and constitution of the country. . . ."

Proclamation prohibiting O'Connell's "monster meeting" at Clontarf, October 1843.

THE short semi-revolutionary Charter strike of August 1842 represented a revolt of industrial workmen against the continuous fall of wages which had been going on unchecked during nearly five years of depression. There had been trouble in the Dudley coal and iron area as early as the beginning of June.[1] In the course of July much more widespread striking was taking place, and yeomanry, constabulary, and troops were "guarding property" extensively.[2] The striking appears to have been largely unplanned and to have been spread by the "turn out" method, a party from one colliery or iron works proceeding to the next and calling out their friends.

Thus the trouble spread from South Staffordshire to Warwickshire and North Staffordshire, where scarcity of coal brought out the Pottery population. The contagion passed on to Cheshire, Lancashire, and Yorkshire, and in Wales, on Tyneside, and in the Lanarkshire mining area of Scotland there were marked repercussions. To explain the trouble in Lanarkshire, where twenty thousand coal and iron miners came out at the beginning of August, Alison, the active historian-sheriff of the county, mentions not only communications from English Chartists, but also wages which in five years had fallen from between 5 and 6 shillings a day to 2s. 6d. or 2s. 9d. To show the men's determination he instances their leaders' open announcement that "they were not going to starve when the country was full of food," and alleges the speedy commencement of "depredations in the fields" over the whole extent of a district twenty miles in length by ten in breadth.[3]

The workmen's case was published in the *Northern Star* of August 13th. "The average wages of the miners of coal and iron," wrote the secretary of one of their unions, "vary from 1s. 7½d. to 2s. 5½d. for putting out one-third more labour than they did one year ago receive 4s. per day for; and at the same time could in many instances get their money when earned, while now we go to our masters' store and take our labour in goods; or if the employer had not a store, he, according to his laws, makes us

---

[1] *Companion to the British Almanac, 1843*, p. 259.
[2] *The Times*, July 19th, 20th. For "great military preparations" at West Bromwich on August 1st, see Graham, the Home Secretary, in *Peel Papers*, Add. MSS. 40449, f. 58.
[3] A. Alison, *Life and Writings*, pp. 486-7

pay one penny for each shilling lifted before per day."[1] It may be surmised, indeed, that truck and wage grievances of the kind here instanced contributed infinitely more to making the mining community the centre of discontent than those conditions of child and woman employment underground which had just allowed Ashley to shock Parliament into passing the Mines Act.

Trouble in the cotton area spread in a manner curiously parallel to that in the mining areas. By refusing to accept a wage reduction on August 5th, the men of Stalybridge made a beginning. On August 7th a large meeting of Lancashire and Cheshire operatives at Mottram Moor resolved on beginning a "national turn out" next day, which should not be ended till the Charter, "the only guarantee . . . for wages," became the law of the land. On August 8th, therefore, the willing operatives of Ashton, Dukinfield, Hyde, and Newton were turned out and on the ninth a vast "turn out" procession advanced on Manchester.[2] As the military there were used with scrupulous constitutional correctitude, virtually all the factories in the cotton capital were soon brought to a standstill. By August 12th the movement had spread much farther, and it was found possible to assemble a large meeting of trade delegates in Manchester who called upon the "people of all trades and callings forthwith to cease work" until the Charter became the law of the land. Next day Burnley was turned out, and there was a grave affray between military and labourers in Preston, where the attempt to stop some factories still running led to the soldiers firing upon the crowd and causing four deaths and many injuries.[3]

By August 14th the news from Manchester was having an electric effect on other industrial areas, especially the West Riding and the Potteries. Indeed, a large Bradford meeting prepared that Sunday for the Yorkshire "turn outs" which began the next day,[4] and at Hanley the gifted Thomas Cooper's eloquence was poured out in a torrent which excited some of his hearers

---

[1] *Northern Star*, August 13, 1842.
[2] *State Trials, 1839-43*, iv, 942 sqq. This is a much safer source than *The Times* or the *Northern Star*, though it involves some balancing of witnesses one against the other in the famous trial of Feargus O'Connor and Fifty-eight Others in 1843.   [3] *Ibid.*, 1000 sqq.
[4] F. Peel, *Risings of the Luddites, Chartists, and Plugdrawers*, p. 341. Because the Chartist strikers of 1842 often drew the plugs of the factory boilers in order to make sure that "turned out" mills would not be promptly restarted, the strike was known in the North as the "Plug Plot."

The Agitations of 1842 and 1843

to meditate the serious arson which soon followed.[1] Cooper was on his way from the Leicester which he had so thoroughly agitated to attend a Chartist Conference at Manchester. It had been arranged before the outbreak of the troubles and was designed to allow the Executive of the National Charter Association to exchange views with a number of delegates from the "localities." The delegates arriving in Manchester on August 16th were, however, to find that the members of the Executive, led by the forceful M'Douall, had been fired by the late events to prepare for a very bold course. A great industrial area was at a standstill all around them, and the trouble was still spreading. August 15th had brought wild scenes not only in the Potteries but in Blackburn, where there had been numerous arrests. On August 16th, again, there was turn out trouble at Stockport and at Cleckheaton in the Yorkshire woollen area. That there might be an opportunity here for Chartist leadership of resource was obvious even though the Government had been able to use the new railways to draft troops up quickly from the South.

The forty to fifty Chartist leaders who assembled in Scholefield's Chapel on August 17th contained only a small minority reluctant to take any risk at all in the attempt to win the Chartist programme by utilising the strike situation.[2] On the other hand, there were not many prepared to assume the risks of trying to stimulate the strikers into revolution. M'Douall, chief of the Executive of the National Charter Association, was one of these, as the firebrand manifesto of his drafting whose placarding was about to be attempted by the Executive amply and plainly shows. But the bulk of the Chartist Conference was not prepared to go as far as M'Douall. They did, however, adopt an address to the nation which recommended the continuance and extension of the strike until the Charter was conceded and which indicated the Executive of the National Charter Association as the proper Chartist organ of leadership. It would appear that according to the law the first overt act of violence which could be connected with their address rendered the Chartist leaders liable to the penalties of treason.[3]

[1] *Life of Thomas Cooper*, p. 187 sqq.
[2] *State Trials, 1839–43*, iv, 1037, gives the voting at 30–6.
[3] Add. MSS. 40447, f. 68, gives Graham's opinion to this effect on a less objectionable address previously issued by the Manchester Trades' Conference. Graham was Home Secretary.

It is the Executive's manifesto, however, which must be quoted in order to illustrate the revolutionary potentialities of the situation.

"Englishmen," ran one section,[1] "the blood of your brothers reddens the streets of Preston and Blackburn, and the murderers thirst for more. Be firm, be courageous, be men! Peace, law, and order have prevailed on our side; let them be revered until your brethren in Scotland, Wales and Ireland are informed of your resolution; and when a universal holiday prevails, which will be the case in eight days, then of what use will bayonets be against public opinion? . . . Intelligence has reached us of the wide spreading of the strike; and now within fifty miles of Manchester every engine is still save the miller's useful wheels and the friendly sickle in the fields.

"Countrymen and brothers, centuries may roll on, as they have fleeted past, before such universal action may again be displayed. . . . Our machinery is all arranged, and your cause will in three days be impelled onward by all the intellect we can summon to its aid. . . . All officers of the Association are called upon to aid and assist in the peaceful extension of the movement, and to forward all monies for the use of the delegates who may be expressed over the country. Strengthen our hands at this crisis; support your leaders; rally round our sacred cause; and leave the decision to the God of justice and of battle."

The perusal of such passages makes it easier to understand the temper in which "Committees of Public Safety" had been erected in some areas before whom appeared applicants for permission to perform "indispensable" tasks.[2]

Though the authorities immediately declared war upon the Executive's manifesto and its authors, the document did not remain without effect, possibly because Chartists took the opportunity of reading it in the newspapers. On the night of August 19th, for example, the Metropolitan Police dispersed a large Chartist meeting at Lincoln's Inn Fields[3] and on the 21st the Home Office was expecting "an expiring effort" on the morrow with "meetings on a large scale" at Barnsley, Birmingham, and around the Metropolis.[4] Large numbers of strikers did not, in fact, give up hope till the end of August; some did not return to factory and pit until September; and in Lanarkshire a stubborn struggle went on until March 1843.[5] It is, nevertheless, plain enough that by the end of August even the stalwarts had virtually

---

[1] *The Times*, August 19th; *State Trials, 1839–43*, iv, 948–50.
[2] *State Trials, op. cit.*, 956-7.   [3] Add. MSS. 40447, f. 80.
[4] *Ibid.*, f. 86.   [5] A. Alison, *Life and Writings*, i, 489–99

The Agitations of 1842 and 1843

dropped the demand for the Charter and were concentrating on immediate wage grievances. The extensive and widespread arrests[1] which had taken place could not but count for much; the great concentration of official force in the shape of troops, yeomanry, police, and special constables for more; and the huge tide of newspaper hostility possibly for most. The newspaper situation, indeed, was during a short period of reaction from the Chartist alarms an uncomfortable one for Radicalism of every kind. The Tory Press led by *The Times* blamed the Anti-Corn Law Radicals for the long inflammatory agitation which, it was claimed, had created a revolutionary temper in the factory districts; the Radical Press blamed the recklessness of O'Connor and his satellites; and the *Northern Star* blamed M'Douall.[2] Had distress and misery not been very real, both the Anti-Corn Law League and O'Connor[3] might have become dangerously discredited with their followings.

In 1842 as in 1839 the uprising of the "millions" was followed by the wholesale bludgeonings of the law. Apart from Assize trials there were Special Commissions for Staffordshire, Cheshire, and Lancashire with numerous cases to try. In Staffordshire, where there had been some arson, no fewer than fifty-four transportation sentences were awarded, and in Cheshire and Lancashire, Lord Abinger, a judicial survival from the High Tory days before 1830, conducted proceedings in a way which reinvigorated all the Radicalisms and moved even Whiggery to fury.

By March 1843, when further batches of delayed Chartist trials were taking place at the Assizes, "public sentiment" was once more dominated by the acute distress phenomena of the time in a fashion which gave Chartist prisoners every facility for putting their case. At Lancaster, where O'Connor and fifty-eight others were charged in one "Monster Indictment" for their part in the Charter strike proceedings of the preceding August, O'Connor made an effective defence well calculated to please

---

[1] *Northern Star*, September 10th, for 377 rioting prosecutions at the Yorkshire Assizes; *Ibid*., October 15th, for 274 prisoners brought before the Staffordshire Commission as presumably the worst among a total of some 800 who had been brought to Stafford Gaol (*Life of Thomas Cooper*, p. 214). One careful estimate of the total arrests is 1,500, with some 800 quickly, released or dealt with by magistrates, and 710 sent to face judges (M. Beer, *History of British Socialism*, ii, 151). [2] *Northern Star*, August 27th.
[3] *Ibid*., September 3rd, for O'Connor on the defensive against O'Brien's *British Statesman*.

his Chartist following, and a number of other Chartist leaders also spoke ably. But the most effective speech of the Assize seems to have been that of Richard Pilling,[1] the plain Stalybridge operative whose energetic agitation had begun the Cotton area strike. Pilling's story of wage-reductions, privations, distress, and death reduced the court to tears, and his whole case furnishes but one instance the more of the restless operative ability for which the existing system had no use and which gave Chartism much of its power. The "Monster Indictment" at Lancaster ended, indeed, in little more serious than verdicts of guilty of exciting dissatisfaction and persuading men to leave work, and such doubts emerged as to whether this was a punishable offence that O'Connor was able to escape imprisonment.[2] Another notable Chartist orator was less fortunate, Thomas Cooper, whose seditious speeches were held to have contributed to the Staffordshire arson. Though he eventually received a two years' sentence, he had the satisfaction of throwing the whole Oxford Circuit out of gear by prolonging his trial for ten days, and he followed this up by haranguing the Court of Queen's Bench for eight hours in London.[3]

While awaiting their trials O'Connor and Cooper had taken part in a second Complete Suffrage Conference with the middle-class Radicals. Very complete preparations had been made to bring together a really authoritative Conference which might produce instant results on public opinion.[4] Each town had been allotted a specific number of delegates, and it had been decided on Lovett's suggestion to do the unenfranchised justice by dividing representation equally among them and the Parliamentary voters gathered in separate meetings.[5] It seems certain that if the 374 delegates who assembled on the morning of December 27, 1842, at the Mechanics' Institute, Birmingham, had been able unitedly to recommend a specific policy, a very marked political effect could have been achieved. The "Sturgeites," indeed, had prepared a "New Bill of Rights" of ninety-nine

[1] *State Trials, 1839-43*, iv, 1097 sqq.
[2] Cf. R. Gammage, *History of the Chartist Movement*, p. 239.
[3] *Ibid.*, p. 240.
[4] Cf. *Morning Advertiser*, September 14th; *Edinburgh Chronicle*, October 1st; *Wiltshire Independent*, October 27th, etc.
[5] *British Statesman*, September 17th. Towns under 5,000 were allowed two representatives; towns over 5,000, four; and London, Edinburgh, Birmingham, Manchester, Glasgow, and Liverpool, six.

The Agitations of 1842 and 1843

clauses and embodying the six Chartist points.[1] This they hoped would be adopted by the Conference and become the common Radical platform of the future. It could be urged in support of such a course that the "New Bill of Rights" was at once more suitably drafted for purposes of Parliamentary enactment than the Charter and less open to the objections of the timid who remembered that the latter document had twice been the centre of popular disorder on a very large scale.

Unfortunately for the prospects of Radicalism in the ensuing years, the middle-class Radicals failed to move the Chartists from their whole-hearted loyalty to the People's Charter.[2] That the Charter must be the basis of any Complete Suffrage alliance was the demand alike of Lovett and O'Connor, a demand which was carried by 193 votes against 94 at the end of the second day of the Conference. As a result of the voting, the Conference split into two ineffective sections meeting in different places and occupied with different activities. The Chartist section, however, was itself disunited. First the Lovett party retired, and then fierce and unworthy wrangling broke out between O'Connor and the Chartist Executive, wrangling which spelt the doom of the National Charter Association in its existing shape.[3] In the reconstruction which was speedily being planned, O'Connor was to become increasingly attracted by the notion of giving Chartism a land-settlement basis borrowed from the Socialists.[4] But paid-up Chartist membership was never again what it had been in 1842.

What makes the disastrous Radical cleavages narrated above the more eventful is the fact that the economic situation in the winter of 1842-3 was desperate enough to have given a united Radicalism considerable chances. Poverty, unemployment, and distress were still increasing to an extent which was, perhaps, not fully revealed till the great debate which Lord Howick opened soon after Parliament had reassembled in February 1843. For

---

[1] *The Nonconformist*, December 31st, pp. 880 sqq.
[2] Henry Vincent was the only prominent Chartist who joined the Sturgeites. For the whole proceedings, see *The Nonconformist*, December 31st, and *These Eighty Years*, by Henry Solly, i, 406 sqq.
[3] Cf. *Life of Thomas Cooper*, pp. 227-8.
[4] "Home colonisation" propaganda by the Socialists had been penetrating Chartism and Trade Unionism since 1840. Hobson, himself a Socialist, had already published for O'Connor a pamphlet, *The Land*, with immense plans for reclaiming waste lands and settling unemployed, etc.

five nights in succession[1] the gloomiest information was poured out as to the state of the industrial areas, and members representing them joined Lord Howick in calling for an immediate inquiry into the contribution which the Corn Law might be making to the restriction of Britain's industrial opportunities. The debate culminated in a furious passage between Cobden and Peel some hours before it ended.[2] Peel's nerves were, perhaps, overwrought by the assassination of a private secretary who less than a month before had fallen to a bullet intended for his chief. He certainly contrived to suggest amid stormy Tory cheering that Cobden's oratory had made him a mark for assassins. In the event he was to find that Cobden was no more to be deprived of importance in the House by such devices than the Anti-Corn Law League had been deprived of importance in the country by Tory charges that its agitation had provoked the troubles of August 1842.[3]

Throughout the Session of 1843, indeed, Peel's Government was in no enviable situation. The Anti-Corn Law League had mobilised practically the entire manufacturing and mercantile middle-class against its fiscal policy, and in returning John Bright for Durham City, a cathedral and county town much under the "influence" of the Ultra-Tory Marquess of Londonderry,[4] the Leaguers were to show that their plans for converting other areas than the manufacturing districts proper were not to be disregarded. The English pauper total, too, which on Lady Day, 1842, was already at the stupendous figure of 1,427,187, had by Lady Day, 1843, mounted still further to 1,539,490.[5] In Scotland, moreover, the destitution problem was of a gravity to give the Government every motive to press forward its preparations for enacting an effective Scottish Poor Law.[6]

[1] *Hansard*, February 13–February 17th.
[2] *John Bull*, February 20, 1843, p. 100.
[3] Add. MSS. 40447, f. 344, for Home Office stimulation of such charges in order to prevent subscriptions to the League's £50,000 Fund, announced in October 1842.   [4] *Durham Chronicle*, July 21, 28.
[5] G. R. Porter, *Progress of the Nation*, p. 90.
[6] "Of all the features of modern society in Britain, none is so peculiar or frightful as the hordes of strong poor, always liable to be thrown out of employment by stagnation of trade. There have been above ten thousand of them in Paisley for more than a year; and a similar cloud darkens every considerable town in Scotland.... The alarming circumstance in their condition is that they have discovered that their number is their force. Instead of resorting to places less distressed, and there getting themselves absorbed obscurely into the ordinary population, they prefer towns, where the magnitude of the evil has terrified the authorities, and produced compulsory subscriptions and earnest

The Agitations of 1842 and 1843

Ireland, again, was causing ever-increasing anxiety throughout the Session. There O'Connell had launched a Repeal campaign to which the response was so great that military repression was being prepared almost from the very first. O'Connell's campaign, it should be remembered, was not merely for the Repeal of the Union and the assembly of an Irish Parliament. Abolition of Tithe, Fixity of Tenure, Encouragement of Irish Industry, Better Poor Relief, Complete Suffrage, and Ballot[1] made up the sum of a programme at once Radical, nationalist, and calculated to alarm all the "interests" on both sides of St. George's Channel to the last degree.

The "respectable classes" were, perhaps, more puzzled by the "Rebecca Riots" in Wales than by the vast Repeal meetings which were soon being reported from Ireland. Irish events had long been explained to a large portion of the respectable as merely illustrating the malevolence of O'Connell and the priests. The gathering of mobs of disguised farmers and pitmen to destroy tollgates on the turnpike roads in Wales was more mysterious.[2] In the distressed mining and iron-working areas there was probably a good deal of Chartism in the motivation of the rioters.[3] But as the riots had begun in the non-industrial sections of Carmarthenshire and Pembrokeshire and remained to the end under the apparent guidance of farmers, its main causation must be sought elsewhere than in Chartism. The proclaimed grievances of the rioters were tollgates, tithes, the New Poor Law, Church Rates, and high rents.[4]

In England and Scotland, meanwhile, the necessarily stiff handling which even the best-intentioned Tory Government brought to State and Church problems made very grave trouble. In the Scottish Church question Aberdeen, Peel's Foreign Secre-

---

applications to Government.... Scarcely one of them enlists.... Hitherto they have behaved peaceably, but they are excellent materials for the demagogue" (*Journal of H. Cockburn*, under February 6, 1843).
[1] *Companion to the British Almanac*, 1844, p. 245. [2] *Ibid.*, pp. 246–51.
[3] W. J. Linton, *Memoir of James Watson*, p. 63, has a curious note to the effect that the "instigator and undiscovered leader" of the Rebecca rioting was the Carmarthen lawyer, Hugh Williams, whose Chartist activities as Secretary of the Working Men's Association had worried the Swansea authorities in 1839 (H.O. 40, 46). It is worth adding that Williams was Cobden's brother-in-law.
[4] *Illustrated London News*, June 24, 1843, p. 432. There are indications in the evidence that it would not be altogether fanciful to see the first stirrings of the later Welsh Radical Nationalism in the movement

tary and the Cabinet's authority, greatly misjudged the intensity of the anti-Erastian feeling which had arisen in the long ten years' struggle against lay patronage. As a result a great disruption took place, and a very powerful Free Church of Scotland was founded with a moral authority altogether superior to that of the State Church rump.[1] The tragedy was the greater from the Tory point of view because the Scottish disruption vastly strengthened the forces making for Disestablishment in all three kingdoms. Yet only a few years before the very leaders of the Free Church had markedly assisted in the revival of Scottish Toryism by their obvious dislike of Whigs who were Latitudinarians and Radicals who were worse.

In England it was Sir James Graham who miscalculated. In 1842 he had shown considerable adroitness in piloting a Bill through Parliament conferring a new five years' lease of life upon the Poor Law Commission.[2] The renewal for five years instead of the ten proposed by the previous Government was itself a concession, and there were such other significantly appeasing clauses as those limiting the number of Assistant Commissioners to nine and allowing the subdivision of large Union areas to facilitate the application for and the administration of Poor Relief. In his proposals for new Factory Legislation, legislation avowedly educational rather than industrial, Graham showed much less discretion. The Children's Employment and the Midland Mining Commissions had, it is true, busily accumulated material in which clergymen, aided sometimes by police officers, magistrates, medical men, and others, had been allowed to compile a terrifying catalogue of the ignorance and debauchery often to be found among working children and the frequent maltreatment to which they were exposed. But a modern eye scanning the Reports of these Commissions or such a notable Parliamentary speech grounded on them as Lord Ashley's of February 28, 1843,[3] sees immediate reason to suspect an unconscious bias towards the omission of relieving touches capable of weakening the impulse

---

[1] W. Hanna, *Memoirs of Thomas Chalmers*, iv, 250 sqq., for the Free Church view. The *Journal of H. Cockburn (1831–1854)* is throughout peculiarly enlightening on Scottish Church questions.
[2] Nicholls, *History of the English Poor Laws*, ii, 377. The Act is 5 & 6 Vict. c. 57.
[3] *Parl. Papers, 1842*, xv, and *1843*, xiii; *Speeches of Earl of Shaftesbury, 1838–67*, pp. 62–86.

The Agitations of 1842 and 1843

towards remedial legislation of a Tory cast. "The soldier and the policeman had done their duty," said the Home Secretary, promising educational measures wherein the place of the Established Church loomed dangerously large from the first, "and the time was come when the moral instructor must go forth."[1] Inevitably Tories tended to assume that the factory districts were Chartist because they lacked adequate provision for that "moral and religious education" which conquered the "improvidence and immorality" to which Chartist misery was ascribed.

From the beginning there were protests from the factory districts against education propaganda which was based on unfair depreciation of their religious and school equipment and unfair exaggeration of their "immorality" in order to accord with Tory prejudices. Indeed, the suspicion was soon expressed that the Tory bias against districts, whose religious and educational equipment could be proved superior to that of the rest of the country taken as a whole,[2] was due to the fact that that equipment was for the greater part in Dissenting hands. Dissenters, indeed, suspected from the first that the Anglican and Tory zeal for factory district education under State auspices concealed sectarian ambitions. Yet had the Tory Government been able to devise an education plan not patently increasing Church influence to a high degree, the factory youth of the country might have been quickly and compulsorily submitted to a "half-time" moral and religious education designed to guard them from future vice, drunkenness, blasphemy, and desire to listen to Chartist and Socialist oratory. But Graham's proposals for organising the rate-supported half-time education of the child worker, so far from being acceptable to the Dissenters, aroused them to the bitterest denunciation of its Church partisanship.

How Graham could have believed that a scheme would be accepted by the Dissenters, which put the suggested rate-aided schools each under a Board of seven trustees with the clergyman as Chairman and his two churchwardens and four nominees of the J.P.s as his co-members, passes comprehension. Nor is it

---

[1] *Illustrated London News*, March 4, 1843, p. 148.
[2] *The Social, Educational, and Religious State of the Manufacturing Districts*, by Edward Baines, Jr., Editor of the mighty *Leeds Mercury*, contains the most detailed evidence on the point, and has been used as the principal source for the Dissenting views given above. W. Cooke Taylor, *Notes of a Tour in the Manufacturing Districts of Lancashire* (1842), tends to confirm Baines's views.

easier to understand how he could have believed that there would be a general welcome for such other proposals as giving the Bishop the approval of the teachers and assistants appointed by the trustees, making the Church Catechism and doctrines a principal subject of instruction (though with leave to Dissenters to stay away) and directing schools to church on Sunday morning and to the study of Church doctrines later in the day. At a time when the Established Church of Scotland was breaking up, and when in England Dissenters' dislike of the Establishment was reinforced by the growth of Puseyite practices which they detested, a new Church impost seemed to be about to be clapped on the country for the purpose of putting all factory children into schools under Anglican control.[1] The measure of Dissenting indignation is given by the speed with which 13,369 hostile petitions were gathered bearing 2,068,059 signatures. Even when Graham had amended his Bill, the thoroughly roused Dissenters pronounced its doom by sending 11,839 more hostile petitions with 1,920,574 signatures.[2] In the excitement Roebuck again ventured to raise the flag of secular education and on May 18th obtained a division of 60 against 156.[3] A week later a Bill abolishing Anglican oaths and subscriptions at Oxford and Cambridge won 105 votes against 175. Quite plainly Graham had stirred up a hornets' nest and seriously weakened the Government. He was less likely than ever to take those thorough measures against the sale of "blasphemous prints and publications" for which the religious zealots were calling indignantly and towards which he had made some approaches.[4]

Yet blessed by a second good harvest in 1843 and profiting, moreover, from the undoubted beginnings of a revival of industry, the Peel Government began to find itself able to take up a more authoritative attitude. In Ireland it certainly brought O'Connell's

---

[1] The fury of the Dissenting opposition may best be studied in the most widely circulated of the Dissenting opposition pamphlets, *Twenty Reasons for Petitioning against and otherwise opposing the Educational Clauses (50–77, 92–4) of the Factories Bill*, by the Rev. W. Thorn, Winchester. It feared not to allege that nine thousand of the twelve thousand parochial priests were Puseyites, and that the Government was intent on "injuring and crushing nonconformity."
[2] Baines, *op. cit.*, p. 76.   [3] *Hansard*, lxix, 564.
[4] That impassioned, well-written, and widely circulated volume *Perils of the Nations* (1843) contains such a demand as part of its remarkable attempt to evangelicise State and Church Toryism. *Illustrated London News*, January 7, 1843, reports that the Metropolitan Police were not only to open a campaign against booksellers, but were also to examine the libraries of the Socialist institutions.

The Agitations of 1842 and 1843

dangerous series of monster Repeal meetings to an end early in October[1] and went on further to order the prosecution of the great demagogue. Shortly afterwards it announced a Royal Commission to inquire into Irish land-tenure and proved that it was disposed to pry deeper into the realities of the Irish situation than had been the wont of the Tory Governments of the past. But Dublin Castle's prejudiced blunderings[2] in arranging O'Connell's lamentably improper trial undid much of the apparent good which the previous display of tempered British firmness was held to have effected. A jury from which all Catholics had been excluded might, after listening to a Chief Justice's unjudicial charge, return a verdict of guilty on all counts on February 12, 1844. But this could not prevent dangerous tension from arising once more amongst aggrieved Catholics nor Hume from leading the Radical cheering which greeted O'Connell's arrival for the Session of 1844.[3] O'Connell was appealing to the House of Lords, and meanwhile his actual presence in the Commons lent an added piquancy to the great nine days' debate on Ireland which was the leading feature of the first part of the Session.

The debate on Ireland was a remarkable affair, and as the subject allowed Whig ex-Ministers to talk in quite Radical tones there was more unanimity on the Opposition side of the House than there was wont to be on other topics. On the New Poor Law and on Factory Hours[4] extreme popular Radicals like Duncombe and Sharman Crawford[5] usually found themselves opposed to

[1] *Annual Register*, 1843, History, p. 234.
[2] *Illustrated London News*, January 20, 1844.
[3] *Ibid.*, February 17th, p. 99.
[4] 1844 was the Session when Lord Ashley's Ten Hours amendments to the Government Factories Bill were a principal political topic. Bright's speech of March 15th (*Hansard*, lxxiii, 1132 sqq.) contains the strongest presentation of the Radical manufacturers' objection to philanthropic Tories attempting to impose humanitarian legislation on their factories while leaving Corn and Sugar duties untouched, and rural districts under Tory landlords in a worse condition of distress than the manufacturing areas. A great part of Ashley's support, it should be remembered, came from Tories anxious for a counter-attack on the manufacturers who were supporting the League.
[5] These two politicians were acting in Parliament, the one as the representative of Chartism and the other as the representative of the Complete Suffrage Association. In the autumn of 1843 Duncombe had even gone on an agitating tour with O'Connor which appears to have helped the reconstituted National Charter Association to increase its membership considerably, if only temporarily (Gammage, pp. 251–2). On the other hand, the Complete Suffrage Association had just made its last important effort to influence the course of politics by calling a metropolitan meeting on January 31, 1844, to consider the possibility of forming a Parliamentary group round Sharman Crawford which

brother-Radicals ready for Universal Suffrage but not for waste of ratepayers' money or bad "Political Economy." On the Corn Law, again, the whole of the Radicals were united but were sundered from the Whigs, who still held to Low Fixed Duty projects[1] as the most likely enactable compromise between the increasingly powerful League and an "agricultural interest" more nervous than ever after Peel's Canada Corn Bill of 1843.[2] But on Ireland in 1844 as on Graham's unfortunate Education proposals of 1843 the entire Opposition could be mobilised effectively without any cross-fighting.

The shrewdest of the broadsides poured into the Government's Irish record was, perhaps, that from Macaulay on February 19th.[3] Macaulay, however, did not confine himself to the miserable pettifogging of the O'Connell trial but arraigned the whole Tory record in regard to Ireland and especially the determined obstruction which had been practised towards the conciliatory efforts of the Melbourne Government. In reviewing at the close of his speech the inadequacy of the Tory case for maintaining the Established Church of Ireland with undiminished wealth and prerogatives, Macaulay pointed anew to the subject which had been the strongest link among the "Reforming" groups of the Parliaments of 1833, 1835, and 1837. The intense agitation of the Anti-Corn Law League, now fighting every possible by-election and attempting to rally farmers against the high rents entailed by the Corn Law and their labourers against the high food prices, might certainly have deposed the Irish Church question from its former primacy among pressing political issues. Yet it should not be forgotten that it was an Irish situation finally which permitted the League to triumph.

would obstruct the supplies until there was "redress of grievances" in a Complete Suffrage sense. O'Connor, attended by a large band of Chartists, was present with Duncombe, who was his own candidate for the Parliamentary leadership of an obstruction campaign. Disorder was the result (*The Times*, February 1st), and the movement collapsed in a way which Chartists were still regretting a year later (cf. Cooper's *Letter to the Working Men of Leicester* dated March 18, 1845).

[1] Cf. *Later Correspondence of Lord J. Russell*, i, 63, 72.
[2] 6 & 7 Vict. c. 29. The "agricultural interest" had undertaken resistance both in the Commons and the Lords (*Annual Register*, 1843, History, pp. 122–32) and Peel reached a dangerous degree of unpopularity with his own supporters.
[3] Macaulay, *Writings and Speeches*, pp. 641 sqq.

CHAPTER XV

RADICALS AND GOVERNMENT POLICY, 1844-6

"Sir, believe me, to conduct the government of this country is a most arduous duty. I may say it without irreverence, that these ancient institutions, like our physical frames, are 'fearfully and wonderfully made.' It is no easy task to ensure the united action of an ancient monarchy, a proud aristocracy, and a reformed constitution. I have done everything I could do, and have thought it consistent with true Conservative policy to reconcile these three branches of the State. I have thought it consistent with true Conservative policy to promote so much of happiness and contentment among the people, that the voice of disaffection should no longer be heard and that thoughts of the dissolution of our institutions should be forgotten in the midst of physical enjoyment."

SIR ROBERT PEEL *in the Debate on the Address, January 22, 1846.*

"Are not lectures at Maynooth cheaper than State prosecutions? Are not professors less costly than Crown solicitors? Is not a large standing army, and a great constabulary force, more expensive than the moral police with which, by the priesthood of Ireland, you can be thriftily and efficaciously supplied? . . . The man who denounces the Catholic religion as an idolatry incurs the frightful hazard of teaching other men to inquire whether the Christian religion itself is not a fable!"

SHEIL *in the Maynooth Debate, April 4, 1845.*

"These are briefly my opinions as a Radical; upon them rests my only claim to your support. If you approve of them—if you are in favour of Free Trade—if you desire a repeal of the Corn Laws—if you are a friend to religious liberty and equality—if you are for the progressive reform of the institutions of your country—and lastly if you would do justice to Ireland, then give me your vote. But if, on the contrary, you are opposed to Free Trade—if you love the Corn Laws—if you would resist extension of suffrage, triennial Parliaments, and vote by ballot . . . and lastly, if you would offer a deadly insult to Ireland by proposing the rescinding of the grant to Maynooth—then I am not the man to represent you."

SIR W. MOLESWORTH *on his successful by-election candidature at Southwark, September 10, 1845.* ("Speeches of Sir W. Molesworth," *pp. 4-5, September 10 and 12, 1845.*)

DESPITE the gravity of the issues raised by the Irish debates of February 1844, the year was to be a prosperous one for the Peel Government. Trade was reviving,[1] great new railway schemes[2] expanded the demand for employment, and improved Government credit permitted the Treasury to undertake a notable Conversion of National Debt to lower interest.[3] The Government's prestige was further enhanced by another triumph on a non-controversial issue. On April 29th a Budget statement was read which showed not only that the long series of deficits was at an end but that there was a huge gross surplus of over four millions. Only minor remissions of taxation were offered to the public for the time, but Exchequer balances were held at heights which denoted that 1845 would be the year when Government would declare whether it would allow the Income-tax to lapse or would suggest other great reductions of taxation instead. Finally, in the bank-note proposals of the Bank Charter Act of 1844, Peel, whose experience of the subject was admittedly unique, offered the country an automatic check against the irresponsible creation of bank-note currency. Such creation had broken the American financial system in 1837, and had done something even in England to necessitate the sudden credit restrictions which had ushered in the long period of bad trade. The whole situation, indeed, was such as to make it unnecessary to enter into detailed explanations of why Chartism ceased to be an explosive force and the Anti-Corn Law League to win by-elections.[4]

In Parliament, Radical criticisms of Peel's financial proceedings were largely confined to the customary attacks of Hume and Williams on the alleged magnitude of the military and naval estimates, and the debating efforts of Muntz of Birmingham and Wallace of Greenock to stay the progress of the Bank Charter Act. On the shoulders of Muntz now lay the currency mantle of

---

[1] G. R. Porter, *Progress of the Nation*, p. 360, gives the following export figures: 1842, £47,381,023; 1843, £52,279,709; 1844, £58,584,292.
[2] *Ibid.*, p. 327, for an increase of authorised issues of railway capital from the £3,861,350 of 1843 to the £17,870,361 of 1844.
[3] *Illustrated London News*, January 6, 1844, reported Consols standing "much higher than . . . at any period during the present century." The Conversion scheme was presented to the Commons on March 8th, was approved by the money market, and was soon being accepted by holders as generous (*Ibid.*, March 23rd). [4] *Ibid.*, June 1st, for a damaging defeat in S. Lancs.

Radicals and Government Policy 1844-1846

Attwood, but a time of prosperity was not the best one for advancing the heretical notions on money which had attracted considerable support in the days of distress. There might have been more serious resistance to the Bank Charter Act if it had confined all note issue to the rigid conditions imposed upon the Issue Department of the Bank of England. But as existing country banks were left with rights to their actual issue practically unaltered, such a division as that of June 24th produced only the sorry figures of 18 against 205.[1]

A Radical crusade which deserves some notice is H. G. Ward's attempt to revive the Irish Church issue on June 11th and 12th.[2] The Whig legislation of 1833 and 1838 had removed the most crying scandals of the Irish Establishment, but the readiness of the Catholic priests to lead their flocks into the Repeal movement showed even Tories that further "concessions" would speedily have to be made. But Tory ideas of concession differed widely from those of the Radicals, and even from those of the Whigs who had long been ready for a very partial disendowment. Indeed, it was because the Tory circles immediately surrounding Peel were felt to be awaiting the right moment to launch a plan of "Concurrent Endowment" for the Catholic priesthood of Ireland[3] that the issue raised by Ward failed to arouse any vivid interest, though it did procure the large division of 179-274.

Turning from Westminster to the country, a very considerable decline is observable in the *tempo* of Chartist agitation. Working men did not abandon the Charter as a political ideal, but some of the most vigorous among them began turning into trade channels the energy and hope which once had gone to Chartism.[4] This is most marked in the mining community which had been so combatively Chartist both in 1839 and 1842. By the beginning of 1844 a Miners' Association of Great Britain and Ireland had not only recruited a powerful membership, supporting a national delegate conference of between seventy and eighty, but it was[5]

[1] *Illustrated London News*, June 29th. [2] *Ibid.*, June 15th.
[3] E.g. Sidney Herbert. Cf. *Illustrated London News*, March 2, 1844.
[4] S. and B. Webb, *History of Trade Unionism*, p. 163, for the revival of the Potters' Union and of the Cotton Spinners' Association in 1843. These crafts had produced the most determined Charter-strikers of 1842. Nor should the Rochdale flannel-weavers be forgotten, some Chartist, some Socialist, whose putting aside of money for the financing of the possible strike which might prove necessary to raise wages led to the epoch-making opening of their Co-operative Store in December 1844 (F. Podmore, *Robert Owen*, p. 583 sqq.).
[5] *Illustrated London News*, January 6, 1844. Cf. Webb, *op. cit.*, p. 164 sqq.

preparing to take action with regard to its grievances. Other trades, too, showed similar if less startling signs of activity; the operative stonemasons, for example, rising in membership from a low point of 2,144 in 1842 to the 4,861 of 1845,[1] and the steam engine makers from a membership of 956 in 1843 to one of 1,352 in 1845.[2] By November 1844, indeed, the *Northern Star* had come to consider it worth while to adopt the style of the *Northern Star and National Trades Journal*, and its readers were being invited to consider the great significance of what was going on in the trades.

"I invite you," wrote O'Connor, "to keep your eye steadily fixed upon the great Trades' Movement now manifesting itself throughout the country, and I would implore you to act by all other trades as you have acted by the colliers. Attend their meetings, swell their numbers, and give them your sympathy; but upon no account interpose the Charter as an obstacle to their proceedings. All labour and labourers must unite; and they will speedily discover that the Charter is the only standard under which they can successfully rally. . . . I assert without fear of contradiction that a combination of the Trades of England under his (Roberts') management and direction would be the greatest move ever witnessed within the last century. It would be practical Chartism."[3]

Like Chartism, the Anti-Corn Law movement could not but be affected by the return of prosperity which had set in during the second half of 1843. Before its results became visible at the beginning of 1844 the League had gone on from strength to strength, and even the once-scornful *Times* had counselled concession.[4] But during the course of prosperous 1844 the hitherto optimistic Cobden was himself to lose some of his confidence in a speedy victory.[5] The enormous aggregations of revenue and power in the hands of the Tory landed class were a discouraging spectacle, and it should be remembered that they were now being wielded with more social charity than had ever been the case before. Both from a desire to beat off the repeated democratic

---

[1] R. W. Postgate, *The Builders' History*, pp. 131-2.
[2] *Annual Expenditure*, 1843-4 and 1844-5.
[3] *Northern Star*, November 16, 1844. W. P. Roberts was the Chartist attorney who was doing remarkable work as the paid "Miners' Attorney General."
[4] *The Times*, November 21, 1843, contained the famous article, "The League is a great fact." On November 14th, after two remarkable Anti-Corn Law by-election victories, the League had made a sensationally successful opening in raising a new £100,000 fund for further propaganda.
[5] J. Morley, *Life of Cobden*, ed. 1903, pp. 294-5.

Radicals and Government Policy 1844–1846

challenges to its leadership,[1] and from the ever-increasing humanitarianism of the time, landlordism was now often striving to take on model qualities.[2] In numbers of cases the matter was passing from interest in the provision of churches and church schools and readiness to subscribe to local charities to embrace also attention to the sanitary and housing questions so prominently brought forward by the work of those Benthamite disciples, Chadwick and Southwood Smith.[3] There were strategically-minded Tory circles, moreover, planning to keep the Radical danger for ever at bay by taking charge of "social reform" themselves, whether by sending Oastler to the factory districts to revive ten-hour agitation[4] or by experimenting with the "Young England" methods so strikingly advocated by Disraeli and his friends.[5]

Cobden early perceived the weakest point of the Tory enemy to lie in the complete and irremediable faultiness of the economic structure of the countryside. He therefore followed up the remarkably successful rural campaigning of 1843 with action in Parliament. His speech of March 12, 1844, asking for a committee to investigate the alleged benefits of the Corn Law to harassed farmers and miserable labourers contained sufficient detail to make it markedly impressive.[6] Indeed, subsequent events were to prove that in a year when every other class in the community was in the enjoyment of prosperity, farm labourers in their hungry misery continued rick-burning and other incendiarism on a formidable scale,[7] and farmers, too, complained loudly of distress and called for relief from their tax burdens. A year of relatively cheap corn prices, that is, put many farmers into immediate

---

[1] Cf. *Memoir of Sidney Herbert*, i, 32. "One has no business to sit idle and let others take one's place."

[2] Cf. *Ibid.*, chapter 5, and *Life of Lord Norton*, chapter 22, for two examples of the younger landlord. Herbert had among other things important Dublin property of growing value, and Lord Norton the increasingly valuable Saltley estate near Birmingham.

[3] Cf. *Perils of the Nation*, a remarkable Tory work of 1843, and Lord Ashley's Sturminster speech of November 1843 (*Speeches, 1838–67*, pp. 87 sqq.).

[4] *Illustrated London News*, March 6, 1844, for the subscriptions, mainly Tory, to the Oastler Fund for repaying the debts for which he had been imprisoned. *Ibid.*, April 13th, for great Leeds and Bradford meetings addressed by Oastler and Ferrand, the notorious Tory M.P.

[5] Cf. *Plea for National Holidays* by Lord John Manners.

[6] *Illustrated London News*, March 16th, p. 166, for significant editorial comment from this non-political paper with the largest circulation of the time.

[7] *Ibid.*, October 19th, p. 244.

difficulties to find their over-high rents, with the result that they pressed upon their labourers with a weight which inevitably led to retaliatory incendiarism. Of all these depressing rural phenomena the League had Corn Law explanations to offer which Peel and some of those around him began to find more irrefutable at the very time when Cobden was making up his mind that League success would not come quickly.

The Anti-Corn Law agitators, indeed, needed considerable pertinacity to keep their movement together between the summer of 1844 and that of 1845. It is possibly a sign of their feeling that it was inadvisable to risk losing the public attention that Cobden and Bright should have consented to a public debate with O'Connor and another Chartist at Northampton on August 5, 1844.[1] The complete bewilderment of local Chartist rank and file as they perceived their leader quite unable to reach his opponents' level makes it clear, however, why the general public maintained an undiminished interest in the League's chief propagandists, and why their brother manufacturers' subscriptions did not fall off. The League, in fact, was confident enough to embark upon the attempt to capture some of the county divisions from "farmers' friends" by promoting the extensive purchase of 40s. freeholds which would confer votes at the next elections. Both in this activity and in that of assisting Free Trade voters with "Registration" very great successes were claimed when the League's great weekly Covent Garden meetings were resumed in the capital during December. The capture of thirty-two seats, it was affirmed, had been made certain with a turnover of sixty-four votes on a division.[2] Leaguers, in short, were strengthening the Radical vote in the constituencies with results that proved important when the next political crisis occurred.

When Parliament reassembled early in February 1845, however, there was no sign of a crisis, and Peel seemed stronger than before. Armed with the certainty of another huge surplus, the Prime Minister laid before the Commons a striking Budget programme which, while offering no Corn Law changes, proposed remarkable approaches to Free Trade at the cost of continuing

---

[1] Gammage, *History of the Chartist Movement*, pp. 253-5, counts the occasion "the greatest victory they (the League) ever obtained." A. Prentice, *History of the Anti-Corn-Law League*, ii, 228-35, for the speeches.
[2] *Illustrated London News*, December 14th.

Radicals and Government Policy 1844-1846

the Income-tax. Four hundred and thirty import duties, relatively troublesome to collect, were to be swept away, and all export duties, including the unwise impost on coal, were also to be removed. There was to be an important reduction in the Sugar Duties valuable to the poor consumer, and the glass excise was to be abolished so that the great glass industry might be freed to give the poor man cheaper window glass and to experiment unshackled with promising new uses for its product. Even the cotton industry, now highly prosperous, was to have its raw material free of duty. Peel had thus again mounted far above the normal struggle of party interests. It is significant that the warmest cheering of his great speech of February 14th came from the Whig and Radical Opposition,[1] and that the next crowded meeting of the League at Covent Garden found its most Ultra-Radical agitator, George Thompson, prophesying that Peel would deal with the Corn Laws next if League pressure continued.[2]

On the Budget, however, two kinds of Radical objection were to be pressed. In moving the exclusion of incomes earned in "trades, professions, and offices" from the operations of the Income-tax, Roebuck led a Radical attempt to confine Income-tax for the future to unearned income. Its defeat by 263 votes against 55 left the Budget underanged.[3] On the Sugar Duties, again, Radical Free Traders protested against a system which disguised the maintenance of a steep degree of Colonial Preference at the expense of the working-class consumer at home under the specious exterior of discriminating against slave-grown sugar. Dividing on their own motion of February 24th the Radicals obtained a vote of 84–211, while when they combined two days later with Whig ex-Ministers the division figures were taken to 142–236.[4]

More perilous to Peel than these Radical objections of detail or the finessing of Whig ex-Ministers, anxious to return to office, was the deep-rooted distrust of the "landed interest."[5] Many of the 430 Import Duties which Peel wished to abolish were, it was claimed, duties on articles which competed with the produce of British agriculture. Their abolition threatened, therefore, to make

[1] *Illustrated London News*, February 15th and 22nd.
[2] *Ibid.*, February 22nd.
[3] *Ibid.*, February 22nd. The division was on February 16th.
[4] *Ibid.*, March 1st.
[5] *Ibid.*, March 22nd, for the debate of March 17th.

English Radicalism 1832–1852

the British farmer's plight even more desperate than Peel's measures of 1842 and 1843 had left it. Moreover, Peel was proposing to spend all his huge Budget surplus on matters helpful to the "manufacturing and mercantile interests," and to devote none of it at all to the relief of the "agricultural interest," specially burdened though that was with poor rates, tithes, and the various species of county rates. Ever since his 1842 Budget, indeed, Peel had come under the increasing suspicion of the coroneted magnates who were regarded as the special voices of the "agricultural interest," and who unswervingly adhered to the view that "agricultural distress" was not due to high rents but to insufficient protection and to the "special burdens placed on the land." Though Cobden,[1] in moving for an inquiry into the alleged agricultural distress, and Ward,[2] in moving for one on the peculiar exemptions and advantages of the landed interest, exposed some of the hollowness of the landowning cry, they naturally failed to end the animus growing up against Peel inside his own party. Only seventy-eight Tories might be ready on March 17th to divide against the Government in pursuance of their demand for the application of £300,000 of Peel's surplus to the relief of county rates. But the vast relish with which many others were greeting Disraeli's famous series of philippics against Peel showed how easily the rot might spread.

It was in April that Peel's increasing departure from the old Tory landmarks brought a still greater storm. On April 3rd he rose to move a vote for spending £30,000 on the reconditioning of the Irish Catholic Seminary at Maynooth, for allotting £26,360 annually to its work, and for taking the future maintenance of its fabric under the official care of the Office of Works.[3] It was Peel's first considerable step to reconcile Ireland and to recapture for Westminster an attention still largely concentrated on O'Connell's Repeal activities and the Young Ireland nationalist movement. Among Orangemen, High Tories, and Tory Evangelicals, however, it raised an enormous storm, and when the Second Reading division came to be taken at 3.30 a.m. on the morning of April 19th the Tory party was split between the 158 Tories who followed Peel in the majority and the 145 who voted against him.[4] But the Maynooth College Bill did more than

---

[1] On March 13th.
[2] On June 3rd.
[3] *Illustrated London News*, April 5th.
[4] *Irving's Annals*, p. 174.

Radicals and Government Policy 1844-1846

antagonise nearly half the Tory party. It provoked a great popular agitation which brought upon Parliament 10,253 hostile petitions with 1,288,742 signatures.[1] Much of this signing was the work of Radical Dissenters, whose first emotions on hearing of the proposal for the State endowment of "Popery" had impelled them to ally even with State and Church Tories in a common Protestant effort to intimidate pro-Maynooth Parliamentarians by gathering at Westminster a hostile Conference of 1,000 deputies from 400 cities and towns. At the Conference, however, it was speedily discovered that the Disestablishment solution of all religious troubles was not expected to be urged, because it would break up "Protestant harmony." There was the inevitable secession, and the successful gathering of another anti-Maynooth Conference also of 1,000 deputies, but on Disestablishment lines.[2] Its views had already been expressed in Parliament by Bright in his most forceful and democratic style. The Maynooth measure's purpose, he claimed, was to tame down the agitators, to throw a sop to the priests. It was to give the Catholic clergy hush-money so that they might not proclaim to the world the sufferings of the Irish population. The measure was meant to separate the priests from the people, to give them a little more Greek and Latin and tame them to the condition of the parsons of Dorset and Suffolk.[3]

The Government's Irish programme was not confined to Maynooth. On May 9th the Government announced another Irish measure which, though enjoying practically unanimous Whig and Radical support, provoked further trouble inside the Tory party. It was proposed to found and endow three colleges for the higher education of Irish youth, but colleges where no prescribed religious instruction would be given as part of the curriculum. It was not, of course, that Peel's Government had become enamoured of Radical notions of secular education. But the colleges were mainly intended to serve the Catholic and Presbyterian youth as the great foundation of Trinity College, Dublin, served the Episcopalians, and any plan of prescribed

[1] *Companion to the British Almanac, 1846*, p. 232.
[2] S. Skeat, *History of the Free Churches of England*, pp. 618-19.
[3] *Hansard*, April 16th, Cobden, however, voted for the Bill as an educational measure, and Hume as one contributing to the appeasement of Ireland. The large majorities for the Bill were due to the virtually unanimous Whig votes in his favour, the Whigs being less divided about its provisions than either Tories or Radicals.

religious instruction would have raised a great inter-denominational controversy fatal to the future of the colleges and possibly to the political tranquillity of Ireland. As matters turned out, however, High Tory opposition to "Godless education" found unexpected assistance from the Irish Catholic prelates who held parallel views as to the dangers of releasing educational processes from close connection with religion.[1] The suggested colleges of Galway, Cork, and Belfast, in fact, proved but little contribution to Irish appeasement, though they were sanctioned by very large Parliamentary majorities including all shades of British Radicalism.

A third Government measure relating to Ireland, a timid Tenants' Compensation Bill, was simultaneously giving the Government trouble in the Lords. Irish landlords, indeed, strongly resisted the Government proposal[2] to appoint a Government Commissioner of Improvements with powers to authorise tenants to undertake building, fencing, and draining for which the landlords would have to give compensation on a change of tenancy. The Government, thereupon, consented to remit the Bill to a Select Committee,[3] and ultimately it was abandoned without the Radicals in the House of Commons having had a chance to insist on its inadequacy. It was a course which assisted the Government to enter upon a long Parliamentary recess with apparently undiminished power. Chartism seemed to have sunk out of all political significance,[4] and even the men of the Anti-Corn Law League to be spending their admitted ingenuity and energy in vain.[5] They had impressed all London with a remarkable industrial exhibition and sale known as the "Free Trade Bazaar" and organised with the support of a host of favourable manufacturing houses in all industries.[6] Yet when they exerted themselves to the utmost to bring that popular and widely known Ultra-Radical, Colonel Perronet Thompson, into Parliament at a Sunderland by-election, whose issue was regarded as significant, they were defeated by a supporter of Peel the practical, George Hudson, the railway promoter.[7]

[1] *Illustrated London News*, May 17, 1845, p. 305.
[2] Opposition was expressed at the Bill's introduction (June 9th), and by the time of the Second Reading (June 24th) was capable of dividing against the Government at 34–48. [3] June 26th.
[4] Cf. Morley's *Life of Gladstone*, ed. 1908, i, 204.
[5] Cf. Disraeli's *Lord George Bentinck*, ed. 1874, p. 7.
[6] *Illustrated London News*, May 10th and 17th. It was in a sense the parent of the Great Exhibition of 1851.   [7] *Irving's Annals*, pp. 180–1.

Radicals and Government Policy 1844-1846

But already the potato disease had been noticed which was to change the course of politics.[1] The failure of the Irish potato crop with parallel failures in England and Scotland rendered it necessary before long to envisage the feeding of three million extra people on foreign grain. To collect the existing Corn Duties in such circumstances Peel recognised as impossible. But a study of his proposals to his Cabinet colleagues in the five successive Cabinet Memoranda of November and early December reveal an increasing desire to use the emergency to free himself permanently from the toils of an orthodox Corn Law theory which he had long been outgrowing.[2] Peel's resolution was strengthened by the famous "Edinburgh Letter" of Lord John Russell, in which the Whig leader virtually called upon the League to organise the popular demonstrations which would force the hesitating Cabinet's hand.[3] Failing, however, to carry a unanimous Cabinet with him, Peel resolved on resignation (December 5th). On December 20th he was fortunate enough to be recommissioned as Prime Minister after a Whig attempt to form a Government had failed.

Though League speakers had treated of such grave constitutional problems as Coalition, Creation of Peers, and General Election,[4] the solution proved less agitating than at one time seemed possible. Peel persuaded all his important colleagues except Stanley to resume office with him, though a formidable revolt of the "landed interest" was expected which would have to be countered with Whig and Radical votes. Meanwhile the League armed itself both against the "landed interest's" energetic attempts to stave off Corn Law Repeal and the Prime Minister's possible refusal to offer a completely satisfactory measure. On December 23rd a new £250,000 fund was announced towards which £60,000 was subscribed at the inaugural Manchester meeting alone.[5] On January 15th Cobden in preparation for the momentous Session approaching expressed the League's attitude

---

[1] *Irving's Annals*, p. 180; *Peel Memoirs*, ii, 108-10.
[2] *Peel Memoirs*, ii, 141-220.
[3] "The Government appear to be waiting for some excuse to give up the present Corn Law. Let the people by petition, by address, by remonstrance, afford them the excuse they seek." Almost simultaneously another Whig ex-Minister, Lord Morpeth, sent a subscription to the League (*Later Correspondence of Lord J. Russell*, i, 85-6. *Ibid.*, p. 84, for H. G. Ward on a new Whig-Radical alliance).
[4] Cf. W. J. Fox, *Collected Works*, iv, 269, for his Covent Garden speech of December 19th. [5] *Irving's Annals*, p. 190.

even more emphatically. "We have nothing to do with Whigs or Tories," he declared. "We are stronger than either of them; and if we stick to our principles we can beat them both."[1]

By its constitution the League was, of course, confined to Radical advocacy in the restricted economic field. But the situation undoubtedly seemed ripening for Radical progress elsewhere. On January 21st, for example, just before the opening of Parliament, there was launched a new daily organ of "advanced Liberalism," the *Daily News*. On the same day, again, the National Association of United Trades, an ambitious organisation which had been formed during the past year to unite the trades for political and economic action, entertained its President and Parliamentary representative, Duncombe,[2] to a pre-sessional "banquet."

The complete plan with which Peel faced Parliament at the end of January 1846 was a very bold one.[3] In a great programme of freer trade, which required the "manufacturing interest" to prepare for the removal or the reduction of the import duties on its foreign competitors, the "agricultural interest" was asked for similar self-denial for the general good. Like the manufacturer, the farmer was to be offered in return the remission of duties on his raw materials, clover-seed, for example, and maize and other cattle-feeding products, and in addition he was to be given a modified Corn Law for a transitional period of three years. Nor was this all. The Exchequer would relieve the pressure of local rates upon the "agricultural interest" by taking over from the Poor Rate half the cost of medical relief, and from the County Rate the cost of conducting prosecutions and maintaining convicted prisoners. The Highway Rate, too, would be lessened by forming 600 highway districts of the 16,000 independent areas, and special advances at low rates of interest would be made available for landlords desirous of undertaking land-drainage which would increase productivity. In sum, Peel's proposals were ingeniously enough balanced to warrant the assumption that but for the surprising emergence of Lord George Bentinck as a passionately earnest Protectionist leader[4] there would have been no long weeks of Tory resistance in the Commons.

[1] *Irving's Annals*, p. 191.   [2] *Ibid.*, p. 191.
[3] *Hansard*, January 27th; *Illustrated London News*, January 31st. That non-party paper concluded: "It is almost hopeless that the Lords will agree to it. Then comes the Dissolution."
[4] B. Disraeli, *Lord George Bentinck*, chapters 5–16.

Radicals and Government Policy 1844–1846

But though a thoroughgoing Opposition was organised in the Commons and the majority in the Lords would eagerly have voted down Peel's proposals had it dared,[1] the League's power to stir the country from end to end was to prove the decisive factor in the Parliamentary situation. The Leaguers were well enough satisfied with Peel's proposals, though they thought fit to urge that total and immediate repeal was a preferable policy.[2] But the essential purpose of their activity, which embraced the promotion of the Repeal petitioning that secured 1,414,303 signatures,[3] was to assist Peel by illustrating the strength of the support enjoyed by much extremer views than his.[4]

What especially delighted Radicals of all kinds in Peel's plans was the care for the poor which they manifested. Peel had spoken the language of true benevolence when proposing the abolition of the duties upon the coarser cotton, woollen, and linen fabrics in which the people were clothed, upon the dressed hides from which their footwear was made, and upon the salt beef, the salt pork, the potatoes, and vegetables which constituted so important a part of their food. In his proposals for compensating the "agricultural interest" Radicals had also found considerable matter for pleasure. In offering to take over the cost of county prosecutions Peel made it plain that he accepted at least partially the Radical criticisms which had been made of the unchecked control of the Justices of the Peace;[5] in undertaking responsibility for part of the medical and all the educational Poor Law salaries he showed his opinion that these services had been much too pinched by some over-economical boards of guardians. Nor did urban Radicals show any displeasure with the Premier's suggestion to relieve the rates of agricultural parishes by allowing legal settlement for Poor Relief purposes to the families which had established an "industrial residence of five years" in a manufacturing centre to which they had migrated from agricultural

---

[1] J. Morley, *Life of Cobden*, pp. 377–8.
[2] *Hansard*, March 2nd and 3rd, for a debate which ended in a division of 78–267. Peel was now so popular with Radicals that men like Hume and Duncombe voted against the League motion in order to strengthen Peel.
[3] *Companion to the British Almanac, 1847*, p. 226.
[4] Morley, *op. cit.*, p. 378.
[5] In Ireland County Rates were also freed from Constabulary contributions, partly to "exclude all power of local nomination and local interference," and partly as special compensation to an overwhelmingly agricultural country. It is another example of the ingenious balancing of a scheme which thus earned O'Connellite support.

parishes of origin. Few parts of Peel's great speech of January 27th seem to have been cheered more warmly or more generally.[1] Another thing which it pleased Radicals to hear was Peel's decisive rejection of the persistent demand from the "agricultural interest" for the levying of local rates not on real property alone but on personal property also.

It was not the Corn and Customs Bills, therefore, which led to Peel's resignation in June. Indeed, they won him such a huge measure of popularity that so clear-sighted a person as Cobden himself urged him to take the opportunity to recast the whole of the party system by appealing to the country against the Protectionists on a "Condition of England" and "Practical Reform" basis.[2] Cobden had a whole programme for such a Government as would concentrate for a time on "Practical Reform"—the complete demolition of Protection, the full adoption of a Free Trade example to the rest of the world, and bold Irish Land proposals. Probably many Radicals besides Cobden would have been prepared to postpone urgent pressure on Suffrage questions to help Peel in such a task. But Peel would only have asked for the Dissolution, which would have thrown the party system into the melting-pot, if he had been defeated on his Corn and Customs measures. Towards the end of June, however, it was obvious that they were about to be accepted even by the Lords, and Peel was therefore ready for resignation on his unfortunate Irish Coercion Bill.

Whatever need there might have been in February for the Irish Coercion Bill then introduced into the Lords, that need certainly seemed to have gone by in June when the measure was at length being advanced nearer its concluding stages in the Commons.[3] It had early been urged from among the Radicals that what Ireland needed was not coercion but Outdoor Poor Relief,[4] and during the course of the Session there had been the plainest proof that Radical distrust of Irish landlordism was amply justified. In some instances destitute tenantries, ruined by the potato failure, were evicted in the most heartless manner,[5]

---

[1] *Illustrated London News*, Supplement, January 31st.
[2] J. Morley, *Life of Cobden*, pp. 394-7.
[3] Cf. *Illustrated London News*, June 6th.
[4] *Hansard*, February 11th, for Sharman Crawford; April 1st, for Poulett Scrope on the second reading of his Bill for the relief of the Destitute Poor.
[5] *Illustrated London News*, April 4th, for an ejection involving 270 persons.

Radicals and Government Policy 1844-1846

and often the Government's Public Works legislation enabling County Grand Juries to create useful employment was disregarded for fear of over-burdening "property."[1] By June, however, Irishmen were so comparatively tranquillised by a burst of fine farming weather and the smoothness with which arrangements for introducing cheap maize, rice, and buckwheat were working that the Government would have been well advised to abandon its Coercion Bill. When it persisted, it became obvious that it was placing itself in mortal peril. Bentinck announced his intention of leading his vindictive agricultural party into the division against the Government; Lord John Russell gave a lead to the Whigs by declaring against a measure which he had supported on earlier stages; and Radicals, though most reluctant to displace Peel, did not deem it right to give him the special powers of the proposed Coercion Bill.[2]

Defeated on June 25th by a singular combination of Protectionist, Whig, Radical, and Irish votes, Peel resigned on June 27th, the day after his Corn Bill became law. The enactment of the Corn Bill led to another notable event—the winding up of the Anti-Corn Law League on July 2nd.[3] True to the undertaking which had been given to the public during the agitation against the Corn Law, the Leaguers ceased their activity at the very time when the most Radical forces in the country would have liked to rally behind them for further struggles against "aristocratic privilege."[4] That Radicalism would only be able to make the most gradual advances was further made clear by the history of Lord John Russell's Cabinet-making. Russell had tried very hard to strengthen his Whig following from among Peel's Ministry.[5] When he had failed he formed a Whig Cabinet of a very aristocratic cast and paid for the Radical support he expected by finding four

---

[1] *Illustrated London News*, April 14th, p. 254.
[2] Cf. Cobden's speech of June 25th, with its warm praise for Peel, but its arguments against Coercion.
[3] *Irving's Annals*, p. 204. A committee was, however, left in being till Peel's measure should have been fully worked out. This would happen in 1849, and till then the Committee was charged with resuscitating the League if there was a danger of Protectionist reaction.
[4] Cf. *The Aristocracy of England*, by John Hampden, Jr., 2nd ed., 1846. When preparing for a possible struggle with the Protectionists in 1846, the Leaguers had certainly taken some drastic steps. Cf. the *League* newspaper, February 7th, 1846, for a firm creating thirty-five voting lots of £40 each for employees on a property near Huddersfield.
[5] *Memoir of Sidney Herbert*, i, 68. Three of Peel's younger Cabinet Ministers were approached.

non-Cabinet posts for Ward, Buller, Milner Gibson, and Hawes. Despite the "advanced Liberalism" of their political professions, the three first-named were of the country gentleman stock whose practical behaviour the Whigs felt they could rely on, and Hawes had already proved himself the most painstaking and obsequious of soap-boilers' sons.

In Russell's private Cabinet-making negotiations, indeed, it had been stressed that "social questions" must take complete precedence of all awkward political questions, even that of the Irish Church.[1] "Social Reform" was just then the popular catch-word with which it was being sought to evade "political reform," and on public education, the treatment of criminals, the sanitary conditions of towns and villages, and Irish distress there certainly seemed the possibility of planning "Practical Reform" of a kind which would stave off serious Radical agitation for years.[2] The close of the Session gave ample proof that the policy planned promised at least temporary success. A reduced flogging schedule for the Army,[3] lower Sugar Duties for the people,[4] and a number of conciliatory steps towards Ireland were all measures enjoying warm Radical approval. Especially in regard to Ireland the Government did well to abandon coercion, and to assume a somewhat severer attitude towards landlordism's dislike of undertaking local Public Works employment schemes burdensome to "property."[5]

Even in so agitated a Session as that of 1846 the factory question had been repeatedly pressed. In Ashley's absence Ten Hour advocacy had fallen to the Radical Fielden, and his Bill for limiting to ten hours the labour of young persons between thirteen and eighteen had won 193 supporters against the Government's 203.[6] As Peel and Graham, his Home Secretary, were both

[1] *Later Correspondence of Lord J. Russell*, i, 108-9.
[2] *Irving's Annals*, p. 204, for Russell's address to his City of London constituents. Further measures of "commercial freedom" and attention to colonial administration are also mentioned.
[3] *Hansard*, August 7th, for Russell's announcement of a new maximum of fifty lashes. It was to meet the renewed Radical pressure for total abolition.
[4] *Ibid.*, July 20th, for the introduction of the Sugar Duties Bill.
[5] *Ibid.*, August 17th, for Russell's announcement that he would empower the Lord-Lieutenant to summon magistrates' meetings in the counties and baronies, which would be required to undertake Public Work programmes superintended by the Government Board of Works.
[6] *Ibid.*, May 22nd, for the division on a Second Reading which had begun on April 29th. Macaulay's speech of the 22nd is a good indication of how a large section of responsible opinion was moving away from a confined "Political Economy" position.

strongly opposed to the Bill, while so prominent a Whig ex-Minister as Macaulay made a very strong supporting speech, the prospects of Ten Hour legislation were probably brighter for the change of Government. The Radicals were still in two camps on the question. On the one hand men like Fielden, Brotherton, Wakley, and Muntz favoured Ten Hour legislation strongly, while on the other Hume, Roebuck, Ward, and Bright represented important sections of middle-class Radical opposition.[1] Duncombe's Lace Factories Bill was in one sense a more extreme measure than Fielden's Ten Hour Bill, for it was based on the principle that it was not merely children and young persons who required hours protection but adults, and even male adults also, as was proved by their decrepitude, disease, and premature death. Aided by a mixed band of Radicals and Anti-Manufacturer Tories, Duncombe obtained a division of 66–151.[2]

It was Duncombe also who acted as the Chartist representative in the Commons. It was in this capacity that on March 10th he presented numerous Chartist petitions for the release of the transported men of Newport, petitions which he erroneously asserted to have been signed by 1,400,000 persons.[3] In 1846 Chartism was much too weak to be capable of so great a petitioning effort. For one thing the position of the *Northern Star* in the world of Ultra-Radical journalism was much smaller than it had been in 1839 or 1842. Not only had its own circulation fallen, but new organs of vast popularity had arisen which, though of Ultra-Radical politics, were very ready to attack O'Connor and were not even committed to the Charter.[4] Even among the kernel of Chartist stalwarts, whose union in the National Charter Association gave them a weight in the working-class world which should not be underrated, O'Connor's fame was not what it had been once. His character and record had been under hot and penetrating attack during 1845,[5] and his Land Scheme to promote

---

[1] Partly *laisser-faire*, partly "anxious not to reduce wages."
[2] *Hansard*, May 20th.
[3] *Companion to the British Almanac, 1847*, p. 226, for the very different figure of 355,403 signatures to 342 petitions.
[4] Especially *Lloyd's Weekly* and the *News of the World*.
[5] Cf. R. Gammage, *History of the Chartist Movement*, pp. 258–60, for the attacks of M'Douall, and *Ibid.*, pp. 260–9, for those of two other members of the Convention of 1839, Carpenter and O'Brien. Carpenter was writing for *Lloyd's*, and O'Brien now again had a newspaper of his own, the *National Reformer*. This ran till 1847, and advocated not merely Chartism, but Land Nationalisation, and remarkable Currency and Credit changes.

the settlement of Chartists on small farms was under damaging journalistic criticism[1] long before the accumulation of small subscriptions allowed him to make a beginning in the summer of 1846. But O'Connor was a man both of persistence and resource. Though he failed to harness the genius of Thomas Cooper to the propagation of the Land Plan,[2] he succeeded better with that of Ernest Jones, the most remarkable Ultra-Radical politician of the next quarter of a century.[3] Though, again, circumstances seemed singularly unpropitious for many months after the Land Plan was launched in April 1845, O'Connor acted with undeniable energy, verve, and imagination.[4] The result was that from the second half of 1846 a good deal of the old Chartist enthusiasm came to be captured for the "Land and the Charter." That fact was to be of singular political importance when a revolutionary wave swept through Europe early in 1848.

[1] Cf. R. Gammage, *History of the Chartist Movement*, p. 267.

[2] *Ibid.*, pp. 272–81, for a long account of the matter which is borne out by the *Life of Thomas Cooper*. The original Land Plan may be found set out in the *Northern Star*, April 26 and May 5, 1845. It proposed to make a beginning through a Chartist Land Co-operative Society, with a capital of £5,000 divided into shares of £2 10s. each, purchasable in weekly instalments of 3d., 6d., 1s., and upwards. A Conference of December 1845 (reported *Northern Star*, December 13th and 20th) showed total receipts of £3,266, but by the end of March £7,000 was in hand, and a second Co-operative Land colony had become possible. The great immediate incentive to share-subscription among working men, dreading unemployment and old age, was not, of course, interest, but the chance of being fortunate in the ballot and receiving the opportunity of taking a 4-, 3-, or 2-acre holding with a new cottage attached. They had the *Northern Star's* assurance that they would be able to thrive on these holdings on the new intensive culture system which it was intended to adopt. Trade Union sentiment was also enlisted because the scheme would put the "surplus labour" which was holding down wages on the land, and Socialist sentiment because of certain co-operative features in the intended arrangements, and the wider "community" possibilities which would open up if the land colonies were successful.

[3] Born 1819 in Germany, and son of Major Jones, equerry to the Duke of Cumberland. He was called to the Bar in 1844, and entered Chartism from the beginning of 1846. He was a most gifted orator and Chartist song-writer.

[4] Cf. *Northern Star*, August 22nd, for the enthusiastic celebrations at the exhibition of the wonders of O'Connorville, the first of the colonies. It was near Rickmansworth.

CHAPTER XVI

PARLIAMENTARY RADICALISM AN INCREASING FORCE

"And now a word with the Irish landlords. For the last three hundred years the British Parliament has been legislating for them as a body against the people of Ireland—has been maintaining them against the people of Ireland—has been permitting them to work for their very personal purposes, the mischief of the people of Ireland . . . and now after centuries of legislation for his (the Irish landlord's) benefit, he comes to England to ask her to maintain, not only himself, but the paupers whom he has created. Now, sir, I say that it is the duty of England—and I especially address myself to English representatives—to insist that the land of Ireland shall maintain the people of Ireland. . . ."

    ROEBUCK *in the Debate on the Address, January 19, 1847.*
    ("Annual Register," *p. 12, which differs considerably from* "Hansard," *lxxxix, iii sqq.*)

"If he was not prepared with a new system to succeed the present one—a new system which would enable every industrious man to live honourably, independently, and happily—he would not give a snap of the fingers for the Charter. (Hear.) But he had studied the question of the rights of labour, both theoretically and practically—he had devoted days and parts of nights to the consideration of the means of elevating the industrious classes, and he was ready, if he had the Charter granted to-morrow, to put every man willing to labour to work, and to earn double and treble the wages he now earned. . . ."

    FEARGUS O'CONNOR *quoted in the Commons, April 10, 1848.*
    ("Hansard," *xcviii, 115–16.*)

"*May 21, 1848.*

"After two months' more experience, I adhere to my statement about the general attachment of the fed classes to our Monarchy and institutions. Since then there has been some violence, and a good deal of extravagance, not only in pauperised England and mad Ireland, but in peaceable Scotland. . . . Chartism has superseded Radicalism, and draws the whole starving discontent of the country in its train. It is far more a matter of food than of principle. Extension of the franchise is the phrase, but division of property is the object."

    "Journal of H. Cockburn."

During the autumn of 1846 it became obvious to all the political world that the course of the next Session of Parliament would be dominated by an ever-deteriorating Irish situation.[1] The potato crop of 1846 had failed even more disastrously than that of 1845, millions of Ireland's inhabitants were starving, and efforts, unprecedented in British history, were being made to find employment for several hundreds of thousands on "public works," mainly roadmaking. Though the Irish barony and county magistrates called for and received a total of Treasury loans which members of Parliament had probably never contemplated when passing the authorising legislation, the pressure from desperate and semi-rebellious Ireland for an early summons of Parliament became very strong. Desiring to avoid interference with an Irish Executive, almost overwhelmed by the immensity of its new administrative burdens, Ministers put off the opening of Parliament until January 19, 1847. But it was at considerable cost. The almost openly revolutionary "Young Ireland" party[2] gained heavily at the expense of O'Connell's "Moral Force" Repeal organisation, and O'Connell himself found it necessary to demand for Ireland a loan of forty millions from the British Exchequer.[3]

When Parliament reassembled the Irish situation gave the Radical Free Traders an important triumph without a contest. The potato failure had been a strong factor in raising the price of grain to heights which were considered dangerous even in Britain.[4] Accordingly the Protectionists, too, were ready to suspend until the next harvest both the Corn Duties and the Navigation Code's restrictions on shipping which carried corn.[5] A further advance by the Radical Free Traders was made on February 9th, when J. L. Ricardo obtained a Select Committee on the Navigation Laws. The vote of 155–61 hardly showed much sign that the "reaction" hoped for by the Protectionists was yet under way.

Meanwhile there had already begun the discussion of Irish

---

[1] *Later Correspondence of Lord J. Russell*, i, chapter 6, "The Irish Famine."
[2] *Illustrated London News*, December 12th, for arming and outrage details.
[3] *Irving's Annals*, p. 213.
[4] *Hansard*, January 21st, for Russell's statement that wheat had risen from the August 1846 price of 49s. to 70s. 3d., and barley in a higher proportion still. The English harvest had been below average, there was a shortage in other European countries, and the Scottish potato crop had failed like the Irish.
[5] *Ibid.*, January 21st and 22nd.

conditions and of the Government's suggested legislative programme to meet them. From the first Ministers were compelled to admit that the "public works" programme, which they had been financing with Treasury loans advanced on the security of local rates, was not developing very satisfactorily.[1] Over 450,000 men were already "employed" on public works by mid-January,[2] and before arrangements could be completed gradually to reverse a system which was leading to a dangerous neglect of cultivation the number had actually increased to over 700,000.[3] The financial costs of these proceedings were so serious, moreover, that it was at once felt to be necessary to offer the "property" of each district the cancellation of responsibility for one-half of the money that had been advanced by the Treasury on the recommendation of its magistrates and on the security of the rates.[4]

Such special solicitude for Irish "property" was by no means to the taste of many Radicals, who felt that the Irish landlords who had so long been the bane of Ireland should not be allowed so readily to transfer their responsibilities to the British Exchequer.[5] But, if there was criticism, there was no revolt until Ministers, having raised a loan of eight millions, proposed to spend part of that sum in making advances to landlords to enable them to give employment. Though Peel lent his great authority to the cause of the Ministers, and starvation and fever deaths were growing at a fearful pace in Ireland,[6] Radical resentment was still strong enough to enable Roebuck to divide at 26–121.[7] His proposition was that the Ministerial arrangement should only be accepted if the Irish landlords were subjected to Income-tax, Assessed Taxes, and a Poor Law of the all-embracing English kind.[8] Too long, held Roebuck, had Irish property been allowed to escape its just burdens.

It was, perhaps, the obvious approach of a General Election which caused a certain revival of Radical party activity during

[1] *Hansard*, January 25th, Lord J. Russell.
[2] *Ibid.*, January 19th, Labouchere, Chief Secretary, Ireland.
[3] *Ibid.*, March 8th, for Peel's figure of 700,000.
[4] *Ibid.*, January 25th, Lord J. Russell.
[5] Cf. *Ibid.*, February 1st and 4th, Roebuck.
[6] *Illustrated London News*, March 13th.   [7] *Hansard*, March 8th.
[8] There was no Outdoor Relief of any kind in Ireland under the Irish Poor Law of 1838, but the Russell Government was now about to make its introduction possible by the Poor Relief (Ireland) Bill. That Bill was very determinedly fought by Irish landowners under Irish Whig leadership (cf. *Hansard*, Lords, May 6th).

the Session. Duncombe renewed the project of amending the Reform Act of 1832,[1] Sharman Crawford and Tennyson D'Eyncourt moved against the Septennial Act, and Ewart and Bowring divided the House at 41-81 on a project of abolishing capital punishment.[2] Fielden's Ten Hour Bill, moreover, was taken through to the Statute Book despite the opposition of a combination of opposites led by Peel, Graham, Roebuck, Hume and Bright, and the Prime Minister's appeal for a preliminary experiment with an Eleven Hour Bill.[3]

The principal subject of "Social Reform" on which strong Radical sections were arrayed against the Government during the 1847 Session was that of popular education. Education and public health were the two subjects of "practical" import which had apparently been best prepared for Ministerial treatment by the newspaper discussions and the philanthropic efforts of the preceding years. Especially was education an activity which the Whigs were moved to encourage, because in their optimistic view educated labourers would be brought more easily to understand the infallibility of McCullochian economics, the folly of Chartism, and the merits of thrift and birth limitation. Accordingly, Kay-Shuttleworth, the notable Secretary to the Committee of Council on Education, had been encouraged to produce in August and December 1846 two famous minutes which were the basis of Lord John Russell's proposals of April 19th to the House of Commons. Extra pay and entry into a pensions scheme was to be offered to those school teachers who were deemed worthy of certificates of merit by the Government Inspectorate. The entry of suitable recruits into teaching work was, moreover, to be secured by subsidising arrangements for an apprenticeship period to be followed in proper cases by a period in a "normal school."[4]

For reasons which will be given below, Radical Dissenters had been organising an attempt to defeat the scheme for months before Lord John Russell spoke, and to save it embarrassing concessions had had to be made to the Wesleyans,[5] who had thus been separated from the bulk of Nonconformity. Among these

---

[1] *Hansard*, February 23rd.   [2] *Ibid.*, March 9th.
[3] *Ibid.*, March 17th, Lord J. Russell. The Bill, it should be remembered, applied not only to children and young persons, but to adult women also.
[4] H. Holman, *English National Education*, pp. 115-19, for a summary of the Minutes.
[5] *Hansard*, April 19th. Cf. E. Hodder, *Life of Shaftesbury*, ii, 214-25.

Parliamentary Radicalism an Increasing Force

concessions was an undertaking that no part of the grant of 1847 was to go to Roman Catholic schools or to schools of other types where the Authorised Version of the Bible was not employed. Though anti-Catholic and anti-Secular prejudices had thus been met, hostile Dissenters were nevertheless numerous enough to send 4,204 petitions signed by 559,978[1] persons to Westminster against the scheme.

Ever since the pro-Anglican education plan of 1843 Dissenters had viewed the Committee of Council on Education with great suspicion. In any case the distribution of more public money through its agency was most unwelcome to them, for according to Lord John Russell's own admission of April 19th Church schools had found the means of absorbing 18s. 9d. of every pound which Parliament had so far voted for education. It was Bright, perhaps, who most vehemently gave voice to anti-Church sentiments when he protested against the further aggrandisement of a Church which was the enemy of liberty and against the increase of its powers to do mischief when Disestablishment was not far removed.[2] Duncombe, who led the opposition, took wider ground. Apart from urging the certainty that the money to be spent would not be divided equitably between the Church and the Dissenters, he criticised the cowardice which the Government had shown in excluding Catholics from the scheme, and argued that the Government plan would involve vast expenditure[3] and turn every schoolmaster into a Government agent relying on Government patronage.

That Ewart, whose zeal for the spread of useful knowledge had placed the Museums Act on the Statute Book in 1845, felt considerable qualms about the scheme is evidence that it contained objectionable features. He seems to have agreed with Roebuck's secularist objections to turning every Government-subventioned schoolmaster into a teacher of religion charged with inculcating the Authorised Version. But like Molesworth and others in that Parliament, Ewart, for all his objections to particular

---

[1] *Companion to the British Almanac, 1847*, p. 214. This was by far the biggest petitioning of the Session. The Ten Hour Bill, for example, which had been the subject of determined campaigning for years, called out 752 favourable petitions with 178,937 signatures, and the Health of Towns Bill 306 favourable petitions with 40,985 signatures. [2] *Hansard*, April 20th.
[3] *Ibid.*, April 19th. Duncombe ventured the figure of two millions annually.

points, was not prepared to refuse the extra money offered to education by the Government. After three days of debate, therefore, the division of April 22nd showed the disappointing figures of 47–372 to the anti-Establishment Radicals, who had been in hopes of repeating their victory of 1843.[1] Those who study Macaulay's well-known speech during the proceedings will understand what effective use had been made of police and wealth-production arguments in winning so relatively easy a passage for the Government proposals. A properly schooled people, argued Macaulay, would not only leave property alone but "merely as producers of wealth" would repay a hundredfold the proposed expenditure. Nor was this all. "For every pound you save in education," he urged, "you will spend five in prosecutions, in prisons, in penal settlements."[2]

The Government's health programme had much more general Radical approval than its programme of education. But the problem of constructing a satisfactory Central Board of Health and Public Works, linked by an Inspectorate to elective local authorities with adequate powers of drainage, nuisance removal, water supply, and smoke abatement, was no easy one, as the Peel Government had already discovered. On July 8th, indeed, the Health of Towns Bill, the Government's main Public Health measure,[3] was withdrawn, and the advent of the water-tap into the homes of the urban poor, to mention only one of the pictures which Lord Morpeth had called up in his opening speech of March 30th, was indefinitely delayed. Anxious to clear the way for a General Election which the whole nation was impatiently awaiting, Ministers felt unable to keep the House sitting discussing the endless amendments of detail which the representatives of local interests insisted on pressing. Ministers may well have been pardoned some anxiety to escape from the enormous labours involved by the enactment of new administrative codes. They had already had much fatiguing work of that kind in connexion

---

[1] When the Government, overwhelmed by a flood of petitions, had given way and withdrawn its proposals.

[2] *Hansard*, April 19th. The main Education debate was on April 19th, 20th, and 22nd. It was renewed by Molesworth on April 26th.

[3] But the Baths and Washhouses Act (1847) made that of the previous year more effective and the immense Town Improvement (Clauses) Act offered an immense budget of good things sanitary from parks and medical officers of health to advanced building and house drainage regulations, which future promoters of Local Acts, Radical or Humanitarian, might try to get adopted.

with Ireland, and they had had also to design a new type of Central Poor Law Authority in place of the Poor Law Commission, totally discredited now by the persistent hostility of *The Times* and the last fatal Andover Workhouse scandal.[1] In regard to the competence of the new Poor Law Board, Humanitarians and Radicals had combined to force one significant change upon the unwilling Government. Married couples over sixty years of age were not to be separated in the workhouse.[2]

The General Election of July and August 1847 was held in circumstances which favoured the gain of greater influence by Radicalism. For one thing the Tory forces which had been led to victory by Peel in 1841 were now in total decomposition in many constituencies, so that even a number of county divisions were resigned without a contest. Cobden, for example, was returned unopposed for the West Riding, and other very Radical personalities also for South Lancashire and East Surrey.[3] Industrial stress, again, had for some time been pressing upon certain of the industrial areas with considerable severity,[4] and the general effect seems to have been to favour the more Radical varieties of candidate. Two Ultra-Radical candidates whose return to Parliament caused a notable raising of eyebrows among the "respectable classes" were George Thompson, who had carried by storm the vastest urban constituency in the country, that of the Tower Hamlets, and W. J. Fox, who had been elected by Oldham. These men had neither the social station of a fellow-Ultra like Colonel Thompson, now returned for Bradford, nor the wealth of a Sir Joshua Walmsley, now member for Leicester. On the contrary, they had taken the wages of the League during the Anti-Corn Law agitation. In sum, the election had resulted in the return of a smaller number of military and naval officers, country gentlemen, and relations of peers, and of a larger number of barristers, merchants, railway contractors, and political writers and lecturers.[5]

[1] Cf. J. L. and B. Hammond, *The Age of the Chartists*, pp. 68–9.
[2] *Hansard*, June 24th, for the first forcing of this amendment upon the Government by 70–58. After further struggles it became part of the 10 & 11 Vict. c. 109.
[3] Cf. C. R. Dod, *Electoral Facts, 1832–1866*, under constituencies.
[4] Though the price of corn, and therefore of bread, was falling from the huge heights to which the universal crop deficiencies of 1846 had finally taken it, the deadness of business during the first half of the year was by no means completely overcome, and the financial situation was actually deteriorating (*Illustrated London News*, x, xi, 1847).
[5] *Quarterly Review*, September 1847, pp. 541–2.

English Radicalism 1832–1852

One of the political writers and lecturers returned had been Feargus O'Connor himself, who was elected for Nottingham. A review of election accounts, indeed,[1] would lead to the conclusion that the opportunities for political demonstration afforded by the General Election had served as a distinct fillip to Chartism[2]—this though none of O'Connor's lieutenants secured the right to accompany his leader back to Westminster. Certainly the Chartist Land Plan continued to attract a surprising volume of financial support[3] despite the hostile Press criticism to which it was being subjected. Indeed, it would almost seem that O'Connor's counter-efforts, seconded by those of Ernest Jones, his lieutenant, and of M'Douall, Kydd, and West, his perambulating lecturers, more than counterbalanced the hostile criticisms in their effects on the mind of the average Chartist sympathiser.[4] Accordingly, O'Connor was able to continue confidently with his land enterprises, and to prepare for a great new Chartist petition also which should bear 5,000,000 signatures. Meanwhile events abroad were already hastening towards the revolutions of 1848, which were to give Chartism another revolutionary impulse similar to those of 1839 and 1842. Both Chartist leaders and rank and file, nurtured on a long course of sympathy with the victims of European autocracies, were particularly liable to catch any revolutionary infection that might be in the air. The famous Engels and Marx[5] looked for years to British Chartism as a movement that might in the end decide the triumph of European democracy.

Meanwhile came the alarming money-market crisis of September and October 1847, which compelled the Government to authorise the Bank of England to disregard the tight currency restrictions of the Bank Charter Act of 1844.[6] The corollary to this extraordinary measure was the summons of Parliament to an

---

[1] R. Gammage, *History of the Chartist Movement*, pp. 283–5.
[2] O'Connor, it should be remembered, defeated a Cabinet Minister, Ernest Jones attacked the Chancellor of the Exchequer's seat, Harney that of the Foreign Secretary, McGrath that of another Minister, and Clark that of two. The defeat of Macaulay at Edinburgh, again, was celebrated by Chartists as due in part at least to Chartist preference for the Radical Cowan.
[3] *Northern Star*, November 13, 1847, for the figure of 42,000 shareholders who had paid £80,000. Meanwhile he had purchased the fourth estate of the Land Company in June, and was later to plan the addition of a fifth.
[4] Gammage, *op. cit.*, pp. 286–90.
[5] Cf. Julius West, *History of the Chartist Movement*, pp. 283–5.
[6] *Illustrated London News*, October 30th.

Parliamentary Radicalism an Increasing Force

unusually early Session in order to consider the Indemnity Act which might become necessary and the whole problem of the "excessive" drain of capital to railway financing that had contributed to bring on the crisis.[1] Though the Government's belated suspension of the Bank Charter Act prevented a complete collapse of the money market, it came too late to prevent the marked repercussions of the money crisis upon the industrial situation of the ensuing months. At the end of October, for example, there was a significant attempt to organise a "general strike" of factory operatives of twenty-four towns in the cotton districts against a threatened 10 per cent wage reduction.[2] On December 20th, again, prior to the adjournment of Parliament, the industrial situation in the Midlands was calamitous enough to lead to protests from Midland members against so distant a reassembly date as February 3rd.[3] In short, the industrial position at home once again favoured the growth of "extreme" political sentiments among the working classes.

The Parliamentary discussions of November and December 1847 had turned not only on "Commercial Distress" but on Ireland. The insurrectionary temper of that country had undoubtedly grown as a result of the removal by death of O'Connell's restraining hand. As winter approached without Repeal, Tenant Right or Exchequer support for the Irish Poor Law, "criminal outrages" commenced on a scale which led the Government to ask Parliament for a Coercion Act almost as soon as it was assembled.[4] It was a situation which enabled O'Connor to act in Parliament as the most determined Repealer there,[5] and so to forward those hopes of allying British and Irish discontents which had been the ceaseless preoccupation of Chartism since 1838. Much more reputable Radicals than O'Connor had strong things to say on the Irish situation that winter. Bright's Third Reading speech on the Coercion Bill of the year, the Crime and Outrage

---

[1] The railway explanation was not sufficient for Currency reformers of various types who attempted in imitation of the Anti-Corn Law League to found a National Anti-Gold Law League (*Illustrated London News*, November 20th).   [2] *Ibid.*, October 30th.

[3] *Hansard*, December 20th, Messrs. Spooner and Newdegate. Birmingham and the Black Country were suffering severely from the cessation of railway orders.

[4] *Ibid.*, November 29th, Sir George Grey (Home Secretary).

[5] *Ibid.*, December 7th, for his motion, which he declined to withdraw on the Home Secretary's appeal, and which was rejected by 23–255.

English Radicalism 1832–1852

Bill, may be taken as a vigorous presentation of the attitude towards the Irish situation of the British middle-class Radical.[1] Regretfully voting for the Bill, Bright demanded legislation which would enable the vast, ill-managed, and decaying masses of debt-encumbered landed estates to be put up for sale. So, he hoped, would commence a revivifying circulation of real property in Ireland which might bring the land into the hands of those with the capital to raise it to English standards of productivity and the tenantry with it to higher standards of efficiency and responsibility. In pressing at the same time for the abolition of primogeniture and entail, the simplification of title, and the reduction of the cost of land-transfer, Bright urged what all the British Radicals had long been doing in regard to the land-system not only of Ireland but of Great Britain also. All these measures they felt were necessary if landholding, and with it much of the political, social, and economic life of the nation, were to be defeudalised.

When Parliament came together early in February the first important question put before it was a Government Jewish Emancipation Bill, which had the warmest Radical support in and out of Parliament.[2] Soon afterwards followed a Budget on which the case was very different. The Government proposed not merely to continue the unpopular Income-tax but formidably to increase it in order to "strengthen the national defences."[3] In the country Cobden had already fought the panic fear of French invasion, which had quickly risen to great heights following on the unauthorised divulgation of the Duke of Wellington's alarmist views.[4] But the issue was distinctly doubtful until it became clear to the large sections of the middle classes, which had been disposed to believe in the instant necessity of great defence measures, that they would be required to pay for them. Then, indeed, there burst forth an outcry[5] which became irresistible when the very monarch against whose possible designs the country had been

---

[1] *Hansard*, December 13th; *Speeches of John Bright*, pp. 153 sqq.
[2] All the Radical newspapers, the *Weekly Dispatch*, *Lloyd's Weekly*, *Daily News*, etc., gave strong support, so that the high figure of petition-signatures is explicable. There were 889 petitions with 302,728 signatures for Jewish Emancipation, and 832 with 56,986 against (*Companion to the British Almanac, 1849*, p. 218). [3] *Hansard*, February 18th, Lord John Russell.
[4] *Cobden's Political Writings*, *The Three Panics*, ii, 225–31.
[5] Cf. *Illustrated London News*, February 26, 1848.

Parliamentary Radicalism an Increasing Force

invited to arm itself was chased from his throne. But Income-tax payers were not satisfied with the Government's abandonment of the projected increase in the Income-tax that was announced on February 28th, four days after the collapse of the throne of Louis Philippe. Urging the unfairness of a tax which mulcted "precarious" trading and professional incomes equally with secure incomes from property, the agitators attempted to enlist the working-class help which would end the Income-tax altogether.[1]

The very vigorous Income-tax agitation, conducted as it was under Radical auspices, provided something of the contagiously excited atmosphere which enabled a semi-revolutionary Chartist movement to be launched. The successive Continental revolutions, the news of which strangely unsettled even the most prosaic of the middle class,[2] had a much deeper effect on working men still suffering extensively from the industrial results of the financial shocks of 1847. On March 2nd an enthusiastic London meeting of the Chartists sent a congratulatory deputation to the Republican Government at Paris, and very soon Stepney Green, Bethnal Green, and Clerkenwell Green, the principal meeting-places of the working-class politicians of the Metropolis, were the scenes of "immense gatherings."[3] That the provincial towns were also overcome by the same excitement became evident from the events of the week beginning on Monday, March 6th. Glasgow especially was for a time in the hands of a mob pillaging provision shops and shouting "Bread or Revolution" and "Vive La République."[4] But it was London's West End which saw the most remarkable Chartist manifestations. For three successive days there were Chartist hostilities with the police in connexion with the ban placed upon meetings in Trafalgar Square, and on one occasion a movement was attempted upon Buckingham Palace.[5]

After this explosive intimation of its revival Chartism engaged in several weeks of mass meetings, sometimes in halls, sometimes on town greens, and sometimes on the waste ground outside or between populous places.[6] Chartists were once more listening to

---
[1] Cf. *Illustrated London News*, February 26th, March 4th.
[2] *Ibid.*, March 4th, for the vastly increased newspaper sales (p. 155).
[3] R. Gammage, *History of the Chartist Movement*, p. 293.
[4] *Illustrated London News*, March 11th, for a very hostile account. Unemployment in Glasgow and, indeed, in all industrial Scotland was very serious. For the grave situation some weeks later, cf. *Illustrated London News*, February 5th.
[5] Gammage, *op. cit.*, pp. 294–5.   [6] *Ibid.*, pp. 296–301.

inflammatory oratory, signing yet another National Petition, and electing yet another Convention. Meanwhile the outbreak of successful democratic revolution even in Berlin and Vienna increased the hopefulness of Chartists and led to much more attention being given by the middle-class Radicals to the problem of forcing on the consideration of Suffrage Extension.[1] But when the new Chartist Convention came together on April 4th after weeks of exciting declamation by a band of the most experienced agitators in the country, hopes of speedy triumph were much too vivid to allow the delegates to consider mere plans of effecting Suffrage Reform through the "People's Party" of Humes and Cobdens sometimes mooted in the Radical Press.[2] Instead the delegates adopted a much more ambitious programme. If the Petition were rejected, the Convention would prepare a memorial to the Queen calling for a Dissolution of Parliament and the appointment of Ministers willing to make the Charter a Cabinet measure. This memorial would be presented to "simultaneous meetings" on Good Friday, April 21st, which would give approval and elect representatives to a National Assembly empowered to sit until the Charter became the law of the land.[3]

Events made the manner of the National Petition's presentation of singular importance. For this Petition over 5,000,000 signatures were now claimed, and the Convention desired that the signature rolls should be accompanied to the Houses of Parliament by a huge procession which was first to be mustered on Kennington Common. In this procession, however, the Government perceived the possibilities of revolution, and invoking an Act of Charles II's time it issued a proclamation declaring the procession illegal and throwing the taint of illegality over the Kennington meeting also.[4] Meanwhile the Duke of Wellington was taking most elaborate military precautions with the soldiery, fashionable society was arranging to fill its West End mansions with "trusty men" fully armed,[5] and the number of special constables sworn in was being raised to over 150,000.[6] The danger against which this huge

---

[1] Cf. T. W. Reid, *Life of W. E. Forster*, i, 220–6, for conditions at Bradford, where five hundred electors and more promised the unenfranchised aid with their Suffrage demands, while "loudly preaching order and abusing violence."
[2] Cf. *Weekly Dispatch*, March 26, 1848.
[3] Gammage, *op. cit.*, p. 309.   [4] *Illustrated London News*, April 8th.
[5] Lord Malmesbury, *Memoirs of an Ex-Minister*, under April 10th. Malmesbury brought up five gamekeepers from the country, and says "a great many have done the same."   [6] *The Times*, April 11th.

Parliamentary Radicalism an Increasing Force

array of force was gathered proved unexpectedly slight. Only some 25,000 working men,[1] sacrificing the day's pay, arrived in orderly processions from various parts of London to hear the feast of oratory prepared for them on Kennington Common by the delegates of the Convention. These had already decided on O'Connor's advice to abandon the procession from Kennington to Westminster but to allow the Petition signatures to go forward unaccompanied after the Kennington proceedings should have ended. The only violence, therefore, that occurred that day was some scuffling between returning demonstrators and the police, who tried to keep Blackfriars Bridge closed far too long.

The story of how O'Connor told the Commons that night that the Petition was signed by 5,706,000 persons, and how the Committee on Petitions engaged a staff to check this statement is well known. On April 13th the Committee was able to inform the House that the total of purported signatures was only 1,975,469; that many of these were fraudulent, seeing that numerous consecutive signatures were in the same handwriting; and that others represented mere outbursts of buffoonery or profanity.[2] Devastating as these revelations proved to the last shreds of O'Connor's personal credit in Parliament, it would be wrong to argue, as so many popular histories have done, that they at once reduced the Chartist movement to insignificance. On the contrary, the Chartist leaders, secure in the unswerving loyalty of the great mass of working-class sentiment, were about to undertake another vigorous course of activity which included an attempt to come to an alliance with the "Young Ireland" movement now preparing for rebellion.[3]

The very frankness, indeed, with which the most varied sections of "public opinion" agreed that popular discontent continued very widespread promoted a powerful middle-class effort at a "New Reform Movement" which should offer a measure of

---

[1] *Illustrated London News*, April 15th, gave the number of 23,000 to 25,000, but made this include processionists and spectators. This paper contains some interesting illustrations of the day's happenings.

[2] *Hansard*, April 13th (Thornley). He mentioned such signatures as Victoria Rex, the Duke of Wellington, Sir Robert Peel, Pugnose, Longnose, Flatnose, Punch, etc. *Companion to the British Almanac, 1849*, p. 218, gives 577 petitions with 2,018,888 signatures for Universal Suffrage. These figures included the "Monster Petition."

[3] Gammage, *op. cit.*, p. 324, for Irish assemblies addressed by special envoys from the Chartist Convention.

281

appeasement. The initiative was taken at Manchester, where the old Anti-Corn Law League circle gathering round George Wilson, their chairman, made a first move which was widely imitated by their former associates in other manufacturing towns. Cobden and Bright were meanwhile securing Hume as the most helpful standard-bearer of the cause, and with Hume the assurance of solid backing from the Parliamentary Radicals, of whom between 80 and 90 ultimately voted against the Government.[1] In the first half of May, therefore, the "New Reform Movement" was already in its stride with an increasing number of meetings, and, as events proved, Radicalism had opened a Suffrage Extension campaign which can hardly be said to have ceased for decades. One thing should be noted in this "New Reform" pressure which was an innovation. The great provincial centres were already very dissatisfied with their representation in the Commons by two members when their population and position entitled them to much greater weight. At Manchester, for example, the claim to seven members was an important factor in winning adherents to the "New Reform," and much the same thing appears to have been true of similar claims in other centres, including the Metropolis.[2]

[1] *The Times*, May 1st, contains an early account of the first steps in the movement.
[2] *Hansard*, June 20th (xcix, 957 sqq.), for unfriendly commentary by Disraeli.

CHAPTER XVII

THE CONTINUED PRESSURE FOR INNOVATION, 1848

"I believe it to be essential to the peace of the world, and to the stability of Governments, that the experiment which is now being made in France shall have a fair trial, and not be embarrassed or disturbed by extrinsic intervention. But at the same time when I look at the social principles which are professed, I must say that I hope the working classes of this country will not be deluded by the doctrines which are held on subjects which intimately concern their labour and employment. If the doctrines there maintained be true—if there be indeed an antagonism between capital and labour—if it be true that all men, without reference to their different capabilities, their different degrees of strength, and their different capacities ought to have the same iron formula applied to them—if, I say, these things be true, then all the experience and all the science of the last 150 years have existed in vain. Let us in that case burn the works of Turgot, of Say, and of Adam Smith. . . . But I do earnestly hope—I have that confidence in the good sense of the working classes in this country which induces me to believe —that no false delusions as to a compulsory sharing of profits, no enmity directed against capital, no destruction of competition, no overbearing of individual energy by Government undertakings at the public expense, will in this country be considered for the benefit of the working classes, or as likely if they prevailed, to be attended with any other result than the fatal one of involving them in misery and ruin. . . ."

PEEL *in the Commons, April 18, 1848.*

"The value of this 'organisation of industry' (co-partnership) for healing the widening and embittering feud between the class of labourers and the class of capitalists must, I think, impress itself on all who habitually reflect. . . . I cannot conceive how any such person can persuade himself that the majority of the community will, for ever, or even for much longer, consent to hew wood or draw water all their lives in the service and for the benefit of others or can doubt that they will be less and less willing to co-operate as subordinate agents in any work when they have no interest in the result: and that it will be more and more difficult to obtain the best work-people, or the best services of any work-people, except on condition of their being made participants in the profits of their own labours. . . ."

J. S. MILL *in* "Principles of Political Economy," *ii, 335.1848.*

THAT Chartism should again have been frightening Whitehall in June 1848, not two months after the "Monster Petition" fiasco of April, needs some explanation. Nor will an explanation suffice that is confined to demonstrating the energy of Chartist leaders like Jones, M'Douall, and Kydd, who, after the "simultaneous meetings" of Eastertide had ended, contrived to hold the National Assembly in spite of the discouraged O'Connor's ban.[1] One factor that should not be forgotten is the continuous stimulation that came from events on the Continent, and especially from Paris, where "Red Republicanism" was singularly powerful and Communistic Socialism was entrenched in the State workshops. It was this stimulation from Continental events, indeed, that had much to do with the revival of Chartist journalism which began at this stage.[2] Another factor to be taken into account in explaining Chartist strength is the industrial distress of the time, a distress largely due to the fast falling off of purchases by the revolution- and war-ridden Continent.[3] Lastly may be noted the excitement of the Irish in the industrial towns following on Government prosecutions of "Young Ireland's" leaders.[4] By the end of May the combined operation of all the forces noted above was undoubtedly contributing to the growth of an insurrectionary temper in the working-class parts of London and some of the principal industrial centres. Of Bradford, for example, a future Radical Cabinet Minister was writing as follows on May 26th: "I find the state of the town most alarming; the physical forcists have gained a strength in my absence which I almost think I could have prevented. Large numbers of men are armed and drilling nightly, and

[1] R. Gammage, *History of the Chartist Movement*, pp. 322–30.
[2] *Ibid.*, pp. 345–6. Gammage allows Bronterre O'Brien's *Reformer* a circulation of 15,000. It is to be noted that new forces entered the fray by the side of O'Brien, O'Connor, Harney, Linton, Holyoake, and others of the "old guard." The most gifted of the new recruits were, perhaps, those remarkable plebeian poets, Gerald Massey and J. B. Leno. That their new "Red Republican" paper, *The Spirit of Freedom*, could be begun with an issue of one thousand as late as April 1849—and in Uxbridge!—suggests how circumscribed must be the acceptance of the traditional textbook view that Chartism "collapsed" in April 1848 (cf. *Autobiography of J. B. Leno* (1892), pp. 42–3).
[3] *Illustrated London News*, May 20th, for Leeds, June 10th for Manchester. Besides unemployment there was wage-cutting as at Sunderland shipyards.
[4] *Ibid.*, June 3rd for London, Manchester, Stockport, Oldham, Leeds, Bradford, etc., demonstrations after a fourteen-years' transportation sentence in Dublin.

The Continued Pressure for Innovation 1848

there is of course much fear and suspicion, and a bitter class feeling."[1]

Meanwhile official and propertied London was growing increasingly nervous of the incessant meetings at Clerkenwell Green and other Chartist rendezvous, and the processions formed in connexion with them.[2] On June 4th, therefore, large bodies of mounted and foot police were used with great vigour against Chartist meetings in the open spaces of Bethnal Green and Hackney, and on June 6th a number of Chartist leaders, including Ernest Jones, were arrested.[3] These measures, it was hoped, would help to defeat the Chartist plan of holding "simultaneous meetings" on Whit-Monday, June 12th. To supplement them, extensive bodies of troops and police were marched on to the Chartist meeting-grounds on Whit-Monday itself.[4]

Similar steps were taken in the provinces, especially at Manchester and Birmingham, so that the only formidable Chartist demonstration that took place that day was in the West Riding, where a great mass meeting was gathered on Toftshaw Moor between Bradford and Leeds. In July and August official alarm grew high once more, and if the expected Irish revolt had not proved abortive, there might possibly have been revolutionary attempts in England. There was actually one such attempt on August 14th at Ashton-under-Lyne, which was rapidly followed by extensive Chartist arrests in Manchester and London of men who were charged with preparing for revolt.[5] There were more arrests in September, and indeed the newspapers were still reporting Chartist trials till just before Christmas.[6]

One not unimportant consequence of the Chartist menace of 1848 may be noticed before attention is turned to the "New Reform Movement" by which the middle-class Radicals hoped to achieve working-class appeasement. A group of scholarly and philanthropic Anglicans, clerical and lay, were moved to make

---

[1] T. W. Reid, *Life of W. E. Forster*, i, 247.
[2] *Illustrated London News*, June 3rd.
[3] *Ibid.*, June 10th. In July Jones and five others received sentences of two years' imprisonment. [4] *Ibid.*, June 17th.
[5] *Ibid.*, August 19th, 26. One of these prisoners was the Chartist leader, Dr. M'Douall, who was speedily sentenced to two years' imprisonment. Some of the London sentences, obtained by the use of a most disreputable *agent provacateur*, were to transportation for life.
[6] *Ibid.*, December 23rd, for a death sentence, four sentences of transportation for life, etc.

the bold attempt to Christianise the vast flood of Chartist discontent and launched the Christian Socialist movement. The Christianity of Maurice and Kingsley, the remarkable clerical leaders of the movement, was profoundly social-democratic as Shaftesbury's *grand seigneur* evangelicism never was. Maurice, for example, when closing the famous weekly series of *Politics for the People* in July 1848, regretfully acknowledged that the comparative lack of success with the working classes had been due to the failure to keep "the relation between the capitalist and the labourer" as the most prominent subject in his pages.[1] Kingsley, again, the vigorous Parson Lot of the *Politics for the People* and the later *Christian Socialist*, had already written *Yeast*, and was to go on to produce that epoch-making and sympathetic study of a Chartist leader, the novel *Alton Locke* (1850).

From the beginnings of 1848 were to come the conferences with Chartist leaders in 1849 which issued immediately in attempts to launch co-operative production,[2] next in the establishment of the Central Co-operative Agency of Vansittart Neale, parent of the huge Co-operative Wholesale activities of to-day, and finally in the winning of legal status for all co-operative societies in the Industrial and Provident Societies Act of 1852.[3] Thus did Christian Socialism most effectively serve Owenites and Chartists, engaged like the Rochdale Equitable Pioneers in building up what measure of co-operative activity was obtainable without political revolution. Christian Socialism's activities, indeed, make a singularly important supplement in the economic field to those working-class efforts represented by the labours of the National Association of United Trades.[4]

It is time to turn to the New Reform Movement of the middle-class Radicals. More lay behind the vigour of the Radical resurgence than mere desire for Chartist appeasement. The aristocracy, Whig and Tory alike, was still felt to be leagued to

---

[1] C. W. Stubbs, *Charles Kingsley and the Christian Social Movement*, p. 106.

[2] Capital was supplied for the opening of co-operative tailors', hatters', and shoemakers' shops, which it was hoped might set the working class a lead. See J. B. Leno's *Autobiography*, pp. 44–9, which also offers an explanation of the breakdown of these and similar enterprises.

[3] C. W. Stubbs, *op. cit.*, pp. 129–45. It should be noted that the Christian Socialists had been stirred anew by the famous series of articles in the *Morning Chronicle* (1849) on "London Labour and the London Poor."

[4] This Association launched its own journal, the *Labour League*, on August 5, 1848. Its "Trades" approach to social and political problems in 1848–9 makes its perusal indispensable.

The Continued Pressure for Innovation 1848

maintain too barbarically costly a Court; the Government services, and especially the Army and Navy, were suspected of being conducted with a profusion very helpful to "younger sons"; and the system of taxation was very widely resented, especially in its collection of Income-tax from "precarious incomes" at the same rate as from the assured incomes derived from land and the funds.[1] If these things were to be altered, if the Protectionist "reaction" was to be guarded against, if a beginning was to be made with the defeudalisation of the countryside by challenging the economic structure imposed upon it by primogeniture and entails, it would be necessary to loosen the landed caste's tight grip on three-quarters and more of the representation. For one thing, Malton and Manchester, Leominster and Liverpool, Shoreham and Sheffield, Wenlock and Westminster could no longer be permitted to weigh equally in the House of Commons.[2]

The resolution moved at the numerous meetings held in support of the "New Reform Movement" during May and June 1848 are, perhaps, the best indication of its scope. At the Middlesex County Meeting of May 17th, for example, the resolutions adopted after peaceably urged Chartist amendments had been outvoted ran as follows:[3]

> That in the opinion of this meeting the Commons House of Parliament as at present constituted does not fairly represent the population, the property, or the industry of the country; that the disclosures made before committees of 1835, 1842, and also during the present session, prove that the return of its members has been extensively influenced by bribery, corruption, coercion, and intimidation; that the Reform Act has not realised the just expectations of the country; that since the passing of that Act the public expenditure has not only been much more extravagant, but has exceeded by many millions sterling the expenditure of the last session of the unreformed Parliament; that the system of taxation is so contrived as to favour the aristocracy, and to

---

[1] *Illustrated London News*, May 20th, for the entry of the Equitable Taxation League into the Reform movement.

[2] Add. MSS. 40452, f. 267 (Peel Papers), contains a letter from the Whig Minister Cornewall Lewis to the Peelite Graham, showing the intense Whig dislike and suspicion of the mooters of the "New Reform Movement." "If the bulk of the upper and middle classes cannot continue to keep on good terms for the next six months," wrote Lewis on April 20th, "a few ambitious and vindictive men may call in the assistance of the working classes in the large towns and overthrow everything. I hear that Bright proposes that the Metropolis should return from fifty to sixty members, and by universal or household suffrage."

[3] *Illustrated London News*, May 20th.

English Radicalism 1832–1852

throw the pressure of its burden unjustly on the industrious classes of the people.

That to secure the stability of the throne, public order and contentment, the constitutional rights of the people, equalisation of taxation, economy of the public expenditure, just laws, and good government, it is indispensable that the elective franchise should be extended to all men who are registered as residents for a limited time; that the duration of parliaments should not exceed three years; that votes should be taken by ballot; and that there should be more equal apportionment of members to population.

It is a very Philistine Radicalism which is here represented with its eyes mainly fixed on reducing the taxation demand.

The introduction of the "New Reform Movement" into Parliament did not go altogether according to plan. Hume had been put in charge by the Radical section of the House, but when the appointed day arrived on May 23rd Lord George Bentinck, who had precedence, took advantage of it in a way which prevented Hume's business being reached till after eleven in the evening. In consultation with other Radicals, Hume decided that it was impossible to bring on so important a matter as the "New Reform Movement" in such circumstances, and that he had best defer it until the first "open day," June 20th.[1] O'Connor thereupon blamed Hume for juggling with the people, and Cobden rose to give the Chartist leader a terrible castigation as one who had done more than any other public man in the country to prevent the working classes obtaining what they wanted by the only means which promised them success. The quarrel between the Radicals and the Chartist seemed to give the Prime Minister a good tactical opportunity for asserting that the masses desired neither the Chartist plan nor that of the Radicals. Straightway Hume appealed to the "Reformers of the United Kingdom" to prove before June 20th what were their wishes, and the angry Radicals followed his advice.[2] A singularly active campaign of meetings and petitions preceded the next bringing on of the Radical Reform motion.[3]

When he rose, therefore, on June 20th Hume spoke with considerably enhanced authority. He advocated not merely the ballot, triennial Parliaments, more equal electoral districts, and

---

[1] *Illustrated London News*, May 27th.
[2] In a widely printed letter dated from the House of Commons, May 23rd, midnight. [3] *Illustrated London News*, June 10th and 17th.

The Continued Pressure for Innovation 1848

abolition of the members' property qualification, but a suffrage extended to embrace all rate-paying householders and all sub-tenants also who should take the proper measures to pay their own rates. This extended suffrage, Hume considered, would add two millions[1] to the voting registers and make for better government.

In his reply Lord John Russell gave evidence that the strength of the New Reform Movement had impressed him. Though he opened by a maladroit attempt to show that many of the meetings of which the New Reformers boasted were attended rather by Chartists than New Reformers, the Prime Minister permitted himself to drop a few observations admitting some imperfection in the suffrage system. But he made it plain enough that the reforms for which the Whigs were prepared were of the scantiest. A vague reference was made to replacing the freemen of corrupt boroughs by the traders and mechanics; another to the possible award of the franchise to savings banks depositors; and a third to the enfranchisement of men who should be elected by "guilds" of their fellow-workers. But all this was still in the "perhaps not distant" future.[2] Meantime, while "erroneous and mischievous views of capital, of labour, and of property" were afloat and threatening danger, it was no time to consider great changes. The terrible street-fighting which the Socialist workmen of Paris began against the military on June 23rd, and continued for three whole days, came usefully to the aid of Whiggish arguments. When the final division was taken on July 6th the Radicals were beaten by 358 votes against 84.[3]

The efforts of the New Reformers were not, however, wasted. Their exposure of the anomalies and injustices of the existing suffrage system had produced the beginnings of concession not only from the Whig Front Bench but from *The Times*,[4] often a greater power. It was plain, too, that if the New Reformers persevered the Chartist following would increasingly become theirs. Meanwhile the course of politics furnished at intervals the small encouragements necessary to keep political crusaders in heart. On August 8th, for example, the Radicals contrived for the first time in history to defeat the Government on a Ballot

---

[1] *Hansard*, xcix, 899. [2] *Ibid.*, p. 929. [3] *Ibid.*, c, 226.
[4] *The Times*, May 27th, June 21st, and July 8th, on which last occasion the policy of "progressive reform" was adopted.

English Radicalism 1832-1852

motion. Their jubilation[1] over a mere division of 86-81 is, however, a proof of how far they still knew themselves to be from power.

It is time to turn to other Radical activities than those on suffrage subjects. Radicalism stood also for the de-ecclesiasticisation of the State, and though Jewish emancipation was now the subject of its principal political efforts in this sphere,[2] State and Church questions of other types were not lacking. One such question which had provoked special interest was brought before the Commons by Bouverie, a younger son of the very Radical Lord Radnor, whom it was soon found convenient to take into the Whig official circle. Since the break-up of the State Church of Scotland various Free Church communities had found it impossible to obtain suitable land, on which to erect their new churches, from irate landowners furious at the schism which their insistence on patronage rights had provoked. In proposing a Bill which made the sale of sites for churches compulsory, Bouverie was in effect merely extending the principle of the Land Clauses Act of 1845, which had already accepted compulsory landlord expropriation against full compensation in such cases as railway construction. Bouverie's Bill was, however, rejected on Third Reading,[3] and a number of Scottish Free Church congregations had to continue meeting in the open air under conditions which a Commons Select Committee of 1847 had condemned.

Bouverie, too, it was who on May 30th urged the need for sweeping away the anachronistic jurisdiction which ecclesiastical courts applying outworn codes and using "inefficient but costly procedure" retained over "some of the most important civil rights of the subject." The matter had excited Radical attention before, as it well might do seeing the manner in which the gentlemen of Doctors' Commons had retained their expensive and antiquated control of the huge legal provinces of Probate and Marriage with Admiralty thrown in. The whole treatment of marriage was in special need of modernisation. For one thing, the prohibited degrees of relationship were widely felt to lack justification in several instances, and the prohibition of marriage

---

[1] *Illustrated London News*, August 12th. *Punch*, still inclined to Radicalism of the Cobden and Hume type, turned Russell's Anti-Ballot speech to ridicule, and made him also the subject of a Ballot cartoon.
[2] The Lords having rejected the Jewish Emancipation Bill (*Hansard*, May 25th), the struggle was far from over. [3] *Hansard*, c, 613.

The Continued Pressure for Innovation 1848

with a deceased wife's sister was especially disregarded with a frequency which had led to the appointment of a Commission of Inquiry only the year before. Then as another relic of the Middle Ages the Ecclesiastical Courts had no power to grant divorce with permission to remarry, but only a separation from bed and board. After having obtained such a separation from the Ecclesiastical Courts an innocent party, wishing to marry again, had to undertake the further expense of promoting a private Act of Parliament. Yet on the Continent some Protestant states had had divorce arrangements since the Reformation, and the French Revolution had served to extend the institution still further. In probate cases, again, on which the ownership of vast properties might turn, the Ecclesiastical Courts provided few of the securities of the Courts of Common Law. There was no oral examination of witnesses, for example, and no jury to give a verdict.[1] According to the Home Secretary, however, the whole subject of the Ecclesiastical Courts bristled with difficulties, and though he recognised the need for change he asked inevitably for delay.

Of the landholding system Radical criticism was particularly vigorous during the Session. Bright was early in the field with a Bill to repeal the Game Laws, which, under the scrutiny of the Select Committee procured by him in 1845, had cut a very sorry figure.[2] That the right to kill and take ground game should be denied even to the tenant-farmers whose crops they were destroying was a very sore point with Radicals, who saw food needlessly wasted and the price of the rest enhanced so that landowners might jealously retain a "sporting rights" monopoly. Moreover, it had been made plain enough to the Committee that hungry, underpaid farm labourers declined to see anything criminal in snaring a hare or rabbit by night, though it might involve savage retribution by interested J.P.s administering an admittedly over-stringent code. The whole game situation had grown worse since landowners had taken to "rearing" game like pheasants and partridges in order to enjoy the sport of subsequent shooting parties. To farmers game-preserving on the part of their

---

[1] *Hansard*, xcix, 100 sqq.
[2] Harriet Martineau, *Autobiography*, ii, 257–8. Miss Martineau was so impressed that she set about to produce the three volumes of *Forest and Game-law Tales*, and afterwards gave the subject ample notice in her very famous *History of the Thirty Years' Peace*. The making of criminals by the Game Laws enforcement was one of the most deplorable features of the countryside.

landlords was especially noxious, for the birds often did great damage to their growing crops, and there was no means of driving them off or obtaining compensation from the landlord. To farm labourers the "reared" game brought new temptations but also corps of gamekeepers, the contest with whom sometimes led to transportation and the gallows. Yet, though Bright secured a long debate on March 23rd, and won an admission from the Home Secretary that there was a case "against the great accumulation of game and its strict preservation," a vote of 87 against 82[1] prevented the matter from being proceeded with.

That those two singularly intelligent Tories, Philip Pusey and Henry Drummond, should have been urging Tenant Right legislation during the Session is a sign that other Radical indictments of the current system of landholding were beginning to be appreciated. Nor would the publication of John Stuart Mill's *Political Economy*, destined as it was to be the economic textbook of the next three or four decades of Parliamentary Radicalism, do anything to weaken the case against the ruling system of land-tenure.[2] With that textbook, indeed, the merits of a system of peasant proprietorship may be deemed to have been admitted into the circle of orthodox economic thought. When contrasted with the system of the large estate, jealously preserved entire by primogeniture and strict settlements, and ultimately cultivated by classes as degraded as the English farm labourer and the Irish cottier, peasant proprietorship had very much to recommend it. Parliamentary politicians, however, even of the sturdiest Radical types, were not yet concerned with such a remote objective as peasant proprietorship. Cobden was thinking far ahead when he hoped to make the abolition of primogeniture one of the results of Suffrage Extension.[3]

---

[1] *Hansard*, xcvii, 962.

[2] *Principles of Political Economy with some of their Applications to Social Philosophy* (1848). Successive editions, too, as they appeared showed no greater friendliness to landlordism, but rather the reverse, as Mill collected more evidence favouring Peasant Properties. W. T. Thornton, Mill's friend, issued his *Plea for Peasant Proprietors* in 1848 also.

[3] Cf. J. Morley, *Life of Cobden*, pp. 491-2. "The great obstacle to all progress both in Ireland and England is the landlord spirit, which is dominant in political and social life. It is this spirit which prevents our dealing with the tenure of land. You would be astonished if behind the scenes in the Committees, and in the confidence of those men who frame bills for Parliament, to observe how vigilant the spirit of landlordism is in guarding its privileges, and how much the legislator who would hope to carry a measure through both Houses, is

The Continued Pressure for Innovation 1848

The Whig Front Bench, meanwhile, was wrestling with Irish difficulties which were driving it, in regard to Irish land at least, to consider policies which would have been regarded as revolutionary before the Famine. In November 1847, for example, Russell was sufficiently alarmed as to what would happen when he asked for Irish Coercion from a Parliament where Radicalism was stronger that he requested his Lord-Lieutenant to consider the following programme: (*a*) An occupant of five years' standing or more not to be ejected without a payment for the tenure of the soil, such payment not to exceed the value of five years' rent. (*b*) A tenant to be allowed to dispose of his tenure with allowance to the landlord in such a case of the full rights of the "Ulster custom." (*c*) In view of the shocking scenes being enacted at the evictions of starving cottier families, evictions by sheriff's officers on landlord demand to be brought under new legal checks.[1] It is almost unnecessary to add that the "practical politics" of 1847 soon forced Ministers to stop thinking along these dangerously Radical lines. They prepared rather to face agrarian outrage and possible rebellion with bayonets than the huge storm which would arise from the landlord world.

Accordingly the great Government measure of 1848 with regard to Ireland was the Encumbered Estates Act, and this was eventually pushed through to the Statute Book, though a Landlord and Tenant Bill enacting a measure of compensation for improvements had to be allowed to fall by the way. But the Encumbered Estates Bill of 1848 was less bold than the original project of

obliged to consult its sovereign will and pleasure. Hence the difficulty of dealing with game laws, copyholds, and such small matters, which grow into things of mighty import in the House of Commons, whilst the law of primogeniture is a sort of eleventh commandment.... If I had absolute power I would instantly issue an edict applying the law of succession as it exists in France to the land of Ireland.... I would so divide the property as to render it necessary to live upon the spot to look after it. But you can do nothing effectual in that direction with our Houses, and therefore I am in favour of letting in the householders as voters, so as to take away the domination of the squires" (Cobden to a correspondent, October 4, 1848).

[1] Spencer Walpole, *Life of Lord J. Russell*, i, 464, for (*a*) and (*b*), which occur in a letter of November 10th to the Lord-Lieutenant himself: (*c*) is mentioned in a letter to the great Irish landlord of the Cabinet, Lansdowne, on November 18th, and doubtless formed the subject of communication with Clarendon also. The procedure Russell was considering was the following: a tenant receiving notice of ejectment was to have an appeal to the assistant barrister; on receiving notice of such an appeal the assistant barrister notified the sheriff, who stopped the ejectment proceedings; the assistant barrister considering the appeal was only to be debarred from discretionary action if more than a year's rent were owing (*Ibid.*, p. 467).

1847, which had allowed a wider variety of interested parties to force the sale of an estate. After that gifted Radical newcomer Torrens M'Cullagh[1] had failed to expand the list of parties capable of forcing action, it was freely prophesied that the Government measure would fail to bring much land on to the market and would need supplementation in the very next Session. Such, indeed, proved the case.[2]

For the time, then, "practical" politicians, including the great body of the Parliamentary Radicals, saw no better hope for Ireland than the breaking up of the most undesirable of the old estates through the operation of an Encumbered Estates Court.[3] The sales ordered by this court were expected to attract into Irish landownership the men of capital and enterprise from all over the United Kingdom, who, it was widely assumed, would quickly undertake the profit-bringing outlays of new capital which would raise Ireland's condition nearer that of Great Britain. So strong, indeed, was current confidence in the inevitable beneficence of the operations of the "men of enterprise" that even politicians like Sharman Crawford and Poulett Scrope,[4] who for years had been goading on the Whig Front Bench in matters of Irish distress, were blind to its possible consequences. They, too, failed to foresee that only too often the "men of enterprise" purchasers of parcels of Encumbered Estate would be country attorneys and tradesmen who either contrived to wring more money out of the cottiers than the old landlords or cleared their land for grazing farms.[5] But if they made no difficulties about the Encumbered Estates legislation, they were still pressing the Whig Front Bench on other matters. Sharman Crawford was urging a Tenant Right Bill, and trying to save patches of a quarter of an acre or less for owners who were starving but could not

---

[1] B. 1813, and now M.P. for Dundalk. In 1868, as M.P. for Finsbury, was to become the father of Public Housing for the Working Classes by carrying the Torrens Act.

[2] The 1848 Act is the 11 & 12 Vict. c. 48. It had to be supplemented by the 12 & 13 Vict. c. 77, of 1849.

[3] Cf. Bright in *Speeches of John Bright*, pp. 155-7 (1847), p. 161 (1848), pp. 169-75 (1849).

[4] Scrope, it should be mentioned, was on Suffrage matters rather a Whig than a Radical. On Poor Law matters, however, he had been ready to attack the Whig Front Bench since the Poor Law Amendment Act of 1834.

[5] M. F. J. McDonnell, *Ireland and the Home Rule Movement*, pp. 56-8; Sir J. O'Connor, *History of Ireland, 1798-1924*.

The Continued Pressure for Innovation 1848

obtain relief while they retained possession.[1] Poulett Scrope was meanwhile pressing for action against the Boards of Guardians in whose areas people were being allowed to die of starvation, and was agitating also for the appropriation of Irish waste lands so that the able-bodied poor might be set to work upon them. Nor was this kind of pressure without administrative and even legislative result.[2]

It was in the Recess, however, rather than in the Session that Ministers were again tempted to consider the most Radical projects of handling the desperate Irish situation. The attempted rebellion of Smith O'Brien might have failed ignominiously, but the country seemed likely to become a heavy military and economic charge indefinitely unless there was a revolution in its administration and economy. Buller proposed such a scheme, which was under the serious consideration of the Cabinet for some time. The scheme included "strong government, abolition of jury unanimity in criminal cases, emigration on a large scale, particularly to the Cape of Good Hope, and the constitution of a Board of Employment and Cultivation who are to borrow money and invest it just as an individual capitalist might do."[3] If such a board had taken compulsory powers to acquire the extensive "waste" but improvable Irish lands from the proprietors, a huge volume of reclamation work might have been created and scores of thousands of families settled on the reclaimed acres on liberal terms. One advanced economic thinker had even suggested a programme as large as the following:[4]

Purchase of 1,600,000 acres at £2 per acre . . .	£3,200,000
Expense of drainage and subsoiling at £5 10s. . . .	8,800,000
Construction of 200,000 cottages at £40 each . . .	8,000,000
Advances to 200,000 cottiers of £20 each	4,000,000
	£24,000,000

---

[1] Cf. *Hansard*, March 7th, for Irish Tenant Right, when Crawford was assisted by Scrope and Bright to get a First Reading; March 9th for the other.

[2] In the administrative sphere the Irish Poor Law Board was to show very commendable activity both in 1848 and afterwards, and negligent local Boards of Guardians were frequently replaced. Assurances on this point were already given to Scrope on February 9th (*Hansard*). In the legislative sphere there was the 11 & 12 Vict. c. 46—*An Act for the protection and relief of the destitute poor evicted from their dwellings in Ireland*. It may be noted that Sharman Crawford's Outgoing Tenants Bill was only lost by 122-145.

[3] The words are from the Greville *Memoirs*.

[4] W. T. Thornton in *A Plea for Peasant Proprietors* (1848).

English Radicalism 1832-1852

It was argued that interest on the capital expenditure would probably be available from the rentals of the improved acres. But even if it was not, the raising of two hundred thousand families from destitution to independence, the relief of the rest of the peasantry from their ruinous competition for potato land, and finally the saving of several annual millions in Poor Relief expenditure were ample enough justification for the activities proposed.

It is hardly probable that Buller's Board of Employment and Cultivation would have gone as far as this. Nevertheless, the Chancellor of the Exchequer declared against it as violating all the orthodoxies. He saw no remedy save allowing the price of Irish land, already brought low by huge Poor Law liabilities and further threatened by Income-tax for paying the Catholic clergy,[1] to sink still lower, to the point, indeed, where it became an excellent investment to persons prepared to sink new money into improving its condition and agricultural equipment. The working of the Encumbered Estates Act, however, was to show how vain were the hopes reposed on their unaided operation. Tenant Right and Assisted Peasant Purchase had eventually to be adopted, and in 1891 a Congested Districts Board for the poorest areas much after Buller's[2] design.

It is necessary to turn from Ireland's tragedy to throw a few rapid glances in other directions. In the latter half of 1848 the bright working-class hopes of immense political and social changes quickly to be achieved were being very rapidly dimmed. The Ultra-Radical "cause" which suffered most severely from the change was the Chartist Land Scheme, whose power to attract financial support quickly declined.[3] By the end of the year, indeed, Chartists were so much without a stimulating activity of their own that the new tax-reduction campaign then launched by

---

[1] *Correspondence of Lord John Russell, Later,* i, 230-3.

[2] Buller, Chairman of the Poor Law Board, was the "philosophic Radical" of 1833 who fitted most easily into the Whig official setting without abandoning his positions. His death later in 1848 produced high praise even in the *Northern Star* for his great abilities.

[3] E.g. *Northern Star*, November 20, 1847, had announced that the preceding week's Land share subscriptions had amounted to £1,678 5s. 2d. The similar receipts announced on December 30, 1848, were £40 8s. 2d. Figures went down almost to vanishing point in 1849, as the over-optimism on which the scheme had been based became clearer. In 1851 a Statute was obtained for the winding up of the Land Company after it had experienced the great difficulties which account in part for O'Connor's ultimate insanity.

The Continued Pressure for Innovation 1848

Cobden conspicuously attracted them.[1] Working-class opinion on fundamentals did not, however, change. On Suffrage matters it remained Chartist, on economic and community organisation Socialist,[2] and on matters of belief very largely indifferent or infidel.[3] If middle-class Radicalism's views were similarly generalised, they could fairly be represented as favouring Household Suffrage or more in enfranchisement matters, *laisser-faire* in economic organisation, and Disestablishment in religious matters. But it should be added that international peace and international free trade were now conspicuously arousing the ardour of middle-class Radicals, and that a large number were already prepared for public secular schools.[4]

[1] Cf. *Reasoner*, January 24, 1849, for the attitude of the People's Charter League, representing the old Hetherington following. The *Northern Star*, December 30, 1848, had considerable good to say of it.
[2] Cf. *Labour League*, the organ of the National Association of United Trades, August 5, 1848, for plans of Government employment of "surplus labour" on useful public works and of Trades' promotion of "self-supporting" industrial colonies.
[3] Henry Dunckley, *The Glory and the Shame of Britain*, pp. 64–102.
[4] The Lancashire Public School Association had been founded in 1847, and it was to be expanded into the National Public School Association in 1850.

Note on "Young Ireland."

As it was "Young Ireland's" readiness for open revolution in 1847-8 which helped forward the production of some of the Irish land schemes mooted in England, a quotation from James Fintan Lalor, the most striking of "Young Ireland's" thinkers, becomes justifiable. The following is a passage from his *Rights of Ireland* (1848):

"Not to repeal the Union, then, but the conquest—not to disturb or dismantle the empire, but to abolish it utterly for ever—not to fall back on '82 but act up to '48—not to resume or restore an old constitution, but found a new nation . . . this is my object. . . .

"The principle I state, and mean to stand upon, is this, that the entire ownership of Ireland, moral and material, up to the sun and down to the centre, is vested of right in the people of Ireland: that they, and none but they, are the land-owners and law-makers of this island; that all laws are null and void not made by them, and all titles to land invalid not conferred or confirmed by them. . . ."

CHAPTER XVIII

THE PROTECTIONIST "REACTION" OVERCOME, 1849-52

"What better proof could be had of the necessity of an alteration of our representative system than is to be found in the simple fact that the Protectionist party are claiming to have public opinion on their side in favour of a revival of the Corn Laws. They tell us to look at the reaction in the late elections for Kidderminster and Reading, where a few hundred men, more or less under influence, returned Protectionists. Now, I would ask, how many members would they return in favour of the bread-tax, if the constituencies numbered, as they ought to do, 10,000 voters at least?"

COBDEN *to Walmsley, President of the National Reform Association, January 7, 1850.* ("Illustrated London News," *January 12th.*)

"The Chartist party became more divided than ever, in consequence of the attempted union with middle-class reformers. O'Connor, who until recently had denounced Cobden, followed him to Aylesbury, where a public meeting was held in the County Hall, and bespattered him with the most fulsome praise as he had previously with the foulest abuse. . . . O'Connor became every day more in love with the Financial and Parliamentary Reformers. A few months ago their movement was nothing but an artful dodge, now he not only approved of the scheme, but had every confidence in its promoters, and he travelled to Norwich, Aberdeen, and other distant towns in order to render them his support. . . ."

R. GAMMAGE, "History of the Chartist Movement," *pp. 350-1.*

"If I can consolidate . . . the now awakened spirit of Protestantism, and at the same time keep the latter within reasonable bounds, I can go to the country with a strong war-cry, . . . 'Protestantism, Protection, and down with the Income Tax.' . . . In my mind, among all its evils and all its dangers, the evocation of the Protestant spirit, which has been aroused, is not without its use. Even the most Radical towns, but especially the constituencies in which Protestant Dissent has any power, are so furiously anti-Papal, that that feeling will neutralise the cheap bread cry. . . ."

The Protectionist Leader, LORD STANLEY, *to Mr. Croker, March 22, 1851.*

IN the preceding chapter attention was almost exclusively focused on the progress of "advanced liberal ideas" in the political and social sphere. It is here necessary to draw attention to the continuance of the struggle between Free Traders and Protectionists which is far too widely assumed to have ended in 1846. The great financial crisis of 1847 with its train of "declining trade and grinding poverty, bankrupt railways and increased taxation,"[1] gave the Tory Protectionists an admirable opportunity of arguing that the whole trend of the commercial legislation which had preceded it must have been mistaken. When farmers learnt that the first nine months of 1847 had shown 100 per cent increase in the import of live animals and provisions, 35 per cent in butter, 15 per cent in cheese, and 300 per cent in grain and flour,[2] their explanation of the crisis was simple. "There is some little difference," triumphantly proclaimed *Blackwood's* for them in January 1848, "between sending thirty millions in twelve months in hard cash to America and the Continent for grain, and sending it to Kent, Yorkshire, Essex, and Scotland."[3] As corn prices were low after the fine harvest of 1847, farmers could be relied on heartily to support any efforts of the "landed interest" to reverse the Free Trade currents prompted by the "Radicals of the Manchester School."

The best Protectionist opportunity of 1848 came in the matter of the sugar colonies, whose plantations were alleged to have been so dangerously affected by the Sugar Duties revision of 1846, that Bentinck obtained a Select Committee of some importance.[4] A very strong case, indeed, could be made out for the view that the Sugar Bill of 1846, so powerfully pressed by the Radicals[5] on the infant Whig Government of that day, had dealt a final blow to the tens of millions of British capital invested in the West Indian plantations, a capital already seriously depreciated by the Abolition of Slavery in 1833 and the end of

---

[1] *The Times*, November 26, 1847.
[2] *Ibid.*, November 24th. The increase was over the corresponding months of 1846.   [3] *Alison's Essays*, i, 411.
[4] B. Disraeli, *Lord George Bentinck*, pp. 376 sqq.
[5] Cf. *Later Correspondence of Lord J. Russell*, i, 176–7, for the attempt of Cobden and Bright to secure an even more Radical Bill than was conceded with Colonial and "free labour" preference to end in 1849 instead of 1851.

English Radicalism 1832-1852

apprenticeship in 1838. Compelled by the Radicals and sentimentalists of Westminster to use the dearest and most unsatisfactory plantation labour in the world, the sugar colonies had been invited in 1846 to prepare to meet the full blast of unfettered slave-plantation competition on a terrifying scale of rapidity. Already Brazilian and Cuban sugar-slaves were being worked with increased savagery and the slave trade from Africa was being mightily encouraged at the very beginning of the five years' sliding-scale path down into the complete equalisation of the duties upon colonial and foreign sugar. When the end of that path should have been reached, the slave-labour and slave trade consequences would be terrible to contemplate. Moreover, though the British consumer might obtain his sugar slightly cheaper, it would be at dangerous cost to the very centres clamouring for Free Trade. The free labour of Jamaica and Mauritius was able to pay for infinitely more cotton fabric than the slave-masters of Cuba and Brazil were likely to allow to their plantation negroes.[1]

Bentinck, in point of fact, had judged his ground very well, and when his Committee reported on May 29th, there was matter in its resolutions to justify his hope that he had discovered how to defeat the "Manchester School." By June 16th, indeed, Whig Ministers, who had opened with a stiff resolve not to make material concessions, had deemed it politic to change their course and were offering to prolong the régime of preferential duties on colonial sugar until 1854.[2] Though this concession brought upon Ministers the criticism of Bright, Cobden, and Villiers, the Protectionists deemed it insufficient and opened an attack in form which seemed likely at one time to bring down the Government.[3] Indeed, not only did the anti-slavery side of the case bring numbers of Peelites and humanitarians into the Opposition camp, but it enlisted even Hume, the veteran Radical, who stressed his conviction that the British colonies would have been able to compete successfully if given equal conditions. Had Peel and Graham now cared to overthrow the Government

---

[1] Cf. Mathieson, *British Slave Emancipation, 1838-49*, chapter 7, for the whole subject of the paragraph; also Disraeli, *Life of Bentinck*, pp. 326-45, for the way the Protectionist case was prepared.
[2] *Hansard*, June 16th, Lord J. Russell.
[3] *Ibid.*, June 19th, 22nd, 26th, 29th. On the 24th Greville felt the Government would fall.

The Protectionist "Reaction" Overcome 1849–1852

they could have done so with ease.¹ But though the Government's sugar proposals should in their opinion have gone further, they gave the Whig Cabinet their aid and helped to save it in the remarkable division of June 29th which ended with 260 votes for the Government and 245 against. They recognised that the installation of a Tory Ministry in England when the Continent was aflame with revolution was dangerous enough in itself. What made it doubly dangerous was the prospect that the middle-class Radicals would revive their League to guard against the fiscal "reaction" to which the Tories were pledged. A Tory Government pitted against Ireland, Chartism, and the League would have been in the most dangerous of positions.²

On June 30th Bright as the representative of the home consumer ventured to divide the House again on behalf of the unyielding Free Trade thesis that there was no call to alter the 1846 settlement. After twenty millions had been expended for emancipation, he urged, and another thirty millions given to the planters in the shape of the protection of the past eleven years, Parliament owed nothing more to the colonial interest but a great deal to the home consumer, so deeply wronged in the past.³ But a vote of 36 against 302 is evidence enough that Bright's thesis was felt in the circumstances to be exaggerated by all but the straitest Free Trade Radicals.

Meanwhile a more fundamental conflict of economic principles even than that engaged on the Sugar question had been opened on May 15th. Resting its case partly on the desire of the colonies to be free to use the shipping of any flag and partly on the danger of foreign retaliation if a change were not made, the Government proposed to throw open to the shipping of the world the hitherto reserved inter-Imperial trades.⁴ The Radical Ricardo, who had obtained the Committee of 1847 which had opened up the question,

---

[1] Cf. Greville *Memoirs*, June 26th, for sixty-nine M.P.s marked as doubtfuls in the Government Whip's list. Most of them had been waiting for Peel's view to become known. Graham's speech of the 26th was an indication which was confirmed by Peel on the 29th.

[2] Cf. Greville, *Memoirs*, June 24th, for Graham descanting on what would follow a Tory Ministry: "the great impetus it would give to reform, and the vast power the Radical and subversive interest would acquire, etc."

[3] *Hansard*, xcix, 1420.

[4] For an anticipatory protest organised by the "shipping interest," see *Illustrated London News*, February 12th. It took the picturesque form of a water-procession of sailors on the Thames to accompany a deputation to the Home Secretary with a memorial for the Queen.

made some enlightening observations on the "shipping interest's" contention that high British building costs and wages gave the shipping industry a claim to be continued in the Navigation Code advantages. He pointed to the fact that it was the Americans with dearer ships and higher wages than England's who were the most formidable competitors, while the Russians with much cheaper ships and much lower wages had been compelled to see the whole even of Anglo-Russian trade pass to British ships.[1] One specially valuable point made by Ricardo was the demonstration of what the needless preservation of inter-Imperial shipping monopoly might mean to the pockets of the numerous emigrants of the time. The British fare to Australia, he stated, was £20 while that from Bremen was £12.[2]

Cobden, one of the most travelled men in the House, contributed a characteristic speech to the debate. He used the published evidence to show that British-built ships were as cheap as foreign and better-made and that British seamen had greater natural aptitude for the sea than their rivals. That American captains and sailors worked their ships better, despatched their business in port more quickly and took better care of their cargoes formed, he thought, a case not for legislative protection but for correcting the drunkenness and insubordination which detracted so much from the British sailor's superior seamanship.[3] But the most characteristic note of "Manchester School Radicalism" came when Cobden was dealing with the arguments for the Navigation Code which were based on its stimulation of British shipping and British seamen for use in a possible war. Was this the time always to be singing *Rule, Britannia*? asked Cobden, and when the Tories cried out in the affirmative, he told them that if they had served with him in the Committee on the Service Estimates they would have had a just idea of the cost of that tune. The constant assertion of maritime supremacy, he continued, was calculated to provoke kindred passions in other nations: whereas if Great Britain enunciated doctrines of peace she would invoke similar sentiments from the rest of the world. Freedom of trade and intercourse, too, would blend the interests of nations and place a most powerful obstacle in the way of war.

As Peelites joined Whigs and Radicals in considering the time had come for ending the restriction of inter-Empire shipping

[1] *Hansard*, xcviii, 1040.   [2] *Ibid.*, 1042.   [3] *Ibid.*, xcix, 616.

The Protectionist "Reaction" Overcome 1849–1852

to the British flag, the first important Navigation division of June 9th yielded a vote of 294–177 in favour of Free Trade. But in view of the pertinacious Tory opposition to be expected, the Government reconciled itself before long to deferring the projected legislation to 1849. The Bill was not, however, carried in 1849 without a severe struggle, especially in the Lords. What made the matter more difficult was the fact that as far as working-class feeling was evident at all, it was against the Bill and in favour of the sailors and shipwrights who were expected to suffer.[1] The hard times of 1847–8 had stirred a good deal of Protectionist sentiment in the considerable sections of the working class exposed to Continental competition[2] and this gave special encouragement to the Tories in their efforts against the Navigation Bill of 1849.[3] Had that Bill been defeated even in the Lords, the Whig Government would probably have been brought down[4] and a Tory combination have received the chance of experimenting with an all-round system of moderate Protection. But even if the Whigs had not resigned, the grievances of Canada, the West Indies, and other Colonies, forced to submit to shipping restrictions without the old compensation of preferential treatment in the British market, would have forced reconsideration of the whole fiscal situation. The political position, indeed, would have become so involved that a new Peel Ministry defending Free Trade in close alliance with the Radicals would very possibly have emerged.[5] But the Tory hot-bloods just failed to force all these matters forward when their Second Reading division in the Lords against the Navigation Bill ended in a vote of 163–173.[6] A considerable number of Conservative Peers had declined to

---

[1] Cf. *Labour League*, March 31, 1849. The Navigation Laws and the Shipwrights. Cf. also *Companion to the British Almanac, 1850*, p. 226, for 125,522 petition signatures against the Government proposals, and 6,437 for them.

[2] Especially in the London luxury trades whose sentiments had some weight with the Metropolitan Trades' Delegates who tried to lead "labour" feeling between 1848–52 (cf. Gillespie, *Labour and Politics in England, 1850–67*, pp. 38–41). Ultimately *The Home*, a Protectionist weekly with some appeal to the working classes, was maintained by Oastler between 1851 and 1855.

[3] *Illustrated London News*, May 5th and June 30th, for the imposing meetings of May 1st and June 26th, in connexion with the "National Association for the Protection of British Industry and Capital."

[4] *Later Correspondence of Lord J. Russell*, i, 193–5.

[5] Cf. *Later Correspondence of Lord J. Russell*, pp. 194–5, for the views of the Prime Minister and of Lord Palmerston.

[6] *Hansard*, May 8th. The Government had to make an unwelcome use of proxies.

risk a constitutional crisis when the Continent was still ablaze with revolutionary fires, Ireland sullen and desperate, the Radicals anxious for a new crusade, and the Chartist movement ready to revive at the first favourable sign.[1]

It is not necessary here to recapitulate the Radical arguments used once more in 1849 on behalf of Free Trade. It is more advisable to turn to the Protectionist counter-attack on the whole Manchester position now, after Lord George Bentinck's death, under the virtual leadership of Disraeli. Disraeli's speech on the Third Reading of the Government's Navigation Bill gives better indications of what he considered the promising line to take than the familiar cry of "agricultural distress" which he had had perforce to raise earlier in the Session and which had been contemptuously rejected in a division of 280–189.[2] During the three years' experience they had had of Free Trade, he urged upon the Commons in the Navigation debate, the Poor Rates had increased 17 per cent, the capital of England had diminished by a hundred millions, and the deposits in the savings banks had declined by one-half.[3] Indeed, Irish distress and the revolutions and counter-revolutions of the Continent were doing no good to British trade, and there were signs of doubt even in the Radical camp as to the absolute validity of the Free Trade theories. In Parliament, for example, Muntz of Birmingham may be found supporting the Government's shipping proposals on the strange ground that their adoption would remove the last excuse which Free Traders might make for any non-verification of their confident prophecies.[4]

By the end of the year 1849 Free Traders could be altogether

---

[1] Cf. *Letters of George Cornewall Lewis*, p. 206, for an estimate of that summer's position made on June 10th. "There is no doubt that a dissolution at the present time would give a great gain to the Protectionists, though not perhaps a majority. The triumph of the Protection party would, however, be short-lived.... There would be a great struggle between the town and country populations, and the former would attempt to gain the superiority . . . by diminishing the number of members for counties and small boroughs, and increasing the number for large towns. In this way they would ultimately succeed...."

[2] *Hansard*, March 15th. It was widely felt that as far as Disraeli had asked for changes they would have benefited not farmers, but landlords (cf. *Illustrated London News*, March 17th). [3] *Ibid.*, April 23rd, civ, 701.

[4] *Ibid.*, March 12th. Cf. *Illustrated London News*, April 14th, for Cobden on the defensive at a West Riding banquet of April 11th: "We never said that free trade in corn would prevent the evils that follow excessive speculation in railways... we never said it would prevent civil war on the Continent... we never said that there would be no potato rot if we had a free trade in corn...."

The Protectionist "Reaction" Overcome 1849–1852

more confident of the justice of their views. There had been a great revival of business activity and a remarkable increase of the Export figures which Protectionists might ascribe to the reopening of Continental markets, the pacification of India, and new-mined Californian gold[1] but which Free Traders looked upon as justifying their theories of commerce. Yet with wheat at 41s. the quarter and meat at 5d. a lb.[2] the cry of agricultural distress became much more formidable, and the Free Traders found themselves facing the possibility of Peelite and even Whig[3] landlords joining in the Protectionist demonstrations for a reduction in the "burdens on land." During the "agricultural distress" debates of March 1849 Cobden had already given the direct Radical negative to proposals for moving the "burdens on land" to the shoulders of the general taxpayer.[4] In a memorable Leeds speech of December 18, 1849, he voiced even more confidently and resolutely the strongest opposition to all suggestions "that the burdens hitherto put upon the land shall henceforth be paid out of the taxes wrung from the agricultural labourer upon his ounce of tea, and the half-starved needlewoman in London upon her half-pound of sugar . . . that the £12,000,000 of local taxes for poor rates, highway rates, church rates, and the rest, shall half of them, if they cannot get the whole—be taken off the land and put upon the Consolidated Fund; that is taken out of the taxes raised upon the necessaries and comforts of the masses of the poor."[5]

Cobden thought fit to go even further on this occasion. He warned Tories meditating a defeat of the Government and a General Election as preliminaries to a return to Protection or a lightening of the "burdens on land" that if he had to lead another fight it would be against the "whole aristocratic system" of landlordism. A class which opposed retrenchment on armaments because it was interested in maintaining "that great preserve of the landlord class for their younger sons, the army and navy," had no claim to release itself from taxation in other ways. Nor

---

[1] *Blackwood's Magazine*, December 1849; article, "Free Trade at its Zenith," in *Alison's Essays*, i, 636.   [2] *Ibid.*, p. 635.
[3] Add. MSS. 40452, f. 407, for a letter from Graham to Peel (December 8, 1849), suspecting "some members of the Cabinet" of a "secret wish to revert to the fixed duty" (on Corn).
[4] *Hansard*, March 15th. The Radicals, however, themselves proposed to abolish the Malt and Hops Excise but by "economy," principally in armaments.
[5] *Cobden's Collected Speeches*, ed. 1908, i, 215.

needed landlords to expect that they would continue to carry the farmers with them without question. Cobden threatened a campaign which would reveal to every farmer, "however dull he may be," that his true resource was not to identify himself with his landlord but to insist on a reduction of rents proportionate to the fall of corn prices.[1]

Cobden even ventured to give a sample of what such a campaign would be when he appeared at an Aylesbury Reform meeting and did some effective propaganda for rent reduction and Game Law abolition in Disraeli's own county.[2] It was a most effective meeting, received much attention from the Press[3] and like parallel activities of Bright on the subject of Irish landlordism[4] helped to give a decided setback to the nation-wide Protectionist activity just then in progress. What, however, was worse for the Tories was the fact that serious fighting broke out at some of their meetings between farmers and the inhabitants of the country towns where the meetings were held. The Stafford meeting of January 10th, for example, finally ended in a storming of the hall by townsmen, the serious injury of Lord Talbot, the Chairman, and the flight of four hundred farmers to the refuge of hotels and the railway station.[5] An East End meeting in London, again, at which a special appeal to the Protectionism of the working classes was attempted, saw Oastler denied a hearing and a Chartist leader taking charge with denunciations of Toryism, primogeniture, and entail, and demands for reduced taxation and a radical reform of Parliament.[6] The failure of the Protectionist campaign to impress the country is, perhaps, best mirrored in *Punch*, which after grimly cartooning the "shameless mendicity" of the landed interest passed on in February to present Cobden and Agriculture as a Valentine's Day couple.[7]

It was possibly because there had been such a display of urban temper that the Protectionist demand as voiced by Disraeli on February 19th was for no more than that the State should take over from local Poor Rates annual charges amounting in all to

---

[1] *Cobden's Collected Speeches*, pp. 216–18.   [2] *Ibid.*, i, 223–9.
[3] *Illustrated London News* (cf.), January 12th.
[4] *Ibid.* The Irish landlords, it may be observed, had embarked on the Protectionist campaign with marked zeal, and Bright's speeches were used against them with special effect (cf. *Ibid.*, January 19th).
[5] *Irving's Annals*, p. 290.
[6] *Illustrated London News*, January 12th.   [7] *Punch*, xviii, 25, 55, 65.

The Protectionist "Reaction" Overcome 1849–1852

about two millions. On this issue Gladstone led a strong Peelite section in favour of making the concessions demanded as a way of laying the Protection issue. Accordingly the division which resulted gave the Protectionists not victory, indeed, but the very encouraging figures of 252 against 273.[1] It was not a good omen for the Radical plan of bringing relief to farmers and others by reducing Service expenditure and therefore the weight of taxation. Cobden's Financial Reform motion of March 8, 1850 was, in fact, rejected by 272 votes against 89.[2] A Budget followed which, though reducing the Stamp Duties on land-transfers and on bricks, permitted Tory lamentations that the passage of the land into other hands should so plainly be foreseen and Tory complaints that it was the towns which would gain from cheaper bricks, for no one was building in the ruined countryside. Protectionist persistence of this type undoubtedly came to exercise a growing influence over Peelite members for county divisions,[3] and this was increased after Peel's untimely death in July.

The Session of 1851, therefore, offered the Protectionists better hopes than had been the case since 1846. These were improved by the great skill which Disraeli showed on February 11th when moving an "agricultural distress" motion.[4] The effect of his appeal for a termination of the "unhappy controversy between town and country" extended beyond Peelites to embrace even the Radical Muntz of Birmingham, and the Government only obtained a division of 281–267.[5] However, Cobden and the Radical host, which had supported the Government on this issue, turned against it on February 20th when a Bill which would have extended the Suffrage was under discussion. The Protectionists saw no reason to support the Government against the Radicals and allowed the Cabinet to be humiliated by a defeat of 100–52. It was a fatal blow to a Government already without credit and drove Ministers to resignation.[6]

For a few days it looked as though the Anti-Corn Law League might have to be reconstructed to fight a Tory Government

---

[1] Cf. Malmesbury, *Memoirs of an Ex-Minister*, under February 22nd and Greville's *Memoirs*, under February 23rd; *Hansard*, February 19th and 21st.
[2] Cobden was proposing to save £5,820,000 on the army, navy, and ordnance votes, and £630,000 on the civil votes.
[3] Cf. *Later Correspondence of Lord J. Russell*, i, 202–3.
[4] Cf. *Malmesbury Memoirs*, under February 15th.
[5] *Annual Register*, 1851, History, p. 27; Malmesbury's *Memoirs*, pp. 201–2.
[6] *Letters of Queen Victoria*, ii, 289.

with a programme of a 5s. wheat duty and some transfer of tax burdens from land to the general taxpayer.[1] A Protectionist Cabinet, indeed, was already nominated under Stanley, when some understandable nervousness in the totally inexperienced personage appointed to the Board of Trade caused the collapse of the plan and smoothed the path of Russell's return.[2] But the Cabinet continued very weak throughout the remainder of the Session, for Radicals and Peelites often dissented from its policies and the Protectionists needed not to recruit many votes to put the Government in a minority. On May 2, 1851, for example, when despite Cobden's advice Hume persisted in moving that the Income-tax be granted the Government for one year only so that the question of a revision of taxation might be forced forward, a Radical–Protectionist combination put Ministers in a minority of 230 against 244. But as Cobden told Hume it was not the Radical ambition of making the Income-tax fairer to earned incomes that the Protectionists were anxious to forward.[3] On June 17th Cobden again showed himself not unfriendly to the Government when pressing his project of Service economies through the medium of a motion inviting the commencement of joint naval disarmament with France. When he obtained a speech from the Foreign Secretary, Lord Palmerston, concurring in the motion's principle and object, he refrained from pressing it to a division.[4]

But the advent of a Protectionist Ministry could not in the circumstances be avoided for ever, and the famous Palmerston dismissal of December 1851 brought it nearer. When Palmerston found the opportunity for "his tit for tat with Johnny Russell" in February 1852, Lord Derby formed the Government of Tory Protectionists whose construction had been beyond his power the year before. With the ensuing resuscitation by the Radicals of their Anti-Corn Law League the fiscal struggle of the mid-nineteenth century entered upon its concluding stage.[5] It was transferred to the Parliamentary sphere when on March 15th

[1] Malmesbury's *Memoirs*, p. 205; *Letters of Queen Victoria*, ii, 292, mentions a 6s. wheat duty. [2] *Ibid.*, pp. 207–8.
[3] *Annual Register*, 1851, History, pp. 85–6.
[4] Cf. Cobden's *Speeches*, i, 263–9.
[5] *Illustrated London News*, March 13, 1852, for the League's first subscription list headed by twenty subscriptions of £1,000, one of £750, and twenty-six of £500.

The Protectionist "Reaction" Overcome 1849-1852

Villiers rose to ask "the principles of that policy upon which the Government has undertaken to regulate the foreign commerce of this country, and more especially that branch of commerce which relates to the food of the people." Though Cobden failed to win either Russell and the Whigs or Graham and the Peelites to the policy of an instant attack upon the equivocal pronouncements of the Government,[1] it was recognised that the Protectionist Ministers were powerless to effect any fiscal changes prior to a General Election. If, however, they should venture to propose any such changes after a General Election nearly certain to give them gains from Peelites and Whigs in rural areas, they would undoubtedly arouse a very dangerous and intensive campaign on the part of the League.[2] Nor would the League be seriously hampered by Chartist hostility as had been the case in the past. It is true that though a tragic fate had overtaken O'Connor, eloquent Chartist leaders like Ernest Jones still commanded vast audiences and a Chartist organisation and Press were still by immense exertions kept in being.[3] But the middle-class Radicals, both by successfully committing the Whigs to Franchise Reform and by fighting against the landlords as defenders of cheap bread, had left themselves little reason to fear the political effects of such criticism of them as might be undertaken by the quarrelling Chartist leaders.[4] Even the normally perilous topic of the general middle-class Radical approval given to Competition and *laisser-faire* was much less troublesome than it would have been in less flourishing times than the summer of 1852, when the influence of the new gold from California and Australia was powerfully fostering trade expansion.[5]

The General Election of 1852, nevertheless, saw an energetic Tory attempt to exhaust all the possibilities of the Parliamentary

---

[1] Morley's *Cobden*, pp. 580-1.
[2] The more dangerous from the fact that Cobden had now acquired a tenant-farmer following with an interesting "five-point Farmers' Charter," including Malt Tax abolition by economy, Tenant Right and the repeal of the Game Laws for all ground game (cf. *Illustrated London News*, June 26th).
[3] The *Northern Star* was still struggling on under Harney's editorship and the title of the *Star of Freedom*, and on May 8, 1852, was joined by Ernest Jones's *People's Paper*. The competition was fatal for the former, which ceased publication in November 1852.
[4] Cf. Gammage, *History of the Chartist Movement*, pp. 383-92, for the quarrels, partly personal, partly the result of different views as to the policy of working with the "middle-class reformers."
[5] Cf. *Illustrated London News*, June 26th.

English Radicalism 1832-1852

system of that day in order to obtain as high a measure of electoral gains as possible. But though the results obtained, by means often far from scrupulous, were very considerable,[1] they were insufficient to allow the Tory Ministers to contemplate helping the "agricultural interest" by means of Corn Duties. Indeed, in the very midst of the elections and in total disregard of a wide variety of Protectionist oratory actually being used by some of his own Ministerial colleagues, Disraeli determined that the time had come to sound the retreat from all manner of Corn Laws and to concentrate upon other means of relief for the "agricultural interest." "No one can suppose," declared he brazenly, "that the present administration has any intention, or ever had any intention, to bring back the laws that were repealed in 1846."[2] But if more Peelites had succumbed in the rural areas and more borough constituencies had yielded to such different manners of Tory wooing as were employed, for example, at Liverpool, Greenwich, and Derby,[3] Disraeli would no doubt have been prepared to use another language. But even as things were, the Tories gained a good deal of strength from the elections, and with some three hundred supporters opposing a congeries of Peelites, Whigs, Radicals, and Irish,[4] their chances of keeping office were by no means negligible.

The inveterate hostility of the Free Trade Radicals, however, prevented Ministerial plans for the gradual absorption of the Peelites and the neutralisation of some at least of the Irish from having any long chance of trial. On November 2nd Cobden announced to 3,000 Free Trade banqueters at Manchester, who included a muster of some 70 M.P.s, that the Tory Government would be compelled to admit that Free Trade did not lower wages, drain the country of gold, and put the land out of cultivation as Ministers had so freely prophesied, but that on the contrary it had promoted the national well-being to its current unprecedented

---

[1] *Russell Correspondence* (Record Office) for a letter from J. Parkes of July 24th summing up: "The Pure Whigs have lost and the Peelites most, the latter all but annihilated." [2] *Illustrated London News*, July 24th.

[3] At Liverpool and Greenwich Anti-Popery sentiment had been employed and at Derby a Tory agent was caught red-handed in bribery transactions involving the Tory Minister, who was distributing the Carlton Club's largesse (*Irving's Annals*, pp. 358–9, 370).

[4] *Illustrated London News*, August 5th, gives an estimate of 299 Ministerialists against 206 Liberals and Whigs, 87 Radical Reformers, 26 newly elected Reformers, and 38 Peelites.

The Protectionist "Reaction" Overcome 1849–1852

heights.[1] It was an eve-of-the Session warning to which the Government somewhat defiantly replied in a Queen's Speech recommending dispassionate consideration of how "to enable the industry of the country to meet successfully that unrestricted competition to which Parliament in its wisdom had decided that it should be subjected."[2]

After such an exchange it was inevitable that Villiers, the old Anti-Corn Law standard-bearer in the House, should be put forward by the Radicals with resolutions allowing not the slightest ambiguity to the Government on the subject of Free Trade. On November 23rd, therefore, the House of Commons was called on to declare "that the improved condition of the country, and particularly of the industrious classes, is mainly the result of recent commercial legislation, and especially of the Act of 1846, which established the admission of foreign corn, and that that Act was a wise, just, and beneficial measure."[3]

In moving this and two later resolutions Villiers made it plain that the Radicals considered that Free Trade had profited the countryside as well as the town. The farmers undoubtedly had a claim for Parliamentary help, but it was in respect to such matters as compensation for unexhausted improvements, the Game Laws, and the Law of Distress.

The Villiers resolutions were met by Disraeli with an amendment accepting "recent legislation" as the main cause of the better conditions of the working classes and offering to confine such "measure of financial and administrative reform" as Ministers should introduce within the limits of Free Trade. On this amendment, however, the Radicals would still have won sufficient support to defeat the Government, and Palmerston, already carving his way to a Premiership needing Tory tolerance, induced Ministers to accept a third form of words from him. On this Palmerston wording, sufficient Whig and Peelite votes were detached from the Radicals to give the Government success in a division of 256–236.[4] But the Ministers who had so fiercely denounced Free Trade since 1845 cut a very poor figure in their chaffer for less "odious" terms in which to praise its results than those put forward by the Radicals.[5] The one justification for the

---

[1] *Illustrated London News*, November 6th. [2] *Ibid.*, November 13th.
[3] *Ibid.*, November 27th. [4] *Hansard*, November 23rd, 25th, 26th.
[5] Cf. *Greville Memoirs*, under December 4th.

English Radicalism 1832-1852

Tories' retention of office at the price of such humiliation was the opportunity that was now promised them of doing something in the Budget for the "agricultural interest."

In his remarkable five and a quarter hours' Budget speech of December 3, 1852, indeed, Disraeli made proposals intended to give the "agricultural interest" some compensations for the definite surrender of Protection. These did not assume the expected form of the taking over by the Treasury of local Poor Law charges in the manner asked for by the Chancellor in the past. As Cobden was to show in his speech of December 13th, farming was now prosperous and the landlords receiving higher rents, so that the Chancellor had to take other ground than when he had been able to talk plausibly of a distressed "landed interest." But to increase the house taxes so that one half of the Malt Tax might be taken off as well as one half of the hop duties, to bring a lawyer's clerk earning £100 a year within the scope of Income-tax while excusing the farmer big enough to pay rent of £299 per annum had too plainly the appearance of doing injustice to the towns.

In some ways the worst feature of the Budget was what Cobden called the "miserable, paltry attempt to get a special benefit for the tenant-farmer" by altering Income-tax procedure and taking one-third instead of one-half of the rent he paid as the measure of his income. The treatment of the townsman and especially of him who earned between £100 and £150 per annum was most unjust by comparison. Subjected for the first time to Income-tax, his House-tax, too, was to be made more burdensome, for only houses under £10 annual value were to be exempt for the future instead of those under £20 annual value and taxation was to be at double the former rate. It took some days, however, for the hundreds of thousands of affected persons to grasp the situation, and for a short time Whitehall even considered that the Budget would make the Tory Ministry stronger,[1] containing as it did the promise of cheaper beer and cheaper tea. But soon increasing anger out of doors[2] settled its fate, and Radicals made part of the majority of 305 which on the morning of December 17th outvoted 286 Tories on the House-tax. With the consequent fall of the Derby Government ended the last attempts of the "landed interest" to force "compensation" for Corn Law Repeal.

---

[1] Cf. *Greville Memoirs*, under December 6th.
[2] Cf. *Illustrated London News*, December 11th.

CHAPTER XIX

SUFFRAGE, EDUCATION, AND NEWSPAPER TAXATION

"Socialist doctrines and principles are far more rife in the great towns of this country than most people are aware of. They are found principally among the artisans and skilled workmen, and specially in the metropolis. These parties aim at a distribution of all the property of those above them, and calculate on measures to prevent in the future all accumulations of wealth in single hands. They do not, I think, look much to physical force; they rely chiefly on the extension of the suffrage. ... The land is their first object ... and many, who are not disposed to go as far as the Socialist party, urge them on to this extent, because they know that a revolution in the tenure, or descent of landed property must speedily extinguish the House of Lords. ... There are three propositions of special danger: the ballot, electoral districts, and shortening the duration of parliaments. I know not how the country could stand the whole of them. ... The country could endure something approximating to universal suffrage much better than it could any one of the three propositions stated above. ..."

Lord Shaftesbury to Lord John Russell, November 15, 1851. (E. HODDER, "Life and Work of Lord Shaftesbury," ii, 372-4.)

"While Churchmen and Dissenters are quarrelling as to how we are to be educated, while Government accords but a paltry grant, and while earnest reformers like yourself acknowledge that a considerable time must elapse before any scheme of national education can be adopted—the least that all these parties can do is to allow us to educate ourselves. We are told that Englishmen are too ignorant to be entrusted with that franchise which is now nearly universal in Western Europe; we demand that ignorance should no longer be compulsory. ... By the penny stamp not only are we debarred from the expression of our thoughts and feelings, but it is made impossible for men of education or of capital to employ themselves in instructing us. A cheap *stamped* newspaper cannot be a good one. ..."

The People's Charter Union to Cobden, January 19, 1849. (C. D. COLLET, "History of the Taxes on Knowledge," pp. 44-5.)

AMONG the general political issues of the period 1849-52 none was more vital to Radicals of every type than Extension of the Suffrage, none was pushed more energetically, and none formed a more likely foundation-ground for the construction of a distinct party organisation. Whether to defend Free Trade or to secure an equitable redistribution of taxation, whether to enforce Government economy in the Services or to promote the International Peace movement, the middle-class Radicals found they needed that wide reorganisation of Parliament which would come from the adoption of democratic principles. That such adoption was most unlikely to imperil the institution of private property seemed proven by the course of Universal Suffrage in France, where it had produced a National Assembly ready to crush the insurrectionary Communism of the Paris poor with terrible severity. Accordingly active middle-class Radicals were ready in 1849 to continue the "New Reform Movement" which had been held out in 1848 as a measure of appeasement to the Chartists.

The Reform agitation of 1849-52 was conducted under the style of a "Financial and Parliamentary Reform Movement" for reasons which are worth a little investigation. An energetic and wealthy mercantile group at Liverpool with allies at the other leading ports had conducted economy and tax-reduction propaganda sufficiently notable to induce Cobden to ally with it at the end of 1848[1] when he was already looking for help in his projected attempt upon the Service Estimates. In alliance with this Liverpool Financial Reform Association Cobden issued a plan for a model "national budget" which received great publicity and attracted much support.[2] Bright was extremely anxious to associate Parliamentary with Financial Reform in the new crusade, and despite Cobden's dislike of a mixed issue he succeeded in having his way when the new movement was formally launched in Manchester.[3] As Cobden, however, had prophesied from his knowledge of some of the men who had supported the old Anti-Corn Law League, the mixture of Suffrage and Economy proved

---

[1] Morley's *Cobden*, pp. 495-6, 502. The Liverpool Financial Reform Association was to continue for many years its chosen line of activity.
[2] Cf. *Punch's* laudatory cartoons, xvi, 6, 49.
[3] Morley's *Cobden*, pp. 502 sqq.

Suffrage, Education, and Newspaper Taxation

an indifferent basis for a second Manchester agitation and the new Commons League which was projected had but little genuine vitality.[1]

In the Metropolis, however, where the energetic, wealthy, and ambitious Sir Joshua Walmsley took charge of Financial Reform, he succeeded somewhat better than Bright in grafting Parliamentary Reform upon it. By the beginning of 1850 the National Reform Association had met with sufficient success in attracting the old Anti-Corn Law following, the middle-class sympathisers with Chartism and a strong Chartist section under O'Connor himself to allow it to chronicle the activities, metropolitan and provincial, which had been undertaken in 1849 and to announce a £10,000 campaign fund for 1850.[2] The Association's three-day National Conference of April 1850 certainly made some appearance with a platform of notabilities which included Cobden, Bright, Hume, and Feargus O'Connor, 130 delegates from all over the country and a string of ambitious resolutions responsibly moved.[3]

In Parliament, meanwhile, Hume had urged Household Suffrage, Ballot, Triennial Parliaments, and More Equal Electoral Districts in a motion of June 5, 1849,[4] which corresponded largely with the programme which the National Reform Association was to adopt. Though supported by personalities as different as Berkeley, who had constituted himself the special proponent of the Ballot, and Feargus O'Connor, who still had a very large Chartist following, by the "Manchester School" in the persons of Bright and Colonel Thompson and the very different strains of Radicalism represented by Bernal Osborne, Locke King, and Page Wood, the Reform motion was rejected by 286 votes against 82. The most conspicuous point in the Home Secretary's unyielding speech was his assertion that the adult males productive of the existing electorate of 800,000 numbered not eight millions, as Hume had claimed, but only four. The Prime Minister in his

---

[1] Morley's *Cobden*, pp. 500–1.
[2] *Illustrated London News*, January 12th. The receipts for the nine months preceding were given as £1,980 7s. Of the £10,000 required for 1850, £1,500 was raised at a meeting of January 5th. It was such financial backing which convinced O'Connor, Reynolds, and Clark among the Chartist leaders that the Association's readiness to receive Chartist support should not be discouraged.
[3] *Ibid.*, April 27th. Reynolds, the Chartist author and newspaper proprietor, failed to obtain the adoption of Manhood instead of Household Suffrage.
[4] *Hansard*, cv, 1171.

turn, stung apparently by Bright's remarks on the over-aristocratic composition of Parliament and the Government, accused the Manchester politicians of narrowness of understanding concerning "the great principles on which our ancestors founded the Constitution of this country, and which we their successors humbly admire and endeavour to follow." Though even moderate opinion found the Whig language irritating,[1] Peelites and Protectionists would have been stiffer still in asserting the wonders of the British Constitution.

The aspect of Parliament, indeed, was unfavourable enough to induce Cobden to put his immediate hopes rather in the Freehold Land movement which he was promoting than in the agitation to induce Parliament to pass a sweeping new Reform Bill. In London, Birmingham, Sheffield, and other centres Radical politicians and their friends were founding Freehold Land Societies[2] which aimed at buying parcels of land suitable for subdivision as building plots, gardens, or allotments. Artisans anxious at once for a good investment and the 40s. freehold vote were encouraged by the readiness of Radical trustees of the highest standing to act, to bring their £20, £30, £40, or £50 of savings to the Societies or else to begin saving as fast as possible.

But strenuously as Cobden and others worked in this movement for years, it seems plain that it made but little appreciable alteration even in the tenure of the county seats most open to this form of Radical attack.[3] The artisans whose position was so secure that they felt able to sink £40 or £50 of savings into freehold ground were not many. In some provincial manufacturing areas, it is true, such a piece of ground might be near enough to a man's work to make it possible for him to dream of erecting his own cottage there when he should have completed the process of saving anew, and in the meantime it might serve him as an

---

[1] *Illustrated London News* (June 9th) and *Punch* (xvi, 241) had immense upper- and middle-class circulations, and yet expressed dissatisfaction.
[2] By 1850 there were eighty societies with 30,000 members. In 1852 there were 130 societies with 85,000 members, 19,500 allotments of sites worth 40s. a year or over had been made, and £790,000 had been paid in (J. E. Ritchie, *Freehold Land Societies, their History, Present Position and Claims*, quoted by F. E. Gillespie, *Labour and Politics*, etc., p. 95 n. 1).
[3] W. Williams, *Address to the Electors and Non-Electors of the U.K.*, December 1849, p. 29: "I fear that much delusion is being created in the public mind as to the importance in a political point of view of the Freehold Land Movement."

Suffrage, Education, and Newspaper Taxation

allotment. But to the unenfranchised London artisan, fired perchance by Cobden's picture of the good which might be done if he possessed himself of a vote, Cobden could but offer the picture of a relatively distant plot with the rent of letting coming in by the penny post.[1] Even if the artisan were prepared for this, the problem of securing registration might involve considerable trouble and expense as might also the actual recording of the hard-won vote when polling-day at length arrived for Middlesex, Essex, Kent, or Surrey. Little wonder then that Cobden was also anxious to press into county-voting service those Dissenters of wider means who had the county qualification or might possess it but neglected to register. Not ten of the actual county members, he urged, were prepared for such an elementary piece of justice as the removal of Church Rates.[2]

It must always remain an open question whether Cobden could not with a more vivid democratic faith have taken the Reform movement of 1849–52 on to partial success before the ugly period of 1853–65 was allowed to settle upon the country. Cobden's standing in politics was now immense,[3] and a vast mass of "moderate" opinion could undoubtedly have been swung out of complacency with the existing electoral system if Bright had been able to persuade his great friend to throw himself into a Suffrage campaign with the ardour he had shown for Corn Law repeal. As is well-known from the great Morley biographer, however, Cobden could never be persuaded to give more than a lukewarm support to the "Walmsley agitation" which even so brought the Whig Cabinet to offer the concessions of the Russell Reform Bill of 1852.[4]

Among the reasons privately offered by Cobden for his reluctance to begin a Suffrage agitation was his conviction that the forces he had led in the Anti-Corn Law struggle were not for the most part to be rallied again for a Suffrage war.[5] Indeed, the conversion of moneyed manufacturedom to Conservatism in all

---

[1] *Cobden's Speeches*, ii, 549–57. [2] *Ibid.*, 556.
[3] Based on a careful survey of the Press of 1849–50, and especially of two non-partisan organs of high circulation, the *Illustrated London News* and *Punch*.
[4] *Illustrated London News*, February 14, 1852. The Bill offered the franchise to the immense numbers in boroughs who were householders of premises between £5 and £10 in annual value. Though no real redistribution accompanied it, and it could, therefore, have done little to alter the balance of forces inside the House of Commons itself, the Tories were very alarmed (*Morning Herald*, February 17th). [5] Morley's *Cobden*, p. 558.

English Radicalism 1832-1852

but name seems to have begun with Corn Law Repeal and to have progressed fast. Yet there was every reason for Cobden to avoid antagonising his former supporters. For one thing, a skeleton League was being maintained which it might be necessary to revive if the threatened Protectionist "reaction" appeared likely to endanger Corn Law repeal. Moreover, manufacturers unenthusiastic for Suffrage extension of the O'Connor or even of the Hume-Walmsley pattern, might still be guided towards freehold land and public education schemes which Cobden considered essential steps on the way.

But political strategy is not the entire explanation of Cobden's backwardness on the Suffrage issue. It is difficult not to suspect that he distrusted the judgment of the uneducated poor on political and economic matters with something of the temper of a Russell or a Macaulay, that the energy with which he flung himself into the Freehold Land movement rather than into the Suffrage Extension movement proper marks his desire to qualify a working-class franchise with the need to prove "character" of a kind permitting the saving of £30, £40, or £50.[1] Cobden, who had had the bitterest experience of O'Connorite political vagaries, can be excused for his distrust of mere mobs, but it must be admitted, nevertheless, that he showed a complete inability to appreciate the industrial evils against which the Chartist mobs had so often protested. Increasingly interested in promoting human happiness through the abolition of armaments, war, and international tariffs, he yet disliked industrial legislation in restraint of the use or rather the misuse of labour by the desperately competitive private interests everywhere in charge of the organisation of production. In 1850, it should be remembered, the "Manchester School" was still engaged in a successful rearguard action against the Ten Hour legislation for textile factories,[2] and Cobden and Bright were strongly opposing a plan, then making much noise, of initiating legal protection for male adult labour in the special case of the oppressed London journeymen bakers.[3]

[1] Morley's *Cobden*, p. 501.
[2] E. Hodder, *Life of Shaftesbury*, ii, 198-211, for the Parliamentary struggle of 1850 by which a 10½-hour factory day was put on the Statute Book. Shaftesbury's weakening brought upon him hot attacks from Oastler and J. R. Stephens, still active in factory matters.
[3] F. E. Gillespie, *Labour and Politics in England, 1850-67*, pp. 64-5.

Suffrage, Education, and Newspaper Taxation

In 1850 the Hume Parliamentary Reform motion was rejected by 242 votes against 96, and the Berkeley Ballot motion incurred the same fate in a division of 176–121.[1] But these figures served to mark some Radical progress, and the Radicals were encouraged besides by the Whig Cabinet's Parliamentary Voters (Ireland) Bill, which contained the greatest departure yet officially entertained from the electoral conditions established in 1832. On the ground of the great impoverishment of Ireland and the alarming decline in the numbers qualified to vote, it was proposed, amid considerable Radical rejoicing, to extend the Irish franchise to all in occupation of land and premises of the rateable value of £8 per annum or more.[2] There were the usual doubts, it is true, from the Radicals as to whether Suffrage Extension without the Ballot would not merely enhance landlord influence. M'Cullagh, again, made himself especially prominent by reviving O'Connell's old case for a £5 franchise in the Irish boroughs. But in the main Radicals looked upon the Government's Irish franchise plans with Bright's pleased anticipation of parallel British plans to follow and gave them the warmest support against determined Tory resistance. In the Lords, however, the key personage of the Government, the great Irish landlord Lansdowne, was permitted to show a singular complaisance towards Tory opposition and to accept a £12 occupation franchise for the counties as a compromise between the £8 originally fixed by the Commons and the £15 desired by the Lords majority.[3] The whole proceedings on the Irish Bill, indeed, made it clear how real were the obstacles which Parliamentary Reform, even of the moderate character attracting Russell himself, would have to overcome in the conservatism of the High Whig section of the Cabinet and in the determination of the Lords majority to allow no Suffrage changes threatening the existing "balance of the Constitution."

In the Session of 1851 Parliamentary Reform was destined quickly to take an apparently decisive turn. Locke King, member for East Surrey, one of the county divisions dominated by the vote of metropolitan suburbs, had been promoting for some

[1] *Hansard*, February 28th, March 7th.
[2] *Annual Register, 1850*, History, pp. 98–104, for summary of the long-drawn-out proceedings in Parliament.
[3] *Hansard*, July 1st, for the substitution of the £15 rating in the Lords. Even after a conference with the Commons on August 1st, an obstinate section opposing the £12 compromise was only beaten (*Hansard*, August 6th) by 126–114.

English Radicalism 1832–1852

time a Radical Bill to give dwellers in the counties the same franchise conditions as those in the boroughs, or in other words to enfranchise the numerous £10 householders in the county divisions who had not the freehold, copyhold, or £50 tenancy qualifications. On February 20th Locke King moved for such a Bill in the House, Hume seconded him, and the Prime Minister concluded a somewhat hesitant reply by undertaking to bring in a Reform measure during the following Session. Though Cobden rose and gave Radical thanks and Locke King was prepared to refrain from a division, it was Hume who took charge of Radical strategy on this occasion. He insisted on a division "else Lord John would withdraw his promise again in a fortnight." As the Tories, weary of being used as anti-Radical pawns in a Whig game, had abandoned the House that evening, the Radicals succeeded in defeating the Government by 100–52. "When the result of the vote was made known," wrote Prince Albert in a memorandum on the Ministerial crisis which supervened, "the shouting and triumph of the hundred was immense."[1]

During the Parliamentary recess in the autumn and winter of 1851 a Cabinet Committee was drawing up a new Reform Bill[2] which could, therefore, be announced in the Queen's Speech of February 3, 1852. At almost any other time during the two decades which had elapsed since 1832 the announcement of a new Reform Bill would have arrested public attention to the exclusion of everything else. But this was not the case in 1852 even among the Radicals, who from the first had a very shrewd idea of how unsatisfactory a Russell Reform Bill would be.[3] To many Radicals there were more exciting topics under discussion than the degree to which the Whig Reform Bill would be found acceptable. The dismissal of Palmerston from the Foreign Office after a tenure which had endangered every autocrat in Europe and made Palmerston himself the hero of the working classes overshadowed the Reform agitation from one angle.[4]

---

[1] *Letters of Queen Victoria*, ii, 289.
[2] *Ibid.*, pp. 332–3, where the Queen notes that the Committee's plans were framed "with a due regard to the importance of not giving an undue proportion of weight to the Democracy." Yet Lansdowne was ready to resign because of his dislike (*Later Correspondence of Russell*, ii, 96).
[3] Morley's *Cobden*, p. 566. Cobden was sure that the Ballot would be left out, and that he would, therefore, be unable to support it.
[4] Cf. *Illustrated London News*, December 27th: "Wherever there is an absolute tyranny in Europe, his Lordship is looked upon with hatred or mistrust;

Suffrage, Education, and Newspaper Taxation

From another it was overshadowed by the panic desire to arm at all costs against the hated Napoleon of the military *coup d'état* of December 2, 1851.[1] The very Radicals who should have been concentrating on Reform at the opening of Parliament were, in fact, divided between those whose hatred of Napoleon led them to cry with the loudest for great preparations against his alleged designs and those who followed Hume and Cobden in denouncing the whole invasion excitement as a baseless panic.[2]

There is evidence enough, nevertheless, that if Russell could have overcome Militia Bill difficulties, all the greater from the fact that a powerful Radical band round Cobden were making trouble in one direction and Palmerston in the other, the Reform Bill might yet have taken the centre of the stage.[3] Certainly the Tory camp as depicted in *Malmesbury's Memoirs* "had been quite knocked down by this Reform Bill."[4] Yet Radicals were far from enthusiastic about Reform proposals, making concessions, indeed, but avowedly such as would not alter what was grandly called the balance of the Constitution, a term by which was meant the control of a large majority in the Commons by the landowning class. Thus the reduction of the borough qualification from £10 to £5 householding would certainly give hundreds of thousands of new persons the right to vote in the great industrial towns, but it was unaccompanied by any scheme of allotting extra members to these new masses of voters or the huge communities of which they formed part. Again, a very considerable accession of village and small-town tradesmen to the county constituencies might be expected from the £20 householding concession in this sphere and a few thousand extra voters might also come from the reduction of the copyholder and long-leaseholder qualification from £10 to £5 annual value. But as the ballot was still being withheld despite Radical protests, it was doubtful whether these county qualification changes could in any case do more than improve the chances of a county-family Whig candidate here

---

and wherever there is a desire for constitutional liberty, repressed by bayonets, or threatened by irresponsible autocrats, there has his Lordship admirers and friends...." [1] *Illustrated London News*, January 17, 1852.

[2] *Hansard*, February 16th, Hume, Cobden.

[3] Reform meetings had been very successfully held after Manchester had seen a great gathering on December 3rd in Free Trade Hall (*Illustrated London News*, December 6th, gives seven thousand as the number present). *Punch* had pro-Reform cartoons on January 3rd, February 7th, and February 21, 1852.

[4] *Memoirs of an Ex-Minister*, under February 13th.

English Radicalism 1832-1852

and there. And if in the more Parliamentary sphere Russell proposed to abolish the property qualification of members and the scandal of the Lords' twenty-year veto upon Jewish M.P.s, he also proposed to remove a check on Ministers which had often been found of value in the closing years of Septennial Act Parliaments, the necessity for promoted Ministers to submit to re-election. It is hard to believe that Radicals would ever willingly have yielded this to Ministerial convenience unless given the compensation of shorter Parliaments.

Triennial Parliaments, indeed, and Ballot were the principal omissions immediately criticised by Hume,[1] but Bright, who allowed himself a wider examination of the Bill, went farther. Moving on from the need of protecting the new borough voters from the influence of manufacturers by giving them the ballot, Bright proceeded to criticise the suggested £20 county occupation franchise and to suggest that a £10 householder in the counties would surely be found as intelligent and as respectable as a £5 householder in the boroughs. Then he turned to deal with the Prime Minister's claim that he had maintained a "balance of interests" in his plan by asserting that the preponderance actually to be retained by the representatives of land and the opponents of Free Trade would mean not a "balance of interests" but a deadlock to the Government.

Bright was referring specifically to the case of the 67 English and Welsh borough constituencies with fewer than 500 voters which were not to be deprived of their members in favour of dense populations elsewhere. According to Russell that would have been to upset the balance of interests established by the Reform Bill, so that his proposal was merely to add to these sixty-seven boroughs adjacent areas calculated to bring their voters above the 500 minimum without altering the "agricultural interest's" virtual supremacy in all of them. Bright insisted that to leave a slightly remodelled Thetford and Harwich returning two members and such boroughs as Manchester, Finsbury, or Westminster no more, could not and ought not to be regarded

---

[1] Russell made his proposals on February 9, 1852, to a "very crowded House" (*Illustrated London News*, February 14th), and Hume was the first of the many speakers to follow. Strenuous Tory resistance was not announced until the Bill had been studied in detail, and the conclusion reached that it would "entirely upset" the balance of the constitution (*Illustrated London News*, February 21st).

as a settlement. He pressed upon the Prime Minister the need of withdrawing representation altogether from the decayed boroughs[1] and of bestowing the seats upon the large constituencies already in existence or the new constituencies which could be shaped out in the populous areas.

But the Radicals were to receive no chance of attempting to revise Russell's measure. Only a few days after the First Reading the Government was defeated on its Militia Bill which the majority of the House considered not to be thorough enough. Russell probably quite expected to be defeated before the Reform Bill became law, but he hardly expected the course which was subsequently to be taken by the stream of national politics. He and his clique appear to have believed that the mooting of the Reform Bill would give him a permanent claim on Radical support in Parliament and out of doors, and that with this his re-installation as Prime Minister could not be long delayed. But he hardly guessed how strong was the Radical dislike of his long course of Whig finessing and how little his Reform Bill had done to overcome it. Accordingly when the Protectionist Government which had replaced his own was brought down, the absence of Radical enthusiasm[2] was certainly one of the factors which prevented his return to the Prime Ministership and allowed the Peelites rather than the Whigs to dominate the Coalition Government of Lord Aberdeen. Though in entering this Government Russell secured permission to continue with his Parliamentary Reform projects, events were long to deny him the possibility of using Reform to force himself back to the Prime Ministership. The Crimean War both forced Reform into the background and Palmerston into the foreground.

[1] Cf. *Illustrated London News*, February 21st, for the rapid hardening even of moderate opinion against Russell on this point: "By the new Reform Bill only two new towns of importance—Birkenhead and Barnsley—are to be enfranchised; but by the same measure at least half a hundred small villages ... are to be tainted with the rottenness of the peccant boroughs to which they are to be annexed, and bribery and corruption are to be provided with fresh material...."

[2] Greville, *Memoirs*, November 3rd, shows the political world to have been discussing "the complete separation between Lord John and Cobden" on the subject of the Ballot, and to have been expecting a prolongation of the Protectionist Government in consequence. In point of fact, Cobden's attitude forced Lord John to abandon his pretensions to the next Premiership, and to offer to work with Palmerston under Lansdowne as Premier. Cf. also, *Later Correspondence of Lord J. Russell*, ii, 108-9, for the Ballot situation with Cobden, and pp. 112-13 for that with Bright.

English Radicalism 1832–1852

Meanwhile the advent of a Tory Ministry in February 1852 had by no means abated Radical Reform efforts. Demonstrations, were, in fact, all the more necessary when a Prime Minister took office who could be quoted by Hume as wishing to "oppose some barrier against the current of democratic influence that is continually encroaching and which would throw power nominally into the hands of the masses, practically into the hands of the demagogues who lead them." The debate on Hume's Radical Reform motion of March 25, 1852, indeed, proved a very interesting one. With characteristic audacity Disraeli, now Leader of the House, produced a set of figures designed to show that the Radical complaint of the under-representation of the industrial populations could be met in kind by the "agricultural interest." North Cheshire, for example, had two members for 156,000 of county population and four members for the 93,000 borough population in Macclesfield and Stockport. South Cheshire, again, had two members for its county population of 178,000 and two for 28,000 in Chester. These and other examples given by Disraeli made most effective debating points which Hume was hardly the right man to counter in his closing speech. More effective was Lord John Russell in taking up Disraeli's remark that the constituency should be changed only from clear necessity. He questioned whether Disraeli did not mean the "clear discontent" which it was dangerous to await. Though Hume's motion, supported only by the Radicals, was defeated by 244 votes against 89,[1] it was of some service in eliciting Government declarations which showed that the Tories, too, would be prepared to contemplate Suffrage Extension of their own if popular pressure should become strong enough. More serviceable still was the division of April 27th on Locke King's motion for giving the county voting qualification to the £10 householder. A vote as encouraging as 149 against 202[2] certainly showed that Reform might yet be brought to the centre of the stage after the current Militia and Protection excitements had been disposed of.

It was obvious, nevertheless, that such a Parliamentary Reform

---

[1] *Illustrated London News*, March 27th. It was Walpole, the Home Secretary, who did not wish to be understood as resisting extension of the suffrage to the "education and industry of the country."

[2] *Ibid.*, May 1st. It may be noted that Henry Drummond, one of the most notable Tory M.P.S, told the Government that by opposing such motions they were helping Russell to return to office.

Suffrage, Education, and Newspaper Taxation

as was desired by the Radical side of the House would only be the result of years of incessant agitation and that the cause would be mightily helped forward if the way could be cleared for a workman's newspaper Press by a new assault on the "Taxes on Knowledge." From the beginning of 1849, indeed, Cobden and Place, the representatives of two different Radical generations, had been doing their utmost for the moderate Chartist group under Dobson Collett which had initiated an agitation destined to last for twenty years.[1] As Cobden had Financial Reform and Disarmament on his hands as well as the Freehold Land movement and the defence of Free Trade, as Bright was interesting himself primarily in Parliamentary Reform and Ireland, Milner Gibson was chosen to lead the Parliamentary agitation against the Excise Duties making the penny newspaper impossible. It was a good choice. Milner Gibson's was a nationally known name, he had held office, and was a Privy Councillor.

Supported by an agitation outside which made it likely that a new unstamped Press might soon make its appearance, Milner Gibson had his first success when Russell conceded him a Newspaper Stamp Committee in 1851. Before this Committee it could be fully demonstrated how newspapers aiming only at local circulations among the poor were prevented from being set up by an Excise system which required a penny stamp per copy and offered in exchange the meaningless privilege of free transmission through the post. Cobden's presence in the Committee, too, meant that a decisive sentence in its Report expressed the members' view that "they do not consider that news is in itself a desirable subject for taxation."[2]

Pending Gibson's raising of the issue even in a completer form in Parliament, ingenious though very troublesome ways of evading the repressive effects of the Newspaper Laws were experimented with in the *Stoke Narrative* and the *Dunfermline Register*. Both were periodical news-sheets particularly well calculated to show what might be the educative influence on the poor of the removal of the Stamp Duty.[3] It was papers of

---

[1] C. D. Collet, *History of the Taxes on Knowledge*, pp. 44 sqq. This group included Hetherington (d. 1849), Watson, and Moore of the old London Working Men's Association, and recruited such Chartist personalities as Thomas Cooper and G. J. Holyoake.
[2] *Ibid.*, p. 82.   [3] *Ibid.*, pp. 85–90.

this type, indeed, needing no great capital for their publication, which Cobden was particularly anxious to see printed and circulated. Through such papers did he envisage the political opinions of the working class becoming as considerable a factor in the State as those of the readers of *The Times* and the *Scotsman*.¹

Unfortunately, many of the established papers, especially those getting good postage value for their penny stamp or fearing the competition of cheap newcomers, were by no means friendly to the agitation for the abolition of the newspaper stamp. There was one particularly plausible argument for the retention of the stamp which won even an unflinching Radical like Roebuck.² In granting perpetual free postage on all stamped copies of newspapers for the penny, the State was said, in effect, to be using the pennies of town-dwellers, whose copies were not sent through the post, in order to subvention the cheap transmission of news even to the most deserted parts of the countryside. In the mouth of its interested defenders, indeed, Newspaper Taxation was nothing but part of a great co-operative educational effort in which town-dwellers, themselves in the heart of affairs, contributed an insignificant something to enable the State to distribute newspapers in the more isolated rural areas.

But it was not only the penny stamp which made the cheap newspaper impossible but also the Advertisement Duty and the Paper Excise. In attacking all three "Taxes on Knowledge" on April 22nd Milner Gibson succeeded in making out a very powerful case, which was not the less strong because moderately urged.³ Evidence he cited, indeed, went to show that working-class improvement was not only suffering from the unnecessary dearness of newspapers but also from the unfair weight with which the Paper Duty bore down on such completely unimpeachable educational publications for working men as Cassell's⁴

---

¹ C. D. Collet, *History of the Taxes on Knowledge*, pp. 110–11, for Cobden's indignation over the suppression of a small paper in his part of Sussex. Cf. E. W. Watkin, *Alderman Cobden*, pp. 140–62. Cobden was watchful against changes of the law which would "create a few big papers throughout the country, and destroy all chance of competition on the part of the second- and third-class journals." ² *Ibid.*, p. 47.
³ *Illustrated London News*, May 1, 1852, gave its tremendous publicity to the speech.
⁴ John Cassell, 1817–65, had, after a course of teetotal oratory as the "Manchester Carpenter," entered publication with the *Teetotal Times*, shown his Radicalism with the *Spirit of Freedom* and the *Freeholder* periodicals, and was actually engaged upon the *Popular Educator*.

Suffrage, Education, and Newspaper Taxation

Popular Educator and Knight's *Penny Cyclopaedia*.[1] On May 12th the debate was resumed, and some significant divisions were taken against a Chancellor who professed fiscal inability to meet the Radical demands but voiced sincere sympathy. On the Newspaper Stamp Duty the Radicals divided at 100–199, on the Paper Duty at 107–195, and on the Advertisement Duty at 116–181.[2] But it was freely prophesied at the time that both the latter duties would very soon be given up. Certainly the "commercial" objections to an Advertisement Duty hindering the normal development of trade and to a Paper Excise which kept a large industry enchained and unable to take full advantage of rapidly growing export opportunities received the amplest publicity in a Press with its own axe to grind.[3] For the newspaper stamp, however, behind which was entrenched both the political partisanship of those who feared the growth of cheap working-class journals and the trade anxieties of existing newspapers, a much longer life was forecast.[4] But this was to reckon without the Crimean War. That struggle, which produced a tremendous bellicosity amongst even the humblest strata of the population and relaxed their pressure for Radical Parliamentary Reform almost entirely, had other strange and important effects. One of them was a wide publication of patriotic sheets of war news in such unrestrainable defiance of the Stamp Laws that in justice to law-abiding journals the Stamp Laws themselves had to be withdrawn.[5]

Against newspaper duties Radicals had moved most effectively when dubbing them "*Taxes on Knowledge*" and ascribing to them the dense and dangerous ignorance of the masses. Universal education at the public expense was also brought nearer by illustrating from the alarming percentages of the unschooled under the existing system what perilous moral, industrial, and political

---

[1] Charles Knight, 1790–1873, the worthiest if not the most successful of an age of remarkable publishers, had told the story in the remarkable *Struggle of a Book against Excessive Taxation*.
[2] *Illustrated London News*, May 15th.
[3] *Ibid.*, April 24th, May 1st, May 15th.
[4] *Ibid.*, May 15th. "The stamp on newspapers is a matter on which, as we have often before observed, public opinion is not sufficiently ripe to justify the hope of speedy, if of any legislation. The other two questions stand upon a different footing, and appeal solely upon fiscal, economical, and commercial grounds to the common sense of Parliament and the country...."
[5] C. D. Collet, *History of the Taxes on Knowledge*, pp. 118–26. The publishers, of course, took the line that papers confined to war-news were not newspapers, and declined to accept the Board of Inland Revenue's view.

English Radicalism 1832–1852

"errors" might take root throughout the lower strata of the population. Unfortunately the school question had become thoroughly enmeshed in bitter sectarian strife, and one Radical section in contending against the very marked advantages obtained by Anglicans from the actual operations of the Committee of Council on Education had committed itself to a fatal policy of denying the State any rights in education at all.[1] For all the pertinacity of Baines[2] of Leeds, however, and the eagerness with which Bright had at one time thrown his powerful voice on that side, the predominant feeling even among those Radicals who had taken a hot share in the Dissenting Voluntaryist campaigns of 1843 and 1847 had come by 1849 to be one of greater readiness to examine the possibility of finding unobjectionable means for the State promotion of education. Elected local authorities would certainly have aroused altogether fewer Dissenting suspicions than the Committee of Council.

As soon, however, as elected local education authorities with rating powers were contemplated, the basis of the moral and religious instruction in the schools which they should construct became a matter of difficulty. It was in vain that the bold urged that public schools would only prove workable on a basis of purely secular instruction and that the churches, chapels, and Sunday schools might be trusted, as in America, to take every care for the religious instruction. The mere mention of "secular" education was sufficient to provoke opposition from those who might be Radical enough to contemplate rate-supported public schools and even compulsory attendance but who wanted at least to make "Bible education" a prominent subject therein as a safeguard against infidelity. In this state of feeling the practical difficulties which a local board containing Anglican, Catholic, and Dissenting elements might have in drafting and working any scheme of religious instruction were altogether underrated.

While Cobden was waiting patiently for Baines and the

[1] Mrs. Salis Schwabe, *Reminiscences of Cobden*, pp. 133–5, contains a regretful summary by Cobden of how this had come about.
[2] Edward Baines, the younger (b. 1800), and as editor and proprietor of the *Leeds Mercury* controlling by far the most powerful provincial newspaper in the country with a wide Dissenter circulation throughout Northern England. Joseph Sturge (d. 1859) was one whose powerful influence was cast on Baines's side, and the Congregationalist hosiery millionaire, Samuel Morley, also spent money and effort lavishly in the "voluntary" cause and against Committee of Council policies (cf. E. Hodder, *Life of Samuel Morley*, pp. 97–105).

Suffrage, Education, and Newspaper Taxation

Voluntaryists to fall into line[1] and permit him to open a united Radical agitation for elected public educational authorities, W. J. Fox brought forward a Bill which was quickly dubbed the Secular Education Bill and so denied any serious legislative prospects. In point of fact, despite Fox's eloquence,[2] earnestness, and careful avoidance of giving offence, his Bill was rejected on June 5, 1850, by 287 votes against 58.[3] Yet how his willingness to compromise with unreason had appeared to J. S. Mill, now since the publication of his famous *Principles of Political Economy* already on the road to becoming the Ultra-Radical major prophet, may best be estimated from the correspondence which passed between them while Fox was preparing his Bill. In his draft plans Fox had sought to propitiate religious opposition by making moral instruction one of the subjects in the public "secular" schools, and by putting forward as a possible model for their organisation the undenominational National Schools of Ireland, where the reading of a book of selections from the Bible provided the only religious part of the curriculum.[4] Mill objected to the "moral instruction" which, he said, would come to mean, under the direction of the men who might be expected as school managers, "cramming the children directly with all the common professions about what is right and wrong, and about the worth of different things in life, and filling them indirectly with the spirit of all the notions on such matters which vulgar-minded people are in the habit of acting on without consciously professing." To imitation of the Irish National Schools' use of the Bible he objected because it taught "the general recognition of that book as containing the system and history of creation and the commands of an all-wise and good being. Any system of instruction which does this," he added, "contains I conceive a great part of all the mischief done by a purely Church or purely Dissenting education."[5]

Radical politicians, however, anxious to teach the lower strata of the population the three R's as quickly as might be, could not

---

[1] Morley's *Cobden*, p. 548, November 9, 1850: "I thought I had given time to Mr. Baines and his dissenting friends to get cool upon the subject. But they appear to be as hot as ever. However, I shall now go straight at the mark. . . ."
[2] *Illustrated London News*, March 2nd, March 9th; *Hansard*, February 26th.
[3] *Ibid.*, June 8th.
[4] *Life and Remains of Archbishop Whately*, pp. 75–6, shows, however, that the system was doing more for "Scriptural knowledge" than Fox perhaps knew. [5] *Letters of J. S. Mill*, i, 150–1.

look at matters so much *sub specie aeternitatis* as the philosopher in his study. In throwing himself warmly into the Education struggle during the course of 1850 Cobden did his utmost to show what America was gaining from the "secular system" and yet how little it prevented religion from flourishing there with greater vigour than in England. In particular he saw to it that the advocates of the "secular school" did not adopt what would have been the fatal designation of the National Secular School Association, and that, when enrolled instead as the National Public Schools' Association, they did not take dangerous decisions with regard to the Bible.[1] Yet even in Cobden's own particular Manchester sphere of influence, his authority was not great enough to prevent a rival association from promoting a Manchester and Salford Education Bill whose avowed purpose was to help schools from the rates, but only such schools as made religion an essential part of their curriculum. Yet Cobden had gone as far to meet his opponents as to be prepared to take over their denominational schoolrooms as "public schools" and even to permit religious instruction in them out of school hours if unsubsidised from the rates.[2] For the bulk even of middle-class Radicals the transition from the idea of schools as annexes to churches and chapels was obviously proving difficult.

Accordingly though the whole of the controlling influences in Manchester and Salford were prepared to give a lead to the nation by asking Parliament for local educational rating, a Manchester and Salford Education Bill of 1852 proved but an occasion of inter-Radical dispute which ended any immediate hopes of legislation.[3] Manchester's educational lead to the nation in 1852 had, therefore, to be confined to the decision to rate itself for the support of a Free Library under the admirable Ewart's Library Bill of 1850.[4] On library matters, at least, the problem

---

[1] Mrs. Salis Schwabe, *Reminiscences of Richard Cobden*, prints three of Cobden's speeches on Education at this stage, p. 122 sqq. Cobden was a practising Churchman, and even some of those rigid secularists who wanted to ban the Bible from the schools did so not because they were infidels, avowed or unavowed, but because the use of the Authorised Version in schools would prevent Catholic attendance.

[2] Mrs. Salis Schwabe, *op. cit.*, pp. 162-76, for the whole situation.

[3] *Hansard*, February 11th, March 17th, when the compromise of a Select Committee of Inquiry was come to. It is interesting to observe that petitioning for "secular"' schools was raised from the 6,803 signatures of 1851 to the 67,311 signatures of 1852 (*Companion to the British Almanac, 1852, 1853*.)

[4] *Irving's Annals*, p. 359, for the overwhelming vote of 3,962 against 40.

Suffrage, Education, and Newspaper Taxation

of the tone, religious or otherwise, to give to the book-collection needed not to split Manchester Radicalism.[1] Even the Radical-minded Ewart himself had finally asked Parliament for no more than rate-provided premises and had left the books themselves to come from voluntary donors. There was the extensive experience of Mechanics' Institutions, therefore, to reassure the pious that the adoption of such a system would not allow infidelity to triumph. Indeed, the comparative failure of the Mechanics' Institutions to attract or to mould the most earnest of the working classes during the Chartist Age is partly ascribable to the timid library policy almost invariably pursued by management committees of philanthropic donors. Men who longed to read discussions on the right and wrong of the existing fabric of Church, State, and Society, sooner or later grew tired of the neutral and mainly scientific pabulum which had been philanthropically provided to help the evolution of minor Watts and Stephensons.[2] Such men founded Chartist, Socialist, and Secularist Associations, busied themselves with Trade Club affairs, and sometimes attempted to set up their own library groups.[3]

---

[1] *Illustrated London News*, May 18, 1850, had prophesied that if Ewart's Bill were successful, "We should have one party vehemently insisting on, and another party as vehemently opposing, the introduction of Hume and Gibbon into the libraries of the people. We should have the ratepayers of our towns ranged into factions upon the morality or Christianity of a Byron or a Shelley. . . ." It is obvious why the idea of rating for books was abandoned.

[2] The best view of the library situation is to be obtained from J. W. Hudson's *History of Adult Education* of 1851 and the *Report of the* (House of Commons) *Select Committee on Public Libraries* of 1849. An invaluable commentary is that of J. L. and B. Hammond in *The Age of the Chartists*, pp. 323–34.

[3] Cf. 1849, *Report of the Committee on Public Libraries*, pp. 80, 157.

CHAPTER XX

RELIGION, LANDOWNERSHIP, AND THE FAMILY

"Those who are capable of broaching their infidelity in a logical form, and of defending it with arguments ... are the aristocracy of the working classes. By dint of unwearied and self-denying effort ... they have attained to general historical views. They have inquired into the theory of government, the rights of man, and the laws of trade, and on these subjects they have adopted settled opinions. They have a general acquaintance with science. ... Whatever promises a measure of social and political reform is sure at once of gaining their hearty adherence. They are often total abstainers from intoxicating drinks, conspicuous members of mechanic institutions, indefatigable promoters of benefit and other societies which tend to improve the economical condition of the working classes; in short, they are usually the patrons of every ameliorative change which does not necessarily include religion. Towards this they are animated with an inveterately hostile sentiment...."

H. DUNCKLEY, "The Glory and the Shame of Britain" *(written 1849), pp. 74–5.*

"Once allow the soil of a country which God made for all its inhabitants, and for all generations born upon it, to be bought up or otherwise monopolised or usurped by any particular section of any one generation (be that section large or small), and that moment your community is divided into tyrants and slaves: into knaves who will work for nobody, and into drudges who will have to work for anybody or everybody but themselves. No subsequent legislation, no possible tinkering or patchwork in the way of remedial measures can sensibly affect a system based on so hideous a foundation...."

BRONTERRE O'BRIEN, "Power of the Pence," *April 21, 1849.*

"It is seldom by the choice of the wife that families are too numerous; on her devolves the whole of the intolerable domestic drudgery resulting from the excess. To be relieved from it would be hailed as a blessing by multitudes of women who now never venture to urge such a claim, but who would urge it, if supported by the moral feelings of the community...."

J. S. MILL, "Principles of Political Economy," *Book. 2, chapter 13, paragraph 2.*

DICEY has told with no little legitimate satisfaction the story of the successful resistance of the Church of England to the Disestablishment pressure of the Dissenters during the years following 1832.[1] And, indeed, a Churchman contemplating the detestation with which the Bishops' Bench was so widely regarded at the close of 1831 or that extraordinary Canterbury outbreak of August 7, 1832, against the Primate himself[2] may well be contented with a survey of the Church position arrived at two decades afterwards. The pleasure is the better founded when it is remembered how largely Churchmen had contributed to their own salvation. The activities of the Tractarians, for example, had admirably served to reanimate faith in the unique God-given functions of the clergy.[3] Only heavy sacrifices, again, on the part of both ecclesiastics and earnest laymen, could have made possible the vast Church extension which is associated with such names as those of Blomfield of London, Hook of Leeds, and Molesworth of Rochdale.[4]

Nor should the expansion of social sympathies be neglected which made Hook get on so well with Leeds Chartists, which drove Shaftesbury on to undertake his unique series of crusades, which permitted the appearance of so startling a Church pamphlet in the distressful days of 1843 as *The Perils of the Nation*,[5] and which allowed one powerful Church group at least to meet the perils of 1848 with the *Politics for the People* periodical.[6] Erastian Whig statesmen, too, had played their part in "preserving the Establishment" with their succession of Reforming Acts to amend the most untenable of the Church's institutions. Pamphlets like the brilliant but perverted *Letters to Archdeacon Singleton*, in which, even a Sydney Smith had resisted Cathedral reform show, when taken in conjunction with a parallel pamphlet by so opposite a Church power as Pusey,[7] how surely all manner of Churchmen

---

[1] A. V. Dicey, *Law and Public Opinion in England during the Nineteenth Century*, pp. 311-60.
[2] *Annual Register, 1832*. Chronicle: "No sooner had the carriage of the Archbishop appeared in sight than the most deafening noises rent the air: and when his Grace arrived at the Guildhall, groans and hisses were tremendous ... missiles of every description (were) hurled ...", p. 106.
[3] As administering the Sacraments. Cf. E. B. Pusey, *Script. Views of Holy Baptism*, preface, p. ix.   [4] Cf. *Dictionary of National Biography*.
[5] Cf. M. Beer, *History of British Socialism*, ii, 140.
[6] Cf. *Ibid.*, pp. 184-5.   [7] Cf. H. P. Liddon, *Life of E. B. Pusey*, i, 225-36

would have provoked a Radical Disestablishment if their advice had been taken by the politicians. It needed a trimming Whig Ministry, riding high seas of Dissenting and democratic wrath, to appreciate the full measure of the Radical storm.

But if the State Church was altogether safer in 1849 than it had been in 1832, the opposition of various brands of Radicalism was still formidable. Popular infidelity, bred on Paine, Owen, and Carlile, was much less truculent, perhaps, in what may be called its Holyoake age than it had been at the Blackfriars Rotunda in 1831. Yet its roots were very deep in the people, so that in 1849, for example, the sixteen-year old Bradlaugh was captured at its open-air meetings[1] and in 1852 the construction of a National "Secularist" organisation was being undertaken with the well-circulated *Reasoner* as its weekly organ.[2] In Holyoake, moreover, popular infidelity had a leader capable of interpreting to the working classes the importance of the intellectual blows which were being delivered upon the old-fashioned religious position from new angles. Indeed, he was in close touch with the increasingly important schools of middle-class sceptics for whom Strauss's *Life of Christ* and Lyell's *Principles of Geology* had opened new avenues of critical thought.[3]

Till Bradlaugh, however, had made combative infidelity an important element in the struggle against the State Church, it was combative Dissent upon which the burden of the fight principally rested. In the history of combative Dissent the year 1843 is of singular importance. After having defended State Establish-

---

[1] A. S. Headingley, *Biography of Charles Bradlaugh*, pp. 6–7. The Chartist and Freethinking meetings at Bonner's Fields, Bethnal Green, were held on Sunday mornings, and were so much the scandal of the pious that the Tory Government of 1852 attempted their suppression. It should be remembered that Chartist halls and Socialist institutions were also available for "Secularist" activities.

[2] *Reasoner*, October 20th and 27th, for the Freethinkers' Conference. The *Reasoner's* circulation had been steadily rising for years, and in 1852 it was selling over three thousand copies per week at 1d. each (*Ibid.*, September 29th).

[3] Holyoake's *Reasoner* was subventioned among others by J. S. Mill and Harriet Martineau. Holyoake, too, was allowed to co-operate on equal terms with that remarkable advanced group which was gathered round the *Leader*, the weekly newspaper (1850–60) which is usually connected with the name of G. H. Lewes, the friend of George Eliot. It will help to display the affiliations of the intellectual Radicals to add that it was George Eliot who was the English translator of Strauss's *Leben Jesu*, that the publication was financially supported by Joseph Parkes, the political lawyer, and that the work took George Eliot on to the assistant-editorship of the *Westminster Review*.

ments as indefensible as the Irish and worried the Melbourne Cabinet for years to obtain public money for Scottish Church Extension, the famous Dr. Chalmers led half the Scottish State Church into revolt. The measure of English Nonconformist sympathy aroused was immense, as was proved by the sums collected in England for the Sustentation Fund of a Free Church having suddenly to organise on a voluntary basis and even to put up new buildings by the hundred as quickly as might be.[1] Indeed, the very success of the voluntary financial efforts which could put the Scottish Free Church on a hopeful basis in less than a year might well have inspired the 1,200 delegates from England, Scotland, and Ireland who gathered in London for the great Anti-State Church Conference which began on April 30, 1844.[2] In changing its name in 1853 from the "Anti-State Church Association" to the "Society for the Liberation of Religion from State Patronage and Control," the permanent organisation issuing from the initiatory Conference of 1844 was certainly taking a much more disarming title.[3]

Much of the future pamphleteering between what came to be known as the Liberation Society and adherents of the State Church was to turn on the comparative numbers of churchgoers and chapelgoers. If the Liberation Society could have proved statistically that the numbers of chapelgoers approached, equalled, or exceeded those who went to church, a strong *prima facie* case for Disestablishment legislation would have been established. As is well known, the Census authorities of 1851 attempted an English "religious census" through forms supplied by their enumerators to the authorities at all places where "religious services were customarily performed." It may be interesting here to give the results obtained.[4] The total of Church of England attendances on the morning, afternoon, and evening of Sunday, March 30, 1851, was 5,292,551 and that elsewhere was 5,603,515. By an involved series of assumptions and calculations these attendances were taken to show that 3,773,474 "separate persons"

[1] W. Hanna, *Memoirs of Dr. Chalmers*, iv, 358.
[2] *Illustrated London News*, May 4th.
[3] Cf. the bitter A. H. Hore's *History of the Church of England*, p. 519.
[4] *Religious Worship in England and Wales*, abridged from the Official Report made by Horace Mann to George Graham, Registrar-General. For Anglican criticism of this Report and the use of it made by Dissenters, see Lord Selborne, *A Defence of the Church of England against Disestablishment*, chapter 15.

English Radicalism 1832–1852

attended Church of England services that day and 3,487,558 "separate persons" attended other forms of service. As another series of assumptions led to the conclusion that 12,540,326 of the English and Welsh population total of 17,927,609 could, if they would, have made at least one appearance at a place of worship that day, the deduction was that 5,288,294 had not cared to. But the Census Report was careful to point out that "habitual neglecters of religious services"[1] were to be estimated as fewer than the 5,228,294. This was probably true enough though there were huge urban populations, especially in the metropolitan area, whose complete disregard of Sunday in the matter of provision-buying, street-trading, and pleasure outings was the despair of the Sabbatarians.

Among things tending to strengthen the Liberationist case against Church of England privilege, the attitude of Anglican stalwarts towards Jewish Emancipation must take a considerable place. Since 1833 a majority of Tory Peers had been blocking the way to the complete emancipation which the House of Commons wished to bestow upon the Jews, and when Baron Rothschild was returned for the City of London in 1847 the matter became acute. Both in 1848 and 1849 episcopal voices called upon the House of Lords to reject the Government Bill for Jewish Emancipation[2] which would have allowed Rothschild to take his seat, and on both occasions the Bill was lost, though the Commons had passed it by considerable majorities. After the Lords' rejection of 1849 Rothschild resigned his seat, but, as he was re-elected by the City, the House of Commons had once more to spend much valuable time in 1850 on his problem. Next year the Greenwich Radicals elected a second Jewish M.P. in Alderman Salomons, but again the Lords rejected a Government Emancipation Bill and thus deprived two English constituencies of their members.[3] As Salomons was pledged to his constituents to attempt to take his seat, he made his way into the Commons and incurred various pains and penalties by voting without having abjured the Pretender on the "true faith of a Christian." In 1852

---

[1] *Mann's Report*, p. cliii.
[2] *Hansard*, June 26, 1849, for speeches by the Archbishop of Canterbury and the Bishops of Exeter and Oxford. The Archbishop of Dublin was on the opposite side.
[3] *Illustrated London News*, July 26th, for Salomons's majority of 2,208–1,311 in the by-election just over.

his case was before the Courts, which were compelled to find him guilty while virtually appealing to Parliament to end an intolerable situation. Meanwhile every Jewish Emancipation debate found Catholics claiming that they, too, needed emancipation from the fetters which had been put upon their Parliamentary action in Anglican interests.[1] By the oath which was tendered to Catholics under the Catholic Relief Bill of 1829, action by them to secure Disestablishment of the Irish Church became a breach of their sworn engagements which it took involved casuistry to argue away.

Another politico-religious grievance which had aroused Radical ire for many years was the Church of England monopoly of the ancient Universities of Oxford and Cambridge. Here, too, there was a long Parliamentary history of baffled effort which James Heywood, the Unitarian member for North Lancashire, seemed to have improved upon when his motion of April 25, 1850, for an inquiry into means of improving the management and usefulness of Oxford, Cambridge, and Dublin brought the Prime Minister's promise of Royal Commissions upon Oxford and Cambridge.[2] The Oxford inquiry was conducted under great disadvantages, for so hot was the local Toryism that the Commission's legality was disputed, and it proved impossible to obtain essential information on the revenues of some of the colleges from whom it was being proposed to remove the dead hand of restricting Foundation Statutes and Donors' Wills. The Reports were, nevertheless, to hand during the course of 1852. But for the hard work, however, which followed by the Liberation Society,[3] the Oxford Act of 1854 and the Cambridge Act of 1856 might have preserved Church privilege more irritatingly than actually proved the case.

Church Rates, again, continued a matter apt to make Radical Liberationists even of normal Dissenters with no great urge to violent politics. Though the Dissenters had now made the levying of Church Rates impossible in all places where, with the aid of the infidel and the indifferent, they could collect a vestry majority, the legal position of such a majority remained in doubt until

---

[1] Cf. *Hansard*, February 19, 1849, J. O'Connell; June 26, 1849, Lord Shrewsbury (Catholic).
[2] *Ann. Reg. Hist.*, *1850*, pp. 147–57.
[3] W. N. Molesworth, *History of England from 1830*, ii, 449.

1853.¹ Even when it was established, Dissenters still demanded a Church Rates Abolition Bill for the protection of those among them who dwelt in districts where the combined influence of squire and parson was not to be overborne in vestry. Burial questions, too, would remain a source of discontent until Dissenting ministers obtained the right to take the burial services of those whose families wanted their ministrations in the parish churchyard. Churchmen, however, clung to churchyard domination with marked tenacity. Indeed, it was to be charged against the Bishops that they showed the greatest dislike even for the Burial legislation initiated in 1852 for Public Health reasons, legislation aimed at ending churchyard burials in crowded areas and substituting burial in extra-urban cemeteries in which the rights of all denominations were provided for.²

The most exposed point of the existing State and Church system remained, however, the position of the Irish Church. The Irish Church Reform of 1833 and the subsequent Whig Tithe Regulation, appointments like that of Whately and grants of Treasury money for Maynooth and the Irish Colleges—these things, it is true, had done something to give conscientious Tory politicians a greater moral assurance in defence. Moreover, the great potato famine and its terrible aftermath had served to lay the Irish Church controversy for several years. In 1850 and 1851, again, when England was resounding with a "Papal Aggression" storm provoked by the tactlessly grandiose language which had been employed in announcing the division of England into Catholic bishopric areas, the time was not propitious for a British Radical attempt to revive the Irish Church issue.

Yet in the autumn of 1852 it was undoubtedly being brought somewhat nearer to the field of immediately controversial politics by the activity of Bright, who had long been devoting special attention to Irish politics.³ The occasion which gave Bright his

¹ *Irving's Annals*, p. 388, for the House of Lords' decision that a rate made by a minority against the will of the majority could not stand. It was the conclusion of twelve years of litigation in connexion with the famous Braintree Church Rate of 2s. in the pound made in 1841.

² The original 1852 Act was for London, the 15 & 16 Vict. c. 85. It was followed by the 16 & 17 Vict. c. 134, the 17 & 18 Vict. c. 87, and the 18 & 19 Vict. c. 79 and 128. Of the attitude of the Bishops the *Examiner* wrote: "The Bishops vehemently opposed the closing of the pestilential old graveyards, and, having happily failed . . . they are now doing their best and their worst to obstruct the opening of new burial grounds. For this purpose no pretext is too frivolous and childish . . ." (1856) (*Life and Labours of Albany Fonblanque*, pp. 323–4).   ³ R. B. O'Brien, *John Bright*, pp. 119–34.

Religion, Landownership, and the Family

opening was the Dublin meeting of the Religious Equality Association held on October 28th. To this meeting Bright directed one of the most important of his political letters which laid down what he considered a politically operable programme in regard to the Irish Church.[1] A Church Property Commission would be created to take over the ten millions of Irish Church property. From this would be allotted a piece of property in each parish "say from ten to twenty acres—made over absolutely and for ever to the Catholics" who would, of course, resign the Maynooth grant. The Presbyterians, again, would no longer look to the State for their *Regium Donum*, but would receive from the Church Property Commission a grant in perpetuity of a sufficient portion of its holding to yield an equal annual revenue. On the Protestants of the Church of Ireland would also be bestowed a sum in perpetuity equivalent in value to the grant made to each of the other two Churches, a grant estimated by Bright at £1,000,000 sterling. Moreover, they would have the additional privilege of retaining their church buildings at nominal rents. Finally, the five to seven millions remaining[2] after these disbursements had been made were "to be reserved for purposes strictly Irish, and directed to the educational and moral improvement of the people, without respect to class or creed." It was a programme, in short, which offered an acceptable aim to the combination of Irish Catholics, Liberationist Dissenters, and political Radicals most likely to be formed on the Irish Disestablishment question as soon as the favourable political moment should come.

Radicals, indeed, might have had ground for hoping that Irish Church Disestablishment was not necessarily so far off when they surveyed the apparently rapid progress which Irish Land Tenure Reform was making. Once Sharman Crawford with his Tenant Right plan of curing Irish ills had been a voice crying in the wilderness as far as the "practical politicians" of both Front Benches were concerned. But the Irish famine, the collapse of Irish land values, the drain of English money to Ireland in relief measures, and the very high proportionate costs of garrisoning and policing Ireland had all contributed to spread the conviction

---

[1] Letter to Dr. Gray in *Speeches of John Bright*, pp. 547–53.
[2] It seems apparent that Bright's calculations of the value of Irish Church property were based on the current very depreciated prices obtainable for the "Encumbered Estates" then being marketed under the legislation of 1848 and 1849.

even among reluctant Tory squires that very much was wrong with Ireland besides the priests and the agitators. In 1852, indeed, it was a Tory Government, anxious to put on as liberal a face as possible,[1] which despite internal difficulties announced an Irish Tenants' Compensation Bill as part of its legislative programme.

In the same programme were announced three other Irish Land Bills showing some appreciation of the ultimate indefensibleness of the existing Irish Land system.[2] One contained large expansions of the principle—already adopted by Peel for the United Kingdom generally—of enlarging the capacity of lifeholders of strictly entailed estates to charge their properties with the cost of money raised for improvements. As a further relaxation of the grip put upon the land by strict entail it had its advantages, though, of course, its ultimate effects were intended to be a strengthening of the "landed interest." A second Bill aimed at promoting the giving of leases, and a third, the Landlord and Tenant Bill, dealt among other things with the burning topic of the law of ejectment. It proposed to forbid Distress proceedings for sums under £5 as well as for rents more than one and a half years in arrear.

This Tory land programme for Ireland announced in November 1852 had some real merits. They were not, of course, lessened by the fact that the "Irish Brigade" at Westminster, some fifty strong, might easily have played the decisive part in giving the Derby–Disraeli Ministry the victory over the hostile Coalition preparing to destroy it. Indeed, it is difficult to believe that there were not ulterior political motives behind the rapid production of an Irish land programme at this stage. Timidly conservative of the real interests of Irish landlordism as it now sounds, there was actually to be some dispute in Parliament as to whether such an un-Tory plan had not been filched from the Tory opponents.[3]

When, however, the most important of the Irish Land Bills, that for Tenants' Compensation, was brought to the Second Reading stage, the "Irish Brigade" found it most inadequate. The Irish elections had been fought on a full-blooded Tenant Right programme,[4] and the Government was offering, instead,

[1] Cf. Moneypenny and Buckle's *Disraeli*, iii, 400-1.
[2] *Hansard*, November 22, Napier.
[3] *Ibid.*, December 7th. A scene of some confusion took place.
[4] Cf. T. P. O'Connor's *Memoirs of an Old Parliamentarian*, i, 382-4.

Religion, Landownership, and the Family

merely some cumbrous guarantees that any proper improvements affected by tenants would be compensable on their leaving a holding. There even seemed a possibility that by omitting to take "Ulster custom" within the purview of their suggested statute, Ministers were endangering Tenant Right where it already existed. Giving way to Irish pressure in a manner that worried some of its Tory supporters, the Government hereupon agreed to refer its own Bill and a rival Tenant Right Bill from the Irish party to a Select Committee.[1] But the Government's days were almost numbered, and the Aberdeen Government, which followed it, succeeded, unwittingly perhaps, in splitting the Irish Tenant Right movement by offering place to three Irish members pledged to refuse office save on condition of Ministerial Tenant Right guarantees.[2] It was but another part of Ireland's sorry nineteenth-century experience of enmeshment in British party politics.

Though kept outside the bounds of "practical politics" by priestly influences, there were, of course, strong forces in Ireland enlistable if the proper opportunity should ever come for something much more Radical than Tenant Right. In Britain, too, anti-landlord sentiment of various degrees and kinds animated virtually all the Radical forces from the middle-class respectability of the Brights and Cobdens to the revolutionary fervour of the Lintons and O'Briens. Bronterre O'Brien, for example, who was still a powerful force among the London working men of 1850, was preaching a programme of which Land Nationalisation and Social Credit were principal features.[3] W. J. Linton, again, a force of some magnitude in Ultra-Radical journalism, was ready to raise from a single tax on landowners all the national revenue required by the English Republic of the future, the Republic for which he began his unique personal campaign in 1851.[4] The

---

[1] *Hansard*, December 7th.   [2] T. P. O'Connor, *op. cit.*, pp. 385–6.
[3] Cf. R. G. Gammage, *History of the Chartist Movement*, for details of this National Reform League gathered round O'Brien on a Chartist-Socialist basis which marks a very important stage in the evolution of Socialism (p. 351). For some time this League was in a flourishing condition, with O'Brien as its lecturer-prophet and the John St. and Eclectic Institutes as its centres. O'Brien was also writing the much-admired series of articles for *Reynolds's Weekly Political Instructor* on the "Rise of Human Slavery," and later edited *Reynolds's Weekly* for a short time.
[4] W. J. Linton (1812–98), the best wood-engraver of his time, had already in 1839 issued that very remarkable and handsome Chartist sheet, *The National*, and between 1848 and 1852 he again undertook a great deal of Chartist activity.

English Radicalism 1832-1852

British urban masses, finally, innocent alike of Ricardo's Radical interpretation of rent on the one hand and the criticisms of Jones and Carey on the other, clung instinctively to the old Spencean view that private ownership of land was but the effect of ancient conquest and tyranny. Land nationalisation, whether with some compensation or without, was now the ideal land solution at which they aimed and it had the added attraction of appearing to offer an infallible remedy for Unemployment. State-supported "Home Colonisation" on the many millions of acres of improvable waste seemed to offer an admirable way of relieving industrial wages of the menace from unemployed "surplus labour."[1] That "surplus labour" itself, moreover, would be spared the hardships and dangers of emigration.

It remains to consider various sides of what may be called the detraditionalisation of personal relationships which were being canvassed in these years against an opposition whose central core was nearly always theological. For the student of sociology few of the properly political contentions in Parliament can have the interest of the determined struggle which was so vainly waged in 1850 for an alteration of that tiny province of the Marriage Law represented by the prohibition of marriage with a deceased wife's sister.[2] Though it had well-nigh universal Dissenting support, it was not a Radical struggle in the strictly party sense. Anglican Peelites consented to head the movement, while so accredited a Radical politician as Roebuck allowed himself to be ensnared by the view that to give a man the right to marry his deceased wife's sister would be to let floods of suspicion loose in families, where wives would suspect their husbands and sisters of wishing them dead. The most vigorous anti-traditionalist speech on the Bill's Second Reading was, perhaps, that from Cobden. He stigmatised the opposition as proceeding from

His most characteristic writing is to be found in the *English Republic* (1851-5), a monthly issued by himself probably at considerable loss, but possessing such friends as Joseph Cowen.

[1] *Labour League*, November 25, 1848, for an Address of the London Trades' Delegates, asking for Land Nationalisation and the establishment of "self-supporting home colonies, to give immediate employment to the numerous but compulsory unemployed...."

[2] The Hon. J. S. Wortley, who had been Peel's Judge-Advocate-General, had strongly interested himself in the matter and his Marriages Bill of 1849 had already had some importance. In 1850 petitioning markedly increased, there being 108,296 signatures favourable to allowing Deceased Wife's Sister Marriages, and 46,250 against (*Companion to British Almanac, 1851*).

Religion, Landownership, and the Family

ecclesiastical feelings and convictions and from the attachment of influential Ritualists to Church canons, English and Roman. To enforce such canons through the civil law was, however, an invasion of the religious liberty of non-Churchmen and a violation of the rights of conscience. As to the assertions that family concord would be broken up by allowing deceased wife's sister marriages, Cobden protested against such a foul and calumnious insinuation against the women as well as the men of England.[1]

Aided by the current of anti-Puseyism then flowing very strongly, the Marriages Bill was in 1850 actually taken through all its stages in the Commons despite the opposition which zealous Churchmen and their allies painstakingly brought to bear. In the Lords, however, the measure had ultimately to be abandoned. For more than half a century, therefore, many thousands of deceased wife's sisters going to bereaved homes to bring up orphan nephews and nieces were condemned to concubinage. The ban was maintained even longer against the deceased wife's niece marriages, which had been included with the others in the proposed legislation of 1849 but abandoned in 1850 to reduce the opposition.[2]

The same forces which barred the road to revision of the list of "prohibited degrees" were the forces certain to be up in arms against suggestions of a general Divorce Law. Indeed, despite some persevering Owenite and Ultra-Radical efforts to agitate the need for a new attitude towards marriage and divorce,[3] such questions were left severely alone by the "practical politicians" of all parties until Palmerston and Bethell ventured on their timid but none the less bitterly contested Government Divorce Bill of 1857. No doubt the storm of abuse which had been successfully raised against the Owenites in 1839 and 1840[4] was no encouragement of boldness of legislative approach to the problems of the family. But the famous judicial protest of 1845 against a

---

[1] *Hansard*, March 6th.
[2] *Ibid.*, February 27th. J. S. Wortley in moving the Second Reading.
[3] In the case of the Owenites, even by such handbills as *To the Public of the Staffordshire Potteries*, December 14, 1839, when their views had been misrepresented. W. J. Linton's *National* also contains some very frank writing (pp. 135–9, March 5, 1839).
[4] Joseph Barker's *The Overthrow of Infidel Socialism* and *The Abominations of Socialism Exposed* reveal how every prejudice was exploited. Barker was to change his opinions, and for a number of years after 1847 to become an important Ultra-Radical force.

343

English Radicalism 1832–1852

system which allowed the rich divorce and remarriage for legal costs of about £1,000 and prosecuted the poor for bigamy when, deserted, they attempted remarriage without such legal expenditure,[1] might have been re-echoed even after the Divorce Bill of 1857. Under that Bill the divorce proceedings of rich people were doubtless facilitated and somewhat cheapened. But for the great mass of the population conditions remained what they had been before. Unhappy couples were left to life-long misery or to alternatives of adultery and flight. By a very parallel piece of social hypocrisy restriction of their multiplication had long been demanded from the poor, and yet a "public opinion" allowed to reign virtually unchallenged which was capable of calling at any time for the suppression of Ultra-Radical birth-control booklets. These booklets, nevertheless, seem already to have been responsible for some family restriction among the upper layers of working-class folk.

Intensely conservative as "public opinion" remained on many of the basic thought-habits of society, it was not allowed to remain stationary. Some of the Radical pressure, indeed, vented itself in such socially unprofitable forms as the passion for phrenology which overtook a Combe[2] or the spiritualism which absorbed a Harriet Martineau. But much of its best elements went into securing a revision of the way in which life and society were expounded in out-moded scriptural terms. For example, Robert Chambers in the very important and abundantly circulated *Vestiges of the Natural History of Creation*, of 1844, went far to laying down a satisfactory hypothesis of natural evolution.[3] From another angle, again, current religious convictions were seriously disturbed by such startling contributions as Froude's *Nemesis of Faith* (1848) and Francis Newman's *Phases of Faith*

---

[1] Cf. *The Question of English Divorce* (1903), pp. 37–8, for Mr. Justice Maule's observations of 1845.

[2] George Combe (1798–1858) was a friend of Cobden's, and a leader in the propaganda for education. His now forgotten *Constitution of Man* was circulated more widely than any other book of its time.

[3] In the preface to the 10th edition of 1853, Chambers, referring to the theological opposition, wrote as follows of his book: "It has never had a single declared adherent—and nine editions have been sold. Obloquy has been poured upon the nameless author from a score of sources—and his leading idea, in a subdued form, finds its way into books of science, and gives a direction to research. Professing adversaries write books in imitation of his, and, with the benefit of a few concessions to prejudice, contrive to obtain the favour denied to him."

Religion, Landownership, and the Family

(1850) from the heart of well-known Church families and W. R. Greg's *Creed of Christendom* (1851) from the heart of similar circles in Nonconformity.[1] In Positivism, finally, the Radical intellectuals of the *Leader* and the *Westminster Review* seemed to themselves to have the clue as to the direction towards which serious cosmological thought was moving. It was certainly moving away very fast from its old Biblical moorings.

Yet the "general public," under the guidance of its favourite newspapers and preachers, was kept in virtually total ignorance of all this until seven courageous Anglicans threw the famous bombshell of the *Essays and Reviews* of 1860. Even then their effort to secure open discussion of the revision necessary in accepted Church views was nearly nullified by an episcopally approved plan of concerted silence. Unfortunately for episcopal hopes, clerical zealots, ignorant of their superiors' aims, forced forward a heresy prosecution against some of the beneficed writers of *Essays and Reviews*. The zealots were cheered on heartily by many in Nonconformity. In some respects, indeed, the great bulk of Nonconformity had been even less prepared by its ministers for revised views on the Bible than the Anglicans.[2]

[1] Cf. J. B. Bury, *History of Freedom of Thought*, pp. 202–3; A. W. Benn, *Modern England*, pp. 243–4.

[2] Thanks to the Earl of Bridgewater's bequest of 1829 to the President of the Royal Society (!) Anglicanism was already throwing up a first line of defence for the Bible in the *Bridgewater Treatises* of 1833–40, two of them by figures as prominent as Whewell and Buckland. In Nonconformity, meanwhile, only the ageing Congregationalist Pye Smith (*b.* 1774), reared as he had been in the tradition of Price and Priestley and disturbed by the new geological hypotheses, could venture on an important piece of apologetics in his *On the Relation between the Holy Scriptures and some parts of Geological Science* (1839) —a work for which he received an F.R.S. (!) But Pye Smith belonged to a dying school of Dissenting Ministry that passed on little or nothing of its scientific power to the Spurgeon age which was already dawning in 1853 with that spell-binding young Baptist preacher's arrival in London.

From its doctrinal positions it might have been thought that Unitarianism was specially suited to mediate a reception for "science" in the Dissenting camp. But the intellectual torpor which had overtaken most Unitarian congregations by the 1850's has been graphically described in the famous *Autobiography of Mark Rutherford*, and their barren intellectual pride in having ventured to deny the Trinity. But Unitarian congregations were havens of philosophy when compared with those of a rapidly growing sect like the Primitive Methodists, who in that age relied on plenty of vigorous hymn-singing and sinners' testimony of salvation on the one hand and good strong "blood and fire" preaching on the other.

PART TWO

CHAPTER XXI

RADICALS AND THE EMPIRE

"We have also negroes in our dominions, who, though about to be entirely surrendered as property, will yet, we fear, be long oppressed as citizens, if the vigilance which has freed them be not as active as ever. I regard the work of vindicating the civil standing of the negroes as more arduous and dangerous than freeing them from the chain and the whip...."
HARRIET MARTINEAU, *June 20, 1838*. ("Autobiography," ii, 223.)

"Every purpose of popular control might be combined with every advantage of vesting the immediate choice of advisers in the Crown, were the colonial governor to be instructed to secure the co-operation of the Assembly in his policy by entrusting its administration to such men as could command a majority; and if he were given to understand that he need count on no aid from home in any difference with the Assembly that did not directly involve the relations between the mother country and the colony."
The Durham Report, February 1839. (*Lucas's edition*, ii, 279-80.)

"The *beau ideal* of the 'systematic coloniser' is the British Constitution, their highest aim is to reproduce in the new settlements they advocate a *facsimile* of English society with its classifications of landlords, parsons, lawyers, doctors, capitalists, and labourers.... Now we think that the creation of bishoprics and rectories, rich idlers and poor labourers in the "bush" is not of itself a very desirable thing...."
"The Labour League" (*Organ of the Trades*), *September 2, 1848.*

"I want you to raise the cry for colonial reform.... If you don't separate yourselves from the dominant class—in their attempt to keep the colonies as a field of patronage for their younger sons, and that the aristocracy may nominate the Government, you will have wars without end with your colonial fellow-subjects...."
COBDEN *to his W. Riding Constituents, April 11, 1849.*
("Illustrated London News," *April 14, 1849.*)

AT the elections of December 1832 to the first Reformed Parliament, there seems scarcely to have been a contest in which the question of the abolition of Colonial slavery did not bulk largely in the proceedings.[1] Radical candidates had no difficulty in giving a pledge to support speedy and total abolition, and the pledges extracted from many, more properly describable as Whigs, did not lag far behind. But Tories, and especially those with West India interest, were in a very different position. The twenty-two year old Gladstone, for example, who was the Duke of Newcastle's candidate for Newark, committed himself to nothing more than the setting-up for the negroes of "a universal and efficient system of Christian instruction" and the provision to them of opportunities to earn freedom "through honest and industrious habits."[2] At the hustings, therefore, Gladstone's reception was a very hostile one, though that did not prevent the Newcastle influence from taking him to the top of the poll. But he was sent to a Parliament in which men of his opinions were a weak minority, opposed to a majority which had committed itself to abolition. The electorate, moreover, agitated by years of Abolitionist propaganda, by dreadful recitals of female floggings and field-gang whippings, was impatient for rapid and Radical legislation.

It would appear, however, that the Whig Government was far from eager to hurry the matter forward, and certainly no mention of Emancipation was made in the King's Speech. Hereupon Fowell Buxton, the Abolitionist leader, threatened a motion, certain of extensive Whig and unanimous Radical support, and a hesitant Cabinet decided to promise the "introduction of a safe and satisfactory measure."[3] Soon the West India interest, sure of the assistance of the Conservative party and the House of Lords, was being summoned to private consultations by the Whig Ministers.[4] A Government plan finally appeared on May 14th, and on May 30th long discussions upon it began. As was inevitable in the circumstances, Radicals found themselves called upon to

---

[1] A. Peckover, *Joseph Sturge*, pp. 18–20, for the Agency Committee, the London, Edinburgh, and Dublin Boards of Correspondence, and the local Anti-Slavery societies which made this possible.
[2] G. B. Smith, *Life of Gladstone*, p. 36.
[3] *Memoirs of Sir T. F. Buxton*, p. 13.
[4] Cf. *Raikes's Journal* February 20th, 26th, March 8th.

Radicals and the Empire

defend both the slaves and the tax-payers from over-generous concessions at their expense to the powerfully-protected "colonial interest." Thus the Whig Ministers, who had begun with ideas of advancing fifteen millions to the slave-owners in order to finance the adaptation of slave-plantations to a "free labour" system, had been pushed into offering an outright payment of twenty millions. Again, even after such a payment there was to be a twelve-year period when "liberated" field slaves were to be compulsorily attached to their old employment while they were being "trained" to freedom as apprentices.

Animated by the formidable Abolitionist protests against these terms which were being made out of doors, some very effective Radical opposition was undertaken in Parliament. This opposition took the double form of criticising the compensation granted to the plantation interest as too large[1] and of demanding that, since such generous compensation was to be persisted in, the proposed "apprenticeship" period should be reduced to a minimum. On July 24th a division, in which Ministers only overcame Radical and Abolitionist opposition to their proposed apprenticeship period by 157 votes against 151, furnished convincing proof that the time had come for concession. Next day it was announced in Parliament that the apprenticeship period for field slaves, the most important class, was to be reduced from twelve years to seven and that for domestic and other slaves from seven years to five.

As had been prophesied during the Debates of 1833, the apprenticeship clauses of the Emancipation Bill proved very difficult to operate satisfactorily, where estate-owners were inclined to pervert them. By 1838, indeed, there was destined to be accumulated so vast an indictment of the system, that Radicals and Abolitionists engaged in a great agitation to bring it to an end immediately, instead of allowing it to run its appointed course.[2] The Dissenting chapels, it should be remembered, had long followed Missionary intelligence from the West Indian Colonies with the greatest attention,[3] and in 1837 they had obtained added

[1] Twelve millions was suggested by one Radical, and another divided at 56–304 for fifteen millions.
[2] Cf. *Baptist Magazine*, January and February 1838, for the beginnings of the agitation. It was conducted by a Central Negro Emancipation Committee, which soon ventured on launching a fortnightly, the *British Emancipator*.
[3] The *Baptist Magazine*, for example, contained every month a *Missionary Herald*, with West Indian items from the Baptist missionaries there.

testimony from two volunteer observers of reputation who had gone out from England on a special mission of investigation.[1] Accordingly it proved possible to launch a great popular movement for immediate emancipation which brought to Parliament more than 3,000 petitions with over a million signatures.

The Whig Ministry felt bound, nevertheless, to honour its bargain with the slave-owners and could, of course, rely on Tory support. But such a House of Commons division as that of March 30, 1838, which brought 205 members to support immediate emancipation against the 269 led by the two Front Benches, was clear proof that the Emancipationists had already profoundly affected public sentiment. Very bitter feelings had been called out by the thought that twenty millions had been given to the slave-owners and yet their "apprentices" remained liable to the plantation "dungeon" and to the treadmill and whip of the horrible Jamaican prisons.[2] Indeed, the Whig Ministers themselves proposed and carried an Act containing such elaborate new safeguards for the apprentices that one Caribbean dependency after another saw its slave-owners decide on surrendering their rights rather than attempt to operate it. Even the mutinous Assembly of Jamaica decreed freedom for hundreds of thousands,[3] though not without a demand for compensation in the shape of lower British duties on sugar imports and the prohibition in Britain of the refining of foreign sugars.

It was not the Home Government's disregard of the demand for compensation that was destined to produce the famous quarrel between Jamaica planterdom and the Melbourne Ministry in which English Radicals played so singular a part. It was the Jamaica Assembly's anger at the West India Prisons Regulation Bill by which the Imperial Parliament had sought to take security that the new freedom should not be left exposed to the collars, chains, cart-whips, and solitary cells of the old punishment

[1] In the *West Indies in 1837*, p. 485, by Joseph Sturge and T. Harvey.
[2] Sturge and Harvey, *The West Indies in 1837*, p. 364: "Females have been, and still are, flogged upon the treadmill. They are publicly worked in the penal gang, chained to each other, and with iron collars on their necks ... the practice on the part of the owners and overseers of punishing negroes by confinement at their own caprice ... is general—the planters have also perpetuated their irresponsible authority by withholding the slave allowances; destroying the goats, poultry, and hogs of the apprentices; pulling down their houses...."
[3] R. M. Martin, *Statistics of the Colonies*, p. 8, for a figure of 310,368. *Baptist Magazine*, August 1838, for Abolitionist rejoicing.

Radicals and the Empire

system. As an alleged invasion of the Jamaica Assembly's rights, however, the Bill aroused a tempest of indignation among the already aggrieved planters and made it more than ever hopeless to expect from the Assembly, which represented them, suitable legislation for the new era of equality between black and white. Indeed, while British Dissenting chapels were following with anxious attention the attempt of the plantation managements to dictate their own scale of wages and hut-rents to the new freemen,[1] the planters themselves were determining to prevent further British interference by declining to pass in the Jamaica Assembly the Annual Bills necessary for the island's normal administration. On April 9, 1839, therefore, Whig Ministers were driven to propose a Jamaica Bill under which the Assembly's rights were to be suspended for five years and the functions of legislation handed over to the Governor and a specially reinforced Council. There seemed no other way of securing the laws which would satisfy even Whig opinion that in such matters as hut-rents, wage-contracts, and freedom of movement the negroes had assurance of equitable treatment.[2]

Though in this particular instance many of the Parliamentary Radicals felt no hesitation in assisting the work of suspending a piece of colonial self-government, a group led by Grote and Hume felt differently. They saw in the Jamaica Bill not the temporary suspension of an Assembly representative of only 2,000 of Jamaica's 400,000 inhabitants, but further proof of a readiness for that Imperial dictation which they had long been resisting in the case of the two Canadas. On May 6th, therefore, a small Radical group[3] voted with the Tories against the Jamaica Bill and brought the Government's majority down to five. The Government thereupon resigned, and though reappointed after

---

[1] Cf. *Baptist Magazine,* October and December 1838. "It cannot be dissembled that many proprietors and managers seem to manifest every disposition to annoy and impose upon the people under them by idle threats of expulsion from their properties, and by disgraceful proposals for their future services" (October, p. 446). "The most recent accounts from the West Indies show that much oppression is still practised ... especially by the demand of exorbitant rents for the huts which the negroes inhabit. These amount, in some cases, to seven or eight shillings per week, and that for each occupant. ... The rate of wages is still a matter of angry dispute ..." (December 1838, p. 559).

[2] James Spedding, *Reviews and Discussions,* pp. 87-120, for his remarkable Jamaica Bill article in the *Edinburgh Review* of July 1839.

[3] *Raikes's Journal,* under May 8th, says: "Ten of their Radical friends voted against them" (the Ministers).

M 353

the "Bedchamber Crisis," saw reason to modify its Jamaica Bill. In the end, indeed, the Jamaica Assembly was not suspended at all, and the further course of time proved that the liberated negro had far more protection than had at first been realised from the mere fact of the desperate need for his labour on the part of the very heavily capitalised plantations. Already in May 1841 Whig Ministers seemed to be confirming the hopes of those Radicals who had declined to sacrifice the Jamaican Constitution because, among other things, they saw no reason why the negroes should not rapidly become voters. The House of Commons was informed that the number of Jamaican freeholders holding less than 40 acres had increased from the 2,014 of 1838 to the 7,842 of 1840.[1] Thousands of negroes had, therefore, already found it possible to buy their cottages and a garden plot.

The affairs of the two Canadas had, meanwhile, been playing a large part in British political controversies, and Radicals, as the declared friends of the widest colonial liberties, had been engaged in a long struggle on their behalf against both Whigs and Tories. As early as 1834 both Hume and Roebuck had pressed Canadian grievances upon the notice of a Parliament the bulk of which was, however, quite incapable of appreciating their gravity. The French majority of Lower Canada, a province whose population had numbered 511,917 in 1831[2] and was still growing rapidly, controlled the popularly elected Legislative Assembly of the province. But nominated Legislative Councillors, mainly of English race, formed a Second Chamber which blocked the Assembly's independent legislative efforts, and the Assembly was quite unable to control the policy of the unpopular Executive Council, composed of the chief administrative officers of the colony and again disproportionately English in race. The French-Canadian politicians, therefore, began a pertinacious pressure for an elective Legislative Council and for an Executive Council responsible like the English Cabinet to the people's representatives. There were numerous other points of difference, besides, both with the local official oligarchy and with Downing Street. In 1833, accordingly, the French-Canadians only voted the Colony's Supply after "tacking" conditions which were rejected; in 1834 they formulated their grievances in 92 resolutions; in 1835

---

[1] *Speeches and Despatches of Earl Russell*, May 7, 1841, ii, 158.
[2] R. M. Martin, *Statistics of the Colonies*, p. 153.

Radicals and the Empire

their continued recalcitrance produced a Royal Commission of Inquiry, and in 1836 the situation had become worse than ever.

How completely incapable Whig statesmanship was of rising above the notion of meeting every difficulty by a petty concession was proved when Lord John Russell gave the Downing Street story of Canadian troubles on March 6, 1837.[1] He was asking the Imperial Parliament to undertake what the Legislative Assembly of Lower Canada had for four and a half years refused in default of a redress of grievances, namely the voting of the Lower Canada Supplies. Very determined resistance, however, came from a strong band of Radical members which included O'Connell, Molesworth, Colonel Thompson, Hume, Ward, and Buller. Among the Radicals, indeed, sentiment was strongly favourable to the grant of the full colony self-government for which the Lower Canadians asked. When they divided the House against the Government's refusal to concede an elective Second Chamber to Lower Canada, they raised 56 votes against the combined Whig and Tory 318.[2] When somewhat later they divided on behalf of a responsible Executive Council for Lower Canada, they raised 46 votes against 269.[3] Nor was the struggle for Canadian liberties merely a Parliamentary one. Working-men Ultra-Radicals took their part in a way which seems to have cheered the Canadians.[4]

Though Roebuck had spoken of the certainty that the Lower Canadians would undertake commercial non-intercourse and extensive smuggling from America, though he had ventured to predict that there would be American sympathy and volunteer support for any eventual Canadian rebellion, there may have been some Radicals who were surprised by the events which followed. After a last abortive meeting of the Canadian Assembly in August 1837, Papineau, the French-Canadian leader, organised expressions of discontent which led in November to the official

---

[1] *Speeches and Despatches of Earl Russell*, i, 473-97.
[2] *Hansard*, March 8th, xxxvii, 138.   [3] *Ibid*., April 14th, xxxvii, 1290.
[4] *Life and Struggles of William Lovett* (ed. 1876), pp. 103-10, for the petition promoted by the London Working Man's Association and the Association's later address to the Canadian People. The petition expressed "the conviction that the colonial policy of England has been fraught with tyranny and injustice," that most colonies "have been originated by means no way justifiable on principles of morality," and that the colonies were treated as "legitimate objects of prey," or "as places where the shoots and underlings of despotism might practise their oppression." The Address hoped that the Canadians might yet know Independence.

issue of treason warrants and so to the successful armed rescue of two prisoners which was the first step of open insurgency. On December 5th the troubles spread to Upper Canada,[1] a province predominently British in race but one where there had long been democratic discontent with the way in which a few United Empire Loyalist families, accepted by successive Governors as the salt of the colony, had been allowed to take command of the Legislative Council, the executive employments, and the colony's good things generally, especially the "waste lands." There were other grievances besides, some common with those of Lower Canada like the huge masses of land reserved for the support of Anglican and Church of Scotland clergy,[2] some special to Upper Canada like the unwarrantably high debt which had been accumulated under the lax administration of the "Family Compact." The seriousness of Upper Canadian discontent is plain from the fact that the first warrants issued on December 5th were for the arrest of well-known citizens of Toronto, the capital. On January 5, 1838, an insurgent force was attempting to capture that city for the second time.[3]

When Parliament first debated the early Canadian news on December 22nd, the Radicals made it clear that they blamed the Government and not the Canadians for what had happened.[4] Indeed, some of the Radicals seemed elated that their prophecies should have come true and prepared with a gusto that shocked the Tories for the grant of Independence.[5] In no part of the world, certainly, did it seem more prudent to apply the Benthamic counsel of "Emancipate your colonies" than in the two Canadas at that moment. On January 4th, moreover, in the absence of all Imperialistic sentiment, the Radicals found it possible to hold a great public meeting in London and to carry resolutions putting the blame for the Canadian situation entirely upon the shoulders of the Whig Government.[6] It was partly, therefore, to allay

---

[1] *Irving's Annals*, p. 9.
[2] R. M. Martin, *Statistics of the Colonies*, p. 199, gives the figure of 3,700,000 cultivable acres in Upper Canada alone, and adds with a gravity that must have infuriated his Radical readers, "by some this is thought not an extravagant provision." [3] *Irving's Annals*, p. 13.
[4] Cf. *Hansard*, December 22nd, Leader, Hume, Harvey, Wakley.
[5] Cf. Molesworth, *Hansard*, xxxix, 1466: "That our dominion in America should now be brought to a conclusion, I for one most sincerely desire, but I desire it should terminate in peace and friendship. . . ."
[6] *Irving's Annals*, p. 13.

Radicals and the Empire

Radical opposition to their Canadian policy, and partly also to offer a conciliatory gesture to the Canadian malcontents, that the Whig Ministers resolved on sending out the Radical Lord Durham to North America as Governor-General and High Commissioner. Durham's appointment undoubtedly did much to reduce the Radical opposition to the suspension of the Lower Canada Constitution which was being enacted in January and February 1838.[1] As the "Family Compact" in Upper Canada and British troops in Lower Canada had, moreover, put the question of Independence outside the realm of political possibilities, Radical opinion relied on Durham to produce a Canadian solution which should be just and acceptable to the colonials themselves. Despite the misadventures of his short proconsulate, therefore, Molesworth, who had been one of the most determined Canadian partisans among the Parliamentary Radicals, played a prominent part in organising Durham's welcome back with what was already known to be a remarkable set of recommendations.[2] If carried out, Canadian liberty and the Imperial connection would no longer be incompatible.

In point of fact the famous Durham Report made a great impression from the moment of its publication in February 1839. It decided many of the vital lines of the Canada Act of 1840 and made it possible for the Governor-General of 1841 to open a Parliament of the United Canadas with a virtual pledge that the Legislative Council and the Executive would be composed of "persons, who by their position and character have obtained the general confidence and esteem of the inhabitants of the province."[3] In 1847 the Durham policy had triumphed so explicitly that Lord Elgin, as Governor of Canada, was instructed "to act generally upon the advice of his executive council, and to receive as members of that body those persons who might be pointed out to him as entitled to be so by their possessing the confidence of the Assembly."[4] In 1848, indeed, the allied "Liberals" of Upper and Lower Canada were able to begin a famous period

---

[1] *Hansard*, January 23rd, xl, 469, for the sinking of the Radical opposition vote to 16 against 262.
[2] There were welcomes to Durham at Plymouth, Devonport, Exeter, Honiton, Totnes, Ashburton, and elsewhere on his road to London. For hostile Tory comment, see F. B. Head, *British Policy, a Strange Story*, in his *Descriptive Essays* contributed to the *Quarterly Review*, i, 219 sqq.
[3] H. J. Robinson, *Colonial Chronology*, p. 140.   [4] *Ibid.*, p. 144.

English Radicalism 1832-1852

of Reform under the Baldwin-Lafontaine Ministry, which the combined ill will of the "Family Compact" in Canada and the Tories at Westminster was unable to stay.[1] Radical assistance in England, moreover, was to be of material assistance to the Canadians in securing in (1853) full control of the huge areas which an Imperial Act of 1791 had reserved as a clerical endowment. Molesworth, it may be noted, struck with special vehemence at a violent Tory opposition which was prepared rather to lose Canada than to relax the Church grip on the "Clergy Reserves" against which the Canadian majority had been protesting for decades.[2]

Meanwhile the pressure of the Parliamentary Radicals had been hastening the progress towards full self-government of other colonies also, notably those of Australasia and the Cape. The Radical elements, which so largely directed the "Colonial Reform" agitation of 1848-52, are divisible into two classes. Molesworth represents the survivors of a Radical school of the 'thirties, which had included Ward, Buller, and Lord Durham himself and which, under the tutorship of the remarkable Gibbon Wakefield,[3] had been able to do much for the development of New South Wales and the foundation of South Australia and New Zealand. Cobden, on the other hand, represents a very different type of "Colonial Reformer." He certainly objected like Molesworth to a Colonial Office anxious only to keep the colonies in leading-strings and capable also of such follies as the 1849 attempt to introduce convicts into the Cape when New South Wales itself was dangerously agitated by the non-cessation of transportation.[4] But while Molesworth was anxious to preserve

---

[1] *Hansard*, May 15, 1849, for Earl Grey's charge that Tory speeches in the Lords, and especially those of the Tory Leader, Lord Stanley, had raised the party feeling in Canada to the current heights.

[2] Cf. *Ibid.*, April 11, 1853, for Henry Drummond's: "It will be a good thing for us, I think, when the colonies who have representative governments are altogether separated from us." The subject of the Clergy Reserves aroused the bitterest party strife in the opening months of the 1853 Session (cf. *Illustrated London News*, March 26, 1853).

[3] Cf. A. J. Harrop, *Amazing Career of Edward Gibbon Wakefield* and *England and New Zealand* for the Wakefield plan of "systematic colonisation" and its history. Cf. also *Hansard*, xlviii, 864 (June 25, 1839), for one of Ward's "systematic colonisation" speeches pointing to Natal, and *Hansard*, lxviii, 500-1 (April 8, 1843), for one of Buller's urging on Cobden the high value of the Free Trade markets obtainable in the colonies if "systematic colonisation" were encouraged. Durham, Villiers, and Hutt were three other Radical Parliamentarians who played a part in the New Zealand Company.

[4] H. J. Robinson, *Colonial Chronology*, pp. 146-7.

Radicals and the Empire

the Imperial connection, it is plain that Cobden had no regard for purely political ties with the colonies. His principal grievance against the Colonial Office, indeed, was its despatch of expensive aristocratic nominees to blunder all over the world, to provoke the colonial dislike or the costly Kaffir and Maori wars which gave their army and navy friends additional justification for existence.[1]

Essentially Cobden would have repeated James Mill's famous indictment of the colonial system of the Waterloo decade as existing because "there is not one of the colonies but what augments the number of places... there is not one of them but what requires an additional number of troops, and an additional portion of navy."[2] Cobden, too, had a habit of making odious comparisons with democratic America which the Colonial Office must have found irritating to the last degree. "The last appointment made by the United States," he told his constituents on April 11, 1849, "was a Governor of California, with a salary of £600; our last appointment was the Governor of Labuan, with £2,000 a year."[3]

The "Colonial Reform" pressure showed very speedy results.[4] In February 1850 the Russell Government was proposing a wide programme of constitution-making designed to allow the rapidly growing colonial populations in Australia and at the Cape greater control over their affairs. In the case of the Cape, for example, a Parliament of two elective Chambers was conceded. The Upper House, that is, was not to be nominated by Authority but was to be elected by the "property" of the colony. In the Australian colonies, on the other hand, nominees were still to be retained, but they were to sit in one-Chamber Legislatures together with twice their number of popular representatives.[5] Inevitably

[1] Cf. *Illustrated London News*, April 14th. "If you don't separate yourselves from the dominant class—you will have wars without end with your colonial fellow-subjects." (Cobden to the West Riding electors at Wakefield, April 11th).
[2] The article *"Colony"* reprinted from the Supplement to the *"Encyclopaedia Britannica,"* pp. 31-2.
[3] *Illustrated London News*, April 14th. "We have five colonial governors and a governor in our North American colonies, with salaries amounting to £17,000 a year, while the United States, with thirty governors, paid only £14,300; our colonies having a population of 2,000,000, and the United States 20,000,000."
[4] W. S. Childe-Pemberton, *Life of Lord Norton*, pp. 69 sqq., is an interesting revelation of how much Gibbon Wakefield was behind this second burst of "Colonial Reform" agitation in which Roebuck, Hume, Cobden, Milner Gibson, and Molesworth were associated in a Society for the Reform of Colonial Government with Wakefield-influenced Tories like Lord Norton.
[5] *Hansard*, February 8th, Lord John Russell.

359

English Radicalism 1832-1852

Radical opposition in Parliament concentrated principally upon the nominations to be allowed to the Australian Legislatures, and by contrast the Cape Legislature was even hailed as a model.[1] The Cape plan certainly ended English interference of a kind peculiarly apt to provoke colonial resentment, and the high property basis for voting to the Upper House seemed the more easily justifiable as it permitted a suffrage qualification for the Lower which would admit voting by coloured folk.[2] Aglionby,[3] one of the Radical friends of New Zealand, was among the Parliamentarians who regretted that that colony was not being given similar constitutional provision at this time. The New Zealand Constitution was, however, ready for debate at the opening of the 1852 Session, and the Whig Government had prepared another ingenious device for a Second Chamber which should avoid Radical criticism. The Second Chamber was to be wholly elected by New Zealand's Provincial Councils, though these six bodies were to contain the nominated element of one-third by which Earl Grey, as Colonial Secretary, set so much apparent store. But the Whig Government fell before the plan was debated, and its Tory successor made considerable alterations. To the average Tory an elected Second Chamber was anathema and full of dark menace to the future of the House of Lords in England. New Zealand, therefore, received a Second Chamber of life-nominees, and the objections of "Colonial Reformers" were overruled in a division of 132-89.[4]

What was giving colonial questions such increasing importance during the years after 1848 was the great growth of emigration. Emigrants who had numbered 25,729 in 1820, 56,907 in 1830, and 90,743 in 1840, totalled 280,843 in 1850. In 1851, again, as many as 335,966 departed from the United Kingdom, 254,970 from England, 18,646 from Scotland, and 62,356 from Ireland.[5] Though the United States, it is true, took a high percentage of

---

[1] Cf. *Hansard*, February 8th, Aglionby; February 18th, Roebuck.
[2] Cf. *Colonial Intelligencer*, August and September 1852, for the determined struggle which was made by certain Cape elements to frustrate the plan on this very account. The Constitution was not put into force till 1854.
[3] H. A. Aglionby's is a name to be seen at the head of most Radical division lists from 1833 to his death in 1854. He sat for Cockermouth.
[4] A. J. Harrop, *England and New Zealand*, pp. 282-5.
[5] *Haydn's Dictionary of Dates* (ed. 1881), p. 276. The 1851 figures for England, it should be remarked, probably include many Irish, who found it better to embark from Liverpool than from an Irish port.

Radicals and the Empire

the emigrants and especially of those from Ireland, very large numbers nevertheless went to British colonies whose rapidly augmenting populations could not, even in Whig and Tory eyes, be safely kept in their old leading-strings. From New Zealand, for example, a colony which for a number of reasons had not yet attracted the poor emigrant, a gifted promoter of the Church of England settlement of Canterbury was in 1851 writing as follows to a friendly Tory Parliamentarian:[1]

> The people come out from England in nowise radical or bitter against authority. After a short apprenticeship of colonial agitation, however, they get bitter, abusive, disloyal, democratic—in short, colonial. This process has made the Wellington and Nelson people Chartists in about eight years; how long will it take to chartise Canterbury? It makes me mad to see this deteriorating machinery (*Colonial Office Government*) at work before my eyes, to see what the end must be, if it be suffered to go on working; to see also, so plainly and clearly, the remedy (*self-government*) without being able to get it applied....

It was in this period, too, between 1848 and 1852 that a perceptible change begins to be observable in the attitude of working-class Ultra-Radicals towards emigration. When the first large plans for officially organised emigration were being considered by the Emigration Committees of the Tory days of 1826 and 1827, Cobbett, fearing landlord plots to remove "paupers" to North America, voiced the strongest opposition to the "transportation ... not of the idlers, not of the pensioners, not of the dead-weight, not of the parsons, not of the soldiers ... but of *these working people*, who are grudged even the miserable morsel they get."[2] In 1830, again, he was expressing the liveliest satisfaction that the substantial emigration stream of the time, which the Government would have liked to direct towards British North America, was flowing rather towards the United States, "another England without its unbearable taxes, its insolent game-laws, its intolerable dead-weight, and its tread-mills." "Those villainous colonies," he wrote of British North America, "are held for no earthly purpose but that of furnishing a pretence of giving money to the relations and dependents of the aristocracy. Withdraw the English taxes, and except in a small part of Canada,

---

[1] W. S. Childe-Pemberton, *Life of Lord Norton*, pp. 97–8. It is a letter from the remarkable J. R. Godley to C. Adderley, M.P., the later Lord Norton.
[2] *Rural Rides*, under date August 30, 1826.

English Radicalism 1832-1852

the whole of those horrible regions would be left to the bears and the savages in the course of a year."[1]

Despite the intervention of the gentlemanly group of Radical "systematic colonisers," there is ample proof that Ultra-Radical sentiment long remained profoundly hostile to the preaching of Empire migration as the cure of all working-class ills.[2] The Ultra-Radicals refused to be regarded as "surplus population" because their pay was low or because they were liable to be thrown out of work by fluctuations of trade.[3] The system was wrong, they claimed, which allowed such things to happen; which permitted idle non-producers to brand workers as "surplus population" and endeavour to thrust them out of the country;[4] which prevented that organisation of Home Colonisation on waste and undercultivated lands that would keep British man-power in the country instead of forcing it out, friendless and penniless, to worse ills in the colonies than those experienced at home.[5] Even in 1850 *Reynolds's Weekly Political Instructor* was strongly opposing a philanthropic scheme to send to Australia batches of England's most oppressed workers, the London Needlewomen and Slopworkers. "Miserable enough ye are in your own country, poor women! . . . but ten thousand times more miserable still would ye find yourselves on board the worthless emigrant ships—ten thousand times more miserable when turned adrift in some colony at the end of the world. . . . The grievances of the masses are not to be propitiated by mock benevolence—nor is Pauperism to be met with a decree of banishment."[6]

---

[1] *Rural Rides*, April 19, 1830.

[2] Cf. Jeremiah Dewhirst, Chairman of the Central Committee of the Worsted Weavers of the West Riding, in the *Poor Man's Guardian*, August 1 and 15, 1835; Sharman Crawford, *Hansard*, April 6, 1843; *Labour League*, August 26, September 2, 1848; *Reynolds's Political Instructor*, January 5, 1850.

[3] *Ibid.* "On no conditions but one, will we consent to emigrate. That condition is that the surplus population . . . shall be submitted to a general ballot of all classes and professions—peers, commoners, clergy, and people, capitalists and paupers, and there shall be no release, no hire of substitutes, but actual and identical transportation."

[4] *Labour League*, August 26, 1848. "No doubt in the course of nature, nations must throw off their surplus population by means of emigration, just as bees throw off fresh hives when there are more bees than cells. But in the first instance, the fact of the redundant has been well ascertained by the bees; and in the next place, the honey is fairly appropriated among the workers. They do not let the drones take it all, and then say to the working bees, 'There are too many of you—go away and leave us to enjoy the honey in comfort.' . . ."

[5] Jeremiah Dewhirst in *Poor Man's Guardian*, August 15, 1835.

[6] *Reynolds's Political Instructor*, January 5, 1850. The scheme was, however, under the most responsible supervision, and *First Report of the Committee of the Fund for Promoting Female Emigration* (March 1851) by no means justifies the Chartist attack quoted.

Radicals and the Empire

Yet already sentiment was subtly changing. For one thing emigration was losing many of its terrors as the new lands acquired greater populations and communications became speedier[1] and more regular. For another the Californian gold discoveries of 1848 had initiated a period of commercial buoyancy and confidence which allowed many working men to save and, if the in creasing emigration figures are a criterion, encouraged the more adventurous to try their fortunes abroad. Finally came the remarkable gold discoveries in Australia in 1851 which sent a veritable gold-fever[2] through the veins even of men who had been brooding on social wrongs in 1839, 1842, and 1848. In 1852 alone 87,881 persons left the United Kingdom for Australasia, and even ports like Sunderland saw direct emigrant sailing to the Southern Seas. A number of Manchester Chartists, meanwhile, were hoping to form a considerable party to sail with Dr. M'Douall, the fiery "physical force" orator of 1839, the would-be revolutionary leader of 1842 and the sedition convict of 1848-50. M'Douall's departure in 1853[3] to seek in Australia the professional competence he had never won in England is no inept reminder of the steady drain on democratic combativeness which emigration had long been making.

This chapter on the Empire cannot be closed without a last glance at a subject specially interesting the Parliamentary Radicals —that of Aborigines Protection. An Aborigines Protection Society had been in existence since 1836,[4] thanks largely to philanthropic Friends, and in 1838 William Howitt, that most combative of Radical Quakers, had in his well-known *Colonisation and Christianity* related in popular form the almost invariably blood-stained history of European contacts with aboriginal races. In March 1847 the Aborigines Protection Society greatly expanded its means of influencing politicians and politics when it commenced the issue of a monthly *Colonial Intelligencer*. Important results followed. Thus when Lord Torrington, a relative of the Colonial Secretary, imposed four new taxes shortly after his arrival in Ceylon as Governor and permitted the ensuing troubles to be

---

[1] *Illustrated London News*, August 21, 1852, for an estimate of a fifty-days' journey from Liverpool to Melbourne in the fast mail steamer *Great Britain*.
[2] *Ibid.*, for the leading article on "Emigration and the Gold-Fever."
[3] R. Gammage, *History of the Chartist Movement*, pp. 401-2.
[4] *Colonial Intelligencer*, May 1847.

English Radicalism 1832–1852

brutally treated by martial law, the *Colonial Intelligencer*[1] was one of the forces which contributed to raise the feeling that eventually necessitated Torrington's recall. Such a feeling as allowed Bright to divide against the Government at 100–109 on February 6, 1850 was not indefinitely to be withstood.

Meanwhile Radicals and philanthropists had been even more profoundly stirred by accounts which had arrived from Borneo. There Sir James Brooke, Governor of Labuan and Rajah of Sarawak, seemed to have played a dubious part in the massacre of between 1,500 and 2,000 alleged pirates by a naval expedition stimulated, doubtless, to such wholesale slaughter by the "head money" awards claimable under British anti-piracy legislation.[2] Cobden, Walmsley, and Hume were among the prominent Radical Parliamentarians who co-operated determinedly with more religiously motivated agitators like Joseph Sturge and the Reverend Henry Richard in endeavouring to rouse public opinion to demand an inquiry and to require Parliament to abolish the head money rewards. The "massacre" had occurred in July 1849;[3] a remarkable public meeting was called in the City of London in January 1850;[4] Hume and Cobden moved Parliament for an inquiry in July 1851,[5] and the *Colonial Intelligencer* was still campaigning in 1852 with the figure of the £20,700 head money awards as a noticeable stimulant.[6] It was plain that British officials even at the end of the world were already under the scrutiny which was to do so much for native races in ensuing years.

---

[1] Its issues of April and May 1849 gave very full details of the haste with which some of the eighteen martial law executions were carried out in August 1848. [2] Cf. Morley's *Cobden*, pp. 519–20.
[3] Cf. *Colonial Intelligencer*, Supplement, January 1850.
[4] *Illustrated London News*, February 2, 1850.
[5] *Hansard*, July 10, 1851. The inquiry was refused by 230–19.
[6] Cf. *Colonial Intelligencer*, February 1852.

CHAPTER XXII

RADICALS AND FOREIGN AFFAIRS

"Louis Philippe is but a mere instrument in the hands of the moneyed classes, whose system he must carry out or else abdicate his throne. In like manner Nicholas of Russia is not much less of a tool.... The crimes of Nicholas are, in fact, the crimes of the Russian Church and aristocracy who make him of a tool-idol for their purposes, while those of Louis Philippe are neither more nor less than the necessary results of the conspiracy which the moneyed classes are carrying on against the rights of industry and the independence of the working classes.... Louis Philippe is the plunderers' king. He is the king of the pot-bellied bourgeoisie."
"Poor Man's Guardian," *November 21, 1835.*

" 'Arbitrate' say the most eminent of the non-interventionists, those who deny national duty and make a mock of national honour. Arbitrate! But there can be no arbitration between Right and Wrong. It is a quarrel to the death.

"What arbitration between Italy or Hungary and the Austrian Emperor; between Rome and the Pope; Naples and the Bourbon or between Poland and the Tsar?

"What arbitration, or say compromise, between Ledru Rollin and Louis 'Bonaparte,' between the oppressed and their oppressor, between Liberty and despotism?

"Do the arbitrators propose to arbitrate in the case of Ireland?...

"There may be such a supreme court of arbitration when *the earth shall be divided into nations* instead of kingdoms, when the world shall be organised, not as now, parcelled out to please the caprices of statecraft without regard to nationality.... But there can be no arbitration till Despotism is no more, no Peace till Justice rules the world.
 W. J. LINTON, "English Republic." (*Ed. Kineton Parkes, pp. 171–2.*)

"The great social idea now prevailing in Europe may be thus defined; the abolition of the proletarian, the emancipation of producers from the tyranny of capital now concentrated in a small number of hands: redivision of productions or of the value arising from productions in proportion to the work performed; the moral and intellectual education of the operative...."
 MAZZINI (?) *in the* "Westminster Review," *April 1852.*

DURING the Reform Bill discussions of 1831-2, foreign politics did not occupy a great place in Radical minds. Yet there was no little disappointment among the Ultra-Radicals as to the course of events in France. There the first bright democratic hopes of July 1830 had been singularly falsified, and the growing exasperation of the populace with the Orleans monarchy was to provoke the heavy Paris street fighting of June 1832. On a shaking throne, facing a hostile Prussia, Russia, and Austria and without any countenance from England save that given by the Whigs, Louis Philippe had perforce to accept the Belgian solution which suited Lord Palmerston, the Whig Foreign Secretary.[1] Had the Orleans monarchy, however, made a wider popular appeal in England, its foreign policy might have been bolder not only in Belgium but in Italy and Germany where it would have liked to save the modest "Liberalism" of 1830 and 1831.

But disappointing though Radicals found French developments, exasperating as were those in Italy and Germany, it was the Russian suppression of Poland which aroused the most violent and most permanent Radical feeling.[2] The Polish rising of November 1830 and the Polish military successes of the first half of 1831 had evoked a Radical enthusiasm which was all the greater because the Russian Tsardom was peculiarly identified with the "Holy Alliance" policies that had been the Radical bugbear since 1815. The cruel circumstances of the Russian suppression which ensued, and the determination shown by the Tsar to end Polish nationhood even in the area that the Congress of Vienna had set up as a Polish constitutional kingdom, provoked a very dangerous anti-Russian temper among British Radicals. That temper was only increased by the conviction that the Tsar had also prompted Austria's suppression of the Liberals of the Papal States and the combined Austro-Prussian "cleansing" of the German Press and Universities.

It was inevitable, therefore, that fierce denunciation of the Tsar should be heard when debates on the Polish situation took

---

[1] Cf. H. L. Bulwer, *Life of Lord Palmerston*, ii, for the story.
[2] Cf. C. M. Wakefield, *Life of T. Attwood*, pp. 251-3, for the Birmingham Polish Association. On November 27, 1847, the London Chartists were still attending meetings celebrating the anniversary of the Polish Insurrection of 1830 (J. West, *History of the Chartist Movement*, pp. 234-5).

Radicals and Foreign Affairs

place in Parliament. In 1832, for example, O'Connell indulged in the luxury of calling the Tsar a "miscreant"[1] and another equally prominent Radical, Joseph Hume himself, improved on this by denouncing the Russian potentate as a "monster in human form."[2] In the following year Attwood, the Birmingham Radical leader, was to join furiously in the Parliamentary assaults on Russian policy. The Polish motion of 1833, indeed, calling for the non-recognition by England of Nicholas's changes in Poland, gained 95 votes against 177[3] even after Palmerston had deprecatingly assured the House that he had already formally denied to Russia the right to make the changes which had been effected in Poland.

Soon the anti-Russian temper was to be reinforced in consequence of a new development arguing Russian designs to take control of the Turkish Empire. The Tsar, who had sent ships and 6,000 troops to the Bosphorus to rescue the Sultan from possible overthrow by his over-mighty vassal of Egypt, had won the Sultan's consent to the conclusion of a very intimate eight-year alliance in the Treaty of Unkiar Skelessi of July 8, 1833. Only three days later, and, of course, before knowledge of the Treaty was available in London, the Radical diplomatist M.P., Henry Bulwer, was attacking the Russian activities in the Turkish Empire and calling for papers. It was, perhaps, fortunate that the British public had no certain intelligence of the full terms of Unkiar Skelessi for a very considerable time and that Palmerston was still capable of withholding them on March 17, 1834, when Sheil, the Irish Radical orator, demanded them.[4] Nicholas had succeeded in committing the Turks to closing the Dardanelles to all foreign warships when Russia should be engaged in hostilities. The first result, therefore, of his increased influence over Turkey had been vastly to reduce the effectiveness of the British and French navies as possible instruments of pro-Polish pressure upon Russia.

---

[1] *Hansard*, xiii, 1137.   [2] *Ibid.*, 1143.
[3] *Ibid.*, July 9, 1833, xix, 463–5.
[4] Cf. *Raikes's Journal*, under November 5, 1833, for Wellington's advice to Russia "to avoid any measure that can lead to a popular war." Wellington apparently shared the conviction of "Liberals" and Radicals throughout Europe that a "popular war" against the absolutist powers waged by England and France, or even by France alone, would raise universal revolution. Attwood, for example, was to tell Parliament in the course of the 1834 Session that England "could at one blow crush the bully (Nicholas) to the dust."

English Radicalism 1832–1852

Before tracing further developments of the growingly serious anti-Russian temper manifest in England, attention must be directed to important and not wholly unrelated diplomatic manifestations elsewhere. Whig diplomacy had long been pitted against Russian in Portugal, where the struggle between the absolutist Dom Miguel and the Liberal Donna Maria for the throne had divided Europe into two diplomatic camps. In 1833 the situation was repeated in Spain, where, before Anglo-French hostility had brought Miguel down in Portugal, there opened a similar contest between the absolutism of Don Carlos[1] and the Liberal régime proclaimed for his niece, the child-queen Isabella. In such struggles, conveniently representable as those of "Liberty" against "Tyranny," Radical sentiment was easily mobilisable behind Whig policy. When Don Carlos proved a tougher opponent than had at first seemed possible, the Whigs even ventured to allow the enlistment of a veritable British army, which served in Spain until 1837 under the Westminster Radical M.P., Colonel De Lacey Evans. Only one extreme Ultra-Radical voice marred the chorus of popular approval, that of the still important *Poor Man's Guardian*. "If Colonel Evans would draw the sword against despotism," it cried, "he need not leave England."[2]

The conductors of the *Poor Man's Guardian*, however, were exceptional men in being ready to interpret a "Liberal" struggle for a Constitution as probably a mere device of "capitalists" to establish their supremacy over landowners and the Church.[3] The more normal Radicalism of the *Weekly Dispatch*, for example, followed the fortunes of Spanish Liberalism with enthusiasm as likely to result in the prompt establishment of a régime based nearly on universal suffrage. It is strange, indeed, to see how many Radicals contrived to link the Spanish troubles and those of other countries, also including their own, with the malevolent activities of a Satanic Tsar. A common hope, in fact, was that a Radicalised England allied to a France, from which the cozening Louis Philippe would have been driven, might soon be able to

---

[1] Cf. *Raikes's Journal*, under November 13, 1833.
[2] *Poor Man's Guardian*, June 27, 1835.
[3] *Ibid.*, June 27th. Also December 19th: "You have heard, my friends, what a clatter has been got up by the 'Liberals' against Don Carlos of Spain, and what efforts have been made for the 'constitutional' Government of the young Queen.... We told you the Queenites were a crew of monied conspirators and adventurers.... Well, what has happened? Why, there are to be 63,000 electors for a population of 13,000,000."

proceed to "the rescue of Poland, Spain, Portugal, Italy, Turkey, and Belgium."[1] In November and December 1835 the *Poor Man's Guardian* was actually trying to prove to its readers that the "tyrannicide" of the Tsar and of Louis Philippe would do no good because the classes of which they were the representatives would not thereby be driven from control. Only the enlightenment of the masses could do that, and meanwhile the first work to hand was in England." Let the people of England busy themselves about their own freedom first," wrote the *Poor Man's Guardian*, "and think of the Poles afterwards. We hate this crusading spirit, which forgetful of domestic oppression, hunts after foreign tyrants to *war against* and after foreign victims to sympathise with."[2] The Tsar, it should be added, had just committed another Polish folly which had infuriated the vast mass of Radicals into demanding war. "No country on earth," wrote the *Weekly Dispatch*, "is so completely at the mercy of another as Russia is at the mercy of England, and yet England succumbs to her in all her turpitude. Ten sail of the line in the Baltic would humble Russia and put the tyrant miscreant Nicholas in his grave."[3]

But it was easier to shout with "public opinion" than against it, and "public opinion" was now, thanks to the remarkable David Urquhart,[4] playing in fascinated horror with all manner of Russian panic patterns which were affecting even sceptical Whig Ministers and a Tory Court.[5] In fact the Ultra-Radical readiness for a war with Russia on behalf of Polish and European liberties

[1] *Publicola* of the "*Weekly Dispatch*" (quoted *Poor Man's Guardian*, December 12, 1835): "Russia supplies her proportion to the Carlists in Spain, to the Miguelites in Portugal, and to the camerillas of clubs and spies employed throughout Europe in favour of despotism. It is generally understood that the bloodthirsty miscreant (Nicholas) pays liberally to the Carlton Club. The resources of this club are beyond calculation—it has its machinery of corruption established in every hole and corner of the kingdom. . . . This general combination against the liberties of all Europe, but especially against the liberties of England, is on the point of effecting great mischief. It is impossible not to augur ill from the state of affairs in Spain and Portugal. . . . The King of France has trampled over the French people. . . . The Russian Prime Minister is now in London. . . ."
[2] *Poor Man's Guardian*, December 12, 1835.
[3] *Publicola* of the "*Weekly Dispatch*" (quoted *Poor Man's Guardian*, November 28th). [4] Gertrude Robinson, *David Urquhart*, pp. 320 sqq.
[5] Cf. *Recollections of a Long Life*, by the Cabinet Minister Hobhouse. On June 17, 1835, he reports: "Even Melbourne himself seemed to think Russia might possibly send a fleet into the Channel and sweep our seas." Under June 27th he writes: "H. M. then went on to speak of Russia, and said that he had heard there was an army of 100,000 Russians ready for embarkation in the Baltic. . . ." He added, "I own they make me shake in my shoes."

generally was a dangerous temptation to Whig and Tory Statesmen growing nervous of the complete derangement which would befall their "Balance of Power" if the threatened Russian absorption of the Turkish Empire should be accomplished. It was the essential unreality, indeed, of the figments with which Ultra-Radicals no less than Whigs and Tories were playing that induced a young Radical manufacturer, Richard Cobden, to issue his two notable pamphlets, the *England, Ireland, and America* of 1835[1] and the *Russia* of 1836. In the former Cobden contended that England's first business was to deal with Irish wrongs and its second to study the means by which the remarkable advance of the United States was being attained. In the latter, after a merciless examination of Turkish decadence and the evil record of the Polish governing classes, Cobden went on to contend that a Russian absorption of the Turkish Empire would probably be a benefit to the world. Even if it were not, England's wisest and surest way of benefiting the Continent was not by fighting but by refraining from war and presenting European populations with the inviting spectacle of a society continually advancing in reform and improvement, in wealth and prosperity.[2] It is well known how heartily Lord Durham, then British Ambassador at St. Petersburg, concurred with these views, sought out Cobden's acquaintance, and prophesied his future political greatness.[3]

Meanwhile, however, Polonophil Radicals had received a new exasperation from the military occupation by Austria at Russian urgency of the tiny independent Polish territory of Cracow, where exiles from Russian Poland had been living.[4] There was another dangerous outburst of anti-Russian feeling when in 1837 the Whig Foreign Office was at odds with Russia over the *Vixen*, a British ship which had been seized by the Russians for trading with the Circassian tribes, then making an heroic fight against Russian annexation.[5] But perhaps the dangerous if

[1] *Cobden's Political Writings* (ed. 1867), i, 3, shows that after the original edition at least six cheap editions were struck off.
[2] *Ibid.*, pp. 335–7. Cobden had stressed the same point in the earlier pamphlet also. Cf. *Ibid.*, p. 44. "England, by calmly directing her undivided energies to the purifying of her own institutions, to the emancipation of her commerce —above all to the unfettering of her press from its excise bonds, would aid more effectually the cause of political progression all over the continent, than she could possibly do by plunging herself into the strife of European wars."
[3] *Ibid.*, i, 160.
[4] Cf. *Raikes's Journal*, under March 23, 1836, for the diplomatic situation.
[5] *Ibid.*, under March 21, 1837.

Radicals and Foreign Affairs

obscure rivalry with Russia, which the British Government was indulging in Afghanistan, represented the worst threat to Anglo-Russian peace, for, if it awoke no popular interest in itself, there would have been interest enough and to spare had an Anglo-Russian war seemed to be approaching. Fortunately the Anglo-Indian meddling in Afghanistan, which after a period of initial success was to terminate in such black disaster, did not lead to the Anglo-Russian tension which might have been expected. Between 1839 and 1841, indeed, Britain and Russia were warmly co-operating to defeat, even at the cost of war, the French plans of winning some advantages in the Near East from the victories of Mehemet Ali of Egypt over his suzerain of Constantinople.

But if Palmerston, with France to checkmate on the one hand and Russia to charm out of the Unkiar Skelessi Treaty on the other, was taking a new tone in European politics, Radical resentment against Nicholas was not thereby ended. In 1840, for example, Chartists still found it easy to assert and apparently to believe that Frost, the Newport leader, had been led into treason by Russian agency.[1] A number of Chartist leaders actually threw themselves with great energy into Urquhart's campaign for convincing the country that it had been betrayed by Palmerston and that Russian gold was precipitating the great Anglo-French war which sometimes seemed close during the course of 1840.[2] Such a war, waged, moreover, with Russia's not very desirable assistance in the Near East, could hardly have been anything but unpopular. Even "responsible" leaders of Parliamentary Radicalism like Hume and Grote condemned Palmerston openly during the debate on the Address at the opening of the 1841 Session.[3] And when after a year of Conservative government Palmerston ventured to laud his own foreign policy at Tory expense, Radical opinion, as expressed by Cobden,[4] Hume, and Ewart, by no means supported him, despite his claims that the improved export figures to the Near East vindicated his diplomacy.

It was not till 1849, however, that the Radical passion against continental autocrats was destined to rise once more to heights

---

[1] Cf. M. Hovell, *History of the Chartist Movement*, pp. 181–2, 185.
[2] R. G. Gammage, *History of the Chartist Movement*, pp. 189–90.
[3] *Hansard*, lvi, 50, 83. Cf. *Ibid.*, for Brougham's "an overwhelming majority of the working classes, the middle classes, and all the Liberal party of the nation would have risen and said to the Government 'the peace with France shall not be broken come what may' " (*Hansard*, lvi, 26). [4] *Ibid.*, lxv, 1290.

English Radicalism 1832-1852

from which, as between 1832 and 1838, a "popular war" would have been easy to wage. In the interval on such subjects as the discreditable opium hostilities with China beginning in 1840,[1] the revengeful and prestige-preserving devastations committed in Afghanistan in 1842[2] and the indefensible Scinde annexation of 1843[3] Radical sentiment, sometimes under the guidance of a Peace Society movement already active, followed its normal instinct of protesting against the armed oppression of the weak. In 1847, again, Cobden began the second stage of a career hereafter to be devoted above all else to Armament Reduction and the substitution of International Arbitration for International War.

Cobden opened with a resounding success when the Government plan for increasing armaments was defeated in 1848 with the aid of angry Income-tax payers from whose heightened contributions the increase was to have been financed. But thereafter there was well nigh continuous failure. In 1848, for example, a large part of the Continent was in arms in a way which rendered Disarmament propaganda peculiarly easy to combat. In 1849, again, there were even more unfortunate results from the success of the armed hosts of Austria, Prussia, and Russia in putting down popular efforts at establishing democratic systems of government and the misuse for a similar purpose even of the nominally Republican hosts of France. It became hopeless for the time to win the masses to "peace principles" when the opponents of these principles could contend that their adoption would leave England at the mercy of Nicholas and his brother despots and exposed also to the Machiavellian schemes of the deeply distrusted Louis Napoleon, President of France.

Indeed, had England been under Universal Suffrage a war against the "liberticides" of the European Continent would have been much easier to launch than an Arbitration Conference. As it was, the diplomatic contests of 1848-50 between Palmerston and the "despotic Powers" gave him a reputation with the masses

---

[1] Cf. *The Charter*, January 19, 1840, on the "unprincipled smugglers who had caused these scenes of internal demoralisation throughout the Chinese Empire."

[2] Cf. *Report of the Manchester and Salford Peace Society*, on whose Committee sat Cobden, Hindley, and Brotherton, Radical M.P.s. (cf. *Hansard*, lxvi, 979, for Hutt, another Radical).

[3] Cf. *Hansard*, lxxii, 580, for Sharman Crawford, Brotherton, and Bowring.

Radicals and Foreign Affairs

which served dangerously to obscure the fact that essentially he stood not for democratic systems of government but for such upper-class controlled systems as the British Constitution.[1] How generally perilous, too, Palmerston's popularity with the populace was to become was already manifested during the Pacifico debates of June 1850. Though the most responsible men of all parties condemned his outrageous bullying of Greece, Radical members of the calibre of Cobden and Bright were threatened with the loss of their seats for their criticism.[2]

To throw some light on the popular temper of the time with regard to foreign affairs, it is essential to remember the enormous enthusiasm which the achievements of some of the Continental revolutionaries of 1848-9 had excited among British working men. Palmerston's popularity, for example, was due more than anything else to the firm stand which he had taken at Constantinople against the Russo-Austrian attempt to force Turkey to surrender the refugee Magyar and Polish leaders of the gallant Hungarian Independence effort of 1848-9.[3] Such an abundantly circulated Chartist journal indeed as *Reynolds's Political Instructor*, when giving its readers weekly portraits of the democratic notabilities of the time, included not only the Magyar, Kossuth, and the Poles, Dembinski and Bem, but even earlier in the series Mazzini, the Roman Triumvir, and Louis Blanc, the most socialist of the members of the Provisional Government of France in 1848.[4] Ledru Rollin, again, and even the whole "Mountain" group of the French National Assembly were also limned and described for British Ultra-Radicals before many of their own native notabilities.

A specimen of Ultra-Radical writing on foreign affairs will, perhaps, serve better than anything else to convey an impression

---

[1] Cf. *Later Correspondence of Lord John Russell*, ii, 125-30, for Palmerston's opposition to the Reform projects of 1853-4. "We have difficulty enough," he wrote to Russell," to maintain our necessary establishments; that difficulty would . . . be much increased in proportion as elections depended on men incapable of taking large views and looking only to penny and shilling gains and losses. . . ."
[2] Mrs. Salis Schwabe, *Reminiscences of Richard Cobden*, pp. 108-14, for the justificatory letter Cobden felt it desirable to issue. Bright, who had also undergone pressure from his constituency, acted similarly.
[3] Cf. *Latter Correspondence of Lord John Russell*, ii, chapter 14. "The Revolution in Hungary."
[4] *Reynolds's Political Instructor*, November 24, 1849, for Mazzini; December 29th, for Louis Blanc, etc.

English Radicalism 1832-1852

of the feelings of the "millions" on Continental politics at the end of 1849.

> Assuredly will the nations of Continental Europe rise again—Ledru Rollin will return to France to assume the reins of office under a veritable Democratic Republic; Mazzini will repair to Rome to accomplish the mighty work of Italian freedom; and glorious Kossuth will hasten back to unfurl the oriflam of liberty in the land of the Magyar.... The wretched impostor, Louis Napoleon Bonaparte, the cowardly but bloodthirsty and perfidious King of Prussia, Austria's imperial stripling who has already feasted with such ravenous zest upon human food, the cruel, heartless, and hypocritical old Pope, who beneath the garments of sanctity conceals all the worst vices and the most odious passions of kings, and the monster-miscreant of the North, the Emperor Nicholas—these will be the first potentates to fall before the popular wrath when the clock shall strike the hour of retribution...."[1]

Chartists, it is plain, liked their reading hotly spiced and their foreign heroes and villains clearly defined, the former in angel white and the latter in fiendish black. But even Cobden, when he opposed the Austrian Loan of October 1849 and the Russian Loan of January 1850, sometimes approached to Chartist language. Of the Austrian loan he said:[2]

> What is this money wanted for? Austria, with her barbarian consort, has been engaged in a cruel and remorseless war; and the Austrian Government comes now and stretches forth her bloodstained hand to honest Dutchmen and Englishmen, and asks them to furnish the price of the devastation which has been committed.

The Russian Loan, floated under the specious appearance of a railway operation, was denounced even more vigorously.[3]

> The Cossack hordes have fulfilled their mission in Hungary: witness her wasted fields, her smoking villages, and her scaffolds flowing with the blood of her noblest patriots; and now the savage instruments of all this devastation and slaughter are clamorous for their wages. Englishmen—ay, the capitalists of London—are, it seems, to furnish the blood-money!

---

[1] *Reynolds's Political Instructor*, December 29, 1849, which also prophesied a great reception for Kossuth if he should ever come to England. In the Fraternal Democrats, it should be remembered, there was an organisation which educated British Ultra-Radicals in the democratic politics of the Continent, and in Harney's *Democratic Review*, a monthly which served very similar ends between June 1849 and September 1850.
[2] Mrs. Salis Schwabe, *Reminiscences of Richard Cobden*, pp. 87-8.
[3] *Illustrated London News*, January 19, 1850.

Radicals and Foreign Affairs

It is no wonder that the City was annoyed and that some even of Cobden's friends were angry at this assault on the principle of "free trade in money."[1]

For years, indeed, the generous interest taken by English Radicals of every type in the fortunes of the Continental democrats was to make London the diplomatic storm centre of Europe. In September 1850, for example, there occurred the mob-attack on the visiting "Austrian butcher," General Haynau, which, though it nearly resulted in his lynching, earned such widespread popular approval[2] that it was perforce left unpunished despite the danger of an Anglo-Austrian breach. The democratic refugee leaders gathered in London represented, moreover, a special source of anxiety to numbers of Continental Governments, who hardly trusted the Palmerstonian Foreign Office's watch over the activities of a Mazzini or a Rollin. Palmerston, meanwhile, was co-operating with America in giving Turkey the assurances which finally permitted that country to brave Austro-Russian ill will and allow Kossuth to depart for the West in September 1851.[3]

There followed the amazing episodes connected with Kossuth's triumphal reception in England during his comparatively short stay between October 23rd and November 21st. Considerable preparations to greet him had been made before his arrival,[4] but it was only when he revealed a remarkable power of English eloquence in his very first speech at Southampton that the full possibilities of his visit became plain. Soon even the most moderate of middle-class "Liberals" were seeking for excuses to join in the popular enthusiasm and finding them abundantly in Kossuth's Protestantism, his fine record as Head of the independent Hungarian Republic, and the essential difference of his social views from those of the "Ultra-Revolutionaries" of France and Germany.[5]

The Kossuth demonstrations, nevertheless, could hardly be

---

[1] *Illustrated London News*, January 19 and 26, 1850.
[2] Cf. *Punch*, September 14, 21, 28, and October 5, 1850.
[3] *Later Correspondence of Lord John Russell*, ii, 18.
[4] Cf. *Illustrated London News*, October 25, 1851.
[5] Cf. *Ibid.*, November 22, 1851. "Many persons with that proverbial ignorance of foreign politics which has long been a reproach to our national intelligence, condemn the Hungarians as they would condemn the Chartists of Kennington Common, or the Red Republicans of the Faubourg St. Antoine."

English Radicalism 1832–1852

anything but Radical displays despite Kossuth's conscientious efforts to make them have no bearing upon the internal politics of the country. Nothing, for example, could be as revealing of the spirit which had been called out by Kossuth's arrival as the demonstration in his honour at Birmingham. There the veterans of the old days of the Political Union declared that even in the most exciting times of the Reform agitation they had never witnessed crowds like those formed by the half-million people who had swarmed into the city on November 10th, the day of the Kossuth reception.[1] The procession is worth recording:[2]

> Six men bearing the arms of England, Hungary, America, Turkey, Italy, and Poland. The old standard of the Birmingham Political Union. Glassblowers and cutters with band. Brass-founders. Jewellers. Saltley workmen and band. Tailors, curriers, saddlers, harness and whip makers. Wire-workers, wire-drawers, and pinmakers. Tinplate workers. Stonemasons and bricklayers. Pearl button-makers and band-tool makers. Coachmakers, brass-cock founders, moulders. Japanners. Odd Fellows with regalia. Leicester brass band. Private carriages and horsemen. Fire brigades. Deputations from Midland towns, large banner, "Eljen Kossuth." Band. Bodyguard on horseback. First carriage and four—Kossuth, G. F. Muntz, M.P., W. Scholefield, M.P., Charles Geach, M.P.; second carriage—M. Pulszki, Mr. Toulmin Smith, and Kossuth's aide de camp. Carriages with committee. Bodyguard on horseback. Gunmakers. Shoemakers. Joiners and carpenters. Band. Carriages, horsemen, etc.

Birmingham, indeed, seems to have eclipsed both London and Manchester in its display of enthusiasm. Yet the Kossuth working-class demonstration in Copenhagen Fields, London, was a very imposing one,[3] and the crowds which greeted Kossuth in Manchester were so dense that a procession would have been impossible.[4] The Austrian Government, in fact, had good reason to be anxious about the effect of Kossuth's reception on English Ministers and the repercussions of that reception on Italy and Hungary.

But even before Kossuth departed for the United States, a large change was being matured on the European Continent, which was destined rapidly to push from the forefront of politics

---

[1] Cf. *Illustrated London News* November 15, 1851.
[2] *Ibid.*, November 15th.
[3] *Ibid.*, November 8th. The London Trades would have liked to take Kossuth to his civic reception at the Guildhall in procession, but this was naturally avoided, and the working-class welcome was staged in Copenhagen Fields. Kossuth, in fact, showed considerable adroitness in avoiding identification with extremism. [4] *Ibid.*, November 15th.

Radicals and Foreign Affairs

the liberation of Hungary, Poland, and Italy. On December 2, 1851, Prince Louis Napoleon, with the aid of the army and in violation of his oath, struck down the National Assembly which had refused to consider an alteration of the Constitution making possible a prolongation of his Presidency. Napoleon's pretext of the necessity of saving society from a "vast demogogical conspiracy" deceived no one in England. Indeed, the treachery shown both by him and his far from reputable clique of intimates immediately caused the greatest concern lest the French Government's concentration of steam battleships in the Channel might not portend another *coup*, and this time against England.[1] "Public opinion," in fact, quickly determined that large army and navy increases were essential, that bold militia plans were needed to supplement them and that in the meantime Volunteer Rifle Clubs were not uncalled for. Moreover, as one tyrannous measure of force succeeded another in France, as the slaughters and arrests of December were followed by the transportations and imprisonments of January and the simultaneous rumours of military plans against Belgium, dislike of the new traitor-despot was not confined to Radicals. Indeed, at the opening of the Parliamentary Session of 1852 the Prime Minister was virtually requesting the Press not to endanger Anglo-French peace.[2]

It was Cobden who had opened the attempt to argue the Press out of its fear of a possible French invasion, but at first he did not meet with any great success. Once again he was warned even by normally friendly organs that his seat was in danger.[3] And though after a short time his contention that a French dash across the Channel was wellnigh impossible found very wide acceptance, the general hatred of Napoleon expressed itself in alarms of a different kind as to the likelihood of French aggression against France's weaker Continental neighbours. Thus the most widely circulated newspaper in the country wrote as follows:[4]

> War is made more imminent than it would otherwise be, by our defencelessness; and whether we find it convenient or not, we cannot be indifferent to the fate of the kingdoms of the Continent—or neutral, should a war arise. It is not alone a descent upon our coasts, which no

---

[1] *Later Correspondence of Lord John Russell*, ii, 89, for the early alarm reigning at the Admiralty, and the resolve to call the Lisbon squadron home if the French added to their concentration. [2] *Hansard*, February 3rd.
[3] *Illustrated London News*, February 21, 1852. [4] *Ibid.*, February 21st.

377

English Radicalism 1832–1852

one considers probable, that would call this nation to arms, but an attack, unfortunately but too probable, upon the independence or the territory of Switzerland, Prussia, or Belgium, that would force us, whether we liked it or not, to throw our whole weight against the aggressor. When the day comes that the states of the Continent shall make war upon each other in defiance of England, her arms, or her remonstrances, it may be a happy day for Mr. Cobden, but on that day the downfall of the great English nation will have commenced. Mr. Cobden may think if "England allows herself to be dragged into the affairs of the Continent, she will richly deserve the calamity of bankruptcy." But the sound heart of the country knows that when England has lost all influence in the battles of the Continent, bankruptcy will not only have been deserved but will have been consummated.

"Liberal" fustian of this kind was the more dangerous in that the Radicalism of the masses, inflamed as it was against Napoleon's treachery, could have been swept with the greatest ease into a "popular war." For the time the Emperor Nicholas of Russia had sunk into a second place among the objects of Ultra-Radical hatred.

The Militia debates of the 1852 Session, however, did a great deal to bring the situation back to rational control. Before long, indeed, Cobden and Hume had recovered their normal leadership of Parliamentary Radicalism and were combating with some success the worst extravagances of House of Commons alarmism. In fact a very large volume of petitioning against the Militia Bill was set on foot,[1] and those exposed to its conscription were forcibly reminded that one of the Radical objections to the Bill was that it rendered them liable to the military discipline of the lash.[2] The temporary renewal of the Free Trade versus Protection controversy, moreover, also served to abate the reign of alarmism. Unfortunately, the assumption of the Imperial title by Louis Napoleon towards the end of the year prompted further querying of French intentions and further suspicion of French armament. Service increases, therefore, were again being voted at the end of 1852 amid Press comments which did little to soothe French feelings. The Parliamentary Radicals, too, had such small confidence of being able to rally any volume of popular support for a case which rested partly on their belief in Napoleon's good faith

---

[1] *Cobden's Political Writings* (ed. 1867), ii, 250, mentions "nearly eight hundred petitions."
[2] A. Somerville, *Cobdenic Policy, the Internal Enemy of England*, p. 6.

Radicals and Foreign Affairs

that they allowed the Service increases of December 1852 to pass without a division.[1]

At Constantinople, meanwhile, the Franco-Russian diplomatic bickerings had already begun which were destined so completely to change the European scene during the course of 1853. But in considering the causes which led to so strange a consummation as an Anglo-French entente against Russia, and an entente which Cobden was quite unable to prevent from plunging into the stupidest war of the nineteenth century, it is necessary to remember the long history of continual agitation upon foreign affairs to which the British public had been exposed. A singularly deep popular animus against "military despotism" had thereby been formed but, as Malmesbury, the Tory Foreign Secretary of 1852, told Napoleon after leaving office, that "Radical animus" operated more against Russia and Austria than against himself.[2] Thanks largely to Cobden's unremitting efforts to prevent an Anglo-French explosion, the British public had never been allowed to forget that "France" meant primarily millions of French people intent on their daily tasks and accepting Napoleon by an immense universal suffrage majority as the Emperor of Peace and Commercial Development.[3] When the Near Eastern situation began bringing the English and French Governments ever closer together for the "protection of Turkey" from "Russian designs," Ultra-Radicals reverted quickly and naturally to the anti-Nicholas obsession which had been theirs almost continuously from 1830 to 1850. In 1853 hope flourished anew that an anti-Russian war might serve to liberate Poland and forward also the emancipation of Hungary and Italy.

[1] *Cobden's Political Writings*, ii, 266.
[2] Malmesbury's *Memoirs of an Ex-Minister*, under March 20, 1853, where a long account of an intimate conversation is given.
[3] The *1793 and 1853* pamphlet which Cobden issued in January 1853 appears to have had a decisive effect in improving Anglo-French relations. Its influence was due not only to its own immense sales, but to its widespread appearance *in extenso* in newspaper columns.

CHAPTER XXIII

RADICALISM AND LOCAL GOVERNMENT

"If they who have the power had the requisite knowledge, they would at once pass an Act giving to every parish both the right and the power to elect their own Vestries annually, giving to each Vestry the power to originate and control all parish matters in every department, compelling them, however, to proceed in one uniform way all over the country, doing everything openly and publishing their audited accounts every three months. . . . I, who have had much to do in managing and conducting of many associations as well as of large, very large bodies of people, and especially of working people, know that they are the most docile and most orderly of all classes."
    Francis Place to Sir J. C. Hobhouse, March 22, 1830 (?)
    GRAHAM WALLAS, "Life of Francis Place," *pp. 155–6.*

"The local government of Birmingham is as close as the closest of Irish municipalities; or as the closest of English municipalities previous to the Act being passed by which they were thrown open. We have our Court Leet and our Bailiffs chosen by themselves; our Town Hall Commissioners, chosen by themselves; working in the dark, unseen by the public eye, irresponsible to the public voice; appointing their own officers, levying taxes at their pleasure, and distributing them, without check or control, as their inclination shall determine. . . ."
    "*Birmingham Journal,*" *October 21, 1837.*

"There are in every county many ratepayers who are as respectable as the magistrates; and it would be nothing but fair that they should have a voice in the appointment, and also in the question as to the establishment of any police at all under the (Local and District Constables) Bill."
    J. FIELDEN *in the Commons, July 24, 1839.*

IN the midst of the Reform excitements of the autumn of 1831 Hobhouse, the Radical member for Westminster, secured the passage of a democratic measure on parochial government whose arrival on the Statute Book in view of the then temper of the Peers must be one of the minor puzzles of the constitutional historians.[1] *The Act for the Better Regulation of Vestries and the Appointment of Auditors*, however, had some virtues even from the Tory point of view. Those parishes going through the prescribed forms could substitute elected Vestry government not merely for government by "Select Vestry" but also for the turbulent direct democracy of many "Open" vestries. Again, the activities of ratepayer-elected auditors of parish accounts could hardly fail to have a salutary effect upon parochial Poor Law, Highway, Church Rate, and similar expenditures. Parish jobbery, indeed, had flourished with particular luxuriance under some of the "Select Vestry" oligarchies.

But to permit all ratepayers, male and female, however low their assessments, perfect equality of voting power, to give them, as did Hobhouse's Act, secret ballot[2] and annual elections,[3] was another thing. In point of fact the Lords were just then contending that something which was as far removed from this democratic completeness as the "Great Reform Bill" would in the national sphere yield nothing but the blackest ruin. It may, however, explain the surprising appearance of these Ultra-Radical provisions on the Statute Book to note that the Hobhouse Act was merely permissive. "Property" was certain to make itself abundantly felt while parochial Radicals endeavoured to make use of an adoption procedure which involved bringing at least half the ratepayers to the poll and securing a majority of two-thirds of those voting.

Before many months had passed, indeed, Hobhouse was unsuccessfully pressing an Amending Bill aimed at making his Act somewhat more usable than it promised to be. Hume,[4] too, in his supporting speech may be found hinting darkly at the

---

[1] J. W. Brooke, *Democrats of Marylebone*, pp. 19–20, shows that the Bill owed its passage through the Lords to the confusion reigning at a critical moment during the Reform struggle when Parliament was about to be prorogued.   [2] 1 & 2 Will. IV, c. 60, xv–xvi.
[3] One-third of the elected vestrymen were to retire annually.
[4] *Hansard*, January 27, 1832.

English Radicalism 1832–1852

unwelcome changes which the Lords had forced into Hobhouse's original proposals. But both were unsuccessful in producing an alteration, and the Act of 1831 remained unchanged with the mere *vis inertiae* promising to render it of little effect. A number of large metropolitan parishes, it is true, with particularly detested "Select Vestries" to shake off saw local Radicals capable of organising sufficient excitement to put the Hobhouse Act into effect.[1] But despite such notable early successes as those obtained in Marylebone and St. Pancras when the Radical Reform tide was still sweeping high, the total effect of the Hobhouse Act was destined to be small. By 1842 only nine parishes were using its democratic elective machinery.[2] There were, of course, other thickly peopled parishes on whom the pre-Reform era had imposed oligarchically controlled vestries.[3] But their local Radicals failed to stir sufficient excitement to be able to put the Hobhouse Act into motion, and the Whigs and the Tories of the Commons, with the notorious examples of Marylebone and St. Pancras before their eyes, declined to give such facilities for further Ultra-Radicalisation as would have been provided, for example, by Wakley's Parish Vestries Bill of 1836.

In the first triumphant flush of Reform success the more enthusiastic metropolitan Radicals had had hopes of forcing their way to some control of the Metropolitan Police. A Marylebone constituency meeting of 1832, for example, had ventured to ask not merely for "the election by the people of their own magistrates," but also for a "sufficient control for the parish authorities over the police force and a reduction in its expenditure."[4] This latter demand referred, of course, to the newly created Metropolitan Police Force whose relatively high costs were levied on the parishes of the Metropolitan Police Area without any form of consent.[5] A State police force was still a great innovation in Britain, and some aspects of its activity were long to be suspect to Radicals who knew what the Home Office had been capable of before it had had such a huge budget at its disposal as that of the Metro-

[1] J. W. Brooke, *Democrats of Marylebone*, p. 26.
[2] T. Erskine May, *Constitutional History of England*, iii, 278 n. 1.
[3] *Hansard*, June 22, 1836, xl, 748, for Wakley's contention that under the Vestry legislation of 1819 and 1823 plural voting gave the owner of property of £150 per annum nine votes, and an occupier of £200 per annum only one.
[4] J. W. Brooke, *Democrats of Marylebone*, p. 141.
[5] A Police Rate of 8d. in the pound, such as was made possible by the Metropolis Police Act of 1829, xxiii and xxiv, was naturally regarded as high.

Radicalism and Local Government

politan Police. In 1833, indeed, Cobbett and some of his fellow-Radicals had to be placated by being put on the Select Committee to inquire into the *agent provocateur* activities of "Popay the Police Spy," who had introduced himself in plain clothes into Ultra-Radical working-class meetings and had foolishly stimulated violent counsels, presumably in order to justify his special employment.[1]

Fortunately, the Home Office and the Metropolitan Police Commissioners, conscious that a strong contingent of Parliamentary Radicals and a powerful Press would be very ready to fall upon them if they made any bad blunders, rapidly developed a laudable political discretion. Possibly the lesson learnt from the Popay troubles was strongly reinforced during the Calthorpe Street excitements of May–July 1833,[2] when a police fatality occurring at what was commonly regarded as a high-handed suppression of an Ultra-Radical meeting ended in a singular Crown failure to obtain a "murder" verdict from both metropolitan juries before whom the facts were laid. Yet that desire for local police independence of the Home Office should have been asserted so strongly by the City as to lead it to choose for its first Police Commissioner in 1839 the well-known Ultra-Radical politician Daniel Whittle Harvey,[3] argues that it was some time before Ultra-Radicals were left alone in their fear of the misuse of a centralised police force, not subject to the control of a local authority. In Birmingham, again, it was not merely the Chartists who objected in 1839 to the organisation of a police force under a Crown Commissioner instead of the Town Council. No single area, indeed, was to show anything but the completest distaste for the Metropolitan Police system.

The Scottish burgh Reform of 1833 was the first of the Radical reorganisations of local government which had meanwhile been undertaken by the Reformed Parliament. As a peculiarly technical Scottish question it did not excite a great deal of attention except from the Scottish members, and these were induced to do most of their debating in a special Scottish Burgh Committee after Second Reading. But that the Minister in charge, Jeffrey of *Edinburgh Review* fame, was exposed there to altogether more

[1] *Popay the Police Spy, or a Report of the Evidence laid before the House of Commons*, was reissued by Cobbett for popular circulation.
[2] Cf. *Working Man's Friend* and *Poor Man's Guardian* during this period.
[3] *Hansard*, July 15, 1839, for House of Commons comment.

English Radicalism 1832-1852

tempestuous Radical currents than his gentle Whiggish soul could well bear is revealed in such a letter as the following:[1]

> They chatter, and wrangle, and contradict, and grow angry, and read letters and extracts from blockheads of town-clerks and little fierce agitators; and forgetting that they are members of a great legislature, and (some of them) attached to a fair ministry, go on speculating, and suggesting, and debating, more loosely, crudely, and interminably, than a parcel of college youths in the first novitiate of disception.

Yet at the elections of 1832 Scottish Radicalism had been conspicuously more content with Whig leading-strings than the Radicalisms of either England or Ireland.

Though they aroused no large volume of general interest, the Scottish Municipal Reforms of 1833 were very important both intrinsically and in the Radical lead they gave for the English and Irish Municipal Reforms which were to follow. As is well known, the conversion of the Scottish Town Councils from close corporations, recruited by co-optation, into democratically elected bodies, rapidly and critically affected the Scottish Church Assembly.[2] The arrival into this Assembly in 1834 of the new democratic type of representative sent by the altered Burgh Councils immediately provided a majority for those attempts virtually to eliminate the lay patronage of the territorial gentry that eventually led on to disruption.

The Poor Law Amendment Act of 1834, which divided Radicals into a Hume camp approving its principal aims and a Cobbett camp denouncing them, nevertheless permitted both camps to unite during its passage against the introduction of anti-democratic features into the machinery for electing Boards of Guardians. Twice during the proceedings of June 9, 1834, for example, the united Radicalisms opposed a voting system which not only permitted property-owners their voice alongside ratepaying occupiers,[3] but allowed them to vote by proxy and on a plural voting scale which must have given many of them, even when non-resident, no fewer than six votes. Yet there were many Radicals who, despite these and other failings, were driven to recognise that the Board of Guardians furnished the only repre-

---

[1] Lord Cockburn's *Life of Jeffrey*, p. 339.
[2] *Annual Register*, 1834, History, p. 220.
[3] On the current assumption of political economy that Poor Rates ultimately represented deductions from rent.

Radicalism and Local Government

sentative authorities available to the greater part of the countryside. From the time almost when the Boards began their work, their use as elective bodies for County Financial Boards or County Councils was being mooted by those who did not expect to see direct ratepayer election of County Councils conceded. The Whigs, it should be remembered, could not easily defend the existing system by which nominated J.P.s taxed the county ratepayer and spent the proceeds on county administration without a representational check. Indeed, they were to give some early encouragement to "moderate" projects of associating representatives of the Boards of Guardians with the J.P.s for the management of county finance and administration.[1]

In 1835 English Corporation Reform was undertaken. Of the majority of the Corporation Commission Parkes had written to Place: "Our Chief, Blackbourne, is an excellent Radical, Ballot, etc., and the majority of our men are Balloteerers,"[2] and certainly the Report which they presented after a long inquiry was one long exposure of unrepresentative municipal oligarchies. The Corporation Bill, therefore, based as it necessarily was on the Commission's Report, was for the most part eminently satisfactory to Radicals. In the judicial sphere, however, there was considerable disappointment that the Radical desire to institute democratic methods of choosing magistrates[3] was not found acceptable. But though the Corporation Bill proposed to put local judicial appointments, stipendiary and unpaid, into the hands of the Crown, security was to be given in the Bill that the Town Council's recommendations would have constitutional weight.

There is no place to discuss the heated struggle which followed on the attempt of the Tory majority in the Lords to dictate vital alterations in the most democratic parts of the Bill. It is sufficient to note that the Tory Peers failed to force into the new Town Councils a strong contingent from the old Corporations to sit for life and that they also failed to force upon the Town Councillors property qualifications of the height which they would have liked. But they secured many victories of detail which infuriated Radicals

---

[1] The beginning of such projects may be found in the *Report of the Royal Commission on County Rates*, 1836.
[2] Quoted S. and B. Webb, *Manor and Borough*, pp. 715–16.
[3] E.g. Place would have liked ratepayer election by ballot, while Roebuck favoured Town Council appointment.

English Radicalism 1832–1852

who would have liked to see the Whig Government fight harder than it did. The most considerable weakening of the democratic principle conceded by the Whig Government was in the judicial sphere. Ale-house licensing was withdrawn from the Town Council's competence and was again to be a Justices' affair. The Town Council, moreover, lost its statutory position in regard to the recommendations for judicial appointments.

As might have been expected after Municipal Reform had had such a history, the new Town Councils largely fell into the hands of the class whom the Ultra-Radicals were long to call "sham Radicals" and "middle-class Radicals." The members of the old Corporations had finally discredited themselves by the eagerness with which they had appealed to the Lords to stand in the way of every proposal to bestow upon townsmen generally all the jealously monopolised privileges of corporationers and freemen.

There were some quarters not affected by the 1835 Act in which municipal privilege still made a fight. The City of London, for example, proved too strong to meddle with, despite a special Report upon its Corporation and its Guilds issued in 1837 and the immense work which could have been done with its enormous and largely wasted endowments. But there was yet no general civic consciousness among Londoners, and parochialism was everywhere so strong that only the exceptional Radical like Place could rise superior to the claims even of the City Radicals that their institutions were popularly and progressively administered. In point of fact the "sham Radicalism" which was then so strong in the City Guilds and even in the City Corporation must be counted as a factor in preserving the City from legislative interference and in leaving it free to retain all the anachronisms which its vested interests desired to defend.[1]

Perhaps the most extraordinary of the resistances to Municipal Reform was in Manchester. Not being a Corporation borough, Manchester, like many other urban areas of its type, had to look

---

[1] *Substance of an Address delivered by Charles Pearson on the 11th, 12th, and 18th December, 1844,* is a "sham Radical" defence of the City's position by the City Solicitor. It is significant that, although he was to become the "advanced Liberal" M.P. for Lambeth at the next elections, he ignores the case for allowing the whole of the Metropolis to gain something from the City endowments. J. Toulmin Smith was another "sham Radical" lawyer, whose passionate hostility to "centralisation" of all types was destined to be of service to City localism.

Radicalism and Local Government

for municipal organisation to a Royal Charter. After great efforts had been made by men like Cobden and a Royal Charter secured,[1] the old manorial authorities, alleging the invalidity of the Charter issued, declined to be superseded. Backed by the Tory elements in the town they affected, indeed, to ignore the whole of the elective municipal machinery set up by the Charter. The resultant litigation was not closed until February 22, 1841, when the Courts, in declaring the Manchester Charter valid, confirmed also by inference the similar Charters of Birmingham, Bolton, and Devonport, and encouraged other non-corporate towns to think of municipalisation campaigns. But after the immense thoroughness and bitterness with which the Tories had waged the fight at Manchester and Birmingham, the "sham Radicals" of other places like Bradford might well be excused some hesitation before launching a campaign for a Municipal Charter. In 1842, for example, Birmingham, whose Charter efforts had begun in 1837, was still after unparalleled humiliations being forced to defend itself in the High Courts from the Tory "aggressions" of the County Justices, while in Parliament it was being compelled to find compensation for their agents.[2]

Meanwhile Hume had in 1836 opened a Radical effort to introduce the representative principle into County government.[3] The County rating authority with an extensive rating competence in regard to gaols, houses of correction, police prosecutions, and other police matters, as well as in regard to "county bridges," vagrancy, and the spread of Poor Rates from an overburdened parish to its neighbours, was the County Bench of Justices. The County Benches were mainly of High Tory composition[4]

---

[1] E. W. Watkin's *Alderman Cobden of Manchester* tells the story.
[2] J. T. Bunce, *History of the Corporation of Birmingham*, i, 104-289.
[3] *Hansard*, xxxiv, 689-93.
[4] A good example is the Staffordshire Bench (Lord Talbot, Lord-Lieutenant), much of whose business may be found treated in the revealing *Diary* of General Dyott, a septuagenarian High Tory, who was still opposing even "National School" education of the poor. When on January 1, 1833, Dyott's brother-Justices resolved to make a concession to local popular demand by auditing the County Accounts in public instead of in private, the General protested. "I took the liberty," records the *Dyott Diary*, "of stating my opinion that no good whatever could arise from the proposed alteration, and that I could see no object likely to ensue, unless to accommodate the penny-a-line gusty editors of newspapers. ... I said I considered the proposed alteration as reflecting on the bench of Justices. ... I shall certainly decline the chair of the gaol committee, as I don't wish to have myself exhibited to read the report in publick court for the editor of the county paper to make his facetious remarks."

English Radicalism 1832–1852

and were long to stay out of touch with the movement of national opinion under the guidance of nominating Lord-Lieutenants like the Earl of Warwick and the Duke of Newcastle, who had been appointed in pre-Reform days. Indeed, his Grace of Newcastle was finally to drive his exasperated Whig brother-magnates of the Government of 1839 to the scandal of a public dismissal by completely ignoring the claims of Dissenters to be recommended for Justiceships.[1] Even Wellington found Newcastle's conduct indefensible.

Hume, of course, had a good constitutional case for proposing to withdraw what was in effect local taxation from nominated Justices to elected County Boards. His case was apparently strengthened by some of the figures of County Expenses which were obtained by a Commission which reported on County Rates in 1836.[2] The Justices certainly seemed to have allowed some types of expense to mount too freely, and the situation was aggravated by the fact that farmers were complaining bitterly of "agricultural distress." The time, indeed, was by no means as unfavourable as it was afterwards to become for suggestions of imitating what had just been done in the towns and giving county ratepayers some influence at least over the expenditure of their money. Thus the County Rates Commission thought fit Whiggishly to report that: "no reason is apparent why persons elected by Boards of Guardians should not satisfactorily conduct the affairs of the county in conjunction with a limited number of magistrates."[3]

In asking for direct democratic election to the County Boards, however, Hume went too far in advance of the Commission to give himself any hope of success. He was in fact proposing to give his popular Boards financial powers which might at once have affected the Justices' discretion in such disputable matters as prosecutions. Though Radicals might believe that prosecutions and imprisonments were much too freely entered upon by the Justices and that their cost bulked too large in the county accounts,

[1] *Irving's Annals*, under May 4, 1839.
[2] In *Parliamentary Papers*, 1836, xxvii.
[3] There was, however, no similar half-concession to the Radical desire to deprive the J.P.s of their judicial functions. The Radicals claimed that the "great unpaid" by the intervals between their Petty Sessions and their Quarter Sessions cost the counties far more in lock-up costs, etc., than would suffice for the maintenance of an efficient stipendiary system. The Radicals were ready, it is clear, to use any argument against the detested Justices.

Radicalism and Local Government

there was on this and other questions of police costs no political force in the countryside capable of compelling the County M.P.s to revise their views of the eminent qualities of the notoriously class-biased "unpaid magistracy." Only farmer support could have helped Hume's County Board project to better divisions than it obtained in 1837 and 1839. But Radical farmers were most unpopular with landlords, and, in any case, the mass of farmers believed their interest lay in a farmer-justice combination against the workings of "discontent" and "agitation" among the labourers.

The question of making county government more representative was revived by Milner Gibson of the "Manchester School" in Bills of 1850, 1851, and 1852.[1] There was by this time considerable public interest in the question, especially in Lancashire with its numerous urbanised areas still under Justices' control, and Milner Gibson was apparently emboldened to advance his first proposals more in the Radical direction. In 1851, for example, his Bill would have constituted the County Rating and Expenditure Boards, half from ratepayers nominated by the Boards of Guardians and half from magistrates nominated by the Quarter Sessions. In 1852, however, he ventured to propose that the County Boards should be entirely composed of nominees of the Guardians, and though he accompanied this ignoring of the Justices with the provision that Board members should have a £30 rateable value qualification the Whig Home Secretary forthwith set his face against the Bill.[2] The Second Reading division of February 18, 1852, may, therefore, be left to tell its own story of coalised Tories and Whigs outvoting the Parliamentary Radicals by a vote of 130–63.[3] Representative County Councils were not, in fact, conceded until 1888, and even then police and police finance were significantly reserved to the "standing joint committee of quarter sessions and county council for the purpose of police."

Questions of police control, indeed, had long been at the heart of the resistance of "property" to the popularisation of local

---

[1] Cf. *Local Government and Taxation in the United Kingdom* (Cobden Club Essays, 1882), pp. 89–90.
[2] *Hansard*, February 18, 1852, Sir George Grey.
[3] In view of the 177–84 division of 1837 (*Hansard*, xxxvii, 1150) on Hume's more Radical measure of that date, the question can hardly be said to have been making Parliamentary progress, despite the three hundred petitions sent to Parliament in 1851 (*Companion to the British Almanac, 1852*, p. 216).

government. In 1839, for example, when the County and District Police Bill gave the Justices power to rate for the construction of professional police forces, there were the bitterest Chartist fulminations outside Parliament and Radical demands inside that popular consent should be indispensable. "I do not think," said, for example, Brotherton of Salford, "it would be wise to trust the absolute power of the police with the magistrates. I think the consent of the ratepayers in vestry assembled, or probably of the poor law guardians of the different unions, might be ob- obtained. It appears to me that if those bodies who are chosen by the public generally were required to be consulted on the question of establishing a police force in any district, the measure would assume a more popular character."[1] Fielden of Oldham went further[2] and asked that the ratepayers should have a voice in the police appointments.

It was the police problem, too, which was at the heart of the Irish Municipal Reform difficulties which were then paralysing Parliament. That no less a person than an Irish Earl should have been assassinated at the beginning of 1839 provided the text not only for Tory orations on the unreliability of the Whig management of that grim force of central police, the Irish Constabulary, but served also to justify the dismal prognostications of what would happen to the "Protestant interest" of the towns if the Irish Municipal Reform were conceded, which had been awaiting enactment since 1835. The Tories, indeed, had hardly attempted to defend the notoriously corrupt and the notoriously exclusive Irish Protestant municipalities actually in power,[3] but they were not prepared to see in their place the Radical Catholic municipalities which would result from any system of election politically adoptable. Their plan for the Irish municipal future was the virtual continuation for life of existing officials, future nomination by the Crown to the town sheriffdoms and magistracies, the vesting of corporation property in Crown-appointed commissioners, and the retention of a mere fragment of municipal powers by local Boards chosen under the General Lighting and Watching Act of 1828. Great cities like Dublin and Cork, which had possessed full county powers, were to content themselves with the machinery devised for the villages and country towns which

[1] *Mirror of Parliament*, July 24, 1839, p. 4262.   [2] *Ibid.*, p. 4261.
[3] Cf. *Hansard*, xxxiv, 365–79, for Peel on June 10, 1836.

had possessed no police powers at all. There were Tory members, indeed, ready to assert that the inhabitants of corporation towns like Galway and Clonmel wanted nothing better than to lay down the flummery of magistracies and corporation powers for the cheaper and simpler pleasures of the General Lighting and Watching Act.

Except in 1836 when Hume and Roebuck, for example, would have been ready to urge the Whig Ministry on to extremities against the Lords,[1] British Radicals had little but their votes to offer their Radical allies of Ireland. O'Connell, of course, was a host in himself, and it was largely due to his pertinacity that British Radicals with much else to press in Parliament besides Irish Corporation Reform resigned themselves to the long Irish Municipal contest with the Lords, which under dispiriting Whig leadership finally allowed the Reform tide of 1832 to ebb fruitlessly away. But even O'Connell, with all his resolution and all his consciousness of how easily Crown-nominated sheriffs, magistrates, and corporation property commissioners for demunicipalised towns might come to stand for little but the old Protestant régime, was compelled to follow a "practical" Whig lead in finding a compromise which the Tory Peers, brigaded by Lyndhurst, could be induced to accept. In the final arrangement of 1840[2] ten of the largest Irish towns were allowed automatically to retain the bulk of their old local government competence under elected corporations while full fifty-seven other corporations were abolished. But even in the ten corporation towns "property" and the "Protestant interest" had taken ample precautions. The municipal franchise was confined to the occupants of premises assessed to the rates as of £10 annual value or over, a very high figure for Ireland and one the more open to the charge of injustice in that all English and Scottish ratepayers, however low their assessments, had been allowed the municipal vote.

This is not the proper place to go into the detailed history either of the enactment of an Irish Poor Law in 1838 or of a

[1] *Hansard*, xxxiv, 1067–107, for the proceedings in the Commons on June 30, 1836, when the Commons majority refused to consider the Lords' amendments.
[2] By the 3 & 4 Vict. c. 108, existing corporations were divided into three schedules, Schedule A, with 10, Schedule B, with 37, and Schedule I with 20, of which only those in Schedule A were to be continued on the elective footing. Those in Schedule B, however, might be continued if a majority of the ratepayers could be organised to ask for it instead of Lighting and Watching Boards.

English Radicalism 1832–1852

Scottish Poor Law in 1845. The English working-class Radical of 1832, it may be noted, gave himself special concern for the Irish case,[1] though so prominent a leader of theirs as Cobbett was aware that the fervent praises lavished by the "feelosopher" economists on Scottish methods of teaching self-reliance to the poor also represented a very serious danger. But then the unceasing flight of the Irish poor from a land where "property" had so far been allowed to leave Poor Relief completely to "Christian benevolence" to one where their readiness to take any wages offered threatened to undermine the bases of British working-class life, was certainly by far the most obvious of the serious problems which faced large categories of British industrial labourers.[2]

It was not finally until 1838 that Irish "property" was required to accept a national Poor Law organisation for the support in rate-maintained workhouses of what Government circles optimistically hoped would not exceed 80,000 paupers. Somewhat incongruously O'Connell led the critics[3] both as a landowner concerned for the heavy extra annual charge to be levied on Irish property and as an Irish Catholic patriot harassed by the thought of the self-reliance which would be taken from the Irish character by Poor Relief and the Christian virtues which would be threatened when children could urge their aged parents into the workhouse instead of supporting them. English Radicals, on the other hand, would have been prepared to go much farther than the official Whig proposals. Attwood, for example, was ready to finance with paper money the largest schemes of settling the Irish poor on uncultivated lands,[4] and Hindley of Ashton-under-Lyne proposed the Out-Door Relief provisions[5] which were not forced upon Irish "property" until 1847, and even then only under the impression that, limited as they were, they would be

---

[1] Cf. *Hansard*, January 23, 1832, for a very large petition from Leeds, which asked for the enactment of an Irish Poor Law and the abolition of Irish tithes.

[2] Cf. Carlyle's *Chartism*, chapter 4: "The condition of the lower multitude of English labourers approximates more and more to that of the Irish competing with them in all markets—whatsoever labour, to which mere strength with little skill will suffice, is to be done, will be done not at the English price, but at an approximation to the Irish price...."

[3] O'Connell, under the stress of British criticism (cf. *Life of General Sir C. Napier*, i, 464–5), had changed his original opposition to lukewarm acquiescence.

[4] *Hansard*, February 16, 1838 (xl, 1231–2).

[5] *Ibid.*, February 5, 1838 (xl, 785).

Radicalism and Local Government

withdrawn after the famine's wreckage had been salvaged.[1] One united Radical gesture was, however, made in 1838 to render the Irish Boards of Guardians more representative. Venturing democratically beyond the English precedent of 1834, the Government Bill had already limited the ex-officio J.P. members of the Boards to one-third of those elected. Forty-four British and Irish Radicals under Hume and O'Connell entered the division lobby against 124 Whigs and Tories to affirm the principle that Boards of Guardians should consist of elected representatives only.[2]

In Scotland the long distressful period beginning in 1837 was to show more and more how tragically inadequate the country's Poor Law machinery and relief standards were to meet a really serious depression. The very activity which had been shown by Presbyterian ministers in the gathering of such "voluntary" parochial relief funds as had made Dr. Chalmers famous had misled the "public" as to the faultiness of the existing situation. Throughout more than five-sixths of Scotland there was no compulsory Poor Law rating, but the rich were coaxed, wheedled, and flattered into allowing their "Christian benevolence" to pay into "voluntary" kirk-door collections the sums which helped to keep the well-to-do proud of their charity and the poor starved into the obsequious misery which was considered only right and proper for them by all save the Ultra-Radicals.[3] It was not, indeed, until the grim medical evidence of Dr. Alison's *Observations on the Management of the Poor in Scotland, its Effects on the Health of Great Towns* (1840) was available that Scottish "public opinion" was shaken out of the complacency with which its own dumb pauperdom and low pauper expenditure had been heretofore contrasted with England's "exigent" paupers and high Poor Rates.[4]

---

[1] Irish "property," indeed, nearly forced the specific limitation of the 1847 Poor Relief provisions to the ensuing year. In the Lords, indeed, the Government was at first defeated on the question by 63–50 (*Hansard*, May 6, 1847).
[2] *Hansard*, xl, 1242–6.
[3] *Cobbett's Weekly Register*, June 21, 1834, pp. 706–24, had given the English Ultra-Radical some insight into the hard niggardliness of the treatment of the Scottish poor, at the very time when the English Poor Law Report was eulogising the "admirable practice" of the Scottish system. Dr. Chalmers's writings on pauperism had had, it is plain, a marked effect in England which Cobbett did well to oppose.
[4] Cf. Dr. Chalmers's *On Political Economy* (1832), p. 403. "In the concerns of private benevolence there is a delicacy felt on the one side, and a discrimination exercised upon the other. . . . But the benevolence of the law holds out

English Radicalism 1832–1852

Dr. Alison's conclusion, in fact, was that the "higher ranks in Scotland do much less for the relief of poverty, and of sufferings resulting from, than those of any other country in Europe which is really well regulated," and that it was essential to spend £800,000 annually in Poor Relief instead of the actual £150,000.

The Poor Law Amendment (Scotland) Act of 1845, which finally emerged from the controversy provoked by Dr. Alison's *Observations*,[1] was that of a Conservative Government, over-respectful of the Scottish lairds who had "prided themselves on the admirable institutions of Scotland[2] where the largest allowance made, even to paupers with large families, was ninepence or a shilling a week, and even that miserable pittance was refused in numberless cases where it was legally due." In view of some of the provisions of the 1845 Act, indeed, it is surprising to find that *Hansard* bears so little record of Radical objections to those things which were to prove so galling to the local Radicalisms of a succeeding generation. Perhaps the creation of a Central Poor Law Authority to supervise the systems by which parishes relieved their aged, impotent, and disabled poor and the provision of what proved in practice to be a disappointingly unreal measure of representation on the newly created Parochial Boards to the occupier as contrasted with the owner class were all the changes that were "practicable" at the time. But the exclusion of the able-bodied poor from all claim to relief in a country containing such huge industrial masses, exposed to trade fluctuations, as did the Scotland of 1845, was by no means far-sighted. Another democratic grievance of the future was to arise from the over-caution of the Central Board of Supervision in allotting so frequently the smallest possible quotas of membership to the elected representatives of the occupiers, though, contrary to Scottish rating practice,

---

a wholesale bounty and temptation to improvidence. It has changed the timid supplications of want, into so many stout and resolute demands for justice. The cry of the distressed few for pity has been strangely transformed by it into the cry of a whole population for the redress and rectification of their grievances. . . . It has in fact vitiated and distempered the whole breath of society in England."

[1] *Life and Writings of Sir A. Alison*, Dr. Alison's High Tory brother, contains some vigorous comments on the partisans of the old system "of starving the poor, veiled under the pretence of a trifling legal and extensive voluntary contribution," and makes it plain that it was English horror which was the decisive factor in securing a Royal Commission of Inquiry (i, 458 sqq.).

[2] *Ibid.*, p. 462.

Radicalism and Local Government

these were being burdened with the direct payment of half the Poor Rate.[1]

Scottish county rating was on a basis which made it harder to develop a Radical movement for elected County Boards than was the case in England where, as has been seen, such a movement had been under responsible sponsorship since 1836. In Scotland the county rating authorities were the Commissioners of Supply, who embraced all the landed proprietors of over £100 per annum as well as the eldest sons of proprietors of over £400 per annum. As the Scottish landowners, however, paid the county police and other rates themselves, it was possible even for Liberal proprietors logically to resist tenant representation much longer than in England, where county rates were levied entirely on "occupiers," or in Ireland, where the same principle virtually ruled for the grand jury and baronial "cesses" which corresponded to county rates. But the Poor Law of 1845, in making "occupiers" responsible for half the parochial Poor Rates, was to give them a steadily increasing desire for some representation among the Commissioners of Supply who, it must be remembered, were the court of appeal in "valuation" disputes. The alleged under-valuation of landowners' seats, parks, woods, deer forests, and shootings for rating purposes was destined, indeed, to become a very contentious subject in rural Scotland.[2]

[1] Cf. *Local Government and Taxation in the United Kingdom* (Cobden Club Essays, 1882), pp. 408-9, 444-7. [2] *Ibid.*, pp. 432-6.

CHAPTER XXIV

THE WORLD OF LABOUR

"I do, before Almighty God and this Loyal Lodge, most solemnly swear, that I will not work for any master that is not in the union, nor will I work with any illegal man or men, but will do my best for the support of wages; and most solemnly swear to keep inviolate all the secrets of this Order; nor will I ever consent to have any money for any purpose but for the use of the Lodge and the support of the trade; nor will I write or cause to be wrote, print, mark, either on stone, marble, brass, paper, or sand, anything connected with this Order, so help me God, and keep me steadfast in this my present obligation; and I further promise to do my best to bring all legal men that I am connected with into this Order; and if ever I reveal any of the rules, may what is before me plunge my soul into eternity."

Builders' Union Oath, 1832–4. From "Character, Object, and Effects of Trades' Unions" *(1834), p. 42.*

"This system of *picqueting* mills has been carried to the greatest extent in Manchester; where the obnoxious factory is always watched by five or six men, unknown in the immediate neighbourhood, and who, on a given signal, can be reinforced to the extent of 300. . . . It is absolutely necessary for the protection of liberty, that some legal means should exist for removing these picquets. Any person connected with the establishment so watched, or police-officer at the request of such person, might be authorised to apprehend, without warrants, any of these picquets, and take them before a magistrate, who should have the power of summarily convicting them in a penalty or three months' imprisonment."

From Ibid., *pp. 118–19.*

"When every trade is organised, then would be the proper time to confederate them in such a bond as would get for labour its fair value, and for the labourer his proper consideration in society."

"The Operative," *October 18, 1851.*

THE collapse of the Grand National Consolidated Trades' Union in the summer of 1834 is the most decisive event in the trades history of the first half of the nineteenth century. It was closely followed by an event hardly less decisive in forcing weakened Trade Societies back into their old isolation, the disintegration of the great Operative Builders' Union whose Owenian ambitions had been only less grandiose than those of the Grand National.[1] Though the Builders' Union had kept out of the immense bustle and disorder of the Grand National's short life, its own constitution, too, proved altogether too far-flung to stand long. Though stonemasons, painters, plasterers, plumbers, carpenters, bricklayers, and slaters had had sufficiently obvious trade ambitions in common to take over 40,000 of them into a general Builders' Union before the end of 1833, it was the most powerful craft of them all, the stonemasons, which led the retreat into isolationism in September 1834.[2] It was a retreat which was probably meant to save the stonemasons' own national cohesion from the effects of a Builders' Union collapse deemed to be inevitable. In this it was successful. While the painters, for example, could organise nothing but unfederated local clubs for the next quarter of a century, while the carpenters and bricklayers, again, declined to very small proportions, the stonemasons numbered 3,611 in February 1837 and, in the course of 1838, 4,953.[3] These were figures which promised no Owenite taking over of Society, of course, but considerable influence over trade conditions. As a nationally organised society, the stonemasons had the advantage of being able to call a strike in an unsatisfactory centre in the full confidence of financing it by levies on their members in the rest of the country. Such a stonemasons' strike, indeed, as raged in London between September 1841[4] and April 1842, tended to become dour enough to arouse general working-class support.

Meanwhile there had occurred the notorious Glasgow Spinners case of 1837-8 which had with good reason excited the whole

[1] Cf. *The Pioneer*, September 21, 1833. For the 275 delegates assembled for the first "Builders' Parliament" and the alleged £3,000 of expense, see *Character, Object, and Effects of Trades' Unions* (1834), pp. 37-8.
[2] R. W. Postgate, *The Builders' History*, p. 111.   [3] *Ibid.*, p. 122.
[4] *Ibid.*, pp. 129-30, for its effect on the building of the Houses of Parliament, Woolwich Dockyard, and Nelson's Column.

English Radicalism 1832-1852

working-class world. Though between 1829 and 1831 the spinners had organised under the remarkable Doherty's leadership the monster trade society of the time and had further built up the first great trades combination,[1] they were in 1838 without a national organisation. Yet both the Manchester and Glasgow Spinners' Associations were sufficiently strong to be recognised as most important factors in determining local wages, and in Glasgow, it seems, there was also a tradition of violent methods against "scabs." During the hot Glasgow wages dispute of 1837, indeed, the whole Cotton Spinners' Committee was arrested;[2] in January 1838 a number of cotton spinners were facing dangerous charges of incitement to violence, arson, and murder for which they were sentenced to transportation; and shortly afterwards a Select Committee of the House of Commons began an investigation into combinations which might well have become dangerous.[3]

The widespread feeling in the operative camp that trade liberties had been in considerable peril during 1838 accounts, it would seem, in part for the general resolve to keep the trades as trades out of direct participation in Chartist politics. It is true, of course, that on special occasions and in special cases nearly every trade club abandoned the normal policy of allowing no politics. The London trades, for example, contributed very widely to Lovett's Defence Fund in 1839, and in 1840, when Collins, Birmingham's shoemaker delegate to the Convention, was released from gaol, the Birmingham trades combined to make his return home the occasion of a vast demonstration.[4] Yet such events were exceptions, and there was fated to be long disappointment among Chartist leaders[5] that trades caution

---

[1] *Report of the Select Committee on Combinations*, 1838, p. 256, for Doherty's own estimate that the National Association for the Protection of Labour had banded at least 100,000 men (First Report).

[2] A. Alison's *Life and Writings*, i, 384 sqq.

[3] Cf. *Report*, p. 253, for suggestions to Doherty that a law might be passed requiring a period of notice from a master before he proceeded to wage reductions, but imposing on the men a similar requirement before undertaking a strike (First Report).

[4] Cf. R. G. Gammage, *History of the Chartist Movement*, pp. 185-6.

[5] Even in the revolutionary atmosphere of May 1839 the violent *London Democrat* (May 18th) had declared: "It won't be the organised masses that will carry the victory. *That* depends upon the poor, outcast, friendless beings who have no home to go to, no food to satisfy the cravings of hunger. The battle will be fought and won by those whom poverty and degradation have rendered outcasts from society. . . ." In 1845, again, the *Northern Star* (November 1,

The World of Labour

robbed their agitation of the prestige of direct trades support and of the enthusiasm and contagious solidarity which would have been excited by the pomp and circumstance of banners, regalia, and the procession behind them of the trades four or eight abreast. But it was not in the nature of things that the trades —the upper sections of Labour for the most part—should show the same revolutionary abandon as starving weavers, destitute stockingers, and ragged Irish general labourers dwelling in cellars.

Sheffield furnishes some particularly interesting examples of the relations between Chartism and Trade Unionism. There the pressure of the local Chartist leaders succeeded in bringing about a conference of trade societies in the summer of 1839 to consider the Chartist request for corporate trade society adhesions to the local Chartist organisation. By a majority of 20 against 12 the trade delegates decided against such a course, and the reasons advanced by the majority are worth noting as indicating sentiments which would normally be held by the directing personalities throughout the trade society world. It was emphasised that though the societies did not oppose the adhesion of their members to Chartism as individuals, the societies as groups existed for the industrial defence of their trades, and the introduction of Chartism would be a cause of division. Moreover, society adhesion to Chartism would bring the danger of renewed consideration being given in Parliament to Anti-Combination legislation.[1]

In August 1842, again, after distress and intense Chartist preparation had won the Manchester trades to the policy of calling a universal strike for the Charter, the Sheffield situation is very interesting to watch. Though a mass meeting adopted the resolution to join in the strike, seven Sheffield trade society secretaries wrote to the local Press denying that the meeting represented the trades. Their successful attempts to prevent a strike found some assistance, moreover, from the normally fire-eating Harney who, declaring his belief that the majority of the Sheffield trades were not convinced Chartists, doubted the efficacy of vainly attempting a universal "turn out."[2]

1845), after a long history of alternate flattery and criticism of the trades, may be found talking of "the pompous trades and proud mechanics who are now willing forgers of their own fetters."   [1] *Charter*, September 14, 1839.
[2] Cf. R. G. Gammage, *History of the Chartist Movement*, pp. 235-6.

English Radicalism 1832–1852

Trade society office-bearers, indeed, must often have been engaged in work of direct immediate importance to their fellows beside which the wordy efforts of Chartist oratory could not altogether have avoided the appearance of singular inefficacy. To read the clearly printed accounts of such an advancing trade as the Steam-Engine Makers' Society, which between 1836 and 1842 increased its branches from 14 to 24, its membership from 525 to 994, and its annual *per capita* levy from 14s. 6¾d. to £1 16s. 1d., is to understand that the cream of the trade society world was frequently occupied with other things than the Charter. While the Steam-Engine Makers' accounts give, in fact, not the slightest indication that any notice was taken of the Chartist agitation at society meetings, they give evidence that the liveliest interest was being taken in the London branches' payment of a 10s. per week unemployment benefit in return for an extra levy of 3d. per week and in the attempts of the Manchester branch to secure permission to experiment similarly. In the lodging and feeding of workmen sent on the "tramp," in collecting subscriptions mounting with the bad times, in administering funeral, sick, and "laming" benefits, in dealing with correspondence and financial accounting involving not only relations with the head branch but with other local branches also, and, finally, in attending delegate meetings[1] trade society leaders were engaged in activities which must often have seemed more important than the mere Chartist prating of some of their friends.

Nor were trade society leaders who were lukewarm or sceptical on the matter of Chartist agitation necessarily denied all possibility of manifesting interest in the wider claims of Labour. Loans and gifts to other trade societies engaged in difficult strikes or overcome by financial difficulties were not infrequent. During the Glasgow Spinners' dispute of 1837, for example, the Manchester Cotton Spinners Association, a society of some 1,060 members, contributed between £200 and £300 to the Glasgow funds, and help in the form of loans came from a number of Glasgow trades.[2] In 1841, again, the bricklayers, a London-Manchester union of some 2,000 members, lent £400 to the stonemasons, who, in their turn, made the bricklayers a gift of

---

[1] *Steam-Engine Makers' Accounts, 1836–1844*, form the basis for this paragraph.
[2] *First Report of the Select Committee on Combinations,* 1838, pp. 45, 280, etc.

The World of Labour

£30 in 1844 and a loan of £150 in 1847.[1] The cotton-spinners' associations, too, were the backbone of the Ten Hour movement,[2] and when the large colliers' unions came to be formed after 1841 it was not long before they were engaged in campaigns for improving the measure of safety in mines, campaigns for which the best hope of success lay in making non-partisan appeals to "public opinion" generally. Indeed, the only things Ultra-Radical in the colliers' unwearied pressure after 1844 for thorough Government mines inspection[3] was the fact that Duncombe usually presented their petitions and W. P. Roberts acted as their attorney.

The Webbs have, in fact, clearly demonstrated good reason to hold the view that more and more working-class energy tended after 1842 to enter the trades field as hopes of a speedy Chartist millennium vanished.[4] In 1844, however, came a reminder of the need of watching the political field when a Master and Servant Bill was nearly slipped through the Commons which, under the guise of clarifying the law of employment, would have added dangerously to the facility with which an employer could have secured an employee's arrest and conviction. Though all types of employee, chargeable with breach of contract, would have been exposed to a sentence of two months' imprisonment inflictable by a single J.P., it was the great new Miners' Association, some 70,000 strong, which, advised by its "Attorney-General," W. P. Roberts, initiated the vigorous trades agitation against the Bill and it was energetically seconded by another vitally interested trade, that of the Potters.[5] The 40,000 Durham and Northumberland miners, indeed, with the consent of the Miners' Association, were just about to begin their famous five-months' strike against a yearly binding which had already been found to give their masters ample legal advantages over them without such new

---

[1] *The Builders' History*, pp. 132, 139.
[2] *Character, Object, and Effects of Trades' Unions* (1834) had charged nine-tenths of the factory clamour (pp. 28–9) upon the cotton spinners' anxiety to make more employment for themselves, and Doherty admitted in 1838 that the spinners had been pursuing short-time ambitions for many years.
[3] Cf. R. N. Boyd, *Coal Mines Inspection*, pp. 71–119.
[4] Cf. *History of Trade Unionism* (S. and B. Webb), pp. 174–82.
[5] S. and B. Webb, *History of Trade Unionism*, pp. 182–6. A strong Potters Union had fought a very determined strike in 1836–7 partly against the yearly employment contract, customary in their trade. In 1838 it still owed £3,275 to societies which had come to its support (*Journal of the Statistical Society*, May 1838, p. 43).

English Radicalism 1832-1852

provisions as those threatened in the Master and Servant Bill.[1] For example, though not guaranteed any work at all during the year for which they bound themselves to their collieries, the miners were yet legally inhibited from seeking work elsewhere during their idleness. Helped, however, by two hundred trades petitions Duncombe successfully undertook to make the Parliamentary passage of the Bill impossible, and on May 1st secured its rejection at the Committee stage in a division of 97-54.[2] It had not merely been a Radical victory. A considerable number of Tory M.P.s, impressed by the trades agitation and, perhaps, also by the already much-discussed Durham and Northumberland strike, had decided that though it might be necessary to secure more efficient justice in cases of breach of contracts of employment, the occasion called not for a private member's measure but for a Government Bill.

Such successful trades co-operation in the political field as that of 1844 quickly led to a movement for organising permanently against Parliamentary dangers of the type which had just been revealed. Moreover, when preparations began for setting on foot a National Association of United Trades for the protection of Labour, some limited recognition was given even by the cautious to the advisability of attempting to use the new organisation to advance the industrial interests and social aspirations of the working classes. But though considerable trade conferences in 1845 and 1846 had laboured hard to devise a constitution which should attract the earnest by its ultimate promise and the cautious by the sobriety of its immediate purpose and language, though the *Northern Star* gave its activities generous publicity, the new body had a difficult birth and a life scarce ever free from trouble. Like the Grand National of 1834 it made a great appeal to those sections of Labour which aimed at speedy wage-increases, and, as in 1834, strikers and would-be strikers were loud in complaint when it was made plain that the money which they had counted on would not be forthcoming.[3]

Despite its earlier troubles, however, and the disheartening non-adhesion of the strongest sections of the trades world—

---

[1] Cf. *Illustrated London News*, April 27, 1844, for strike pictures.
[2] *Ibid.*, May 4, 1844, reports that the result was greeted with "much cheering." Yet the Home Office had supported the Bill.
[3] Cf. S. and B. Webb, *History of Trade Unionism*, p. 193.

The World of Labour

builders' labourers joining, for example, but not stonemasons[1] or cotton spinners—the energetic efforts and perambulations of three or four paid organisers gradually built up the National Association of United Trades to considerable strength.[2] It even began issuing its own newspaper, the meritorious *Labour League*, in August 1848. At this stage the Association had the following aims:

> The protection of industry against the unreasonable aggressions of capital by means of mediation, arbitration, and where necessary pecuniary support, derived from the subscriptions of the trades composing the association, which is formed on the basis of a Mutual Assurance Society, each member receiving benefits in proportion to his payments.
>
> The employment of that surplus labour, which constitutes the reserve in the competitive market by means of which wages are always kept down to the lowest subsistence level (this employment was to be furthered by raising among the trades a £50,000 Employment Fund to be "devoted to the formation of self-supporting industrial colonies").
>
> To cause the employers ... wherever practicable, to provide properly lighted and ventilated workshops.
>
> Regulation of the hours of labour in all trades, with a view to equalise and diffuse employment.
>
> The employment of the surplus labour of the country by the Government in useful public works.
>
> Sanitary regulations and the appointment of a Minister of Labour.[3]

The programme, indeed, sounds somewhat more advanced than was the Association's actual conduct of its business, which in the matter of trade disputes affecting those who had insured for its strike benefits leaned heavily on the side of conciliation through one of its staff and against the resort to strikes save as a last necessity. Recruiting mainly the weaker trade groups looking for outside support in case of need, groups like the Sheffield Sickle and Reap Hook Forgers, the Dewsbury Scotch Carpet Weavers, the Sunderland Joiners, the Maidstone Boot and Shoe Makers, the West Bromwich Miners No. 2, the Todmorden Bobbin Turners, the Leek Silk Twisters, and the South Stockton

---

[1] Cf. R. W. Postgate, *The Builders' History*, pp. 133-8, With 6,000 members and £2,000 of reserve funds, the stonemasons were not inclined to share their strength with others' weakness.

[2] *Labour League*, August 5, 1848, announces the coming campaign of Mr. Humphries in Northants and Staffs; of Mr. Parker in Whitehaven, Carlisle, Wearside, Tyneside, and Halifax; of Mr. Williams in the West and Wales, and of Mr. Peel among the "railway interest."

[3] *Ibid.*, August 5, 1848.

Potters,[1] the National Association had necessarily to show the greatest caution before approving of strikes.

Yet that so administratively cautious an organisation should emphasise so strongly in its programmes the problem of "surplus labour" reveals a "Labour" atmosphere in which there must have been the strongest Owenite and Chartist currents afloat. It is no surprise, in fact, to find the *Labour League* bitterly upbraiding Cobden and Bright for their "unmitigated hostility" to the Chartist Land Plan for removing "surplus labour" to self-help in the countryside.[2] Nor is there anything but criticism for the "systematic colonisation" of the Wakefield school as a means of removing "surplus labour." The Home Colonisation, which had long been advocated by Owenites and Chartists, is put forward instead as the ideal solution.[3]

Home Colonisation figured also in the list of aims of another national organisation of trades which was being projected for propaganda purposes by delegates of the London trades. This organisation was not intended to compete with the National Association of United Trades, whose main activities were necessarily in the industrial field. As envisaged by the London trades, however, the National Organisation of Trades would lead trade opinion in the political field. The programme suggested by the London trade delegates in November 1848 was, as might have been expected, a very Ultra-Radical one. Land Nationalisation, Universal Suffrage, Scientific and Secular Education, Currency Expansion, and a Single Graduated Property Tax were in the programme, together with the Home Colonisation and Ministry of Labour which had already figured among the aims of the National Association of United Trades. The Labour Ministry of the trade delegates, it should be noted, was foreseen as an authority of central superintendence over local boards of trade, composed half of masters and half of men.[4]

The most interesting feature, however, of the "Labour" opinion of 1848–9 was its industrial protectionism. In drawing up their programme for a National Organisation of Trades the London trades delegates declared that "foreign manufactures . . . ought

---

[1] These are representative names taken from the columns of the *Labour League* during the latter part of 1848.   [2] *Ibid.*, February 3, 1849, p. 205.
[3] *Ibid.*, August 26, September 2, 1848.
[4] *Ibid.*, November 25, December 2, 1848.

The World of Labour

not to be introduced into the home market except upon such conditions as will secure the tradesman and artisan from the ruinous consequences of foreign competition."[1] Week after week, again, through "Free Trade's" critical period of 1848-9 the *Labour League* voiced a steady hostility. The following is a typical passage from the *Labour League* when it was opposing the Free Trade pressure against the Navigation Laws because of its anxiety for British shipwrights:[2]

> However true and beautiful this Free Trade policy may appear in theory, to thus force it upon the country, while our present iniquitous national debt and all our other iniquitous imposts are constantly increasing in severity is absolute destruction to the industry of the country. . . . Every department of British industry which has been brought into competition during the Free Trade mania has been nearly destroyed for the special advantage of annuitants, pensioners, placemen, and capitalists. . . . The splendid shops and bazaars of the metropolis are crammed with French, German, and American manufactured goods while our own neglected, deserted workmen are literally starving in the streets.

Another economic subject on which the organ of the National Association of United Trades was at fierce odds with the politicians of the "Manchester School" was that of Government "economy." That James Wilson, editor of the *Economist*, was a member of the Government aroused fears that the Government dockyards might adopt the *Economist's* plan of saving money by putting their employees on the piecework against which a great part of the trades world was struggling.[3] Cobdenite pressure, again, for an immediate reduction of 10,000 men in the army and 3,000 in the navy aroused the immediate query of "What is to become of these men? They are no doubt to *widen* the *Margin* of surplus labour which by its wholesome competition is the *secret* of *success* in our private manufacturing system and is henceforth to be the *National Principle*." The best, indeed, that the *Labour League*

---

[1] *Labour League*, November 25, 1848.   [2] *Ibid.*, March 31, 1849.
[3] Cf. R. W. Postgate, *The Builders' History*, p. 149, for the Stonemasons' Secretary in April 1850: "It has come to our notice that tasking (piecework) is creeping in amongst our trade in various parts of England. . . . If there is any chance of succeeding, grovelling employers will try the tasking system. Perhaps they will at first allow somewhat liberal prices. . . . The system being once established, the worthy employer begins to grumble at the high wages they are making, and a reduction of prices will soon follow: then reduction after reduction until it reaches starvation."

English Radicalism 1832-1852

could say for the Cobdenite Budget suggestions so plentifully discussed in the opening months of 1849 was the following: "We are quite willing to admit that five or ten millions struck off from the annual taxation of the country would be so much less of the produce of wealth applied unproductively for governmental purposes; but the question with us is, would any portion of the amount thus saved fall to the share of the working man; would it not rather be absorbed by the profitmonger?"[1]

It seems plain enough that even where the ardent Trade Society man was prepared to admit that middle-class Radicalism offered a nearer approach to political justice than any other political school powerful at Westminster, a vast gulf of economic suspicions sundered him from Cobdenism. The long period of doubt between 1848 and 1850, wherein many factory owners put unjustifiable interpretations on the Ten Hours Act of 1847[2] and with the help of legal decisions procured instead the Compromise Act of 1850, is full of expressions of bitter operative hostility to Bright,[3] the most determined opponent of legislative interference with the factory but the most powerful Parliamentary force ready to crusade for a wide measure of Suffrage Extension. In regard to Free Trade, again, it is obvious that some of the London luxury trades particularly exposed to French competition endeavoured for years to reverse the Cobdenite current. The London trades delegates showed marked activity in this direction. Even after the elections of 1852 seemed finally to have disposed of protectionism, their organisation was still sending out a protectionist "Proclamation of the Working Classes of Great Britain."[4]

It is worth noting, however, that there were already powerful forces at work tending to bring the upper ranks of the Trade Society world more and more into a large acceptance of the middle-class Radical attitude towards politics and society. The powerful temperance agitation, stressing as it did how much an artisan's welfare depended on his own self-control, had been exercising a steadily increasing influence on Trade Society habits and ideals for a generation. As early as 1840 a number of London Trade Societies were in alliance with Parliamentary

[1] *Labour League*, February 17, 1849, p. 221.
[2] Cf. *Ibid.*, March 10, 1849.   [3] Cf. *Ibid.*, September 9, 1848.
[4] Cf. F. E. Gillespie, *Labour and Politics in England, 1850-67*, p. 41.

The World of Labour

Radicals like Wakley and Bowring to finance the building of a trades hall which should free them from dependence on publicans' hospitality.[1] It was a dependence which involved some societies in expending as much as one-third of the weekly contributions in "refreshment." By 1850, however, such a society as the Ironmoulders' may be found reporting that the advance of temperance was causing disgruntled publicans to refuse the society the use of their club-rooms. The way was, indeed, clearing for that large abolition of liquor allowances to members and Committee which was to mark the next decade of Trade Society history.[2]

Another force working in the same direction as temperance propaganda was that of the extremely powerful printing-presses of W. and R. Chambers and Charles Knight. Already in 1834 it was being realised that the enormous circulations of *Chambers's Edinburgh Journal* and of Knight's *Penny Magazine*[3] were nullifying the hopes of the conductors of the Ultra-Radical Press. In subsequent years the appeal of cool, matter-of-fact "Useful Knowledge" literature of the Knight tone and cheapness and of magazine writing of the Chambers quality and verisimilitude served probably as the strongest brake on a mass conversion of the hard-headed of the Trade Society world to revolutionary courses in politics and industry. Such literature powerfully reinforced the middle-class advocacy of temperance and thrift, of diligence in acquiring knowledge, and of enterprise in using it which had in any case a strong attraction for some of the solidest elements in the trades. Indeed, a very surprising attitude towards strikes occasionally became vocal in the Trade Society world of the latter 'forties. When in 1849 finance discussions were going on among the stonemasons, the Liverpool lodge may be found proposing the prohibition of strikes and the Portsmouth lodge even favouring the prohibition of their very mention. For the exhausting and wasteful strike was to be substituted the operation of a Society Emigration Fund which would continually send abroad the "surplus labour" of the trade.[4] The iron-moulders had already

[1] Cf. *Southern Star*, March 15, 1840, pp. 14-15. In 1841, again, the stonemasons' policy of building Masons' Halls was being pushed for reasons from which temperance was not absent (*Builders' History*, p. 145).
[2] S. and B. Webb, *History of Trade Unionism*, II., pp. 203-4.
[3] Knight claimed that the *Penny Magazine* reached a circulation of 200,000 at one stage of its career, and for *Chambers's* the figure of 90,000 has been given as the peak circulation.
[4] R. W. Postgate, *The Builders' History*, p. 151.

in 1846 resolved on freer approaches to employers as a method of avoiding strikes and had altered their constitution in order to confine the strike-authorising power to their Executive Committee.[1] A close inspection of the evidence would nevertheless suggest that the Webbs' famous *History of Trade Unionism* has tended to give the unwary reader an exaggerated impression of the pacific temper of the "New Spirit" of the Trade Society world of 1850.[2] Dislike of strike action was often the result of financial difficulties, and abstention from wage-strikes implied no diminution of hostility to the introduction of piecework, new machinery, or an increased proportion of apprentices. For all the pacific citations of the Webb history, moreover, virtually no society acceptance is to be found of the fundamental competition economics of middle-class Radicalism. If trade thought had really been converted to some approach to Manchester economics, the next instalment of Parliamentary Reform could not have been delayed till 1867, and the epoch-making engineers' dispute of 1852 would never have taken place. In 1850 and 1851 a junction of engineering unions had been effected which produced a new Amalgamated Society with a membership of 12,000 and a capital fund of over £20,000. Yet the engineers' new strength, far beyond anything attained even by the stonemasons and the ironfounders,[3] was quickly thrown into courses which by the standards of the time were markedly aggressive.[4] So much was this the case that a widespread masters' lock-out was arranged even in a very busy season, and despite the pertinacious resistance of the men the amalgamation was thoroughly defeated.

It is interesting, however, to observe that "public opinion" was not ranged as decisively against the men as might have been expected.[5] Thanks to the currents of thought set up by J. S. Mill

[1] S. and B. Webb, *History of Trade Unionism*, pp. 198–9.
[2] Cf. S. and B. Webb, *op. cit.*, pp. 202–3. Yet the stonemasons, whose temporary anti-strike temper of 1849 has been noted above, were to be engaged in a constant succession of small strikes from 1853 onwards.
[3] The ironfounders' strength in 1851 was 4,585 (G. Howell, *Conflicts of Capital and Labour*, p. 514). The ironfounders were also called the iron-moulders.
[4] *Illustrated London News*, January 10, 1852, for example, gives the engineers' demands for the cessation of overtime, the abolition of piecework, and the discharge of non-unionists (this withdrawn), the attention of a hostile leading article making free use of terms like "tyranny," "wicked," "incredible," etc.
[5] The best short history of the dispute is in the well-known *Report of the Committee on Trade Societies*, issued by the Social Science Association in 1860.

The World of Labour

and the Christian Socialists, the "public" now contained influential elements ready to show sympathy for a body like the engineers, who refrained from "outrages," held great and orderly meetings, issued reasoned social explanations of their conduct, and made punctual disbursements of strike-pay. Indeed, in 1853 the "public" was to show almost a general tolerance for the great "wages movement" of that year, though it led to much varied striking.[1] Part of the tolerance was, of course, due to the great rapidity with which the wealth of the upper and middle classes was growing, and proved quite unable to withstand the onset of depression. But part was a permanent gain, the result of a dawning appreciation of the immense cultural advances which had been made by large sections of the artisan class.

Such a situation as has been pictured hardly lent itself to the vigorous revival of Chartism to which Ernest Jones was setting all his great energy and talent. Indeed, he saw reason to complain not only of the political indifferentism with which the engineers' struggle was waged, but the similar neglect of Universal Suffrage aims by those sections of former Chartists who were occupied in rearing a new generation of successful Co-operative stores. Ernest Jones was doubtless right in ascribing the decline of Chartism to operative absorption in Trade Society and Co-operative development.[2] But such absorption was inevitable after long years of repeated Chartist failure and was, in fact, to yield a fine new order of operative leader capable of most effective work in the Suffrage Extension campaigns of 1865–7.

[1] Cf. *The Illustrated London News*, August 20, 1853, for a long and arresting article on "The Working Classes and their Strikes." It achieved almost a judicial tone.   [2] *Notes for the People*, p. 805.

CHAPTER XXV

THE NEWSPAPER PRESS

"When Whigs of the first water, and newspapers which at that time found it convenient to support, or affect to support, the Duke of Wellington's administration, held language of such ferocity—such insolent and vulgar exultation (as did *The Times* and the *Edinburgh Review* over the fall of Charles X of France in July 1830), it may be imagined what would proceed from the professors of scurrility, the sedition-mongers, the licensed dealers in blasphemy, treason, . . . these skunks and foumarts of the press. . . . The works of 'Paine, Voltaire, Volney, Shelley, and others,' are advertised as to be sold, or lent to be read; and another dealer in impiety and sedition, which go hand in hand together, announces the first number of a 'New Family Library, containing Paine's "Rights of Man," both parts, complete.' . . . 'Penny Papers for the People' also were published. 'Designed to restore justice and overthrow oppression; the editor particularly recommending them to coffee-houses and the new beer shops, and every other place which the poorer and labouring classes of society frequent."

"Quarterly Review," *January 1831, pp. 298 sqq.*

"Deafen the 'royal ears' with your cries of distress; thunder out lustily for 'CONSTITUTIONAL REFORM'—shout for 'NO HOUSE OF PEERS,' 'NO ARISTOCRACY'; demand 'EQUAL *representation for all persons arrived at years of discretion*'; insist on '*no more public sinecures,*' *no more public pensioners or placemen,*' '*no more vexatious taxation,*' but 'ONE GRADUATED PROPERTY TAX,' '*no more Church abuses,*' '*no more clerical cormorants,*' 'NO MONOPOLIES'; petition for 'A GENERAL NATIONAL INDEPENDENT GUARD'; tell him '*if he will assist the people. the people will assist him*'; and above all, desire him to 'read the PEOPLE'S PENNY PAPERS.' "

"Penny Papers," *November 1830.*

"All went well until January 1842, when the great hosiery houses announced that orders had ceased. . . . The sale not only of the *Northern Star*, but of my own *Extinguisher*, declined fearfully. . . . We had no organ for the exposure of wrongs—such as the attempts of some of the grinding 'masters' to establish the Truck system, extraordinary acts of 'docking men's wages,' and so on. So I now issued another paper and called it the *Commonwealthsman*. . . . I had a good sale for the earlier numbers—for they were sold for me by agents at Manchester, Sheffield, Birmingham, Wednesbury, Bilston, Stafford, and the Potteries. But trade grew bad in other towns; and the sale soon fell off. In Leicester everything looked more hopeless."

"The Life of Thomas Cooper," *chapter xvi.*

IT was in 1830 that newspaper power of a modern type was first exhibited in politics, and if in 1831-2 Tories failed to defeat or emasculate the Reform Bill " the almost unanimous and wholly unprecedented violence of the newspapers" was rightly made responsible.[1] It may be conceded that such Whig Ministers as Durham and Brougham understood very much better than Wellington the art and need of "managing" the Press.[2] Yet independent altogether of management, the Toryism of 1830 was much too narrowly and selfishly based not to make it inevitable that newspapers selling even at 7d. and 8½d. should represent an infinitely wider world. But for the crippling newspaper taxation, indeed, deliberately laid on to force newspaper prices to these heights, journalistic forces would already long have been able to compel Parliamentary Reform. As it was, such Reforming and Radical names as those of James Perry of the *Morning Chronicle*, James Montgomery of the *Sheffield Iris*, Edward Baines of the *Leeds Mercury*, Robert Rintoul of the *Dundee Advertiser*, William Cobbett of the *Weekly Political Register*, John and Leigh Hunt of the *Examiner*, Charles Maclaren of the *Scotsman*, Charles Sutton of the *Nottingham Review*,[3] and Archibald Prentice of the *Manchester Times* must be left to indicate how gradually the effective political journalism had been reared which seemed so powerful in 1831.

[1] *Quarterly Review*, July 1831, xlv, 535.
[2] In 1831 the very energetic James Silk Buckingham, founder of the *Athenaeum*, was being employed as the Whig Press agent.
[3] The *Nottingham Review*, founded in 1808, is an especially interesting paper to follow in making a judgment on the gradually increasing strength of Reforming pressure. By 1829, though now a principal advertising and mercantile organ in the Midlands, it was repledging itself to its Radical faith in the following terms (December 25th): "To our readers generally we shall briefly observe that the great principles which have ever marked the career of the *Nottingham Review* will be undeviatingly persevered in. . . . Less than a quarter of a century ago, the commencement of such a paper was deemed little short of an act of madness: yet such has been the progress of these principles, the much sneered at but real march of intellect, that not less than six newspapers on similar principles have sprung up in our once exclusive district. We hail them. . . ." In September 1830, after having enthusiastically reported the French Revolution of the time and the Nottingham meeting to elect a deputation of congratulation to proceed to Paris, the *Nottingham Review* was further stirred by the Belgian Revolution. On September 10, 1830, it was encouraging its public to believe that great changes were unavoidable in England also. "We have a confident expectation," it wrote, "that the first session of the new Parliament will be signalised by some mighty measures, that will cause a great sensation throughout the country." It was the expectation aroused by articles of this kind which in the ultimate analysis drove Wellington from power.

English Radicalism 1832-1852

The greatest journalistic force in politics was, however, *The Times*.[1] Long elevated by its wonderful organisation for securing rapid foreign intelligence into a more influential organ than all the other four London morning journals and the several evening sheets put together, *The Times*, while keeping ostentatiously free from Ministerial influence, had nevertheless for decades prior to 1830 willingly and sometimes truculently affirmed its general faith in the existing political order. As the Whigs' *Edinburgh Review* said in 1823: "It takes up no falling cause, fights no uphill battle, advocates no great principle, holds out a helping hand to no oppressed or obscure individual—it is ever strong upon the stronger side."[2]

Yet in *The Times* editorial chair there sat, when the Grey Ministry took office, the famous Barnes, an ex-Radical of the Byron-Shelley literary generation who still apparently possessed a measure of Radical sympathy and who was no doubt acutely aware that a decisive turn was taking place in national politics which, if he failed to follow, might have disastrous results for his paper. In John Black of the *Morning Chronicle*, moreover, there was a rival who had never shed his Radicalism, and who, tutored by James Mill and Brougham, would have been delighted to take sole morning charge of Radical Reform and of the power and profits that course seemed likely to bring. It was a situation, indeed, very apt to remind the owner of *The Times*, the second John Walter, of the successes which the *Morning Chronicle* had once won in a similar case under James Perry, and to make him more ready to accommodate himself to a Reform advocacy which was, perhaps, in view of his later political record, not excessively congenial.[3] Despite repeated Tory representations, therefore, *The Times* supported all three Reform Bills, sometimes with a violence which frightened and disgusted the famous Greville.[4]

The adoption by *The Times* of the cause of Reform was of great immediate importance, but of relatively little ultimate sociological significance. *The Times*, after all, was merely living

[1] Described by the hostile *Quarterly Review*, June 1831, xliv, 296, as "the most influential, though at the same time, the most notoriously profligate of the London newspapers, and the most impudently inconstant in everything, except in malice and mischief."
[2] *Edinburgh Review*, May 1823, xxxviii, 364.
[3] F. Knight Hunt, *The Fourth Estate*; J. Grant, *The Newspaper Press*; and H. R. Fox Bourne, *English Newspapers*, all tell the story.
[4] *Greville Memoirs*, under December 19, 1830, November 21, 1831.

The Newspaper Press

up to its reputation of "being strong upon the stronger side." What was assuredly an altogether more significant national phenomenon than the direction in which Barnes instructed "Thunderer" Sterling to hurl his bolts, was the appearance of a working-class Press with a combative class-consciousness of which even Cobbett's *Register* was innocent. In introducing the subject of the "Unstamped Press" it is important not to omit a mention of William Carpenter, the issue of whose *Political Letters* in October 1830 at first seemed likely to make journalistic history. Though eclipsed by the greater figure of Henry Hetherington, Carpenter was the more typical representative of the struggling Radical journalist of the time. The story of his editorships and sub-editorships, which includes activity on *The True Sun* in 1834, *The Charter* in 1839, and *Lloyd's Weekly News* in 1844, will be found almost as revealing of the social and political issues of the decades following the Reform Bill as the journalistic career of a W. J. Fox, or of the brothers Mayhew.[1]

Though issued without the 3½d. revenue stamp because Carpenter claimed they were not newspapers, Carpenter's *Political Letters* were still priced at 4d., and devoured though they might be at taverns and beerhouses, were hardly purchasable at that price by working men. It is this which gives such significance to Henry Hetherington's issue of the smaller and more ultra *Penny Papers for the People*. Under the later designation of the *Poor Man's Guardian*, this first journalistic venture of Hetherington's was to surpass in importance not only all others by himself from the halfpenny *Republican* to the *Twopenny Dispatch*, but also such formidable Ultra-Radical rivals as Carlile's *Prompter* and Watson's *Working Man's Friend*. The resource which Hetherington showed in his war with the Revenue was remarkable.[2] Combined with the truculent Universal Suffrage and Anti-Property politics which his principal organ advocated, it sufficed to gain him hosts of willing working-class allies to assist in the distribution of the many thousands of unstamped *Poor Man's Guardians*, which were undoubtedly being sold weekly during the Reform Bill excitements, and for a considerable time afterwards.[3]

---

[1] *Dictionary of National Biography.*
[2] J. Grant, *The Newspaper Press*, i, 302-4; F. K. Hunt, *The Fourth Estate*, ii, 75-80.
[3] J. Grant, *op. cit.*, reports the Fleet Street tradition of a circulation "Not far below 100,000." This figure is incredible in view of the police obstacles.

English Radicalism 1832-1852

The revolutionary fervour of the Hetherington Press stood out almost at once. "It is the cause of the *'rabble'* we advocate," wrote Hetherington on November 3, 1830. "The poor, the suffering, the industrious, the productive classes! . . . We will teach this rabble their power—we will teach them that they are your masters, instead of being your slaves! Go to—can you cultivate the earth for yourselves—make your own clothes, build your own houses?—and shall they do all this for you as ye shall please to direct—shall they work harder, and be more patient than your very asses . . . and, in reward for this, be spit upon as 'rabble'!! Oh! mercy, mercy for them, while yet ye have the power to grant it! take off their heavy chains, or they themselves will break them, and with their accumulated weight crush the paltry oligarchy that has spent so many centuries in forging and imposing them. . . .

" 'The outrages' in Kent continue, and are spreading rapidly; the aristocracy are beginning to quake. . . ."

Tories became particularly alarmed during 1833 when the "Destructive" Press seemed to be increasing in power. In September of that year their leading newspaper ventured the following estimate of the Unstamped Press of London alone:[1]

	Average Circulation
Poor Man's Guardian	16,000
This is printed by Hetherington, an Irish Papist and an ex-student of Maynooth [sic].	
Destructive	8,000
Printed by the same. It is scarcely necessary to mention the principles of these publications; they are Jacobinical of the deepest and bloodiest dye.	
Gauntlet	22,000
The conductor of this is the notorious Carlile. His name is enough.	
Cosmopolite	5,000
Editor, Detroisier. Principles, Owenite and Republican.	
Working Man's Friend	7,000
Editor, Watson. Principles, Republican.	
Crisis	5,000
Conductors, Mr. Owen and Morgan.	
The Man	7,000
Principles, Spencean and Republican.	
Reformer	5,000
Editor, Lorymer. Principles, Republican and Revolutionary.	

---

[1] The *Standard*, September 10, 1833.

The Newspaper Press

In point of fact, however, the immediate prospects of the most violent kinds of journalistic extremism were already on the decline, and the decline continued so markedly during three years of great industrial prosperity (1833–6) that even the *Poor Man's Guardian* was given up at the end of 1835.[1] Amalgamating it with their *Twopenny Dispatch*, Hetherington and his remarkable editor, Bronterre O'Brien, hoped to concentrate their energies on what was now proving the most remunerative Ultra-Radical field, the newspaper full of "news." Indeed, despite all police measures, Ultra-Radical "Unstamped" weeklies sold well below the normal 8½d. charged for the "legal" Press had been gaining ground in 1835, and the 7d. dailies, too, were nervous of projects to launch an "Unstamped" 3d. rival. These facts make it clearer why the Exchequer gave way to pressure from the Parliamentary Radicals and, braving Tory resistance, reduced the Newspaper Stamp from 3½d. to 1d. in 1836. Even Hetherington was induced to accept this as the best solution possible for the time, and to convert himself into a legal publisher.

Before turning to the new journalistic era which opened when the standard price of the weekly was brought down from 8½d. to 6d. and that of the daily from 7d. to 5d., a brief review must be made of the field of "legal" Ultra-Radical journalism between 1830 and 1836. Thanks to the demand from the beer-houses and public-houses, the poor man's libraries, Ultra-Radicalism was capable of maintaining a London daily, the *Morning Advertiser*, and for years after 1833 an ambitiously-launched evening sheet, the *True Sun*, was kept on foot in the hope of consolidating parallel support. Though the enterprise was eventually given up, it had certainly forced the rival *Sun* forward to something more popular than "moderate" Radicalism. But the greatest power in Ultra-Radical journalism was the *Weekly Dispatch* with political columns which specialised in highly-spiced attacks upon Bishops, Peers, Parsons, the Pension List, and *hoc genus omne*, and with news columns which were never so popular as when tricking out luscious Court accounts of the drunkenness or sexual misbehaviour of the wealthy. Even at the 8½d. price ruling before the Stamp Duty reduction of 1836, it had acquired a monster circulation of 30,000.[2] When the price was reduced to 6d. its circu-

[1] By this time its circulation had fallen to between 4,000 and 5,000 (*Poor Man's Guardian*, December 19, 1835).
[2] H. R. Fox Bourne, *English Newspapers*, ii, 101.

English Radicalism 1832-1852

lation went on increasing until in 1842 it was at the stupendous height of over 66,000.[1] What gives such figures the more significance is the fact that thousands of these copies went to public-houses and made the favourite reading matter of their customers.[2]

The world of the politicians proper had meanwhile been seeing the most important newspaper activities. After *The Times* had "ratted" to Peelite Conservatism at the end of 1834, "Liberal" and Radical politicians of the Parliamentary majority had striven keenly to bring about its decline. For a time the *Morning Chronicle* gained steadily at its expense, and with the reduction of the Newspaper Duty in 1836 a strong group of writers, full of the "advanced Liberalism" which had been dominating literary London for many years,[3] found the financial support to launch another "advanced Liberal" daily as the *Constitutional*. But this was too ambitious, and the *Constitutional* had to be given up after less than a year of life (1836-7). Its career had proved that the "advanced Liberals" or "moderate Radicals"[4] of the professions and the business world could not support two dailies in addition to their weeklies, the *Spectator* and *Examiner*, and their Review, the *London and Westminster*. The trouble, of course, was that most of them found it impossible to dispense with *The Times*, which, after suffering considerably, began in 1838 to return to its old-time domination as the most powerful organ of attack upon the discredited Whiggery led by

---

[1] Charles Knight, *London*, v, 351-2. As head of a great publishing enterprise, Knight can be relied upon for accurate handling of the Newspaper Stamp returns which have their traps for the unwary.

[2] Some idea of the social penetration of the Press may be obtained from occasional newspaper statistics published in the *Journal of the Statistical Society*. In December 1838 a specially interesting list was printed of the newspapers found in the Coffee, Public, and Eating Houses of three Westminster parishes by members of a group of Social and Statistical Inquirers. Among the morning papers there were 264 copies of the *Morning Advertiser*, 110 of the *Morning Chronicle*, 81 of *The Times*, and 6 of the High Tory *Morning Post*. Among the evening papers there were 82 copies of the "advanced Liberal" *Sun*, 39 copies of the Whig *Globe*, and 13 of the Tory *Standard*. In the list of the weekly sheets, the *Weekly Dispatch* had 238 copies, the more moderate *Sunday Times* 54, and the sporting *Bell's Life* 85. Toryism was hardly represented.

[3] Such names as those of Byron, Shelley, Leigh Hunt, Hazlitt, Landor, and Fonblanque may be cited in evidence. Thackeray, it may be mentioned, found employment with the *Constitutional* at a time when Dickens was working for the *Morning Chronicle*.

[4] These terms were almost synonymous and were intended to denote something more popular and less oligarchical than Whiggery. Yet those who, shying at the term "Radical," called themselves "Liberals" exclusively, may be taken as obedient henchmen of Whig Cabinets.

The Newspaper Press

Melbourne. In vain did the *Spectator* in 1837 and the *Morning Chronicle* in 1839 endeavour by revolt to force the Whig Cabinet forward to the concessions to Radicalism, which might bring a popularity counterbalancing the dangerous hostility of *The Times*. Supported by the Whig territorial families and the Court, the position of the inner Cabinet Junto was just too strong to be forced.

Meanwhile the 1836 reduction of the Newspaper Tax had been forwarding the foundation of numbers of new journals.[1] Among them were some which were destined to transform national politics by helping working-class Ultra-Radicalism to create a Chartist party. As Chartism was a most important political force for two decades after 1838, the working-class Press which reared it deserves special attention. But it is important to remember that middle-class Radical journalism also gained in power from the wider circulation which followed on the reduction of price, made possible by the 1836 lowering of the Newspaper Duty. Thus the *Leeds Mercury* became more influential than ever as the favourite Dissenting newspaper throughout a large part of the North and Midlands, the *Manchester Times* played an essential part in bringing the Anti-Corn Law League to effective life, and the *Birmingham Journal* and the *Leeds Times* served in their respective large spheres of influence to prevent middle-class Radicalism from forgetting the artisan's claim to the suffrage. Inevitably also the reduction of price made newspapers like the *Leicester Mercury*, the *Northampton Mercury*, the *Cheltenham Free Press*, the *Wiltshire Independent*, and the *Stamford and Lincoln Mercury* better able to maintain a "Liberal" tone helpful to Whig and Whig-Radical M.P.s threatened by the "Tory reaction." The share of papers of this class in the politics of the time may be easily underrated.

It is certainly time to deal with the Ultra-Radical foundations of 1837. Though the *Northern Liberator*, established at Newcastle by the moneyed and violent Augustus Beaumont, and the Cobbettite *Champion*, established at Manchester, acquired spheres of influence with some rapidity,[2] they were outdone by the *Northern*

---

[1] *The Journal of the Statistical Society*, July 1841, iv, 113 has a set of statistics according to which the number of newspapers was 397 in 1836, 458 in 1837, 445 in 1838, 516 in 1839, and 493 in 1840.

[2] Industrial Scotland was the sphere of influence of the Glasgow *Liberator*, a paper edited by Dr. Taylor, the later Chartist leader, and financed partly by the Glasgow Cotton Spinners' Association.

English Radicalism 1832-1852

Star launched in Leeds by the Ultra-Radical ex-M.P., Feargus O'Connor. O'Connor's energetic demagogy, indeed, quickly took his 4½d. *Northern Star* to astounding circulation heights[1] at a time when slackening employment, falling wages, and dear bread increased working-class dread of the application of the harsh New Poor Law of 1834 to the Northern Industrial areas and their unemployed.

Another crop of Ultra-Radical newspaper foundations took place in the closing months of 1838 and the opening months of 1839. The Chartist movement had now been launched, and all was hope and confidence in the Ultra-Radical camp. The most remarkable of the new foundations was that of the *Charter*. The way for this had been carefully laid by the famous Lovett and his friends of the *London Working Men's Association*.[2] It opened with a circulation of 5,000, and under Carpenter's editorship was most responsibly and intelligently conducted, giving, indeed, in its sixteen large pages at 6d., a very wide variety of Sunday reading besides the political intelligence from the Convention, Parliament, and the Chartist constituency. The eventual breakdown of this enterprise in March 1840 revealed the scanty financial resources mobilisable behind responsible Chartist writing, capable of winning middle-class respect. Worse still, it left the Chartist newspaper field dominated by the blackguardism of the *Northern Star*. This was more than ever the case when, after the collapse of the *Operative*, the *Champion*, and the *London Dispatch* in the course of 1839, the *Southern Star* and the *Northern Liberator* ceased publication during 1840.

Though such a Chartist as Gammage believed that the *Northern Star* at one time attained a circulation of nearly 50,000,[3] it was impossible in the nature of things for a sale even approaching this volume to continue except in such periods of extravagant hope as the early summer of 1839. 4½d. was a very serious sum even for the most enthusiastic Chartist operative to expend for a private copy, and though the swollen sales of 1839 were partly

---

[1] In its seventh month it was circulating 9,822 copies and had outdone the *Leeds Mercury* (*Northern Star*, June 2, 1838).

[2] Add. MSS. (British Museum) 27820, ff. 381-3. The London Trades had been thoroughly canvassed and some middle-class support also secured from men like Place.

[3] R. G. Gammage, *History of the Chartist Movement*, p. 18. M. Hovell's *Chartist Movement* gives an average sale of 48,000 between February and May 1839, and one of 35,559 for the whole year (pp. 173, 269).

The Newspaper Press

due, no doubt, to these private purchases by individuals, the stamp returns of 1840, 1841, 1842, and 1843 show that individual purchases must have been falling off steadily. It may be that the weekly average sale of 18,780 obtained in 1840, or, indeed, that of 13,580 in 1841, and of 12,500 in 1842[1] still left O'Connor ample means for political activity, and a readership not diminished proportionately to these numbers, but one resorting increasingly to "clubbing" or the beer-house for the *Northern Star*. Such an average, however, as the 9,000 of the closing quarter of 1843[2] must have been most disconcerting to the conductors of the paper. The transfer from Leeds to London effected late in 1844 and the change of title to the *Northern Star and National Trades Journal*, show O'Connor's growing realisation of the need to recruit new Trade Union support in order to arrest the unceasing decline of his influence and income denoted by these circulation figures.

The fact, indeed, was that the *Northern Star* was becoming exposed to a new type of journalistic competition which was to prove more and more dangerous. There was already the difficult competition for the workman's scanty pence with the attractive non-political productions of the Chambers brothers, Charles Knight, and others in fields similar to theirs, and there was, besides, the whole tribe of Police Gazettes and lurid romances specially prepared to be almost irresistible to the operative who wanted more vivid reading.[3] But in 1842 the launching of the *Illustrated London News* opened a new series of newspaper foundations full of peril to the *Northern Star*. It was not the *Illustrated London News* itself which especially threatened the *Northern Star*, for, though its plentiful pictures made it as attractive to the Chartist as to the shopkeeper, its price of 6d. was more beyond the workman's pocket than even the $4\frac{1}{2}$d. of the *Northern Star*. But the phenomenal success of the *Illustrated London News* attracted into the newspaper field the inevitable projector of an illustrated paper more adapted to the operative's means. *Lloyd's Illustrated London News*, it is true, was not long issued, but it prepared the way for *Lloyd's London Weekly News*, a journal which began a momentous career in the Sunday news-

[1] *Parliamentary Papers*, 1843, xxx, 544, quoted by M. Hovell.
[2] *Ibid.*, 1844, xxxii, 419.
[3] J. L. and B. Hammond, *The Age of the Chartists*, contains a mine of the most valuable information on this aspect of the time.

paper world early in 1843, attained a circulation of 30,000 in its first three months, and thereafter, despite growing competition, commenced climbing towards the 100,000 which it was near when the *Northern Star* collapsed in 1852.[1]

Lloyd's, of course, professed advanced Radical views on politics, as did also the *News of the World*, which was launched in October 1843 to compete for the newly discovered 3d. market for Sunday Ultra-Radicalism, and rapidly achieved circulation figures as astounding as those of *Lloyd's*. It would, however, be wrong to assume that the continuous expansion of *Lloyd's* and the *News of the World* meant pure gain to Ultra-Radicalism's strength. Marked set-off must be made for the damage which this expansion inflicted on the *Weekly Dispatch* and the *Northern Star*. For example, Publicola of the *Weekly Dispatch* had long been the greatest single foe of the Church in the country. Now undermined on the shopkeeper side by the "family" appeal of the *Illustrated London News*' pictures and its cleverly opportunistic milk-and-water Liberalism,[2] the *Weekly Dispatch* began to lose heavily on the operative side. The *Northern Star*, again, had never been run purely for profit, and anything which weakened it weakened not only Chartism but the pressure which the Parliamentary Radicals were able to bring for Household Suffrage, by urging the need of offering Chartist discontent some compromise. It was fortunate for Ultra-Radicalism, suffering increasingly from the growing weakness of the *Northern Star*, that its newspaper strenuousness was reinforced in 1850 by the appearance of *Reynolds's Weekly*. The competition of *Reynolds's* certainly did something to excite more political earnestness in *Lloyd's* and the *News of the World*.

Early in 1846, meanwhile, the *Daily News* and *Evening Express* had been launched in the Metropolis with a view to their becoming the morning and evening organs of the Radical public of the capital and even of the nation. An eminent printing firm was interested in the venture, Radical capital was available from men

[1] Cf. H. R. Fox Bourne, *op. cit.*, ii, 122 sqq.; J. Grant, *op. cit*, iii, 88 sqq.

[2] When, in the course of 1842-3, the *Illustrated London News* claimed to be overtaking the circulation of the *Weekly Dispatch*, it described the latter as a "journal whose church is the tap-room, whose drawing-room is the stable-yard, whose religion is blasphemy," and asserted that its "peculiar influence among the low, the abandoned, and the profligate" was one "which no honest or respectable paper would either exercise or accept" (*Illustrated London News*, June 17, 1843).

The Newspaper Press

like Sir Joshua Walmsley, and the immense reputation of Charles Dickens was enlisted for the opening editorship. But for several years its inner financial history seems to have been a troubled one, and a total amount of capital to have been called for well beyond the original estimates of the projectors, who might never, indeed, have ventured had they really understood the full risks. It was still obviously dangerous to expect a very wide public to expend 5d. on a Radical morning newspaper as the mere 4,000 readers obtainable at that figure quickly showed. Yet the attempt thereafter made to produce a marketable journal at $2\frac{1}{2}$d. rather than at 5d. must have proved a financial failure, for if 22,000 readers were obtainable at that price the 5d. figure was reverted to before long. Despite the rising Radical tide, therefore, in the years following its foundation, it was doubtful whether the position of the *Daily News* was really a perfectly secure one until after the Stamp Duty Repeal of 1855, for which it had insistently pressed, allowed a lowering of price.[1]

No word has yet been said of the strong Irish Press whose unceasing hostility to the Irish State Church and unceasing suspicion of Irish Protestant landlordism made it one of the prominent factors in the Radical war on privilege. Nor is there need to do more than note that the disruption of the Scottish Church in 1843 produced a "Free Church" Press. Both these were natural allies of the strong Dissenting movement in England for Church Disestablishment, a movement always capable of becoming the centre of a wider and sterner crusade against Conservatism than almost any other. In Miall's *Nonconformist*, indeed, a weekly founded in 1841 and never enjoying more than a few thousands of circulation among Dissenting ministers and politicians, may be found proof positive of the strength of Disestablishment as a Radical issue. In the very first year of the *Nonconformist's* life as a journal pressing more determinedly for Disestablishment than any other yet possessed by Dissent, Miall was able to provoke the remarkable Complete Suffrage agitation of 1842 among middle-class Radicals. To follow his later activities down to his persistent attempt to force the Gladstone Ministry of 1868–74 to walk the proper Radical path, is to appreciate how large a component Disestablishment feeling formed of that totality of anti-privilege sentiment best denominated as Radicalism.

[1] H. R. Fox Bourne, *op. cit.*, ii, 141–9.

English Radicalism 1832-1852

To attempt a summary and authoritative judgment on the nature and extent of the political influence of the Newspaper Press between 1832 and 1852 is, of course, beyond the wit of man. It would first be necessary, for example, to construct for each organ a formula representing the degree of deviation from its "principles" imposed by circulation and advertisement considerations. Yet something can be gained from an examination of the figures of newspaper sale. Though in 1842, for instance, Westminster was in the hands of such a Tory majority as would have been forecast by few in 1832, the newspaper figures indicate that this reigning Parliamentary majority was very insecurely perched on a relatively small proportion of the population. In the last quarter of 1842 the average weekly circulation of the Ultra-Radical *Dispatch* was 66,666, while the somewhat more moderate Radicalism of the *Weekly Chronicle* obtained 17,083[1] purchasers. The *Northern Star*, again, though now selling only a weekly average of 12,500 copies,[2] very probably represented a larger number of readers per copy than any other journal in the kingdom. On the Tory side, however, there were no similar nationally circulated political organs with their roots deep in the populace. *Old Bell's Messenger* with a country circulation of 17,333[4] was little more than a farmer's paper, and if the prim *Britannia* with a circulation of some 5,000[3] was much more definitely a party weekly, it is hard to believe that it penetrated much lower in the social scale than the upper ranks of Anglican shopkeeperdom. The newspaper situation would seem, indeed, to reveal a most dangerous gulf dividing the industrial masses from Conservatism even of the Peelite order. Too much can easily be made, it is plain, of the Conservative Operative Societies with club and newspaper rooms attached, which Tory tacticians had been founding or financing.[4]

It seems doubtful, in fact, whether without the peculiar journalistic appeal which *The Times* had for such large portions of the professional and upper mercantile ranks, a Conservative Govern-

---

[1] Charles Knight, *London*, v, 351-2. Charles Knight's treatment of the Stamp Returns may be fully relied upon.
[2] *Parliamentary Papers*, 1843, xxx, 544.   [3] Charles Knight, *London*, v, 351-2.
[4] W. Paul's *History of the Origin and Progress of Conservative Operative Societies* (Leeds, 1838), is apt to be misleading on the real interests involved. Hill's *Toryism and the People* (1929), pp. 47-57, comes reluctantly to the conclusion that Tory interest in Operative Societies was wont to be connected with electoral considerations and even electoral corruption.

The Newspaper Press

ment could have been brought into office in 1841 or maintained there for any length of time. The unique position of *The Times*, indeed, is apt to give a misleading impression of the political leanings of many of its 20,000[1] purchasers, who might need the paper's information and admire its skilful and vigorous writing, but yet dissent from its views. How much of professional-class "Liberalism" *The Times* must have served to neutralise becomes clear when the tone and temper of the "opinion-making" weeklies of the age are studied and the considerable volume of their circulation observed. Toryism had virtually nothing to pit against the *Examiner* with its 6,312 circulation, and the *Spectator* with its circulation of 3,750,[2] both of them Whig-Radical forces of moment with important followings in the Inns of Court, the City, the world of commerce and manufacture, and the "Liberal" newspaper offices. These last, indeed, even in the case of organs as important as the *Manchester Guardian* and the *Liverpool Mercury*, must often have needed strengthening against the sin of "moderating" Liberal advocacy almost to the point of extinction in order not to forfeit various types of revenue-bringing allegiance. After its foundation by James Wilson in 1843, the *Economist* rapidly became another opinion-making organ against which the Tories had nothing similar to set.

The passage of the years was only to increase the disharmony between the growingly influential Press Liberalism and such Tory politicians as were placed in office in 1852. When even the vast host of readers of the *Illustrated London News* was treated to some mild derision of the Tory Cabinet,[3] the attitude of the vaster and drabber multitudes represented by *Lloyd's*, *The News of the World*, and *Reynolds's* can be imagined.

Newspaper influences, in fact, effectively counteracted the artificial Parliamentary strength which the political system allowed to a few hundred members of the Carlton Club, and the bulk of the population, led by its newspapers, refused to believe that the Tory Ministry of 1852 was anything but an interim Government and a "Cabinet *pour rire*."[4] Schemes of increasing

---

[1] *Parliamentary Papers*, 1844, xxxii. Stamp Returns, 1843.
[2] These are Charles Knight's figures in *op. cit.*, v, 351-2. The *Atlas* may also be mentioned as a less important weekly of their class with a circulation of 2,400.   [3] Cf. February 28, 1852; May 29, 1852.
[4] And *Punch*, founded in 1841 and now an important organ of "advanced Liberal" banter, was there to lead the laughter.

English Radicalism 1832–1852

Tory newspaper influence were, of course, incessantly considered, but the Tory party needed to become altogether broader-based before Tory newspapers in the capital and the great centres of population could be anything but the organs of small minorities. A mere Land and Church Toryism, indeed, was to become more dangerously obsolete than ever after some able Radical generalship, and the public thirst for Crimean War news combined to force the end of newspaper taxation in the course of 1855. A vast new field had been opened to the cheaper newspaper all over the country, and in the capital the first Radical penny daily, the *Daily Telegraph*, was launched in 1855, and in 1856 the Cobdenite *Morning Star* and *Evening Star* followed. In 1860 actively Liberal newspapers were reckoned at 397 and actively Conservative at 193,[1] and if the circulation figures had been available Tory inferiority of newspaper strength would have seemed very much more striking.

[1] *Journal of the Statistical Society*, xxiii, 549. In addition to these numbers 106 papers are given as Independent and 334 as Neutral.

CHAPTER XXVI

RADICALISM'S SEARCH FOR LEADERSHIP AND PARTY ORGANISATION

"My father and I had hoped that some competent leader might arise; some man of philosophic attainments and popular talents, who could have put heart into the many younger or less distinguished men that would have been ready to join him—could have made them available, to the extent of their talents, in bringing forward advanced ideas before the public—could have used the House of Commons as a rostra or teacher's chair for instructing and impelling the public mind; and would either have forced the Whigs to receive their measures from him, or have taken the lead of the Reform Party out of their hands. Such a leader there would have been, if my father had been in Parliament. For want of such a man the instructed Radicals sank into a mere *Côté Gauche* of the Whig Party."

J. S. MILL, "Autobiography," *pp. 112–13*.

"The advice (of Lord Melbourne) is at once to send for the Duke of Wellington. Your Majesty appears to Lord Melbourne to have no other alternative. The Radicals have neither ability, honesty, nor numbers. They have no leaders of any character. Lord Durham was raised, one hardly knows how, into something of a factitious importance by his own extreme opinions, by the panegyrics of those who thought he would serve them as an instrument, and by the management of the Press, but any little public reputation which he might once have acquired has been entirely dissipated and destroyed by the continued folly of his conduct in his Canadian Government. There is no party in the State to which your Majesty can now resort, except that great party which calls itself Conservative. . . ."

Lord Melbourne resigning and warning Queen Victoria against a Durham Radical Ministry, May 7, 1839 ("Letters of Queen Victoria," ii, *155*)

"However unprepared the public may be for our views on the land question, I am ready to incur any obloquy in the cause of economical truth. And it is, I confess, on this class of questions, rather than on plans of organic reform that I feel disposed to act the part of a pioneer.

"The extension of the suffrage must and will come, but it chills my enthusiasm upon the subject when I see so much popular error and prejudice prevailing. . . ."

Cobden to Bright, October 1, 1851. (MORLEY'S "Life," *pp. 561–2.*)

BEFORE the meeting of the first Reformed Parliament in 1833 very varied estimates were passing to and fro as to its political composition. It was no easy task, indeed, to attempt a judgment, for the proportion of new members was astonishingly high, and many even of the old had been compelled to make declarations of policy unusually Radical. According to the Tory Lord Mahon, Conservatives might be reckoned at 150 against 320 Whigs, and not less than 190 "thick and thin Radicals, Repealers from Ireland, members or friends of the Political Unions, and so forth."[1] But Tories were at first inclined to overestimate the amount of innovation for which many of the new members were prepared, and to read their election addresses and hustings declarations too alarmedly. Silk Buckingham, for example, one of the most daring would-be innovators among the new M.P.s, classified the 508 non-Conservatives of the 1833 House of Commons into 408 Whigs, 96 Liberals, and 4 Independents.[2] Events were to prove that many even among the ninety-six, whom he had in the Continental fashion dubbed Liberals, were often readier to follow what seemed a practical official Whig lead than to make Radical difficulties. Parker, Buckingham's own colleague in the representation of Radical Sheffield, may be found relapsing into so acquiescent a mood from the first that he was a Lord of the Treasury by 1836.

Yet in the constant political storms of the 1833 Session, storms raging inside and outside Parliament, ample proof was given that if Radicalism had no conscious ambition of seating Cobbett or Attwood, Hume or Tennyson d'Eyncourt on the Treasury Bench, it was urged on by very definite desires to force Whig Ministers to democratise their political standards and their political programme. On several critical occasions during the 1833 Session, Parliamentary Radicalism rose to match the fevered Radical atmosphere outside by recording anti-Whig votes of between 120 and 160. All it seemed to lack to become the domi-

---

[1] C. S. Parker, *Sir Robert Peel*, ii, 209-10.
[2] *Parliamentary Review*, i, 31. The question of party nomenclature is an interesting one. Despite the readiness of numbers of "respectable" M.P.s to carry the name of Radical, its association with the whole schools of Hunt and Carlile, Spence and Thistlewood was too much for others who for decades preferred the style of "advanced Liberals," which, be it mentioned, aroused fewer antagonisms among Dissenters.

Radicalism's Search for a Party Leader and Organisation

nating force in the country was a leader of high station who should throw over the movement the shelter of "respectability" and responsibility. More and more, therefore, the Earl of Durham was destined to be marked out as the Radical nominee for a Prime Ministership which should inaugurate a new age of democratic politics after the apparently tottering Whig system should have tumbled to ruin.

Durham, it may be observed, not only desired the part, but had all the apparent qualifications. In the spring of 1833 he had resigned from the Grey Cabinet, but had left behind him in Administration circles a band of influential friends not unwilling to consider that he might in certain circumstances make a suitable successor as Prime Minister to his father-in-law, Lord Grey. Durham was immensely wealthy, extremely popular in the North-Eastern Colliery areas, and had earned his name of "Radical Jack" both from the character of the advanced Reform Bill he had introduced when a Commoner in 1821 and from the large measure of his responsibility for the Reform Bill of 1832.[1] After he made his Gateshead speech of October 23, 1833, there was no disguising the fact that a Durham Premiership might become a possibility if the Grey Government broke up under the strain of popular dissatisfaction with its undemocratic temper and policy.[2] In this speech Durham hesitated not to declare that the original draft of the Reform Bill had been "free from many of those imperfections" now the subject of bitter popular complaint, and gave his support to the pressure for removing the disfranchisement created by the rate-paying and registration clauses. His sympathy with the Radical impatience of the time he expressed in the following terms: "I believe and admit that a spirit of restless discontent is abroad, which requires great prudence, great skill, great discretion, and great statesmanship to allay. But my opinion is, that the best mode of allaying it—the only mode of allaying it—is for the crown and government to go cordially along with the people." The "loud and long-

---

[1] Both J. S. Reid's *Life and Letters of Lord Durham* and C. W. New's later biography contain important sections on Durham's earlier political course. See especially New's chapters 4 and 6.
[2] The *Quarterly Review*, for example, which had closed 1832 in the conviction that the first Reformed Parliament at least would be controllable by the Whigs (xlviii, 544), was in April and July 1833 fearful of control slipping out of Ministerial hands (xlix, 274-81, 556-8).

English Radicalism 1832–1852

continued cheers"[1] which the Gateshead meeting bestowed upon this democratic pronouncement were re-echoed throughout the country.

During the 1834 Session the Grey Government failed to regain any popular favour. In Parliament, moreover, Radicals were completely antagonised by its policy of continuing Irish Coercion without undertaking that examination into the possibility of reducing Irish Church revenues which would have gone far to lay Irish discontent. The whole issue as between Radicals and advanced Whigs on the one side and the Government's pro-Church wing on the other was forced forward by the famous Irish Church motion which H. G. Ward had set down for May 27th. Ward was widely supposed to be acting as the mouthpiece of Durham, who was anxious to return to a Cabinet which he would have had good chances of dominating if the pro-Church wing could have been driven out.[2]

Four Cabinet resignations actually took place on May 27th, but when Grey reconstructed his Ministry Durham was excluded, despite Radical indignation and the protests even of *The Times*. It would appear, however, that several further resignations from the Cabinet would have been tendered to Lord Grey had Durham been invited to return, and for such a situation the weary Premier was not prepared. Palmerston was possibly the most vehement of the successful objectors to Durham, stressing his "extreme opinions" and the "decidedly new character" which would be given to the Government by his coming in.[3] But the new Cabinet did not stand long. Torn between the desire to appease Radicals by offering some modification of Irish Coercion and the fear of weakening government in Ireland too much, its members involved themselves in shabby shufflings which allowed O'Connell to make the fatal revelations producing the final break-up of July 1834.

It was such a chance as Durham and a large section of the House of Commons had been awaiting, and if he had received a Ministerial mandate a "movement" Government might have been formed with momentous results on nineteenth-century developments. But William IV was not the sovereign to make

---

[1] Taken from the *Examiner's* report in A. Fonblanque's *England under Seven Administrations*, ii, 387.
[2] Cf. H. Bulwer, *Life of Palmerston*, ii, 197.   [3] *Ibid.*, p. 195.

Radicalism's Search for a Party Leader and Organisation

a Radical opportunity, and, in fact, attempted to bring about a Whig-Tory Coalition strong enough to deny all the Radical demands. This was altogether to misjudge the temper of the House of Commons and of the populace, which was still combatively Radical enough to make such a course dangerously provocative. Indeed, when Melbourne, as the safest of the old Whig rump, finally received a Whig commission, he thought it wise to meet the Radicals by bringing four "movement" men into his Cabinet as compensation for the continued exclusion of the masterful Durham.[1] It was a typical Whig half-measure certain to lead to trouble with the Tories without satisfying the Radicals.

Trouble, in fact, came very fast, Convinced that a "patchwork" Government, out of favour with the mass of Reformers in the country, could be defied with impunity, the House of Lords rejected the Bill for admitting Dissenters to the Universities, and another Bill which would have reduced Irish Tithes. As one triumphant Peer wrote to a friend: "We have bearded the Dissenters, the Catholics and the House of Commons to the teeth."[2] Such conduct, however, was only to give Durham the opportunity of issuing a Radical call to arms which produced another strong movement of Radical combativeness.

Durham was given his chance at the great dinner which Edinburgh Reformers held on September 15th to honour Lord Grey. After expressing his "perfect confidence" in the newly enfranchised classes, Durham turned to deal with Brougham, who was also present, and had complained of the popular impatience. Rapturous applause greeted the famous sentence in which Durham identified himself with the impatient: "I will freely own to you that I am one of those who see with regret every hour which passes over the existence of acknowledged but unreformed abuses." Somewhat later came the remarkable passage which was to rekindle Radical enthusiasm and hope as it traversed the country. It ran as follows[3]:

> I do not object to the deliberation with which reforms are conducted; but I object to the compromise of principles. I object to the clipping,

---

[1] Who had been the *Morning Chronicle's* candidate for the Premiership.
[2] *Raikes's Journal*, under August 14th.
[3] *Speeches of the Earl of Durham delivered at public meetings, etc., in 1834*, pp. 5-6.

English Radicalism 1832-1852

and the paring, and the mutilating, which must inevitably follow any attempt to conciliate enemies, who are not to be gained, and who will requite your advances by pointing out your inconsistency, your abandonment of your friends and principles, and then ascribe the discontent created in our own ranks by these proceedings, to the decay of liberal feelings in the country. Against such a course of proceeding I must ever protest, as pregnant with the worst consequences, as exciting distrust and discontent, where enthusiastic devotion is necessary, as creating vain hopes, which can never be realised; and above all, as placing weapons in the hands of those, who will only use them for our destruction and the great and important interests committed to our charge.

The great response which was given to Durham's call may be judged not merely from the overwhelming cheering at the Edinburgh dinner, but from subsequent proceedings in ensuing weeks at Dundee, Melrose, Kelso, Newcastle, and Glasgow.[1] The Glasgow happenings on the occasion of Durham's admission to the freedom of the city on October 29th were veritably sensational. "The whole of the mills and factories of every kind were stopped for the day," and according to one report there was a multitude of 120,000 from Glasgow and the surrounding neighbourhood assembled in or near Glasgow Green to witness Durham receiving a very Radical address from the Trades of the town. If the choice of Premier could have been made by popular acclaim, there is not the slightest doubt as to who would have been chosen in the autumn of 1834.

By the time Durham made his next resounding oration at Newcastle on November 19th—that oration which contained the famous "I know there is as much sound sense, as much true honour, and as much real independence to be found under the coarse working jacket of a mechanic as beneath the ermined robe of a peer"[2]—the situation had been vitally changed by the precipitate dismissal of the Melbourne Ministry and the royal summons to the Tories. A glance at the pamphlet literature issued against the Tories—at such Radical productions as Bulwer's *The Present Crisis*, or William Carpenter's *Can the Tories become Reformers?*—reveals at once the abundant respect entertained for Peel's political prowess on the one hand, and

---

[1] *Speeches of the Earl of Durham delivered at public meetings, etc., in 1834*, pp. 5-6.
[2] *Ibid.*, p. 105. Of the Newcastle speech a Durhamite pamphlet, *The State of Politics in 1835 by a member of the Church of England*, was to report that "35,000 copies were sold in an incredibly short time."

Radicalism's Search for a Party Leader and Organisation

on the other the hopes that Reformers, reinvigorated by a struggle against all the "influences," might contrive to bring Durham nearer the centre of affairs. In his Tamworth Letter, however, Peel judged the temper of the restricted electorate with such shrewdness that wellnigh half the House of Commons was returned to support him. Though driven from office in April 1835, Peel, with three hundred followers in the Commons, retained a commanding position in national affairs which served indirectly to strengthen the ability of the restored Whig Cabinet to resist Radical pressure. Melbourne was again able to exclude Durham from power,[1] and to offer him in compensation the dignity but remoteness of the St. Petersburg Ambassadorship of 1835–7.

At this stage in the account of Radicalism in search of a leader it seems desirable to follow up Durham's career to its tragic end, for in no one else could Radicals see speedy hopes of their views taking command of the Cabinet. The fact that that acute politician, Joseph Parkes, kept in the closest touch with Durham throughout his Russian Ambassadorship, that the "movement" Whigs held Durham in reserve for such a burst of Ultra-Radical impatience as should break up the ever-tottering Melbourne Cabinet without letting in the Tories, is as significant as the speculations which were sometimes heard of the friendly feelings supposed to be entertained towards Durham by the Princess Victoria and her mother, the Duchess of Kent.[2] Though at Victoria's accession Lady Durham became one of the Queen's ladies, Melbourne it was who was in a special position to gain her confidence, and who could use the election results of 1837 to justify his course of refusing to meet Radicalism half-way. To Durham was merely offered the perilous North American Governor-Generalship of 1838.

Yet Durham was too big a figure in the country to be capable of easy elimination, and even his return from Canada, in what should by Whig standards have been disgrace, was by Radical effort converted into a triumph.[3] Indeed, in the Cabinet crisis of May 1839 Durham was once again the candidate of Radicals and "movement" men for a Premiership which could still have

---

[1] *Melbourne Papers*, p. 267, shows his determination.
[2] Cf. *Courts and Cabinets of Willaim IV and Victoria*, ii, 125–6.
[3] Cf. J. S. Mill's *Autobiography* (ed. 1908), pp. 123–4, for his part.

English Radicalism 1832–1852

been epoch-making, and Melbourne thought fit to demolish his claims in the course of recommending the summons of Wellington to the Palace.[1] Finally, after Durham's tragic death in July 1840 H. G. Ward, the acutest tactician among the Parliamentary Radicals, may be found writing to his Sheffield constituency in the following strain[2]:

> You have, I am sure, lamented with me Lord Durham's loss. It will be felt more later, but to us it is irreparable. We have literally no one to take his place or to keep things together in the event of an onward move. There is nothing of this kind, however, to be thought of at present, and I do not see what is to cause it, unless the Corn Laws do. This again depends much upon the harvest, for if it be plentiful agitation will cease.

The death of Lord Durham was the more unfortunate for the Parliamentary Radicals in that their groups in the Commons were still without the slightest party cohesion. Attempts to construct a party had been made in 1833 and 1835, but they had completely failed. In 1833 one of the new Sheffield members, whose adhesion might have been expected, was giving instead an almost uniform support to the Whig Front Bench because of the "necessity of supporting some government against some successors—if Tory not to last a month; if Ultra-Radical, without influence enough or talent or character or practical experience to hold the reins of the smallest island in the habitable globe. In short, such a Cabinet which would go to loggerheads, the first evening, and to downright blows the second of their deliberations, and in the meantime the funds would go down to forty."[3] That there were numbers of others from Radical constituencies whose working Radical faith was no stronger must be held to explain the failure of 1833 to form an organised party.

In 1835, again, though the construction of a "Radical brigade" was taken in hand by the most reputable of the Parliamentary Radicals, the plan came to nothing, despite the hopes which had been entertained of erecting an organised party of between seventy and eighty able to pursue an independent course.[4] The fact was that the Radical membership of 1835 and long after-

---

[1] *Letters of Queen Victoria, 1837–61*, i, 155.
[2] *Political History of Sheffield* (1884), letter dated August 16, 1840.
[3] *Ibid.*, p. 7.
[4] Cf. Fitzpatrick's *Correspondence of O'Connell*, i, 520, for the plan of the British Radicals as outlined to the Irish leader. Mrs. Fawcett's *Life of Moles-*

wards was singularly unhomogeneous, singularly hard to unite on any practical course, and singularly given to riding individual hobby-horses.[1] Only a most commanding figure, capable of arousing national enthusiasm outside Parliament and keen intellectual respect inside, could have converted such a membership into a Radical party of potency. Hume fell lamentably short of this standard, as did Grote also, while Roebuck, H. G. Ward, Molesworth, and Charles Buller had even more serious deficiencies.

If the electoral system of 1832 had allowed the Parliamentary Radicals the steadying prospect of power, their utility would undoubtedly have been greater, and the necessary party cohesion and party leader have been more easily produced. But the lack of the Ballot permitted "property" virtually to extinguish county division Radicalism at the elections of 1835 and 1837, and in numbers of small and medium-sized boroughs also it allowed the "independent" voter to be gradually worn down to that acquiescence in the politics of his betters which helped to produce the Tory majority of 1841.[2] The heavily over-represented section of the population which voted in this type of borough was, moreover, living so much in a Conservative-made atmosphere that where "Liberal" candidates appeared they tended in default of special circumstances to be almost as "sound" as the Tories on the basic principles of society. Even on Church Rates and Corn Duties, Ireland and Education, the "Liberal" needed to walk most warily, and if he desired to be successful he had also to lay aside the nicer notions on corruption for which Tories, animated by the fervour of their Church and Property crusade, had in practice but little use.[3] Indeed, there were large towns

worth, p. 73, gives the expected numbers, and adds that youthful politician's prophecy: "This is the commencement of a party which will one day or another bring destruction upon both Whigs and Tories."

[1] Cf. Morley's *Life of Cobden*, p. 191, for his observation soon after entering Parliament in 1841, that "there are a great many busy men of our party who like to see their names in print, and who therefore take up small matters continually; they are very little attended by the House."

[2] *Abridgement of the Evidence given before the Select Committee Appointed in 1835 to consider the most effectual means of preventing Bribery, Corruption and Intimidation* is a mine of information on the subject. It is significant that by 1836 Molesworth had given up hopes of holding his Cornish county seat, and H. G. Ward his seat for St. Albans. As Radicals of social status they found it possible to take refuge in Leeds and Sheffield, but they were unusually fortunate.

[3] Cf. *Abstract of Evidence before the Commons Select Committee appointed to inquire into . . . the last Return for the Borough of Warwick* for the conduct

English Radicalism 1832–1852

also from which the efforts of Tory money did not shrink, so that in 1835, for example, Bristol and Norwich[1] were completely "True Blue," and Liverpool and York had one Conservative apiece. In short, the Radical electoral field which had appeared so illimitable in 1832 had by 1841 shrunk most markedly, and was capable of even further shrinkage if Chartist hustings hostilities against "middle-class Radicalism" were developed on a formidable scale in the manufacturing areas.

The Anti-Corn Law struggle, however, was destined completely to alter the face of politics. In Cobden and in Bright, moreover, it produced the first of the Radicals who impressed far-seeing Whigs as possibly the heralds of a new class of politicians better fitted to force their way to Downing Street than had been the Cobbetts and the Attwoods, or even the Humes and the Grotes.[2] The elections of 1847, indeed, seemed to give proof of this, and it is not unlikely that if Cobden had led a Household Suffrage crusade with some of the spirit and ability which he had used against the Corn Law the aspect of British politics might have been changed surprisingly fast. But Cobden's heart was hardly in this type of crusading, nor yet in the mere forcing of a Radical group into the Cabinet which would probably have ensued. He preferred to crusade for International Disarmament and International Free Trade on the one hand, and for "Public Schools" and Freehold Land Societies on the other. Despite Bright's remonstrances, Suffrage campaigning as such was

---

of the Earl of Warwick's agents in 1832. Not only were fraudulent votes created and labourers brought into the town to enact election riots, but public-houses were "opened" to such an extent that after £4,274 of expense at twenty-six public-houses had been ascertained by the Committee, fourteen other inns or beer-houses involved were left unexamined. This was, of course, a gross, if not unparalleled case, but it is nevertheless true that Radical efforts to inaugurate a régime of electoral purity in 1832, involving in some cases constituency subscriptions to return members "free of expense," were far from matched on the Tory side, either then or afterwards.

[1] Leicester and Ipswich were two other considerable towns where the Commons Select Committee of 1835 found that "Blue" money had been at work producing "Conservative reaction." At Ipswich the corruption was sufficiently brought home to the candidates themselves to permit of their being unseated even under the loose standards of the day.

[2] Grey had urged Cobden's being taken into the Government in December 1845 and Clarendon in July 1846. In August 1847 Russell's Chancellor of the Exchequer was again urging "you must consider betimes what Cobden's position in parliament will be, and how his conduct may affect us," and Russell prepared to make a second Cabinet offer to the Free Trade leader (cf. *Later Correspondence of Lord J. Russell*, i, 180–1).

Radicalism's Search for a Party Leader and Organisation

willingly left to Walmsley and the Chartists, with no great expectation and no excessive desire for their success.[1]

To the construction of a Radical Parliamentary party Cobden brought the same discouraged listlessness which he showed towards Suffrage campaigning. It was not apparently an end which seemed to him to warrant neglecting the more precious interests which he was forwarding. The following is Roebuck's account of one of the occasions when joint Radical strategy was discussed:

> We had a dinner last night at Sir Joshua Walmsley's with the leading Radicals—Hume, Milner Gibson, Charles Villiers (a fish out of water), Cobden, Bright, Rev. W. J. Fox, and a Colonel Sawley. The object was to see if any combined system of action could be devised and it soon became plain that amongst these men, a leader or a system was impossible. Villiers came there to prevent any such result, ditto Milner Gibson. Cobden is a poor creature with one idea—the making of county voters. He is daunted by the county squires, and hopes to conquer them by means of these votes. Little Fox . . . was about as much fit for a political chief as I am for a ballet dancer. The only man of metal and pluck was Bright, the pugnacious Quaker. . . .[2]

Roebuck had a sharp eye as well as a sharp tongue, and the passage gives some insight into the reason why Radical Parliamentarians were still a loose disjointed *Côté Gauche* of the Whigs, from which "Liberal" Cabinets picked now and then a capable and amenable personality for a minor post. When such a muzzled personality quickly tended to come to grief in a "popular" constituency, the Whigs opined not that they themselves were out of touch with the people, but that "popular" constituencies were fickle, their representatives virtually ineligible for the Front Bench and small boroughs vitally necessary for the working of the Constitution.[3]

After the General Election of 1852 the Parliamentary strength of the parties in the House of Commons was estimated by one Tory Cabinet Minister to be as follows: Derbyites 292, Peelites

---

[1] Cf. Morley's *Life of Cobden*, chapter 20.
[2] Leader's *Life and Letters of Roebuck*, Letter of July 1849.
[3] Cf. W. R. Greg's *Essays on Political and Social Subjects* for the *Edinburgh Review*, articles of January and October 1852 on the "Expected Reform Bill" and "Representative Reform," and the article of May 1852 in the *North British Review* entitled "Prospects of British Statesmanship."

30, Whigs 130, Radicals 160, and Irish Brigade 50.[1] On the defeat of the Derby Government, nevertheless, it proved possible for the Peelites and the Whigs to do all the Cabinet-making for the Coalition Government which succeeded, and to feel secure that the distribution of some minor offices among tractable Radicals and Irish would prevent all real trouble from those groups whose votes were being counted on, though they were not being taken into consultation. Such Radical impotence to play any part in an apparently promising situation requires further explanation than has yet been given. The explanation, too, would throw some light on Radical prospects as they appeared to the "practical" politicians of January 1853.

One obvious objection to virtually all the Radical members and one whose strength was widely recognised was their lack of that administrative and official experience which the Peelites and Whigs had in such embarrassing plenty. To the more obvious Radical candidates for office, again, further objections had been early advanced. One Whig review, for example, picking upon Cobden, Bright, Molesworth, and Roebuck as the most considerable of the Radical politicians of 1852, had proceeded to demolish their claims to statesmanship with malicious readiness.[2] Roebuck had an "unmanageable independence of view"; Molesworth was "rich and lazy"; Bright lacked "education," and Cobden wanted "that indescribable enlargement and refinement of the intellect, the faculty for understanding other minds and appreciating hidden wants and sympathies which is indispensable to those who would aspire to govern a nation of cultivated men."

Of Bright and Cobden this was hypercriticism indeed, but it was the more dangerous in that the standing of these politicians as "practical men" was also under attack owing to their Peace and Disarmament activities. In effect, such Whig criticisms as have been cited must be taken as part of the inevitable efforts of Whiggery to prevent the disturbance of the artificial political situation which had allowed its handful of clans the immense

---

[1] Malmesbury, *Memoirs of an Ex-Minister*, p. 287. Cf. *Letters of Queen Victoria, 1837–61*, ii, 412, for Derby's figures, which allowed the Whigs and Radicals something less, the Whigs 120, and the Radicals 150.
[2] *North British Review*, May 1852, Article "Prospects of British Statesmanship"; W. R. Greg, *Essays on Political and Social Subjects*, ii, 375–6, reproduces the passage.

Radicalism's Search for a Party Leader and Organisation

power they had been wielding since 1830. Even the Russell Reform Bill of 1852 must be viewed from one aspect as a device for prolonging Whig control. It promised considerable strengthening of the Whig Parliamentary contingent at the expense of the Tories, but, denying as it did both Ballot and Redistribution, it offered Radicalism only Suffrage Extension without the chance of gaining seriously in Parliamentary numbers. The virtually complete preservation of the small borough representation, moreover, was intended not merely to keep the "populous areas" under-represented, but also to facilitate the production of "statesmen." No view of nineteenth-century politics, indeed, is complete which fails to stress the Whig and Tory advantage in their ability to launch their "statesmen" young into the political world, often enough from small boroughs under influence. Seasoned Parliamentary and official veterans at an age when the normal "advanced Liberal" from the "popular constituency" was calculating whether his fortune in manufacturing, commerce, banking, or the law was sufficient to permit of political activity, these lucky "statesmen" were fated to dominate Tory and "Liberal" Cabinets alike for the rest of the century. Russell, Palmerston, and Gladstone, the "key" figures of the Liberalism of the second half of the nineteenth century, had all thus been launched, and the same was fated to be true of Lord Salisbury, Lord Randolph Churchill, and Mr. Balfour, the Tory "statesmen" who experimented so successfully with "Tory democracy." The very concatenation of such names and such personal histories suggests how far away from social fundamentals, and for how long the "old hands" were destined to keep the struggles of party politics.

During the Cabinet-making of December 1852 Bright let it be known that neither he nor Cobden was a candidate for office. Their time had not yet come they thought. When by his unique Reform campaigns of 1866–7 Bright at length succeeded in bringing the Radical day somewhat nearer, his victory was largely ascribable to indispensable support from the "Organised Trades." No help of such potency was available in 1852. There was no organised Trades activity in politics, Chartism could develop no steady strength, and Walmsley's semi-Chartist National Reform Association had already begun to decline. In December 1852, indeed, Bright may be found plying Lord John Russell privately with "hideous" details of electoral corruption and depravity in an effort to win him to making some concession on the Ballot.[1] It was probably as useful a democratic activity as any other to which he could have set his hand.

[1] *Later Correspondence of Lord John Russell*, ii, 112-13.

SELECT BIBLIOGRAPHY

MANUSCRIPT SOURCES

1. The Place Manuscripts in the British Museum, especially:
   Additional MSS. 27789–27797. Narratives of Political Events in England 1830–5.
   Additional MSS. 27819–27822, 27835. Collections on working men's associations.

2. The Place Collection at the Hendon Repository of the British Museum:
   Set 56. Twenty-nine volumes of newspaper cuttings, placards, handbills, manuscript notes, etc. Reform 1836–47.

3. London Working Men's Association Minutes:
   Additional MSS. 37773–37776. (British Museum.)

4. Correspondence and Papers of the General Convention of the Industrious Classes 1839.
   Additional MSS. 34245 A and B. (British Museum.)

5. The Peel Papers in the British Museum:
   Additional MSS. 40446–40452. Correspondence of Sir Robert Peel as Prime Minister with Sir J. R. G. Graham, Home Secretary 1841–6.
   Additional MSS. 40442. Correspondence with Lord Lyndhurst 1841–9.

AT THE PUBLIC RECORD OFFICE

6. Home Office. Disturbances Correspondence 1838–40, especially:

H.O. 40, 37	(1838–9)	Lancashire (Manchester and Rochdale)
H.O. 40, 38	(1838)	Lancashire
H.O. 40, 43	(1839)	Hereford, Kent, Leicester, Manchester
H.O. 40, 44	(1839)	Lancaster, Bolton, Leicester, Middlesex
H.O. 40, 45	(1839)	Monmouth
H.O. 40, 46	(1839)	Montgomery, Northumberland, etc.
H.O. 40, 49–50	(1839)	Warwick (includes Birmingham)
H.O. 40, 51	(1839)	York and Wales
H.O. 40, 53	(1839)	Military Dispatches and Chartist intercepted letters.
H.O. 40, 55	(1840)	Leicester, Stafford
H.O. 40, 57	(1840)	Scottish and Welsh Miscellaneous

7. Home Office. Disturbances Entry Books:
   H.O. 41, 13–19 (1837–52) Provinces
   H.O. 41, 26 (1820–48) London
   H.O. 41, 30 (1840) Socialists

English Radicalism 1832-1852

AT THE BISHOPSGATE INSTITUTE

8. G. J. Holyoake's Letter Book (1837-41); Log Books (1835-46); Lecture Notes (1838, etc.); Diaries (1847 onwards).

AT THE PUBLIC RECORD OFFICE

9. The Russell Papers:
   G.D. 22.
   2-10. Correspondence and Papers (1836-53) of Lord John Russell.

AT THE BRITISH MUSEUM

10. Add. MSS. 41567 L. Important Home Office and magistrates' correspondence bearing on the Dorchester Labourers' Case of 1834.

PERIODICALS (ULTRA-RADICAL)

Dates	Name	Editorship
1793-5	Pig's Meat	Thomas Spence
1795-6	The Tribune	John Thelwall
1802-35	The Political Register	William Cobbett
1817-24	The Black Dwarf	T. J. Wooler
1819-25	The Republican	R. Carlile
1830-1	Political Letters	William Carpenter
1830-5	The Poor Man's Guardian	Hetherington and O'Brien
	(begun as Penny Papers for the People)	
1832-4	The Crisis	Owenite
1833-4	The Pioneer	James Morrison
1833	The Working Man's Friend	James Watson
1835-6	Pamphlets for the People	J. A. Roebuck
1837-52	The Northern Star	F. O'Connor, etc.
1837-40	The Northern Liberator	A. Beaumont, etc.
1838-9	The Operative	J. B. O'Brien
1839-40	The Charter	W. Carpenter
1839	The National	W. J. Linton
1839	The London Democrat	J. Harney, Coombs
1839	The Western Vindicator	Henry Vincent
1840	The Southern Star	O'Brien and Carpenter
1841	The Nonconformist	Edward Miall
1841-3	The Oracle of Reason	G. Southwell
1843-5	The Movement	G. J. Holyoake
1845-6	The Herald of Progress	Owenite
1846-72	The Reasoner	G. J. Holyoake
1847-8	The Labourer (Monthly)	O'Connor and Jones
1848	The Cause of the People	Linton and Holyoake
1848-9	The Spirit of the Age	Alex. Campbell
1848-9	The Labour League	Nat. Assoc. of U. Trades
1849-50	Reynolds's Political Instructor	G. W. M. Reynolds
1849-51	The Democratic Review	G. J. Harney

Select Bibliography

Dates	Name	Editorship
1850	The People's Review (Monthly)	G. J. Holyoake
1850-2	The Operative	William Newton
1851-5	The English Republic	W. J. Linton
1851-2	Notes to the People	Ernest Jones
1852-8	The People's Paper	Ernest Jones

OTHER PERIODICALS

The Edinburgh Review; The Quarterly Review; (from 1838) The Quarterly Journal of the Statistical Society; The British Almanac and Companion; The Annual Register; (from 1841) Punch; (from 1842) The Illustrated London News.

PERIODICALS OCCASIONALLY CONSULTED

The Times; The Morning Chronicle; The Weekly Dispatch; Lloyd's Weekly Newspaper; The News of the World; Reynolds's Weekly Newspaper; The Weekly Times; The Monthly Magaine; The New Monthly Magazine; The Westminster Review; The London and Westminter Review.

PARLIAMENTARY PAPERS

Date	Volume	Report
1833	XIII	Select Committee Reports on the Metropolitan[1] Police and the Coldbath Street Fields Meeting
	XV	Select Committee Report on Public Walks
	XX-XXI	Royal Commission Report on Factories
1834	VIII	Select Committee Report on Drunkenness
	X	Select Committee Report on Handloom Weavers
	XXVII	Royal Commission Report on the Poor Laws (Appendices in XXVII-XXIX)
1835	VIII	Select Committee Report on Bribery,[2] Corruption, and Intimidation at Elections
	XXIII	Royal Commission Report on Municipal Corporations (England and Wales)
	XXVII-XXVIII	Royal Commission Report on Corporations (Ireland)
	XXIX	Royal Commission Report on Corporations (Scotland)
1836	XXII	Select Committee on Military Punishments
	XXVII	Royal Commission Report on County Rates
	XXX	Royal Commission (Third) Report on the State of the Poorer Classes in Ireland
1837	XVII	Select Committee on the Poor Law Amendment Act Report (Parts 1 and 2)

---

[1] A Radical version of the evidence was specially issued by Cobbett under the style of *Popay the Police Spy*.
[2] An *Abstract of the Evidence* for cheap circulation was issued as part of the Ballot activities for 1837.

English Radicalism 1832 1852

Date	Volume	Report
1837	XXV	Municipal Corporation Commission, Reports on London, Southwark, and the London Companies
1837–8	VII	Select Committee Report on the Education of the Poorer Classes
	VIII	Select Committee Reports on Combinations of Workmen
	XVIII	Select Committee Report on the Poor Law Amendment Act (Parts 1, 2, and 3)
	XXIII	Select Committee Report on the Civil List and on Pensions
1839	XX	Poor Law Commissioners' Report
	XIX	Royal Commission Report on Constabulary
	XLII	Reports from the Assistant Handloom Weavers Commissioners
1842	XV	Royal Commission Report on Children's Employment (Mines)
1843	XIII–XV	Royal Commission Report on Children's Employment (Trade and Manufactures)
1844	XVII	Royal Commission Report on the State of Large Towns and Populous Districts
	XX–XXVI	Royal Commission Report on Poor Law (Scotland)
	XXXII	Newspaper Stamp Returns
1845	XV	Report of the Commissioners appointed to inquire into the Condition of the Framework Knitters
	XIX–XXII	Royal Commission Report on the Occupation of Land (Ireland)
1846	IX	Select Committee Report on the Game Laws
1847–8	XX	(Lords') Select Committee Report on the Navigation Laws
1849	XVII	Select Committee Report on Public Libraries
1850	XIII	Select Committee Report on the County Rates and Expenditure Bill
1851	XVII	Select Committee Report on Newspaper Stamps
1852	V	Select Committee Report on Coal Mines

OTHER PAPERS

| 1831–52 | Hansard's Parliamentary Debates |
| 1842 | Reports on the Sanitary Condition of the Labouring Population of Great Britain (issued by the Poor Law Commission) |

BIOGRAPHY, RADICAL AND ULTRA-RADICAL

Attwood, Life of Thomas, C. M. Wakefield. 1885
Baines, Life of Edward, Sir E. Baines. 1861
Bamford. Passages in the Life of a Radical, Samuel Bamford. 1839–42

Select Bibliography

Bentham Memoirs (In collected works), John Bowring. 1843
Bright, Life of John, G. M. Trevelyan
Buckley, John, A Village Politician, ed. J. C. Buckmaster. 1893
Burdett, Sir Francis and His Times, M. W. Patterson. 1931
Carlile, Life and Character of Richard (pp. 40), G. J. Holyoake. 1849
Cartwright, Life and Correspondence of Major, Miss F. D. Cartwright. 1826
Cobbett, Life of William, G. D. H. Cole. 1924
Cobden, Life of Richard (ed. 1903), John Morley. 1881
Cobden. Alderman Cobden of Manchester, Sir E. W. Watkin. 1891
Cooper, Life of Thomas (ed. 1873), by himself. 1872
Duncombe, Life and Correspondence of T. S., T. H. Duncombe. 1868
Fonblanque, Life and Labours of Albany, E. B. de Fonblanque. 1874
Fox, William Johnson (pp. 41), Graham Wallas. 1924
Frost. Forty Years' Recollections, Thomas Frost. 1880
Grote, The Personal Life of George, Mrs. Grote. 1873
Hardy, Memoir of Thomas, by himself. 1832
Hetherington, Life and Character of Henry (pp. 16), ed. G. J. Holyoake. 1849
Holyoake. Sixty Years of an Agitator's Life, G. J. Holyoake. 1892
Hunt. Memoirs of Henry Hunt, Esq., by himself. 1820–2
Jones, Life and Labours of Ernest (pp. 31), D. P. Davies. 1897
Linton. My Memories, W. J. Linton. 1895
Lovett, Life and Struggles of William, by himself. 1876
Martineau. Harriet Martineau's Autobiography, Maria W. Chapman. 1877
Miall, Life of Edward, A. Miall. 1884
Mill, Life of James, A. Bain. 1882
Mill, J. S. Autobiography (ed. 1906). 1873
Mill, J. S., Letters, ed. Hugh Elliott. 1910
Molesworth, Life of Sir W., Mrs. M. G. Fawcett. 1901
Napier. Life and Opinions of Gen. Sir C. J. Napier, Sir W. Napier. 1857
O'Connell, Life and Times of Daniel O'Connell, John O'Connell. 1846
O'Connell, Correspondence of Daniel, W. J. Fitzpatrick. 1888
Owen, Life and Labours of Robert, Lloyd Jones. 1889
Owen. Life of Robert Owen, Frank Podmore. 1906
Parkes. Joseph Parkes of Birmingham, Miss J. M. Buckley. 1925
Place, Life of Francis, Graham Wallas. 1898
Roebuck, Life of J. A., R. E. Leader. 1897
Somerville. Autobiography of a Working Man, Alexander Somerville. 1848
Spence, Thomas, and His Connections, Olive Rudkin
Stephens, Life of J. R., G. J. Holyoake. 1884
Sturge, Memoirs of Joseph, Henry Richard. 1864
Thelwall, John, Charles Cestre. 1906
Wakley, Life of Thomas, Sir S. S. Sprigge. 1889
Watson. James Watson, A Memoir, W. J. Linton. 1879

A Dictionary of Free Thinkers, J. M. Wheeler, for notes on the leading Socialists and Owenites, not given in the Dictionary of National Biography

English Radicalism 1832-1852

MORE IMPORTANT MINISTERIAL CORRESPONDENCE AND POLITICAL JOURNALS

1. *The Croker Papers*, ed. L. J. Jennings. 1884
2. *The Greville Memoirs*, ed. Henry Reeve. 1888
3. *Correspondence of William IV and Lord Grey*, ed. Henry, Earl Grey. 1867
4. *The Melbourne Papers*, ed. L. C. Sanders. 1889
5. *Memoirs of Sir Robert Peel*, ed. Mahon and Cardwell. 1856
6. *The Peel Papers*, ed. C. S. Parker. 1891-9
7. *A Portion of the Journal kept by Thomas Raikes 1831-47*. 1856-7
8. *The Later Correspondence of Lord John Russell 1840-78*, ed. G. P. Gooch. 1925
9. *The Letters of Queen Victoria 1837-61*, ed. A. C. Benson and Viscount Esher. 1908

MORE IMPORTANT MINISTERIAL AND OPPOSITION BIOGRAPHIES, ETC.

1. *Memoir of Lord Althorp*, Sir D. Le Marchant. 1876
2. *Lord George Bentinck* (edn. 1874), B. Disraeli. 1851
3. *Life and Times of Lord Brougham*, by himself. 1871
4. *Life of Disraeli*, Moneypenny and Buckle. 1910-20
5. *Life and Letters of the First Earl of Durham*, J. S. Reid. 1906
6. *Life of Durham*, C. W. New. 1929
7. *Life of Gladstone*, J. Morley. 1903
8. *Memoir of Sidney Herbert*, Lord Stanmore. 1906
9. *Recollections of a Long Life* (J. C. Hobhouse's), Lady Dorchester. 1909
10. *Life and Letters of Lord Macaulay*, Sir G. O. Trevelyan. 1876
11. *Memoirs of an Ex-Minister* (1885), Lord Malmesbury. 1884
12. *Memoirs of Lord Melbourne* (1890), W. M. Torrens
13. *Life of Lord Palmerston*, Sir H. L. Bulwer and E. Ashley. 1870-4
14. *Life of Lord John Russell*, Sir Spencer Walpole. 1891
15. *Speeches and Despatches of Earl Russell*. 1870
16. *Life and Work of Lord Shaftesbury*, E. Hodder. 1886

OBSERVERS' AND FOREIGNERS' DESCRIPTIONS

BASTIAT, C. F.: Cobden et la Ligue. 1845
BEAUMONT, G. DE: Ireland—Social, Political, and Religious (translated from the French 1839). 1839
BULWER, E. L.: England and the English. 1833
BURET, E. F.: De la Misère des Classes Laborieuses en Angleterre et en France. 1840
CARUS, C. G.: The King of Saxony's Journey through England and Scotland in 1844 (translated from the German). 1846

Select Bibliography

COBBETT, W.: Rural Rides. 1821–32
ENGELS, F.: The Condition of the Working Class in England in 1844 (German original 1845). 1892
FAUCHER, L.: Études sur l'Angleterre (collected edn.). 1845
Manchester in 1844 (translation of one part). 1844
GUIZOT, F.: An Embassy to the Court of St. James's in 1840. 1862
HAUSSEZ D' BARON: Great Britain in 1833 (translated from the French).1833
KAY (KAY-SHUTTLEWORTH), J. P.: The Moral and Physical Condition of the Working Classes employed in the Cotton Manufacture in Manchester. 1832
KAY, J. P.: Social Condition and Education of the People in England and Europe. 1850
KOHL, J. G.: Ireland, Scotland, England, and Wales (translated from the German). 1843–4
LAING, S., Jun.: National Distress. 1844
LAING, S.: Observations on the Social and Political State of the European People in 1848 and 1849. 1850
LEDRU-ROLLIN, A. A.: The Decline of England (translated from the French). 1850
MAYHEW, H.: London Labour and the London Poor. 1850
MILLER, HUGH: First Impressions of England and its People. 1846
RAUMER, F. VON: England in 1835 (from the German). 1836
England in 1841 (from the German). 1842
COOKE TAYLOR, W.: Notes of a Tour in the Manufacturing Districts of Lancashire. 1842
TICKNOR, G.: Life, Letters, and Journals of. 1876

SOME WORKS SPECIALLY ILLUSTRATIVE OR FORMATIVE OF RADICAL AND ULTRA-RADICAL THOUGHT
1832–52

BAXTER, G. R. W.: The Book of the Bastilles. 1841
BENBOW, W.: Crimes of the Clergy. 1823.
Grand National Holiday and Congress of the Productive Classes. 1831
BENTHAM, J.: An Introduction to the Principles of Morals and Legislation. 1780–9
Official Aptitude Maximised, Expense Minimised. 1830
BRAY, J. F.: Labour's Wrongs and Labour's Remedy. 1839
CARPENTER, W.: Advantages of Trade Unions. 1831
The New Black Book. 1835
COBBETT, W.: History of the Protestant "Reformation" in England and Ireland. 1824–7
Legacy to Labourers. 1834
Legacy to Parsons. 1835
COBDEN, R.: England, Ireland, and America. 1835
Russia. 1836

English Radicalism 1832–1852

DURHAM, LORD: Speeches of the Earl of Durham in 1834. 1835
ELLIOTT, EB.: Corn Law Rhymes. 1827
GODWIN, W.: Political Justice. 1793
HODGSKIN, T.: Labour Defended against the Claims of Capital. 1825
HOWITT, W.: A Popular History of Priestcraft. 1833
    Christianity and Colonisation. 1838
    A History of the Aristocracy of England. 1846
JONES, ERN.: Chartist Songs. 1846–
LOVETT, W.: The People's Charter and Addresses of the London Working Men's Association. 1836
LOVETT, W., and COLLINS, J.: Chartism, a New Organisation of the People. 1840
MILL, JAMES: Ballot, Colonies, and Government Articles. 1820–30
MILL, J. S.: Principles of Political Economy. 1848
MORGAN, J. M.: Revolt of the Bees. 1826
O'CONNELL, D.: Speeches and Letters (at 1d. each). 1835
O'CONNOR, F.: Practical Work on the Management of Small Farms. 1846
OWEN, ROBERT: Report to the County of Lanark. 1821
    Lectures on the Marriages of the Priesthood. 1835
    Book of the New Moral World. 1836
OWEN, R. D.: Moral Physiology (New York 1831). 1832
PAINE, TOM: Rights of Man. 1791–2
    Age of Reason. 1794–5
    Agrarian Justice. 1795–6
SPENCE, T.: The Rights of Infants. 1797
SPENCER, H.: Social Statics. 1851
THOMPSON, T. P.: Catechism on the Corn Laws. 1827
THOMPSON, W.: Inquiry into the Principles of the Distribution of Wealth most conducive to Human Happiness. 1824
Rules and Regulations of the National Association of United Trades (Seventh edition). 1853
LONDON TRADES' COMBINATION COMMITTEE: Combinations Defended. 1839

OTHER SIGNIFICANT WORKS BY CONTEMPORARIES

ALFRED: The History of the Factory Movement. 1857
ALISON, A.: Essays (Contributions to the Tory *Blackwood's Magazine* 1831–49). 1850
    Principles of Population. 1840
ANON.: Character, Objects, and Effects of Trade Unions (anti-Union). 1834
ANON.: Perils of the Nation (Anglican Tory). 1843
ANON.: Stubborn Facts from the Factories (anti-League). 1844
ARNOLD, DR.: Miscellaneous Works (includes Journalism 1831–41). 1845
BUCKINGHAM, J. SILK: National Evils and Practical Remedies. 1849

Select Bibliography

CARLYLE, T.: Chartism. 1839
  Past and Present. 1843
  Latter Day Pamphlets. 1850
CHALMERS, DR.: On Political Economy in connexion with the moral state and moral prospects of society. 1832
  Lectures on the Establishment and Extension of National Churches. 1838
CHAMBERS, R.: Vestiges of the Natural History of Creation. (Anon. till 12th edn. 1884). 1844
COCKBURN, H.: Memorials of his time. 1856
  Journal of. 1831–54
DICKENS, C.: Oliver Twist. 1837
DYOTT, W.: Diary 1781–1845 (High Tory). 1907
DISRAELI, B.: Sybil. 1845
FONBLANQUE, A.: England Under Seven Administrations. 1837
GAMMAGE, R. G.: History of the Chartist Movement. 1854
GASKELL, MRS.: Mary Barton. 1848
HANNA, W.: Memoirs of Dr. Chalmers. 1852
LOVELESS, G.: Victims of Whiggery. 1837
MACAULAY, T. B.: Essays (Republished). 1843
MARTINEAU, H.: Illustrations of Political Economy; Illustrations of Taxation; Poor Laws and Paupers. 1832–4
  Deerbrook. 1839
  Forest and Game Law Tales. 1845
  A History of the Thirty Years' Peace 1816–46. 1849
McCULLOCH, J. R.: Principles of Political Economy. 1825
  Statistical Account of the British Empire. 1841
PORTER, G. R.: Progress of the Nation. 1850
PRENTICE, A.: History of the Anti-Corn Law League. 1853
  Historical Sketches of Manchester. 1851
SCROPE, G. P.: Principles of Political Economy. 1833
STANLEY, A. P.: Life of Dr. Arnold. 1844
THORNTON, W. T.: A Plea for Peasant Proprietors. 1848
WADE, J.: History of the Middle and Working Classes. 1833
WILSON, J.: Influences of the Corn Laws (3rd edn.). 1840
  Fluctuations of the Currency, Commerce, and Manufactures referable to the Corn Laws. 1840

LATER WORKS SPECIALLY VALUABLE

BEER, M.: A History of British Socialism. 1921
BENN, A. W.: The History of English Rationalism in the Nineteenth Century. 1906
CARPENTER, S. C.: Church and People 1789–1889. 1933
CLAPHAM, J. H.: An Economic History of Great Britain 1820–50. 1926
GILLESPIE, F. E.: Labour and Politics in England 1850–67. 1927
HALÉVY, E.: History of England 1830–41. 1924

English Radicalism 1832–1852

HAMMOND, J. L. and B.: The Age of the Chartists 1832–54. 1930
HOVELL, M.: The Chartist Movement. 1918
JEPHSON, H.: The Platform, Its Rise and Progress. 1892
POSTGATE, R. W.: The Builders' History. 1923
WEBB, S. and B.: History of Trade Unionism (new edn.). 1920
WEST, J.: A History of the Chartist Movement. 1920

APPENDIX A

LIST OF 216 M.P.s VOTING "AYE" ON GROTE'S BALLOT MOTION OF JUNE 18, 1839

(Cf. pp. 155, 205.)

Abercromby, G. R. Stirling Co.
Aglionby, F. Cumberland E.
Aglionby, H. A.* Cockermouth
Alcock, T. Ludlow.
Anson, Col. Staffs. S.
Anson, Sir G. Lichfield.
Archbold, R. Kildare Co.
Attwood, T.* Birmingham.

Bainbridge, E. T. Taunton.
Baines, E. Leeds.
Barnard, E. G. Greenwich.
Barron, H. Waterford.
Barry, G. S. Cork Co.
Beamish, F. B.* Cork.
Bellew, R. M. Louth Co.
Berkeley, hon. H. Cheltenham.
Bernal, R. Rochester.
Bewes, T. Plymouth.
Blake, M. J.* Galway
Blake, W. J. Newport (I. of W.)
Blewitt, R. J. Monmouth.
Blunt, Sir C. Lewes.
Bodkin, J. Galway Co.
Bowes, J. Durham Co. (South).
Brabazon, Sir W. Mayo Co.
Bridgeman, H.* Ennis
Brodie, W. B. Salisbury.
Brotherton, J.* Salford.
Browne, R. D.* Mayo Co.
Bryan, G. Kilkenny Co.
Buller, C. Liskeard.
Bulwer, Sir E. L. Lincoln.
Busfield, W. Bradford.
Butler, hon. Col. Kilkenny Co.
Byng, G. S. Chatham.

Callaghan, D. Cork.
Campbell, Sir J. Edinburgh.
Cave, R. O. Tipperary Co.
Chalmers, P. Montrose, etc.
Chapman, Sir M. L. Westmeath Co.
Chester, H. Louth Co.

Chichester, J. P. B. Barnstaple.
Clay, W. Tower Hamlets.
Clive, E. B. Hereford.
Codrington, Sir E. Devonport.
Collier, J. Plymouth.
Collins, W.* Warwick.
Conyngham, Lord A. Canterbury.
Craig, W. G. Edinburgh Co.
Crawford, W. London.
Currie, R.* Northampton.

Dashwood, G. H. Wycombe.
Davies, T. H. Worcester.
Denison, W. J. Surrey W.
Denistoun, J. Glasgow.
D'Eyncourt, C. T. Lambeth.
Divett, E. Exeter.
Duke, Sir J.* Boston.
Duncombe, T.* Finsbury.
Dundas, C. W. D. Flint, etc.
Dundas, F. Orkney and Shetland.
Dundas, hon. J. C. York.

Easthope, J.* Leicester.
Eliot, hon. J. E. Roxburgh Co.
Ellice, Capt. A. Harwich.
Ellice, E. Coventry.
Ellis, W.* Leicester.
Erle, W. Oxford.
Euston, Earl of.* Thetford.
Evans, Sir D. L. Westminster.
Evans, G.* Dublin Co.
Ewart, W. Wigan.

Fielden, J.* Oldham.
Fenton, J. Rochdale.
Ferguson, Sir R. Nottingham.
Ferguson, R. Kirkcaldy, etc.
Finch, F.* Walsall.
Fitzgibbon, hon. R. Limerick Co.
Fitzroy, Lord C. Bury St. Edmunds
Fleetwood, Sir P. H. Preston.
Fort, J. Clitheroe.

English Radicalism 1832-1852

Gillon, W. D. Falkirk, etc.
Gordon, R. Windsor.
Grattan, H. Meath.
Grey, Sir E. Devonport.
Guest, Sir J. Merthyr Tydvil.

Hall, Sir B. Marylebone.
Hallyburton, Lord. Forfar Co.
Harvey, D. W.* Southwark.
Hastie, A. Paisley.
Hawes, B. Lambeth.
Hawkins, J. H. Newport (I. of W.)
Hayter, W. G. Wells.
Heathcoat, J. Tiverton.
Hector, C. J.* Petersfield.
Hindley, C.* Ashton-under-Lyne.
Hodges, T. B. Rochester.
Hodges, T. L.* West Kent.
Hollond, E. Hastings.
Horsman, E. Cockermouth.
Howard, F. J. Youghall.
Hume, J.* Kilkenny.
Humphery, J. Southwark.
Hutt, W. Hull.
Hutton, R. Dublin City.

James, W. Cumberland E.
Jervis, J. Chester.
Jervis, S.* Bridport.
Johnson, Gen.* Oldham.

Kinnaird, hon. A. F. Perth.

Lambton, H. Durham, Co., N.
Langdale, hon. C. Knaresborough.
Langton, Col. W. G. Somerset E.
Leader, J. T.* Westminster.
Lister, E. C. Bradford.
Lushington, C.* Ashburton.
Lushington, Dr. S. Tower Hamlets.
Lynch, A. H. Galway.

Macaulay, T. B. Edinburgh.
M'Leod, R. Inverness, etc.
Macnamara, Maj. Clare Co., etc.
M'Taggart, J. Wigtown, etc.
Marshall, W. Carlisle.
Marsland, Maj. H.* Stockport.
Maule, hon. F. Elgin, etc.
Molesworth, Sir W.* Leeds.
Murray, A. Kirkcudbright
Muskett, G. A.* St. Albans

Norreys, Lord. Oxfordshire.

O'Callaghan, hon. C. Dungarvan.
O'Connell, D.* Dublin City.
O'Connell, J.* Athlone.
O'Connell, M. J. Kerry Co.
O'Connell, Maurice. Tralee.
O'Connell, Morgan. Meath.
O'Connor, Don. Roscommon Co.
O'Ferrall, R. M. Kildare Co.
Ord, W. H. Newcastle-upon-Tyne.

Paget, Lord A. Lichfield.
Paget, Capt. F. Beaumaris, etc.
Palmer, C. F. Reading.
Parker, J. Sheffield.
Parnell, Sir H. Dundee.
Parrott, J. Totnes.
Pattison, J. London.
Pechell, Capt. G. R. Brighton.
Pendarves, E. W. W. Cornwall W.
Philips, M. Manchester.
Philpotts, J. Gloucester.
Pigot, D. R. Clonmel.
Ponsonby, hon. J. Derby.
Power, J. Waterford or Wexford Co.
Pryme, G. Cambridge.

Ramsbottom, J.* Windsor.
Redington, T. N. Dundalk.
Rice, E. R. Dover.
Rich, H. Knaresborough.
Rippon, C. Gateshead.
Roche, E. B.* Cork Co.
Roche, W. Limerick.
Roche, Sir D. Limerick.
Rundle, J.* Tavistock.
Russell, Lord. Tavistock.
Russell, Lord C. Bedfordshire.

Salwey, Col.* Ludlow.
Sanford, C. A. Somerset W.
Scholefield, J.* Birmingham.
Scrope, G. P. Stroud.
Seale, Col. Dartmouth.
Sharpe, Gen. Dumfries, etc.
Sheil, R. L. Tipperary Co.
Shelbourne, Earl of. Calne.
Smith, Benj. Norwich.
Somers, J. P. Sligo.
Somerville, Sir W.* Drogheda.
Speirs, A. Richmond.
Standish, C. Wigan.

Appendix A

Stanley, E. J.   Cheshire N.
Stanley, M.   Pontefract.
Stanley, W. O.   Angleseyshire.
Stansfield, W. R. G.   Huddersfield.
Steuart, R.   Haddington, etc.
Stewart, J.   Lymington.
Stuart, Lord J.   Ayr etc.
Stuart, V.   Waterford Co.
Strickland, Sir G.   Yorks W. Riding
Strutt, E.   Derby.
Style, Sir C.   Scarborough.

Talfourd, Sergt.   Reading.
Tancred, H. W.   Banbury.
Thomson, rt. hon. C. P.   Manchester.
Thornely, T.   Wolverhampton.
Troubridge, Sir E. T.   Sandwich.
Turner, W.*   Blackburn.

Verney, Sir H., Bart.   Buckingham
Vigors, N. A.*   Carlow Co.
Villiers, hon. C. P.*   Wolverhampton.
Vivian, Maj.   Bodmin.
Vivian, J. H.   Swansea, etc.

Vivian, rt. hon. Sir R. H.   Cornwall E.

Wakley, T.*   Finsbury.
Walker, R.   Bury.
Wallace, R.*   Greenock.
Warburton, H.*   Bridport.
Ward, H. G.   Sheffield.
White, A.   Sunderland.
White, H.   Longford Co.
White, S.   Leitrim Co.
Wilde, Sergt.   Newark.
Williams, W.*   Coventry.
Williams, W. A.   Monmouthshire.
Wood, Sir M.*   London.
Wyse, T.   Waterford.

Yates, J. A.   Carlow Co.

Tellers.

Grote, G.*   London.
Worsley, Lord.   Lindsey.

Paired.

Hill, Lord M.   Evesham.
Martin, J.*   Tewkesbury.

* On the division of July 12, 1839, all those M.P.s marked with a star (and Viscount Milton, M.P. for Malton) favoured the House of Commons going into Committee on the Chartist National Petition.

APPENDIX B

LIST OF M.P.s WHO DEFEATED THE GOVERNMENT ON A "RADICAL" COUNTY FRANCHISE MOTION, FEBRUARY 20, 1851

(Cf. p. 320.)

Adair, H. E. Ipswich.
Adair, R. A. S. Cambridge.
Alcock, T. Surrey E.
Anderson, A. Orkney and Shetland.
Anstey, T. C. Youghal.

Bass, M. T. Derby.
Blake, M. J. Galway.
Blewitt, R. J. Monmouth.
Bright, J. Manchester.
Brocklehurst, J. Macclesfield.
Brotherton, J. Salford.
Brown, W. Lancs. S.
Bunbury, E. H. Bury St. Edmunds.

Calvert, F. (?) (Sic. V. Hansard.)
Carter, J. B. Winchester.
Chaplin, W. J. Salisbury.
Clay, J. Hull.
Clifford, Col. H. M. Hereford.
Cobden, R. Yorks (W. R.).
Colebrooke, Sir T. E. Taunton.
Collins, W. Warwick.
Crawford, W. S. Rochdale.

D'Eyncourt, rt. hon. C. T. Lambeth.
Drummond, H. Surrey W.
Duncan, Visct. Bath.

Ellis, J. Leicester.
Evans, Sir De L. Westminster.
Evans, W. Derbyshire N.
Ewart, W. Dumfries, etc.

Fagan, W. Cork.
Forster, M. Berwick.
Fox, W. J. Oldham.

Gibson, rt. hon. T. M. Manchester.
Granger, T. C. Durham City.

Hall, Sir B. Marylebone.
Hanmer, Sir J. Flint, etc.
Harris, R. Leicester.
Hastie, A. Glasgow.
Hastie, A. Paisley.
Headlam, T. E. Newcastle-upon-Tyne.
Henry, A. Lancs. S.
Hodges, T. L. Kent W.
Howard, P. H. Carlisle.
Humphery, Ald. Southwark.
Hutt, W. Gateshead.

Jackson, W. Newcastle-under-Lyme.

Keating, R. Waterford Co.
Kershaw, J. Stockport.

Langston, J. H. Oxford City.
Lawless, hon. C. Clonmel.
Lennard, T. B. Maldon.
Locke, J. Honiton.
Loveden, P. (?) (Sic. V. Hansard.)
Lushington, C. Westminster.

Mackie, J. Kirkcudbright.
M'Cullagh, W. T. Dundalk.
M'Gregor, J. Glasgow.
M'Taggart, Sir J. Wigton burghs.
Meagher, T. Waterford.
Mangles, R. D. Guildford.
Moffatt, G. Dartmouth.
Molesworth, Sir W. Southwark.
Moore, G. H. Mayo.
Muntz, G. F. Birmingham.

O'Connor, F. Nottingham.
O'Flaherty, A. Galway.
Osborne, R. B. Middlesex.

Appendix B

Pechell, Sir G. B.   Brighton.
Perfect, R.   Lewes.
Pilkington, J.   Blackburn.
Pinney, W.   Somerset E.
Power, Dr.   Cork Co.

Rice, E. R.   Dover.
Robartes, T. J. A.   Cornwall E.

Salwey, Col.   Ludlow.
Scholefield, W.   Birmingham.
Scrope, G. P.   Stroud.
Shafto, R. D.   Durham N.
Sidney, Ald.   Stafford.
Slaney, R. A.   Shrewsbury.
Smith, rt. hon. R. V.   Northampton.
Smith, J. B.   Stirling, etc.
Stansfield, W. R. C.   Huddersfield.
Strickland, Sir, G.   Preston.
Stuart, Lord D.   Marylebone.
Sullivan, M.   Kilkenny.

Tancred, H. W.   Banbury.
Tennison, E. K.   Leitrim.
Thicknesse, R. A.   Wigan.
Thompson, Col.   Bradford.
Thornely, T.   Wolverhampton.
Trelawny, Sir J. S.   Tavistock.

Villiers, hon C. P.   Wolverhampton.

Wakley, T.   Finsbury.
Walmsley, Sir J.   Bolton.
Wawn, J. T.   S. Shields.
Williams, J.   Macclesfield.
Williams, W.   Lambeth.
Wilson, M.   Clitheroe.
Wood, Sir W. Page.   Oxford City.

Tellers.

King, hon. J. P. Locke.   Surrey E.
Hume, J.   Montrose burghs.

INDEX

Aberdeen, Lord, 323
Aberdeenshire, 170
Abolition (of Slavery) agitation, 86–7, 299, 350–1
Aborigines Protection Society, 363
Afghanistan, 372
Aglionby, H. A., M.P., 360
Albert, Prince, 320
Alison, A. (Sheriff), 165, 179, 237, 393–4
Althorp, Lord, 75, 116, 124, 130
Amalgamated Society of Engineers, 408
Annual Parliaments demanded, 13, 17, 25, 48, 168
Annual Register, The, 104
Anti-Corn Law League, 148, 156, 168, 181, 212, 215–16, 221, 224–35, 244, 250, 252, and G. Wilson 282, 307–8, 312, 417, 434
Anti-Gold Law League, 277 n.
Anti-State Church Association, The, 335
Apprenticeship (of ex-slaves) agitation, 86–7, 352–3
Arming (Chartist), 186, 192–3, 199, 203, 206, 208–9, 211
Army (and Navy) flogging condemned, 67, 89, 141, 146, 266
"Army Reform," 36, 67, 158
Arnold, Dr., quoted 62, 113
Ashley, Lord (*see also* Shaftesbury), 173, 216
Ashton-under-Lyne, 172, 174, 195 n., 199 n., 238, 285
Assessed Taxes agitation (*see also* House and Window Duties), 65, 69 n., 84–5
Attwood, Thomas, M.P., 26–7, 77–8, 131, 165, 169, 194, 200, 253, 367, 392, 426
Australian Constitutions (1850), 359–60
Ayrshire, 198

Baines, E., M.P., 411
Baines, E., 247 n., 328
Ballot agitation, 23, 69, 72, 133–4, 137, 147 n., 155–6, 164–5, 168, 205, 289, 319, 322, 433, 437

Bank of England, agitation against, 89–90, 191
Bank Charter Act (1844), 252–3, 276–7
Baptists, 111 n., 145 n., 351 n., 353 n.
Barnes (of *The Times*), 412–13
Barnsley Chartism, 193, 201, 240
Bath Radicalism, 78, 152–3, 229
Beaumont, A., 169, 174
Belfast, 52, 260
Bem (Polish refugee), 373
Benbow, William, 20, 41
Bentham, Jeremy, 20, 35–7
Benthamite Radicals, 77–8, 82, 142, 157
Bentinck, Lord G., 262, 265, 288, 299, death of 304
Bentinck, Lord W., M.P., 120, 146 n.
Bethnal Green, 172, 211, 279, 285, 334 n.
Birmingham, 19, 37, 43, 45, 49, 164 sqq., 194 sqq., 202, 207 n., 376, 380, 387
Birmingham Journal, The, 165, 183, 188–9, quoted 380, 417
Birmingham Political Union, 81, 164–5, 169, 183, 376
Birth limitation, 28, 36, 124, 160 n., 344
Bishops, agitation against, 33, 37, 38, 69, 71, 116, 333, 338 n.
Black, J., 412
Black Book, The, 91, 101
Blackburn, 239, 240
Blanc, Louis, 373
Blandford, Marquis of, 23
"Blasphemy," 23–4 n., 248, 334 n.
Board of Employment and Cultivation (Ireland), 295–6
Bolton, 182, 201, 387
Bonnymuir, 20
Bouverie, E. P., M.P., 290
Bowring, Dr., M.P., 133, 141, 163, 272, 467
Bradford, 173 n., 207, 209 n., 210, 212 n., 238, 284–5
Bradlaugh, C., 334
Bray, J. F., quoted 157, 176 n.
Brewster, Rev. P., 188, 229
Bright, Jacob, 112

454

Index

Bright, John, 117, 244, 255–6, 272–3, 277, 282, 300, 306, 315, 318, 322, 338–9, 341, 364, 373, 404, 434, 436
Brighton Radicals, 76, 152
Bristol, 38, 57, 192, 434
Britannia, The, 422
Brooke, Sir J., 364
Brougham, Lord, 23, 36–7, 46, 52, 89, 129, 411–12
Brotherton, J., M.P., 76, 267, 390
Buckingham, J. S., M.P., 77, 411, 426
Builders' Union, The, oath quoted 396, 397
Buller, C., M.P., 78, 266, 295–6, 355, 358, 433
Bulwer (Lytton), M.P., 75, 430
Bulwer, H., M.P., 367
Burdett, Sir F., M.P., 19, 64, 150
Burial Laws agitation, 113, 144, 338
Burke, 15
Burnley, 238
Bury, 184, 191

Cambridge University, 116, 137, 144, 337
Canadas, grievances of the, 354–8
Canning, George, 22
Capital attacked, 13, 25–8, 106–8, 403
Capital Punishment agitations, 67, 152, 272
Carlile, Richard, 21, 32, 334, 413
Carlisle, 172, 180, 199
Carlos, Don, 368
Carlyle, Thomas, quoted 157, quoted 203, 217
Carpenter, W., 188, 200, 413, 418, 430
Cartwright, Major, 15, 20, 25
"Catholic Emancipation Bill," 60, 337
Catholic Marriages Bill (1836), 145
Cato Street, 20
Chambers's Edinburgh Journal, 407
Chadwick, Edwin, 36, 88, 121–2, 217, 255
Chalmers, Dr., 335, 393–4
Chambers, R., 344, 419
Chambers, W., 407, 419
Champion, The, 169, 188, 417–18
Chandos, Marquis of, 98
Charter, The People's, 166, quoted 168, 171, Union quoted 313
Charter, The (newspaper), 413, 418

Chartists, 15, Chaps. ix–xii *passim*, 227, Nat. Petition, 232, 237, 252–4, 256, 267–8, 276, and the "Monster Petition," 281, 284–9, 296–7, 309, 399–400, 409, 435
"Cheap Justice" demanded, 62, 89, 157
Cheltenham Free Press, The, 417
Child Employment, 217, 238, 246
Christian Socialism, 286
Church abuses, 66 *sqq.*, 113, 333–4
Church rate disputes, 66, 112, 116–17, 149, 216, 337–8, 381
City, The, 44, 68–9, 336, 383, 386
Civil List opposition, 101, 154
Civil Registration of Births, Marriages, and Deaths, 143
Clay, W., M.P., 65
Cleave, T., 160, 163
Clerkenwell, 195 n., 198, 285
Cobbett, William, 20–1, 26–7, 33, 67, 76, 78, 82–3, *Pol. Reg.* quoted 104, and Poor Law 127, *Legacy to Labourers* 128, 131, 361, 383, 384, 392, 411, 426, 434
Cobbett, J. P., 189, 191
Cobden quoted 171, quoted 220, 227, 244, 254–64, 275, 278, 282, quoted 298, 300, 302, 305–10, 312, 314–26, 328–30, 341–3, quoted 349, 358–9, 364, 370–4, 375, 377–9, 387, 404, quoted 425, 434–7
Cockburn, H., *Journal of*, quoted 30, 179, 269
Coercion Bills (Ireland), 85, 118, 264, 277
Collet, Dobson, quoted 313, 325
Collins, John, 166, 169, 206, 214, 226, 229, 398
Colonial Intelligencer, The, 363–4
"Colonial Reform," 358–60
Colonisation and Christianity, 363
"Complete Suffrage" agitation, 228–30, 242–3, 249–50 n.
Congregationalists (Independents), 111 n., 328 n., 345
Constitutional, The, 416
Cooper, Thomas, quoted 203, 238–9, 242, 268, 410
Co-operation, 105, 286, 409
Co-operative, communities advocated, 26, 105, 181, 268 n., 403, 404
Cork County, 48, 50, 52, 56, 58

455

English Radicalism 1832–1852

Corn Law of 1815, 22, 91–2; of 1828, Chap. v *passim*, 224–5; of 1842, 232–3
Corporation Act, 22
Cotton spinners, 24, 178–9, 398
County Boards demanded, 387–9
Crawford, Sharman, M.P., 141, 163, 221, 230, 249, 272, 294, 339
Creed of Christendom, 345
Creevey, T., quoted 80
Crimean War, 323, 327, 424
Crisis, The, 110–11
Croker, J. W., 80
Cumberland, Duke of, 136
Currency agitations, 26–7, 81, 165–8, 252–3, 267 n., 277 n., 404

Daily News, The, 262, 420–1
Daily Telegraph, The, 424
De Lacey Evans, Lt.-Col., M.P., 65, 140, 151, 368
Dembinski, Gen., 373
Derby, 38, 107–8, 227
Derby, Lord (*see* Stanley)
Derby-Disraeli Ministry, 340
Devonport, 170, 387
D'Eyncourt, Tennyson, M.P., 70–2, 75, 82, 272, 426
Dicey, Prof., 333
Dickens, Charles, 421
Disestablishment, 33, 62, 114, 132, 145 n., 152, 174, 181, 248, 259, 274, 333–6
Disraeli, B., 152, 223, 255, 304, 306–7, 310–12, 324
Dissenters' grievances, 111–17, 247–8, 334–5
Dissenters' marriages, 143, 144, 247–8, 334, 342
Divorce Law, 291, 343–4
Doherty, John, 34, 100, 398
Dorchester Labourers' agitation, 110–11, 141
Douglas, R. K., 165–7, 182–3, 188–9, 191
Drummond, H., M.P., 292
Dudley Political Union, quoted 139
Duncannon, Lord, 75
Dunckley, H., quoted 332
Duncombe, T. S., M.P., 136, 140, 231, 249, 262, 267, 272, 401–2
Dundee, 52, 76, 430
Dundee Advertiser, The, 411

Durham, Lord, 40, 53, 129, 152, 224, and Canada 357–8, 370, 411, 426–32
Durham (and Northumberland) miners, 401–2
Durham Report, quoted 349
Dyott (Gen.), quoted 236

East India Co. attacked, 69, 77, 89–90
Ecclesiastical Courts attacked, 290–1
Economist, The, 405, 423
Edinburgh, 21 n., 179 n., 212 n.
Edinburgh Review, The, 383, 412
Education, National, 67, 80, 82–3, 181, 205, 246–8, 272–4, 328–30
Education, "Secular," 82–3, 248, 273, 328–30, 404
Eldon, Lord, 101
Elgin, Lord, 357
Ellice, E., M.P., 75
Elliott, Ebenezer, 93, 181
Emigration, 360–3
Empire, The, 349–64
Engels, F., 276
Essays and Reviews, 345
Evans, Lieut.-Col. (*see* De Lacey Evans)
Evening Express, The, 420
Evening Star, The, 424
Ewart, W., M.P., 75, 152, 272–3, and the Library Bill 330–1, 371
Examiner, The, 142, 416, 423

Factory Act (1833), 34, 87, 173; (1847), 406; (1850), 318, 406
"Family Compact," The, 357–8
Fielden, John, M.P., 76, 107, 194, 200, 223, 266–7, 272, quoted 380, 390
Finsbury, 65–6, 140
Fonblanque, A., 97, quoted 98
Fox, W. J., 161, 275, 329, 413
"Freehold Land" movement, 256, 316–18
Free Trade, Chap. xviii *passim*
Friends of the People, 162
Frost, John, 207–11
Froude, J. A., 344
Fryer, R., M.P., 69 n.

Game Laws agitation, 33, 291, 306, 311
Gammage, R., quoted 171, quoted 298, 418
Gaskell, D., M.P., 152

Index

General Lighting and Watching Act, 390
George III, 14
Gibson, Milner, T., M.P., 266, 325–6, 389
Gillon, W. D., M.P., 52
Gladstone, W. E., 307, 350
Glasgow, 30, 129, 168, 198, 279
Glasgow spinners, 397, 400
Godwin, W., 26
Graham, Sir James, Bart., 40, 94, 246–8, 266, 272, 300, 309
Grammar Schools Act, 218
Grand National Consolidated Trades' Union, 75, 82, 106, 108, 110–11, 397, 402
Grattan, H., 204
Greg, W. R., 345
Greville, C. C. F., quoted 91, 109, 113, quoted 120, 412
Grey, Lord, 24, 37, 38, 43, 46, 117, 188, and Irish Coercion 119, 120, 158, 427, 429
Grote, George, M.P., 68–69, 78, 82, 122, 133, and Ballot 205, 353, 371, 433
Grote, Mrs., quoted 139
Gully, J., M.P., 76

Hackney, 285
Halévy, Prof., 75, 111
Halifax, 180 n., 192
Hardy, T., 15–16, 18
Harney, Julian, 176, 190, 399
Harvey, D. Whittle, M.P., 101–2, quoted 103, 133, 140, 154, 383
Hawes, B., M.P., 71–3, 163, 266
Health of Towns Bill, The (1847), 274
Henley, Lord, 72, 113
Hetherington, Henry, 24, 32, 41, 159, 188, 212, Charter Union, 213, 229, 413–15
Hetherington's Dispatch, 169
Heywood, Abel, 177
Heywood, James, M.P., 337
Hill, M. Davenport, M.P., 77
Hill, Rev. Mr., 177
Hindley, C., M.P., 163, 392
History of the Protestant Reformation (Cobbett), 127
History of Trade Unionism (Webb), 408
Hobhouse, J. C. (Sir), M.P., 19, 46, 64, 66, 75, 87, 381–2

Hobson, Joshua, 177
Hodgskin, Thomas, 13, 23
Holland, Lord, 142
"Holy Alliance," The, 366
Holyoake, G. J., 334
Home Colonisation, 404
House and Window Duties agitations, 65, 69 n., 84–5, 312
Household Suffrage, 55, 157, 165, 222, 289, 434
Hovell, Mark, 177
Howick, Lord, 75, 243–4
Howitt, W., 112, 363
Hudson, George, 260
Hume, Joseph, M.P., 23, 67, 72, 75, 78–9, 89, quoted 91, 98, 100, 122, 133, 136, 154, 163, 221, 225, 249, 252, 267, 272, 282, 288, 289, 300, 308, 315, 318, 320, 324, 353–4, 355, 364, 367, 371, 378, 381, 384, 387–93, 426, 433
Humphery, Alderman, M.P., 69
Hunt, Henry, 20, 25, 27, 55, 67
Huskisson, 22

Illustrated London News, The, 419–20, 423
Income Tax agitations, 220, 233–4, 256–7, 278, 308, 312
India (*see* East India Co.)
Infant Felons Act, 218
"Infidelity," 21, 23 n., 42, 77, 153 n., 248, 328, 332, 334, 344–5
International Arbitration, 372
Irish Church, 85, 86, 135–7, 143, 338
Irish Church Disestablishment, 337, 339
Irish Coercion Bills (1833), 85; (1834) 118–19; (1846) 264–5; (1847) 277–89, 293
Irish Constabulary, 263 n., 390
Irish Corporation Reform Bills, 137, 143, 148, 156, 391
(Irish) Dublin Police Bill (rejected Lords), 136
(Irish) Dublin University, 51–2
Irish Encumbered Estates Act, 293–4
Irish Encumbered Estates Court, 294
Irish Land Tenure, etc., 339–41, Chap xx *passim*
Irish Landlord and Tenant Bll (1848), 293, Chap. xx *passim*

457

Irish Marriages Bill (rejected Lords), 136
Irish Maynooth Seminary, 258-9
Irish Municipal Reform, 143, 145, 156, 189, 206, 218, 384, 390-1
Irish "National Schools," 329
Irish Poor Law, 154, 391
Irish Queen's Colleges, 259-60
Irish Reform Bill, 48, 51-2
Irish Registration Bills (Stanley), 218-19, 222-3, 226
Irish Suffrage, 51-2, 60, 218-19, 319
Irish Tithe Commutation Bill (1834), 114-16, 119; (1835) 135-6; (1836) 143, 145; (1837) 148; (1838) 155
Isabella, Queen of Spain, 368

Jacob, W., 95
Jamaica Bill (1839), 352-4
Jeffrey, Lord, 383
Jewish Emancipation agitation, 33, 336-7
Joint Stock Banks, 90, 148, 150 n., 181
Jones, Ernest, 211, 268, 276, 284-5, 309, 342, 409
J.P.s criticism of, 106, 191, 195, 291, 380, 387-9

Key, Sir J., M.P., 78
King, Locke, M.P., 315, 319, 324
Kingsley, Rev. C., 286
Kinloch, G., M.P., 76
Knight, Charles, 407, 419
Kossuth, Louis, 373-6
Kydd, Samuel, 276, 284

Labour League, The, quoted 349, 403-5
Lambeth, 70-72
Lanarkshire, 198, 237, 240
Lancet, The, 140
Land Laws agitation, 26-8, 89, 96, 255-6, 258, 260, 269, 292-6, 305-6, 313, 339-42
Land Nationalisation, 341-2
Lansdowne, Lord, 142, 158
Leader, The, 163, 345
Leeds, 22, 49, 51
Leeds Mercury, The, 221, 411, 417
Leeds Times, The, 221, 417

Legacy to Labourers (Cobbett), 127
Leicester, 225 n., 234, 239, 275, 410
Leicester Mercury, The, 417
Liberation Society, The, 335
Lichfield, 135 n.
Life of Christ, The (Strauss), 334
Linton, W. J., 341, quoted 365
Liverpool, 57, 99, 152, 181, 242, 310, 434
Liverpool Financial Reform Association, 314
Liverpool Mercury, The, 423
Lloyd's Illustrated London News, 419
Lloyd's Weekly News, 413, 420, 423
Lloyd's Weekly London News, 419
London, City of, 44, 68-9, 336, 383, 386
London Corresponding Society, 15-19
London Democrat, The, 197
London Democratic Federation, 190
London Dispatch, The, 108, 418
London and Westminster Review, The, 416
London Working Men's Association, 160-4, 179, 181, 418
Lords, House of, attacked, 32, 38, 120, 136-7, 139, 146, 152, 158; and Peers' Proxies, 145
Lot, Parson, 286
Loughborough, 186, 193, 209 n.
Louis, Napoleon, 372-4, 377-9
Louis Philippe, 366-9
Loveless, George, 108
Lovett, W., 105, 160-1, 188, 199, 202, 206, 214, 227, 229, 242-3, and "Defence Fund" 398, 418
Lushington, Dr., M.P., 65
Lyell, C., 364
Lyndhurst, Lord, 134, 143, 147, 151, 391

Macaulay, T. B., 51, 97, 231, 250, 267, 274, 318
Macerone, Col., 42, 192
Malt Tax agitation, 84, 96, 140, 153, 312
Malthus, Rev. T., 123-4
Malthusianism, 123-4, 176 n.
Manchester, 16, 22, 181, 209, 221, 282, 310, 330-1, 386-7, 399
Manchester and Salford Education Bill, 330
Manchester Guardian, The, 423

Index

"Manchester School," The, 299–300, 302, 318, 389, 405
Manchester Spinners' Association, 398, 400
"Marcus," 175–6
Maria, Donna, 368
Marriage Laws criticised, 290–1, 342–5
Marshall (of Leeds), 142, 221
Martineau, Harriet, 344, quoted 349
Marx, 413
Marylebone, 65–8, 382
Master and Servant Bill, 402
Maurice, Rev. F. D., 286
Mayhew, 413
Maynooth (see Ireland)
Mazzini, 373–4, 375
M'Cullagh, Torrens, 294, 319
M'Douall, Dr., 199, 239–41, 276, 284, 363
Mechanics' Institutes, 331
Mehemet Ali, 371
Melbourne, Lord, 109, quoted 110, 118, 130–1, 142, 145, 148, 151, 158, 165, 194, 250, 352, 430, 431
Methodists, 143–4, 272, 345
Metropolitan Police Force, 382–3
Mexborough, Lord, 76
Miall, E., 229, 421
Miguel, Don, 368
Militia, 160 n., 377–8
Mill, James, 25, 27, 35–6, 359, 412
Mill, J. S., 31, 38, 63, 80, 142, 224, quoted 283, 292, 329, quoted 332, 408–9, quoted 425
Milton, Lord, 75, 94
Miners' Association, 253, 401
Mines Act (1842), 238
Mines Commission, 246
M'Nish, 166
Molesworth, Sir W., M.P., 78, 142, 154–5, 158, 159, 218, quoted 251, 273, 333, 355, 357–8, 433, 436
Molyneux, Lord, 75
Monmouthshire Chartism, 193, 195 n., 207–9
Montgomery, J., 411
Montgomeryshire Chartism, 195 n., 206
Morley, Samuel, 317
Morning Advertiser, The, 415
Morning Chronicle, The, 125, 142, 191, 411–12, 416–17
Morning Star, The, 213, 424

Morpeth, Lord, 140, 274
Mudie, G., 105
Muir, T., 17
Mulgrave, Lord, 140
Municipal Corporation Commission, 88, 385
Municipal Reform Act, 1835, Chap. vii *passim*, 133, 140, 385–6
Muntz, G. F., M.P., 165, 252, 267, 304, 307
Museums Act, 275
Mutiny Bill (1833), 89

Napier, Gen. Sir C., 40, 153, 192–3, 197, 199, 211
Nassau, Senior, 121
National Assembly (1848), 284
National Association of United Trades, 286, 402–4
National Convention, The, (1839) Chap xi, (1842) 231, (1848) 280
National Debt holders criticised, 26–7, 33, 405
National Equitable Labour Exchange, 105–6
National Petition, The (1839), 167–8; (1842) 230–2; (1848) 276, 279–81
National Trades Journal, 254, 419
Navigation Act controversy, 270, 301–4, 405
Neale, V., 286
Nemesis of Faith, 344
Newcastle and Tyneside, 136, 139, 169, 180 n., 187, 193, 199, 202, 209
Newcastle, Duke of, 350, 388
Newman, Francis, 344
New Moral World, The, 221
"New Reform Movement," 282, 285–9
New South Wales, 358
New Zealand, 358–61
News of the World, 420, 423
Newspaper Taxes (Taxes on Knowledge), 99, 140, 146–7, 160, 325, Chap xxv *passim*
Nicholas, Tsar, 366–71, 372, 374, 378–9
Nonconformist, The, 228, 421
Northampton Mercury, The, 417
Northern Political Union, 180 n., 202, 212
Norwich, 57, 183, 190, 434
Nottingham, 38, 39, 201, 211, 232, 276
Nottingham Review, The, 411

459

Oastler, Richard, 171-3, quoted 173, Chap. x *passim*, 255, 306, 318 n.
O'Brien, J. Bronterre, 177, 189, 201, 229, quoted 332, 341, 415
O'Brien, Smith, M.P., 295
Observations on the management of Poor in Scotland, and its effects on the Health of Great Towns, 393
O'Connell, Daniel, 22-3, 48, 51, 60, 67, 69, 79, 82, 85, 115, quoted on Irish Coercion 118, 119, 136-7, 146, 150-3, 163, quoted 204, and the Charter 209-5, 221-2, and Repeal Campaign 245, 258, 270, 355, 367, 391-3, 428
O'Connor, Feargus, 58, 76, 161, 169, Chap. x *passim*, Chap. xi *passim*, 213, 222, and "Suffrage Union" (Sturge) 229, 230, 241-3, 249, quoted 254, 267, and Land Scheme 268 and 276, quoted 269, 276-7, 281, 284, 288, 309, 315, 418-19
Old Bell's Messenger, 422
Oldham, 76, 161 n., 236
Operative, The, quoted 396, 418
Osborne, Bernal, M.P., 315
Owen, Robert, 26, 87, 105, 111, 161, 334, 343
Oxford University, 116, 337

Pacifico, Don, debates, 373
Paine, Tom, 15-16, 21, 24, 33, 36, 51, 66, 334
Palmerston, Lord, 308, 311, 320, 323, 343, 366-7, 371-5
Pamphlets for the People, 136
Papineau, 355
Parker, J., M.P., 32, 426
Parkes, J., 31, 88, 134, 385, 431
Parnell, Sir Henry, 75
Paulton, A. W., 212
Payment of Members demand, 165, 168
Peace Society, 372
Pease, J., M.P., 76
Peel, Sir Robert, 22, 46, 50, 64, 74, 79, quoted memoirs of 130-1 ff., 132, 135, 142, 144, 151-2, 194-5, 204, 206, 225, and Repeal of Corn Laws and Income Tax 233, 244-5, quoted 251, and Bank Charter 252-3, and Anti-Corn Law 254-65, and Budgets 256-7, and Ireland 258-60, 271, quoted 283, 300, death of 307, 431

Penny Magazine, The, 407
Penny Papers for the People, 410-13
Pension List, Chap. v *passim*, 154
People's Charter, The, 166
Perils of the Nation, The, 333
Perry, J., 411-12
Peterloo, 20
Petitions, 18, 92, 114, 126 n., 133, 147, 205 n., 211, 218 n., 222 n., 248, 267, 273 (*see also* National Petition)
Phases of Faith, 344-5
Phillips, C. M., quoted 186
Pioneer, The, 107-8, 110
Place, F., 19, 24, 26, 32, 37, 39, 44, 46, 63, 134, 147, 161, 177, quoted 380, 385-6
Police, agitation concerning, 67, 185, 190-1, 198-9, 206, 380, 382-3, 389-91
Polish risings, 366
*Political Economy (Principles of—*J. S. Mill), 292, 329
Political Letters, 413
Political Unions, 23, 31, 32, 37, 41, 46, 49, 54, 62, 81, 82, 129 n., 139
Politics for the People, 286, 333
Poor Law Amendment, 98, Chap. vii *passim*
Poor Law Amendment Bill, 125-6
Poor Law Commission and Science and Art Dept., 125, and Committee of Council on Education 125, and Central Health Board 125, 148, 173-6, Chap. x *passim*, 179-80, 275, 384
Poor Law Commission (Inquiry), 88, Chap. vii *passim*
Poor Law Commissioners, Chap. x *passim*
Poor Law (Ireland), 33, 391-3
Poor Law (Scotland), 244, 393-5
Poor Man's Guardian, The, 32, 42, 62, 100, 107, quoted 120, 131, quoted 365, 368-9, 413, 415
Popay, the Police Spy, 383
Portman, E. B., M.P., 66-8
Post Office, 145, 150
Potter, R., M.P., 77
Potteries, The, 235, 237-9
Prentice, A., 411
Presbyterians (Ireland), 259-60, 339
Preston, 55, 182, 240
Primogeniture, attacked, 32-3, 292
Principles of Geology, 334

Index

Prisoners' Counsel Bill, 145
Prompter, The, 413
Property, private, disliked, 25-8, taxation demanded 16, 81, 85, 405
Property Qualifications, agitation against, 57-8, 61, 67, 158, 164, 165, 385
Pryme, G., M.P., 77
Pusey, E. B., 292, 333, 343

Quakers (Friends), 76, 228, 363
Quarterly Review, The, quoted 410

Raikes, T., quoted 74, 76, 155 n.
"Ratepaying Clauses" agitation, 58-9, 156, 157
Reasoner, The, 334
"Rebecca Riots," 245
Reform Bills (Pitt's), 15 (1832), Chaps. i and ii
Regium Donum, 339
Repeal (of the Union), 245-58
Repository, The, 142
Republican, The, 413
Republicanism, 13, 17, 32, 37, 284
Reynolds's Weekly Newspaper, 420, 423
Reynolds's Weekly Political Instructor, 362, 373, quoted 374
Ricardo, J. L., M.P., 95, 96, 270, 301-2, 342
Rice, Spring T., M.P., 147, 149
Richard, Rev. H., 364
Richmond, Duke of, 13
Rights of Man, The, 16, 25
Rintoul, R., 411
Roberts, W. P., 401
Rochdale, 117, 186, 236
Rochdale Equitable Pioneers, 286
Roebuck, J. A., M.P., 78, 82, quoted 120, 136, 150, 152-3, 165, 221, 231, 234, 256, 267, quoted 269, 271-2, 326, 342, 354, 391, 433, quoted 435, 436
Rollin, Ledru-, 373-4, 375
Rothschild, Baron Lionel de, 335
Russell, Lord J., 54-6, 75, 112, 115, 117, 130, and Municipal Reform 133, 144, 200, 205-6, and "Edinburgh Letter" 261, 265, 272, 289, 293, 308-9, 317-18, 320, 322-5, 359, 436-7
Rutland, Duke of, 77

Sabbatarianism, 153, 336
St. Pancras, 65-7, 382
Salisbury, Lord, 437
Salomons, David, M.P., 336
Salt, H. S., 165, 188, 189, 191
Scholefield, J., M.P., 77, 165
Scholefield's Chapel, 239
Scinde, 372
Scotsman, The, 326, 411
Scottish Burgh, Reform, 384
Scottish Poor Law, 392-5
Scottish Reform Bill, 52, 59-60
Scrope, Poulett, M.P., 394-5
Secular Education Bill, 329
Settlement Laws, 121
Shaftesbury, Lord, quoted 313, 333 (*see also* Ashley, Lord)
Sheffield, 16, 18, 27, 192, 201, 235, 399
Sheffield Iris, The, 411
Sheil, R. L., M.P., 74, quoted 220, quoted 251, 367
"Short Parliaments," 62, 64, 71, 164, 313
Sinecures, Chap. v *passim*
Slavery, abolition of (*see* Abolition)
Smith, Southwood (Dr.), 36, 84, 88, 217, 255
Smith, Sydney (Rev.), 212, 333
Soap Tax, 140
Socialism, 105 *sqq*., 181 n., 243 n., 268 n., 313, 343 n.
Somerville, A., 198
Southern Star, The, 418
Spectator, The, 416, 423
"Speenhamland," 121
Spence, Thomas, 26, 96
Stamford and Lincoln Mercury, The, 417
Stamp Duty, 415, repeal of 421
Stanley, Hon. E., later Lord Stanley and Earl of Derby, 55, 75, 222, 226, 308
Steam-Engine Makers' Union, 400
Stephens, J. R. (Rev.), 174, Chap. x *passim*, Chap. xi *passim*, 206
Stepney Green, 279
Stockport, 199, 226, 284 n., 324
Stonemasons, 397, 407
Strauss's *Life of Christ*, 339
Strutt, E., M.P., 142
Sturge, Joseph, 228-9, 364

461

Suffrage Extension agitation; 1841–4 (see "Complete Suffrage"), 1848 (see "New Reform Movement"), 1849–52; Chap. xix
Sunderland, 229, 284 n.

Tait's Magazine, 142
Tamworth Letter, 130–1, 132, 431
Taylor, Dr., 178, 199
Temperance agitation, 406–7
Ten Hours Act, 406 (see also under Factory Legislation)
Thompson, G., M.P., 256–7
Thompson, Poulett, M.P., 99
Thompson, T. Perronet, M.P., 92–3, 141, 152, 163, 221, 260
Times, The, 125–6, 130, 137, 142, 147, 182, 254, 275, 289, 326, 412, 416, 423
Tithes, agitation for Abolition (England), 62, 67, 71, 72, 112, (Wales) 245, (Ireland) 61, 69, 119, 131, 143, 157, 245
Tolpuddle (see Dorchester) Labourers, 108–9
Tooke, Horne, 17–18
Tooke, William, M.P., 77, 152
Torrington, Lord, 363–4
Tower Hamlets, 65–6, 99, 198
Trade Unions, 106–10, Chap. xxiv
Trevelyan, G. M., quoted 186, quoted 236
Triennial Parliaments demand, 23, 55, 69, 82, 139
True Sun, The, 413, 415
Twopenny Dispatch, The, 413, 415

"Ulster Custom," 293, 341
Uniformity, Act of, 22
Unitarians, 345 n.
University of London, 77, 112, 152
University Reform, 158
University Tests and Dissenters, 116, 119, 337
Unkiar Skelessi, Treaty of, 367, 371
Urquhart, David, 369, 371

Vestiges of the Natural History of Creation, 344

Vestries Act (1831), 66
Victoria, Queen, 151–2, 154, 195, 204, 431
Villiers, C. P., M.P., 141, 300, 309, 311
Vincent, Henry, 163, 192, 202, 206, 208, 229
Vixen, The, 370

Wakefield, Daniel, 71–2
Wakefield, E. Gibbon, 358
Wakley, T., M.P., 140–1, 154, 223, 267
Wallace, R., M.P., 382, 407
Walmsley, Sir J., M.P., 275, 315, 317–18, 364, 421, 435, 437
Walpole, Spencer, quoted 139
Walter, John, 412
Warburton, H., M.P., 75, 142
Ward, H. G., M.P., 117, 253, 432, 433
Warwick, Earl of, 388
Watson, J., 159–60, 413
Webb, S. and B., 408
Weekly Chronicle, The, 422
Weekly Dispatch, The, 368, 369, 415, 420, 422
Weekly Political Register, The, 411, 413
Wellington, Duke of, 23–4, 44–5, 64, 130, 194, 278, 280, 388, 411, 432–3
West India Prison Regulations, 352
West, J. (Chartist), 276
Western Vindicator, The, 207, 210
Westminster, 19, 63–5
Westminster Review, The, 345
Whalley, Sir S., M.P., 58, 68, 338
Wilkes, John, 14
William IV, 151, 164, 428
Williams, William, M.P., 252, 316 n.
Wilson, George, 282
Wilson, James, 405, 423
Wood, Page, M.P., 78, 315
Working Classes, National Union of the, 27, 39, 42, 159
Working Man's Friend, The, 413
Wyse, T., M.P., 141

"Young Ireland," 270, 281, 284, 297 n.

For Product Safety Concerns and Information please contact our EU
representative GPSR@taylorandfrancis.com
Taylor & Francis Verlag GmbH, Kaufingerstraße 24, 80331 München, Germany

www.ingramcontent.com/pod-product-compliance
Lightning Source LLC
Chambersburg PA
CBHW071234300426
44116CB00008B/1024